THE POLITICS OF INTERNATIONAL LAW

Today international law is everywhere. Wars are fought and opposed in its name. It is invoked to claim rights and to challenge them, to indict or support political leaders, to distribute resources and to expand or limit the powers of domestic and international institutions. As a professional vocabulary and an expression of popular aspirations for a better world, international law is deeply enmeshed in international politics. It is part of the way political (and economic) power is used, critiqued, and sometimes limited. Despite its claim for neutrality and impartiality, it is implicit in what is just, as well as what is unjust in the world. To understand its operation requires shedding its ideological spell and examining its actual operation with a cold eye. Who are its winners and who are its losers? How – if at all – can it be used to make a better, or at least a less unjust, world?

In this collection of essays Professor Martti Koskenniemi, a well known practitioner and one of the great theorists and historians of international law, examines the recent debates on humanitarian intervention, collective security, protection of human rights and the 'fight against impunity' and reflects on the use of the professional techniques of international law to intervene politically. The essays both illustrate and expand his influential theory of the critical role of international law in international politics. The book is prefaced with an introduction by Professor Emmanuelle Jouannet (Sorbonne Law School) which locates the texts in the overall thought and work of Martti Koskenniemi.

D1344463

The Politics of International Law

MARTTI KOSKENNIEMI

·H A R T·
PUBLISHING

OXFORD AND PORTLAND, OREGON
2011

Published in the United Kingdom by Hart Publishing Ltd
16C Worcester Place, Oxford, OX1 2JW
Telephone: +44 (0)1865 517530
Fax: +44 (0)1865 510710
E-mail: mail@hartpub.co.uk
Website: http://www.hartpub.co.uk

Published in North America (US and Canada) by
Hart Publishing
c/o International Specialized Book Services
920 NE 58th Avenue, Suite 300
Portland, OR 97213-3786
USA
Tel: +1 503 287 3093 or toll-free: (1) 800 944 6190
Fax: +1 503 280 8832
E-mail: orders@isbs.com
Website: http://www.isbs.com

British Library Cataloguing in Publication Data
Data Available

ISBN: 978-1-84113-939-5

Typeset by Hope Services Ltd, Abingdon
Printed and bound in Great Britain by
Lightning Source UK Ltd

PREFACE

I

The chapters in this book examine different ways in which the intervention by international law in particular contexts – diplomatic crises, governance problems as well as academic disputes – takes on a contested, political appearance. They survey international law's operation *as* a (vocabulary for) politics and are thus eminently not about international law *and* politics. The conjunctive form would suggest a meeting of two separately identifiable entities whose action upon each other would then be subjected to analysis. As the two 'theoretical' chapters at the beginning expressly argue, I do not think there are such separate entities. Nothing in this book participates in the sometimes fashionable enquiries of international law's 'impact' on politics or vice-versa. Such an enquiry would be like examining Christianity's relationship to religion. The relationship (if that is the correct word) is not one of two entities colliding against each other but one of identity. International law is an *expression* of politics much like Christianity constitutes one type of expression of religious spirituality. Both also operate as technical languages that are resorted to by trained professionals and lay persons alike in order to communicate human aspirations, fears and ambitions. In the case of international law, such sentiments are invoked so as to support or criticise particular actors or practices in the contexts of action we like to call 'international' or today perhaps 'global'.

Nor is there any discussion of the nature of 'politics' or the 'political' in this book – at least not the kind of political theory discussion that used to preoccupy (German) intellectuals during the inter-war era and has resurfaced every now and then in the analyses of the conditions of international and domestic order. The 'politics of international law' refers to no jurisprudential thesis about the *real nature* of politics or (international) law. Instead, it points to the experience of a certain fluidity and contestability that most people – lawyers and non-lawyers – have when they enter the world of international law and find themselves in the presence of alternative and often conflicting rules, principles or institutional avenues between which they are expected to choose and realise that it is by no means self-evident how to justify that choice. Topics such as the intervention by the North Atlantic alliance (NATO) in Kosovo in 1999, the operation of the Strasbourg human rights institutions, the trial of former President Milosevic, or the 'fragmentation of international law', discussed below, all involve choice and the experience that more is involved in that choice than applying a pre-existing principle. The essays below take that experience seriously and not just as an effect of a technical or communication failure that could be corrected by 'interpretation'. International law, they suggest, is not about operating an algorithm but about deciding between alternative types of action each of which may, with some ingenuity be brought within the conventions of plausible legal argument. The question 'who will win, who will lose' is never far from the surface of such choices and it is to that question the following chapters seek to give a sense of concreteness and urgency.

The 'politics of international law' in this book connotes the intervention of what is sometimes labelled a 'prejudice' or a 'bias' in legal work. Nothing pejorative is meant thereby. As I have elsewhere explained in detail, and as I hope to make clear in chapters 1, 2 and 12, indeterminacy, decision and bias are inevitable aspects of all work in international law, from giving legal advice to drafting judgments of international tribunals, from academic system-construction to the argumentative interventions by activists.[1] They give meaning and applicability to abstract standards, and make the legal vocabulary 'tick' by directing it to the defence or critique of alternative positions. To speak of 'politics' is intended to highlight the reality of choice in international law and to contrast it with the technical production of the justification for it. In this way, I hope to convey a realistic view of the operation of international law as a *practice* of decision-making that interferes in peoples' lives instead of a theoretical exercise in deduction-subsumption from abstract rule-formulations, principles of 'justice' or the 'policies' of international institutions. We need the legal vocabulary to justify our decisions and to support or critique the choices of others. But the vocabulary does not decide on our behalf. We remain responsible. If there is an underlying critical motif in these chapters, it is directed at the point where the experience of choice is lost and where standard interpretations begin to appear as inevitable results of an impartial legal reason or where institutional routine has become so entrenched that it is no longer recognised as the contingent result of past choices that it is. That international law itself tends to become, to use a well-worn phrase, 'part of the problem', is often a consequence of the emotional and political intensity of its vocabularies. Expressions such as aggression, genocide, torture or right to life, among others, are key parts of the professional language and make powerful appeals for choosing in particular ways. But they speak to the heart so that the mind may find it indecent to object.[2] To lose the experience of contestability even of such words, however, and thus one's distance from the institutional commitments one has made, is to be complicit in the way the world is.

Many of the chapters here highlight the strategic dimensions of legal work: how to argue for particular positions? How to find a legal justification – or to attack the justification by one's adversary? But I will also ask the question of the limits of such

---

[1] See the 'Epilogue' in my *From Apology to Utopia. The Structure of International Legal Argument Reissue with a New Epilogue* (Cambridge University Press, 2005).

[2] I have discussed this especially in my 'International Law in Europe: Between Tradition and Renewal', 16 *European Journal of International Law* (2005) 113–24. See also David Kennedy, *The Dark Sides of Virtue. Reassessing International Humanitarianism* (Princeton University Press 2005).

a view. Is there an independent 'politics' of a legal formalism that insists on process rather than outcome? I think there is. But as I argue in chapter 8, I also think that there is a point at which formalism will break down under the weight of other considerations. If neither formalism nor anti-formalism will save us, then focus will inevitably turn back to ourselves as lawyers, activists or academics, and our sensitivity to what is important in the practical contexts in which we act. It is true that institutional practices are often well-entrenched and hard to change – not to mention that their very fixedness may make us lose the sense that any large transformation is at all possible. The power of cynicism may also achieve that even the identification of complacent hypocrisy goes no way to eradicating it. And how useful is it, really, to open the imagination if all it does is to make one even more conscious of the enormous distance between present reality and utopian hope? These are hugely important existential questions that a book on 'the politics of international law' cannot pretend to resolve. But at least such a book can give expression to the experience of fluidity and contestability and provide tools for the cool-headed analysis of what our participation as legal language-users in our professional contexts does to the world and to ourselves.

II

The original essays on which the chapters below are based were written over a time-span of 20 years. I have updated or slightly modified many of them so as to make them suitable for this book. That they appear in a largely (though not completely) chronological order is a coincidence that reflects the way my attention and professional engagements have shifted from one subject to another. Part I of the book – chapters one and two – lays out the argument about the operation of the 'politics of international law' and serves as a kind of general introduction to the rest. Those interested in human rights, collective security, criminal law or 'fragmentation', for example, may go directly to the relevant chapters. Nevertheless, all the chapters illustrate in different ways the operation of the argumentative structure presented at the beginning and a full grasp of this book may require at least some slight attention to the discussion of the operation of the legal grammar presented there.

Part II examines collective security as a platform for the use of legal argument in the context of the first Iraq crisis in 1990–91 and in the anxious debates among European lawyers during the 1999 Kosovo crisis. If the latter offers an exemplary case of the over- and under-inclusiveness of the legal vocabularies of the use of force, intervention and self-defence, the former provides a sketch of an institutional context where those vocabularies became surprisingly fixed in legal terms. The two chapters together examine both the effects and the limits of formal legal argument conducted under the terms of Chapter VII of the UN Charter. They seek to refute both the (political realist) view that law has nothing to say when vital interests of states are at issue, and the (legal deductivist) position that law actually dictates how we should behave in those situations.

The work of ambition and uncertainty, innovation and stasis in the human rights field constitutes the subject of Part III. It seems clear that the much-debated rise of human rights in international institutions in the 1980s and 1990s came about as a response to the perceived weakness and retrograde politics of statehood that people tended to identify at the heart of 'traditional' international law. But the effort to replace old diplomatic languages by aiming directly at the 'good' values of human rights did not free us from the experience of uncertainty and choice. It did not take long before the institutionalisation of human rights law opened the argumentative avenues to the familiar logics of conflicting rights, rules versus exceptions, and the whole business of interpretative controversy. None of this speaks in favour of departing from rights as a professional vocabulary. There is no other language (at least no other language *now*) that would do better what rights-language tried to do. Therefore I have joined the critique in chapter 5 with a constructive discussion in chapter 6.

Part IV juxtaposes the operation of international law in 'limit situations' – in the context of crimes against humanity and nuclear weapons – with more routine types of institutional work and legal argument. Chapters 7 and 8 analyse the effect of massive ideological and emotive pressures in the fight against impunity and the debate on nuclear weapons on the legal vocabulary and points to the operation of *power* behind moral indignation and commitment. Chapters 9 and 10 are about power, too, but this time as it appears through the routine use of the law in struggles over jurisdiction to decide. They examine international law as a 'universalisation project' within which particular interests come to seem generally shared and enquire into the possible contribution that law makes in contrast to, say, religion or economics as alternative languages of universalisation.

Part V – The Spirit of International Law – joins together four chapters that turn back to the subject who operates the law and to the specificity of the legal language. What are the emotional consequences of committing to a profession as fragile and uncertain about its premises and effects as international law? How to be professionally conscious of the contested basis of one's professionalism? The essay on 'miserable comforters' reminds us that the grass is no greener on the other side of the academy, however, and just as there is no distinction between international law and politics, there is no significant difference between 'doing' international law or doing international politics, either. The question is always 'how' one does this, with what sense of immersion in or distance from one's vocabulary and its institutional alignments? Based on the Chorley Lecture given at the London School of Economics in 2006, the last chapter was inspired by my participation in the debates on the 'fragmentation of international law', and can be read as a personal assessment of the conditions within which 'the politics of international law' takes place today.

III

Practically all of these chapters have been inspired by the contexts of diplomatic or academic practice in which I have been involved over the years. There is a strong autobiographical aspect to them and no doubt it is possible to see there a certain development – even if the core ideas, outlined schematically in the first two chapters, may not have changed much. Therefore I should really thank all the friends and colleagues who have accompanied me in these debates during two decades, who have heard these chapters as spoken lectures or read and made comments on them after their original publication. The context of 'critical' or 'new approaches' to international law has of course been important, whether their centre has been located at Harvard, London, New York, Paris, Melbourne, Cambridge or – as I like to think – at the Erik Castrén Institute of International Law and Human Rights at the University of Helsinki (ECI). I am grateful for the many friends at those places; without the global context of conversations they have provided, these chapters and this book could never have been written. For this book specifically, I need to thank Emmanuelle Jouannet for her wonderful Introductory Essay, Richard Hart for agreeing to take this book to be published in English, following up on an earlier French version. Many people at ECI have participated in the revision and the technical reproduction of these essays. They include Sanna Villikka, Ilona Nieminen, Johannes-Mikael Mäki and Margareta Klabbers. I thank them all.

Helsinki, February 2011
MK

ACKNOWLEDGEMENTS

The chapters were published in their unamended form as:

Part I: *The Politics of International Law*

1) 'The Politics of International Law' (1990) 1 *European Journal of International Law* 4–32.
2) 'The Politics of International Law. Twenty Years Later' (2009) 20 *European Journal of International Law* 7–19.

Part II: *The Law and Politics of Collective Security*

3) 'The Place of Law in Collective Security' (1996) 17 *Michigan Journal of International Law* 455–90.
4) 'The Lady Doth Protest too Much: Kosovo, and the Turn to Ethics in International Law' (2002) 65 *The Modern Law Review* 159–75.

Part III: *The Politics of Human Rights*

5) 'The Effect of Rights on Political Culture' in Philip Alston (ed), *The European Union and Human Rights* (Oxford University Press, 1999) 99–116.
6) 'Human Rights, Politics, and Love' (2001) *Mennesker & Rettigheter* 4, 33–45.

Part IV: *Limits and Possibilities of International Law*

7) 'Between Impunity and Show Trials' (2002) 6 *Max Planck Yearbook for United Nations Law* 1–36.
8) 'Faith, Identity and the Killing of the Innocent. International Lawyers and Nuclear Weapons' (1997) 10 *Leiden Journal of International Law* 137–62.
9) 'International Law and Hegemony: A Reconfiguration' (2004) 17 *Cambridge Review of International Affairs* 197–218.
10) 'What is International Law For?' in Malcolm D Evans, *International Law* (Oxford University Press, 2003) 89–114 (2nd edn 2006) 57–81.

Part V: *The Spirit of International Law*

11) 'Between Commitment and Cynicism: Outline for a Theory of International Law as Practice' in *Collection of Essays by Legal Advisers of States, Legal Adviser of International Organizations and Practitioners in the field of International Law* (United Nations, NY, 1999) 495–523.

12) 'Letter to the Editors of the Symposium' (1999) 93 *American Journal of International Law* 351–61.
13) 'Miserable Comforters. International Relations as a New Natural Law' (2009) 15 *European Journal of International Relations* 395–422.
14) 'The Fate of International Law. Between Technique and Politics' (2007) 70 *The Modern Law Review* 1–32.

While every care has been taken to establish and acknowledge copyright, and to contact copyright owners, the publishers apologise for any accidental infringement and would be pleased to come to a suitable agreement with the rightful copyright owners in each case.

CONTENTS

Contents

Koskenniemi: A Critical Introduction

E Jouannet

I think international law has a wonderful political and intellectual potential (this is why I am interested in its history) but that it has in the 20th century become – *malgre soi* – a small bureaucratic discipline at law schools. My project is to try to revive a sense of its original mission, its importance. I suspect I am creating a myth (for it probably never was much better) – but myth-creation is an important aspect of political activity and activism.

(Martti Koskenniemi, commenting at a Conference at the Law Faculty of the Sorbonne, February 2004.)

I

MARTTI KOSKENNIEMI IS now well-known throughout the world, not only as a result of his position as the President of the International Law Commission's study group on the fragmentation of international law, but also on the basis of his doctrinal work. Both *From Apology to Utopia*[1] and *The Gentle Civilizer*[2] are truly remarkable intellectual achievements, each exceptionally powerful in its own way, as they have profoundly revolutionised the ways in which we can understand both international legal discourse (*From Apology to Utopia*) and its history (*The Gentle Civilizer*). In doing so, they move from a structuralist approach to one based upon historical narration and contextualisation; a progression driven not by chance, but on the contrary by the desire to clarify the object of our discipline and its effects on the international plane. Koskenniemi has never intended to produce a 'theory of international law'; indeed, he would object to the

---

[1] M Koskenniemi, *From Apology to Utopia; the Structure of International Legal Argument* (1989) (Re-issue with a new Epilogue, Cambridge University Press, 2005) 683. I will refer here to the recently published second edition, which contains an extremely important new epilogue in which the author himself puts his work into perspective and discusses the criticisms that have been made. The first edition, now out of print, was published in 1989 by the Finnish Lawyers' Publishing Company.
[2] M Koskenniemi, *The Gentle Civilizer of Nations: The Rise and Fall of International Law 1870–1960*. Hersch Lauterpacht Memorial Lectures (Cambridge, Cambridge University Press, 2002) 569.

very term itself, as his goal has never been to be perceived as a legal theoretician or philosopher, but rather and above all as an international lawyer addressing other international lawyers. In doing so, he has sought to illustrate the ways in which international legal discourse is articulated, the ways in which it operates, and to illuminate and improve our practice of international law in full awareness of both its limits and its promise.

Indeed, when we read Koskenniemi we, in my view, become the privileged witnesses of an extremely powerful and lucid account of the linguistic and contextual reality of international legal discourse. It is, moreover, an account that is always in motion, undermining itself insofar as it cannot be exempt from the ambiguities and other difficulties that Koskenniemi is constantly seeking to overcome (as is, for example, attested to by the new epilogue to the reissue of *From Apology to Utopia*).[3] Often, we academics, after having staked out our initial arguments, are so inclined to repeat ourselves that we continue, simply restating in another form that which we said at the outset. Yet, if Koskenniemi's thought has remained deeply conditioned by his first book (and by the first of the texts in the present volume), or perhaps more accurately, by the paradigm upon which it was based, we cannot but admire the manner in which he has progressed without ever appearing constrained by any of the frontiers that often limit academic thought. Koskenniemi is an author without frontiers – personal or intellectual – and this, I think, is one of the reasons for his incredible productivity, and for the versatility and innovation of his thought. When we read many of his innumerable works, and the texts collected in this volume, we see that Koskenniemi – who speaks at least four languages – genuinely seems based at the intersection between the three great traditions that formed the three pillars of *The Gentle Civilizer*: the Anglo-Saxon, the German and the French. This intersecting of traditions and familiarity with the work of foreign authors is evident in *From Apology to Utopia*, not merely in the vast range of literature cited, but also in the very reasoning of the book itself. Although this work unquestionably reflects the influence of the Critical Legal Studies (CLS) movement in the United States, it draws, in doing so, directly on the source of French structuralism, borrowing its analytical method from the work of Levi-Strauss; it is thus less influenced by the 'Derridean' strands of CLS so popular in the United States.

That the author is familiar with these three major cultures should not come as a surprise, and can be explained in part by his education in Finland, and in part by his own personal trajectory. At the time, legal education in Finland largely followed the German tradition: Kelsen was, of course, studied; as were Laband, Gerber, Jellinek, Weber and the Frankfurt School. Curiously, however, very little in the way of Anglo-Saxon thought and, of course, even less of French international legal thinking was taught there. It was thus at University that Koskenniemi became immersed in the German jurists, and in the culture of Scandinavian realism dominated by Olivecrona and Ross. The influence of the hard realism of the

---

[3] Koskenniemi, *From Apology to Utopia* (2005) 562–617.

Scandinavians is also perceptible in Koskenniemi's work (he devoted an article to the subject), but he was equally able to make a very firm break with that heritage.[4] He developed a more profound knowledge of the Anglo-Saxon and French legal cultures a little later, during the year he spent at Oxford from 1982–83, and as a result of his work at the Finnish Ministry for Foreign Affairs, which led to him spending some time in France and considerably more in the world of UN multi-lateral diplomacy. During his travels, he discovered in particular the thought of the American critical legal scholars – and above all that of Roberto Unger, and Duncan and David Kennedy – whose direct influence can be seen so strongly in his work.

Through his education, his reading and his travels, Koskenniemi has thus become thoroughly transdisciplinary; and we can see in him an embodiment of the advantages that studying law in a manner free from disciplinary barriers can bring. Koskenniemi's thought is without such barriers, without any intellectual taboos; the different texts collected in this volume show a multi-talented author prepared to venture across all of the different landscapes of the law and its adjacent fields, into which he increasingly interweaves history, literature and the human sciences.

On one reading, a number of his works such as, for example, 'The Lady Doth Protest Too Much: Kosovo, and the Turn to Ethics in International Law' or 'International Law and Hegemony: A Reconfiguration' demonstrate that Koskenniemi has transcended the Anglo-Saxon/Continental cultural divide, and thus also that between realism and formalism: precisely the kinds of classic dichotomies from which he has sought to escape. From this particular perspective, Koskenniemi's work strikes me as unclassifiable; his piece entitled 'Perceptions of Justice: Walls and Bridges between Europe and the United States' (not included in the present volume) illustrates well his knowledge of, attachment to, and critical perspective on these two worlds, European and American, that he knows so well.[5] Thinking of Koskenniemi, I am reminded of what someone once said of Paul Ricoeur: 'he strikes out along ridges'. All of Koskenniemi's thought is located on such 'ridges': exposed to the open air and to multiple horizons, vibrant, strong, fertile, never restricted within its own confines or inward-looking, but on the contrary in constant interrelation with other worlds, other cultures, and other authors.

It would, however, be a mistake to think that by using this interdisciplinarity, these cultural intersections, Koskenniemi would lose himself on these borrowed paths among an increasing range of perspectives and theories. On the contrary, his work rests upon certain fundamental presuppositions through which he has forged his own concepts and practices, following a rigorous method of reasoning that is entirely particular to him. I will return below to certain key themes within these foundations; at this early stage, however, it suffices to note that one of the most notable elements is without doubt the inseparability of theory and practice in his work, as is shown by the numerous concrete examples to which he refers

---

[4] M Koskenniemi, 'Introduction: Alf Ross and Life Beyond Realism' (2003) *European Journal of International Law* 14, 653–59.
[5] M Koskenniemi, 'Perceptions of Justice: Walls and Bridges between Europe and the United States' (2004) *Heidelberg Journal of International Law* 64, 305–14.

throughout the texts collected in this volume. He always seeks to come back to practice – not in order to illustrate some deductive, theoretical argument, but rather to draw out inductively the lessons that can be learned from the practice itself, as he explains in his piece entitled 'Style as Method Letter to the Editors of the Symposium'.[6] This inextricable association between theory and practice, intrinsic to his thought, corresponds to the broader goal that Koskenniemi has chosen to pursue: not, as noted above, the production of a general theory of law, but rather the clarification of practice and discourse of international lawyers – or perhaps more accurately, the discourses and the practices that appear to him simply as different styles that we can adopt depending on circumstance, but by which we are also inevitably constrained.

This association between theory and practice has been further reflected in his working life: a scholar, and now Professor with the University of Helsinki, who has always at the same time been a practitioner. Employed as a legal counsellor in the Department of Foreign Affairs in his home country, he was, as a result of the small size of the legal department, quickly given important responsibilities. In particular, he participated in a number of United Nations Environment Programme (UNEP) working groups, and was for a number of years a member of the Finnish delegation to the Sixth Committee of the UN General Assembly. From 1989–90, including the start of the first Gulf War in Iraq, Finland was a member of the Security Council; and Koskenniemi took away from these years an insider's experience that later informed his article on 'The Place of Law in Collective Security'.[7] He was also a counsellor on legal affairs in his Foreign Ministry, working in a number of different areas, such as relations with the USSR at the time of the dissolution of the Soviet empire,[8] and a Co-Agent of Finland in the Case Concerning Passage Through the Great Belt before the International Court of Justice (he has continued this activity – also pleading for Finland in the recent Kosovo advisory opinion (2009). This constant activity in the service of his country made a lasting impression upon him, and thus something he often reflects upon in his doctrinal writings. This intimate knowledge of, and desire to remain connected to, practice accounts for the fact that Koskenniemi has never approached the study of international law in an external manner, but has always sought to conduct an internal exploration of international legal discourse, be it in terms of its structure, its operation in theory and practice, or its historical development. Here we find another of the strengths of his work. 'Normative' theories of law, international or otherwise, take as their object principles rather than rules or institutions. However, in Koskenniemi's view, the true principles of international law cannot be discovered through some sort of a priori ideological self-justification, but rather within the internal conceptualisation of international legal practice – in the way in which

---

[6] See chapter 12 in this volume.

[7] Chapter 3 in this volume.

[8] Amongst other writings on this experience, see M Koskenniemi et PM Eisemann, *La succession d'Etats : la codification à l'épreuve des faits* (Académie de droit international de La Haye, La Haye, Nijhoff, 2000) 1012 et M Koskenniemi et M Lehto, 'La succession d'Etats dans l'ex-URSS, en ce qui concerne particulièrement les relations avec la Finlande' (1992) AFDI 905–47.

international lawyers conceive of that which they actually do. Thus, in his piece entitled 'Between Commitment and Cynicism: Outline for a Theory of International Law as Practice', he notes that 'International law is what international lawyers do and how they think.'[9]

Moreover, in his essay on 'The Place of Law in Collective Security', Koskenniemi again insists upon the necessity of this internal perspective, denouncing external critiques such as those offered by the more radical Anglo-Saxon realists. For him, the external point of view is completely irrelevant for the decision-makers themselves. It has no comprehension of their situatedness as participants instead of observers in the process – their need to find some language to justify their action in view of concerns that they find relevant for their professional context.[10] Deferring to a strictly internal viewpoint does not, however, signify uncritically accepting and systematising the self-definition of international lawyers and legal institutions in order to render it intelligible. Yet neither is it a case of breaking entirely with this discourse and adopting a purely external perspective, attempting to comprehend it from the outside and totally ignoring the pre-understanding that international lawyers and other relevant actors have of their object and of their discipline: to do so would be to remain entirely unaware of that which imparts all particularity, all specificity to law. Nothing could be further from Koskenniemi's approach. Instead, he occupies a space between these two positions, adopting what François Ost and Michel van de Kerchove have called, following Hart, a 'moderate external point of view' – that is, a perspective that '[takes] account of the point of view internal to law without adopting it', and without seeking to furnish it with its ultimate justification.[11]

His multicultural perspective and his 'moderate external' mode of reasoning aside, is it possible to discern a consistent thread running throughout Koskenniemi's work, notwithstanding the fact that he himself vigorously resists the idea of developing a systematic theory? A priori, the search for such a thread seems ill-fated: having emphasised the richness and the constant movement and innovation of his thought, it might easily be concluded that its originality is to be found not at one but at multiple points. At its core, his work is simultaneously located on a number of different levels, which it can on occasion be somewhat difficult to disentangle: it presents itself as at once an analysis of the discursive practices of international lawyers; as a theory of society and of politics; as a critique of liberalism and of modernity; as a re-interpretation of the history of international law; and even as an analysis of memory and truth. One purpose of the present volume is precisely to bring together the various aspects of this protean oeuvre in order to better grasp both its eclecticism and the full extent of its complexity. Reading the different texts collected here, however, it is possible to gradually discern the connecting thread

---

[9] See chapter 11 in this volume.
[10] See chapter three in this volume.
[11] See M van de Kerchove and F Ost, *Legal System between Order and Disorder* (Oxford, Clarendon Press 1994) 9. Here, as elsewhere, where I used an official translation of a French text for a direct quote, I will cite the English official translation used.

that enables this body of work to retain its structure and coherence across these many and varied fields of investigation. Indeed, it is perhaps even easier to discern this thread in this volume than it is in reading the two major intellectual monuments to which I referred at the outset, *From Apology to Utopia* and *The Gentle Civilizer*: as, leaving aside the obvious differences in form and genre, the general trajectory remains the same whether we are inclined towards his major books or whether we focus instead on his shorter, more accessible studies. The thesis presented in *From Apology to Utopia* is succeeded by that of *The Gentle Civilizer* in order to progress towards a specific horizon; just as the author has selected the articles included in this volume in order to progress towards a particular epilogue. The key decisions of the author are again evident in this volume, and we can see Koskenniemi's work develop in a manner that runs counter to the major trends in contemporary thought: neither positivist nor strictly realist, but structuralist, deconstructivist and anti-liberal.

So much so, indeed, that we might be tempted to suggest that the connecting thread in Koskenniemi's work might be that of rupture itself. His versatile and fertile intellectual trajectory could be presented as constructed around a succession of ruptures: a rupture with dogmatics and with the classic, logical manner of approaching international legal discourse by subjecting it to a deconstructive critique; a rupture with the classical, canonical history of international law, which has been called into question by his particular re-reading of the international legal project; and finally, a rupture with liberalism – the preferred option of the majority within the international legal world – against which he has set himself in favour of a progressive, leftist stance. It would not, it seems to me, be false to present Koskenniemi's trajectory in this manner: he is a committed international lawyer who has developed precisely through his opposition to a number of the traditional – conservative and academic – ways of understanding international law. Nevertheless, it is not this thread that I will focus on here in interpreting his work. Although rupture has certainly been one of the driving forces behind his thought, to me it seems overly reductive to make of the themes of opposition and fracture the connecting threads of his work. To do so would be to suggest that he only defines himself in opposition to dominant existing theories, whereas what he has sought to do has rather been to deconstruct the opposition between these theories and to understand their underlying foundations, in order to shed light both on the 'machinery' of international law and on 'its wonderful potential'. As Christian Descamps has noted, 'deconstruction is not destruction';[12] rather, it is to bring to the surface meanings that the play of language and the structures of thought have hidden or forbidden. We can thus choose another way of interpreting the thought of Koskenniemi: in my view, he has sought less to 'oppose' than to 'make sense', while remaining profoundly critical and thus 'committed'.

---

[12] C Descamps, *Quarante ans de philosophie française* (Paris, Bordas, 2003) 150 [*déconstruire n'est pas détruire*].

To make sense is, according to Ricoeur, a basic aspiration of all human beings; and Koskenniemi makes sense for the world of international law in a series of particularly brilliant steps, in many different ways (including, of course, the application of critical and deconstructive approaches) and constantly confronting the difficulties – practical and theoretical – to which international law gives rise. He 'makes sense' in this regard through his dual insight – that international law is at once a language and a site of politics – and then again through his use of this insight as a basis for commitment. In his major books, as in all of the texts collected in the present volume, Koskenniemi seeks to show that international law is above all a language characterised by a precise grammatical structure. This is the original and foundational point of departure for his entire approach, a condensed version of which is offered in the first article of this volume ('Between Apology and Utopia: The Politics of International Law') and constitutes the basic element of his work without which, in my view, we cannot understand anything that has come since. Law, however, is not only a language for Koskenniemi; international law is also politics. His revelation of the argumentative structure of international legal discourse should not, according to the author himself, create the impression that we are somehow trapped by this underlying structure; rather, it should lead us to the realisation that our very knowledge of the existence of such a structure can free us from ourselves, and prime us for our necessary – yet now lucid and fully understood – return to the politics of international law. Hence the title of the present volume.

II

Koskenniemi's work marks a genuine turning point in our understanding of international law. He is among those rare international lawyers who have managed to truly integrate the linguistic turn into their thought (and thus the work of Saussure, Wittgenstein, Peirce and Austin), also taking into consideration Perelman's theory of legal argumentation, the critical approaches of Foucault in France and the CLS movement in the United States, and the anthropological work of Lévi-Strauss. Drawing on these different sources, on his own impressive erudition and his in-depth professional experience, Koskenniemi succeeds in developing, from the first article in this volume onwards, a thesis that is at once profound, original and provocative: that the discourse of international lawyers corresponds to an argumentative structure from which there is no escape – regardless of the particular vision of international law to which we subscribe. In his view, this discourse oscillates – interminably, necessarily – between two poles of argumentation: the abstract utopianism of the idealists and the power apologism of the realists. It is inescapable because, as he illustrates with numerous examples, the more normative an argument is, the less it can be justified by reference to what actually exists in the world, and thus the more vulnerable it becomes to the charge of utopianism.

Conversely, the more an argument seeks to root itself in concrete reality in order to evade the charge of utopianism, the closer it comes to simply reflecting power and rendering it indistinguishable from the interests of the actors, and thus becoming susceptible to the charge of apologism. Put otherwise, international legal discourse is somehow trapped in between these two opposing yet intersecting poles of argumentation. The constraints inherent in the art of argumentation, in the play of language itself, in effect force each side to defend its viewpoint by borrowing, recurrently and unremittingly, the argumentative premises of the other.[13]

> Following mainstream structuralism, I described international law as a language that was constructed of binary oppositions that represented possible – but contradictory – responses to any international legal problem. I then reduced international legal argument – what it was possible to produce as professionally respectable discourse in the field – to a limited number of 'deep structural' binary oppositions and transformational rules. To this matrix I added a 'deconstructive' technique that enabled me to demonstrate that the apparently dominant term in each binary opposition in fact depended on the secondary term for its meaning or force. For example, the principles of self determination and of *uti possidetis* are at once mutually exclusive and mutually dependent: self-government is only possible within a fixed territory; and the authority of existing power can only be justified by reference to some idea of self-government.[14]

It is this that results in the fundamental indeterminacy of legal argumentation – an indeterminacy that cannot be resolved by reference to law alone. Only a political choice (a politics of law or of rights) can determine a solution. This does not mean that this is necessarily negative or 'bad', or totally arbitrary; and there is an awareness of this in the profession itself, an awareness expressed in the mundane way every doctrine always turns from determinative rules to the search for an 'equitable' solution. For Koskenniemi, this is an everyday demonstration of the profession's silent knowledge that its premises are always political in nature. Koskenniemi's demonstration of this point was both audacious and striking, enabling him to carry out his deconstruction of our major theoretical controversies and of all the dichotomies (positivism/natural law, consent/justice, autonomy/community, etc) that have long haunted our disciplinary repertoire, as all of these dichotomies are at once logically opposed and inevitably interlinked, and no solution thereto can have any decidable legal foundation. This deconstruction is itself based upon a structural – as opposed to a causal or logical – explanation of international legal discourse, within which we find the analytical frameworks that are fundamental to Koskenniemi's thought: the theme of identity-opposition within international legal discourse; the indeterminacy of norms and their formal predictability; the reversibility of arguments and the instability of the positions they support; and finally the inevitable and necessary reliance of each position upon its apparent opposite.[15]

---

[13] This argument is developed in the first of the texts collected in this volume, 'Between Apology and Utopia: The Politics of International Law', which is itself a condensed reworking of his major work cited above, Koskenniemi *From Apology to Utopia* (2005).

[14] See chapter 12 in this volume.

[15] See chapter one in this volume.

Clearly, such an approach to law is not common in Europe, despite the fact that the specificity of legal language, the indeterminacy of norms and the related problem of interpretation have become staples of international legal thought. Neither, however, is it so common to be 'banal' in other settings. The strength of this understanding of international law as a language lies in its ability to integrate that which is commonly referred to today as the 'linguistic turn', whilst also drawing on the contribution of the American CLS movement and the work of the French structuralists. The profound originality of Koskenniemi's work lies in his illumination of the underlying 'structure' of the discourse of international lawyers, whether they be academics or practitioners, and of the indeterminacy that results, ad infinitum, from that structure.

It is useful, in order to better understand both the origin and the impact of Koskenniemi's work, to recount briefly the characteristics of linguistics and structuralism and the contribution that they made to his thought. What is meant, first of all, by the term 'linguistic turn'? It is not simply an approach that understands law as a particular language (an old idea, established at least since Savigny), but rather one that seeks to explore in a more decisive fashion the relation between language and thought,[16] and the 'power of words';[17] to insist of the impact of language upon thought and upon social practices such as law. Since Saussure, contemporary linguistic theory has demonstrated that individuals are constrained by their languages and discourses, which form arbitrary and autonomous systems from which there is no escape. Language is not, however, merely a system of signs; it is also a social activity. This social dimension was emphasised above all in the work of Wittgenstein, who described the 'pragmatic' dimension of language (*Philosophical Investigations*, 1936–49).[18] Drawing on this pragmatic, social dimension of language, Wittgenstein introduced the notion of 'language-games' in order to illustrate the irreducibility of every discursive practice: each type of discourse refers back to a (social, historical, collective) practice that has its own rules and its own specific grammar. These language-games are social facts constructed upon implicit conventions. The pragmatic dimension of language also helps us to understand, thanks to the works of authors such as JL Austin, that our legal-linguistic utterances are not simply descriptive propositions, but also actions. Austin's famous book, *How To Do Things With Words*,[19] showed that when we formulate a legal argument, we are performing an act, an action; and that these acts, these actions, produce certain effects. The 'linguistic turn' also reminds us, in particular through the play of argumentation, that language is dialogue, and that dialogue is unique to humans. Language for humans is not, as it is for animals, a simple tool of communication; rather, it is that which gives individuals the capacity to think and to represent. To speak is to formulate ideas, and to accept that these are exposed to criticism. Thus, it is also to foresee objections and to test the

---

[16] D Nicolet, *Lire Wittgenstein. Etude pour une reconstruction fictive* (Paris, Aubier, 1989) 21.
[17] *La pratique de la philosophie* (Paris, Hatier, 2000) 120.
[18] L Wittgenstein, *Philosophical Investigations* (New York, Macmillan, 1953).
[19] JL Austin, *How To Do Things With Words*, 2nd edn (Oxford, Oxford University Press, 1976).

strength of our arguments. Of course, Plato had already stressed above all else the importance of dialogue; however, the contemporary linguistic turn constituted a powerful reintroduction of this dialogic and discursive dimension, which is constitutive of the human being.

With Saussure, writing at the beginning of the twentieth century (*Course in General Linguistics*,[20] 1907–11), the linguistic turn was simultaneously structuralist. Language was thus conceived as a system of signs in which each is defined not in isolation but in relation to the others: the meaning of each is determined by its position in the system as a whole.[21] Put otherwise, the whole – the structure – prevails over each individual element. The structuralist element of the discourse would later be contested, but it nevertheless altered to a degree our understanding of the language of law. While, previously, mastery of this language had conveniently represented the implicit possibility of rational discussion on the law, today it has come to signify equally that which eludes such a discussion. It signifies that which is inherent to the language of law in its social usage – which cannot be altered at will by individuals, politicians or international lawyers – but also that which ensnares them in the play of argument and counter-argument. It is, in any event, amusing to note here the intellectual detour taken by Koskenniemi in integrating structuralism into the language of international law, as he first came to structuralist analysis through the anthropological work of Lévi-Strauss and not that of the linguists.[22] In many ways, this provides a further reason for the link between the structure of language and the analysis of a particular social group – in this case, international lawyers – in Koskenniemi's work, even if the analysis of that group in a given context ultimately led him to move in a certain sense beyond a structuralist analysis.

All of this forms a particularly rich theoretical background to Koskenniemi's work on the discourse of international lawyers: it presents us above all with international law as both discourse and as social fact, as a particular language-game whose grammar he uncovers for us (in particular in the first text in the present volume). It is important, however, to understand precisely what the result of Koskenniemi's discourse-based critique is: it has an extremely powerful unmasking effect, which has not always been appreciated due to the fact that his critique is situated at the level of the structure of the discourse itself, and not that of the indeterminacy of norms or the ambivalence of words.[23] Indeed, Koskenniemi has often been accused of exaggerating the indeterminate nature of rules or legal

---

[20] F de Saussure, *Cours de linguistique générale*, edited by C Bally and A Sechehaye (Lausanne and Paris, Payot, 1916); translated by W Baskin, *Course in General Linguistics* (Glasgow, Fontana/Collins, 1977).

[21] ibid 431 [*conçue comme un système de signes se définissant les uns par rapport aux autres et non pas isolément : le sens d'un élément est déterminant par sa position dans l'ensemble du système*].

[22] Levi-Strauss himself borrowed his method of structuralist analysis from linguistics, granting primacy to the system over its various different elements and revealing in this manner the permanence of a certain type of arrangement of human relations.

[23] See Koskenniemi *From Apology to Utopia* (2005) 590, where Koskenniemi sets out all of the distinctions that follow.

terminology, even though his analysis is not primarily concerned with that issue, but rather is situated at an even more fundamental level. Put simply, legal norms might be absolutely 'clear', but they would nonetheless remain – always and inevitably – imprisoned within the structure created by the play of legal argumentation; a structure that renders them interdependent, and within which each is defined not in isolation but in relation to the others. Koskenniemi often takes the example of the play of restrictive and expansive interpretations of rules (which in turn decide which cases are and are not included within the rule in question), or that of the rule and the exception, as in both of these configurations each position necessarily refers to its opposite. When we are confronted by dramatic cases (such as the prohibition on the use of nuclear weapons) that pose the problem of the 'unthinkable exception' par excellence, and that thus seem to imply an absolute prohibition defined in its own terms and not in relation to other rules, our only option is to move beyond the play of legal language altogether – as demonstrated well by Koskenniemi in his analysis of the 'silence' of the International Court of Justice in the Nuclear Weapons advisory opinion ('Faith, Identity and the Killing of the Innocent: International Lawyers and Nuclear Weapons').[24] It is thus above all important not to mistake structuralist deconstruction of legal argumentation for, or to confuse it with, the classical question of the indeterminacy of norms or the problem of interpretation; Koskenniemi's work, even if it analyses the configuration of norms through the play of issues such as exception and inclusion, is simply not situated at that level. Rather, it is the relations between norms (and doctrines and principles) that are fundamental, and that together constitute the 'structure' of international legal discourse, not the individual elements thereof (norms, doctrines, principles) taken in isolation. There is thus stability to this 'highly formal and predictable' structure of relations, which forms across the great fluidity of possible arguments and positions.

Having shown this, however, Koskenniemi goes even further still as, in uncovering the structure of international legal discourse, he is able to deduce the general indeterminacy of the play of argumentation in law (which is different from the question of the indeterminacy of norms) – that is, the impossibility of resolving controversies on the basis of law alone, due to the way in which relations between the different norms, principles and doctrines are structured. It is important, in this regard, to read the new epilogue to *From Apology to Utopia*, in which Koskenniemi discusses in detailed and illuminating fashion what he calls 'the nature of indeterminacy'.[25] If this general indeterminacy is not the same as the issue of the indeterminacy of norms then it stems from the structure of the language; and yet it does not necessarily imply the indeterminacy of actual experience, or the unpredictability of solutions to particular controversies. Controversies are resolved every day; judicial decisions are handed down, following methodologies and modes of justification that are predictable to all those who have mastered the

---

[24] See chapter eight in this volume.
[25] Koskenniemi *From Apology to Utopia* (2005).

language of international law and who are familiar with the institutional practices and the players involved. Put simply, the solutions adopted and decisions taken no longer find their ultimate justification in the formal language of law; rather, they belong to the actual world of politics – which is that of determination and commitment, just as it is that of manipulation and exploitation.

This possibility of concluding legal debate and finding a solution by means of a political choice moves us from a pure linguistic structuralism to a theory of political action and of freedom, the seeds of which were already present in *From Apology to Utopia* but which were developed in more detail in his subsequent works.

III

The fact that international law is a specific social discursive practice, imbued with its own structure, leads Koskenniemi to draw a number of conclusions that are in fact quite far removed from radical structuralism, and demonstrate rather his affiliation with both the US CLS movement and with the Frankfurt School.[26] There is thus a second fundamental thesis developed in *From Apology to Utopia* (and in the first of the texts collected in the present volume), which is intimately related to, but ultimately moves beyond, the structuralist thesis, as it is situated at a different level than that of structural analysis: the critical exposure of the effects of political liberalism on international law. According to Koskenniemi, 'international law reproduces the paradoxes and ambivalences of a liberal theory of politics'.[27]

Liberal thought, which was born almost at the same time as international law itself, has constantly sought to defend the idea of the primacy of law over politics, in order to neutralise 'the passions' and to allow for conciliation between the different subjective values held by the members of international society. It has taken different forms, from natural law to positivism, objectivism to subjectivism, formalism to realism; it has left its mark on the different conceptions of sources and rules that we have inherited today; yet it has always sought to maintain the ideal of the primacy of law over politics.[28] The desire to do so has, however, a considerable perverse effect: it has masked the inevitable social and political conflicts that are the very heart of the international sphere, necessary to its evolution.

> In this article, however, I shall extend the criticism of the liberal idea of the Rechtstaat, a commonplace in late modern western society, into its international counterpart. I shall

---

[26] The Frankfurt School brought together, from 1923 onwards, at the Institute for Social Research in Frankfurt, a whole group of major German thinkers who tasked themselves with renewing Marxist analyses of society and denouncing all contemporary forms of totalitarian domination, including Max Horkheimer, Walter Benjamin, Theodor Adorno and Herbert Marcuse. Jürgen Habermas is the best known representative of the 'second generation' of this School, and has given it a less Marxist turn.

[27] Koskenniemi *From Apology to Utopia* (2005) xiii.

[28] See chapter one of this volume.

attempt to show that our inherited ideal of a World Order based on the Rule of Law thinly hides from sight the fact that social conflict must still be solved by political means and that even though there may exist a common legal rhetoric among international lawyers, that rhetoric must, for reasons internal to the ideal itself, rely on essentially contested - political - principles to justify outcomes to international disputes.[29]

In this way, the link between Koskenniemi's two theses – that is, between his account of the language of international law as imbued with a highly determinate argumentative structure and his political critique of liberalism – is immediately clear: in bringing the argumentative structure of international legal discourse to the fore, he was able to show that the idea of the primacy of law over politics is pure illusion. In effect, no legal theory, norm or principle is ever capable of furnishing the means of its own justification: the argumentative structure of the discourse renders each and every position fundamentally undecidable. The ultimate determination of the 'best' argument is never grounded upon purely legal criteria alone, but is rather inevitably made on the basis of an underlying political choice – to the extent that the political neutrality sought by liberal internationalism since the inception of modern international law is a mere delusion, profoundly harmful in as much as it encourages the supremacy of experts and bureaucrats to the detriment of genuine political decision-making. Koskenniemi's goal has thus been to demonstrate the importance of politics within international law, and to rehabilitate the former at the expense of the so-called 'neutrality of law' and the liberal idea of the primacy of law. He has also been concerned to expose the hegemonic political project at work behind the strategies of universalisation of international law. An echo of this point, which is distinct from the simple rehabilitation of the political moment in law, can also be found in the work of Lévi-Strauss who, in the aftermath of the two World Wars and the Vichy regime, had extremely good reasons for doubting international law, and for his belief that the much-vaunted universalism of law and of values represented an excellent means of masking ethnocentrism and Western colonialism (*Tristes Tropiques*, 1955).[30]

This double focus (on language and politics) which constitutes, in fact, a single, two-sided thesis has been the subject of innumerable commentaries, such is the richness, strength and originality of the manner in which it brings together the critique of political liberalism and the structuration of international legal discourse.[31] It is also, however, a deeply provocative approach, as that which Koskenniemi refers to as 'liberalism' in international law covers the positions of the vast majority of international lawyers. As noted above, political liberalism in Koskenniemi's work corresponds in effect to a very broad idea of the primacy of law over politics, and over the subjective values of states. In fact, Koskenniemi at this point picks up arguments advanced by authors such as Roberto Unger and

---

[29] ibid.

[30] C Lévi-Strauss, *Tristes tropiques* (New York, Penguin, 1992 [1955]).

[31] See, eg the essays in 'Special Issue: Marking Re-Publication of From Apology to Utopia' (2006) 7 *German Law Journal* 977–1108.

Timothy O'Hagan,[32] developed in the context of domestic civil societies dominated by political liberalism, and makes them his own, transposing them to international society, and integrating them into the contemporary movement within both domestic and international society towards 'contextual justice' (the balancing of interests, appeals to notions of equity, etc) in which outcomes are not predetermined by rules. On this point, Koskenniemi's position has been subjected to inevitable criticism – even from within the international legal realist current in the United States – as he does not claim that international law, in the final instance, boils down to the political interests of states; rather, he refutes the idea that a solution founded upon law alone can exist. There is thus a radical element to his critique, which will be rejected or accepted depending upon each individual's own particular perceptions of the international legal project and of international law.

In any event, it would be a mistake to think that this claim implies a devalorisation of law that brings Koskenniemi's position closer to that of the Anglo-Saxon realist international relations specialists, some of the more radical deconstructionists or certain orthodox continental Marxist thinkers. There is, of course, a realist underpinning to his conception, the origins of which can be attributed to the influence of the CLS movement, and perhaps Scandinavian realism, too; however, his critique of liberalism, and the rehabilitation of the political that he advocates with regard to the ultimate choice that must be made in adopting any given position, are not made at the expense of international law, but rather in order to give back to each – to law and to politics – its particular role and purpose.

> A better metaphor than pigeon-holing for the law/politics relationship might refer to the contemplation of a landscape. In the morning, we see the colours of the trees and the reflection of the leaves on the water; in the evening, we notice the outline of the cliffs against the grey sky, and the shadow of the forest stretches far into the sea. The landscape is the same, the messages it conveys are different. The images are equally self-contained and full. We can reproduce both separately, but we cannot mix them. Likewise, law and politics seemed coherent and separate, yet related to one single reality.[33]

In doing so, Koskenniemi has also sought to illustrate at what points law and politics are consubstantial, intrinsically linked to each other like the two opposing faces of Janus, and how ignorance of this link can explain the trends towards bureaucratisation and technocratisation that he decries, along with the political liberalism that produces them. This is particularly evident when we read his two articles on human rights. The first of these ('The Effect of Rights on Political Culture')[34] seeks to criticise, in a manner typical of CLS scholarship (but also close to that of the Frankfurt School), the technocratic banalisation of human rights discourse and the perverse effects of this, while the second ('Human Rights,

---

[32] RM Unger, *Law in Modern Society: Toward a Criticism of Social Theory* (New York, Londres, Free Press, Collier Macmillan, 1976) 309; T O'Hagan, *The End of Law?* (Oxford, Blackwell, 1984) 183.

[33] See chapter three in this volume.

[34] See chapter five in this volume.

Politics and Love')[35] sets out in a much more optimistic fashion the ways in which rights and politics can, in the metaphor of the impossibility of love, be brought together. His critical, deconstructive approach enables him to expose the subjective presuppositions and the extent of the political powers exercised by the legal authorities, in particular judges, that lie beyond the apparent impartiality and neutrality of rights discourse; yet his own position leads him to equally emphasise the necessary and positive character of that discourse.

The denunciation of political liberalism within international law also reflects one possible principle driving the evolution of Koskenniemi's thought since *From Apology to Utopia*, a more complex development than can be accounted for by structuralism alone. The discourse is not self-contained, it is not only structure; international law cannot be analysed as a language alone. It is also a set of utterances that produce social effects; it is an instrument that can be manipulated; and it is a practice that can be the bearer of much promise. It is not only a language; it is also a discourse. It is a politics every bit as much as it is a language; and this political dimension opens up new perspectives that become, for Koskenniemi, new fields of investigation. Law is politics just as law is culture; law is alive. It is not the metaphor of the game, so commonly used today, that is appropriate to describe the manner in which Koskenniemi conceives of international law; rather, it is without doubt – as his works make clear – the old metaphor of the 'tongue' that is best suited to this task; a tongue by now moulded by many centuries of culture, religion and history; a common tongue, constructed progressively, that has enriched other domains even as it has sombrely colonised them. Law belongs to the realm of the tongue, of lived experience, of history. To compare it to a game or to a system of rules, or even to a set of networks would without doubt appear reductionist to Koskenniemi, as it would be to ignore that in law which goes beyond the rules and the systems, beyond the networks, beyond the instruments used.

As the author himself explains in his new epilogue to the re-edition of *From Apology to Utopia*, the grammar that he revealed through his analysis of the linguistic structure of international legal discourse remains a given for him; it is that which he now refers to as 'the condition of possibility of international law', without which international law would cease to be itself and become something fundamentally different. However, we might also think that, since the publication of *From Apology to Utopia*, Koskenniemi has moved from a sort of 'optimistic structuralism' (corresponding symbolically to the more optimistic nature of international relations during the 1990s, when he wrote that book) towards a sharper awareness of the limitations of this type of analysis in allowing him to develop a more pronounced contextualism, at once historical and social. He has refused to allow himself to become locked within an ahistorical perspective of the sort that his structural analysis of international legal discourse could readily lead to, and to reduce the meaning of international law to the mere practice of combining different arguments. It is this that led him to show, in a more precise and altogether remarkable manner,

---

[35] See chapter six in this volume.

the limits of our discourse on death in, for example, 'Faith, Identity and the Killing of the Innocent: International Lawyers and Nuclear Weapons'[36], with regard to the Opinion of the International Court of Justice on the use of nuclear weapons. These limits are discussed again in different contexts: for example, when the discourse on death becomes judicial and aspires to historical truth, as it did in the Milosevic case (see 'Between Impunity and Show-Trials')[37]; when it becomes banalised in the context of human rights (see 'The Effect of Rights on Political Culture')[38]; or when it ignores the dramatically unequal realities of international society (see 'International Law and Hegemony: A Reconfiguration').[39] These considerations have also led Koskenniemi to study in an in-depth (and internal) fashion the different discursive practices and behaviour of different types of international lawyer, as the play of argumentation only derives its sense from the perspectives of the actors immersed within their practices and cultures ('Between Commitment and Cynicism: Outline for a Theory of International Law as Practice'). The behaviour of the international lawyer, whether the lawyer is a legal advisor, a human rights advocate, a judge or an academic, is conditioned both by the lawyer's social and cultural environment and by the discursive structure of the activity that the lawyer conducts.

It is also for this reason that Koskenniemi has sought to define the various methodological approaches to international law as different 'styles' that are valid according to the specific contexts within which they are adopted. None (formalism, realism, feminism, third-worldism, etc) is 'correct', because all methodological approaches to international law are dependent upon a particular context:

> It was a merit of this theory, however, that it demonstrated that to achieve these strategic goals, the contexts of legal practice offered many different styles of argument. It was sometimes useful to argue as a strict positivist, fixing the law on a treaty interpretation. At other times it was better to conduct an instrumentalist analysis of the consequences of alternative ways of action – while at yet other times moral pathos seemed appropriate. Each of these styles – or 'methods' in the language of this symposium – was open-ended in itself, amenable to the defense of whatever position one needed to defend. None of them, however, gave the comfort of allowing the lawyer to set aside her 'politics', her subjective fears and passions. On the contrary, to what use they were put depended in some crucial way precisely on those fears and passions.[40]

Put simply, this means that we move beyond the analysis of international legal language as a structural system in order resituate that language within a precise historical, cultural or social context that also imbues it with meaning; with the consequence that the active will of the international lawyer ultimately prevails over the linguistic structure. Just as *From Apology to Utopia* was followed by *The Gentle Civilizer*, the texts presented in this volume follow this same guiding thread.

---

[36] See chapter eight in this volume.
[37] See chapter seven in this volume.
[38] See chapter five in this volume.
[39] See chapter nine in this volume.
[40] See chapter 12 in this volume at 299.

Meaning is no longer sought simply through an exposition of the grammar of international legal language, but rather through an understanding of this language as a discourse addressed by some individuals to others in specific and unique circumstances. Put otherwise, the meaning of an utterance is not produced by the structure of the relations between signs alone, the meaning of any given dialogue is not the product of the play of developed argumentation alone; rather, these result from the intention – or if not indeed a conscious 'will', then at least an externally conditioned 'intent' of the speaker – with reference to the historical, economic and social reality within which the speaker is situated. It is important to understand, however, that Koskenniemi is not here calling into question the argumentative structure that he unmasked previously; he is, on the contrary, continuing to pursue, in different ways, the same project set out in *From Apology to Utopia* – a project that developed and matured in the course of his subsequent texts. Since *From Apology to Utopia*, Koskenniemi has time and again drawn attention to irreconcilable disagreements (as, for example, in 'The Lady Doth Protest Too Much' and in 'Perceptions of Justice')[41]; his goal, however, has not been to reduce the tension between these opposing poles, but rather to show that this very tension is constitutive of the discourse and practice of international lawyers. In doing so, he seeks to show that although we present our theories and our arguments as being indissolubly tied to one single perspective, they in fact draw their strength from confrontation with opposing theories and arguments – to which they are thus inextricably linked. Yet from the moment that this has been successfully shown, the polemics to which they give rise become of little interest, as both poles of argumentation are at once true and false. This is not, for all that, mere empty rhetoric, as it remains decisive within and constitutive of international law. However, because these theories and arguments, these rules and principles, remain indeterminate, devoid of any ultimate, rational foundation in law, it is necessary to move onto the terrain not only of politics, but also of history, society and culture. It is these terrains that can impart some consistency to different arguments, and enable us to make a choice between them.

It is in this manner, therefore, that we can understand the general evolution of Koskenniemi's thought between *From Apology to Utopia* and *The Gentle Civilizer*: after having uncovered the argumentative structure of international legal discourse in the former, he then proceeds, in the latter, to situate that discourse in its historical context. And while, in *From Apology to Utopia*, he had in a certain manner demonstrated the exhaustion of the discourse (its 'end' in the philosophical sense of the term), in *The Gentle Civilizer* he detailed the exhaustion and the failure of the international legal project – understood as a liberal, humanist project born in the nineteenth century with the first great professionals of the discipline – itself. The act of re-situating international law within its liberal and history has enabled Koskenniemi to shed light on the hopes and the errors to which it has given rise up until the present day; a point in time at which, in his view, a

---

[41] See chapter four.

pragmatic and technocratic culture – detrimental to any project of advancing emancipation through law – has come to dominate. Despite this, however, Koskenniemi lapses neither into cynicism nor into disenchanted detachment with regard to his discipline and its object. This is the last general characteristic that I want to underline here: that his is a 'committed' approach to international law.

IV

Koskenniemi's critical analyses have not led him to the cynicism practiced by certain Anglo-Saxon realists; neither, however, have they led him to the neutrality of the more continental formalist jurists, nor to militant activism. He does, on occasion, adopt a sceptical perspective; but only as a barrier against dogmatism, not as a definitive suspension of judgment. For me, the sense that ultimately emerges from Koskenniemi's work is that of a positive, if profoundly critical, commitment; a commitment towards a new 'politics of international law'. The author himself has written a brilliant study, contained in the present volume, on commitment and cynicism in international law as two intrinsically linked professional attitudes within the international legal field ('Between Commitment and Cynicism: Outline for a Theory of International Law as Practice'):[42]

> In this chapter I want to argue, however, that no middle position is available; that to practice international law is to work within both strands of tradition: a sentimental attachment to the field's constitutive rhetoric and traditions, an attachment that I like to call 'commitment', and a pervasive and professionally engrained doubt about the profession's marginality, or even the identity of one's profession, the suspicion of its being 'just politics' after all, a doubt that I will call 'cynicism'.[43]

In this piece, he analyses the social activity of international lawyers, drawing on the notion of 'field' developed and used by the French sociologist Pierre Bourdieu in order to characterise the practices specific to different sectors of activity that result from the social division of labour. Individuals (agents) within these sectors consider as self-evident the interests and issues specific to their own 'field', despite the fact that they might be of no interest whatsoever to those in another. These very individuals are at once interdependent and in competition with each other within their own field in defining the legitimate contours of that field. Drawing on this idea, Koskenniemi was able to describe the two attitudes of commitment and cynicism as the two basic dispositions of all those working in the field of international law. In any event, his own theoretical presuppositions lead him here to a more general form of commitment, as an author who makes choices, who takes up direct positions on the most fundamental issues of our time, and who rejects the

---

[42] See chapter 11 in this volume.
[43] ibid 272.

illusion of positivist neutrality. It is a commitment against the 'non-committal legal rationality'[44] that, in his view, characterises contemporary international law.

How best to precisely define this commitment? A non-conformist both as an intellectual and as an international lawyer, Koskenniemi above all rejected the hermeneutics that he had been taught while at the same time setting himself against the tide of positivist and liberal thought dominant in international law – often provoking, perhaps predictably, some lively reactions against his position. Yet he has on each occasion put forward his case, calling for a renewal of the political within international law and denouncing the false axiological neutrality of legal discourse espoused by liberalism and positivism; calling for the rejection of the ventures into technocratic governance to which, in his view, strict positivism and strict realism both lead; and challenging the banalisation of particular discourses on law, either the all-too-comfortable closure offered by legal formalism or the hegemonic manipulation to which the pragmatism of the powerful leads.

There can be no doubt that, for Koskenniemi, this aspect is absolutely fundamental; both the necessity and the nature of this commitment can be readily observed running throughout his entire oeuvre. The theoretical elements of his thought rest upon a set of strong, pre-existing convictions that function as a sort of motive, underpinning and directing both his practical action and his theoretical work. Two elements thus remain constant in his work: the fact that the international sphere is profoundly unjust in its distribution of wealth and power; and the fact that international law alone cannot remedy this, as it is itself part of the problem. We too often think of international law as a means of prohibiting certain forms of behaviour, forgetting that, as a result of its discursive structure, it can also, and perhaps above all allow, authorise and legitimise any type of behaviour: each state, each tyrant, each economic actor in a position of power can find in international law the legitimation of their public policies or private interests. Each of them can turn to the opinions of legal advisors, enabling them, through the play of rules and of argumentation, to provide their positions with an aura of legal respectability. Hence the necessity to move beyond the framework offered by the legal discourse of the law, to move beyond the strictly 'legal' sphere, in order to take the struggle to the realm of politics, which alone renders us capable of founding a commitment, of taking a decision, and of fighting against injustice.

As all of the texts collected in the present volume attest, the vitality of Koskenniemi's thought has been harnessed in service of this type of commitment; a commitment that nevertheless remains essentially critical in nature, based upon a very precise analysis of our discursive practices (Koskenniemi is an author who seems to prefer describing international legal practice to reimagining or reinventing the whole field). Nor does he display the moralism of certain militants, who so often confuse morals with politics. To advocate for politics is not necessarily to

---

[44] To paraphrase H Albert, *La sociologie critique en question* (Paris, PUF, 1987) [*rationalité juridique sans engagement*].

advocate for 'the good'. Where this distinction is elided, it is perhaps too easy to arrive at a clear conscience or feelings of righteous indignation; whereas acceptance of the political is also to accept its violence, its flaws and thus also a certain amorality. Moreover, as Raymond Aron emphasised, in limiting ourselves to moral discourse we can avoid compromising ourselves with the political – but only at the cost of remaining ineffectual in the world. Koskenniemi constantly decries the faults of the international sphere, the profound rift between a powerful periphery and a centre that grows ever more impoverished. An expert on Marxism and sympathetic to the Frankfurt School,[45] he conceives of law as always profoundly anchored within an international social practice, the terrible inequality of which he never ceases to denounce, even if he subscribes neither to the Marxist logic of dialectical materialism nor to the project of the Frankfurt School, which would without doubt appear to him to be too rationalistic. Yet there is also something nostalgic about this commitment, a nostalgia that draws strength from his intimate knowledge of the history of international law, and of that period in the nineteenth century during which a small group of liberal, humanist internationalists embraced the ideals of an internationalist faith, without at that time understanding the negative consequences that this faith could lead to, or the fact that it already contained the seeds of its own destruction. *The Gentle Civilizer* is a brilliant and penetrating description of the slow decay of a dream, on the basis of which the author offers us a reflection on law, politics and history within the field of international law; a reflection that implicitly informed the texts that followed the publication of this second major work.

What, however, is the path proposed by Koskenniemi today? In order to discern this, it is necessary to return to the different conclusions that punctuate his various studies, and in which we find something that recalls the 'tragic optimism' of Sartre. Koskenniemi does not believe in either the capacity of reason to provide us with ultimate foundations, or in the Kantian ideal of peace through law – meaning that our lived experience is necessarily that of anxiety, uncertainty and incompletion:

> History provides little support for the belief that revolution or happiness could survive the first moments of enthusiastic bliss. The morning after is cold, and certain to come. And as we pick up the pieces of yesterday's commitment, we might perhaps fight tomorrow's cynicism by taking ourselves lightly, for a change.[46]

At the same time, the existential background to Koskenniemi's work lends a certain optimism to his latest writings, born from the conviction that individual freedom can be an act of creation, of rupture with the conditions in which we find ourselves; that freedom itself consists in the acts for which we are all – as international lawyers, men, women, victims and perpetrators – absolutely responsible.

---

[45] For Koskenniemi's position on Marx, see 'What Should International Lawyers Learn from Karl Marx?' (2004) *Leiden Journal of International Law* 17, 229–46; and in terms of his work closest to a critical social science perspective, see his article inspired by the work of Herbert Marcuse entitled 'Legitimacy, Rights and Ideology: Notes towards a Critique of the New Moral Internationalism' (2003) *Associations. Journal for Legal and Social Theory* 349–74.

[46] See chapter 11 in this volume at 293.

There is, ultimately, nothing else upon which we can genuinely count; yet, if this freedom is a goal, a commitment, it must be exercised with lucidity and, with regard to international lawyers, with a better understanding of the law for which we are striving, of the discipline within which we evolve, and of the international world within which we are situated. This implies, for Koskenniemi, not only a culture of politics and of responsibility, but also a culture of formalism. Although the latter may seem surprising, the author, in presenting liberty as the solution, evidently does not intend, in the manner of the more extreme forms of realism, to give free rein to the freedom of the strong against the weak; he thus ultimately returns to the formal barriers that the law can set up against this. It would thus be an error to conclude that Koskenniemi rehabilitates politics in order to dissolve the formal specificity of law. Indeed, it is for precisely this dissolution of law in politics that he criticises realist and instrumentalist approaches in his piece entitled 'The Place of Law in Collective Security', which contains a concrete and internal – and extremely convincing – demonstration of the specificity of the sophisticated, formal and normative language of law. Although he might appear very Kelsenian from this perspective, he is in fact even closer to the position of Max Weber in his concern to preserve the specificity of the object of his discipline and to maintain the distinction between legal and natural facts.

> That the United Nations has dealt with the humanitarian crisis in Bosnia in an insufficiently effective manner because the resources, interests, or policies of the great powers have militated against full-scale involvement may or may not be true. But its truth or falsity is not a sufficient response to the question of whether the United Nations has been justified in acting in the way it has, or what might be the right course of action to proceed in the future.[47]

Of course, Koskenniemi is not seeking here to defend a formalism whose goal is neutrality, masking political choices and conflicts; he is not proposing a positivistic formalism, but rather a committed, political and cultural formalism:

> Because formalism is precisely about setting limits to the impulses – "moral" or not – of those in decision-making positions in order to fulfil general, instead of particular interests; and because it recognises the claims made by other members of that community and creates the expectation that they will be taken account of. Of course, the door to a formalism that would determine the substance of political outcomes is no longer open. There is no neutral terrain. But against the particularity of the ethical decision, formalism constitutes a *horizon* of universality, embedded in a *culture* of restraint, a *commitment* to listening to others claims and seeking to take them into account.[48]

The result is that international law becomes an unsurpassable horizon in Koskenniemi's work; not only as a highly formal common language but also as a potential site of emancipatory struggles and of individual recognition.

---

[47] See chapter three in this volume at 94.
[48] See chapter four in this volume. The culture of formalism receives a fuller discussion in Koskenniemi, *The Gentle Civilizer of Nations* (2002) 494–509.

V.

Clearly, therefore, Koskenniemi is a 'committed' international lawyer, with his own personal method of exploring international law that he brings to bear on all of the fundamental themes of our discipline, very often placing him in the vanguard of debates. As a result, however, he inevitably finds himself more intellectually exposed than others, and his thought gives rise to some important further questions. Despite their exceptional force, Koskenniemi's arguments are not themselves free from difficulties, ambiguities even, of their own. Here, I want to briefly outline a number of these, before concluding with some reflections on the 'conditions of possibility' of his own discourse.

We might note from the outset, as others have done, that Koskenniemi seems on occasion to deliberately caricature opposing theories, presenting their positions in absolutist terms in order to make the task of critiquing them easier. This was the criticism levelled at him by, for example, Philip Alston, in the context of his presentation of human rights as 'trumps', and by Pierre-Marie Dupuy in response to his analysis of the European tradition of international law.[49] Koskenniemi is, of course, perfectly capable of putting across ideas that are foreign to him and formulating his own critical observations; it is, however, true that, on occasion, he does appear to resort deliberately to somewhat reductive polemics or to the use of irony in a manner intended to disconcert. The difficulty here lies less in the resort to polemics itself (which can, in fact, be greatly beneficial insofar as it provokes genuine reflection) than it does in the actual tenor of his discourse. Reliance upon caricature can lead to distorted conclusions, or cause the author to fall into the trap of reductionism.

Yet, a priori, Koskenniemi appears profoundly opposed to all reductionism: he never seeks to minimise positions, rules or institutions, or to reduce their contradictions, but rather to simply take full account of their tensions as a constitutive fact of international law. It is worth recalling also that his aim is above all to help those who specialise in our discipline to better conceptualise and structure their arguments through unmasking the internal structure and the historically-situated nature of their discourse. In this sense, he remains very close to the approach adopted by Wittgenstein, insofar as he understands his theoretical activity as simply a practice of problem-clarification and leaves entirely to one side any extravagant pretensions to resolving foundational problems. To leave problems to one side is not, however, to resolve them; and, if dealt with in this manner, they can subsequently reappear indirectly. Here I want to set out explicitly some of the issues that Koskenniemi omits from consideration; issues that can give rise to much debate. The strength of his claims is remarkable; yet, on occasion, his vision of law, of rationality, and of methodology can appear too narrow, or apt to give rise to a number of somewhat problematic consequences.

---

[49] P-M Dupuy, 'Some Reflections on Contemporary International Law and the Appeal to the Universal Values: A Response to Martti Koskenniemi' (2005) *EJIL* 16 131–38.

Consider the question of the foundation of international law, which is, in a certain sense, at the root of all of the analyses collected in the present volume. Koskenniemi demonstrates that it is the absence of an ultimate foundation for law in the modern era that explains the indeterminacy of all possible positions and the need, ultimately, to have recourse to subjective and political solutions. He set this out clearly in terms of the 'liberal internationalist' turn, which has led jurists to abandon all idea of an objective foundation of international law; and it is undoubtedly true that international lawyers have for the most part abandoned this line of thought since the 1950s. In doing so, however, he has simply remained comfortably within the internal discourse of international lawyers and left completely to one side the entire contribution of an important element of contemporary legal theory, which presents the question of objective foundations in a different manner, basing it on the idea of intersubjectivity. From the deconstruction of law that he performs, Koskenniemi retains only the idea that legal discourse is a form of power, a very precise social argumentative practice, and a dialogue; but he dismisses any possibility of an intersubjective foundation for human rights or international law. He does not reject the idea that there can be a serious, deliberate and successful use of international law, claiming only that any such use is of necessity political and contingent. His entire approach to the foundation – or lack thereof – of law is summarised in typically exemplary fashion in his discussion of Philip Alston's views in 'The Effect of Rights on Political Culture',[50] in which the only idea of objective foundation that he entertains is in the form of a neo-natural law conception (of the type of which Dworkin sometimes seems to espouse), and the only universalisation that he envisages is that which results from a policy of hegemony (which can, of course, be the case). The possibility of basing it upon contemporary, intersubjective agreement is never considered.[51] This, however, is to ignore the entire recent discussion (led by figures such as Apel, Habermas, Rawls, Renaut, etc) on the possibility of an intersubjective foundation for ethical principles, including those of law, and in particular of human rights. Of course, these new contributions can be contested, in particular as being overly liberal; it is, however, difficult not to discuss them in a reasoned manner, simply claiming instead that these questions inevitably lead us back to problematics that we have now moved beyond. Indeed, the attempt to shed light on the argumentative structure of international legal language (that is, discourse as dialogue and as the play of argumentation) can accord perfectly with the contemporary themes of communicative ethics or neo-Kantian intersubjectivity, which allow for the rational re-foundation of legal claims in a manner that fully integrates the 'linguistic turn'.

We can, moreover, further clarify the issues at stake in this debate by reference to the more general turn in the philosophy of law taken at the same time as the turn to liberal positivism in international law; indeed, the two are, it seems to me, interlinked. The philosophy of law was strongly devalued in favour of a general

---

[50] See chapter five in this volume.

[51] See P-M Dupuy's discussion of this issue, Dupuy, 'Some Reflections on Contemporary International Law and the Appeal to the Universal Values' (2005).

theory of the Kelsenian sort, viewed by the positivists/normativists as the sole scientific possibility. More generally, however, positivism deprived itself of the possibility of furnishing a complete solution to the question of foundations, referring that question back instead to philosophy. The key point here, however, is that the field of philosophy has remained very much divided on this issue. On the one hand, the post-Heideggerian heritage has cultivated historicism, relativism, the deconstruction of rationality and legal anti-humanism – to the extent that this area of philosophy (of which the deconstruction movement was part) has in fact come to indirectly reinforce legal positivism in its rejection of all critical perspectives based upon ideas of justice, and in its affirmation that no principle can claim to be genuinely universal. On the other hand, a significant section of contemporary philosophy has, in reaction against this post-Heideggerian movement, struck out on the path towards a re-foundation through an examination not of the object of the concept of law, but rather of the concept itself – and thus of its conditions of possibility in its universal dimension, and its disassociation from fact on one hand and morality on the other. These reflections led to an appreciation of the decisive role played by practical rationality and intersubjectivity. This contemporary philosophy of practical rationality, necessarily post-Kantian, has succeeded in integrating the linguistic and hermeneutic turn, allowing for the foundation of a formal universality that enables us to make a choice based upon something more than simply endlessly reversible ideas. We can thus adopt a position that is in this sense no longer 'fluid' or contingent, but that moreover is neither naïve nor metaphysically charged as was previously the case. Such a position can provide us with new foundations for reason and for a certain universality of values after the deconstructive work carried out in the various post-Heideggerian currents, such as those of Foucault, of Wittgenstein, of Derrida, etc.

In reality, Koskenniemi is fully aware of the different elements of this debate, although he of course only considers them in relation to the premises of his own conception of language and of politics. He is prepared to accept that a certain degree of intersubjectivity can be effectively practiced in the elaboration of norms, but insists that from the moment at which the play of argumentation itself begins, the practice of intersubjectivity inevitably becomes a simple argumentative strategy for claiming objectivity and thus a struggle to ensure the hegemony of one's personal position.

It is also worth noting that the conception offered by Koskenniemi of the different 'methods' within international law ('Letter to the Editor of the Symposium') – which he seeks to recast as culturally situated 'styles' – give rise to the same kinds of difficulties; here also his argument risks appearing somewhat reductive, as it seems to assume that international lawyers still claim to be able to attain genuine scientific objectivity through the application of their methods.[52] To do so, however, is to fail to acknowledge that our understanding of what constitutes the 'truth' of law has evolved considerably since Descartes; that the issue of scientific

---

[52] See chapter 12 in this volume.

objectivity within the domain of the human sciences such as law has changed, and that jurists are now much more conscious of the limits of their scientific work. Koskenniemi is, on the other hand, entirely convincing – and rightly so – when he shows that although the classic methods are most often presented as neutral forms of knowledge, disinterested in social conflicts, there is always a historically and socially situated interest in the application of each. It is also true that this neutral and disinterested knowledge is presented as a guarantee of access to a certain truth – a truth that is, however, no longer presented as absolute. However, does the revelation of the social and cultural interests concealed behind the apparent neutrality of the positivist necessarily mean that what were previously 'methods' become mere 'styles'? In addition, if methods are indeed only styles, does Koskenniemi not simply offer us a choice between the different styles to be made on the basis of our cultural traditions, just as the organisers of the symposium asked a number of international lawyers to set out their methodologies in order to compare their respective merits? Moreover, does not the critical approach, in revealing the irreducible particularity of each 'style', ultimately have the same results as the liberal approach that seeks to encompass the plurality of 'methods'? Koskenniemi, of course, claims to have deliberately broken with this methodological liberalism by changing style and writing a letter instead of a study on his method. Moreover, he makes no claim to be able to make an impartial comparison of the merits of each. To propose nothing is, however, still to suggest something: it is to claim that there is no underlying justification for choosing one approach over the others – the worst or the best. It is thus to propose here scepticism and relativism and thus equally to guide choices.

This problem doubles in difficulty when we reach the level of the final political decision. As we have seen, the solution to legal questions stems from a political decision and not from a reasoned choice – or, at least, this is the position that Koskenniemi generally adopts:[53]

> The decision always comes about, as a political theorist Ernesto Laclau has put it, as a kind of 'regulated madness', never reducible to any structure outside it. A court's decision or a lawyer's opinion is always a genuinely political act, a choice between alternatives not fully dictated by external criteria. It is even a *hegemonic* act in the precise sense that though it is partial and subjective, it claims to be universal and objective.[54]

If Koskenniemi at times appears to resemble Hannah Arendt in the manner in which he conceives of politics as freedom and the capacity to innovate, he is very unlike her in his refusal to consider it as the constitution of a plural public space for deliberation and for the emergence of power without domination. He does not argue that all decisions are entirely externally conditioned, but neither does he believe in the possibility of a political praxis capable of generating a common good through the mutual respect – spontaneous or imposed – of those involved in the

---

[53] In chapter 10 in this volume, Koskenniemi mentions discussion and argumentation; he only does so very briefly, however, and without really dealing with the question of choice.

[54] See chapter nine of this volume, at 259–60.

discussion, as for him conflict is the fundamental reality of the social world and political decision the only available means of defusing it. Yet, if one of his many contributions has been to demonstrate that placing too much confidence in the deliberations of legal actors can on occasion mask problems of hegemonic obstruction or manipulation, he himself is unable to avoid a political decisionism that brings with it a number of problems of its own.

Decisionism is often darkly associated with the Nazi German thinker Carl Schmitt but has become a much more general problem, of central concern to a large number of German thinkers such as Niklas Luhman, Hans Albert and Hermann Lübbe (of whom neither the past nor the authority is contested).[55] Schmitt criticised the political and economic liberalism of his time in calling for a new order founded upon the political; and, in doing so, handed down a set of analyses of the meaning and the existence of the political decision that have become classics on the subject. In his view, liberalism promotes the rule of law in order to destroy political power. The essence of the political lies in the decision that determines and applies the norms and that, in doing so, expresses not objective justice but rather the existential and vital will of a people. Politics is thus a matter of decision, not of discussion; and it is independent of any foundation in rational argument, as it is always inscribed within the tragic context of the struggle for survival against the enemy. The risk here is not, of course, that Koskenniemi is seeking to defend a decisionism in the style of Schmitt. Such a suggestion would do him a profound injustice,[56] as he clearly does not espouse a power-based vitalism or an apology for war; and even less does he display the fundamental, detestable bad faith of the German author. On the contrary, he proposes an ethic of responsibility that brings him closer to the decisionism of figures such as Max Weber.[57] We shouldn't ignore the fact that political decisionism can bring to the fore the type of enigmatic moments in international politics highlighted by Raymond Aron, evoking the image of the President of the United States when confronted with the decision to launch a nuclear weapon.[58] That which can be called the 'decisionism' in Koskenniemi's thought is, in any event, not necessarily of that order. Certainly, he refers on occasions to 'the existential moment of the foreign policy "decision"';[59] however, his idea of political choice far more often recalls the pragmatic manner in which the judge or even the advisor weigh up the two contradictory arguments before them before coming to a 'decision' that aims

---

[55] S Mesure, 'Rationalisme et fallibilisme' in A Renaud (dir), *Histoire de la Philosophie politique*, T. 5 (Paris, Calmann-Lévy, 2000) 150.

[56] As P-M Dupuy emphasises, Koskenniemi sometimes criticises Schmitt explicitly. He also, however, has carried out some very in-depth analyses of Schmitt's work: 'International Law as Political Theology: How to Read the Nomos der Erde' (2004) *Constellations: An International Journal for Critical and Democratic Theory* 11, 492–511; and 'Carl Schmitt, Hans Morgenthau and the Image of Law in International Relations' in Michael Byers (ed), *The Role of Law in International Politics* (Oxford, Oxford University Press, 2000) 17–34, in which he argues that all international relations theory in the US was constructed upon Schmittian foundations. See also Koskenniemi (n 2) 474–94.

[57] See, in this regard, chapter four and chapter three in this volume.

[58] Mesure, 'Rationalisme et fallibilisme',154.

[59] See chapter four in this volume.

to strike a certain balance between the interests involved with regard to the context in question.

> Few international lawyers think of their craft as the application of pre-existing formal rules or great objectives. What rules are applied, and how, which interpretative principles are used and whether to invoke the rule or the exception – including many other techniques – all point to pragmatic weighing of conflicting considerations in particular cases.[60]

He even refers to this process as one of 'contextual prudence'.[61] We are thus some considerable distance here from the Schmittian sovereign who decides upon the exception in the name of the national will, even if Koskenniemi does on occasion seem to endorse this image in other situations.[62] We thus find in Koskenniemi's work the premises of all forms of decisionism: '1) the incompatibility of fundamental viewpoints, 2) the impossibility of resolving these conflicts through genuinely rational argument, and thus 3) the need to make a choice';[63] and the disadvantages that stem from these, such as a complete relativism with regard to the solutions adopted, and a radical conventionalism and contextualism close to that of the later Wittgenstein. As there is no possible rational foundation (that is, founded in reason) capable of determining the political decision, everything can appear reduced to a matter of tastes, interests, cultural preferences, and often hegemonic will, as if nothing – other than resistance movements – could oppose the hegemony of the most powerful: 'If law is also inevitably about the subjective and the emotional, about faith and commitment, then nothing prevents re-imagining international law as commitment to resistance and transgression.'[64]

Yet, if everything is contingent and relative, what is it that legitimates resistance movements rather than the hegemonic powers in their use of international law? What is it that enables us to differentiate effectively between the phenomenon of resistance and that of power? If everything is relative and cultural, what is it that makes a political culture of formalism more desirable than an instrumentalist political culture? On what grounds can this formalist culture be opposed to Anglo-Saxon instrumentalism? Can we really content ourselves with saying, as Koskenniemi does, that we can establish distinctions in the same way as 'we distinguish between kitsch and non-kitsch'.[65] Indeed, beyond its ironic formulation, does such a stance not once again simply render this distinction nothing more than a matter of taste, and thus essentially subjective and contingent?

Koskenniemi's response to these questions is more nuanced than it at first appears, and criticisms of this sort can miss their mark if they argue that he espouses an absolute subjectivism – at least, he himself would firmly reject such

---

[60] See chapter 10 in this volume at 253.
[61] Mesure 'Rationalisme et fallibilisme'.
[62] See chapter four in this volume.
[63] Mesure 'Rationalisme et fallibilisme' 153.
[64] See chapter four in this volume.
[65] Koskenniemi, 'International Law in Europe: Between Tradition and Renewal' (2005) *EJIL* 16, 123.

a suggestion. Koskenniemi does not believe that there exists any genuine subjectivism or objectivism in the positions we adopt, any more than – in his view – there exist any purely subjective or objective values. Indeed, he rejects the idea that we can rely upon a clear distinction between the subjective and the objective as, from his deconstructivist perspective, these represent simply two opposing poles of the same game of argumentation, and are thus relative and interdependent. In this sense, there is no more 'pure' subjectivity than there is 'pure' objectivity in Koskenniemi's thought, as we can perceive these terms, always and inevitably, only through language games and the play of argumentation, thus as already internalised through language and socialisation. There is something circular in this that must always be borne in mind in order to understand Koskenniemi's thought: international legal language is at once a structure that is structured by the implicit social conventions in use within a given group, and a structure that itself structures our behaviour. In a sense, we inhabit this structure; and this is also why, according to Koskenniemi, we 'are in decisionism'; it is imposed upon us, and we are forced into taking a decision if we want to differentiate between 'kitsch' and 'non-kitsch'.

In making this move, however, it can seem that the difficulties have not been resolved, but merely displaced; the problem of human liberty as choice-making subjectivity has not been dealt with at a fundamental level, and nor has the fact that this liberty is not determined by choices rationally founded in law, but rather in accordance with personal preferences, tastes, and even environmental conditioning. Whatever the ways in which it is conditioned by language and by socialisation, the taking of a decision remains a moment at which it is no longer the language of law that governs the choice, but rather what we must call, in one way or another, a 'human subjectivity', which frees itself from all normative obligations and which thus becomes in a certain sense absolute, 'deciding' according to the value system of the actor and the social group in which he or she has developed. There are, in effect, only two alternatives: either we can liberate ourselves sufficiently from the structure of language and make a choice, or we are conditioned and do not thus make a genuine choice. Yet Koskenniemi seems caught between the two: he presents us with the disconcerting idea not only of the necessity of making a choice, but of a choice that remains conditioned. This position is extremely complex and difficult to understand, and contains a curious ambiguity. It is here that an internal difficulty, specific to Koskenniemi's thought, begins to take shape, resulting from his structuralism, which at once reinforces and undermines his decisionism. The key question is whether these are genuinely compatible: decisionism, of any sort, always presupposes a moment of liberty in which a free choice can be made; it presupposes a 'subject'. It presupposes a decision that remains irrational, not in the sense that it is taken blindly or without reflection, but in the sense that, even if well-considered, it remains free – that is, not constrained by reason or language. However, can such a decisionism go hand in hand with a structuralism that always presupposes the conditioning of that liberty by structure and by language, and that seems to lead to precisely the erasure of the 'subject'? This remains an open question; and Koskenniemi maintains the enigmatic quality of this tension, without resolving it, as he situates his own viewpoint strictly at the level of the actor immersed in practice. It may even be supposed that he would accept this aporia as impassable, and as constitutive of non-dogmatic, fallible thought.

Be that as it may, even if we overlook this obstacle and accept Koskenniemi's 'subjective' political decision, do we not in any event run up against the aporia of an increasing 'subjective' politicisation of the international sphere, which goes hand in hand with a denunciation of the instrumental and pragmatic bureaucratic gigantism of international law? If law comes down to the individual policies of different actors, is there not a risk of an inevitable dilution of law in politics, thus turning international law into the law of the most powerful? Certainly, Koskenniemi constantly refers back to the formal autonomy of law as a particular discourse; yet international law remains an instrument for the contingent realisation of the particular interests that are expressed through it. In order, therefore, to understand the meaning of legal acts and norms, it is necessary to go back, beyond the norms themselves, to the play of historically and socially situated interests that sought expression through the laws in question. In doing so, however, it is difficult to see in what way the formal autonomy of law is preserved; indeed, we might well ask whether we are not witnessing a rather more insidious negation of law itself.

In other words, in insisting too much on the critique of international legal liberalism (an approach whose focus on law without doubt leaves it impoverished politically), the risk is that Koskenniemi is unable to genuinely oppose utilitarianism, instrumentalism or the hardest forms of realism – and thus traps himself within a singular paradox. And yet is liberalism not also human rights which Koskenniemi acknowledges are as 'necessary' as they are 'impossible'?[66] This formulation appears both enigmatic and paradoxical, but it in fact represents a profound expression of his thoughts on, and a powerful critique of, rights discourse. At the same time, it conveys a certain ambivalence on Koskenniemi's part with regard to liberalism:

> . . . while the rhetoric of human rights has historically had a positive and liberating effect on societies, once rights become institutionalized as a central part of political and administrative culture, they lose their transformative effect and are petrified into a legalistic paradigm that marginalizes values or interests that resist translation into rights-language. In this way, the liberal principle of the 'primacy of the right over the good'[67] results in a colonization of political culture by a technocratic language that leaves no room for the articulation or realization of conceptions of the good.[68]

If we understand Koskenniemi's critique here, we might also point out that this passage illustrates the implicit necessity of conserving a certain form of liberalism, which provides the basis for fundamental rights (they are necessary) even as it condemns its other, bureaucratic and technocratic form (they become impossible

---

[66] 'Human rights are like love, at once necessary and impossible' in chapter six in this volume.
[67] J Rawls, *A Theory of Justice* (Oxford, Clarendon Press, 1971) 31.
[68] See chapter five in this volume at 133.

to preserve as such). Yet is this really so impossible? Has Koskenniemi implicitly become, like Weber before him, a 'disappointed liberal'?[69] Does his own conception of liberalism not mask certain essential differences between different types of liberalism at the international level? Liberalism was not really born with Hobbes, but rather with Locke, who theorised the idea of the individual subject, endowed with inalienable individual rights that could be opposed to authority. Liberalism thus originally confronted absolutism and the tyranny of power; and this original basis of liberalism can be neither denied nor forgotten, even when transposed into international law. Indeed, the connection between liberalism and certain forms of legal humanism is evident at the international level, with the inscription of human rights within positive law after 1945, and their reactivation during the 1990s.

Hence the equally problematic character of what can appear as a latent anti-humanism in Koskenniemi's writing, resulting from his critique of liberalism and of rights. However, one must proceed with caution here: legal humanism, like political liberalism, is a multifaceted and ambiguous concept. If, then, there is a legal anti-humanism in Koskenniemi's thought, it would be deployed not in order to undermine 'human dignity' but rather to preserve it through illustrating the dehumanising effects of an excess of legalism, technical reason and bureaucracy in dealing with rights and humanitarian issues. After all, is not a certain type of liberalism equally associated with the culture of formalism that Koskenniemi ultimately defends, against those who adopt instrumentalist standpoints (that is, the fact that the legal form can both encompass and give voice to the values and the 'subjective objectives' of all)?

> The form of law constructs political adversaries as equals, entitled to express their subjectively felt injustices in terms of breaches of the community to which they belong no less than their adversaries – thus reaffirming both that inclusion and the principle that the conditions applying to the treatment of any one member of the community must apply to every other member as well. In the end, competent lawyers may disagree about what this means in practice. But the legal idiom itself reaffirms the political pluralism that underlies the Rule of Law, however inefficiently it has been put into effect; or, more accurately still, it is the primacy of the formal rule that makes possible this political pluralism.[70]

Does Koskenniemi not here return to the very liberal idea, which he had already condemned, of the primacy of law over subjective values? Of course, as a result of his deconstruction of the subjective/objective couplet, his view is that there exists no genuinely 'subjective values'; and it is also true that he defines this formal primacy as a cultural style. These caveats do not alter the fact, however, that he defends this principle on many occasions, and that he thus here begins on a journey back to the primacy of law that may seem paradoxical.

It is clear, however, that all of these difficulties or ambiguities, which have a

---

[69] To use the expression of WJ Mommsen in *Max Weber et la politique allemande, 1890–1920* (Paris, PUF, 1985) 478 [*libéral désespéré*].

[70] See chapter 10 in this volume at 257.

number of implications for Koskenniemi's thought, are ultimately less linked to what has been perceived as radicalism or reductionism in his work than they are to his desire to maintain international law as at once and intrinsically, constitutively, a horizon of meaning and an instrument of hegemonic politics; as potentially both an emancipatory language and an instrument of domination:

> But although international law, too, in this way is a hegemonic politics, 'it is nonetheless a form of politics that has some particular virtues' . . . it is possible to see the expanding practice of making political claims in legal language by an increasing number of international actors in the human rights field, in trade and environment bodies, in regional and universal tribunals and organizations and, not least, in the struggles over the meaning and direction of globalization, as parts of a process of construction of a universal political community.[71]

Moreover, it is this that makes Koskenniemi's approach particularly attractive: as I emphasised above, he refuses to endorse the scepticism of certain legalists, the cynicism of the realists or even the systematic devalorisation of law by critical authors such as Foucault, to whose work he on other occasions appears very close. However, in rejecting the possibility of reducing the oppositions that are generated by this basic double stance, is he not thereby trapped by the tensions that result from them? Is that which he suggests is a constitutive tension of international law not in reality a genuine contradiction of the basic principles thereof? Also, perhaps more profoundly still, upon what can he base the critical dimension of his approach?

Koskenniemi's post-modern (non-rationalist) anxiety perhaps makes him one of the last (of the new?) romantics of international law; a lucid, romantic author who has retraced for us the structure and the history of international law so brilliantly that his work has come to form part of the acquis of international legal thought, but who – like all other romantics before him – believes that we should allow ethical and legal rationality to be carried away by the stream of international legal history. There remains, however, one last path that can be taken, which necessitates an appreciation of the importance of direction itself. Meaning is not exhausted by the significations that can be drawn from structure and historical narrative; it is also about the orientation of our behaviour in practice. It is international law in the sense of an 'ought', as a model for behaviour. Is it possible to provide this path with new foundations after Koskenniemi's work? One of his most important contributions has been the desire to rehabilitate the genuinely political moment located at the very heart of the international legal world. However, could we not conceive of a politics for the international realm which is not that of decisionism and the exception but rather, as Koskenniemi himself on occasion suggests, one that can better accompany the emergence of a contemporary global society that functions normally as a space for discussion as much as it

---

[71] See chapter nine in this volume at 239.

does a site of conflict? A politics that makes room for the 'reasonable decision',[72] the result of a critical discussion on what should be done?[73] If so, might there not also be a rational justification for a coherent and critical liberalism, characterised by solidarity, which goes beyond the previous liberalism internationalism and its incapacity to limit the excesses of technical legal reasoning?*

---

[72] This is the expression used by R Aron in his introduction to M Weber, *Le savant et le politique* (Paris, Plon, 1959) 230 [*décision raisonnable*].

[73] See E Jouannet, 'La communauté internationale vue par les juristes' (2005) *AFRI* VI, 21s.

* This introduction was translated from the French language by Euan Macdonald.

Part I

The Politics of International Law

1

Between Apology and Utopia: The Politics of International Law

This is an early summary of the structuralism expounded in my *From Apology to Utopia. The Structure of International Legal Argument* (Helsinki 1989). It was published in the first issue of the European Journal of International Law 1990 and lays a foundation for the reading of all my later work. The article is inspired by writings in the Critical Legal Studies tradition in the United States, above all by those of Professor David Kennedy (Harvard Law School). However, it also draws upon structural linguistics (Saussure), argument theory (Perelman) and the mélange of analytical hermeneutics and critical theory that formed the orthodoxy in Finnish legal theory in the 1980s. The main point here is to show how indeterminacy works in international legal argument. The article works towards an immanent critique of international law: that is, a critique based on premises that are themselves accepted in professional international law discourse. As there is no necessary closure to this discourse, but arguments continue interminably, any closure must come from outside the structures of law itself and such closure may be characterised as a politics of international law.

The Flight from Politics

IT MAY BE a matter of some controversy among historians as to when one should date the beginning of the modern states-system.[1] Less open to debate, however, is that somehow the idea of such a system is historically as well as conceptually linked with that of an international Rule of Law. In a system where the units are assumed to serve no higher purpose than their own interests and which assumes the perfect equality of those interests, the Rule of Law seems indeed the sole thinkable principle of organisation – short of the *bellum omnium*. Since

---

[1] For example, AF von der Heydte, *Geburtstunde des souveränen Staates* (Regensburg, Josef Habbel, 1952) 41–43 suggests the turn of the fourteenth century, while FH Hinsley argues that one cannot properly speak of a states-system until the eighteenth century, *Power and the Pursuit of Peace* (Cambridge University Press, 1962) 153.

the publication of Emerich de Vattel's *Droit des gens ou principes de la loi naturelle appliquées à la conduite et aux affaires des nations et des souverains* in 1758, jurists have written about international matters by assuming that the liberal principles of the Enlightenment and their logical corollary, the Rule of Law, could be extended to apply in the organisation of international society just as they had been used in the domestic one.[2]

Notwithstanding the historical difficulty with dates and origins, the connexion between the Rule of Law and the principles of the Enlightenment appear evident. Of the latter, none seems more important than that of the subjectivity of value.[3] Hobbes writes: 'For one calleth wisdom what another calleth fear and one cruelty what another justice; and prodigality what another magnanimity . . . And therefrom such names can never be ground for any ratiocination'.[4] However much later liberals may have disliked Hobbes' substantive conclusions or his political realism, the one thing which unites them with Hobbes is their criticism of relying upon natural principles to justify political authority. Appealing to principles which would pre-exist human society and be discoverable only through faith or *recta ratio* was to appeal to abstract and unverifiable maxims which only camouflaged the subjective preferences of the speaker. It was premised on utopian ideals which were constantly used as apologies for tyranny.

From the simple denial of the existence of principles of natural justice – or at least of our capacity to know them – follow the three liberal principles of social organisation: freedom, equality and the Rule of Law. If human beings are not born to a world of pre-existing norms, then they are born free; if there are no antecedent principles establishing the relative worth of individuals, the individuals must be assumed equal. Finally, freedom and equality are guaranteed only if social constraint is governed by public, verifiable and determining rules: 'A free people obey but it does not serve; it has magistrates but not masters; it obeys nothing but the laws, and thanks to the force of laws, it does not obey men'.[5]

The fight for an international Rule of Law is a fight against politics, understood as a matter of furthering subjective desires, passions, prejudices and leading into an international anarchy. Though some measure of politics is inevitable (as we

---

[2] The analogy is explicit in JJ Rousseau, *The Social Contract* (translated and introduced by Maurice Cranston) (Harmondsworth, Penguin, 1986) bk I ch 7, 63; J Locke, *Two Treatises on Government* (introduced by WS Carpenter) (London, Everyman's, 1984) Second Treatise, 183, 211. For commentary, see, eg P Vinogradoff, *Historical Types of International Law* (Leiden, Brill, 1920) 55–57; ED Dickinson, *The Equality of States in International Law* (Cambridge, Harvard University Press, 1920) 29–31, 49–50, 97–98, 111–13. See also M Walzer, *Just and Unjust Wars* (New York, Harper and Collins, 1980) 58–63; C Beitz, *Political Theory and International Relations* (Princeton, Princeton University Press, 1979) 74. For useful analysis of the effect of the analogy to the conception of a state's (territorial) rights, see A Carty, *The Decay of International Law?* (Manchester, Manchester University Press, 1986) 44–46, 55–56.

[3] My discussion of this principle is influenced by RM Unger, *Knowledge and Politics* (1975) 76–81, and A MacIntyre, *After Virtue; A Study in Moral Theory*, 2nd edn (Notre Dame, University of Notre Dame Press, 1984) 6–35.

[4] T Hobbes, *Leviathan* (edited and introduced by CB Macpherson) (Penguin, 1982) ch 4, 109–10.

[5] J-J Rousseau, 'Oeuvres complètes, Pléiade' (vol III, 842) quoted by Cranston (Introduction to Rousseau, *The Social Contract* (1986) 32).

commonly assume), it should be constrained by non-political rules: '. . . the health of the political realm is maintained by conscientious objection to the political'.[6]

The diplomatic history of the nineteenth century is a history of such a fight. Since the Vienna Congress of 1814–15 and the defeat of Napoleon, the relations between European powers were no longer built on one power's search for primacy but on a general pursuit of the maintenance of the balance of power, guaranteed by complicated legal procedures and alliances.[7] As contemporaries increasingly saw Europe as a 'system' of independent and equal political communities (instead of a *respublica Christiana)*, they began to assume that the governing principles needed to become neutral and objective – that is, that they should be understood as law.

The legal scholarship of the nineteenth century interpreted and systematised diplomatic practice into legal rules. It assumed that the behaviour of European states was determined and explicable by reference to a body of (European) public law. The plausibility of this assumption relied on the procedural character of that law. Containing mainly rules concerning diplomatic and consular contacts, procedures for attaining statehood, territory or neutral status, it did not severely restrict the ends which European sovereigns attempted to pursue. In particular, it renounced theories of the just war; war now became one political procedure among others.[8] Though the professional lawyers of the nineteenth century did speak about justice in the conduct of the sovereigns' affairs, they no longer thought of justice as material principles. Woolsey put the matter adroitly:

> By justice, however, we intend not justice objective, but as it appears to the party concerned or, at least, as it is claimed to exist. From the independence of nations it results that each has a right to hold and make good its own view of right in its own affairs.[9]

Although twentieth century lawyers have not looked too kindly upon the scholarship of the preceding century, they never rejected the ideal of the Rule of Law. On the contrary, the reconstructive scholarship which emerged first from the catastrophe of the First World War and then in the 1950s and 1960s accused the pre-war doctrines of *not going far enough* to uphold the Rule of Law. Wherever attempts by jurists to construct a solid framework of public law had faltered, it had done so not because of some defect in the liberal assumptions behind this project but because jurists had deviated from them.

The vision of a Rule of Law between states (which re-emerged for example in United Nations General Assembly Resolution 44/23 [15 November 1989] declaring the period 1990–99 as the 'United Nations Decade of International Law') is yet another reformulation of the liberal impulse to escape politics. So strong is the grip

---

[6] M Wight, 'Western Values in International Relations' in W Butterfield (ed), *Diplomatic Investigations; Essays in the Theory of International Politics* (London, Allen and Unwin, 1966) 122.

[7] See, eg Hinsley, *Power and the Pursuit of Peace* (1962) 186–271.

[8] See, eg H Wheaton, *Elements of International Law* (Text of 1866 with Notes, Carnegie Endowment, Classics of International Law, No 19) (Oxford, London, Clarendon Press, Milford, 1936) 313–14.

[9] TD Woolsey, *Introduction to the Study of International Law; Designed as an Aid in Teaching and in Historical Studies*, 5th edn (London, Low, Marston, Searle and Rivington, 1879) 183.

of this vision that the representative of the Soviet Union at the same session of the General Assembly explained that in his view to restructure the basis of international relations there was a need to 'arrive at a comprehensive international strategy for establishing the primacy of law in relations between states'.[10] With the end of the Cold War, strengthening the Rule of Law nationally and in the international world has now become a widely supported series of UN projects.[11]

Throughout the twentieth century, reconstructive doctrines have claimed that what merits criticism is the corruption of the Rule of Law either in the narrow chauvinism of diplomats or the speculative utopias of an academic elite. If only the Rule of Law can be fortified to exclude these contrasting distortions, then the jurist's part in the construction of a just world order has been adequately executed.

In this chapter, however, I shall extend the criticism of the liberal idea of the *Rechtstaat*, a commonplace in late modem western society,[12] into its international counterpart. I shall attempt to show that our inherited ideal of a World Order based on the Rule of Law thinly hides from sight the fact that social conflict must still be solved by political means and that even though there may exist a common legal rhetoric among international lawyers, that rhetoric must, *for reasons internal to the ideal itself,* rely on essentially contested – political – principles to justify outcomes to international disputes.[13]

The Content of the Rule of Law: Concreteness and Normativity

Organising society through legal rules is premised on the assumption that these rules are objective in some sense that political ideas, views, or preferences are not. To show that international law is objective – that is, independent from international politics – the legal mind fights a battle on two fronts. On the one hand, it aims to ensure the *concreteness* of the law by distancing it from theories of natural justice. On the other hand, it aims to guarantee the *normativity* of the law by creating distance between it and actual state behaviour, will or interest. Law enjoys independence from politics only if both of these conditions are simultaneously present.

---

[10] UNGA 'Memorandum: On Enhancing the Role of International Law' UN Doc A/44/585 (2 October 1989).

[11] See, eg the documents in the UN website on the Rule of Law at www.unrol.org/.

[12] For the ensuing text, particularly relevant are criticisms stressing the internal tensions of liberal theory. See generally Unger, *Knowledge and Politics* (1975) 63–103 and, eg A Levine, *Liberal democracy; A Critique of its Theory* (New York, Columbia University Press, 1981) 16–32; Fishkin, 'Liberal Theory and the Problem of Justification' *NOMOS* XXVD1 207–31.

[13] This article is a condensed version of some of the themes in M Koskenniemi, *From Apology to Utopia; the Structure of International Legal Argument* (Re-issue with a new Epilogue, Cambridge University Press, 2005).

The requirement of concreteness results from the liberal principle of the subjectivity of value. To avoid political subjectivism and illegitimate constraint,[14] we must base law on something tangible – on the actual (verifiable) behaviour, will and interest of the members of society – states. The modern view is a *social conception of law*.[15] For it, law is not a natural but an artificial creation, a reflection of social circumstances. As such, its contents can be impartially rarified by studying those circumstances closely.

According to the requirement of normativity, law should be applied regardless of the political preferences of legal subjects. It should not just reflect what states do but should be *critical* of state policy. In particular, it should be applicable even against a state which opposes its application to itself. As international lawyers have had the occasion to point out, legal rules whose content or application depends on the will of the legal subject for whom they are valid, are not proper legal rules at all but apologies for the legal subject's political interest.[16]

Stated in such a fashion, I believe that the requirements of legal objectivity vis-à-vis political subjectivity are met. For if the law could be verified or justified only by reference to somebody's views on what the law *should* be like (ie theories of justice), it would coincide with their political opinions. Similarly, if we could apply the law against those states which accept it, then it would coincide with those states' political views.

This argumentative structure, however, which forces jurists to prove that their law is valid because it is concrete and normative in the above sense, both creates and destroys itself. For it is impossible to prove that a rule, principle or doctrine (in short, an argument) is both concrete and normative simultaneously. The two requirements *cancel each other out*. An argument about concreteness is an argument about the closeness of a particular rule, principle or doctrine to state practice. However, the closer to state practice an argument is, the less normative and the more political it seems. The more it seems just another uncritical apology for existing power. An argument about normativity, on the other hand, is an argument which intends to demonstrate the rule's distance from state will and practice. The more normative (ie critical) a rule, the more political it seems because the less it is possible to argue it by reference to social context. It seems utopian and – like theories of natural justice – manipulable at will.

The dynamics of international legal argument are provided by the constant effort of lawyers to show that their law is either concrete or normative and their becoming thus vulnerable to the charge that such law is in fact political because it is either apologist or utopian. Different doctrinal and practical controversies turn

---

[14] For a typical argument stressing the political character of natural law see, eg S Sur, *L'interpretation en droit international public* (Paris, LGDJ, 1974) 25–32 or JHW Verzijl, *International Law in Historical Perspective* (Leiden, Sijthoff, 1968) vol I, 391–93.

[15] 'C'est à une conception fonctionnelle de pouvoir, à une conception sociale du droit que s'attache notre enseignement', De Visscher, 'Cours général de principes de droit international public' (1954) 86 *Recueil des Cours de l'Académie de droit international de la Haye* 451.

[16] See, eg H Lauterpacht, *The Function of Law in the International Community* (Oxford, Clarendon Press, 1933) 189 and passim.

out as transformations of this dilemma. It lies behind such dichotomies as 'positivism'/'naturalism', 'consent'/'justice', 'autonomy'/'community', 'process'/ 'rule', etc, and explains why these and other oppositions keep recurring and do not seem soluble in a permanent way. They recur because it seems possible to defend one's legal argument only by showing either its closeness to, or its distance from, state practice. They seem insoluble because both argumentative strategies are vulnerable to what appear to be valid criticisms, compelled by the system itself.[17]

This provides an argumentative structure which is capable of providing a valid criticism of each substantive position but which itself cannot justify any. The fact that positions are constantly taken and solutions justified by lawyers, demonstrates that the structure does not possess the kind of distance from politics for which the Rule of Law seems to posit. It seems possible to adopt a position only by a political choice: a choice which must ultimately defend itself in terms of a conception of justice – or then remain substantively unjustified. We accept it because *that is what we do.*

Doctrinal Structures

Two criticisms are often advanced against international law. One group of critics has accused international law of being too political in the sense of being too dependent on states' political power. Another group has argued that the law is too political because it is founded on speculative utopias. The standard point about the non-existence of legislative machineries, compulsory adjudication and enforcement procedures captures both criticisms. From one perspective, this criticism highlights the infinite flexibility of international law, its character as a manipulable *façade* for power politics. From another perspective, the criticism stresses the moralistic character of international law, its distance from the realities of power politics. According to the former criticism, international law is too *apologetic* to be taken seriously in the construction of international order. According to the latter, it is too *utopian* to the identical effect.

International lawyers have had difficulty answering these criticisms. The more reconstructive doctrines have attempted to prove the normativity of the law, its autonomy from politics, the more they have become vulnerable to the charge of utopianism. The more they have insisted on the close connexion between international law and state behaviour, the less normative their doctrines have appeared. Let me outline the four positions which modem international lawyers have taken to prove the relevance of their norms and doctrines. These are mutually exclusive and logically exhaustive positions and account for a full explanation of the possibilities of doctrinal argument.

[17] For an alternative but similar type of exposition, see D Kennedy, *International Legal Structures* (Baden-Baden, Nomos, 1987).

Many of the doctrines which emerged from the ashes of legal scholarship at the close of the First World War explained the failure of pre-war international doctrines by reference to their apologist character. Particular objects of criticism were 'absolutist' doctrines of sovereignty, expressed in particular in the *Selbstverpflichtungslehre*, doctrines stressing the legal significance of the balance of power or delimiting the legal functions to matters which were unrelated to questions of 'honour' or 'vital interest'. Writings by Hersch Lauterpacht, Alfred Verdross and Hans Kelsen among others, created an extremely influential interpretation of the mistakes of pre-war doctrines.[18] By associating the failure of those doctrines with their excessive closeness to state policy and national interest and by advocating the autonomy of international legal rules, these jurists led the way to the establishment of what could be called a *rule approach* to international law, stressing the law's normativity, its capacity to oppose state policy as the key to its constraining relevance.

This approach thinks of law in terms of rules and insists on an objective, formal test of pedigree (sources) which will show which standards qualify as legal rules and which do not. If a rule meets this test, then it is binding. Although there is disagreement between rule approach lawyers over what constitutes the proper test, there is no dispute about its importance. The distinctions between hard and soft law, rules and principles, regular norms and *jus cogens,* for instance, are suspect: these only betray political distinctions that undermine the law's objectivity and verifiability.[19] Two well-known criticisms have been directed against the rule approach. First, it has remained unable to exclude the influence of political considerations from its assumed tests of pedigree. To concede that rules are sometimes hard to find while their content remains, to adopt HLA Hart's expression 'relatively indeterminate'[20] is to undermine the autonomy of the rules from 'evaluation' which the rule approach stressed. Second, the very desire for autonomy seems suspect. A pure theory of law, the assumption of a *Völkerrechtsgemeinschaft* or the ideal of the wholeness of law – a central assumption in most rule approach writing[21] – may simply betray forms of irrelevant doctrinal utopianism. They achieve logical consistency at the cost of applicability in the real world of state practice.

The second major position in contemporary scholarship uses these criticisms to establish itself. A major continental interpretation of the mistakes of nineteenth

---

[18] Lauterpacht, *The Function of Law* (1933); A Verdross, *Die Verfassung der Völkerrechtsgemeinschaft* (Wien, Springer, 1926); H Kelsen, *Das Problem der Souveränität und die Theorie des Völkerrechts* (Tübingen, Mohr, 1920).

[19] This approach is best illustrated in G Schwarzenberger, *The Inductive Approach to International Law* (London, Stevens, New York, Oceana, 1965). Many of its points are forcefully made in P Weil, 'Towards Relative Normativity in International Law' (1983) 77 *American Journal of International Law* 413–42. For further references on this and the other approaches, see Koskenniemi, *From Apology to Utopia* 2005 182–218.

[20] HLA. Hart, *The Concept of Law* (Oxford, Clarendon, 1961) 132.

[21] See, eg Lauterpacht, 'Some Observations on the Prohibition of "Non Liquet" and the Completeness of Law', *Symbolae Verzijl* (1958) 196–221 and the 'realist' criticism by Stone, 'Non-Liquet and the Function of Law in the International Community', (1958) XXV *British Year Book of International Law* 124–61.

century lawyers and diplomats explains them as a result of naive utopianism: an unwarranted belief in the viability of the Congress system, with its ideas of legality and collective intervention. It failed because it had not been able to keep up with the politics of emergent nationalism and the increasing pace of social and techno-logical change. Lawyers such as Nicolas Politis or Georges Scelle stressed the need to link international law much more closely to the social – even biological – neces-sities of international life.[22] Roscoe Pound's programmatic writings laid the basis for the contemporary formulation of this approach by criticizing the attempt to think of international law in terms of abstract rules. It was, rather, to be thought of 'in terms of social ends'.[23]

Since the inter-war years this approach – the *policy approach* – has become widely practiced especially in the United States, especially under the influence of legal realism and its various offshoots such as the 'process school' or 'rational choice'. According to it international law can only be relevant if it is firmly based in the social context of international policy. Rules are only trends of past decision which may or may not correspond to social and instrumental necessities. 'Binding force' is a juristic illusion. Standards are, in fact more or less effective and it is their effectiveness – their capacity to further social goals – which is the relevant ques-tion, not their formal 'validity'.[24]

But this approach is just as vulnerable to well-founded criticisms as the rule approach. By emphasizing the law's concreteness, it will ultimately do away with its constraining force altogether. If law is only what is effective, then by definition, it becomes an apology for the interests of the powerful. If, as Myres McDougal does, this consequence is avoided by postulating some 'goal values' whose legal impor-tance is independent of considerations of effectiveness, then the (reformed) policy approach becomes vulnerable to criticisms which it originally voiced against the rule approach. In particular, it appears to assume an illegitimate naturalism which – as critics stressing the liberal principle of the subjectivity of value have noted – is in constant danger of becoming just an apology of some states' policies.[25]

The rule and the policy approaches are two contrasting ways of trying to estab-lish the relevance of international law in the face of what appear as well-founded criticisms. The former does this by stressing the law's normativity, but fails to be

---

[22] G Scelle, *Précis de droit des gens. Principes et systématique I–II* (Paris, Sirey, 1932, 1936); N Politis, *Les nouvelles tendances du droit international* (Paris, Hachette, 1927).

[23] R Pound, 'Philosophical Theory and International Law' (1923) I *Bibliotheca Visseiana* 1–90.

[24] For a famous formulation, see MS McDougal, 'International Law, Power and Policy: A Contemporary Perspective', (1953) 82 *Recueil des Cours de l'Académie de droit international de la Haye* 133–259. For useful analysis, see B Rosenthal, *L'étude de l'œuvre de Myres Smith McDougal en matière du droit international public* (Paris, LGDJ, 1970). See further the essays by Wiessner & Millard, O'Connell and Abbott in SR Ratner and A-M Slaughter, *The Methods of International Law* (Washington DC, ASIL, 2004).

[25] For such criticism, see, eg P Allott, 'Language, Method and the Nature of International Law' (1971) 45 *British Year Book of International Law* 123–25: Boyle, 'Ideals and Things: International Legal Scholarship and the Prison-House of Language' (1985) 26 *Harvard Journal of International Law*, and G Fitzmaurice, 'vae Victis or Woe to the Negotiators !' (1971) 65 *American Journal of International Law* 370–73.

convincing because it lacks concreteness. The latter builds upon the concreteness of international law, but loses the normativity, the critical force of its law. It is hardly surprising, then, that some lawyers have occupied the two remaining positions: they have either assumed that international law can neither be seen as normatively controlling nor widely applied in practice (the sceptical position), or have continued writing as if both the law's binding force as well as its correspondence with developments in international practice were a matter of course (idealist position). The former ends in cynicism, the latter in contradiction.[26] The late modem mainstream often situates itself between the rule and the policy approaches. In Richard Falk's words, the task of an adequate doctrine today is to establish: '[a]n intermediate position, one that maintains the distinctiveness of the legal order while managing to be responsive to the extralegal setting of politics, history and morality'.[27]

But such a movement towards pragmatic eclecticism seems self-defeating. There is no space between the four positions, rule approach, policy approach, scepticism and idealism. Middle-of-the-road doctrines may seem credible only insofar as their arguments, doctrines or norms are not contested. But as soon as disagreement emerges, such doctrines, too, must defend their positions either by showing their autonomous binding force, or by demonstrating their close relationship with what states actually do. At this point, they become vulnerable to the charge of being either utopian or apologist.

The result is a curiously incoherent doctrinal structure in which each position is ad hoc and therefore survives only. Mainstream doctrine retreats into general statements about the need to 'combine' concreteness and normativity, realism and idealism, which bear no consequence to its normative conclusion. It then advances, emphasising the contextuality of each solution – thus undermining its own emphasis on the general and impartial character of its system.

International law's contradictions force it into an impoverished and unreflective pragmatism. On the one hand, the 'idealist' illusion is preserved that law can and does play a role in the organisation of social life among states. On the other, the 'realist' criticisms have been accepted and the law is seen as distinctly secondary to power and politics. Modern doctrine, as Philip Allott has shown, uses a mixture of positivistic and naturalistic, consensualist and non-consensualist, teleological, practical, political, logical and factual arguments in happy confusion, unaware of its internal contradictions.[28] The style survives because we recognise in it the liberal doctrine within which we have been accustomed to press our political arguments.

A final point is in order. Each of the main positions reviewed, as well as their combinations, remain distinctly modern. Each refuses to develop its concept of

[26] For reference, see Koskenniemi, *From Apology to Utopia* (2005) 197–200, 209–18.

[27] R Falk, 'The Interplay of Westphalia and Charter Conceptions of the International Legal Order' in R Falk, C Black (eds), *The Future of the International Legal Order* (Princeton, Princeton University Press, 1969) vol I, 34–35.

[28] Allott, 'Language, Method and the Nature of International Law' (1971) 100–05, 113.

law in terms of some material theory of justice. Each assumes that law is an artificial, human creation which comes about through social processes and that an adequate concept of law is one which provides a reliable description of those processes and their outcomes. Moreover, each bases its claim to superiority vis-à-vis the other on that very description. The point at which they diverge is their theory on how to interpret those processes, how to understand what goes on in social life in terms of law creation and law application.

The difficulty in choosing between a rule and a policy approach is the difficulty of defending the set of criteria which these put forward to disentangle 'law' from other aspects of state behaviour. For the rule approach lawyer, the relevant criteria are provided by his theory of sources. For the policy approach, the corresponding criteria are provided by his theory of 'base-values', authority or some constellation of national or global interest and need. As it is these criteria which claim to provide the correct description of social processes, they cannot be defended without circularity in terms of social processes themselves.[29] To decide on the better approach, one would have to base oneself on some non-descriptive (non-social) theory about significance or about the relative justice of the types of law rendered by the two – or any alternative – matrices.[30] Such a decision would, under the social conception of law and the principle of the subjectivity of value, be one which would seem to have no claim for objective correctness at all. It would be a political decision.

Substantive Structures

It is possible to depict the tension between the demands for normativity and concreteness in two contrasting methods of explaining the origin of the law's substance. From the perspective of concreteness, this substance comes about as a consequence of the fact of sovereignty of the state. One aspect of sovereignty is the liberty to 'legislate' international norms which bind oneself. Wherever particular norms have not been thus established, the metaprinciple of sovereign liberty – the 'Lotus principle' – remains valid.

It is equally possible to understand the law as a consequence of the functioning of normative criteria for law-emergence. From the perspective of normativity, there must be assumed criteria – 'sources' – which allow us to distinguish between the fact of the existence and behaviour of certain centres of power (states) and the

---

[29] The point about conceptual matrices, scientific theories, 'paradigms', interests of knowledge or prejudices, if not strictly determining what we can know of our social world at least significantly influencing our perception, is a common theme in much modern epistemology. See further Koskenniemi, *From Apology to Utopia*, (2005) 522–32 .

[30] On choosing significant features for description, see, eg J Finnis, *Natural Law and Natural Rights* (Oxford, New York, Clarendon Press, 1980) 3, 9–18. See also A MacIntyre, 'The Indispensability of Political Theory' in D Miller and L Siedentop (eds), *The Nature of Political Theory* (Oxford, New York, Clarendon Press, 1983) 19–33.

law. In this sense, all international legal substance is dependent on the content of those criteria. These explanations seem radically conflicting and appear to provide exhaustive but incompatible methods for elucidating the origin and character of international law. Indeed, much of the dispute between 'idealists' and 'realists', or the rule and policy approaches, seems captured in this contrast, reflected also in the organisation of the substance of standard textbooks. One style consists of preceding the law's substance with an analysis of the character of statehood and that of the international order – the 'political foundations'. Another starts out by listing the sources of international law and lets the law's substance follow therefrom.

Despite their initially contrasting outlook, both 'methods' rely on each other. 'Realist' doctrines use criteria to distinguish between law and coercion which fall short of a doctrine of sources only by not bearing that name. 'Idealist' programmes end up pointing to state practice to defend the relevance of their sources and to verify the content of the law they support.[31] The fact that the available outlooks provide identical substantive systems and that both remain vulnerable to well-rehearsed criticism further explains the late modern turn to doctrinal pragmatism.

In the practice of international dispute resolution, the lack of a satisfactory explanation for the origin of legal rules has led lawyers to abandon seeking justification for solving interpretative controversies from any of the suggested explanations. Behind ritualistic references to well-known rules and principles of international law (the content of which remains a constant object of dispute), legal practice has increasingly resorted to solving disputes by a contextual criterion – an effort towards an equitable balance. Although this has seemed to work well, the question arises as to whether such practice can be adequately explained in terms of the Rule of Law.

Sovereignty

There is a body of doctrine which addresses itself to the questions: what are the character and normative consequences of statehood? It deals with such themes as the acquisition and loss of statehood, the justification and extent (limits) of territorial sovereignty, the rights of states, the delimitation of competing jurisdictions, etc. The rhetorical importance of this doctrine has varied, but its urgency within the liberal doctrine remains unchallenged. In some ways, sovereignty doctrine plays a role analogous to that played by individual liberty in domestic legitimation discourse. It explains what it is to be a legal subject, and then sets down basic conditions within which the relations between legal subjects must be organised.

The character and consequences of sovereign statehood might, however, be explained from different perspectives. One explanation holds sovereignty as basic in the sense that it is simply imposed upon the law by the world of facts. Sovereignty and together with it a set of territorial rights and duties are something external to the law, something the law must recognise but which it cannot control. I shall call

---

[31] Compare also Kennedy, *International Legal Structures* (1987).

this the 'pure fact view'.[32] Another explanation holds sovereignty and everything associated with it as one part of the law's substance, determined and constantly determinable within the legal system, just like any other norms. This might be called the 'legal view'.[33]

Normative argument within the different realms of sovereignty doctrine uses the contrast between these explanations to constitute itself. One party argues in terms of pure facts (of effectiveness, for example), while the other makes its point by reference to a criterion external to facts (general recognition, for example). However, neither position is sustainable alone. Relying on the pure fact of power is apologist.[34] Relying on a criterion independent of effectiveness is both abstract and question-begging.[35] It is question-begging as it merely raises the further question about whose interpretation of the criterion or its application should be given precedence. A defendable argument seems compelled to make both points: it must assume that sovereign rights are somehow matters of pure fact as well as of some criterion external to those facts themselves.

The development of the positions of Norway and Denmark during the *Eastern Greenland* case (1933) illustrates this. Originally, Norway based its rights to the disputed territory on its effective occupation. Relying on the views of other states would have violated Norway's sovereign equality. Denmark based its own claim on general recognition and challenged Norwegian title on the absence of such recognition. As the title was to be valid *erga omnes*, it could not be dependent on Norway's acts. In their subsequent arguments both states replied assuming their adversary's first position: Norway argued that its occupation was sanctioned by a generally recognised rule which based title on occupation. Denmark aimed to show that Norway in fact could not have occupied the territory because it had already been effectively occupied by Denmark.[36]

Neither claim could be preferred by simply preferring the 'pure fact' or the 'criterion' of general recognition because both states argued both points. Consequently, the Court affirmed both argumentative tracks. To support its view that Denmark had sovereignty, it argued from Danish occupation as well as general recognition and denied both in respect of Norway.[37] To reach this conclusion, the Court had to make interpretations about the facts (effective occupation) as well as the law (the extent of general recognition) which, however, were external

---

[32] G Jellinek, *Allgemeine Staatslehre* (3 Aufl) (Berlin, Haring, 1925) 337, 364–67 and, eg M Korowicz, 'Some Present Problems of Sovereignty' (1961) *Recueil des Cours de l'Académie de droit international de la Haye* 102.

[33] See, eg Verdross, *Die Verfassung der Völkerrechtsgemeinschaft* (Vienna, Springer, 1926) 35, and eg C Rousseau, 'Principes de droit international public' (1958) 93 *Recueil des Cours de l'Académie de droit international de la Haye* 394.

[34] See, eg H Lauterpacht, *International Law* (Cambridge, Cambridge University Press, 1979) vol I, 341–44.

[35] See, eg *Island of Palmas* case, II *Reports of International Arbitral Awards* 839, 843–46.

[36] These points are belaboured at length in the written proceedings. See *Eastern Greenland* case PCIJ Rep Series C No 62 and C No 63 and the parties' oral arguments, C No 66. For more detailed analysis, see Koskenniemi *From Apology to Utopia*, (2005) 288–93.

[37] *Eastern Greenland* case PCIJ Rep Series A No 53, 45–62.

to the applicable facts and the law and which were difficult to justify against Norway's conflicting sovereign interpretation of them. The crucial point in the judgment was the Court's discussion of the famous 'Ihlen declaration', which allowed the Court to protect Norwegian sovereignty by denying its possession in reference to the construction according to which Norway itself had already 'recognised' Danish sovereignty in Eastern Greenland.[38]

The same structure can be detected in all territorial disputes. In each, the 'pure fact' and 'legal' approaches dissolve into each other in a way which makes it impossible for the court or tribunal to solve the case by merely choosing one over the other. There are two difficulties. First, the need to make both points loses the initial sense of both: the pure fact view was premised on the assumption that the law follows from what facts say. The legal view assumed that the sense of facts was to be determined by rules. In argument, both points claim to defer, or *overrule* each other. To assume that they could be valid (determining) simultaneously makes both meaningless. Second, that the 'pure fact' and the 'legal' approaches show themselves indeterminate compels the decision-maker to look closer into the relevant 'facts' and the relevant 'legal' criterion. Decisions turn on contextual interpretations about the facts and the law – interpretations which, by definition, can no longer be justified by reference to those facts or criteria themselves.

Late modern practice of solving sovereignty disputes pays hardly more than lip service to the traditional bases of territorial entitlement. Deciding such questions is now thought of in terms of trying to establish the most equitable solution.[39] The point is that the various interpretations and pragmatic considerations, as well as the final appreciation of the equity of the proposed solution, cannot be justified by reference to legal rules. On the contrary, recourse to the kind of justice involved in such appreciation can only mean, from the perspective of the Rule of Law, capitulation to arbitrariness or undermining the principle of the subjectivity of value, required in the pursuit of a Rule of Law. Let me take another example. It was often argued that the existence of states is a 'matter of fact' and that 'recognition' was only 'declaratory' and not 'constitutive' of statehood. If states were created by an external act of recognition, this would introduce for existing states a political right to decide which entities shall enjoy the status of legal subjects. This conflicts with the principles of self-determination and equality, which are both logical consequences from the rejection of a natural law.[40]

Yet, even such an apparently realistic and democratic view needed to assume the existence of some kind of pre-existing criteria whereby it could be ascertained whether statehood was present in some entity or not. The problem was never really that anyone would have seriously contested that the emergence of states was a factual, sociological process. The problem was – and remains – that people view

---

[38] ibid 64–74.

[39] See *Burkina Faso – Mali Frontier case*, [1986] ICJ Rep 567–68 para 28 (and n 48).

[40] The classic remains T-C Chen, *The International Law of Recognition* (London, Stevens, 1951). See also L Kato, 'Recognition in International Law; Some Thoughts on Traditional Theory, Attitudes of and Practice by African States' (1970) 10 *Indian Journal of International Law* (1970) 299–323.

the normative consequences of social process through different criteria and arrive at irreconcilable conclusions even when using the same criteria.

There is, however, a measure of common agreement on a matter as important as statehood. However, it has very little to do with factual power or effectiveness. Rhodesia, Transkei and Taiwan were never regarded as states, whereas Tuvalu and Monaco were. But, to explain these 'anomalies' – as well as other apparently puzzling cases of statehood – simply by reference to the 'constitutive' view is equally unsatisfactory. The original objections against the imperialistic character of this theory remain just as valid as Lauterpacht's middle-of-the-road position about a duty to recognise when the legal criteria have been fulfilled remains question-begging:[41] if a state refuses to recognise an entity because it says that this fulfilled the relevant criteria, there is little point to insist upon the existence of the duty. The matter turns on the interpretation of either the factual circumstances or the content of the relevant norm. The real problem is that it is impossible, within liberal premises, to overrule any participant interpretation in a legitimate fashion. Under those premises norms are 'auto-interpretative' and each state must be presumed to have the liberty to interpret the sense of factual events around it.[42]

These anomalies of statehood as well as the resurgence of the time-honoured practice of non-recognition after the *Namibia* Opinion (1971), suggest that the attainment of statehood territorial title – at least if the matter is of some import-ance – has a relationship to what is decided externally.[43] However, they also show that to believe that such decision can be understood as 'following a rule' requires either a rule or an imagination so flexible that neither the legal nor the pure fact view can take much credit in trying to establish itself upon it.

If the presence of the quality of sovereignty in some entity is difficult to explain in terms of pure facts or legal rules, it is even more trying to do this in respect of the consequences of sovereignty. That the boundaries of domestic jurisdiction are shifting, and that 'sovereignty' has seemed compatible with a state's hermetic iso-lation as well as extensive integration, indicates that whatever rights or liberties this quality may entail is, as the Permanent Court of International Justice observed, a 'relative matter' – dependent on the content of the state's obligations at any given time.[44] In other words, nothing determinate follows from sovereignty as a matter of 'pure fact' – on the contrary, the content of sovereignty seems determinable only once we know what obligations the state has.

Lawyers adopting the 'legal view' sometimes believe that the above conclusion fully vindicates their position. 'Sovereignty' is not a matter outside but within the law, a convenient shorthand for the rights, liberties and competences which the

---

[41] H Lauterpacht, *Recognition in International Law* (Cambridge, Cambridge University Press, 1948).

[42] For a useful restatement of this (liberal) point, see B Cheng, 'Custom, The Future of General State Practice in a Divided World' in R St J Macdonald and DM Johnston (eds), *The Structure and Process of International Law: Essays in Legal Philosophy Doctrine and Theory* (The Hague, Martinus Nijhoff, 1983) 513, 519–23.

[43] *Namibia* case [1971] ICJ Rep 51, 54 paras 112, 117, 119.

[44] *Nationality Decrees* case PCIJ Rep Series B No 4, 24.

law has allocated to the state – and which can be retrieved at any time.[45] To solve a sovereignty dispute it suffices only to look at the body of legal rules, and see if the state has the capacity which it claims by a legislative allocation.

The problem with such a conclusion, however, is that on most areas of state conduct no definite legislative act can be found which would establish the state's competence to act in some particular way. Moreover, and here is another paradox, the most important rules of general application seem to be precisely those rules which lay down the right of exclusive jurisdiction, self-determination, non-intervention and sovereignty. It is not only that if sovereignty were reduced to a non-normative abstraction, then international law would appear as a huge *lacuna*, we would also lack a connected explanation, an interpretative principle to solve differences of opinion about the content or application of the few particular rules which we could then discern.

In most areas of non-treaty-related state conduct, specific obligations are, or can be, plausibly made to seem either ambiguous or lacking. In such case, the state's sovereignty – its initial liberty – will re-emerge as a normative principle in its own right: in the absence of clear prohibitions, the state must be assumed free. This principle – the *Lotus* principle[46] – is not only a convenient rule of thumb. It encapsulates the assumption that the mere fact of statehood has a normative sense (right of self-determination) and that in the absence of unambiguous legislative prohibitions any attempt to overrule the liberty inherent in statehood can only appear as illegitimate constraint.

The difficulty with the *Lotus* principle is twofold. First, all the rules and principles are more or less indeterminate in their content. If the mere fact of the existence of differing interpretations were sufficient to trigger the presumption of liberty, then the binding force of most rules would seem an illusion. The even more important difficulty is that the principle is useless if the case involves a *conflict* of liberties. However, if it is assumed – as is inevitable if the idea of a material natural law is discarded – that the liberties of one state are delimited by those of another, then any dispute about the rights or obligations of two or more states can be conceptualised in terms of a conflict of their liberties and, consequently, would not seem soluble by simply preferring 'liberty' – because we would not know which state's liberty to prefer.

At that point, legal practice breaks from the argumentative cycle by recourse to equity – an undifferentiated sense of justice.

Continental shelf disputes are one example. The International Court of Justice (ICJ), as is well-known, started out with the assumption that the entitlement to continental shelf was a matter of giving effect to the coastal state's *ab initio* and *ipso facto* right. It was not a matter of 'abstract justice' but of (objective) fact.[47] However,

---

[45] G Schwarzenberger, 'The Forms of Sovereignty' (1957) 10 *Current Legal Problems* 248; HLA Hart, *The Concept of Law* (1961) 218.

[46] *Lotus* case PCIJ Rep Series A No 10, 30. See further Koskenniemi, *From Apology to Utopia* (2005), 255–58.

[47] *North Sea Continental Shelf* cases [1969] ICJ Rep 22–23 paras 19–20.

this view has proved unhelpful. Which facts are relevant – the decisive problem – is decided by the Court ad hoc and it is not inscribed in some transcendental code *ex ante*. Later delimitations have even ceased paying lip service to the *ipso facto/ab initio* theory and understood 'arriving at an equitable result' as its proper task.[48] The history of the argument in continental shelf cases is the history of the Court first noting the lack, or at least the ambiguity of the relevant rule, it then making appeal to a pure fact (*ipso facto*) view; then abandoning that view (because no 'fact' can be normative without an anterior criterion) in favour of a legal view (equity *infra legem*[49] as the correct rule) and the whole cycle ending in the content of that rule being dispersed into justice – a justice which can, under the principle of subjective value and the Rule of Law, only be seen as arbitrary.[50]

Transboundary pollution, to take another example, involves the juxtaposition of the freedoms of the source-state and the target-state: on the one hand, there is the former's sovereign right to exploit its natural resources in accordance with its own environmental policies; on the other hand, there is the victim's sole right to decide what acts shall take place in its territories.[51] The former's liberty to pursue economically beneficial uses of its territory is contrasted with the latter's liberty to enjoy a pure environment. The conflict is insoluble by simply preferring 'liberty', or some right inscribed in the very notion of sovereignty. Balancing seems inevitable in order to reach a decision.[52]

A similar structure manifests itself everywhere within sovereignty doctrine. While sovereign immunity is usually stated either in terms of the (pure fact of) sovereignty or a systematic necessity for international communication, legal practice tends to construct the foreign sovereign's exemption from local jurisdiction by balancing the two sovereigns' interests vis-à-vis each other.[53] The same seems true in cases dealing with the determination of the allowable reach of a state's extraterritorial jurisdiction.[54] The law on uses of international watercourses[55] and fishery resources,[56] as well as conflicts concerning foreign investment between the

---

[48] *Tunisia–Libya Continental Shelf* case [1982] ICJ Rep 59 para 70; *Gulf of Maine* case [1984] ICJ Rep 312 para 155; *Libya–Malta Continental Shelf* case [1985] ICJ Rep 38–39 para 49.

[49] *North Sea Continental Shelf* cases [1969] ICJ Rep 20–22 paras 15–20.

[50] For this criticism, see, eg Gros, dissenting opinion *Tunisia–Libya Continental Shelf* case [1982] ICJ Rep151–56 and *Gulf of Maine* case [1984] ICJ Rep 378–80.

[51] See Principle 21, UN Conference on the Human Environment, Stockholm 5–16 June 1972 UN Doc A/CONF48/14.

[52] See, eg M Koskenniemi, 'International Pollution in the Systems of International Law' (1984) 17 *Oikeustiede-Jurisprudentia* 152–64; J Lammers, '"Balancing the Equities" International Environmental Law' (1984) *Recueil des Cours de l'Académie de droit international de la Haye* 153–65.

[53] J Crawford, 'International Law and Foreign Sovereigns, Distinguishing Immune Transactions' (1983) 54 *British Year Book of International Law* 114–18.

[54] W Meng, 'Völkerrechtliche Zulässigkeit und Grenzen der wirtschaftsverwaltungsrechtlichen Hoheitsakte mit Auslandswirkung' (1984) 44 *Zeitschrift für ausländisches öffentliches Recht und Völkerrecht* 675–783; AV Lowe, 'The Problem of Extraterritorial Jurisdiction: Economic Sovereignty and the Search for a Solution' (1985) 34 *International & Comparative Law Quarterly* 730.

[55] S Schwebel, 'Third Report on the Non-Navigational Uses of International Watercourses' (1982/ II/I) *Yearbook of the International Law Commission* 75–100.

[56] *Fisheries Jurisdiction* cases [1974] ICJ Rep 30 paras 69–70.

home state and the host state,[57] entail the drawing of a boundary between the two sovereigns, a determination of the extent of their sovereign liberty. In the absence of determinate rules, and being unable to prefer one sovereign over another, legal practice has turned to equity in order to justify the delimitation of the two sovereignties vis-à-vis each other.

The substance of the law under sovereignty has dispersed into a generalised call for equitable solutions or 'balancing' whenever conflicts arise. Standard academic justifications of state rights, either as a consequence of the pure fact of statehood or as laid down in legislative enactments, have no application. Nor can they have application because neither 'facts' nor 'rules' are self-evident in the way liberal lawyers once believed. The facts which are assumed to establish title do not appear 'automatically' but are the result of choosing a criterion from which facts may be invested with normative significance.[58] However, rules, too, are always subject to interpretation. In order to link itself to something tangible, interpretation should refer back to some kind of facts. To establish the sense of facts, we must take the perspective of a rule; to decide interpretative controversies about the rule, we must – under the social conception – look at facts. Hence the late modem silence about theoretical justifications and the leap to ad hoc compromise.

Sources

Despite its original emphasis on actual power, the doctrine of sovereignty seemed unworkable because of the abstract and arbitrary way in which its normative content was determined. It is possible to make a fresh start and imagine that international law might just as well be described not as a consequence of statehood but through a set of normative criteria – sources – for law-creation and identification.

Not surprisingly, sources doctrine is riddled with dualisms which express in different ways the conflicting pull of the demands for concreteness and normativity. The very doctrine is often understood from two perspectives: as a description of the social processes whereby states create law (concreteness) and as a methodology for verifying the law's content independently of political opinions (normativity). By integrating both explanations, sources doctrine can maintain its apparent objectivity. On the one hand, something would not be law merely as a result of the value of its content but as a result of a social process. On the other hand, the existence of sources as a constraining methodology creates the needed distance between it and whatever states might will at any one moment.

Although there is no major disagreement among international lawyers about the correct enumeration of sources (treaties, custom, general principles), the rhetorical

---

[57] The *LIAMCO* Award [1981] 20 ILR 76–77 paras 150–51.

[58] 'In the realm of law there is no fact in itself, no immediately evident fact; there are only facts ascertained by the competent authorities in a procedure determined by law'. H Kelsen, *Principles of International Law* (edited and revised by RMTucker) (New York, Holt, Rinehart and Winston, 1966) 388.

force of sources ('binding force') is explained from contrasting perspectives. Their importance is sometimes linked with their capacity to reflect state will (consensualism). At other times, such binding force is linked with the relationship of sources arguments with what is 'just', 'reasonable', 'in accordance with good faith', or some other non-consensual metaphor.

Standard disputes about the content or application of international legal norms use the contradiction between consent and justice-based explanations. One party argues in terms of consent, the other in terms of what is just (reasonable, etc). However, neither argument is fully justifiable alone. A purely consensual argument cannot ultimately justify the application of a norm against non-consenting states (apologism). An argument relying only on a notion of justice violates the principle of the subjectivity of value (utopianism). Therefore, they must rely on each other. Arguments about consent must explain the relevance and content of consent in terms of what seems just. Arguments about justice must demonstrate their correctness by reference to what states have consented to. As these movements (consent to justice; justice to consent) make the originally opposing positions look the same, no solution can be made by simply choosing one. A solution now seems possible only by either deciding what is it that states 'really' will or what the content of justice 'really' is. Neither question, however, is answerable on the premises of the Rule of Law.[59]

For the modem lawyer, it is very difficult to envisage, let alone to justify, a law which would divorce itself from what states think or will to be the law. The apparent necessity of consensualism seems grounded in the very criticism of natural norms as superstition. Yet, the criticisms against full consensualism – its logical circularity, its distance from experience, its inherent apologism – are well-known.[60] Consensualism cannot justify the application of a norm against a state which opposes such application unless it creates distance between the norm and the relevant state's momentary will. It has been explained, for example, that although law emerges from consent, it does not need every state's consent all the time, that a general agreement, a *volonté générale* or a *Vereinbarung* is sufficient to apply the norm.[61]

However, these explanations violate the principle of sovereign equality – they fail to explain why a state should be bound by what another state wills. This can, of course, be explained from some concept of social necessity. However, in such case we have already moved away from pure consensualism and face the difficulty of explaining the legal status of the assumed necessity and why it should support one norm instead of another.

A more common strategy is to explain that the state has originally consented (by means of recognition, acquiescence, by not protesting or by 'tacitly' agreeing), although it now denies it has. Such an argument is extremely important in liberal

---

[59] See also Kennedy, *International Legal Structures* (1987), 11–107.
[60] Koskenniemi, *From Apology to Utopia* (2005), 309–13.
[61] For the classic, see H Triepel, *Völkerrecht und Landesrecht* (Leipzig, Hirschfeld, 1899) 27, 51–53.

legitimation discourse. It allows defending social constraint in a consensual fashion while allowing the application of constraint against a state which denies it consent.[62] However, even this argument fails to be convincing because it must ultimately explain itself either in a fully consensual or fully non-consensual way and thereby becomes vulnerable to the objections about apologism or utopianism.

Why should a state be bound by an argument according to which it has consented, albeit 'tacitly'? If the reason is stated in terms of respecting its own consent, then we have to explain why we can know better than the state itself what it has consented to. Even consensualists usually concede that such knowledge is not open to external observers. However, even if it were possible to 'know better', such an argument is not really defensible within the premises of the Rule of Law. It contains the unpleasant implication that we could no longer rely on the expressed will of the legal subject. It would lose the principal justification behind democratic legislation and justify the establishment of a Leviathan – the one who knows best what everyone 'really' wills. It is a strategy for introducing authoritarian opinions in democratic disguise.

Tacit consent theorists usually explain that the question is not of 'real' but of 'presumed' will. However, what then allows the application of the presumption against a state denying that it had ever consented to anything like it? At this point the tacit consent lawyer must move from consensualism to non-consensualism. Tacit consent – or the presumption of consent – binds because it is 'just' or in accordance with reasonableness or good faith, or it protects legitimate expectations or the like.[63] Now the difficulty lies in defending the assumed non-consensual position. However, under the principle of subjective value, 'justice' cannot be discussed in a non-arbitrary way.[64] Were this otherwise, the Rule of Law would be pointless if not outright harmful. One might, of course, say that a notion of reasonableness is justified because the state in question has itself accepted it. However, this defence will re-emerge the problem of how it is possible to oppose a consensual justification against a state denying its validity and so on, *ad infinitum.*

In the *Gulf of Maine* case (1984), Canada argued that the United States was bound to a certain line of delimitation as it had not protested against its de facto use. Relying on absence of protest reflected, Canada explained, on the one hand, US consent to be bound and, on the other hand, gave expression to good faith and equity. It argued in terms of consent as well as justice. The Chamber of the Court accepted both explanations. It started out with the latter, non-consensual one. What is common to acquiescence and estoppel is that '. . . both follow from the fundamental principle of good faith and equity'.[65]

---

[62] See, eg the argument in A Bleckmann, *Grundprobleme und Methoden des Völkerrechts* (Freiburg, Alber, 1982) 81, 184–89. On the tacit consent construction generally, see Koskenniemi, *From Apology to Utopia* (2005), 325–33.

[63] See, eg JP Müller, *Vertrauenschutz im Völkerrecht* (Cologne, Heymann's, 1970); A Martin, *L'estoppel en droit international public* (Paris, Pedone, 1979).

[64] 'Le principe de bonne foi est un principe moral et rien de plus'. E Zoller, *La bonne foi en droit international public* (Paris, Pedone, 1977) 345.

[65] *Gulf of Maine* case [1984] ICJ Rep 305 para 130.

Had it followed this understanding, it should, because not all silence creates norms, have had to enter a discussion of whether or not the conditions of good faith or equity were present to bind the United States now. However, there was no such discussion. This is understandable, as arguing from non-consensual justice seems so subjective and abstract. Instead, it moved to a consensual understanding of relying on absence of protest and went on to discuss whether the 'Hoffmann letter' sent by the US administration to Canadian authorities was evidence of the United States' acceptance of the Canadian equidistance. It was not: '. . . facts invoked by Canada do not warrant the conclusion that the U.S. Government thereby recognized the median line . . .'[66]

In other words, the United States was not bound because there was no subjective intent to be (regardless of considerations of good faith or equity). How did the Court arrive at this conclusion? Not by relying on (the absence of) real US intent to be bound; this would have been apologist and in violation of Canadian sovereignty. The Chamber's conclusion did not concern lack of 'real' intent but rather of 'constructive' US intent. On what principles was that construction based? Mainly on inconsistency in the facts and on the low governmental status of the authorities involved.[67] However, what justified this choice of relevant facts and their ensuing interpretation? What made the Court's construction better than the Canadian one? The argument stops here. The principles of construction were left undiscussed.

In theory, the Chamber could have used two principles of construction: 1) a construction is justified if it corresponds to intent; 2) a construction is justified if it reflects non-consensual justice. These are exclusive justifications. However, neither was open to the Chamber. The former was excluded by the previous argument which ruled out the possibility of knowing real US intent and using it against Canada. The latter was excluded because it would have involved arguing in a fully non-consensual way against Canadian non-consensual justifications. This would have assumed the correctness of an objective justice and would have conflicted with the Chamber's previous refusal to think of acquiescence-estoppel in a fully non-consensual way. The Chamber simply took another interpretation of US conduct than Canada. Why it was better was not discussed as it could not have been discussed. The decision was, on its own premises, undetermined by legal argument.

An identical argumentative structure is present in treaty interpretation. Particular interpretations are traced back either to party will or to some idea of good faith, reasonableness, etc.[68] As 'real' party will cannot be identified and justifiably opposed to a party denying such intent, and because the content of what is a 'just' interpretation cannot be determined in a legal way, late modern doctrines usually concede the aesthetic, impressionistic character of the interpretative process.[69] Controversial

---

[66] ibid 307 para 138.

[67] ibid.

[68] For this contrast generally, see, eg, Zoller, *La bonne foi* (1977) 205–44.

[69] Sur, *L'interprétation en droit international public* (1974). See also McDougal, 'International Law, Power and Policy' (1953) 149–57.

points about party will clash against equally controversial points about the justice of particular interpretations.

In the case *Concerning the Interpretation of the Algerian Declarations of 19 January 1981*, the Iran-United States Claims Tribunal was to decide whether article II of the Claims Settlement Declaration included a right for Iran to press claims against United States' nationals. The majority held that it could not be so interpreted. A 'clear formulation' of that article excluded Iranian claims from the Tribunal's jurisdiction. This clear formulation had authority because it was the clearest evidence of Party consent.[70] The minority argued that a literal construction failed to give effect to the settlement's reciprocal character. According to the minority, reciprocity had been the very basis on which Iran had entered the agreement. By excluding reciprocity, the majority had violated Iranian consent and unjustifiably preferred the justice of literality to the justice of reciprocity.[71] Both sides invoke consent and justice but are unable to address each others' views directly. Neither side argues on the basis of 'real consent.' However, while the majority sees consent manifested in the text, the minority sees consent in reciprocity. Both sides say their interpretative principle is better as it better reflects consent. However, deciding the dispute on these arguments would require a means of knowing consent independently of its manifestations – a possibility excluded as reference was made to manifestations because of the assumption that real consent could not be known. Moreover, neither can the two sides argue that their justice – the justice of literality or the justice of reciprocity – is better without arguing from a theory of justice which seems indefensible under the Rule of Law. Ultimately, both interpretations are unargued. A doctrine which excludes arguments from 'knowing better' and natural justice has no means to decide on the superiority of conflicting interpretations.

Attempts to explain why states should be bound by unilateral declarations meet with similar problems. In the first place, as the ICJ observed in the *Nuclear Tests* case (1974), such statements might be held binding '(w)hen it is the intention of the state making the declaration that it should become bound according to its terms'.[72] However, their binding force cannot be fully consensual because then the state could be freed simply by a further act of will. Therefore, the Court also noted that

> (o)ne of the principles governing the creation and performance of legal obligations . . . is the principle of good faith . . . Thus interested states may take cognizance of unilateral declarations and place confidence in them, and are entitled to require that the obligation thus created be respected.[73]

Now the declaring state is bound regardless of its will, by the simple fact of the statement and others' reliance.

---

[70] Iran – United States Claims Tribunal, 'Interpretation of the Algerian Declaration of 19th January 1981' [1982] 62 ILR 599–600.
[71] ibid 603–606.
[72] *Nuclear Tests* cases [1974] ICJ Rep 267 para 43.
[73] ibid 268 para 46.

The necessity of making both arguments seems evident. The Court's first – consensual – argument justified holding France bound by its statements. However, it was also threatening because it implied that France could modify or terminate this obligation at will. This would violate the wills and sovereignty of the Applicants (Australia and New Zealand). The second – non-consensual – argument about good faith and legitimate expectations was needed to protect the latter. The decision was consensualist and non-consensualist at the same time. It allowed basing the applicable norm on protecting the sovereignty of each state involved. Simultaneously, it seemed to give effect to what justice seemed to require.

However, the decision also remains vulnerable from each perspective. How could the Court base its norm on French consent in the face of express French denial of any such consent? It leaves unexplained how it can protect the Applicants' reliance, as they denied having relied. It also leaves its theory of justice unexplained, which says that *these* statements and actions in *these* circumstances bind because that is in accordance with good faith.

The structure, importance and weaknesses of tacit consent is nowhere more visible that in the orthodox argument about customary international law.

According to this argument, binding custom exists if there is a material practice of states to that effect and that practice is motivated by the belief that it is obligatory. This 'two-element theory' gives expression to the principle of liberal sociology, for which the meaning – law or not law? – of social action lies neither in its external appearance nor in what someone thinks about but is a combination of the two: an external (material) and an internal (psychological) element.[74] The function of the former element is to ensure that custom can be ascertained without having to rely on states' momentary, political views. The point of the latter is to distinguish custom from coercion.

The problem with the two-element theory is that neither element can be identified independently of the other. Hence, they cannot be used to prevent the appearance of Mr Hyde in each other.

Modern lawyers have rejected fully materialistic explanations of custom as apologist, incapable of distinguishing between factual constraint and law. If the possibility is excluded that this distinction can be made by the justice of the relevant behaviour, then it can only be made by reference to the psychological element, the opinio juris. However, as many students of ICJ jurisprudence have shown, there are no independently applicable criteria for ascertaining the presence of the opinio juris. The ICJ has simply inferred its presence or absence from the extent and intensity of the material practice it has studied.[75] Moreover, it does not even seem possible to assume the existence of such criteria and that the opinio thus received

---

[74] See Hart, *The Concept of Law* (1961) 91. For discussion, see M Koskenniemi, 'The Normative Force of Habit; International Custom and Social Theory' (1990) 1 *Finnish Yearbook of International Law* 77.

[75] See, eg M Sørensen, *Les sources du droit international* (Copenhague, Munskgaard, 1946) 108–11; M Virally, 'The Sources of International Law' in M Sørensen (ed), *Manual of Public International Law* (London, New York, Macmillan, St Martin's Press, 1968) 134–35; H Günther, *Zur Enststehung von Völkergewohnheitsrecht* (Berlin, Duncker & Humblot, 1970) 70. See further, Koskenniemi *From Apology to Utopia* (2005) 428–29.

could be opposed to a non-consenting state. That would be an argument about 'knowing better'. In other words, although it seems possible to distinguish 'custom' from what is actually effective only by recourse to what states believe, such beliefs do not seem capable of identification regardless of what is actually effective.

One might try to avoid the above circularity by assuming that some types of behaviour are by their character – 'intrinsically' – such as to generate (or not to generate) normative custom. However, attempts to single out lists of such types have been unsuccessful. A 'flexible' concept of material practice has emerged: any act or statement may count as custom-generating practice if only the states wish so.[76] (Indeed, any other conclusion would manifest an illegitimate naturalism and violate the principles of liberal sociology: it would fail to have regard to the 'internal aspect'.) Using this criterion (what it is that states wish), however, would assume that we can know the opinio independently of the act in which it is expressed. However, this possibility was already excluded by our previous argument about the need to look at material practice in the first place. Indeed, were it so that we could know state intentions regardless of what states do, the whole two-element theory would become unnecessary: we could simply apply those intentions. Custom would coalesce with (informal) agreement. (In which case, of course, we would face the difficulty of having to interpret the content embedded in any such agreement by further reference to the parties' 'real' wills or to some notion of justice, as explained above.)

Customary law doctrine remains indeterminate because it is circular. It assumes behaviour to be evidence of states' intentions (opinio juris) and the latter to be evidence of what behaviour is relevant as custom. To avoid apologism (relying on the state's present will), it looks at the psychological element from the perspective of the material; to avoid utopianism (making the distinction between binding and non binding usages by reference to what is just) it looks at the material element from the perspective of the psychological. It can occupy neither position in a permanent way without becoming vulnerable to criticism compelled by the other. The very assumptions behind customary international law provide the mechanism for its self-destruction.

For late modern international practice the standard theory is increasingly a camouflage for what is really an attempt to understand custom in terms of a bilateralised equity. The ICJ, for instance, has always been somewhat ambiguous as to the character of the rules of non-written law which it has discerned. The Court's argument about the relevant custom in the *Anglo Norwegian Fisheries* (1951) as well as *Fisheries Jurisdiction* (1974) cases already looked upon the matter more in terms of the relevant interest at stake than trying to find some general rule to 'apply'.[77] The several maritime boundary cases further extended this move. The

---

[76] See, eg L Ferrari-Bravo, 'La coutume internationale dans la pratique des Etats' (1985) 192 *Recueil des Cours de l'Académie de droit international de la Haye* (1985) 243, 261 and Koskenniemi *From Apology to Utopia* (2005), 431–32.

[77] *Anglo–Norwegian* case [1951] ICJ Rep 133; *Fisheries Jurisdiction* cases [1974] ICJ Rep 30–33 [69]–[79].

judgment in the *US Military and Paramilitary Activities* case (1986) did not even seriously attempt to justify its four customary rules – non-use of force, non-intervention, respect for sovereignty and especially the relevant humanitarian rules – in terms of material practice and the opinio juris.[78] Many have been dissatisfied with the modern strategy of arguing every imaginable non-written standard as 'custom'. Sir Robert Jennings, among others, has noted that what we tend to call custom 'is not only not customary law: it does not even faintly resemble a customary law'.[79] However, if a non-written standard is not arguable in terms of material practices or beliefs relating to such practices then it can only exist as natural law – being defensible only by reference to the political importance of its content. In fact, much ICJ practice in the relevant respect remains *ex cathedra*: the Court has 'instituted a system of decision-making in which the conclusion reached is determined by the application of rules largely treated as self-evident'.[80] To be sure, often there is consensus on such rules, for instance, on the 'elementary considerations of humanity' invoked by the Court in the *Corfu Channel* case (1949). However, the problem is clearly less to explain why people who agree are bound, than also why those should be bound who do not agree, and how one should argue if interpretative controversies arise.

The Politics of International Law

The idea of an international Rule of Law has been a credible one because to strive for it implies no commitment regarding the content of the norms thereby established or the character of the society advanced. It was possible for nineteenth century European powers to start thinking of their relationships in terms of legal rules because they formalised inter-sovereign relationships and no sovereign needed to feel that their substantive policies were excluded by them. It was possible for the UN General Assembly to accept by consensus the Declaration on the 'Decade for International Law' in 1989 for precisely those same reasons. This is strikingly highlighted by the fact that the Declaration contained no substantive programme. The Declaration merely called for the promotion of respect for the principles of international law and the peaceful settlement of disputes and for the encouragement of the development and dissemination of international law. For what purpose the law was to be put or what kinds of rules it should promote was not addressed by it.

Modern international law is an elaborate framework for deferring substantive resolution elsewhere: into further procedure, interpretation, equity, context, and so on. The 1982 Law of the Sea Convention is a typical example: in place of a list

---

[78] *US Military and Paramilitary Activities* case [1986] ICJ Rep 97–115 [183]–[220].

[79] R Jennings, 'The Identification of International Law' in B Cheng (ed), *International Law, Teaching and Practice* (London, Stevens, 1982) 5.

[80] C Kearney, 'Sources of Law and the International Court of Justice' in L Gross (ed), *The Future of the International Court of Justice* (Dobbs Ferry, Oceana Publications, 1976) vol I, 653.

of do's and don'ts it establishes a framework for delimiting sovereign powers and allocating jurisdictions – assuming that the substantive problems of the uses of the sea can be best dealt with through allocating decision-power elsewhere, into context and usually by reference to 'equitable principles'.[81] The success of international law depends on this formality; this refusal to set down determining rules or ready-made resolutions to future conflict. Although there is a distinctly legal 'process' – and in this sense a relatively autonomous and coherent system which can be abstracted in academic treatises – there are no determining legal standards. Let me explain this somewhat schematically.

The Rule of Law constitutes an attempt to provide communal life without giving up individual autonomy. Communal life is, of course, needed to check individualism from leading either into anarchy or tyranny. Individualism is needed because otherwise it would remain objectionable for those who feel that the kind of community provided by it does not meet their political criteria. From their perspective, the law's communitarian pretensions would turn out as totalitarian apologies.[82]

The law aims to fulfil its double task by becoming formal: by endorsing neither particular communitarian ideals nor particular sovereign policies. Or, conversely, an acceptable legal rule, argument or doctrine is one which can explain itself both from the perspective of enhancing community (because it would otherwise seem apologist), as well as safeguarding sovereignty (because its implications would otherwise remain totalitarian). The problem is that as soon as any of these justifications are advanced to support *some particular kind of communal existence or some determined limit for sovereign autonomy*, they are vulnerable from an opposing substantive perspective. So, while an advocate justifies his or her preferred substantive outcome by its capacity to support community, it becomes simultaneously possible for his or her counterpart – not sharing the same communal ideal – to challenge the very justification as totalitarian. Correspondingly, a rule, principle or solution justified by resource to the way it protects sovereignty may – for someone drawing the limits of 'sovereignty' differently – be objected as furthering egoism and anarchy.

Take the case of transfrontier pollution, for example. Noxious fumes flow from state A into the territory of state B. State A refers to its 'sovereign right to use its natural resources in accordance with its national policies'. State B argues that A has to put a stop to the pollution. It interprets A's position to be an egoistic one while it makes its own argument seem communitarian. It might refer to a norm of 'non-harmful use of territory', for example, and justify this by reference to analogies from rules concerning international rivers and natural resources, as well as precedents and General Assembly resolutions.[83]

---

[81] See generally P Allott, 'Power Sharing in the Law of the Sea' (1983) 77 *American Journal of International Law* 1–30.

[82] See further the seminal article by D Kennedy, 'The Structure of Blackstone's Commentaries' (1979) 18 *Buffalo Law Review* 205.

[83] For both arguments, see Principle 21 of the Stockholm Declaration (n 51) and further Koskenniemi, 'International Pollution in the System of International Law' (1984), 100–03.

State A can now retort by saying that norms cannot be opposed to it in such a totalitarian fashion. A is bound only by norms which it has accepted. It has never accepted the analogies drawn by B. This would force B either to argue that its preferred norm binds irrespective of acceptance – in which case it stands to lose as its argument would seem utopian – or to change ground so as to make its position seem protective of sovereignty as well. State B might now argue that the pollution violates its own freedom and constitutes an interference in its internal affairs as Australia did in the *Nuclear Tests* case.[84] B's position would now seem both communitarian (in respect to A) and individualistic (in respect to B itself).

To counter this last argument by B, A needs to make a communitarian point. It may argue that there is a norm about friendly neighbourliness, for example such as that observed in the *Lake Lanoux* case (1957), which requires that states tolerate minor inconveniences which result from legitimate uses of neighbouring states' territories.[85] B cannot demand complete territorial integrity. A's position is now both individualistic (in respect of A itself) and communitarian (in respect of B).

The argument could be continued. Both parties could support the communitarian strand in their positions by referring to equity, general principles and the like, to deny the autonomy (egoism) of their opponent. They could also support the sovereignty-based arguments by further emphasis on their independence, consent, territorial integrity, self-determination, etc to counter their adversary's communitarian (totalitarian) arguments. As a result, the case cannot be decided by simply preferring autonomy to community or vice-versa. Both arguments support both positions. The case cannot be solved by reference to any of the available concepts (sovereignty, non-harmful use of territory, territorial integrity, independence, good neighbourliness, equity, etc) as each of the concepts may be so construed so as to support either one of the claims. Also, the constructions have no *legally* determined preference. A court could say that one of the positions is better as a matter of equity, for example. Or it might attempt to 'balance' the claims. However, in justifying its conception of what is equitable, the court will have to assume a theory of justice – a theory, however, which it cannot justify by further reference to the legal concepts themselves.

Another example concerns the relations between a foreign investor and the host state. The view which emphasises individualism, separation and consent may be put forward to support the host state's sovereignty – its right to nationalise the corporation without 'full, prompt and adequate' compensation. However, the same position can equally well be derived from communitarian points about justice, equality or solidarity or the binding character of the new international economic order, for example.[86] The home state's case may be argued in a similar way, by laying emphasis on that state's freedom, individuality and consent – as expressed in the acquired rights doctrine – or the non-consensually binding character of the *pacta sunt servanda* norm, good faith or other convenient conceptions of justice.

---

[84] *Nuclear Tests* cases ICJ Pleadings I 14.

[85] *Lake Lanoux* case XII UNRIAA 316.

[86] Both justifications for this right may be read, for example, from the Charter of Economic Rights and Duties of States, UNGA Res 3281 (XXIX) (12 December 1974).

To make a choice, the problem-solver should simply have to prefer one of the sovereignties – in which case sovereign equality is overruled – or it should use another theory of justice (or equity) which it cannot, however, justify by reference to the Rule of Law.[87]

The relationship between the principles of self-determination and territorial integrity, both having been enshrined in countless UN General Assembly Resolutions, has remained a puzzle.[88] The problem, as we can now understand it, is that neither of the conflicting principles can be preferred because they are ultimately the same. When a people call for territorial integrity, they call for respect for their identity as a self-determining entity and vice-versa. In order to solve the conflict, one should need an external principle about which types of human association entail this respect and which do not. This seems to involve arguing on the basis of contested, political views about the type of organisation the law should materially aim at.

The formality of international law makes it possible for each state to read its substantive conception of world society, as well as its view of the extent of sovereign freedom into legal concepts and categories. This is no externally introduced distortion in the law. It is a necessary consequence of a view which holds that there is no naturally existing 'good life', no limit to sovereign freedom which would exist by force of some historical necessity. If this kind of naturalism is rejected – and since the Enlightenment, everybody has had good reason to reject it – then to impose any substantive conception of communal life or limits of sovereignty can appear only as illegitimate constraint – preferring one state's politics to those of another.

It is impossible to make substantive decisions within the law which would imply no political choice. The late modern turn to equity in the different realms of international law is, in this sense, a healthy admission of something that is anyway there: in the end, legitimising or criticising state behaviour is not a matter of applying formally neutral rules but depends on what one regards as politically right, or just.

Conclusion

Theorists of the present often explain our post-modern condition as a result of a tragedy of losses. For international lawyers, the Enlightenment signified loss of

---

[87] 'A solution therefore should recognize the home state's and the host state's sovereign right to the investment concerned and should endeavour to find an equitable balance between them', I Seidl-Hohenveldem, 'International Economic Law. General Course on Public International Law' (1986) 198 *Recueil des Cours de l'Académie de droit international de la Haye* 54.

[88] See UNGA Res 1514 (XV) 14 December 1960; 2625 (XXV) 24 October 1970 and comments, eg in M Pomerance, *Self-Determination in Law and Practice; the New Doctrine in the United Nations* (Boston, Nijhoff, 1982), 43–47 and passim.

faith in a natural order among peoples, nations and sovereigns. To contain political subjectivism, nineteenth and twentieth century jurists put their faith variably on logic and texts, history and power to find a secure, objective foothold. Each attempt led to disappointment. One's use of logic depended on what political axioms were inserted as the premises. Texts, facts and history were capable of being interpreted in the most varied ways. In making his or her interpretations, the jurist was always forced to rely on conceptual matrices which could no longer be defended by the texts, facts or histories to which they provided meaning. They were, and are, arenas of political struggle.

However, the way back to Vitoria's or Suarez' unquestioning faith is not open to us. We cannot simply start assuming that politics – justice and equity – could be discussed so that in the end everyone should agree. This teaches us a lesson. As the world, including lawyers' views about it, is conflictual, any grand design for a 'world order' will always remain suspect. Any legal rule, principle or world order project will only seem acceptable when stated in an abstract and formal fashion. When it is applied, it will have overruled some interpretation, some collective experience and appear apologist.

Social theorists have documented a recent modern turn in national societies away from the *Rechtstaat* into a society in which social conflict is increasingly met with flexible, contextually determined standards and compromises.[89] The turn away from general principles and formal rules into contextually determined equity may reflect a similar turn in the development of international legal thought and practice. There is every reason to take this turn seriously – though this may mean that lawyers have to re-think their professional self-image. For issues of contextual justice cannot be solved by the application of ready-made rules or principles. Their solution requires venturing into fields such as politics, social and economic causality, which were formally delimited beyond the point at which legal argument was supposed to stop in order to remain 'legal'. To be sure, we shall remain uncertain. Resolutions based on political acceptability cannot be made with the kind of certainty post-Enlightenment lawyers once hoped to attain. And yet, it is only by their remaining so which will prevent their use as apologies for tyranny.

---

[89] See, eg RM Unger, *Law in Modern Society. Toward a Criticism of Social Theory* (New York, London, Free Press, Collier Macmillan, 1976); T O'Hagan, *The End of Law?* (Oxford, Blackwell, 1984).

2

The Politics of International Law – 20 Years Later

This chapter examines some of the changes in my own thinking about the politics of engaging in international law since the original publication of the article that opened the first issue of the *European Journal of International Law* in 1990. The chapter points to the change in focus from indeterminacy (to which I am as committed as ever) of legal arguments to the structural biases of international institutions. It then discusses the politics of definition, that is to say, the strategic practice of defining international situations and problems in new expert languages so as to gain control over them. It attacks the increasing 'managerialism' in the field and ends with a few reflections about the significance of the moment of the establishment of the Journal 20 years ago.

From Doctrines to Institutions

THE ARTICLE THAT opened the *European Journal of International Law* 20 years ago made the point about the inevitability of 'politics' in the profession of public international law.[1] It did this by analysing in some detail doctrinal problems – sovereignty, sources, history, case law – familiar to all international lawyers. It was, of course, written in the vein of 'criticism'. Its style and outlook followed those of legal realism and critical legal studies, mainstream structuralism, and aspects of legal hermeneutics – but it tried to keep its methodological commitments below the surface so as to speak directly to the field. It had been inspired by a thorough-going frustration with the isolation of public international law from developments in legal theory and method and the conviction that the naïvety of the profession was anything but innocent – that it was somehow responsible for the implication of public international law in the perpetuation of the very problems that it officially claimed to alleviate. The article was not very clear about what its target was, apart from lack of professional imagination, and it left quite open its own commitments, what it wanted to 'achieve' (apart from more complexity, more self-awareness within the profession). Nor did it explain what it

---

[1] M Koskenniemi, 'The Politics of International Law' (1989) 1 *European Journal of International Law* 1, 1–38 (above, Chapter 1).

meant by 'politics' in its title beyond the kind of issues that lawyers had always pointed to when they discussed the use of 'discretion' in the law.

The article may itself have been somewhat naïve in its assumption that the demonstration of the contradictory and inconsequential nature of legal argument, the way everything about the law deferred to contested ('political') assumptions, about the world would make the scales fall from the eyes of the professionals; that it would compel a process of self-examination that would transform the preferences of international institutions in support of 'progressive' causes. The kind of immanent critique of which it was part does not really work like that. Above all, it is powerless against the experience that legal experts may themselves fail to take the claims of determinacy and coherence all that seriously: '[o]f course we know that it is not that simple. Of course more is at work out there'. In such a case, the critical intervention only confirms what everybody already (secretly) knows – and fires back against the critic as an accusation that the latter has simply missed the boat. Moreover, drawing attention to incoherence and conflict seems to assume that international law is an *intellectual* discipline that would (or should) pay much regard to logical problems. That may be altogether wrong. As craft, it may simply by-pass its intellectual ambitions as an inessential:

> We deal with serious problems of peace and war, governance, and distribution. And you are worried about coherence. As if *that* were somehow progressive! And if coherence and determinacy are never to be attained anyway, why would *your* incoherence be any better than ours?

A demonstration that 'it all depends on politics' does not move one inch towards a *better* politics.

Now, many of these problems have been discussed and highlighted in novel ways in the course of the past two decades. A new generation of lawyers has taken stock of the power and weakness of the critiques and my own responses and revisions have been published in many places, the fullest version in the Epilogue to the 2005 edition of *From Apology to Utopia* and in a lecture at the London School of Economics in 2007.[2] There is today much more readiness to engage in reflection on international law's political roles, its dark and bright sides, than 20 years ago. Students with intellectual ambition are increasingly engaging with themes first laid out in the work of David Kennedy and continued by him along with many others. The directions of new work have been explored elsewhere.[3] A particularly import-

---

[2] M Koskenniemi, *From Apology to Utopia; the Structure of International Legal Argument* (1989) (Re-issue with a new Epilogue, Cambridge University Press, 2005) and chapter eight in this volume. For detailed comments by readers, see especially the essays in the special issues marking the publication of the new edition of *From Apology to Utopia* in (2006) 7 *German Law Journal.*

[3] See, eg D Cass, 'Navigating the Newstream' (1996) 65 *Nordic Journal of International Law* 341; S Ratner, A-M Slaughter (eds), *The Methods of International Law* (Washington, ASIL, 2004).; A Orford, *International Law and its Others* (Cambridge, Cambridge University Press, 2006); M Koskenniemi, 'International Legal Theory and Doctrine' in *Max Planck Encyclopedia of International Law* (2008), available at: www.mpepil.com. See also E Jouannet, H Ruiz-Fabri, and J-M Sorel (eds), *Regards d'une nouvelle génération sur le droit international* (Paris, Pedone, 2008) and S Marks (ed), *International Law on the Left: Re-examining Marxist Legacies* (Cambridge, Cambridge University Press, 2008).

ant facet of the new approaches in the field is how they deal with post-colonial themes and often come from students in the Third World, even if educated in the universities of the North. In any case, it often seems that the greatest political stakes are in whether a new generation of Third World intellectuals is able to combine legal professionalism with a new strategic awareness of the limits and possibilities offered by international law for political engagement.

The article of 20 years ago dealt with the structure of international legal language. The most significant addition to the original piece is emphasis on *structural bias* that moves from doctrinal analysis to a discussion of institutional practices, the way in which patterns of fixed preference are formed and operate inside international institutions. A demonstration of the lack of coherence ('politics') of legal argument is only a preface to the more important point that although all the official justifications of decision-making are such that they may support contrary positions or outcomes, in practice nothing is ever that random. Competent lawyers know that the world of legal practice is actually quite predictable. As Susan Marks recently put it, alongside the demonstration of 'false necessity' – by now a classical critical theme – what needs demonstration is 'false contingency', the idea that because the argumentative structures are open anything goes in fact.[4] Recent debates of global governance and especially international law's fragmentation have well demonstrated the emergence and operation of structural bias. Through specialisation – that is to say, through the creation of special regimes of knowledge and expertise in areas such as 'trade law', 'human rights law', 'environmental law', 'security law', 'international criminal law', 'European law', and so on – the world of legal practice is being sliced up in institutional projects that cater for special audiences with special interests and special ethos. The point of creating such specialised institutions is precisely to affect the outcomes that are being produced in the international world. Very little is fully random out there, as practising lawyers know very well, directing their affairs to those institutions where they can expect to receive the most sympathetic hearing.

This is why much about the search for political direction today takes the form of jurisdictional conflict, struggle between competing expert vocabularies, each equipped with a specific bias. If such regimes are bold in ambition, and able to rely on the support of some powerful sector of the political world, then they may succeed in changing the general bias in the law. For example, the rise of the bilateral investment treaty has certainly transformed the relationship between the private investor and host state from what it was 20 years ago. On a smaller scale, the effort by the International Criminal Tribunal on Former Yugoslavia in the *Tadić* case to hold outside states responsible for the behaviour of parties in a civil war on the basis of the overall control they exercised over the latter, is another example of a (perhaps failed) effort to change in the law in support of the 1990s project 'against impunity'. Other examples come from the re-interpretation of general legal vocabularies such as 'human rights' in terms of the preferences of new sectoral

---

[4] S Marks, 'False Contingency' (2010) 62 *Current Legal Problems* 1–22.

interests – say, the interests of private ownership or security. As 'human rights', like any legal vocabulary, is intrinsically open-ended, what gets read into it (or out of it) is a matter of subtle interpretative strategy. If a British court is able to read the indefinite detention of a person in Iraq as a human rights measure, then that decision will become part of a shifting pattern of outcomes produced by institutions having recourse to human rights vocabularies.[5]

More modest but not necessarily less effective is to refrain from attacks on the old bias, and argue 'only' in terms of a patterned exception. This is how novel preferences usually are consolidated. The argument is that owing to 'recent developments' in the technical, economic, political, or whatever field (typically linked with some sociological language about 'globalisation'), new needs or interests have emerged that require a new treatment. The new regime – say, a regime of environmental protection or security – seeks to respond to new 'challenges' not by replacing the old rule but merely by creating an 'exception' to it. Sometimes, however, the exception may gain more ground until it becomes the new rule. 'Human rights' and 'trade' have certainly behaved like that. The fact that many US law schools (and some European ones) have replaced courses on 'public international law' by courses on 'international environmental law', 'international business transactions', 'international criminal law', or 'law and globalisation' suggests that the centre may have completely collapsed, its place taken by a plethora of specialisations, each with its own preferred idiom, career prospects, and, of course, structural bias. This is why the most important political conflicts in the international world are often legally articulated as conflicts of jurisdiction and applicable law. Topics such as 'trade and environment', 'security and human rights', 'development and investment' give name to some such conflicts, while notions such as 'sustainable development', 'responsibility to protect', or 'human security', among a host of others, single out fragile compromises in areas where the struggle between opposing groups of experts and their preferences has not (yet) been taken to the end. They also indicate cutting-edge themes within which ambitious lawyers increasingly like to intervene for political effect. All this is based on the insight that it is anything but irrelevant to know, regardless of what the law is, which institution gets to decide – for example, whether a problem about pollution from a nuclear reprocessing plant is dealt with under a universal law of the sea regime or a regional economic integration scheme; whether the management of fishery stocks is directed to food and agricultural officials (Food and Agriculture Organisation (FAO)), trade experts (World Trade Organisation (WTO)), or conservationists (Convention on International Trade in Endangered Species (CITES)); or whether the activities of military officials

---

[5] For the former example, see Case CO/3673 *The Queen (on the application of Hilal Abdul-Razzaq Ali Al-Jedda) v Secretary of Defence* [2005] EWHC 1809 (Admin), (2007) QB 621 [104]. In the same vein, see the discussion of the arguments of Australia's Attorney-General concerning counter-terrorism measures as an implementation of human rights in Carne, 'Reconstituting "Human Security" in a New Security Environment. An Australian, two Canadians and Article 3 of the Universal Declaration on Human Rights' (2006) 25 *Australian Year Book of International Law* 1.

in conflict-zones ought to be assessed through the prism of human rights or humanitarian law.[6]

Political intervention is today often a politics of redefinition, that is to say, the strategic definition of a situation or a problem by reference to a technical idiom so as to open the door for applying the expertise related to that idiom, together with the attendant structural bias. Here, only imagination sets the limit. Think about an everyday international occurrence such as the transport of hazardous chemicals at sea. This can be conceptualised at least through half a dozen vocabularies accompanied by the same number of forms of expertise and types of preference: law of trade, law of transport, law of the environment, law of the sea, 'chemical law', and the law of human rights. Each would have something to say about the matter. Each would narrate it as part of a different set of human pursuits, values, and priorities. Trade law might focus on trade agreements between the countries and their relations with third parties. Transport law might highlight the legal-technical relationships between the different parties to a single contract of carriage and allocate jurisdiction differently between the legal systems to which they adhere. Environmental law might examine the nature of the cargo and the properties of the environment through which it is passing. Law of the sea might fix on the jurisdiction of the coastal state and the port state, or perhaps on the relevant International Maritime Organisation (IMO) standards, while 'chemical law' would examine it from the perspective of the best practices, standard operation forms, and the economic position of the industry. Finally, the law of human rights might concentrate on the dangers of the voyage to the persons involved in it, the conditions on board the ship and during the off-loading of the cargo to the local populations, and so on. Each such vocabulary is likely to highlight some solutions, some actors, some interests. None of them is any 'truer' than the others. Each renders some aspect of the carriage visible, while pushing other aspects into the background, preferring certain ways to deal with it, at the cost of other ways. What is being put forward as significant and what gets pushed into darkness is determined by the choice of the language through which the matter is looked at, and which provides the basis for the application of a particular kind of law and legal expertise. That this choice is not usually seen as such – that is as a *choice* – by the vocabularies, but instead something natural, renders them ideological. If 20 years ago it seemed intellectually necessary and politically useful to demonstrate the indeterminacy (and, thus, political preference) within the idiom of public international law, today's critique will have to focus on the clash of different idioms – public international law just one competitor among many to global authority – and

---

[6] The first example is that of the MOX plant. For my comments on this see M Koskenniemi, 'Constitutionalism, Managerialism and the Ethos of Legal Education' (2007) 1 *European Journal of Legal Studies* 1–18; for the latter see MA Young 'A Legal Framework for Regime Interaction: Lessons from International Trade and Fisheries Regimes' (Talk at the Lauterpacht Centre of International Law, Cambridge, 21 November 2008). For a recent plea to apply human rights (over humanitarian law) standards in international conflict, see A Orakhelashvili, 'The Interaction between Human Rights and Humanitarian Law: Fragmentation, Conflict, Parallelism, or Convergence?' (2008) 19 *European Journal of International Law* 161.

highlight the way their competing descriptions work to push forward some actors or interests while leaving others in the shadows.

The politics of redefinition is about shifts in the production of types of outcome within international institutions, reflecting efforts by the native language speakers of some local idiom to raise the status of that idiom to a kind of Esperanto. This is what the emphasis on 'universality' in our profession is looking after. It may not be sufficient simply to occupy the place of decision. One may also want to ensure that the decisions seem to emanate from some external logic or method that is neutral among the participants, that what is at work is not really 'one's' method but the universal (or 'scientific') method – or, even better, that at work is not a 'method' at all but *reality* itself.[7] There is nothing that would be new or out of order in this process – apart from the fact that the struggles are described in the neutral language of expertise.[8] This hides or obscures the contingent nature of the choices made, the fact that at issue is structural bias and not the application of some neutral economic, environmental, human rights, or security *reason*. To this extent the vocabularies act as 'ideologies' in the technical sense of reifying, making seem necessary or neutral something that is partial and contested. Awareness of bias in this sense suggests two conclusions in regard to teaching students, writing articles, or co-operating with colleagues. One is to examine the strategic choices that are opened by particular vocabularies of global governance more closely. The other concerns the proper attitude to take with regard to the managerialism underlying today's international legal debates.

Practice: An Eye to Strategic Choices

International law today offers a wide variety of specialist vocabularies and institutions with which we engage in legal practice. Very often, as David Kennedy has observed, we commit to them without reflecting on their effects in the world of outcomes.[9] There is the sense that doing 'international law' or 'human rights' or 'free trade', or by working for institutions that are committed to 'refugees', 'humanitarian law', or 'human security', is *by itself* a progressive move, and that joining the native speakers of those idioms is automatically a beneficial move to accomplish. However, if the critique of indeterminacy of 20 years ago is right, then that cannot be automatically the case. On the contrary, the vocabularies and institutions must themselves appear as sites of controversy and compromise where

---

[7] I describe this in terms of struggle for hegemony in chapter nine of this volume.

[8] See further D Kennedy, 'The Mystery of Global Governance' (1 Kormendy Lecture, Ohio Northern University, Petit College of Law, 25 January 2008), available at: www.harvard.edu/faculty/faculty-workshops/kennedy.workshop.pdf.

[9] D Kennedy, *The Dark Sides of Virtue. Reassessing International Humanitarianism* (Princeton, Princeton University Press, 2005).

prevailing 'mainstreams' constantly clash against minority challengers. Broad agreement on institutional objectives among lawyers in the same field often leads to complete disagreement about how the objectives should be understood and what might be the best way of bringing them about in a particular situation; there is a Left and a Right of trade law, as well as conservative and anti-conservative ways to speak about human rights. Globalisation may have shifted the *locus* of political engagement from 'sovereign states' to 'functional regimes'.[10] However, it has hardly transformed the dynamics of such engagement. It is still about conquering the decision-making position within one's institution, and then laying out the agenda of reform.

It is useful to think of the 'functional regime' by analogy to the 'sovereign state' that existed once upon a time. Like the latter, regimes are characterised ideologically by solipsism and imperialism, both self-absorption and the urge to translate everything on sight into their own preferred idiom. Yet, they are not 'billiard balls' but are divided as regards their point and purpose and the right strategic choices to be made in view of any particular situation as nation-states are. By now we have learned that possessing some particular national identity is indeterminate. It does not commit to particular ways of thinking or behaving, at least not unless one unreflectively assimilates in some phantasm of the 'national spirit' – something international lawyers have been, by profession, well buttressed against. Analogously, functional vocabularies are indeterminate, coexisting with the most varied ways of thinking and acting in the world. Economists, environmentalists, and human rights experts are just as divided among themselves as Finns, Frenchmen, or Fijians about how to understand the world and what to do with it. The regimes, institutions, and vocabularies offered to lawyers as languages to manage 'globalisation' do not have automatic consequences: to join an institution or to choose a professional language is no more to close oneself in an iron cage than to be the national of Finland, France, or Fiji. The critique of 20 years ago demonstrated the indeterminacy of public international law. Today, critical analysis will have to do the same in regard to such alternative vocabularies.[11] This is good news inasmuch as the prospects of a meaningful professional life are concerned: many things are open for redefinition and innovation inside the vocabularies themselves. However, to take advantage of this requires adopting a more nuanced attitude to the jurisdictional conflicts and the attendant choices about distributionary effects. It is seldom self-evident what side one should take in disputes about competence: the trade idiom may be used to bind and to liberate, just as is the environmental idiom. This demands increasing sensitivity for the strategic choices.

---

[10] See G Teubner and A Fischer-Lescano, *Regime-Kollisionen. Zur Fragmentierung des globalen Rechts* (Frankfurt, Suhrkamp, 2006).

[11] Nothing is easier than this, and much work has been done, for example, to show the indeterminacy of human rights, security, and environmental vocabularies – and thus to point to the political choices preferred or downplayed by those types of discourse. So far, the biases of the trade regime have been rather more assumed than rigorously demonstrated. A useful beginning is, however, A Orford, 'Trade, Human Rights, and the Economy of Sacrifice' in Orford, *International Law and its Others* (2006), especially 166–92.

Let me take a familiar example. Human rights activists and security experts frequently choose strategies for 'mainstreaming' to increase their influence in trade policy, government of failed states, or development co-operation.[12] If the strategy is successful, the object institution will make increasing use of human rights or security language in its official documents and new administrative positions will be opened for 'human rights experts' or 'security experts'. While all of this may indeed empower human rights activists or security professionals, it is still very far from having any effect in institutional outcomes. In the first place, as I have tried to argue above, *any* policy may with some ingenuity be described in 'human rights' or 'security' terms owing to the openness of those terms. If the institutional outcomes are not changed, then the change of vocabulary will only end up stunning the capacity for transformation that was originally sought. However, it is frequently unclear what the 'human rights preference' or the 'security concern' might entail. In development projects, for example, human rights may be put forward to support private indigenous ownership but also in order to establish state-supported co-operatives. They may be invoked to attack or to support some large-scale agricultural project, depending on whether priority is put on concerns for food production or pollution prevention. Also, what about massive attacks on suspected 'terrorist outposts' in formally neutral countries? Do they actually limit or increase terrorism? The point is not that such questions could not be answered; only that applying some particular language may not yet bring clear directives for action. One needs to know *whose* understanding of 'human rights' or *which notion* of security ought to be preferred and, once that preference is fixed, what type of action will best support it.[13]

It is a familiar experience that the more activists participate in administrative management, the more they will feel the difficulty of identifying those policies that will actually support the interests they wanted to support as they started out. The openness of professional vocabularies to disputed choices will push lawyers to increasingly detailed analyses of economic efficiency, administrative appropriateness and social causality. The more pressing such questions become, however, the more legal work will become indistinguishable from the activity of those *other* experts, economic experts, administrative co-ordinators, sociologists, and so on. In the end the question arises whether there is (or *can be*) *any* distinct commitment to 'human rights' or 'security' – or indeed 'law' – that would not be a commitment to a *particular* theory of economic development, fairness in distribution, or administrative appropriateness.

It is hard to see how the dangers in seeking to transform institutional reformers into mainstream administrators could be avoided without taking critical distance

---

[12] Two studies on such strategies with which I have been recently associated include S Seppänen, *Possibilities and Challenges of the Human-Rights Based Approach to Development* (Helsinki, The Erik Castrén Institute, 2005) and T Pajuste, *Mainstreaming Human Rights in the Context of the European Security and Defence Policy* (Helsinki, The Erik Castrén Institute, 2008).

[13] Another recent study published in Helsinki makes some of these points: see P Niemelä, *The Politics of the Responsibility to Protect. Problems and Prospects* (Helsinki, The Erik Castrén Institute, 2008).

from 'mainstreaming' altogether. There is much to be said in favour of critical voices staying *outside regular administrative procedures*, as critics and watchdogs, flagging the interests and preferences of those who are not regularly represented in international institutions. This protects them from the need to make the kinds of mundane choices that administrators have to make on a routine basis and that call for a downsizing of one's preferences into pragmatic thumb-rules that are streamlined with existing practices. Yet, this risks marginalisation, irrelevance, or even the hubris of martyrdom and can no more be recommended in general terms than its counterpart. The choice whether to participate or not is an ever-present dilemma of any institutional politics and it cannot be resolved by a general formula. Only strategic sensitivity and the pursuit of critical distance can be recommended – qualities that are opposed to full immersion in the administrative culture in which one is called upon to work, that is, opposed to managerialism.

Theory: Against Managerialism

Since that early article, much has happened in the international legal academia. There is now a growing body of critical writing that uses the kinds of techniques that it displayed and embodies the same kind of transformative urge, but is perhaps clearer in what it rejects and what it wants to achieve in the world. The critical project has been extended to human rights law, international criminal law, environmental law, post-conflict governance, state-building, and 'intervention', among others. New writing has sought links with new thinking in comparative law, private international law or private law *tout court*, law and development, as well as legal history.[14] Work on institutional (instead of merely argumentative) practices of international actors (the United Nations, intergovernmental organisations, expert regimes and networks) has focused on the gap between promise and achievement.[15] It has become common to adopt a feminist, or a third world, or post-colonial, or even a Marxian vocabulary, and thus to foreground the political commitments of the analysis.[16] It is not at all alien to see legal writings peppered

---

[14] This work is too extensive to be adequately reflected here. For some examples, see, eg A Riles (ed), *Rethinking the Masters of Comparative Law* (Oxford & Portland/Oregon, Hart Publishing, 2001); K Knop, R Michaels, and A Riles (eds), 'Transdisciplinary Conflicts of Laws' (2008) 71 *Law and Contemporary Problems*; D Trubek and A Santos, *The New Law and Economic Development* (New York, Cambridge University Press, 2006); Orford (n 3); A Anghie, *Imperialism, Sovereignty and the Making of International Law* (Cambridge, Cambridge University Press, 2004); N Berman, *Passions et ambivalences. Le colonialisme, le nationalisme et le droit international* (Paris, Pedone, 2008).

[15] See, eg R Wilde, *International Territorial Administration. How Trusteeship and the Civilizing Mission Never Went Away* (Oxford, Oxford University Press, 2008); N Bhuta, 'Against State-Building' (2008) 15 *Constellations* 517.

[16] See, eg C Chinkin and H Charlesworth, *The Boundaries of International Law. A Feminist Analysis* (Manchester, Manchester University Press, 2000); Anghie, *Imperialism, Sovereignty and the Making of International Law* (2004); Marks (ed), *International Law on the Left* (2008).

by anthropological, sociological languages, or references and insights carried over from international relations, political theory, or political economy.

But 'interdisciplinarity' often comes with a dubious politics.[17] I am particularly thinking of the kind of 'managerialism' that suggests that international problems – problems of 'globalisation' – should be resolved by developing increasingly complicated technical vocabularies for institutional policy-making. One encounters this often in the suggestion to replace international law's archaic *mores* by a political science-inspired language of 'governance', 'regulation', or 'legitimacy'. The managerial approach is critical of the formal aspects of the legal craft that it often sees as an obstacle for effective action. Its preference lies with informal 'regimes' and its focus is on (the fact of) 'compliance', rather than (normative) analysis of what there is to comply with. Managerialism wants to realise 'actors" (often identified as billiard-ball states) more or less unproblematic 'interests'. For it, the objectives of institutional action are given and the only remaining questions concern their manner of optimal realisation. The fantasy position of the managerialist is that of holding the prince's ear – hence the anxious concern for concrete results, insistence on the policy-proposal at the end of the article.[18] For the managerialist, normative questions about the ends of action or about the right order between conflicting ends appear only in the language of 'legitimacy' that translates them into empirically manoeuvrable 'feelings' in the audience.[19] As behaviour is not caused by law but by 'coincidence of interest and coercion', the managerialist can only view 'interdisciplinarity' as a path to academic takeover: 'There is a more sophisticated international law literature in the international relations subfield of political science.'[20]

The more one conceives of international law in those terms, however, the sillier it begins to look. The world's causalities are too complex, the strategic simplifications too crude. The functional 'interest' is not a solid policy datum to 'apply' but an object of interpretative controversy, stable neither in place nor in time and just as indeterminate as the 'rule' that it was to replace – although of course accompanied by a different bias, that of the policy-science elite. This is not only a problem about the anachronism of a suggested return to a time (of innocence?) before the *Positivismusstreit* of the 1960s and 1970s, that is to say, before the collapse of the idea that normative social science ought to be constructed through the idiolect of behavioural explanation and prediction.[21] Of course, empirical and technical

---

[17] Not to say anything about the way it serves to *strengthen* disciplinary boundaries by taking them for granted and by perpetuating the disciplinary identifications of participants by casting them as 'representatives' of particular academic orientations.

[18] I have discussed this in M Koskenniemi, 'Constitutionalism as Mindset. Reflections on Kantian Themes about International Law and Globalization' (2007) 8 *Theoretical Inquiries in Law* 9. See also chapter 13 of this volume.

[19] See further M Koskenniemi, 'Legitimacy, Rights and Ideology: Notes towards a Critique of the New Moral Internationalism' (2003) 7 *Associations. Journal of Legal and Social Theory* (2003) 349.

[20] J Goldsmith and E Posner, *The Limits of International Law* (Oxford, Oxford University Press, 2005) 15.

[21] For an introduction, see T Adorno (ed), *The Positivist Dispute in German Sociology* (London, Verso, 1976).

knowledge have their uses. They sharpen analysis and give a clearer sense of the available alternatives for action. However, they have nothing at all to say that would be of normative and even less of emancipatory interest.[22] Yet, managerialism has its concealed normativity that privileges values and actors occupying dominant positions in international institutions and who therefore have no reason to take a critical attitude to those institutions. It solidifies the sense that questions of distribution and preference have already been decided elsewhere, so all that remain are technical questions, questions about how to smooth the prince's path.

On the other hand, the more I think about the traditional (European) jurisprudence of exegesis and the managerialism that seeks to challenge it, the more the two appear to inhabit the same conceptual space. The search for the right interpretation of a concept and the optimal derivation of a policy from some notion of 'interest' appear equally fixated to the search for a right answer, and the belief that this is accessible by technical reasoning, in the one case through interpretation, in the other by 'rational choice'. Both are equally insistent on downplaying the role of will and randomness, passion and ideology in the way the world is governed, and their own implication in it. Although both fall modestly back on the contextuality of each solution they offer, each still thinks of itself as a *general* theory or method. With this, they allocate decision-making powers to the native speakers of their attendant vocabularies, and thus attain subtle shifts in the pattern of institutional decision and outcome. At their best, both illuminate some participant experience of the world, and thus enable us to plan and communicate professionally within international institutions. At their worst, they obscure the way power works and make particular intellectual or social hierarchies appear as natural aspects of our lives.

This suggests that the juxtaposition between European constitutional formalism and the 'imperial' challenge to international institutions by the United States in the past years – the subject of much academic hand-wringing – may be somewhat off the mark. To believe that commitment to 'law' would be an automatically progressive choice is no less crude a directive to policy than the belief that all needs to be streamlined for the attainment of imperial preference. The question always remains: what kind of (or whose) law, and what type of (and whose) preference? Constitutionalism and empire go well together, as testified both by nineteenth century European experience and today's American one. Of course, the constitutionalism put forward especially from German universities today is culturally connected with (or has a bias for) transparency and accountability that are valuable aspects of institutional lives.[23] However, these are no proof for becoming a facade

---

[22] For another introduction, see J Habermas, *Knowledge and Human Interest* (Cambridge US, MIT Press, 1976).

[23] For the politics of constitutionalism see now 'The Exercise of Public Authority by International Institutions', Special Issue of the German Law Journal (edited by A von Bogdandy, R Wolfrum, J von Bernstorff, P Dann, and M Goldmann) (2008) 9 *German Law Journal* 1375. For the turn to administrative vocabularies, see B Kingsbury, N Krisch, and RB Stewart (eds), 'The Emergence of Global Administrative Law' (2005) 68 *Law & Contemporary Problems*.

for stasis, and the question always needs to be asked, what is included in the constitution, and what is left out (as 'private', for example, or as 'scientific'), and whom does the present constitution lift to decision-making positions? I totally approve of the political move to redefine the managerial world of international institutions through constitutional or administrative vocabularies – not because of the intrinsic worth of those vocabularies, however, but for the critical challenge they pose to today's culture of a-political expert rule, and perhaps for the appeal of the (Kantian) perfectibility that they set up as a regulative goal for human institutions.[24] However, law is no panacea. Problems in the 'war on terror', for example, do not emerge from the absence of 'law' or 'rights' – in fact, a huge amount of law and regulation enables and directs the activities of those implicated.[25] This means that merely by making something 'legal' or a matter of 'right' will not suffice as assurance for the beneficiality of one's choice. Would a Security Council authorisation to the Iraq war really have changed the way we thought of it? Should it have done so? Again, one cannot avoid recourse to strategic choices. Or, more realistically, one cannot avoid oscillating between figuring out the right strategic choice and falling back on institutionally conventional ways of acting as proper thumb-rules about appropriate policy.

One antidote to exegesis and managerialism lies in a turn to history so visible in international law recently. This may have been inspired by a purely historiographical concern: the sense that not enough has been done to elucidate the often ambivalent role that law and lawyers have played in policy-making and conflict or that standard histories have either erred on the side of hagiography or have squeezed the world's causalities into excessively homogenous epochal narratives. New histories have tried to create a live sense that the profession is not only about *limiting* the use of power, but enabling and facilitating the use of power. Often they have been inspired by a normative concern, particularly the gut feeling that some aspect of today's policy is best understood as a washed-up version of some past pattern of privilege (typically Eurocentrism, colonialism, or the 'civilising mission').[26] *Historia magistra vitae* may be a methodologically dubious basis on which to make the point about the importance of history. As a style of legal writing, however, historical narrative liberates the political imagination to move more freely in the world of alternative choices, illuminating both its false necessities and false contingencies.

---

[24] See Koskenniemi, 'Constitutionalism' (2007), above note 18, 33–36.

[25] See D Kennedy, *Of War and Law* (Princeton, Princeton University Press, 2006); Johns, 'Guantanamo Bay and the Annihilation of the Exception' (2005) 16 *European Journal of International Law* 613.

[26] See especially the works by Berman, *Passions et ambivalences. Le colonialisme, le nationalisme et le droit international* (2008) and Anghie, *Imperialism, Sovereignty and the Making of International Law* (2004) and, eg, the extensively historical C Mieville, *Between Equal Rights: A Marxist Theory of International Law* (Leiden, Brill, 2005) and E Jouannet and H Ruiz-Fabri, *Imperialisme et droit international en Europe et aux Etats-Unis* (Paris, Société de Législation compareé, 2007).

European Journal of International Law

Some years ago I published an account of the establishment of the first international law journal, the *Revue de droit international et la législation comparée* in 1869 and the first professional international society, the *Institut de droit international* in 1873, as part of the European liberal entrenchment after a period of progress in Europe as clouds of the coming crisis had begun to appear on the political horizon.[27] International law was born from a move to defend a liberal-internationalist project in a time of danger and opportunity. The men of 1873 knew what Lenin knew, namely that a journal is not only a collective propagator or a collective agitator but also a collective organiser. There was, I suppose, much of that also in the setting up of the *European Journal of International Law* in 1989 and the European Society of International Law some years thereafter. Twenty years ago, like at the end of the nineteenth century, lawyers, animated by what the 'men of 1873' called their *esprit d'internationalité*, responded to ongoing changes in the world by a turn to intensified professionalism with modernising ethos.[28] That response would be organised from a variety of distinctive locations. In 1873 the key locations were Columbia University, Ghent, Heidelberg, and Geneva; in 1989 Florence, Munich, again Geneva, and Greenwich Village. The point was to turn a position of privilege into progressive causes (and inevitably the other way around). The *European Journal* has since then become one of the more interesting publications in the field and New York University has come to be regarded as the home of the world's most prestigious European law school. However, it is harder to say whether that translates into political influence, or what direction that influence might have had. The fact that the Journal no longer accepts French manuscripts speaks much about the 'Europe' in its title. However, meaningful political projects are not necessarily linked with a determined territorial base, a *Nomos*. The arguments made above suggest that labelling one's project under the title of 'Europe' may evoke all kinds of ambivalent cultural and political associations. It is a strategic choice that cannot be reduced to alignment with an inherent utopian ethos in that overburdened name. Yet, one should bear in mind that what that choice achieves in the world cannot continuously be rethought in strategic terms. Like any name or a concept, it receives independence; it becomes an autonomous carrier of a bias and we adopt it as second nature, a home and a faith, a prison and an open door.

---

[27] M Koskenniemi, *The Gentle Civilizer of Nations. The Rise and Fall of International Law 1870–1960* (Cambridge, Cambridge University Press, 2001) 11–97.

[28] Indeed, it often seemed, during and after 1989, that the international change was backwards, towards a future that should have been *then*.

Part II

The Law and Politics of Collective Security

3

The Place of Law in Collective Security

Having worked as legal adviser in the delegation of Finland in the UN Security Council in 1989–1990, I had been struck by the ambivalent role that law played in the Council debates during the time from Iraq's occupation of Kuwait in August 1990 to the first Gulf War in 1991. On the one hand, legal arguments seemed to be everywhere. On the other hand, nobody believed that anything about the activities of the various parties would have been determined by law. This prompted me to make the argument – perhaps familiar in itself, but frequently in neglected in 'international relations' oriented debates on the role of law – that law's significance did not reside in the causal explanation of behaviour. Instead it was expressed in the practice of institutional justification that enabled the analysis and critique of decisions taken by reference to the standards of the relevant community (in this the UN) . This chapter, written originally in 1996 and now slightly revised, is a critique of 'legal realism' – the idea that the indeterminacy of legal rules means that law is only a passive reflection of power. Even as the examples here come from the early 1990s, it is astonishing to what extent the points made here have preserved their validity in the analysis of events around the Kosovo crisis in 1999 and the Iraq War in 2003, as well as the war on terrorism in the past and present decade. As treated here, law does not exist as a causal variable of politics. Instead law 'frames' politics, makes it understandable and enables both actors and observers to take positions and move about in the political world.

I T MAY SEEM anachronistic to suggest that law might have something to do with the high politics of international security. The period between the two world wars has, of course, been credited precisely by a mistaken reliance on such an idea. Confidence in the League of Nations' ability to deter aggression did not only, we are told by Realists of the post-war order, prove an academic error, it was positively harmful in directing attention away from the need to prepare for the inevitable aggression when it came.

This is the understanding that most of us, as diplomats, political theorists, or lawyers, have cultivated through most of the past five decades. We have labelled belief in the ability of rules and institutions to deter aggression 'formalism', or even worse 'legalism', highlighting its abstract, utopian character, its distance from the flesh and blood of the application of power by states to fulfill their interests. Only some years ago, Stanley Hoffmann commented on the state of world order studies:

> Nobody seems to believe anymore in the chances of collective security; because of its constraining character, it is too contrary to the freedom of judgement and action implied

in sovereignty; and . . . it is in conflict with the imperative of prudence in the nuclear age, in which the localization or insulation of conflicts appears far preferable to their generalization.[1]

In this chapter, I want to examine the place of law in our thinking about and sometimes participation in decision-making regarding international security. After the end of the Cold War, and particularly since the United Nations' reaction to Iraq's occupation of Kuwait in 1990–91, an academic debate concerning the possibility of collective security has arisen anew.[2] My intention is not to take a definite view in that controversy. Instead, I shall suggest that the debate has been framed so as to obscure the role of normative considerations, including law, in the production or construction of collective security. A theoretical-instrumental bias produces competing descriptions of the conditions of international 'security', but fails to provide an understanding of the actual contexts of decision-making on 'security'. For an internal or cultural examination of collective security, a distinctly legal approach seems not only useful, but unavoidable.

Rebirth of Collective Security?

The collective security system of the UN Charter is based on two elements. First, there is the prohibition of inter-state threat or use of force under article 2(4). The second element is the UN Security Council's 'primary responsibility for the maintenance of international peace and security, . . . [expressed in both the members' agreement] that in carrying out its duties under this responsibility the Security Council acts on their behalf'[3] and in those Charter provisions which establish a legal obligation on members to carry out the Council's decisions.[4]

Collective security, often academically distinguished from balance of power politics, is seen as invoking an 'automatic' reaction against any potential aggressor.[5] Collective security under the UN Charter system, however, involves little automation. Under the Charter, the decision of whether and how to react is vested with the Council, which itself has broad discretion. Whether this makes the Charter system

[1] S Hoffmann, 'Is There an International Order?' in Janus and Minerva (eds), *Essays in the Theory and Practice of International Politics* (Boulder, Westview, 1987) 85, 117. The essay was originally published in French in 1985.

[2] See, eg R Betts, 'Systems for Peace or Causes of War? Collective Security, Arms Control, and the New Europe' (1992) 17 *International Security* 5; H Freudenschuss, 'Between Unilateralism and Collective Security: Authorizations to Use Force by the Security Council' (1994) 5 *European Journal of International Law* 492; A Hurrell, 'Collective Security and International Order Revisited' (1992) XI *International Relations* 37.

[3] UN Charter art 24 (1).

[4] ibid arts 25, 48. Also relevant in this context is art 2(5), which requires Member States to 'give the United Nations every assistance in any action it takes in accordance with the present Charter', and requires that no assistance be given to any state against which preventive or enforcement action is being taken pursuant to the terms of the Charter.

[5] See, eg Betts, 'Systems for Peace or Causes of War?' (1992) 16; J Mearsheimer, 'The False Promise of International Institutions' (1994/95) 19 *International Security* 5, 29–32.

something other than collective security under some definition is uninteresting. No system of rule application is 'automatic', as envisioned by the academic distinction between collective security and balance of power. The point is that under the Charter, Member States have renounced some of their freedom of action by vesting the Council with competence to decide on collective action on their behalf and are (legally) bound by the decisions the Council has made. The United Nations system has a strong bias against unilateralism and broad directives to guide the Council as it exercises its competence.

The fact that the Cold War made it impossible to apply the security system embedded in chapter VII of the Charter is, of course, well-known.[6] The procedure for collective reaction in articles 39 through 42 was set aside in favour of the balance of power strategies employed by the great powers outside the United Nations. The little enforcement activity that remained with the Security Council was limited to decolonisation issues that did not bear upon great power relations. Appeals by the General Assembly to activate collective security under the Charter system came to nothing.[7]

Judged against the Council's historical record, its reaction to Iraq's invasion of Kuwait from August 1990 onwards was clearly something new, even though paradoxically described as a 'return' to the original concept of chapter VII of the Charter. In his 1992 *Agenda for Peace*, the Secretary-General made several references to 'collective security'. He explained:

> an opportunity has been regained to achieve the great objectives of the Charter – a United Nations capable of maintaining international peace and security, of securing justice and human rights and of promoting, in the words of the Charter, 'social progress and better standards of life in larger freedom'. This opportunity must not be squandered. The Organization must never again be crippled as it was in the era that has now passed.[8]

During the first 40 years of the history of the UN (1946–86), the Council had made only two determinations of 'breach of the peace' under article 39.[9] Two states (Israel and South Africa) had been condemned for 'aggression', while the Council had recognised the existence of a 'threat to international peace and security' seven times.[10] During the first 45 years of the United Nation's history, the Council had resorted to military force three times,[11] and to binding non-military sanctions twice.[12] In the

---

[6] For analyses, see, eg ND White, *The United Nations and the Maintenance of International Peace and Security* (Manchester, Manchester University Press, 1990).

[7] See UNGA Res 159 (1986) UN Doc A/RES/40/159; UNGA Res 119 (1983) UN Doc A/RES/38/119.

[8] B Boutros-Ghali, *An Agenda for Peace. Preventive Diplomacy, Peace-Making and Peace-Keeping: Report of the Secretary-General*, A/47/277 (1992).

[9] UNSC Res 502 (1982) UN Doc A/RES/40/502, Falkland; UNSC Res 82 (1950) UN Doc S/1501, Korea.

[10] UNSC Res 573 (1985) UN Doc S/RES/573, Israel's attack on PLO headquarters in Tunis; UNSC Res 418 (1977) UN Doc S/RES/418, South Africa; UNSC Res 353 (1974), Cyprus; UNSC Res 307 (1971) UN Doc S/RES/307, Pakistan; UNSC Res 232 (1966), South Rhodesia; UNSC Res 161 (1961) UN Doc S/4741, Congo; UNSC Res 54 (1948) UN Doc S/902, Palestine.

[11] Korea, The Kongo, South Rhodesia. The last was an authorisation for Britain to patrol Beira harbour in Mozambique to prevent oil from reaching Rhodesia. UNSC Res 221 (1966) UN Doc S/RES/221.

[12] The economic blockade of Southern Rhodesia (1966–79) and the arms embargo of South Africa (1977–94).

light of the perhaps 73 inter-state wars that had broken out during this same period,[13] the data shows the dramatic extent of the Council's paralysis.

In 1990, the situation suddenly began to look altogether different. During 1990–94, collective measures had been taken in respect of eight situations – Iraq, Liberia, Former Yugoslavia, Somalia, Libya, Angola, Haiti and Rwanda. The Council had authorised the use of military force five times in a total of 19 resolutions.[14] In each of the eight situations, the Council had recourse to binding, non-military sanctions. Since that period of some euphoria, the level of the Council's activity has not returned quite to the level of the mid-nineties, but is still more intense than in the early years. Between 2004 and 2007, for example, the Council identified special or generic 'threats to the peace' in 19 situations through a total of 141 resolutions. At the same time, the Council authorised enforcement action four times with respect to the United Nations peacekeeping missions.[15] It had five times recourse to the language of 'all necessary measures', 'all necessary means', or 'all necessary action' within the framework of chapter VII.[16] This was in addition to an enforcement action for the first time by a joint African Union/United Nations hybrid operation.[17] The Council also imposed or modified sanctions regimes in nine situations, as well as imposing a number of judicial measures.[18] For comparison, consider the following statistics: in 1988, there were five peacekeeping operations, by 1994, the number was 17, and at the end of 2009 the number of ongoing operations was 15; in 1988, the Council adopted 15 resolutions, in 1994, the Council adopted 78, and in 2009 the number of adopted resolutions by the Council was 48. From 1988 to 1994, the number of annual informal consultations among Council members rose from 62 to 273, and in 2007 this number was 169.[19]

A qualitative development has likewise taken place in the Council's understanding of its task of 'maintaining international peace and security'. Traditionally, collective security – and with it, the Council's competence – was seen as a military

---

[13] White, *The United Nations* (1990) 47.

[14] UNSC Res 940 (1994) UN Doc S/RES/940, Haiti; UNSC Res 929 (1994) UN Doc S/RES/929, Rwanda; UNSC Res 836 (1993) UN Doc S/RES/836, Former Yugoslavia; UNSC Res 814 (1993) UN Doc S/RES/814, Somalia; UNSC Res 794 (1992) UN Doc S/RES/794; UNSC Res 678 (1990) UN Doc S/RES/678, Iraq . For a full analysis of the resolutions, see Freudenschuss, 'Between Unilateralism and Collective Security' (1994) 493–522.

[15] UNSC Res 1545 (2004) UN Doc S/RES/1545, Burundi; UNSC Res 1528 (2004) UN Doc S/RES/1528 Côte d'Ivoire; UNSC Res 1529 (2004) UN Dic S/RES/1529, Haiti; UNSC Res 1590 (2005) UN Doc S/RES1590, Sudan.

[16] UNSC Res 1575 (2004) UN Doc S/RES/1579, Bosnia and Herzegovina; UNSC Res 1671 (2006) UN Doc S/RES/1671, Democratic Republic of the Congo; UNSC Res 1778 (2007) UN Doc S/RES/1778, Chad and the Central African Republic; UNSC Res 1744 (2007) UN Doc S/RES/1744, Somalia; UNSC Res 1529 (2004) UN Doc S/RES/1529, Haiti.

[17] In Darfur (UNAMID); 'Repertoire of the practice of the Security Council. Supplement 2004–2007. Chapter XI: Consideration of the provisions of Chapter VII of the Charter' (New York, United Nations), available at http://un.org/en/sc/repertoire/2004-2007/04-07_11.pdf.

[18] 'Repertoire of the practice of the Security Council. Supplement 2004–2007', available at www.un.org/en/sc/repertoire/2004-2007/04-07_11.pdf.

[19] Global Policy Forum, 'Tables and Charts on Security Council, Council Meetings & Consultations: 1988–2008 – Table and Graph', available at www.globalpolicy .org/images/pdfs/Z/Tables_and_Charts/mtngsconsults.pdf.

matter, concerned with the prevention of inter-state violence and, in particular, the transboundary use of force. However, most modern large-scale violence does not involve formal armies marching across boundaries. As *Agenda for Peace* never tires to remind us, and countless reviews of post-Cold War peacekeeping keep repeating, the greatest proportion of large-scale violence that presents a threat to international peace and security is home-brewed violence – civil war. Whatever conceptual difficulties tackling with non-international conflicts might pose for traditional applications of collective security,[20] the limitation of violence within one state has not prevented the Security Council from using its mandate during recent years:

> Of the five peace-keeping operations that existed in early 1988, four related to inter-State wars and only one (20 per cent of the total) to an intra-State conflict. Of the 21 operations established since then, only 8 have related to inter-State wars, whereas 13 (62 per cent) have related to intra-State conflicts . . . Of the 11 operations established since January 1992, all but 2 (82 per cent) relate to intra-State conflicts.[21]

Moreover, it has long been argued that war can only effectively be prevented by tackling its root causes, that war is merely the external manifestation of the violence of the social institutions, that peace follows only from domestic enlightenment and justice.[22] Modern liberals have continued to make the same case. Peace starts at home, from the eradication of poverty, social injustice and the violation of human rights.[23] Today, 'non-military threats to security' and the 'comprehensive concept of security' are rooted in the vocabulary of diplomats and politicians throughout the political spectrum. At one euphoric moment in 1992, the Security Council, in its first meeting at the level of heads of state and government, stressed that: '[t]he non-military sources of instability in the economic, social, humanitarian and ecological fields have become threats to peace and security.'[24] It is not clear whether this much-quoted sentence should be taken at face value; that is, as an indication of the Council's readiness to use its collective security powers under chapter VII of the Charter to deal with economic, social, humanitarian, or ecological developments which, in its opinion, are sufficiently grave to warrant such treatment. Nevertheless, a leading commentator has recently concluded that at least the Council 'has consistently taken a wide view of "threat to the peace" and has been prepared to identify such a threat as arising out of internal conflicts such

---

[20] See also Hurrell, 'Collective Security' (1992) 38–39.

[21] See UNSC 'Report of the Secretary-General on the Work of the Organization' (2 September 1994) UN Doc A/49/1 5; UNSC 'Supplement to An Agenda for Peace: Position-paper of the Secretary-General on the Occasion of the Fiftieth Anniversary of the United Nations' (1995) UN Doc A/50/60 (1995) § 11.

[22] See I Kant, *To Perpetual Peace: A Philosophical Sketch, in Perpetual Peace and Other Essays on Politics, History, and Morals* (Ted Humphrey trans, Hackett Publishing Co 1983, 1975) 107 especially 112–15: the 'First Definitive Article of Perpetual Peace: The Civil Constitution of Every Nation Should Be Republican[,]'.

[23] For a programmatic discussion, see F Tesón, 'The Kantian Theory of International Law' (1992) 92 *Columbia Law Review* 53.

[24] UNSC 'Note by the President of the Security Council' (1992) UN Doc S/23500.

as those in the DRC and Somalia, overthrow of democratic government as in Haiti and refusal to act against terrorism in the cases of Libya, Sudan and the Taliban regime in Afghanistan'.[25] The unlimited nature of the language of Article 39, coupled with the statement of 1992 and the virtual impossibility of judicially challenging any determination under article 39 do suggest an image of the Council as a post-Cold War Leviathan; not only as police but as judge,[26] or perhaps a priest,[27] of a new world order.

Collective Action or Power Policy?

However, there is controversy about the correct understanding of these developments. While many agree with the Secretary-General that the Council's newly found activism should be seen as a 'return' to the 'original' Charter conception, others have been more doubtful. Several factors complicate a reading of the Council's recent activity as an application of collective security.

The first problem relates to the Council's notorious selectiveness.[28] Why Libya, but not Israel? Why the Council's passivity during most of the eight-year Iran-Iraq war? Why has the Council's reaction in Africa been so much less vigorous and effective than in the Gulf? Why the discrepancy between the Council's forceful attack on Iraq (an Islamic country) and its timidity to defend the Muslims of Bosnia-Herzegovina? The choice of targets, as well as the manner of reacting has certainly not been automatic. The argument is made that the Council has not reflected the collective interests of United Nations members as a whole, but only the special interests and factual predominance of the United States and its Western allies within the Council.

This point seems particularly potent in relation to the form of the Council's recourse to military force. The Kuwait crisis of 1990 presented a unique opportunity to activate the integrity of the Charter's collective reaction machinery. This would have included not only a decision on military action against Iraq, but also the conclusion of 'special agreements' under article 43 between the Council and Member States for the submission of national military contingents to the Council, as well as the activation of the military staff committee as envisioned in article 47. However, none of this was done. The Council merely gave its 'authorisation' for a

[25] Christine Gray, 'The Use of Force and the International Legal Order', in MD Evans, *International Law* 2nd edn (Oxford, Oxford University Press, 2006) 606.

[26] J-M Sorel, 'Rapport general. L'élargissement de la notion de menace contre la paix' in *Le Chapitre VII de la Charte des Nations Unies* (SFDI, Pedone, 1995) 52 et seq; K Harper, 'Does the United Nations Security Council have the Competence to Act as Court and Legislature?' (1994) 27 *New York University Journal of International Law and Policy* 103.

[27] See M Koskenniemi, 'The Police in the Temple. Order, Justice and the UN: A Dialectical View' (1995) 6 *European Journal of International Law* 325.

[28] See O Russbach, *ONU contre ONU. Le droit international confisqué* (Paris, Découverte, 1994).

coalition led by the United States to attack Iraq while absolving itself from the operational command and control of the coalition action.[29]

Lawyers have been at pains to find a plausible legal basis for this novel formulation: collective security or unilateral action in (collective) self-defence – or *excès de pouvoir*?[30] The debate has been largely inconsequential. Since 'Operation Desert Storm', the same formulation has been used in a number of other situations (eg Somalia, Former Yugoslavia, Rwanda, Haiti, East Timor, Macedonia and Afghanistan in which the Council decided to use military force. In each, the acting party was a powerful member or a coalition led by a powerful member (the United States, except for 'Operation Turquoise' in Rwanda, which was carried out by France and the INTERFET operation by Australia in East Timor).[31]

It is equally difficult to interpret the 'new generation peacekeeping' or its many cognates, including 'peace-making', and 'peace-building' as well as the now fashionable 'Responsibility to Protect', as collective security devices. True, the appearance of blue helmets with increasing frequency in the context of actual fighting, and sometimes with a mandate to use limited force, has seemed a step toward collective enforcement of pre-established standards of behaviour. However, a closer study of the cases so far (for example those of UNPROFOR in Krajina and Bosnia, UNOSOM II in Somalia and INTERFET in East Timor) shows that there is very little that is predictable about such operations. They are authorised for a varying set of purposes that range from carrying out humanitarian assignments to assisting in State-building.[32] An early examination of resolutions in which the Council has either authorised Member States to take military action or otherwise expanded the mandate of peacekeeping forces prompted one observer to conclude that 'a new instrument has been carved out of the need to fill the gap between an invocation of an inapplicable and inopportune right of collective self-defence and the unwanted application of the system of collective security.'[33] Whether the various Council activities that are popularly labeled 'humanitarian intervention' or 'peace-building' by observers (the Council tends to avoid this type of language) are

---

[29] UNSC Res 678 (1990) UN Doc S/RES/678.

[30] There is a great deal of literature on the subject. See eg R Lavalle, 'The Law of the United Nations and the Use of Force, under the Security Council Resolutons of 1990 and 1991, to Resolve the Persian Gulf Crisis' (1992) 23 *Netherlands Yearbook of International Law* 3, 33–46; O Schachter, 'United Nations Law in the Gulf Conflict' (1991) 85 *American Journal of International Law* 452; C Warbrick, 'The Invasion of Kuwait by Iraq' (1991) 40 *International & Comparative Law Quarterly* 482, 486–87; M-C Djena-Wembou, 'Reflexions sur la validité et portée de la resolution 678 du conseil de securité' (1993) 5 *African Journal of International and Comparative Law* 34, 44–49; R Zacklin, 'Les nations unies et la crise du Golfe' in B Stern (ed), *Les aspects juridiques de la crise et de la guerre du Golfe* (Paris, Montchrestien, 1991) 57, 69. See now also C Calliess, G Nolte and P-T Stoll, *Coalitions of the Willing: Avant-Garde or Threat?* (Göttingen, Heymanns, 2007).

[31] See eg UNSC Res 940 (n 14), US-led military intervention in Haiti 'to facilitate the departure from Haiti of the military leader'; UNSC Res 929 (n 14), French action to 'achieve . . . humanitarian objectives' in Rwanda; UNSC Res 836 (n 14), NATO air strikes to support peacekeepers; UNSC Res 794 (n 14), Operation 'Restore Hope in Somalia; SCR 1264 (1999), East Timor, UN Doc S/RES/1264.

[32] See UNSC Res 836 (n 14), limited use of force to protect the 'safe areas'; UNSC Res 814 (n 14), limited use of force mandate for the UNOSOM II.

[33] Freudenschuss 'Between Unilateralism and Collective Security' (1994), 522.

signs of welcome legal humanitarianism or merely novel types of neo-imperial policy in a collectivist disguise remains to be seen. There is hardly a more controversial topic today among legal academics – though little of it has had any direct influence in the Council itself.[34] The activities themselves, in their almost infinite variety and ad-hoc-ness, tend to lend themselves to political realist – even super -realist – interpretations about the determining force of great power interests inside the UN. Clearly there is little 'rule-application' here.

Moreover , recourse to economic sanctions by the Council has not been automatic in a way that would have clearly distinguished it from an interest-governed exercise of economic power. True, most states implemented the early Iraqi sanctions diligently, transforming the Council's decisions into acts of national law.[35] Yet, the Council's failure to manage its economic statecraft in a rational way has made it increasingly doubtful whether Member States should continue to take its use of sanctions seriously. In the early 1990s there was neither antecedent planning of the measures nor an evaluation of their effects on the target states' economy or political decision-making. The objectives of sanctions themselves were very unclear: change of policy or change of regime? Or perhaps just an effort to 'do something' short of going to war. How to measure their effectiveness in such situations? After the effects of the sanctions on the Iraqi population and the corruption relating to the 'Oil for Food' program came to public knowledge, Council actions have been increasingly targeted against particular individuals and some slight rule of law guarantees have been inserted in the process.[36] As is well-known, however, and graphically manifested in the *Kadi* cases in the European Court of Justice, huge legal problems still remain.[37] Moreover, sanctions are administered by committees consisting of diplomats of the Member States of the Council who have neither the interest, time or resources to do the job properly. Unlike in the early South Rhodesian situation (in which of course there was a much greater ideological agreement among the members) the committees work in secret, not even reporting substantially to the Council itself . They follow partly differing procedures resulting in differing interpretative decisions on, for example, the

---

[34] The literature is too vast to be reflected here. Useful critical works include A Orford, *Reading Humanitarian Intervention. Human Rights and the Use of Fore in International Law* (Cambridge, Cambridge University Press, 2003) and S Chesterman, *You, the People. The United Nations, Transitional Administration , and State-Building* (Oxford, Oxford University Press, 2004). For a useful review of some recent literature on the UN exercise of territorial authority, see A Orford, 'Jurisdiction without Territory: From the Holy Roman Empire to the Responsibility to Protect', (2009) 30 *Michigan Journal of International Law* 981.

[35] See DL Bethlehem (ed), *The Kuwait Critis: Sanctions and their Economic Consequences* (Cambridge, Cambridge University Press, 1991).

[36] The latest of these has been the creation of the post of a sanctions ombudsman in December 2009, see UNSC Res 1904 (2009), S/RES/1904. A good overview of the legal problems that led to the establishment of this position is B Fassbender, *Targeted Sanctions and Due Process: The Responsibility of the UN Security Council to Ensure that Fair and Clear Procedures are Made Available to Individuals and Entities Targeted with Sanctions under Chapter VII of the UN Charter* (20 March 2006), available at http://untreaty.un.org/ola/media/info_from_lc/Fassbender_study.pdf

[37] Joined Cases C-402/05 P and C-415/05 P; *Yassin Abdullah Kadi and Al Barakaat International Foundation v Council and the Commission* (3 September 2008).

application of the humanitarian exemptions.[38] The Council has failed to react to widely publicised violations of sanctions by individual states (for example the Islamic states' non-application of the Libyan boycott in force since 1992) and the practice of including individuals in its black lists remains erratic. The old problem of how to alleviate the problems of vulnerable third states remains unresolved.[39]

The Realist Critique of Collective Security

These various critiques seem to support two conclusions usually associated with political Realism. First, they suggest that the Council's activity should not be understood in terms of a functioning collective security system. It does not involve rule application in the way that would differentiate it from 'normal' hegemonic or balance of power policy. All aggressors are not, in fact, being hit by the system. Some actors that are not aggressors are being hit by it because that seems to be in the interests of the hegemonic powers. I call this critique the *interpretative thesis*. Its point is that we cannot interpret or understand the recent UN actions as an application of collective security.

Second, the critiques also support the more general Realist position according to which collective security is impossible – that it simply cannot work (the case of the Cold War) or works only as a camouflage for power policy. Whether peace exists is not dependent upon the presence or absence of rules about collective reaction, but upon the application of power by those states in a position to do so in the advancement of their interests. I call this critique the *causal thesis*.[40]

The two theses rely on a clear differentiation between legal 'rules' and political 'interests' and on the priority of the latter over the former. Since the great powers' interests are protected by articles 24 and 27 of the Charter, the mechanism seems already defined so as to defer to them. Nor are other interests irrelevant. It is not difficult to conceive of cases in which the interests of a Member State that has a special relationship with the target State or which is vulnerable to retaliation seem so important as to override conventional obligations.[41] Jordan's continuous and widely accepted breach of sanctions against Iraq during the 1990s is one example.

---

[38] See Koskenniemi, 'The Police in the Temple' (1995) 345–46.

[39] Some of these difficulties were taken up by the Secretary-General as early as 1995. See 'Supplement to An Agenda for Peace (1995) § 66–76. The Council responded by indicating certain measures to 'make the procedures of the Sanctions Committees more transparent' UNSC 'Note by the President of the Security Council' (1995) UN Doc S/1995/234 (1995).

[40] For a forceful reformulation, see Mearsheimer, 'The False Promise of International Institutions' (1994/95) 28–33.

[41] The doubts about the reality of the American nuclear umbrella in case of an attack on Western Europe, and its consequent readiness to set itself as a target for a similar attack, illustrate this point. So does the hypothesis of a Russian attack on the Ukraine. It is not plausible to believe that small European states will risk their safety by joining a campaign to support the Ukraine's independence.

A variation of this theme links it to the logic of state behaviour. Whatever ratio-nally calculable long-term advantage there might be for a state to abide by a col-lective measures norm will not offset the more immediate harm that it will seem to suffer as a result of obedience. So even if a purely rational calculation of interests might speak in favour of obedience, considerations relating to, for example, the unwillingness of political elites to make 'hard decisions' will overrule such calcula-tions. This is a variant of the argument from the 'tragedy of the commons' – that even if it were rational for all participants in a common good ('security' in this case) to take action to safeguard it against danger, there are always some who choose to become free-riders – with the effect that it will appear rational for others to choose a similar policy as well.[42] Collective security, Realists have insisted, relies upon trust between the partners. In the absence of trust (a fact that defines the condition of international 'anarchy'), it seems both rational and responsible to place immediate self-interest before an uncertain and fragile common interest.[43]

Moreover, procedural difficulties may seem daunting. Within an agreement to react to aggression some members will receive more protection than others. Selectivity is unavoidable. Much may depend on whether the aggressor is able to invoke the support of a permanent member. Even if members of a security pact had parallel interests, a collective reaction procedure could still not be applied consistently. Political choices will have to be taken when interpreting, for example, who the aggressor is, or whether there has been a 'threat to the peace'. We are not entitled to assume that the historic, ethnic, or political, affiliations or hostilities between particular members of such a pact are irrelevant when making those choices. However, even if there were no divergent affiliations, we may hardly hold as irrelevant factors such as the likelihood that retaliatory action against one aggressor would expose pact members to attack by another aggressor or drive the aggressors into each others' arms, a fear that hampered the League's sanctions policy against Italy in 1935–36. Who decides when to react, and how? Who pays for reaction or the costs of preparation? Who will command the collective force or decide on the objectives of common action and when they have been attained?[44] If everything depends on the particular facts and circumstances, the rule-governed character of the procedure will disappear and, with it, the system's deterrent force. It will start to seem like just another context for politics.[45]

---

[42] See J Joffe, 'Collective Security and the Future of Europe: Failed Dreams and Dead Ends' (Spring 1992) *Survival* 36, 42.

[43] See also the discussion in J Rosenberg (ed), *The Empire of Civil Society. A Critique of the Realist Theory of International Relations* (London, Verso, 1994) 27.

[44] See VA Roberts, 'The United Nations and International Security' (Spring 1992) *Survival* 3, 23–26.

[45] These questions reflect the different position in which members to a collective security pact are vis-à-vis each other. Some will have to lead, others will have to follow. It is not self-evident that parties will be ready to accept the assessment of the largest potential contributor – but if they do not, will the contributor contribute?

The Limits of Realism: Theory v Engagement

The above theses are powerful. They show that decision-making within the Security Council cannot be described as rule application in the abstract fashion in which 'collective security' has often been portrayed in the more legalistic accounts of it. However, the theses are also limited. They operate within a very narrow notion of 'rule application' and fail to see to what extent their determining concepts such as 'interest,' 'power,' or 'security' are themselves defined and operative within a normative context.

Realism receives its strength from its focus on empirical-instrumental questions such as 'what happened?' or 'what can be made to happen?' But it avoids posing normative questions such as 'what should happen?' or 'what should have happened?' or more accurately, Realism deals with the latter set of questions on the basis of its responses to the former. Having committed itself to a descriptive sociology of the international world characterised by the struggle for 'power' by 'states' in the pursuit of 'national interests', Realism marginalises normative questions into issues of 'ethics,' oscillating between the private (and thus inscrutable) morality of individual statesmen and the public morality of states in which it seems necessary sometimes to dirty one's hands in order to prevent the system's collapse into anarchy. Realism is avowedly instrumentalist, that is, concerned with the effects of particular policies on the world. However, its instrumentalism is not that of the situated participant but that of the external observer, the rational calculator, the theory-builder. To the external observer, the statesmen and states are atomistic subjects, equipped with a predetermined bag of interests or 'values,' standing outside the international polity on which they seek to employ various diplomatic, economic, and military management techniques. However, since the basic tenets of its sociology turn out to be normatively loaded, Realism seems compelled to defend itself on normative terms: one's 'security' will appear as another's domination, one's 'intervention' as another's 'protection of sovereignty'.[46] In this debate, there is no privileged realm of pure description.

The Normative in the Empirical

The *interpretative thesis* argued that law or political principles 'are not sufficient to explain either the past history of collective security or the course of events in the Gulf'.[47] The determinant factors in recent Council actions were not Charter

---

[46] For this latter theme, see Cynthia Weber's collapsing of the two apparent opposites into a single term she refers to as 'sovereignty-intervention', a term which can characterise any conceivable interstate relationship. C Weber, 'Simulating Sovereignty: Intervention, the State and Symbolic Exchange' (1995) 37 *Cambridge Studies in International Relations* 123–27.

[47] Hurrell 'Collective Security' (1992) 49.

provisions or international law, but the new rapport between the United States and the Soviet Union/Russia, the strategic and economic significance of Kuwait to the Western allies, and so on. I have no great problem with this thesis. It opens a critical perspective that refuses to take at face value the suggestion that United Nations' action represents communal interests merely because it has been decided by the Security Council. Nonetheless, the thesis' usefulness remains limited precisely because its hermeneutic suggestion excludes reference to international norms.

During the past years, the foundational character of the hard facts of state power and interest to our understanding of international politics has been questioned from a wide variety of perspectives. The 'level of analysis' approach already modified Realism's strong reliance on *states* as the basic units by which international acts should be explained.[48] Structural constraints and non-state actors seemed to create effects as well. Yet, even structural Realism's analytical priority for states may seem like an ideological move, justifying conservative policy and failing to account for the determining agency of class, economic system, or religious faith in the geopolitical, just as in the national, space.[49] Perhaps less controversially, liberal internationalists have long insisted that the 'globalisation of politics' has formed interest groups and lines of battle that cannot be reduced to the application of power by states.[50] To 'explain' United Nations action in Somalia, for instance, in terms of a power play between members of the Security Council would undermine the extent to which humanitarian perceptions, institutional programmes and ambitions, the legacy of East African colonialism, and the character of the Siad Barre regime account for the relevant events. Aside from states, we see both metropolitan (United Nations) and peripheral (Somali) actors, ideas and interests as relevant.[51] To argue that things went so bad because there was no clear national interest to protect is a *non sequitur:* things went as they did because the events showed factors other than a 'national interest' as relevant.

The concept of 'power' is likewise contested. Realists' over-identification of power with military power was undermined by the end of the Cold War. Inasmuch as 'power' is seen in larger terms of structure and knowledge, its embedment in other *explicanda* becomes evident.[52] Power is a matter of perspective. It receives meaning as threat or support depending on how we relate to it. It is applied as a

---

[48] The level of analysis approach, however, is only a temporary resolution of the problem of adjusting theory to observable facts. A more fundamental problem relates to the constructive aspects of observation itself: whether we tend to see states, economic systems, ideologies, individuals, or transnational communities as the relevant actors seems dependent on our prior choice of the relevant 'level' (matrix). The choice of the level, however, must be independent from the thing to be explained, ie on a pre-empirical evaluation of significance.

[49] See generally Rosenberg, *The Empire of Civil Society* (1994).

[50] The ideas of 'common security' and 'comprehensive security' seek to capture this image. For one recent reformulation, see Commission on Global Governance, *Our Global Neighbourhood* (Oxford, Oxford University Press, 995) 78–84.

[51] The argument draws inspiration from MW Doyle, *Empires* (Ithaca, Cornell University Press, 1986) 22–30.

[52] A Wendt, 'Constructing International Politics' (Summer 1995) *International Security* 71, 73–75.

means to an end different from itself. A study of ends, however, introduces norma-tive elements into the explanatory matrix that cannot be grasped by the sort of empiricism that Realists espouse.[53] The establishment of economic sanctions on Libya by the Security Council in 1992 as a result of Qaddafi's unwillingness to extradite the suspects for the 1988 Lockerbie terrorist attack could clearly be seen as an application of power by the Western allies. However, this is more the starting point than the end of the analysis. It would be difficult to understand the action without further reference to the role 'terrorism' played and still plays in Western political discourse, enabling the taking of extraordinary means – in this case the non-application of a valid treaty (the 1971 Montreal Convention against aerial terrorism) and the overrunning of the International Court of Justice. It is the normative construct of a specific 'terrorism discourse' that made possible the organisation and application of physical power against Libya.[54]

The concept of 'national interest' is no more transparent. Whose interest is that? States, just like individuals, live in a network of partly overlapping, partly incom-patible interests. Choosing an interest to base a policy is, as feminists have always argued, a normative act, and not something one automatically discovers after one has decided to further national interests. In any case, the assumption of a unitary national interest fails to account for, and even less articulate, the contrasting inter-est of a local population, minority, or women, for instance.[55] To say that Yemen supported Iraq in the Council during 1989–90 because that was in its interests is not only questionable insofar as Yemen's economic or diplomatic position was concerned (and undermines the effect of the ideological and religious links involved), but lifts the policy of a Yemeni male elite to representational position inimical to other Yemeni interests.[56] In fact, a reference to 'interests' is often no more than a sweeping gesture toward the truism, present since Vattel, that states act in accordance with their self-interest. However, the important point is that even '[s]elf-interest cannot be an unproblematic concept if the self is conceived as a set of constructed identities that need not be stable over time.'[57]

Arguing that normative factors are either irrelevant or only marginally relevant to Security Council action undermines the degree to which any social action, including international activity, makes constant reference to normative codes,

---

[53] For the expanding literature challenging the empiricist/positivist bias of international relations studies and stressing the need to undertake normatively focused analyses, see generally C Brown, *International Relations Theory: New Normative Approaches* (New York, Columbia University Press, 1992); M Frost, *Towards a Normative Theory of International Relations* (Cambridge, Cambridge University Press, 1986); MA Neufeld, *The Restructuring of International Relations Theory* (Cambridge, Cambridge University Press, 1995).

[54] See I Porras, 'On Terrorism: Reflexions on Violence and the Outlaw' (1994) *Utah Law Review* 119.

[55] A Orford, 'The Politics of Collective Security' (1996) 17 *Michigan Journal of International Law* 373; see generally DG Dallmayer (ed), *Reconceiving Reality. Women and International Law* (American Society of International Law, Studies in Transnational Legal Policy, (Washington, ASIL, 1993) fn 25.

[56] The point is strikingly illustrated by the fact that in the first post Gulf War elections in Kuwait in October 1992, only 14% of the country's 600,000 citizens were eligible to vote, Orford, 'The Politics of Collective Security' (1996) 390.

[57] R Price, 'A Genealogy of the Chemical Weapons Taboo' (1995) 39 *International Organization* 73, 88.

rules, or principles. Political events are never simply physical acts or people behaving empirically in this way or that.[58] They exist in relation to a shared normative code of meaning. Sending troops in another country is not a full description of an event: normative terms such as 'aggression,' 'self-defence,' 'counter-measure,' 'territorial sovereignty,' or 'peace-keeping' are not solely disinterested descriptions of the events. They refer back to more general, systemic theories, assumptions, world-views, and prejudices that provide the implicit matrix that makes description possible. An account of the 1991 Gulf War, for example, that made no reference to such notions but is content to refer to United States' military or economic interests would be no understanding at all. It would fail to grasp the difference between that sequence of military moves and those to which they were a response, or between Kuwait and Panama, or Kuwait and the Soviet attack on Finland in 1939. The distinctions are normative and characterised as such by the various participants involved.

Let me illustrate these remarks by reference to the comprehensive conception of security. That an understanding of 'security' should not be limited to military security, but should also encompass non-military threats to states and people, has become commonplace in post-Cold War diplomatic language.[59] This expansion of the operating concept of 'security' highlights the fact that explaining international action by reference to 'security needs' remains an empty phrase unless 'security' is first given a meaning. This involves an appreciation as to what is significant to the identity of political communities called 'states'.[60] Again, an answer to that question depends on whether we see a state's identity in territorial, economic, institutional, ideological, gendered, religious or constitutional terms.[61] Besides, the links between security and statehood are increasingly questioned, and diplomatic rhetoric has resorted to notions such as 'common security', 'comprehensive security', or even 'human security' to describe the objectives of international policy. A reference to 'security needs' as an explaining factor or an agreed principle of policy encounters, on the Realist side, the same difficulties that the attempt to define 'aggression' has always (and famously) met on the Idealist side: the notions remain both overdetermining and underdetermining. On the one hand, every event that modifies the State's external environment poses a threat to the State, and may therefore be deemed to constitute 'aggression' or 'intervention'. On the other hand, no event can permanently remain within these categories since the principle of inclusion may always be challenged by constructing the State's identity or its

---

[58] See P Winch, *The Idea of Social Science and Its Relation to Philosophy* (London, Routledge, 1958) 108–11, and more recently, with special reference to modern international theory, Neufeld, *The Restructuring* (1995) 70–94.

[59] See G Evans, *Cooperating for Peace. The Global Agenda for the 1990's and Beyond* (Sydney, Allen and Unwin, 1993) 15–16; Commission on Global Governance, *Our Global Neighbourhood* (Oxford, Oxford University Press, 1995) 80–82; B Buzan, 'New Patters of Global Security in the Twenty-First Century' (1991) 67 *International Affairs* (1991) 431, 439–51.

[60] See, eg JA Tickner, 'Re-Visioning Security' in K Booth and S Smith (eds), *International Relations Theory Today* (London, Polity, 1995) 175; O Waever, 'Identity, Integration and Security: Solving the Sovereignty Puzzle in EU Studies' (1995) 48 *Journal of International Affairs* 389.

[61] B Buzan, *People, States & Fear*, 2nd edn (New York, Harvester, 1991) 57–107.

sphere of sovereignty in a novel fashion. The controversy is therefore normative – 'what is significant for the identity of this State or for the furtherance of this type of policy?' – and not empirical.[62]

The matrix that describes the international world in terms of statal power policy has been challenged by interdependence theory and more recent research into the role of culture, class, gender, and tradition for international affairs.[63] Nonetheless, as RBJ Walker notes, 'a large proportion of research in the field of international relations remains content to draw attention to contemporary innovations while simply taking the modernist framing of all spatiotemporal options as an unquestionable given'.[64] This is partly a result of the fact that Realism encapsulates deeply entrenched commonsense assumptions. In part, it also follows from a real difficulty to see how the 'innovations' would inform political practices. After all, as I have argued elsewhere, one can reimagine the structures of the international world only now and then. For the rest of the time we seem compelled to act within an actual political community.[65]

For present purposes, it suffices to note that the need to choose the matrix highlights the normative element hidden in Realist premises, an element sometimes revealed in private positions Realists have taken on moral or political issues.[66] By failing to take its normative commitments seriously (even at best marginalising them into a problem of 'ethics and international relations'), Realism opens itself to a political criticism which alleges that Realism lacks the instruments to defend itself. Moreover, lack of sensitivity for the non-descriptive undermines the instrumentalism upon which Realism bases its claim for superiority. The kind of tragic heroism embedded Realism's attempt to confront power and vice directly, without the mediating vessels of ethics/ideology, is undermined by the equally ideological character of that posture itself; the posture being equally a role within

---

[62] The same point may be made by highlighting the degree to which the debate about the United Nations' or individual states' competence to intervene in internal crises constantly redefines the basis of sovereign statehood. Whether we believe 'sovereignty' to be located in the 'people', in the Head of State, or in the State's institutions will provide us with different, and often contradictory, justifications for or against intervention. From this perspective, statehood provides no limit to intervention. On the contrary, it is an effect of our assumptions about the right form of government. See Weber, 'Simulating Sovereignty' (1995). The resuscitated 'constitutivist' approach to the recognition of states, which conditions statehood on domestic democracy and guarantees for minority protection, works, of course, in the same direction. See European Community: *Declaration on Yugoslavia and on the Guidelines on the Recognition of New States* (1992) 31 ILR 1485.

[63] For a particularly strong anti-statal matrix using the 'deep-structure' of the capitalist world-system in which nationalism and universalism appear as historical or local instances, see I Wallerstein, *Geopolitics and Geoculture: Essays on the Changing World-System 139–237* (Cambridge, Cambridge University Press, 1991) (discussing the role of 'culture' and 'civilization' as the 'intellectual battlegrounds' of post-Cold War policy).

[64] RBJ Walker, *Inside/Outside: International Relations as Political Theory* (Cambridge, Cambridge University Press, 1993) 7.

[65] M Koskenniemi, 'Book Review' (1995) 89 *American Journal of International Law* 227, 230 (reviewing Dallmayer (ed), *Reconceiving Reality* (1993)).

[66] The two standard examples being Morgenthau's opposition to the Vietnam War and Martin Wight's private pacifism. For a discussion, see J George, 'Realist "Ethics", International Relations, and Post-Modernism: Thinking Beyond the Egoism – Anarchy Thematic' (1995) *Millennium. Journal of International Studies* 195, 205–07.

the drama of international diplomacy that it pretends to 'describe', a role that, however logically compatible with fighting the noble fight (for a lost cause), too easily becomes a justification for complacency.

The Engaged Perspective

For Realists, reference to norms, such as the obligation to participate in common action under articles 2(5) or 48 of the UN Charter, in an explanation of international politics appears as it appeared to the American legal Realists of the 1930s; namely, as transcendental nonsense, an 'attempt to exorcise social evils by the indefatigable repetition of magic formulae'.[67] Obligations are both causally ineffectual and unamenable to scientific inquiry. By contrast, the process whereby states apply power to advance their interests seem more firmly linked with observable reality and may therefore appear amenable to causal hypotheses whose verity can always be checked by experience.[68]

That Realism is the *genre* of theory, and not engagement, is clear from its emphasis on causality. The acting subject is the external observer, the policy-scientist, possibly employed by a government office to 'predict' the future course of international policy in order to formulate scenarios for appropriate response. In the previous section, I argued that Realism's causal models were dependent on, or could not be applied in abstraction from, normative choices regarding desirable courses of action. Here I make the point that causal description fails to grasp the ('internal') perspective of diplomats or lawyers working within an institutional environment such as the Security Council. For them, the argument that the Council's policy is caused by interests well-represented in the Council is as relevant or interesting a point to make as the argument to government officials that governments tend to propose legislation that advances the interests represented by the governmental coalition. Such statements, whatever their status otherwise, raise at least three points. First, neither statement has a necessary bearing on whether the proposed legislation or policy is *justified*. That the United Nations has dealt with the humanitarian crisis in Bosnia in an insufficiently effective manner because the resources, interests, or policies of the great powers have militated against full-scale involvement may or may not be true. However, its truth of falsity is not a sufficient response to the question of whether the United Nations has been justified in acting in the way it has, or what might be the right course of action to proceed in the future.

Second, neither statement is helpful when it is precisely what those interests are or what kind of action best serves them that need examination. To some extent, at least, the United Nation's hesitation at the outset of the crisis in the Former

---

[67] H Morgenthau, 'Positivism, Functionalism, and International Law' (1940) 34 *American Journal of International Law* 260, 260.

[68] ibid 260–284; see also JS Watson, 'A Realistic Jurisprudence of International Law' (1980) *Yearbook of World Affairs* 265, 266–67, reprinted in M Koskenniemi (ed), *International Law* (Aldershot, Dartmouth, 1992) 3, 4–5.

Yugoslavia during 1991 reflects this problem. Was it in the Western allies' interests to prevent or to facilitate dissolution? This is not only a technical question. Often, interests cannot even be identified without a prior political choice. Will participation in a Common European Defence be in the interests of traditional military neutrals such as Austria, Finland, or Ireland? An answer to this question depends on an earlier choice regarding whether the 'natural home' of these countries is within or without a Western political community.

Third, and most fundamental, Realism's theoretical-empirical bias compels it to treat justification as a process of 'façade legitimation', the dressing of the technically necessary policy in the garb of generally acceptable norms. This leads Realism into supporting manipulative diplomatic practices, approaches to negotiation that presume the primacy of the hegemonic powers. This is not simply ethically questionable, but also bad policy. For, inasmuch as 'interests' or 'security' are not facts of nature but social constructions, the effects of language and political preference, they cannot be distinguished from the justifications that seek to realise them. Whether or not dealing with an international humanitarian crisis (such as Liberia in 1992 or Rwanda in 1994) should be seen as a matter of collective security, and thus the object of concerted action, cannot be adequately discussed by invoking a presumed causal chain from the crisis to the sovereignty of other states (through the resulting refugee problem, for instance), but involves a prior redefinition of the community itself – who are 'we' as subjects of security?

In order to grasp the 'internal' or engaged perspective on collective security, let me discuss the Security Council's reaction to the Iraqi attack on Kuwait in the fall of 1990 in the light of personal recollections of the role of legal argument seemed to play in the process.

During 1989–90, Finland was one of the elected members of the Security Council. I was posted at the Finnish Permanent Mission in New York at the time and assigned to serve as legal advisor to the Finnish Council team. The nine-member team was headed by the Permanent Representative who was not only Ambassador and Under-Secretary of State, but also a former professor of Political Science in Finland. Most of the team came from the political department of the foreign service. My position in the delegation was relatively humble, somewhere around the middle of the list. This corresponded closely to the place of my opposite numbers, the lawyers in the other 14 delegations. We were neither among the leading policy-makers nor among the youngest rapporteurs.

I had no formal instructions to obey as the lawyer of the team. Of course, there were general guidelines applicable to all the members, regarding the direction of Finnish United Nations policy, plus some more specific instructions in particular crises. However, while it seemed evident for everyone that there had to be one lawyer (indeed, one was certainly enough) among the nine, there was no articulated explanation for this certainty. The same applied, I believe, to my colleagues at least in the 'Western European and Others' Group' (WEOG) delegations. None of us had any specific 'legal' instructions. The place of law in the Security Council was in this respect obscure. It was perhaps assumed that as we had done quite a bit of international law previously, we would know what to do at the right moments. Our role arose from a shared professional background, not from conscious planning.

Much of the lawyer's work was identical with that of others: sitting at informal and formal meetings, participating in recurring consultations headed by the month's president, and reporting home on a daily basis. The lawyer concentrated on textual aspects of resolutions, on those aspects of particular crises that involved legal status (such as the situation in the Palestinian occupied territories) plus on the negotiation of generally formulated, 'legislative' resolutions (such as a resolution on plastic explosives and on terrorism[69]). From a policy perspective, these issues were neither quite central, nor fully marginal: my diplomatic placing corresponded to the level of my tasks.

In routine matters, the law's (lawyer's) role in the Council during 1989–90 arose from two informal considerations embedded in the working culture of the Council. First, the jurist was expected to assess the domestic and constitutional implications of particular resolutions. Second, particular geographically limited disputes that had been on the Council's agenda for a long time were allocated to political officials experts on the region or on the dispute itself. Contrary to received wisdom, law's role seemed the most limited in routine issues on which everyone had fixed positions and no dramatic moves were or could reasonably be expected. Where the political framework was stable, the lawyer was the handmaid of the politician, helping out if new language for negotiation and consensus was needed. That role depended on pragmatic considerations, not on any shared or articulated theory regarding the delimitation of legal and political matters.

However, things looked different when a non-routine issue emerged. On the night of 2 August 1990, Iraqi troops invaded Kuwait. I was on holiday in Finland on that day but returned to New York very soon thereafter. By the time of my return, the Council had demanded immediate withdrawal of Iraqi troops, established the obligation of non-recognition on Member States, and implemented the first full-scale economic embargo on any state since the League of Nations' action against Italy in 1935–36.[70]

I have been trained as a Finnish career diplomat in the belief that in matters concerning the existence of states – such as the Kuwait crisis – Finland's vital interests, as determined by the political leadership, become the basis for our diplomatic action. Trained in the spirit of post-war Realism, I had little difficulty accepting that legal norms should in such cases defer to political requirements. Indeed, Finland's own experience with the League in 1939 seemed the best argument for this necessity.

As I returned to New York in the middle of August 1990, however, I was struck by the enthusiasm with which my 'political' colleagues in the delegation had immersed themselves in a controversy about the legal status of the various courses of action taken by or available to the Council and to my own delegation. How

---

[69] UNSC Res 638 (1989) UN Doc S/RES/628; UNSC Res 635 (1989) UN Doc S/RES/635.
[70] UNSC Res 661 (1990) UN Doc S/RES/661; UNSC Res 660 (1990) UN Doc S/RES/660.

should sanctions be administered? What about the blocking of Iraq's ports? What was the status of Western troop concentrations in Saudi Arabia? What law applied to the Embassies in Kuwait City or in Baghdad? The delegation, as well as Helsinki, clearly believed that legal viewpoints were not only somewhat relevant, but in some respects central to devising a national position.

The headquarters acted in a similar way. I found permanent representatives and political colleagues grouping in the corridors with the little blue book – the UN Charter – in their hands, quarrelling about the meaning of the various parts of chapter VII of the Charter, giving contrasting interpretations about the extent of the right of self-defence under article 51, and disagreeing about whether article 42 (military sanctions) needed to be applied in conjunction with articles 43 and 47 on the provision of national contingents and on the role of the military staff committee respectively. Even Prime Minister Thatcher at one point took pains to argue that the concentration of coalition troops in Saudi Arabia before the Council had authorised the use of military force had been a perfectly legitimate application of the right of collective self-defence under article 51.

How should we understand the fact that in the midst of one of the most serious cases of aggression in the post-war order, diplomats at the United Nations started invoking legal norms and arguing as if whatever action the United Nations or its Member States could take was dependent on rules of law? A first point to make is that I do not think anyone saw the Council's role akin to a penal court, acting in Montesquieu's image as '*la bouche qui prononce les paroles de la loi*'. Although necessary, nobody thought it sufficient to establish what the law said. Of course, this would also have been bad law. The Council is not a court. It is not obliged to react in any predetermined way to any 'breach of the peace, threat to the peace or act of aggression'. Nor do these concepts spell out an 'international crime' akin to 'theft' under national law that would require the Council to order a 'sanction'.[71] The Council may react even in the absence of unlawfulness; and a violation of the law does not by itself trigger Council competence. Besides, as every national judge knows, Montesquieu's image is pure fiction. There is always choice and policy involved in law application, the relevant norms being open-textured and open to exceptions. This was a fact that was easy to agree upon in the Council.

A second possibility is to think that delegations agonised over international law in the fall of 1990 not because they felt they had to find the 'one right answer' but because they needed to determine what limits were imposed by the law upon Council 'discretion'. This would be a liberal and a realistic response, imagining Charter provisions as a neutral framework leaving ample room for political manoeuvre. However, this is not really psychologically plausible. 'Law' and 'discretion' did not exist in separate pigeon-holes in our minds. The legal debate did not 'stop' at any point to leave room for a separate political choice; political choices were posed the moment the legal debate started.

---

[71] For the juristic discussion about the nature of chapter VII 'sanctions' as police measures, see, eg H Kelsen, *The Law of the United Nations: A Critical Analysis of Its Fundamental Problems* (New York, Prager, 1951) 732–37.

A better metaphor than pigeon-holing for the law/politics relationship might refer to the contemplation of landscape. In the morning we see the colours of the trees and the reflection of the leaves on the water; in the evening, we notice the outline of the cliffs against the grey sky, and the shadow of the forest stretches far into the sea. The landscape is the same, the messages it conveys are different. The images are equally self-contained and full. We can reproduce both separately, but we cannot mix them. Likewise, law and politics seemed coherent and separate, yet related to one single reality.

And yet reality has a temporal dimension: morning turns into day and the evening begins sooner than we had noticed. In the Security Council, law and politics developed analogously into each other. As the debate progressed, each successive moment added something to our understanding, until the original image had turned into its counterpart. We saw the landscape first in the brightness of legal language: aggression, sanctions, blockade, and non-recognition. This language was used to give expression to the contrasting positions of the delegations. These were positions of the evening, visible only in an obscure, shadowy form, impossible to reach in description. The further the debate progressed, the clearer became the interdependence of light and shadow, law and politics, and focus was increasingly on the boundary. The amount of time available determined the point at which debate had to finish and action had to be taken. Thereafter, that action, and its justifications, turned into precedent, calling for formal consistency in future behaviour. Legal and political simultaneously, the long line of resolutions in the fall of 1990 sought to give effect to the ambitions of the drafters as well as to the Charter. In retrospect, we interpret them from both perspectives, yet we can do this fully only from one perspective at a time, by keeping the other outside our gaze.

There is, of course, a third possible understanding about the sense of these debates; namely, that they served only to camouflage the play of ideologies, power, and interests that were 'really determining' behind a *legalistic façade*. What may appear as the brightest day is in truth the darkest night! There are two versions of this understanding. First, it may be assumed that part of diplomatic training is to learn to lie about one's true aims. Under this version, the debate in New York was a fraud. It is difficult to prove or disprove this suggestion which speaks about the real, although hidden, intentions of diplomats at the United Nations. Although I have to make allowance for the odd exception, I find this psychologically implausible. Most of the diplomats 'honestly' felt that arguments about the Council's competence to order a blockade of Iraq's ports, for instance,[72] had intrinsic relevance. In any case, this criticism misses the point. These are arguments whose validity in no way presupposes honesty in making them. The legality of the blockade has nothing to do with the state of mind of the person invoking it. A day is a day if it looks like one. There is no deeper reality that might prove it otherwise; even our watches provide only a conventional temporal interpretation.

---

[72] For the Council's actions regarding the blockade, see UNSC Res 665 (1990) UN Doc S/RES/665.

The same is true of the second version which provides that, notwithstanding the states of mind of delegation members, the legal debate was intrinsically without a consequence. Under this view, the diplomats were acting under a false consciousness, a legalistic ideology which camouflaged the fact that what was going on was use of power to further national interests. This kind of 'Realism' is very common and presents an extremely critical picture about the United Nations, assuming that diplomats do not really understand their job but act under a legalistic spell. I find it hard to support this understanding on an intuitive basis. The Finnish delegation, for instance, was *en block* trained as hard-headed Realists. If there had been indoctrination, it was surely not of the legalist sort. The architect of post-war Finnish foreign policy, President Paasikivi, once remarked famously that the Kremlin is no Court of Law, meaning (among other things) that sound legal arguments are a poor substitute for clever policy when it comes to Finland's relations with its Eastern neighbour. Although the historic background is of course different, I believe this applied to the non-lawyers in the other delegations as well.

More importantly, however, is that this criticism presents an exclusively external perspective on the events. Legal arguments camouflage the determining force of political or economic power. That is their very point. In the morning we see light. But we know it is inevitable that darkness will fall, and can examine it later, but not at the same time. However determining political power may be, it is irrelevant for delegations struggling to find public justification for Council action. It may be true that 'international government is, in effect, government by that state which supplies the power necessary for the purpose of governing'.[73] Such a causal assumption provides, however, nothing for those examining the justifiability or proposed courses of action within an institutional structure.

This is my point about the role of law in the Kuwait crisis. In 1990, the traditional patterns of Council decision-making had become irrelevant and inapplicable. There was no anterior political agreement, no long-standing negotiation with fixed positions, and no routine language to cover the events. The situation was canvassed nowhere but in the Charter itself. As the debate took on a legal style and an engaged aspect, the rest of formalism followed suit: the search for precedent (Southern Rhodesia for the management of economic sanctions) and consistency (in the formulation of the resolutions during the autumn of 1990), the concern for human rights, diplomatic inviolability, and humanitarian law were all strikingly central for the resolutions. Placing the argument in the context of law, there seemed to be no halfway house. The Council could not just apply some law in the Kuwait crisis, leaving the rest unapplied. Long shadows would have been inconsistent with the place of the sun in our landscape. After all, this was the same time as the signing of the 'Charter of Paris' by the Conference on Security and Cooperation in Europe (CSCE) which stressed the need for the rule of law in the management of political societies.

---

[73] EH Carr, *The Twenty Years' Crisis 1919–1939: An Introduction to the Study of International Relations* 2nd edn (London, Macmillan, 1994) (1946) 107.

It is an uninteresting truism that delegations couch decisions in legal garb to make them look more respectable. That is the point of law. Clearly, both the United States and the Yemeni delegations, like those of Finland, Canada and Romania, sought interpretations that would be in line with their (partly differing) policies. No delegation wishes to report to its capital that it cannot pursue the instructed policy because it cannot defend it in legal terms. Those terms will be found. However, although this may appear to support the Realist critique about 'façade legitimation', it fails to appreciate how legitimation or justification always has a 'façade' aspect to it without this making it any less useful or even necessary. Justification is only more complex, tentative, and fragile than the Realist straw-man image of 'rule application' would suggest. Newton may have come up with the theory of gravity by sitting under an apple tree and being struck by a falling apple. This causal account of the events, however accurate, is no explanation of his genius or even a beginning of a theory of gravitation defensible in the scientific community. Newton's genius was in the skill of his justifying his intuition to his fellow scientists in the form of a coherent theory in accordance with the rules of scientific discourse, not in the process which causally produced it.

The engaged perspective that looks for justification differs from the construction of theories about determining causes by assuming the existence of and invoking an inter-individual, international, political community in which the speaker is situated. Saying that 'I believe this is aggression because it suits me to think so' emerges from a solipsism in which others exist only as objects of want-satisfaction. By contrast, saying that this is 'aggression' under article 39 of the Charter invokes a 1945 agreement and a polity in which the speaker situates his or herself and every person to whom the statement is directed. The road to an undistorted communal life is of course not thereby created. Much more would be needed for that purpose. Without justifying discourse, however, social life would be reduced to manipulative relationships: security will be the security of the king while no problem will seem too small for the intervention of the security force!

Law's contribution to security is not in the substantive responses it gives, but in the process of justification that it imports into institutional policy and in its assumption of responsibility for the policies chosen. Entering the legal culture compels a move away from one's idiosyncratic interests and preferences by insisting on their justification in terms of the historical practices and proclaimed standards of the community. Even if it does not, as both Formalists and Realists may have thought, lift the burden of substantive choice, it implies a recognition of the existence of a world beyond the speaker's immediate subjectivity. Only in this way can 'security' maintain its beneficial, altruistic orientation, instead of invoking the somber association with the security police – arrests after midnight, featureless officials, and insulated cellars. As opposed to technical-instrumental rationality, a legal culture involves a 'situational ethics',[74] encompassing not only rules and

---

[74] R Jackson, 'The Political Theory of International Society' in Booth and Smith (eds) *International Relations Theory Today* (London, Polity, 1995) 110, 124–27.

principles (after all Realists were right in stressing their indeterminacy) but a fairness of process, an attitude of openness and a spirit of responsibility that implicitly or expressly means submission to critique and dialogue with others about the proper understanding of the community's principles and purposes – in a word, its identity.[75] Law is what lawyers do, said Max Weber in one of the most adept definitions of it. He was of course thinking about national societies with a high degree of professional specialisation. In the international context, law is what diplomats do when they debate the meaning of the UN Charter, the competence of the Security Council, or Libya's duties under particular Council resolutions. There is nothing *substantive* that would distinguish those debates from political *Diktat*. An enlightened despot or a monkey might sometimes succeed in reciting the right Charter article. What makes these debates *legal* is the manner in which they are conducted: by open reference to rules and principles instead of in secret and without adequate documentation; by aiming toward coherence and consistency, instead of a selective bargaining between 'old boys'; by an openness to revision in light of new information and accountability for choices made, instead of counting on getting away with it.

Realism's theoretical-empirical bias would not be too serious if Realism remained content with its status as expert knowledge. It does not, however. Realists stress the practical character of their particular language, its role in the formation of policy and statecraft. Thereby Realism itself becomes a sociological problem. Even as it readily concedes the (theoretical) separation of 'is' and 'ought' as a matter of practical consequences, it answers questions about the latter by reference to its responses to the former. It thinks about peace, security and social order in terms of 'jobs' to be carried out, or a series of 'problems' to be resolved. It hopes to do this by employing resources in accordance with advice from technical, intelligence, and military experts whose expertise is limited to the narrowest possible range of relevant 'issues': nuclear deterrence, arms control, peacekeeping, diplomacy. The tricky and eminently political question of the meaning of 'peace' in particular circumstances, indeed, the delimitation of the circumstance itself, is never raised and *cannot be raised without immediately posing the question of the qualifications of the experts charged to deal with it.* Was the 'issue' in the Gulf War the old boundary disagreement between Iraq and Kuwait? The internal regime of these countries? Peace in the Middle East? Or was the 'issue' access to strategic resources? It was treated as an 'aggression' of one United Nations Member State against another because that is the language of the Security Council, but it was managed through a military operation because 'hard' issues of sovereignty are deemed to fall ultimately under the soldiers' realm of competence. In contrast, genocide in Rwanda would trigger principally the competence of relief workers and refugee organisations.

Difficulties in reaching political agreement at the global scale (which is the United Nations' scale) on the right characterisation of local political events (do

---

[75] For a useful redefinition of Weber's 'ethics of responsibility' so as to involve a dialogical relationship between the responsible agent and the person to whom the agent is responsible, see D Warner, *An Ethic of Responsibility in International Relations* (London, Rienner, 1991) 104–16.

they implicate 'security'?) and priorities for action has led to an international culture of functional specialisation and compartmentalisation. This is nowhere more visible than in the separation of the United Nations' hard core political activities from its economic and social activities, with each body and each department in the Secretariat jealously guarding its individual allotment of problems to solve. The justification for a particular action is always given by the non-political, technical competence of the body dealing with it. Indeed, it often seems that the crucial decision about some particular policy is which organ or department is empowered to deal with it (or succeeds in monopolising it). Once we know the organ or department, we already have a good idea about what sort of action will be taken.

In contrast, a legal culture is never only about *how* to get there. It also poses the question of what there is to get to. The lawyers' anxiety about the proper legal basis of a Security Council resolution always implicitly refers to the institutional teleology of the United Nations. It has two aspects which a purely instrumental debate lacks. First, it implies recognition of situatedness in a political community and openness to dialogue with other members of the community. To put one's argument in terms of articles 42, 43 and 47 of the Charter is to reaffirm the institutional character of the problem, a readiness to bind oneself to a policy vis-à-vis the others, and an assumption of the responsibility for so doing. Second, it entails a redefinition of the institution (the United Nations') constitutive principles and objectives. Legal argument is never deduction from self-evident rules. It always adds to our understanding of the law, and thus of the identity, objective, and principles of the institution. The periodic fluctuations of the United Nation's image between that of an economic and social development organisation and that of the guarantor of 'peace and security' reflect a constant redefinition of the organisation's identity as a result of its institutional policies.

There is in fact not much difference between standard Realism and its traditional rival, Institutionalism. Both are concerned about causes and effect in a description of the international world juxtaposing uniform agents (states) within a structure of international policy in which 'power' is deployed for the attainment of 'interests' and in which the aggregate result is characterised in terms of 'peace/war'. Where Realists assume that the best causal model reproduces the structure of the balance of power, and that any institutional policy must defer to this, Institutionalists agree but argue that the best way for the balance to operate is to defer to institutions.[76] Accordingly, any description of the international world is capable of supporting both positions: the absence of peace may always be explained either as the absence of the balance of power, or as the absence of adequate institutions through which the balance could realise itself!77]

[76] CA Kupchan and CA Kupchan, 'The Promise of Collective Security' *International Security* (Summer 1995) 52 (a response to the criticism by Mearsheimer (n 5).

[77] The same applies to international lawyers' standard response to the Realist challenge. To argue that most states do follow most of the rules most of the time may seem to rescue international law's 'relevance' by showing the wide scope of application of its rules – but it does this only at the cost of their normative nature. The result is a description of international reality that underwrites both politics and law – yet distorting the normative aspects of both in the process. M Koskenniemi, *From Apology to*

This indeterminacy of the Realist/Institutionalist debate is one result of the theoretical-instrumental bias on both sides. The anterior choice of the determining structures in a causal description of the international world is left unaddressed in both theories and the conclusions are hidden in their premises. Realist descriptions win if one already believes in the superiority of an understanding of the world in terms of atomistic and egoistic states obsessed by a power-maximising urge. Institutionalist portrayals seem more compelling if one sees the world in terms of an underlying structural causation that views states as instruments for an underlying historical, economic, or military logic. To repeat: any fact situation can always be described in terms of either matrix while the choice of the matrix – indeed, the question whether the choice is more apparent than real – seldom enters the picture.

The Work of the Security Council

The European Congress system that was set up after the Napoleonic wars during 1814–15 is usually regarded as the first attempt at collective security. It was based on a statist ideology that held all threats towards the status quo as security threats to be counteracted by collective force. Even Castlereagh was able to defend Austrian intervention against the revolution in Naples in 1820, which evoked much sympathy in Britain, by reference to Austrian security interests that had been sanctioned by the Alliance. The main interest was an undefined 'security' to which other normative concerns had to defer. The fundamental problem of that system was clearly explained in an early British memorandum:

> The idea of an 'Alliance Solidaire', by which each State shall be bound to support . . . all other States from violence and attack, upon condition of receiving for itself a similar guarantee, must be understood as morally implying the previous establishment of such a system of general government as may secure and enforce upon all kings and nations an internal system of peace and justice. Till the mode of constructing such a system shall be devised the consequence is inadmissible, as nothing would be more immoral or more prejudicial to the character of government generally than the idea that their force was collectively to be prostituted to the support of established power without any consideration to what extent it is abused.[78]

During the Cold War, issues of legitimacy and justifiability such as those raised in this memorandum could not arise as it was clear that there was no such 'system of general government' to which they could be dealt by reference. In the 1990s, however, the situation appeared to have changed. The vocabulary of the CSCE Paris

---

Utopia; the Structure of International Legal Argument (1989) (Re-issue with a new Epilogue, Cambridge University Press, 2005) 143–53.

[78] R Albrecht-Carrié, *The Concert of Europe* (London, Macmillan, 1968) 42 (quoting a memorandum on the Treaties of 1814 and 1815 submitted by the British Plenipotentiaries at the Conference of Aix-la-Chapelle, October 1818).

Charter of 1990[79] or of the Security Council summit declaration of 1992 suggested that at least governmental rhetoric had moved to a level that had prompted observers to speak about an 'emerging right to democratic governance'.[80] It appeared that the Security Council was now in a position to enforce the public morals of a new order.

Many of the Council's recent actions have been seen in this light, especially its readiness to intervene in civil wars[81] and its increasing resort to statements about the illegality of particular forms of state behaviour.[82] Closely related are the Council's decisions to set up two war crimes tribunals[83] and a war reparations procedure,[84] as well as the authorisation to use force to apprehend criminals.[85] The Council has demarcated and guaranteed boundaries,[86] enforced its own decisions by recourse to economic sanctions,[87] and authorised the use of force to ensure the departure of a military regime.[88] It has set up territorial administrations in post-conflict situations[89] and, in the aftermath of 2001, it even legislated anti-terrorism measures on the world.[90] All of this seems justified through a redefinition of 'security' (often as 'human security') by reference to a background conception of a public morality that has become the Council's business to enforce.

---

[79] *Conference on Security and Co-operation in Europe: Charter of Paris for a New Europe* (1991) 30 ILR 190, 193–208.

[80] TM Franck, 'The Emerging Right to Democratic Governance' (1992) 86 *American Journal of International Law*. 46.

[81] See, eg UNSC Res 929 (n 14) pmbl para 10 ('[d]etermining that the magnitude of the humanitarian crisis in Rwanda constitutes a threat to international peace and security in the region'); UNSC Res 794 (n 14) pmbl para 3: ('[d]etermining that the magnitude of the human tragedy caused by the conflict in Somalia, further exacerbated by the obstacles being created to the distribution of humanitarian assistance, constitutes a threat to international perace and security'); UNSC Res 788 (1992) UN Doc S/RES/788 pmbl para 5: ('Determining that the deterioration of the situation in Liberia constitutes a threat to international peace and security.')

[82] On the illegality of forcible territorial acquisitions and on the violation of the 1949 Geneva Conventions, see, eg UNSC Res 836 (n 14); UNSC Res 780 (1992) UN Doc S/RES/780; see also UNSC Res 941 (1994) UN Doc S/RES/941 (all declarations concerning property made under duress are void). For an extensive overview of the Council's practice in condemning violations of international humanitarian law, see SD Bailey, *The UN Security Council and Human Rights* (New York, St Martins Press, 1994) 59–89.

[83] UNSC Res 955 (1994) UN Doc S/RES/955; UNSC Res 827 (1993) UN Doc S/RES/827. It is particularly noteworthy that these resolutions also contain the statutes of the two tribunals (on former Yugoslavia and Rwanda) that define what law should be applied – a real legislative power.

[84] UNSC Res 692 (1991) UN Doc S/RES/692; UNSC Res 687 (1991) UN Doc S/RES/687; UNSC Res 674 (1990) UN Doc S/RES/674.

[85] UNSC Res 837 (1993) UN Doc S/RES/837; see also UNSC Res 978 (1995) UN Doc S/RES/978 (call for all states to apprehend suspects accused of participating in the Rwandan massacres).

[86] UNSC Res 833 (1993) UN Doc S/RES/833.

[87] UNSC Res 687 (n 84).

[88] UNSC Res 940 (n 14).

[89] See eg UNSC Res 1244 (1999) as well as analysis of the whole practice and the literature accompanying it, Anne Orford, 'Book Review Article: International Territorial Administration and the Management of Decolonization' (2010) *59 International and Comparative Law Quarterly 227–249*.

[90] UNSC Res 1373 (2001). The issue of the Council's 'legislative powers' has been the subject of much discussion. See eg C Denis, *Le pouvoir normative du Conseil de sécurité de Nations Unines: Portée et limites* (Brussels, Bruylant, 2004).

One of the most remarkable actions in this respect was the Council's much-belaboured economic boycott to force Libya to extradite two Libyan citizens suspected of the terrorist attacks on the Pan Am flight over Lockerbie in December 1988 and on the French UTA flight over Niger in September 1989.[91] The Council defined Libya's refusal to extradite the two men 'as a threat to international peace and security'.[92] There was no threat or use of force by Libya against any state. Libya's policy was simply too unacceptable, and therefore definable as a security threat, a position that overruled the provisions of an international convention in force between all the parties that would have allowed Libya to refuse extradition.[93] In 2003, as a result of an agreement between the interested parties, Libya agreed to withdraw the case from the Court and the sanctions were eventually dropped. [94]

For the Realists, these developments are just more power policy in disguise. As the world remains as it was in Castlereagh's day, it would be illusory to think that the Council is acting to enforce some new code of morals or law. But as I argued in the foregoing section, this is certainly not so from an engaged perspective. Whatever the Council does appears as an institutional activity and calls for an institutional justification. In fact, the Council knows this well and has therefore begun to invoke a justification based on some enlarged and morally coloured notion of a 'wide understanding' of peace and security. However, as recent debates on this notion, and hence of the Council's competence have shown, how such justification should be construed is by no means clear. Lawyers have sought normative limits to Council authority from an interpretation of articles 1, 2, 24(1) and 39 of the Charter, laying down the purposes and principles of the organisation and the formal competence of the Council to try to create a link between them.[95] But the principles and purposes of the Charter are many, ambiguous, and conflicting. In particular, they are no less indeterminate than the original concept of a 'threat to the peace' that they pretend to clarify. If the Security Council takes action, does that not, by *fiat*, suffice to determine the issue? What more is there to say? For this reason, some have embraced the Kelsenian point that '[i]t is completely within the discretion of the Security Council to decide what constitutes a "threat to the peace"'.[96] However,

---

[91] UNSC Res 731 (1992) UN Doc S/RES/731.

[92] UNSC Res 748 (1992) UN Doc S/RES/748 preamble.

[93] *Questions of Interpretation and Application of the 1971 Montreal Convention Arising from the Aerial Incident at Lockerbie* (*Libya v United States*) [1992] ICJ Rep 126–27 [hereinafter Lockerbie Case]. For background and comment, see F Beveridge, 'The Lockerbie Affair' (1992) 41 *International and Comparative Law Quarterly* 907, 907–09.

[94] See eg P Daillier, M Forteau, A Pellet, *Droit international public* 8th edn (Paris, LGDJ, 2009) 1106.

[95] Lockerbie Case (n 93) 155–56 (Judge Bedjaoui, dissenting); ibid 170–75 (JudgeWeeramantry, dissenting). Of the large commentary on the Lockerbie Case see, eg J Chappez, 'Questions d'interprétation et d'application de la Convention de Montréal du 1971 resultant de l'incident aérien de Lockerbie' (1992) *Annuaire Français de Droit International* 468, 477–79; B Greafrath, 'Leave to the Court What Belongs to the Court: The Libyan Case' (1993) 4 *European Journal of International Law* 184, 186–87; See generally O Schacter, *International Law in Theory and Practice* (The Hague, Nijhoff, 1991) 399–400; R-J Dupuy (ed), *The Development of the Role of the Security Council: Peace-Keeping and Peace-Building*; Hague Academy of International Law (1992).

[96] Kelsen, *The Law of the United Nations* (1951) 727; see also M Akehurst, *A Modern Introduction to International Law*, 6th edn (London, Routledge,1992) 219.

others have pointed out in impeccable legal logic that 'the United Nations is a creation of a treaty and, as such, it exercises authority legitimately only in so far as it
deploys powers which the treaty parties have assigned to it'.[97]

In this controversy law and politics keep deferring to each other in an endless
search for authority and normative closure: texts constrain (law) – but need to be
interpreted (politics); interpretative principles need to be applied (law) – but they
are conflicting and ambiguous (politics); the International Court of Justice could
perhaps decide the matter (law) – but the Court has no jurisdiction in 'political'
matters (politics); but is not the possibility for such judicial control implied in the
Charter (law) – well, that depends on how it is interpreted, and so on.[98]

Yet, the question about the justifiability of Council action under chapter VII
does not really pose itself in the abstract tone of whether or not the Council is
'bound' by legal principles. It is much more concretely linked to the Council's
handling of particular problems. If there is a problem about the legitimacy of
Council action, as many argue,[99] it is precisely in its practical approach to its task,
in the absence of what might be called a legal culture within it. This is visible in
many ways[100]

The first one is secrecy. Since the late 1980s the Council's practice of holding
informal consultations has expanded rapidly.[101] Today, practically all the Council's
substantive discussions take place outside the official meetings. Council delegations meet at the horseshoe table in front of the public only when substantive
agreement has already been attained or proved impossible. There is in general no
access to the *travaux preparatoires* of particular resolutions. Secrecy is, of course, a

---

[97] TM Franck, 'The Security Council and "Threats to the Peace": Some Remarks of Remarkable
Recent Developments, The Hague Academy of International Law', in *The Development of the Role of the
Security Council* (n 95) 83.

[98] It is interesting how all the parties in the Lockerbie Case subscribed both to the view that law and
politics were part of the same hierarchical structure as well as to their being hermetically isolated from
each other. Libya claimed that the Council's resolutions 'infringe . . . the enjoyment and the exercise of
the rights confered on Libya' Lockerbie Case [1992] ICJ Rep 125, and that there is 'no competition or
hierarchy between the Court and the Security Council, each exercising its own competence[,]' ibid 126.
The former argument assumes that law and politics are part of the same structure, and that law (namely
the law of the Montreal Convention) predominates – the second assumes that law and politics are separate, and that the Court should only be concerned with the former. The United States claimed that
protecting Libya's rights 'would run a serious risk of conflicting with the work of the Security Council[,]'
ibid, and that 'Libya has a Charter-based duty to carry out the decisions in the resolution', ibid. The
former argument assumes again that law and politics are separate and that it is precisely because they
are separate that they may conflict – and it is the Court's business to avoid such conflict. The latter argument links both into a hierarchical structure where law predominates – this time the law of the Charter
(instead of that of the Montreal Convention). Neither party answers its opponent directly: If law should
prevail, should it be the law of the Charter or that of the Montreal Convention? If law and politics are
distinct, does this mean that the Court should ignore the possibility of conflict or prevent it?

[99] See, eg, Legal Consequences for States of the Continued Presence of South Africa in Namibia
(South West Africa) Notwithstanding Security Council Resolution 276 (1971) ICJ 16, 293–94 (June 21)
(Judge Fitzmaurice, dissenting); DD Caron, 'The Legitimacy of the Collective Authority of the Security
Council' (1993) 87 *American Journal of International Law* 552.

[100] See also Koskenniemi, 'The Police in the Temple', (1995) 345–47.

[101] See GR Berridge, *Return to the UN: UN Diplomacy in Regional Conflicts* (London, Macmillan,
1991) 3–11; see M Reisman, 'The Constitutional Crisis in the United Nations' (1993) 95 *American
Journal of International Law* 83, 86.

general problem of the political activities of the United Nations. As already mentioned, the Sanctions Committees established for the management of the sanctions regimesdo not publish their records or even their interpretative decisions. Nor do they report substantively to the Council. As a result, there is no access for Member States or the public to data that is crucial for an evaluation of the success of the economic measures, with the further implication that they will continue to be used as an article of faith, not as a rational policy measure.[102]

But there are also many other procedural problems, especially relevant when the Council is acting in a judicial or quasi-judicial role. For example, its determination of Libya's guilt for complicity in the Lockerbie terrorist attack and its liability in Resolution 731 in January 1992 fell below all standards of procedural fairness.[103] Nor did the Council take into account Iraq's claims when in 1993 it determined the place of the long-disputed Iraq-Kuwait boundary.[104] In addition, the basis on which the Iraqi Compensation Commission distributes compensation is far from clear.[105] It has traditionally been argued that it is not the Council's business to engage in the material settlement of disputes. Practice has shown, however, that in cases where an argument can be found based upon the Council's primary responsibility to uphold or restore peace and security, even the imposition of a binding settlement does not fall outside the Council's competence. Of course, such problems have not escaped public notice and in the mid-1990s suggestions to review the Council's working patterns were dealt with by various UN bodies and the Council itself initiated minor, but still beneficial, amendments to its procedures.[106] The General Assembly stressed the need to increase the transparency of the Council's activity and requested more detailed information from the Council for this purpose.[107] A working group was set up to look into the composition and working practices of the Council. While the representativeness problem proved, in 1994 and 1995 as intractable as in the past, with no agreement on how the Council's composition could be amended, a number of proposals were presented on the secrecy issue the thrust of which was to include non-members and especially 'interested states' in the Council's deliberations. Some of such proposals had

---

[102] For descriptions and criticisms, see P Conlon, 'Legal Problems at the Centre of United Nations Sanctions' (1996) 65 *Nordic Journal of International Law*; M Koskenniemi, 'Le comité des sanctions (crée par la résolution 661 (1990) du Conseil de Sécurité)' (1991) *Annuaire Francais de Droit International* (1991) 119; MP Scharf – JL Dorosin, 'Interpretating UN Sanctions: The Rulings and Role of the Yugoslavia Sanctions Committee' (1993) 19 *Brooklyn Journal of International Law* (1993) 771.

[103] See B Graefrath, 'Leave to the Court' (1993) 187–91, 196, 204.

[104] UNSC Res 833 (n 86).

[105] See *Report of the Secretary-General Pursuant to Paragraph 19 of the Security Council Resolution 687*, S/22559 (1991).

[106] These include regular briefings by the president of the Council to the president of the Assembly and the chairmen of regional groups, consultations with troop-contributing and other 'interested countries', daily publication of the agendas of the Council's informal consultations, monthly circulation among the permanent missions of its programme of work, 'orientation debates' open to all members as the Council begins the consideration of new items, and the reconsideration of the format of its reports to the Assembly. *Questions of Equitable Representation on and Increase in the Membership of the Security Council*, A/49/965 (1995). Not all of these have, however, yet been implemented .

[107] UNGA Res 264, (1994) UN Doc A/RES/264(1994).

already been adopted by the Council, others underlined the need to clarify the division of competence among the Council and other United Nations bodies, to review the practice of economic sanctions, and to update and make permanent the Council's provisional rules of procedure.[108] The proposals did not seek to modify the statist image of collective security, though they did go some way towards strengthening legal culture within the Council. Yet, none of this has fundamentally affected the role or operation of the Council. Adopting the realist voice, Thomas Weiss has pointed to the illusionary aspects of debates about Security Council reform: it all depends on what Washington thinks as useful for the attainment of its objectives. This may be true but that, too, is an engaged perspective – namely imaginary engagement on the side of a powerful actor, not necessarily a preface to a job application but a literary effort to imagine one is more than – well – just an academic.[109]

Another group of problems is relative to the Council's lack of commitment to the policies it has chosen. The weakness of its reaction in the former Yugoslavia or in the African crises are famous. The practice of authorising Member States to take military action on the Council's behalf might seem like another abdication from responsibility; however, many delegations explain it as a lack of resources on the United Nations' part. The same explanation is given for the Council's lack of adequate political and material support to the two war crimes Tribunals. Much publicity concentrated on the situation of the Yugoslavian and the Rwandan war crimes Tribunal in the 1990s. For example, by the end of August 1995, some 16 months after the genocide, the work of the war crimes Tribunal had not even commenced, while 51,000 prisoners were being held in Rwandese prisons in facilities meant for 12,500.[110] A technical reason, such as lack of resources, is a poor justification here inasmuch as resources do exist in Member States but are not allocated for a purpose that might seem marginal or risky for potential contributors. The tribunals have been unable to close their operations and although the overall situation may have been improved, in part owing to the establishment of the International Criminal Court (ICC) in 1998, the 'fight against impunity' has stalled since the early nineties, especially owing to tensions in North-South relations. relates to the Council's lack of accountability within the United Nations system and beyond.

Finally, there is the much-belaboured question of the representativeness of the Council, as reflected in its composition. Most Member States and many observers view this as the Council's main problem, and suggest amending the Charter so as to enhance its democratic legitimacy. Aside from the diplomatic impossibility to agree on the amendment, I am uncertain about the suggestion itself. As I have argued more fully elsewhere, the Council's role is to co-opt military power for the

---

[108] ibid.

[109] TG Weiss, 'The Illusion of UN Security Council Reform 26 *The Washington Quarterly* (2003), 147–61.

[110] *Letter Dated 29 August 1995 from the Secretary-General addressed to the President of the Security Council*, S/1995/762 (1995); see also *Third Report of the Secretary-General Pursuant to Paragraph 5 of Security Council Resolution 955*, S/1995/741(1995).

service of the organisation. Enhancing its democratic image supports even more expanded powers for it, a consequence which I find objectionable.[111] Inasmuch as it makes sense to speak of democracy in a statist international political system (which is by no means a self-evidently beneficial rhetorical strategy), it is surely the job of the General Assembly to imagine the political community whose boundaries then are to be policed by the Council. Much discussion has centered on the possibility of judicial control over the Council's actions by the International Court of Justice. It is no doubt more relevant for the General Assembly to use its powers, for instance its budgetary powers, to seek to influence or override the policy of the Council.[112] But a revitalisation of the 'right of last resort' of Member States, touched upon in the discussions over the 'Kadi' case in the EU, would surely constitute a non-negligible means to enhance the Council's accountability.[113]

Security and Law as Institutional Cultures

If there is any single point on which Realism agrees with Institutional formalism, it is expressed in this one sentence by the most paradigmatic of the formalists, Hans Kelsen: 'By its very nature, collective security is a legal principle, while the balance of power is a principle of political convenience.'[114] Realists embraced this definition and rejected collective security precisely as the kind of legalistic Utopianism whose failure seemed the single most important lesson from the League of Nations experiment. *De maximis no curat praetor.* Today, most lawyers have accepted that if law has a role to play in matters of security, it is as a handmaid to state power and interest, a facilitator for politics to take its natural course 'by rationalizing and stabilizing the existing and improvised means of collaboration between [the] Powers'.[115] The favourite metaphor invokes traffic regulation: the law's role is based on its usefulness for states in the same way as rules of the road are useful to motorists. 'But it is precisely in the vital realm of power relations that it is at its weakest.'[116]

The assumed primacy of policy over law implies both the existence of fixed and verifiable state security interests and the presence of reliable information on the causal chains that allow their realisation. In this image, shared by Realists and

---

[111] Koskenniemi, 'The Police in the Temple', (1995).

[112] For a sceptical view in this respect, however, see F Delon, 'L'Assemblée générale peut-elle contrôler le Conseil de sécurité?' in *Le Chapitre VII de la Charte des Nations Unies* (n 26) 239.

[113] See D Ciobanu, *Preliminary Objections. Related to the Jurisdiction of the United Nations Political Organs* (The Hague, Kluwer, 1975) 173–79 (discussing a state's right of last resort under the laws of the United Nations).

[114] H Kelsen, *Collective Security and International Law* (Naval War College International Law Series 49, 1954) 42.

[115] GW Keeton and G Schwarzenberger (London, Stevens, 1946) 96 (making this point about the United Nation's role).

[116] Hoffmann, 'Is There an International Order?' (1987) 89.

Institutionalists alike, law is purely external and instrumental, something that decision-makers choose to ignore or apply at their will when seeking to fulfill interests and values. This is the modern image of the 'gardening state', the image of public policy in the service of human betterment.[117] In this image, international security appears as a function of bureaucratic management skills in the combination of unilateral with institutional policies.

However, much of our late modern experience suggests scepticism about the ability of public decision processes to reach their goals. In the first place, there is uncertainty about those goals – whether their familiar rhetorical forms actually encapsulate shared values or interests. The present consensus about a new 'world order' is not immune from the observation by EH Carr, that: 'as soon as the attempt is made to apply these supposedly abstract principles to a concrete political situation, they are revealed as transparent disguises of selfish vested interests'.[118] Second, even if there were agreement on such values or interests, we seem to lack information about how they can be reached. Our science and technology no longer seem reliable guides for action. Sometimes the solution of problems creates new, unforeseen, and often more serious problems, making the very process of policy as 'problem-solution' inherently suspect.

For such general reasons, there is room for scepticism about the instrumental nature of law, its ability to express and to realise values, interests or, indeed, 'security'.[119] The vocabulary of 'security' is a terrain of conflict and struggle: whose interest will attain the label of being a 'security interest' – and who will pay for that by the sense of increased insecurity? This scepticism is in no way diminished by a reason specific to the law, such as the indeterminacy of its rules and principles. Instead of being an external, objective instrument for policy, law is enmeshed with the same uncertainties as policy – its application remaining simultaneously a political act.

Realism and Institutionalism both imagine the law as an instrument for political purposes. This, I argued earlier, is an offshoot of their theoretical-empirical bias, that bias itself being inseparable from the modern image of the 'gardening state' and supporting an international culture of technical expertise in the manipulation of 'power' for the enhancement of 'interests'. I want to contrast that with my favourite quote from George Kennan who once depicted international law as having 'the unobtrusive, almost feminine, function of the gentle civilizer of national self-interest[.]'[120] Despite the intended irony, the quote reveals an important truth about international law as a cultural instead of an instrumental phenomenon, highlighting the engaged aspect of the law, its being 'inside' social practices instead of 'outside' them as an objective language or a formal procedure. From that aspect, law acts as a spirit or an attitude that involves recognising the

---

[117] Z Bauman, *Modernity and Ambivalence* (London, Polity, 1991) 20, 26–39.

[118] Carr, *The Twenty-years' Crisis 1919–1939* (1946) 87–88.

[119] For one useful discussion of the significance of such (and other) anti-instrumental themes for legal practice, see G Binder, Beyond Criticism (1988) 55 *University of Chicago Law Review* 888.

[120] G Kennan, *American Diplomacy 1900–1950* (Chicago, University of Chicago Press, 1951) 54.

institutional situatedness of the speaker: hence its curious, yet typical, ability to engage the practitioner in political action while seeking distance from anyone's idiosyncratic interests. Engaging in the formalism of the legal argument inevitably makes public the normative basis and objectives of one's actions and assumes the actor's institutional accountability for what it is that one is justifying. It is the antithesis of a culture of secrecy, hegemony, dogmatism and unaccountability.

For a brief moment in the autumn of 1990, the political context within the Security Council seemed open and institutional culture might have been revised. By early 1991, that momentum was gone. The Council met only once during Operation Desert Storm, and even then in a closed session. There is no longer much debate around the meaning of collective self-defence, or the relationship among articles 42, 43 and 47. Indeed the new cultures of security that arose to institutionally decisive positions after 2001 may have seemed to put legalistic concerns momentarily on the side – though they did re-emerge powerfully as a language to condemn the Bush-Blair war on Iraq in 2003. The long list of procedural problems within the Council, however, that remains under discussion in the General Assembly as well as, to some extent, in the Council itself, remain relevant for the development of legal culture within the Council. Many factors work against such development. The background of diplomats at the United Nations who serve in the Council has traditionally focused on the 'hard realities' of power politics – one does not get into a Council delegation by having served in development assistance! The routines and composition of the political secretariat of the United Nations are equally resistant to legal culture, so are its administrative inertia, lack of resources, recruitment policies, and the relative isolation of the office of legal affairs from the political centre.

For me, it seems clear that law has a place in collective security as a working culture of the 'gentle civilizer' by opening conceptions and practices of 'security' to public debate, and by enhancing the accountability of governmental and international institutions for what goes on under the label of 'security policy'. That security has expanded beyond its military and statist component highlights its political and constructive aspects and the inadequacy of the practices within the United Nations (and elsewhere in international organisations) through which 'security matters' have been handled. Security can no longer be seen in terms of expert knowledge managed through secret bureaucratic routines, but as one theme among others that seek to articulate the political values on which we claim to base our communal identities. The question is never about security versus something else, but about 'whose security', and 'at what cost'?

4

'The Lady Doth Protest Too Much': Kosovo, and the Turn to Ethics in International Law

The bombing of Serbia in the spring of 1999 gave me occasion to restate the analysis of legal indeterminacy in a somewhat novel language. It also enabled me to criticise the turn to 'ethics' that I found was increasingly creeping into the argumentative practices of the profession – a counterpart of its attempt to turn to 'realism', analysed in the previous chapter. This text tries to accomplish three things: (a) to restate the functioning of legal indeterminacy in respect of a particular set of facts; (b) to focus on the existential moment of foreign policy 'decision', and (c) to introduce the larger theme of international law as a vocabulary of the social that makes some things visible while rendering others invisible.

IN A FAMOUS talk nearly 40 years ago, Professor Martin Wight of the London School of Economics posed the question about why there was no international theory. One of the reasons he found is the fact that it would have to be expressed in the languages of political theory and law. However, these were languages that had been developed in the thinking about the state and about the control of social life in normal conditions:

> Political theory and law are maps of experience or systems of action within the realm of normal relationships and calculable results. They are the theory of the good life. International theory is the theory of survival. What for political theory is the extreme case (as revolution or civil war) is for international theory the regular case.[1]

The distinction between the normal and the exceptional came to be part of the Realist explanation for why international law was such a weak structure. In the domestic context, situations are routine. Political normality by far outweighs the incidence of the exception – that is, ultimately revolution. By contrast, the international context was idiosyncratic, and involved 'the ultimate experience of life and death, national existence and national extinction'. It was not the realm of the regularised search for happiness or avoidance of displeasure: it was the struggle for

---

[1] M Wight, 'Why is There is no International Theory?' in H Butterfield and M Wight (eds), *Diplomatic Investigations. Essays in the Theory of International Politics* (London, Allen and Unwin, 1966) 33.

survival. Political theories would not apply and legal rules would not work because the need for survival far outweighed the need for compliance.

Lawyers are not, of course, insensitive to the distinction between the normal and the exceptional. 'Hard cases make bad law' we say. Few would fail to distinguish between the law regulating the provision of parking tickets to diplomats and the law concerning the use of force. In the recent *Nuclear Weapons* case (1996), the International Court of Justice came very close to admitting that no law could govern the case of self-defence when the very existence of the state was at stake.[2] During the Cold War, international lawyers largely gave up any attempt to conceive of the balance of power in terms of legal rules or principles. The dark passion of Great Power politics overwhelmed law's rational calculations. Thus, many have understood the post-1989 transformation as a move from an *exceptional* situation to a *normality* where the rules of civilised behaviour would come to govern international life. The limitation of the scope of law during the Cold War had been an anomaly; now it was possible to restart the project of organising the administration of the international society by the Rule of Law in the image of the liberal West. Collective enforcement under the UN Charter 'would function in a regular and non-selective manner each time that circumstances required it, thus providing an institutional guarantee to the broad core of constitutional principles'.[3] Sovereignty would lose its exceptional force as a barrier against the enforcement of human rights, democracy or the requirements of the global market. The indictment of *Pinochet* and *Milošević* would imply a rejection of the 'culture of impunity' that seemed such a violation of normal legal accountability.[4] The creation of the ad hoc war crimes tribunals on the Former Yugoslavia and Rwanda and the establishment of the International Criminal Court in Rome in 1998 would augur a 'new world order based on the rule of international law'[5] and continue the constitutionalisation of the international order, celebrated as a major implication of the new dispute-settlement system under the World Trade Organisation.[6]

---

[2] ICJ, *Legality of the Threat or Use of Nuclear Weapons*, Advisory Opinion, Reports 1996, [90]–[97] and [105 E] (dispositif).

[3] G Abi-Saab, 'Whither the International Community' (1998) 9 *European Journal of International Law* 264.

[4] Out of the wealth of writings on the matter, see JM Sears, 'Confronting the "Culture of Impunity": Immunity of Heads of State from Nuremberg to *ex parte Pinochet*' (1999) 42 *German Yearbook of International Law* 125–46.

[5] A Cassese, 'On the Current Trend towards Criminal Prosecution and Punishment of Breaches of International Humanitarian Law' (1998) 9 *European Journal of International Law* 8. The establishment of war crimes tribunals as an aspect of liberal legalism's projection of domestic ideals at the international level is usefully discussed in GJ Bass, *Stay the Hand of Vengeance. The Politics of War Crimes Tribunals* (Princeton NJ, Princeton University Press, 2000) especially 16–36.

[6] See E-U Petersmann, 'The WTO Constitution and the Millennium Road' in M Bronkers and R Quick (eds), *New Directions in International Economic Law. Essays in Honour of John H Jackson* (The Hague, Kluwer, 2000) 111–33 and ibid 'Constitutionalism and International Adjudication: How to Constitutionalize the UN Dispute Settlement System?'(1999) 31 *New York University Journal of International Law & Politics* 753–90. Astonishingly, many international lawyers continue to interpret the UN Charter as a 'constitution of mankind', eg B Simma and A Paulus, 'The "International Community" Facing the Challenge of Globalization' (1998) 9 *European Journal of International Law* 274.

The completion of the international legal order by bringing 'exceptional' situations within its compass has taken place through an increasing deformalisation, accompanied by a turn to ethics in the profession. To illustrate this, I shall examine the legal argument about the bombing of Serbia by the North Atlantic Treaty Organisation (NATO) in 1999. This enables me to provide a focused genealogy of modern international law as it moves, in a familiar succession of argumentative steps, from formalism to ethics, in order to capture within law a great crisis that under the old, 'realistic' view would have fallen beyond its scope. But it also allows me to argue that the obsession to extend the law to such crises, while understandable within a historical perspective, enlists political energies to support causes dictated by the hegemonic powers and is unresponsive to the violence and injustice that sustain the global everyday. The 'turn to ethics' is profoundly conservative in its implications. Many critics have observed the 'ideological' character of 'Kosovo'.[7] What I wish to do is to generalise from that incident to the state of the discipline as it struggles to find credibility and critical voice in the conditions of increasingly imperial politics.

I

The bombing of Yugoslavia in the spring of 1999 caused around 500 civilian casualties.[8] From the perspective of the Western Alliance, these deaths were perhaps a tragic but unavoidable collateral damage. For international lawyers, they are an agonising puzzle: humanity's sacrifice for the gift of the Rule of Law or the consummation of a blatant breach of the UN Charter? Part of the agony stems from the difficulty to think that those are the only alternatives. In some ways, formal law seems unable to deal with Kosovo. So, many prefer to describe it through the discourse of diplomatic or military strategy: you could not negotiate with *Milošević*, the only language he understands is force! Others seek to encompass those deaths within the frame of historical causality: it has always been bad down there, it could not be changed overnight – what is important is the creation of the conditions for a more democratic Yugoslavia, and a more humane international order. But most commentators have envisaged Kosovo as a moral or ethical issue, a matter of rights or principles. It is this perspective that tends to separate Kosovo from the old world of the Cold War. While 'then' it was all a calculation of military force and balance of power, 'now' it has become a matter of moral ideals, self-determination, democracy and human rights. When the Secretary-General of NATO announced that the attack on Serbia had commenced, he did this in the following terms: 'We

---

[7] See especially O Corten, 'Les ambiguités de la reference au droit international comme facteur de légitimation portée et signification d'une déformalisation du discours légaliste' in O Corten and B Delcourt, *Droit, légitimation et politique exterieure: l'Europe et la guerre du Kosovo* (Bruxelles, Bruylant, 2000) 223–59 and A Orford, 'Muscular Humanitarianism: Reading the Narratives of the New Interventionism' (1999) 10 *European Journal of International Law* 679–711.

[8] There is no reliable exact number to the civilian deaths of 'Operation Allied Force'. The Human Rights Watch estimates that about 500 civilians were killed in approximately 90 incidents. See Amnesty International, *NATO/Federal Republic of Yugoslavia. 'Collateral Damage' or Unlawful Killings? Violations of the Laws of War by NATO during Operation Allied Force* (Amnesty International, June 2000) 1.

must stop the violence and bring an end to the humanitarian catastrophe now taking place in Kosovo. We have a moral duty to do so.'[9]

What is the relationship between 'moral duty' and the question about the lawfulness of the killing of the 500? A simple answer would be to relegate the former into a matter of the private conscience, or describe it as part of the foreign policy debate about the pros and cons of Western involvement. But this would be uncomfortably close to Cold War Realism and would counteract the urge to think about the international world, too, in terms of the 'theory of the good life'. Now there have, of course, been lawyers who have claimed that there is no reason why the law should not be applicable to any international matter, including the high politics of survival. This conclusion has been sometimes received from the nature of law as a complete system.[10] NATO was either entitled to bomb Serbia or it was not. *Tertium non datur.* Surely, it is an essential part of the Rule of Law that society contains no corner of outside-the-law. Surely, it would seem strange if the law had nothing to say about the civilian casualties in Serbia. But what does the law say, and with what conviction?

After a decade of debate, the positions are well known. For some, 'Kosovo' was a formal breach of the UN Charter and there is nothing more to say about it. Others read their moral intuitions as part of the law: because the intervention was morally necessary, it was also lawful. However, most lawyers – including myself – took the ambivalent position that it was both formally illegal and morally necessary.[11] Such schizophrenia tears wide open the fragile fabric of diplomatic consensus and exposes the aporia of a normative structure deferring simultaneously to the impossibility of ethical politics in a divided and agnostic world and the impossibility not to assess political action in the light of some ethical standpoint. The agony of lawyers that paraded through conferences and symposia on Kosovo and manifests itself in the odd view that brings law and ethics together by assuming that the Council 'legalised' the NATO action ex post facto,[12] suggests that whichever conclusion one holds, it remains a rather secondary rationalisation in view of the speciality of the events.

To think of Kosovo as law is to move it from the realm of the exceptional to that of the routine. It becomes a 'case' of a 'doctrine' – the law of humanitarian

---

[9] NATO Press release (1999) 041 (14 March 1999).

[10] The completeness of international law was the focus of much of the inter-war reconstructive jurisprudence. For Hans Kelsen, completeness was an outcome of the formal principle of the exclusion of the third. More influential has been the theory of material completeness that forms the heart of one of the most important books of twentieth century international jurisprudence, H Lauterpacht, *The Function of Law in the International Community* (Oxford, Clarendon, 1933).

[11] This argument is expressly made eg in A Cassese, '*Ex iniuria ius oritur.* Are We Moving Towards International Legitimation of Forcible Humanitarian Countermeasures in the International Community?'(1999) 10 *European Journal of International Law* 23–30. For nuances, compare B Simma, 'NATO, the UN and the Use of Force: Legal Aspects' (1999) 10 *European Journal of International Law* 1–22. For particularly useful discussions of the international lawyers' reaction, see S Schieder, 'Pragmatism as a Path towards a Discursive and Open Theory of International Law' (2000) 11 *European Journal of International Law* 663, 691–98 and O Corten, 'Les ambiguités de la reference au droit international comme facteur de légitimation portée et signification d'une déformalisation du discours légaliste' in: O Corten and B Delcourt, *Droit, légitimation et politique exterieure: L'Europe et la guerre du Kosovo* (Brussels, Bruylant, 2001) 223–59.

[12] See A Pellet, 'Brief Remarks on the Unilateral Use of Force' (2000) 11 *European Journal of International Law* 389.

intervention. To the extent that we then wish to take account of its special aspects, and admit various informal arguments to characterise it, it moves us in the direction of the idiosyncratic, personal – until at the end it becomes the single situation that appeals to us not through the rational rhetoric of the rules but its singular meaning, as it were, through our souls. In this way, I suggest, Kosovo has invited international lawyers to throw away dry professionalism and imagine themselves as moral agents in a *mission civilisatrice*. A particularly shallow and dangerous moralisation that forecloses political energies needed for transformation elsewhere. This is why my title picks up the spontaneous cry – 'the Lady protests too much, methinks' – that Shakespeare put into Queen Gertrude's mouth. The debates reveal that 'Kosovo' is not only about what happened 'out there' – in the play that Hamlet had staged for his mother to watch – but also, and importantly, about what took place 'in here', the audience. Reacting to the play, Queen Gertrude was reacting to her own guilt which, of course, was the *real* subject being dealt with. Analogously, Kosovo has come to be a debate about ourselves, about what we hold as normal and what as exceptional, and through that fact, about what sort of international law we practice.

II

Let me now trace the eight steps through which international lawyers are transformed into moralists by the logic of the argument from humanitarian intervention, which also traces modern international law's odyssey for 'policy-relevance'.

Step 1: (Formal law stricto sensu – *law as pure form).* Lawyers who held the bombing illegal based this on the formal breach of article 2(4) of the UN Charter that was involved. As is well-known, the article admits of only two principal exceptions: authorisation by the Security Council and self-defence under article 51. Neither was present. *Ergo*, the bombing was illegal. Although there is little doubt of the professional correctness of this conclusion, it still seems arrogantly insensitive to the humanitarian dilemmas involved. It resembles a formalism that would require a head of state to refrain from a pre-emptive strike against a lonely submarine in the North Pole, even if that were the only way to save the population of the capital city from a nuclear attack from that ship – simply because no 'armed attack' had yet taken place as required by the language of article 51. But does the law require the sacrifice of thousands for the altar of the law? Surely the relevant texts should be read so as to produce a 'reasonable' result. If it is the *intention* of the self-defence rule to protect the state, surely it should not be applied in a way to bring about the destruction of the state.

But how does one know whether self-defence is applicable? Clearly, this cannot be determined independently of a definition of the relevant 'self'. For the North Atlantic Alliance it may not be implausible to think of European security as a matter for its own security. Or perhaps the relevant 'self' was the Albanian population in Kosovo – in which case the NATO attack might have been lawful assistance for a people struggling for self-determination under the 1975 Friendly Relations Declaration.[13]

---

[13] UNGA Res 2625 (XXV) (24 October 1970).

To what extent might such considerations offset the requirement of prior armed attack? In order to give sense to the normal meaning of the language of the relevant instruments, and solve hierarchical controversies, it is necessary to move to interpretation, that is beyond the pure form of articles 2 (4) and 51.

Step 2: (Formal law lato sensu – *law as representative for 'underlying' social, historical, systemic, or other such 'values').* Although it is difficult (though by no means impossible) to sustain humanitarian intervention as a formal custom,[14] many might receive it from the object and purpose of the UN Charter, supported by a series of General Assembly resolutions plus the residual custom that contains a principle of proportionality and perhaps no longer sustains sovereignty against massive human rights violations. In the case of the Charter, recourse to its object and purpose is 'of special significance' due to its constitutional nature and extreme difficulty of carrying out formal revisions.[15] There is no doubt that the violent oppression of ethnic Albanians in Kosovo by the Milošević regime was against the Charter. If the Charter prohibits such oppression then surely it must also provide the means whereby it is discontinued. Remember the non-recognition of South Rhodesia by the UN during 1965–79, the sanctions against South Africa, or the official international community's silence after India's intervention in East Pakistan in 1971. If sovereignty is an expression of communal liberty and self-rule, then surely it cannot be permitted to destroy them.[16] '[A] jurist rooted in the late twentieth century can hardly say that an invasion by outside forces to remove [an usurper of power] and install the elected government is a violation of national sovereignty'.[17]

Notice that the argument in the opposite direction occupies the same terrain. Why would it be necessary to stick closely to the formal prohibition of force and the narrow understanding of the exceptions thereto? Well, surely because of the dangers of abuse and selectivity, the fact that '[m]ilitary enforcement raises the spectre of colonialism and war'.[18] There is no space of 'innocent' literality. If challenged, a restrictive view – even if motivated by bona fides concerns of intellectual rigour – is immediately called upon to produce a substantive defence and will thus

[14] Unsurprisingly, the customary law argument enjoys wide support among US lawyers such as Lillich, McDougal or Reisman. The problem with that argument is that it has to be made against the authority of ICJ, *Nicaragua Case (Nicaragua v US)* (Merits) [1986] ICJ Rep 109. Apart from Kosovo, practice is still scarce of cases in which the acting state itself would have understood (or justified) its action as humanitarian intervention. See D Kritsiotis, 'Appraising the Policy Objections to Humanitarian Intervention' (1993) 19 *Michigan Journal of International Law* 1010–14. For a balanced overview and assessment, see S Chesterman, *Just War or Just Peace? Humanitarian Intervention and International Law* (Oxford, Oxford University Press, 2001) 53–86.

[15] See G Ress, 'The Interpretation of the Charter' in B Simma (ed), *The Charter of the United Nations. A Commentary* (Oxford, Oxford University Press, 1995) 42–43.

[16] This is the argument in M Walzer, *Just and Unjust Wars. A Moral Argument with Historical Illustrations*, 2nd edn (New York, Basic Books, 1992) 101–08.

[17] M Reisman, 'Sovereignty and Human Rights in Contemporary International Law' in G Fox and B Roth, *Democratic Governance and International Law* (Cambridge, Cambridge University Press, 2000) 245.

[18] TM Franck, *The Empowered Self. Law and Society in the Age of Individualism* (New York, Oxford University Press, 1999) 272. For the policy objections, see Kritsiotis, 'Appraising the Policy Objections' (1993) 1020–34.

reveal its underlying ideology.[19] At that point we have irrevocably left formalism for hermeneutics. Law is now how it is interpreted. As the 'deep-structural' values which the interpretation is expected to reveal do not exist independently of human purposes, we are down the slippery slope of trying to identify those purposes. This might be accomplished in different ways.

Step 3: (Instrumentalism). As human activity, international law is not a mechanic transformation of a piece of textual information into action. It is, rather, activity with a point, oriented towards a human purpose. The point of criminal law is to maintain social peace; the point of contract is to exchange goods. Without such point, the law and the contract would seem utterly meaningless or aspects of some strange metaphysics. This is how a Martian might feel trying to interpret what parliaments and businessmen do in abstraction of any point: the raising of the hands, the filing of the ballot, and the exchange of pieces of paper – exotic rituals indeed, which we understand as the point-oriented activities of legislation or trade. The same is true of international law, of course. The point of the UN Charter is to attain peace, human rights, economic welfare. We do not appreciate the Charter because of some mystical quality of its text or the aura of its authors. The Charter is not God. We honour it because we believe it leads us to valuable secular purposes.

This is also how many lawyers understand the sacrifice of the 500 Serbs.[20] The sacrifice is justified by the point of the Charter, to prevent aggression, to bring peace to the Balkans, to protect human rights and self-determination. Or conversely it was mass murder because the Charter seeks to prevent aggression, protect sovereignty, to channel disputes into UN organs. If human activity is an activity with a point, and the UN is a human activity, then to understand it – and not simply to apply its formal text – we must examine whether the point of the Charter and the point of the sacrifice do or do not coincide. But now a formidable problem emerges.

If law is thoroughly instrumental, we should be able to ascertain what it is an instrument for. However, if we *do* know that, we already have access to an objective moral world of what 'we' as UN members want (or what is 'good') and no longer need (formal) law at all – except as a practical guide on how to get there. However, – and here is the difficulty – if law is just a 'practical guide' to reach a point, *then we have no need for it if we already know the point*. We have then silently stepped out of the melancholy agnosticism of legal modernity, and entered an earthly paradise in which (1) we can think of ourselves as (again) capable of knowing the good in some inter-individually valid way without the necessary intervention of any authority, or mediator; and (2) the things we know are good are coterminous with each other, there is no conflict between them, and consequently no need for rules on conflict resolution. Morgenthau was wrong: human life is not

---

[19] P-M Dupuy, 'L'enfer et le paradigme: libres propos sur les relations du droit international avec la persistance des guerres et l'objectif idéal du maintien de la paix' in *Mélanges offerts à Hubert Thierry* (Paris, Pedone, 1998) 199–200.

[20] See P-M Dupuy, 'L'obligation en droit international' (2000) 44 *Archives de philosophie du droit* 218.

tragic, utopia is available. Morgenthau was right; it does not include a binding, formal law.[21]

The 'object and purpose' test is not just a technique; it is a replacement of the legal form by a claim about substantive morality. It thus involves difficulties of philosophical anthropology and epistemology that bring us to the edge of modernity, and maybe beyond. But it also meets with the practical obstacle that people – and States – still do disagree on what is good, and, by extension, how the Charter should be interpreted. Far from resolving the problem of Kosovo, hermeneutics restates that problem in another vocabulary: the sacrifice was necessary for the same reason that it seemed necessary for Abraham to kill Isaac, because that is what God said.[22] Verbal uniformity may sometimes reflect or bring about substantive agreement. However, often it veils disagreement, and when it does, merely to insist on 'strict compliance' with the rule is pointless as the disagreement is about what there is to comply with in the first place.[23]

Step 4: (Utilitarianism). Well, you might think, it is true that formal law does not solve the issue, and that God is not available for guidance, but that this is to exaggerate the difficulty. Perhaps, you think, all that is needed is to balance the stakes, to calculate. Is it not the purpose of political action to attain the greatest good of the greatest number? If intervention can save more lives than it might destroy, then it must be carried out. The 500 were sacrificed for the greater good. Many of us often reason this way. Much recent international regulation has refrained from laying down substantive do's and don'ts and instead referred to an *ad hoc* balancing of interests in a contextual, deformalised fashion, in order to attain the greatest overall utility.[24] But many of us are also aware of the problems, familiar as they have been since John Stuart Mill's adjustment of Benthamite 'pig-philosophy'. Which items are included in the calculation? How are those items weighed against each other? Would massive destruction of nature be part of the package – how might it compare to civilian deaths? What about the formal status of the victims: surely the cost of 10 dead pilots – by flying lower in order to hit only true military

---

[21] The view that human interests or wants are essentially compatible and that social problems are thus ('ultimately') problems of scientific or technical co-ordination, lies at the heart of the traditional (liberal) interdependence-based explanations of the possibility of international law. It is precisely that assumption – the harmony of interests – that was the basis of the 'Realist' critique of international law and the tragic view of the human predicament propagated by leading 'Realists'. See EH Carr, *The Twenty-Years' Crisis 1919–1939*, 2nd edn (London, Macmillan, 1946) especially 40 et seq, 80–88 and H Morgenthau, *Scientific Man vs Power Politics* (Chicago, University of Chicago Press, 1946).

[22] For this familiar parable, see also chapter 8 in this volume.

[23] This is what makes the recent obsession about 'compliance control' with international agreements so frustrating: in the interesting cases, non-compliance is not a technical or a bad faith problem but a political one: substantive disagreement about what the party accused of non-compliance undertook to comply with. For a more sustained argument on this, see M Koskenniemi, 'Comment on Compliance with Environmental Treaties' in W Lang (ed), *Sustainable Development and International Law* (London, Dordrecht, Boston, Nijhoff, 1995) 91–96.

[24] A good example of this is the 1997 UN Convention on the Law of the Non-Navigational Uses of International Watercourses (8 July 1997) UN Dec A/RES/51/229. The Treaty merely lays down a general standard of 'equitable and reasonable utilization' that reserves the determination of permitted and prohibited uses to an open-ended multi-factor calculation, 'taking into account the interests of the watercourse States concerned, consistent with the adequate protection of the watercourse' (article 5(1) *in fine*).

targets – might have been a more acceptable offer for the Rule of Law than 500 Serbian civilians? But what is the ratio and which are the relevant values? What about accepting the death of 1000 soldiers in a ground campaign to spare 500 civilians as an offshoot of an air war? However, at some point it becomes abominable to count heads in this way. The targeting of old Serbs in order to save young Kosovar Albanians might work as an effective deterrent in which the ratio in terms of saved years would clearly be in favour. However, it would make banal the value of lives, and inculcate an insensitive and dangerous bureaucratisation that lowers the threshold towards killing if only that might seem rational under some administrative reason. Besides, it presumes full knowledge of the sacrifice that is going to be required and the consequences of alternative scenarios. But we know now that NATO knew precious little of the actual effects of its bombing on the ground – and had still less idea about the political results. As Thomas Nagel put the point:

> Once the door is opened to calculations of utility and national interest, the usual speculations about the future of freedom, peace, and economic prosperity can be brought to bear to ease the consciences of those responsible for a certain number of charred babies.[25]

Step 5: (Rights). Due to such formidable difficulties, many would say that law or morality is not just about head-counting: surely they are also about justice, in particular about rights. Rights, in this version, act as 'trumps' that prohibit the carrying out of policies that would otherwise seem to provide an aggregate benefit.[26] Indeed, article 6 of the 1966 UN Covenant on Civil and Political Rights lays down the right to life without provision for exception. As there is no derogation from right to life, the bombing was illegal. But the right to life is, of course, not absolute in this way: the provision prohibits only the 'arbitrary' deprivation of life and what is 'arbitrary' is to be defined *in casu*. Killing in war or in self-defence does not qualify as a breach of article 6.[27] But the point is larger. Rights are always consequential on a prior definition of some benefit as 'right' and on contextual appreciation where rights-language is given a meaning (especially in terms of somebody's enforceable duties). Likewise, conflicting rights can only be put to a hierarchy by reference to some policy about the distribution of entitlements under conditions of relative scarcity.[28] In other words, rights depend on their meaning and force on the character of the political community in which they function.[29] This applies also to the right to life. Abortion and euthanasia, for instance, receive normative status only once we know the society that is our reference-point. In the practice of international institutions – that is to say, within the 'thin' culture of public cosmopolitanism – rights turn

---

[25] T Nagel, *Mortal Questions* (Cambridge, Cambridge University Press, 1979) 59. For a good account of the problems of utilitarian arguments about killing in war, see R Norman, *Ethics, Killing and War* (Cambridge, Cambridge University Press, 1995) 44–50.

[26] The idea of rights as 'political trumps held by individuals' is famously defended in R Dworkin, *Taking Rights Seriously* (Cambridge MA, Harvard University Press, 1977).

[27] ICJ, *Threat or Use of Nuclear Weapons* (Advisory Opinion) Reports 1996 [24]–[25].

[28] See chapter five of this volume.

[29] See C Brown, 'Universal Human Rights: A Critique' in T Dunne and NJ Wheeler (eds), *Human Rights and Global Policies* (Cambridge, Cambridge University Press, 1999) 111–14.

into effects of utilitarian calculations. Far from 'trumping' policies, rights defer to them. To believe otherwise is to accept some policy about rights as binding in an absolute, non-political way – that is to say, to believe it was given to human society instead of created by it, like God's words.[30]

Step 6: (Legislative discourse). But if humanitarian intervention involves deference to political principles or balancing calculations, then it threatens to degenerate into a pretence for the use of power by those who have the means. After all, Hitler, too, intervened in the *Sudetenland* to protect the German minority there. To avoid this, many have suggested the establishment of criteria for such intervention that would check against the possibility of political misuse. If those criteria were clear enough it would be possible to ascertain objectively – automatically – whether an intervention was justified or not.[31] However, this is to restate the difficulty with rules. However enlightened, peaceful and rational the appliers are, rules cannot be applied in the automatic fashion that their proponents suppose. This is because any rule or criterion will be both over and under-inclusive. It will include some cases that we did not wish to include and it will appear to leave out some cases that we would have wanted to include had we known of them when the criteria were drafted. Say the criterion allows intervention if 500 are killed. From the perspective of a devout Catholic nation, this would allow, perhaps even call for intervention to prevent the thousands of cases of abortion routinely practised in the secular West. Surely that would seem over-inclusive. After all, it would not apply in a case where only 400 were killed. But would this not be quite arbitrary? Should there really be no difference between the case where the 400 were military men, killed in combat, or newborn babies, charred to death in their cradles because they belong to an ethnic minority?

A very precise ('automatic') criterion would be undesirable for the reason Julius Stone pointed out in a related context, namely because it would be a 'trap for the innocent and a signpost for the guilty'.[32] It would compel the well-meaning state to watch the atrocity being committed until some in itself arbitrary level has been attained – and allow the dictator to continue until that very point. A criterion is always also a permission. *This is how far I can go!* It is precisely for this reason that the attempts to define 'aggression' have either failed or ended up in parody. When the General Assembly in 1952 started to look for a definition, its concern was to check political misuse by the Security Council of its broad enforcement powers under chapter VII. A definition was finally adopted by the Assembly in December 1974.[33] In an operative part that contains eight articles and takes a good two sheets

---

[30] Which is how they are defended, eg in MJ Perry, *The Idea of Human Rights. Four Inquiries* (Oxford, Oxford University Press, 1998) 11–41. For the classical critique, see E Burke, *Reflections on the Revolution in France* edited by JCD Clark (1790, Stanford, Stanford University Press, 2001) 217–21.

[31] For a long list of references to academic studies that propose the development of 'criteria', see P Malanczuk, *Humanitarian Intervention and the Legitimacy of the Use of Force* (Amsterdam, Spinhuis, 1993) 30 and 69 fn 298. See also Krtisiotis, 'Appraising the Policy Objections to Humanitarian Intervention' (1993) 1022–24.

[32] J Stone, *Conflict through Consensus. UN Approaches to Aggression* (Sydney, Maitland, 1977).

[33] UNGA Res 3314 (XXIX) (14 December 1974).

of the space of a regular UN document, the definition lists as 'aggression' not only 'first use of armed force by a State in contravention of the Charter', but also other kinds of 'invasion', 'bombardment', 'blockade', 'sending of armed bands', as well as 'substantial involvement' in such actions. After the long – but non-exhaustive – list of examples, the definition then provides that 'the Security Council may determine that other acts constitute aggression under the provisions of the Charter'. The very point of such an exercise was to limit Security Council discretion, but ended up defining as aggression whatever the Council chose to regard as such!

Little is to be expected of legislation. The more precise the proposed criteria, the more automatic their application, the more arbitrary any exclusion or inclusion would appear. This would be arbitrariness not just in regard to some contested policy but to the humanitarian point of the rule. This is why it would be a mistake to assume that the definition of aggression failed due to the scheming malevolence of diplomats. Everyone participated in the exercise with two legitimate aims: (1) whatever you agree, do not end up curtailing the action of your home state when action is needed to defend its essential interests, and (2) try as best you can to prevent action that might be prejudicial to the interests of your state. Now when everyone participated in the debate on such instructions, the result could only be meaningless: language that is both absolutely binding and absolutely open-ended.

An exercise to draft criteria for humanitarian intervention within the UN would end up as the definition of aggression. As an absolute criterion such as '500' allows the slow torturing to death of 499, flexible terminology is needed. The situation should be such that 'fundamental human rights are being or are likely to be seriously violated on a large scale and there is an urgent need for intervention'.[34] Like the definition of aggression, this seems both sensible and inconsequential. It is responsive to the humanitarian urge and avoids the danger of absolutism – but only by simultaneously opening the door for military action in dubious cases, and facilitating the tyrant's hypocrisy. We are back in the original situation. As soon as the rule is no longer automatic, but involves discretion, the possibility of abuse that was the point of the rule to eradicate reappears.[35] Why?

The proposal to legislate over responses to massive human rights violations brings forth the very problem that Martin Wight pointed out and with which I opened this essay: namely that formal rules work well in a domestic normality where situations are routine and the need to honour the formal validity of the law by far outweighs incidental problems in its application. The benefits of exceptionless compliance offset the losses. Think about the organisation of popular vote. Most societies have an absolute rule about the voting age – often 18. Why do they have such a rule? Because it is thought that only mature people should be entitled

[34] 'Humanitarian Intervention', Report by the Dutch Advisory Council on International Affairs (AIV) and the Advisory Committee on Public International Law (CAVV) No 13 (April 2000) 29. For a much more sceptical discussion, see Danish Institute of International Affairs, *Humanitarian Intervention. Legal and Political Aspects* (Copenhagen, 1999) 103–11.

[35] See also TM Franck, *The Power of Legitimacy Among Nations* (Oxford, Oxford University Press, 1990) 67–80.

to participate in the direction of political community. However, the rule is clearly both over and under-inclusive. It allows some people to vote who are immature – your middle-aged alcoholic neighbour who gambled his family's savings, for example. It also excludes others that clearly are mature – your 17-year-old daughter who just had a straight A from her social science class. Note again that the problem is not an external distortion: the inclusion and the exclusion appear problematic because they contradict the point of the rule. But we still insist to apply the rule. Why? Because the only alternative would be to condition voting rights directly on the substantive criterion of 'maturity'. However, this would allocate the decision on the delimitation of the electorate to those who have been put in the position to assess the 'maturity' of the voters. Now you might think that is all right if it is *you* who sits in the 'maturity board' – but it is more likely to be *your neighbour.*

In domestic normality it is possible to live with automatic rules because the alternative is so much worse. The occasional injustice is not too dramatic and will be dispelled: your neighbour falls in love and sobers up; your daughter votes in the next election. No threat to the legal order emerges. Revolution will not take place. But this is otherwise in an international emergency of some gravity. An injustice caused by the law immediately challenges the validity of a legal system that calls for compliance even against self-interest. The point of the rule (that is, the need to prevent serious and large scale violations of fundamental human rights) is more important than its formal validity. In the domestic situation, the rule is applied perhaps in millions of situations. Automaticity excludes political manipulation and the connected routine brings about an overall result that is more valuable than any (small) injustice that is being caused. In the international situation, on the other hand, and especially if the situation is defined as a 'serious violation of fundamental rights', the need to uphold the formal validity of the law cannot be compared to the weight of the impulse to act now.[36] If the rule does not allow this, so much worse for the rule. Any appeal for passivity in the interests of upholding a general sense of law-obedience will ring hollow, even cynical.

Step 7 (Law as Procedure). After all such problems, you might conclude that international law's role lies less in offering substantive rules, whether absolute or flexible, than in providing a decision process that allows a controlled treatment of the situation. It would channel the problem to institutions and bodies – *regimes,* in a word – in which interested parties could agree on the right interpretation, or the correct course of action, if possible under conditions of transparency and accountability.[37] This would be a democratic way to deal with the problem.

---

[36] The way in which the legislative choice between (automatic) rules and (evaluative) standards is influenced by the frequency of the conduct being regulated has been much debated in law and economics, including international trade law. The point is that the less frequent the behaviour, the less appropriate automatic rules for regulating it are. J Trachtman, 'Trade and . . . Problems: Cost-Benefit Analysis and Subsidiarity' (1998) 9 *European Journal of International Law* 37.

[37] This move is usefully described in F Kratochwil, 'How Do Norms Matter?' in M Byers (ed), *The Role of Law in International Politics. Essays on International Relations and International Law* (Oxford, Oxford University Press, 2000) 37–42.

However, what would the correct procedure be? For some, it was precisely the procedural side-stepping of the Security Council where the illegality of the bombing lay. For others, NATO decision making offered enough 'collectiveness' to account for lawfulness. Some would retort, of course, that how can a regional body arrogate to itself the power to decide on a matter entrusted by the Charter to a universal one? To those, however, seasoned observers would respond in the way Morgenthau commented on the UN's first efforts to deal with the crises in Greece, Spain, Indonesia and Iran. They 'provided opportunities for exercises in parliamentary procedure, but in no occasion has even an attempt been made to facing the political issues of which these situations are surface manifestations'.[38] One need not share Morgenthau's distaste of liberalism to admit that institutional procedures in the UN and elsewhere often provide more of an excuse for non-action than a reasoned technique for solving acute crises. Even if political theorists might seek 'ideal speech situations' to account for institutional legitimacy, what is 'ideal' will remain open for controversy and empirical evidence of it is largely absent from the international scene. The argument of the Uniting for Peace Resolution in 1950 that justifies overtaking the Security Council if the Council is 'unable to act' was then, and remains, a contested re-description of following the Council's rules of decision-making as a violation of the political *point* of the Charter. This is an incident of the over-exclusiveness of article 27 (3) of the Charter: it sometimes excludes action in cases where some people think action is needed. There may well be, as intimated in the UN Secretary-General's General Assembly speech in September 1999, good reason to set aside the correct procedure in order to act.[39] But although to explain this as an implementation of the 'deep' logic of the Charter is a part of the diplomatic practice never to say one is actually breaking the law, it still remains the case that a beneficial illegality today makes it easier for my adversary to invoke it tomorrow as precedent for some sombre scheme of his. Hence, of course, the anxiety of Western lawyers about Kosovo.

Step 8: (The Turn to Ethics). For such difficulties, many people believe that even as law is not just formal texts and precedents, its informality cannot be reduced to utilitarian calculations, absolute rights or procedural techniques either. The relevant considerations are situational. One version of such attitude follows Max Weber's analysis of the failure of legal formality in the conditions of complex modernity, and highlights the way bureaucratisation focuses on the decision-maker's preferences or alliances. To grasp decision-making in an environment deprived of determining rules, Weber made his famous distinction between an ethics of ultimate ends and an ethics of responsibility. According to him – and to many others – it was the latter that provided the more appropriate framework for decision-makers in a case such as now

---

[38] Morgenthau, *Scientific Man vs Power Politics* (1946) 119.

[39] 'If . . . a coalition of states had been prepared to act in defence of the Tutsi population, but did not receive prompt Council authorisation, should such a coalition have stood aside and allowed the horror to unfold?' UN Press release SG/SM/7136, GA 9596.

exemplified by Kosovo.[40] The argument might be – and I have myself sometimes made it in this way – that in the context of 1999, with the experience of passivity in Kigali and in Srebrenica, Western European officials had to take action. If formal law is anyway unclear and cannot be separated from how it is interpreted, then much speaks for the individualisation of Kosovo. A decision has to be made and that decision – as one of Weber's close readers, Carl Schmitt, the *Kronjurist* of the Third Reich, the theorist of the exception would say – is borne out of legal nothing.[41] What counts is the experience of the decision-maker and his or her sensitivity to the demands of the situation. The problem is not about criteria or process, but about something that might be called 'wisdom'.[42]

The merit of this flight to decisionism/ethics of responsibility (or love) lies in the way it discounts Kosovo as precedent. Kosovo – the killing of 500 – is so important that it cannot be captured by rules or procedures. But the problem lies in the implied suggestion that the proper realm of the important lies in the personal, subjective, even emotional – and in particular in the conscience of those whom the dictates of power and history have put in decision-making positions. Let me paraphrase Schmitt again. For him, legal normality was dependent on the power of the one who could decide on the exception: legal normality, rules and processes, was only a surface appearance of the concrete order that revealed its character in the dramatic moment when normality was to be defended or set aside. Behind the tranquillity of the *pouvoir constitué* lay the founding violence of the *pouvoir constituant* – a *coup d'état*, a revolution.[43] From this perspective, the bombing of Serbia was the exception that revealed, for a moment, the nature of the international order which lay not in the Charter of the United Nations nor in principles of humanitarianism but in the will and power of a handful of Western civilian and military leaders. The sacrifice of 500 civilians would then appear as a violent reaffirmation of the vitality of a concrete international order created sometime after the Second World War and in which what counts as law, or humanitarianism, or morality, is decided with conclusive authority by the sensibilities of the Western Prince.

III

However, to reduce the nature of social order to the mental activities or moral states of Princes – the 'purity of heart' that St Thomas held an indispensable ingredient of the just war – is to blind oneself to the suffering that is produced by social normality. To credit the decision-makers as having been involved in an emotional process

---

[40] For the strong recommendation for statesmen to shun from absolute principles and to act on an honest appreciation of the concrete effects of one's decision, see M Weber, 'Politics as Vocation' in *From Max Weber: Essays in Sociology*, translated, edited and with an introduction by HH Gerth and C Wright Mills (London, Routledge, 1967) 77–128. For the application in international relations, see D Warner, *An Ethic of Responsibility in International Relations* (Boulder CO and London, Rienner, 1991).

[41] C Schmitt, *Political Theology* (Cambridge, MA, MIT Press, 1985) 31–32.

[42] H Morgenthau, *Politics among Nations* (New York, Knopf, 1948) 444. An excellent analysis of the way Western argument in Kosovo went beyond positivism but fell short of natural law 'theory', is in Corten (n 7) 233–59.

[43] Schmitt, *Political Theology* (1985) 5–15.

about their moral obligations is to make precisely that mistake of fact (of being in a position of power) for right for which Rousseau once accused Grotius: 'it is possible to imagine a more logical method, but not one more favourable to tyrants'.[44] 'Man was born free and he is everywhere in chains', Rousseau also wrote, bearing in mind the religious binds of an *ancien régime* that were finally loosening in his time. The Enlightenment that we associate with him sought freedom through rational rules and public decision-making processes, and relegated morality into one's conscience. To extrapolate the nature of the international order from the moral dilemmas – however real – of the statesmen involved in great events makes us blind to the political and moral problems of a normality that has lifted those people in decision-making positions in the first place and leaves the rest as passive spectators or sometimes sacrificial victims on the altar of their superior moralities.[45]

This leads me to observe an ironic reversal of the relations between the normal and the exception. For the classical realists, the founding violence of law – the violence which could not be encompassed by law because it was its precondition – was an act of physical force, sending in the military to occupy a territory or to overthrow (or uphold) a government, war, aggression, sovereignty: great moments of historical significance. These were the a priori on which the law was based and that could not, therefore, be captured within law. How different it all seems today. It is hard to think of a more central concern for the profession than Kosovo, a more normal conference topic or item of polite conversation than war, crisis management and peace enforcement, punishment and sanctions. The wide concept of security promoted by UN officials and European crisis managers has blurred the line between military and civilian matters – thus expanding the jurisdiction of military experts, making talk about forcible intervention a matter of bureaucratic normality. If every concern is a security concern, then there are no limits to the jurisdiction of the security police.[46] Every international lawyer today negotiates genocide and war crimes and learns to speak the language of moral outrage as part of a discipline relearning the crusading spirit, and the civilising mission.

What this new normality has done, like every normality, is to relegate its own founding violence into the shadow. Undoubtedly, a sacrifice of 500 is important. However, what about the violence of a global system in which, according to the United Nations Development Programme (UNDP) report of 2000, more than 30,000 children die every day of malnutrition and the combined wealth of the 200 richest families in the world was eight times as much as the combined wealth of the 582 million people in all the least developed countries.[47] We deal with military intervention, peace enforcement, or the fight against terrorism in the neutral language of legal rules and humanitarian moralities, and so come to think of it in terms of a

[44] J-J Rousseau, *The Social Contract* (Harmondsworth, Penguin, 1968) 51.

[45] For the ideological nature or standard narratives about humanitarian intervention that 'depend upon the acceptance of gendered and racialized metaphors', see Orford, 'Muscular Humanitarianism' (1999) 701, 689–703.

[46] See M Koskenniemi, 'The Police in the Temple. Order, Justice and the UN: A Dialectical View' (1995) 6 *European Journal of International Law* 325–48.

[47] UNDP, *Human Development Report 2000* (Oxford, Oxford University Press, 2000) 73, 82.

policy of a global public realm – forgetting that it is never Algeria that will intervene in France, or Finland in Chechnya. The peace that will be enforced will not be racial harmony in Los Angeles and the terrorism that shall be branded as the enemy of humanity will not be an intellectual property system that allows hundreds of thousands of Africans to march into early death by sexually transmitted disease. Our obsessive talk about Kosovo makes invisible the extreme injustice of the system of global distribution of wealth, reducing it to the sphere of the private, the unpolitical, the natural, the historically determined – just like war used to be – a 'social', 'cultural' or 'economic' *condition* of law which therefore cannot be touched by law.[48]

So, it is precisely at the moment when we celebrate the capture of exception of military force into the Rule of Law that all ambition has been renounced to attain a critical grasp of the concrete order of global distribution of power and wealth. It is tempting to think that the very condition that has made it possible to articulate Kosovo in the language of international law has also made it impossible to deal with that other founding violence. If international law is centrally about the informal management of security crises by diplomatic and military experts, then of course it is not about global redistribution: it is about upholding the status quo and about directing moral sensibility and political engagement to waging *that* battle. Kosovo and its civilian deaths spell anxiety, a recognition of the insufficiency of existing rules and principles, a call for moral sensibility. Hunger and poverty do not. The more international lawyers are obsessed by the effectiveness of the law to be applied in 'crises', the less we are aware of the subtle politics whereby some aspects of the world become defined as 'crisis' whereas others do not. Despite the rhetoric of universal international law, and of *ius cogens*, only the tiniest part of the world is encompassed by international law. Even as law now arrogates to itself the right to speak the language of universal humanitarianism, it is spoken only by a handful of experts fascinated about matters military and technological, the targeting of missiles and press conferences with uniformed men who speak clearly. Should their moral sensibilities now be the lawyers' greatest concern?

IV

What alternatives are there? The eight steps traced above might seem to describe a logic which, after successive failures to attain normative closure, leads into the spontaneous and the private: 'moral duty' compels Kosovo. Such an understanding celebrates the emotional immediacy of the inner life as the sanctuary of the true meaning of dramatic events that cannot be captured within law's technical structures. This would, however, involve an altogether groundless belief in the primacy of the subjective, or the ability of emotion (in contrast to 'reason') to grasp some authentic form of life to be contrasted to the artificial structures of the law. However, the conventions of the subject, and the related disciplines of psychology and identity politics are no closer to or distant from 'authentic reality'

---

[48] For this argument in a more general form, see D Kennedy, 'Putting the Politics Back in International Politics' (1998) IX *Finnish Yearbook of International Law* 19–27.

than the conventions of public life, including formal law, sociology or market. Moreover, as I have argued elsewhere, the very claim that one is arguing from the position of authenticity – for example, a given notion of human right, or self-determination – involves an objectionable attempt to score a political victory outside politics.[49] The subjective and the spontaneous form a symbolic order just like the realm of the objective and rational. Neither occupies an innocent space that would be free from disciplinary conventions and ambitions and at which international lawyers could finally grasp the authentic.

The merit in the 'turn to ethics' lies in the way it focuses on the indetermination of official behaviour by rational standards and criteria and thus, inevitably, brings to the fore the *political* moment in such decisions. It reveals the way such decision-making is an aspect of social antagonism, instead of something neutral or 'rational' in the way liberal internationalism has often assumed. Intervention remains a political act, however much it is dressed in the language of moral compulsion or legal technique. On the other hand, however, that cannot be the end of the matter, either, although this is how many critics of liberalism – including Carl Schmitt and Hans Morgenthau – have often suggested. Neither the opposition between the friend and the enemy, nor the lust for power shares the character of a final, foundational truth about society or politics. Existentialism, too, is just a symbolic order, a language.

So the turn to ethics, too, is a politics. In the case of international law's obsession about military crises, war and humanitarianism, it is a politics by those who have the means to strengthen control on everyone else. The Kosovo Albanian is worthy of humanitarian support as long as he or she remains a helpless victim – but turns into a danger the moment he or she seeks to liberate his or herself.[50] In such a situation, insistence on rules, processes, and the whole culture of formalism now turns into a strategy of resistance, and of democratic hope. Why? Because formalism is precisely about setting limits to the impulses – 'moral' or not – of those in decision-making positions in order to fulfil general, instead of particular, interests; because it casts decision-makers as responsible to the political community; and because it recognises the claims made by other members of that community and creates the expectation that they will be taken account of. Of course, the door to a formalism that would determine the substance of political outcomes is no longer open. There is no neutral terrain. But against the particularity of the ethical decision, formalism constitutes a horizon of universality, embedded in a *culture* of restraint, a *commitment* to listening to others' claims and seeking to take them into account.[51] The

---

[49] M Koskenniemi, 'The Wonderful Artificiality of States' (1994) *ASIL Proceedings* 22–28.

[50] As pointed out in S Žižek, *The Fragile Absolute. Or Why is the Christian Legacy Worth Fighting For?* (London, Verso, 2000) 59–60.

[51] The arguments here draw inspiration from recent debates about the possibility of a left universalism that would not only recognise but enhance claims of identity and the reality of politics as ('agonistic') struggle. Out of a flourishing recent literature, see C Mouffe and E Laclau, *Hegemony and Socialist Strategy* (London, Verso, 1985) and J Butler, E Laclau and S Žižek, *Contingency, Hegemony, Universality. Contemporary Dialogues on the Left* (London, Verso, 2000). I have discussed the culture of formalism at more length in my *The Gentle Civilizer of Nations. the Rise and all of International Law 1870–1960* (Cambridge, Cambridge University Press, 2002) 449–509.

reference to 'moral duty' in the justification of the bombing of Serbia was objectionable because it signified a retreat from such commitment into the private life of the conscience, casting the Serbs as immoral 'criminals' with whom no political community could exist and against whom no measures were excessive.[52] By contrast, a commitment to formalism would construct the West and Serbia as political antagonists in a larger community, whose antagonism can only be set aside by reference to what exceeds their particular interests and claims.

In a related context, David Kennedy has characterised analogous arguments in terms of modernity's 'eternal return', the way they reduce professional history into the repetition of familiar moves: from formalism to anti-formalism and back, from interpretation to literality and back, from emotion to reason and back, from sociology to psychology and back, from apology to utopia and back – with 'no exit and existential crisis'.[53] If this were all, then a move to formalism like the move to ethics would indeed only repeat certain modernist tropes that we have seen over the years being performed with some regularity in art, philosophy, politics, as well as in law. But this need not be so. Modernity is unstable, and every move it makes is always already split by reflexivity against itself. Formalism can no longer be blind to its own politics. Having shed the pretensions of objectivity it must enter the political terrain with a programme of openness and inclusiveness, no longer interpreted as effects of neutral reason but of political experience and utopian commitment, as *articulation* of what might be called the 'sedimented practices constituting the normative framework of a certain society'.[54] To be sure, formalism can no longer believe that it merely translates this framework to particular decisions. This is why it does not suffice only to provide a hearing to the claims of the political other, but also to include in political contestation the question about *who* are entitled to make claims and *what kinds* of claims pass the test of validity. Without such self-reflexivity formalism will freeze into the justification of one or another substantive policy – just like democracy may do. Such a formalism lives on a paradox, split against itself inasmuch as it recognises itself as 'culture' – an aspect of the human, dependent on psychology and politics, uncertain and partial, yet also seeking to articulate something universal and shared. This 'split' holds up its utopian moment, suggesting an exit from the anxiety of the 'eternal return' and redeeming cosmopolitanism and emancipation as aspects of a properly political project.

For many years now, international lawyers have been called upon to assume the role of technical policy-advisers, participants in a global culture of effectiveness and control that underwrites the objectives projected onto the unipolar world by those in hegemonic positions. Now their ethical commitment has been directed to military enforcement as part of the gradual naturalisation of an economic system

[52] This 'Schmittian' point is also made in Žižek, *The Fragile Absolute* (2000) 56–60.

[53] See D Kennedy, 'The Nuclear Weapons case' in L Boisson de Chazournes and P Sands (eds), *International Law, the International Court of Justice and Nuclear Weapons* (Cambridge, Cambridge University Press, 1999) 468–72.

[54] E Laclau, 'Identity and Hegemony: the Role of Universality in the Constitution of Political Logics' in Butler, Laclau and Žižek, *Contingency* (2000) 82–83.

that sustains the hegemon. However, the turn to ethics has also revealed a vulnerable spot in the latter. If law is inevitably always also about the subjective and the emotional, about faith and commitment, then nothing prevents re-imagining international law as commitment to resistance and transgression. Having learned its lesson, formalism might then re-enter the world assured that whatever struggles it will have to weigh, the inner anxiety of the Prince is less a problem to resolve than an objective to achieve.

Part III

The Politics of Human Rights

5

The Effect of Rights on Political Culture

Human rights intervene in Western law at the moment when the critique of legal formalism has done its work and legal practice turns from 'applying rules' to seeking 'reasonable' outcomes or 'balancing the interests'. This move seems dangerous as it transfers social power from legislators to law-appliers and creates the need for something solid and non-negotiable – 'rights' – to limit the ensuing discretion of public officials. I try to show here that rights, too, are vulnerable to the anti-formal critiques and therefore cannot avoid the 'politicisation' of public administration. On the other hand, the absoluteness of rights rhetoric makes it tempting for political actors to describe their interests in rights-terms and thus to make them appear non-negotiable. In this way, the turn to rights is adverse to a political culture of negotiation and critique.

I WISH TO make two arguments. First, while the rhetoric of human rights has historically had a positive and liberating effect on societies, once rights become institutionalised as a central part of political and administrative culture, they lose their transformative effect and are petrified into a legalistic paradigm that marginalises values and interests that resist translation into rights-language. In this way, the liberal principle of the 'priority of the right over the good'[1] results in a colonisation of political culture by a technocratic language that leaves no room for the articulation or realisation of conceptions of the good.

Second, I will argue that rights-rhetoric is not as powerful as it claims to be. It does not hold a coherent set of normative demands that could be resorted to in the administration of society. To the contrary, despite its claim for value-neutrality, rights-rhetoric is constantly reduced to conflicting and contested arguments about the political good. The identification, meaning and applicability of rights are dependent on contextual assessments of 'proportionality' or administrative 'balancing' through which priorities are set among conflicting conceptions of political value and scarce resources are distributed between contending social groups. Inasmuch as such decision-making procedures define what 'rights' are, they cannot themselves be controlled by rights. To this extent, the 'priority of the right over the good' proves an impossible demand, and insisting upon it will leave political discretion unchecked. The problem lies in how to move from an uncritical postulation of legal rights into a political culture in which delegated authority would be

---

[1] J Rawls, *A Theory of Justice* (Oxford, Clarendon Press, 1971) 31.

133

actively controlled by a condition of civic public-mindedness in the community at large.

Let me stress that I do *not* claim. I do not hold the Benthamite view that rights talk is 'nonsense upon stilts'. I do not think that rights have absolutely no value or that they encapsulate a bourgeois ideology in contrast to some deeper truth. In a thoughtful contribution, Klaus Günther once argued that rights have significance inasmuch as they open political culture to experiences of injustice and fear, and provide a voice through which the pain of torture, for example, can be articulated and listened to and the social practice of torture condemned and perhaps eradicated.[2] I have no quarrel with that. Günther concedes, however, that rights sometimes degenerate into 'human rights talk' that aims at legitimation of the status quo. However, while he thinks that this is a marginal problem, I shall argue that this is the central weight of human rights in Europe today: the banal administrative recourse to rights language in order to buttress one's political priorities. The experience of pain and injustice are again on the margins- – as partly history, or embedded in Europe's geographical fringes (former Yugoslavia) – while the anxious question must be: might such banalisation at some point do away with the ability of human rights language to convey any sense of pain and injustice? The strength of Günther's argument lies in its being made at a philosophical level. I shall counter it by drawing on the practice of European institutions in order to highlight the mundane experience of rights constantly deferring to political priorities.

The usefulness of rights lies in their acting as 'intermediate stage' principles around which some communal values and individual interests can be organised. As the German and Italian Constitutional Courts, in a series of well-known cases in the late 1960s, challenged the supremacy of European Community (EC) law over the fundamental rights provisions included in the constitutions of those Member States, this was precisely so as to distinguish and emphasise national core values, the overriding of which by a European-wide community policy seemed inadmissible. But rights often remain insufficiently normative to ground a sense of community and insufficiently concrete to be policy-orienting. The majority of United Nations (UN) Member States, for instance, have no difficulty in subscribing to most of the annual resolutions of the UN Commission of Human Rights and the Third Committee of the General Assembly without this indicating that we are any nearer to a world federation than, say, 50 years ago.

Finally, a political culture that officially insists that rights are foundational ('inalienable', 'basic'), but in practice constantly finds that they are not, becomes a culture of bad faith. A gap is established between political language and normative belief that encourages a strategic attitude as the proper political frame of mind, as well as cynical distance to politics by the general population. Human rights are erected as a façade for what has become, on the one hand, a technical administration of things and, on the other, a struggle for power and jurisdiction between

---

[2] K Günther, 'The Legacies of Justice and Fear: A European Approach to Human Rights and their Effect on Political Culture' in P Alston e al (ed), *The European Union and Human Rights* (Oxford, Oxford University Press, 1999) 117–44.

different organs entrusted with policy-making tasks.[3] So, while rights-rhetoric does form an important and occasionally valuable aspect of political life, it covers only a part of it and, if allowed to colonise the whole, will have a detrimental effect on politics and critique.

The Point of Rights

Rights are grounded in a profound mistrust of conceptions of the good society. Such conceptions are assumed to bring forth conflicts of subjective value and of political passion that cannot be settled by reason. The liberal Enlightenment aimed at constructing a political order that would no longer be dominated by such passion, conducive as it was to civil war (Hobbes) and tyranny (Locke, Rousseau, Mill). It was assumed that '[t]he health of the political realm is maintained by conscientious objection to the political'.[4]

In the public realm, the mechanism for attaining this was the separation of legislation and administration (adjudication) by reference to the subjective/rational scheme. Where legislation was the proper field of value and power (of subjectivity), those elements needed to be purged from administration. How administration was to be constrained by what is rational and non-subjective has been conceptualised in different ways and has engendered a series of losses of faith.

For early liberals, constraint was initially received from an autonomous '*reason*' (naturalism) that delimited the sphere of individual freedom as against the social order in a universally homogenous way, and provided apolitical principles that constrained those in administrative positions without relying on anybody's political preferences. As faith in the self-evidence of reason started to seem doubtful, constraint was sought from legal rules and *textual form* (positivism). Rules and texts, however, soon seemed unable to take account of life's 'real necessities' and appeared vulnerable to interminable interpretative controversy. Loss of faith in formalism was followed by calls for recourse to the social ends ('utility', effectiveness) that were assumed to lie behind rules, and 'balancing' of the conflicting interests of social groups and classes (realism).

The use of *rights* in the political discourse of liberal societies in the 1960s and 1970s should be seen as a further move of liberalism's efforts to constrain politics, now against the realist emphasis on social utility and interest-balancing that seemed just a camouflage for making (contested) policy-decision by those in administrative positions. Ronald Dworkin's famous thesis of rights as 'trumps' is

---

[3] This is precisely the criticism made against the European Court's development of its fundamental rights doctrine in countermove to the critiques by the German and Italian Supreme Courts in the influential article by J Coppell and A O'Neill, 'The European Court of Justice: Taking Rights Seriously?' (1992) 29 *Common Market Law Review* 669–92.

[4] M Wight, 'Western Values in International Relations' in H Butterfield and M Wight, *Diplomatic Investigations; Essays in the Theory of International Politics* (London, Allen & Unwin, 1966) 122.

directed precisely at limiting administrative discretion by recourse to realist 'policies'.[5] Contrary to 'policy', rights were assumed to be unpolitical in that they were *universal* (ie independent of time and place; unamenable to political controversy) and '*factoid*' (ie self-evidently 'there' – 'fact-like' – with compelling consequences – unlike the consequences of a statement such as 'do good').[6]

Rights arguments detach the interests of individual right-holders or groups of right-holders from political subjectivity and 'restate the interests of the group as characteristics of all people'.[7] In this way, they may seem to avoid partaking of the political subjectivity that 'raw' interests possess.[8] Claims of right can be recast as claims of an objective reason, reflected in the fact that rights 'straddle' between legal positivity and naturalism. To demonstrate their independence from the political passions of the day, rights appear as ahistorical and universal. Yet, to disclose their concrete (and democratic) content, they are translated into positive constitutions (fundamental rights) and other legal enactments. Hence, the extraordinary rhetorical power of rights: on the one hand, they are 'outside' the political community in the sense that the legislators's task is merely to declare their presence in positive law, not to create them. On the other hand, they are also 'inside' the community by being fixed in constitutions and other positive legal enactments and thus amenable to objective confirmation.

Yet, this duality creates an ambivalence: the more we insist on the ability of rights to impose an external standard for the community, the more rights start to resemble theology, and the more difficulty we have in aligning them with the ideal of popular sovereignty with which, as Jürgen Habermas has shown, rights have emerged.[9] To fall back on constitutional or other positive law standards, again, questions the universalism with which rights are associated and focuses on the procedural aspects of the constant struggle about where to draw the line between community interests and individual preferences.

Translation Problems

Social morality cannot, however, be translated exhaustively into rights language. Such language is based on an ideal of individual autonomy that perceives social conflict in terms of interpersonal relationship: for every right, there is a correlative

---

[5] 'Individual rights are political trumps held by individuals. Individuals have rights when, for some reason, a collective goal is not a sufficient justification for denying them what they wish': R Dworkin, *Taking Rights Seriously* (Harvard University Press, 1977) xi.

[6] See D Kennedy, *A Critique of Adjudication (fin de siècle)* (Harvard University Press, 1997) 305–06.

[7] ibid 307.

[8] Because there is no essential conception of a right, it seems difficult to object to the common practice in Western societies, whereby beneficiaries of a policy dress their interests in the fulfilment of that policy in terms of their 'human rights'.

[9] J Habermas, 'Human Rights and Popular Sovereignty. The Liberal and Republican Versions' (1994) 7 *Ratio Juris* 2–6.

duty; and for every duty, there exists a correlative right.[10] However, in existing societies, many people are confronted with normative demands that cannot be reduced into right-duty relationships. Religions, for instance, typically impose duties on people without the assumption that somebody is in a possession of a correlative right. Nor can aspirations for virtue or personal excellence plausibly be translated into rights-language.[11] If a morality seeks to regulate a person's private behaviour, a right-duty relationship can only be constructed by the tenuous fiction of envisaging the holder of the right and duty to reside in the same person.[12] The priority of the right over the good leaves little room for political value: citizenship is reduced to private reliance on right. Civic virtue, public-mindedness and political participation become a profession that seems indissociable from the advancement of private interests, and object of contempt and a source of popular cynicism.[13]

More generally, the notion of some things as intrinsically praiseworthy cannot find a place in rights-language and yet, there are a number of contexts in which the very identity of a community depends on a conception of non-instrumental, intrinsic value. Nationalism provides one example. Typical claims of justice embedded in controversy about nationhood envision nations – or a particular nation – as an uninstrumental good, worthy of more than the human lives that inhabit it. As they are not reducible to claims of rights by individuals, liberal theory tends to think of religion and nationalism as fundamentally irrational.[14] Hence, as Nathaniel Berman has argued, international efforts to find a compromise in nationalist conflicts, such as those involving Jerusalem, have failed. The passions of the parties, of the Arabs and the Israelis, cannot find their way into any of the proposed 'rational' schemes for the city's administration. The antagonists do not see themselves as rational right-claimants in the way liberal theory assumes in order to operate towards a rational balance.[15] Or think about indigenous societies that construct their sense of identity by a special relationship to land. Members of such societies may have duties to the land that has traditionally belonged to the community; yet no one thinks of himself or herself as an individual right-holder. A legal system that can conceptualise a lien with land only in terms of property and

---

[10] On individual autonomy as the social ideal informing rights, see C Nino, 'Introduction' in C Nino (ed), *Rights* (The International Library of Essays in Law & Legal Theory: Schools; 8 1992) xxvi–xxvii. The correlativity of rights and duties (or powers/liabilities, immunities/disabilities, claims/no-rights, etc) is a familiar theme of analytic jurisprudence. Although one may, from a conceptual point of view, question the necessity of such correlativity, the point is that rights seem socially effective (and, as such, 'real') often only inasmuch as they are reflected in somebody's (legally enforcible) duties.

[11] See J Raz, *The Morality of Freedom* (Oxford, Oxford University Press, 1988) 196–97.

[12] The argument may of course be made that there is no reason for the law to regulate private behaviour. This, however, is not a value-neutral view, but one that builds upon the kind of individualistic premises that characterise one distinct type or liberal theory, and the question remains as to the criteria whereby what is 'private' is delimited.

[13] See C Mouffe, *The Return of the Political* (London, Verso, 1993) 82–88.

[14] In the manner of, eg E Kedourie, *Nationalism* (London, Hutchinson, 1960).

[15] N Berman, 'Legalizing Jerusalem or, of Law, Fantasy and Faith' (1996) 45 *The Catholic University of America Law Review* 823–35.

contract (and thus through a basic relationship between the right of the property-owner and the duties of others) cannot articulate the normative reality of such a community. Or think about the solidarity of friendship: there may be a duty between friends to compensate the loss of something even if nobody has committed a wrong. Such duty is independent of the existence of any right in anyone; yet, in terms of friendship, it makes perfect sense to say that the loss ought to be compensated by a person who was involved in bringing it about and has the resources to do so.

In a similar way, and famously, the relationship between the employer and the wage-labourer, or the sexual relations between man and woman, can only with a loss of meaning be described in rights language, for which the focus is on the terms of the contract concluded between two fully rational and autonomous individuals, assumed to trade their rights from a decontextualised negotiating position. The quality of the overall relationship, the purposes for which the work or the sexual act was carried out, or the contract's effects on third parties (eg within the family) cannot find articulation. Of course, late modern law includes a plethora of informal considerations that are taken account of in the assessment of such relationships. However, these considerations reflect substantive ideals about the labour market and the quality of family life that override and delimit what can justifiably be concluded by reference to the rights of the relevant community members. Only through them does it become possible to assess whether or not the literal terms of the contract should be honoured. The deformalisation of contract law by notions of reasonableness, good faith, and public order famously presume the presence of a perspective of the good society from which the rights established by the contract may be evaluated.[16]

The power and the weakness of rights is that they focus on the need to protect the individual against oppression and injustice by the community or the state, as explained usefully in Klaus Günther's essay referred to above. Although 'rights-talk' has of course spread beyond individual rights to characterise various kinds of economic, social, and cultural objectives, as well as different collective goods (right to peace, right to the environment), the latter differ from the former in the all-important sense in which they are understood to be ('merely') programmatory; setting guidelines to the legislators and policy objectives to governments instead of creating legally enforceable claims (or powers, immunities) for any person or group of persons.[17] To the extent that such rights may be thought of to create legally enforceable claims, they too portray social conflict as *ultimately* having to do with

---

[16] For the (Weberian) argument about the destructive effects to liberal legalism of such deformalisation, see RM Unger, *Law in Modern Society. Towards a Criticism of Social Theory* (New York, Free Press, 1976) 192–200.

[17] It may be conjectured that economic and social rights entered political language as a (left) counter-move to invest (left) social objectives with the same kind of dignity or prima facie absoluteness that 'bourgeois' objectives in the field of civil and political rights had managed to attain by recourse to rights rhetoric.

the rights of individuals.[18] In such a case, the relevant social goods worthy of protection are reduced to private interests: I have a right inasmuch as somebody else has a duty not to violate my (legally protected) interest (ie right). Since Marx, such a view has been criticised as a formalist, 'alienating' vehicle for the perpetuation of the liberal-capitalist society. The projection of society as merely so many individuals behaving and forming their conceptions of justice from behind a 'veil of ignorance' of their particular character, abilities, desires, and histories is, as later communitarians have insisted, an ideological fiction, examining social normativity

> not by investigation of human beings as we find them in the worlds, with their diverse histories and communities, but by an abstract concept of the person that has been voided of any definite cultural identity or specific historical inheritance.[19]

For our purposes, the relevance of this critique lies in the fact that an abstract personhood and the conception of individual rights that goes with it cannot address the sense of injustice that arises, for example, from structural (economic/social) causation or from the sense of belonging to an oppressed minority. But posing the normative issue in terms of individual rights fails to grasp its social meaning in many other contexts. To take an example from Joseph Raz: I may own a painting by Van Gogh. Nonetheless, I may have a duty not to destroy it even if nobody has a correlative right. The value of art, in this case, cannot be expressed in rights language – just as little as, for instance, the value of a clean environment in a conflict concerning the carrying out of a contract for a large industrial project.[20]

Yet, rights are not foundational but depend on collective goods that are evaluated independently from the rights through which we look at them. Freedom of speech is dependent on and intended to support the collective good of the system of political decision-making and public information that prevails in society. The protection of the freedom of contract presumes the existence of, and is constantly limited by, the conditions of the market. Rights protect personal autonomy but 'autonomy is possible only if various collective goods are available'.[21] In a society that offers no choices, autonomy is meaningless. The extent of the availability of such collective goods again is a pure issue of political value; of struggle and compromise between alternative views about what a good society would be like.

That rights refer back to contested notions of the political good is reaffirmed daily in the public decision-processes in which rights-discourse is being waged. A famous example is the *Handyside v United Kingdom* case, in which the European

---

[18] This is implied in scholarly discussion about the enforceability of such rights. See M Scheinin, 'Economic and Social Rights as Legal Rights' in A Eide, C Krause, and A Rosas, *Economic, Social and Cultural Rights* (Boston, Nijhoff, 1995) 41–62. Likewise, Bercusson, 'Fundamental Social and Economic Rights in the European Community' in A Cassesse, A Clapham, and J Weiler, *Human Rights and the European Community: Methods of Protection* (Baden-Baden, Nomos Verlagsgesellschaft, 1991) 200–01.

[19] J Gray, *Enlightenment's Wake. Politics and Culture at the Close of the Modern Age* (London, New York, Routledge, 1995) 2.

[20] Raz, *The Morality of Freedom* (1988) 212–13.

[21] ibid 247. See J Finnis, *Natural Law and Natural Rights* (Oxford, Oxford University Press, 1980) 210–18. Likewise, Mouffe, *Return of the Political* (1993) 30–32 and M Tushnet, 'An Essay on Rights' (1984) 62 *Texas Law Review* 1364–71.

Court of Human rights discussed the margin of appreciation available to national authorities in the field of free speech. The Court affirmed the national authorities' competence to set limits to free speech (regarding a matter of publications that might offend the sensibilities of the reading public) inasmuch as there did not seem to exist 'a uniform European conception of morals'.[22] The importance of such affirmation is not so much in who the Court saw as the relevant decision-maker, the national or the international judge (though the fact that its focus was on *jurisdiction* is not irrelevant for the argument of this chapter), but that it expressly spelled out the fact that freedom of speech was a matter of moral assessment, itself independent from the conflicting rights (of free speech and privacy) to which it set a determined boundary.

The insufficiency of rights-rhetoric becomes evident as we try to seek justification or limits to rights. Here a curious paradox emerges. To the extent that rights are assumed as foundational (and this was the argument behind the view of rights as 'trumps'), there can exist no perspective from which to justify (or examine/criticise) them. Any justification would relegate the right to a secondary position, as an instrumentality for the reason that justifies it. If the reason is not present, or not valid, then the right is not valid, or applicable, either. Thus, recourse to rights remains an irrationalist strand of liberal theory – or perhaps a bad faith irrationalism ('well, we know we cannot really defend them'). For rights are constantly examined, limited and criticised from the perspective of alternative notions of the good. This is evident particularly as we examine the four persistent problems that turn recourse to rights into enforcement of invested political preferences, namely the problems of field constitution, rights and exceptions, conflicts between and the indeterminacy of rights.

Field Constitution

Whether or not a conflict is seen as a rights problem and what rights may seem relevant depends on the language we use to structure the normative field in focus. Examining the question whether the concept of fair trial included the right to legal counsel, Judge Fitzmaurice put his finger on the relevant problem:

> Both parties may, within their own frames of reference, be able to present a self-consistent and valid argument, but since there frames of reference are different, neither argument can, as such, override the other. There is no solution to the problem unless the correct – or rather acceptable – frame of reference can first be determined; but since matters of acceptability depend on approach, feeling, attitude, or even policy, rather than correct legal or logical argument, there is scarcely a solution along these lines either.[23]

---

[22] *Handyside v United Kingdom* (1976) Series A no 24, 22; *Müller v Switzerland* (1988) Series A no 133, 22.

[23] *Golder v United Kingdom* (1975) Series A no 18 dissenting opinion of Judge Fitzmaurice [23].

In other words, the choice of the relevant language ('frame of reference') – whether the normative field is seen in terms of 'human rights' or, for example, 'economic development' or 'national security' – reflects upon a prior political decision independent of the language finally chosen, often having to do with which authority should have the competence to deal with a matter.

A good example of field constitution is provided by the development of a fundamental rights jurisprudence by the European Court of Justice. As is well known, after a period of reluctance in applying human rights,[24] the Court changed its attitude in response to the challenge by the German and Italian Constitutional Courts and asserted its jurisdiction to examine the compatibility of Community instruments with fundamental rights as inspired by Member States' constitutions (*Stauder v City of Ulm; Nold KG v Commission; Hauer v Land Rheinland-Pfalz*[25]). Thereafter, such power of review was extended also to (some) Member State legislation in the field of Community law (*Rutili v Minister for the Interior; Wachauf v Germany; Society for the Protection of the Unborn Child v Grogan*[26]). As a result of the Court's wish to reassert its jurisdiction as against that of (some) Member States, to borrow a phrase from Ian Ward, '[a]ll sorts of things are bandied around as potential fundamental or human rights',[27] including various political rights (freedom of information), administrative and procedural rights, and rights in the area of social law.[28] The Court has, in a particularly striking way, also reconstituted the field of economic activity in terms of human rights: '[i]t should be borne in mind that the principles of free movement of goods and freedom of competition, together with freedom of trade as a fundamental right, are general principles of Community law of which the Court ensures observance'.[29]

While the Court has re-described entitlement to property and land, as well as the confidentiality of business information in fundamental rights language,[30] no such language has been used to describe problems relative to immigration or asylum, racial discrimination, minorities or environmental protection. Such selectivity is of course not dictated by any 'essential' nature of those problems. It is a matter of (political) preference: which interests, which visions of the good merit being characterised as 'rights' and thus afforded the corresponding level of protection, and which do not? What moves are needed to ensure jurisdiction and

[24] See Case 1/58 *Stork v High Authority* [1959] ECR 17.

[25] Case 29/69 *Stauder v City of Ulm* [1969] ECR 419; Case 4/73 *Nold KG v Commission* [1974] ECR 491; Case 44/79 *Hauer v Land Rheinland-Pfalz* [1979] ECR 3727.

[26] Case 36/75 *Rutili v Minister for the Interior* [1975] ECR 1219; Case 5/88 *Wachauf v Germany* [1989] ECR 2609; Case 159/90 *Society for the Protection of the Unborn Child v Grogan* [1991] ECR I-4685.

[27] I Ward, *The Margins of European Law* (Basingstoke, New York, Macmillan Press, St Martin's Press, 1996) 142.

[28] See G de Búrca, 'The Language of Rights and European Integration' in J Shaw and G More, *New Legal Dynamics of European Union* (Oxford, Clarendon, 1995) 30–39.

[29] Case 240/83 *Procureur de la République v Association de défense des brûleurs d'huiles usages* [1985] ECR 531, 548.

[30] See Case 44/79 *Hauer v Land Rheinland-Phalz* [1979] ECR 3744–50. See also Case 168/91 *Konstandinidis v Stadt Altensteig, Standesamt and Landesamt Calw* [1993] ECR I-1191 in which the general principles of Community law were restricted to apply only in the economic field.

control?[31] Today, every interest, every preference tends to present itself in rights-language so that the critical power of that language is largely lost. In the 'war against terror', for example, efforts to control the expansive jurisdiction of security concerns and security experts were originally opposed in the language of individual rights. By now, however, security concerns are themselves addressed as human rights concerns so that even an indefinite detention may be justified by reference to the human right to security of the detained person's prospective victims.[32] The point is not that this is perverse; it is that this is formally *correct*: the rights of many *may* depend on the limitation of the rights of some. The only (political) questions to ask are: whom do we believe, what values do *we* want to prefer and which we are ready to override?

In its advisory opinion on the *Legality of the Threat or Use of Nuclear Weapons*, the International Court of Justice reconstituted the field of possible uses of nuclear weapons in the language of human rights, protection of the environment, humanitarian law, and national self-defence. The decisive concerns, it seems, came for the field of national security that led to the Court's unprecedented *non liquet*.[33] One is left wondering whether that would have been the result had the Court restricted itself to characterising the use of nuclear weapons in human rights terms (particularly by reference to article 6 of the 1966 UN Covenant on Civil and Political Rights[34]). The point here is that the choice of the relevant legal field – human rights/environmental law/humanitarian law/self-defence – was crucial for the outcome of the decision, but that this choice, unarticulated though it seemed, could only follow from an external preference about which kinds of concerns are most significant in relation to nuclear weapons.[35]

Conflicts Of Rights

In every important social conflict, it is possible to describe the claims of both sides as claims for (the honouring of) rights. One typical generic form of rights-conflict is that between right-as-freedom and right-to-security. If, for example, the State's authority to intervene for the prohibition of rape in marriage is conceptualised in terms of a 'right to privacy', then the husband's right to (sexual) freedom is privileged against the wife's right to security. Such a conflict cannot be resolved by mere

---

[31] As Weiler puts it, the Court's language is that of human rights while the deep structure is that of supremacy, in 'Methods of Protection: Towards Second and Third Generation of Protection' in Cassese, Clapham, and Weiler, *Human Rights and the European Community* (Baden Baden, Nomos, 1991) 580–81.

[32] Case CO/3673/2005 *The Queen (written application of . . . Ali Al-Jedda) v the Secretary for Defence* [2005] EWHC 1809 (Admin) 104 and chapter 14 in this volume.

[33] *Legality of the Threat or Use of Nuclear Weapons* (1996) 35 ILM 809 (Advisory Opinion of 8 July 1996).

[34] International Covenant on Civil and Political Rights, adopted by UNGA Res 2200 A(XXI) (1966) in United Nations, *A Compilation of International Instruments* (1994) i part 1, 20.

[35] See further chapter eight below.

rights-talk. The boundaries of freedom and security cannot be drawn from any intrinsic or essential meaning of the relevant 'rights'. On the contrary, the debate over where such boundaries should lie reflects back on culturally conditioned ways of thinking about family relationships and the function of the State.

Justification for the imposition of constraint in a morally agnostic society may often seem to lie in the need to limit freedom by the freedoms of others. If your use of your freedom creates harm for me, such use is prohibited. However, the formal principle of preventing 'harm to others' merely shifts focus to the concept of 'harm' and fails to indicate which of the competing conceptions of 'harm' should be preferred.[36] Think of the problem of public intervention in rape in marriage again. Here, 'harm' for the woman is constituted by the husband's physical aggression, while the 'harm' the husband will suffer follows from the outside intervention on his sexual liberty that he had purchased in the act of marriage. The politically and culturally conditioned character of the notion of 'harm' is perhaps easiest to see in the classic debates about matters of sexual morality. For while most liberals would today feel that homosexual acts between consenting adults should not be taken to 'harm' society,[37] the practice of prostitution or pornography might seem degrading and, as such, harmful for women at large.

However, this is just one aspect of the right to freedom/right to security conflict. Embedded in the former in most cases is the ideology of laissez-faire, while embedded in the latter is a communal ethic of responsibility, and the dilemma is that 'any effort to keep the state out of our personal lives will leave us subject to private domination'.[38]

It does not follow, however, that rights conflicts could be solved simply once we have decided whether to prefer individualism or altruism; neither is unmitigated good. Individualism is the Dr Jekyll to the egoism of Mr Hyde. Communal ethic grounds also suffocating, totalitarian practices. But if there is no general recipe for the solution of rights conflicts, no single vision of the good life that rights would express, then everything hinges on the appreciation of the context, on the act of ad hoc balancing, that is to say, on the kind of politics for the articulation of which rights leave no room.

European human rights organs repeatedly deal with conflicts involving an individual's right to privacy and the right of other individuals to security that the State has been tasked to guarantee. Are prison authorities, for instance, authorised to censor prisoners' letters? Again, the matter turns on policy, or 'striking a balance

---

[36] This is of course John Stuart Mill's famous doctrine:'[t]he only purpose for which power can rightfully be exercised over any member of a civilized community, against his will, is to prevent harm to others': JS Mill, *On Liberty* (Oxford, Oxford University Press,1859/1974) 68. For the point that'harm' cannot be defined in a morally neutral way, see N MacCormick, 'Against Moral Disestablishment' in N MacCormick, *Legal Right and Social Democracy: Essays in Legal and Political Philosophy* (Oxford University Press, 1982) 28–30.

[37] On the classic debate between Hart and Lord Devlin on the Wolfenden Report on abolishing the criminality of homosexual practices, see HLA Hart, *Law, Liberty and Morality* (Stanford, Stanford University Press, 1963) and P Devlin, *The Enforcement of Morals* (Oxford, Clarendon, 1959).

[38] F Olsen, 'Liberal Rights and Critical Legal Theory' in C Joerges and DM Trubek, *Critical Legal Thought: An American-German Debate* (Baden-Baden, Nomos, 1989) 251.

between the legitimate interests of public order and security and that of the rehabilitation of prisoners'.[39]

However, obviously, there are no technical means of calculating the relative weights of the two kinds of interests. Any 'balancing' will involve broad cultural and political assumptions about whether the good society should prefer the values of public order or those of rehabilitation. It is hard to think of a more openly politico-cultural divide than that. In the *Society for the Protection of the Unborn Child v Grogan* case involving the prohibition of dissemination of information on abortion in Ireland, the Advocate-General of the European Court perceived a conflict that required 'balancing two fundamental rights, on the one hand the right to life as defined and declared to be applicable to unborn life by a Member State, and on the other the freedom of expression'. This was to be dealt with by reference to the Strasbourg Court's criteria of whether any restriction had a legitimate aim and was necessary in a democratic society, criteria which were 'analogous to the principle of proportionality used in Community Law'.[40] Summarising the task, he concluded:

> The correct justification under general principles of Community law is public policy and/or public morality, because the rule at issue here is justified by an ethical value-judgement which is regarded in the Member State concerned as forming part of the bases of the legal system.[41]

Alternatively, think of environmental policies. The rights of the upstream industrial user of a common watercourse may conflict with the right of the downstream user to clean water. Neither right enjoys an absolute preference. Any balancing will have to invoke the values of either economic prosperity or clean environment without any expectation that the attained outcome would manifest some sort of an inherent or non-political equilibrium between them.

Another rights conflict is that between formal equality and substantive equality; or equality of opportunity and equality or result. For the women's movement, it has often seemed important to argue from the right to equality (equality of voting rights, for instance), while in other cases the fact that formal neutrality may advance male interests has seemed to compel arguing in favour of (reverse) discrimination. From the perspective of a universalising rights-rhetoric, this appears as incoherence; while from the perspective of political struggles, incoherence translates into a political necessity.

The resolution of rights-conflicts (and every social conflict is amenable to a description of such) presumes a place 'beyond' rights, a place that allows the limitation of the scope of the claimed rights and their subordination to

> some pattern, or range of patterns, of human character, conduct and interaction in community, and the need to choose such specification of rights as tends to favour that

---

[39] *Silver v United Kingdom*(1987) Series B no 51, 75–76, (1983) Series A no 61.
[40] Case 159/90 *Society for the Protection of the Unborn Child v Grogan* [1991] ECR I-4685. Opinion of the Advocate- General [34].
[41] ibid [35].

pattern, or range of patterns. In other words, we need some conception of human good, of individual flourishing, in a form (or range of forms) of common life that fosters rather than hinders such flourishing.[42]

What this pattern might be in Community law was famously stated by the European Court in *Wachauf* as follows:

> The fundamental rights recognized by the Court are not absolute, however, but must be considered in relation to their social function. Consequently, restrictions may be imposed on the exercise of these rights, in particular in the context of a common organization of the market, provided that these restrictions in fact correspond to objectives of general interest pursued by the Community and do not constitute, with regard to the aim pursued, a disproportionate and intolerable interference impairing the very substance of those rights.[43]

The point here is not, of course, that the Court's statement should be seen as a mistaken or cynical position about rights, but that recourse to the language of 'functions', 'objectives', 'general interests' and 'proportionality' which seems so far removed from our intuitive association of rights with their absoluteness, or 'trumping character', against social policies, is simply unavoidable. A right is, often, a policy and must be weighed as such against other policies. Here there is no question of Klaus Günther's memories of pain and injustice that would seek articulation. The European Court's judicial everyday is the banal exercise of coping with conflicts of (most commonly economic) interests, and allocating scarce resources. The fact that those interests are dressed in rights language does not change this pattern, but it does obscure the political nature of the task.

Right-Exception Schemes

One example of this concerns the historical vicissitudes of the right of free speech in the United States, in which that right is always conditioned by the balancing test of the First Amendment and the 'clear and present danger' standard. One of the limitations has been to allow free speech only in places that are 'public forums', excluding for instance leafleting in shopping-centres and prohibiting the posting of signs on city-owned buildings in a way that reflects deeply ingrained political assumptions of American culture.[44]

---

[42] Finnis, *Natural Law and Natural Rights* (1980) 219–20.

[43] Case 5/88 *Wachauf* [1989] ECR 2639. Likewise in Case 44/94 *The Queen v Ministry of Agriculture, Fisheries and Food, ex p National Federation of Fishermen's Organizations, Federation of Highlands and Islands Fishermen* [1995] ECR 3115; Case 22/94 *Irish Farmers Association v Minister for Agriculture, Food and Forestry, Ireland, and the Attorney General* [1997] ECR 1809. As the Court stated in *Nold*: 'if rights of ownership are protected by the constitutional laws of all Member States . . . the rights thereby guaranteed, far from constituting unfettered prerogatives, must be viewed in the light of the social function of the property and activities protected thereunder': Case 4/73 *Nold* [1974] ECR 491.

[44] See D Kairys, 'Freedom of Speech' in D Kairys (ed), *The Politics of Law. A Progressive Critique* (revised edition, New York, Pantheon, 1990) 262–63.

Within the European system, the relations between rights and the power to derogate from them are in principle conditioned by the criterion of what may be 'necessary in a democratic society'. As Susan Marks has shown, this is a criterion that is heavily contextualised in the political self-understanding of post-war Western societies.[45] There is nothing a-historical (or unpolitical) in the conclusion, for instance, that if a person loses his or her opportunity to work because of the disclosure by public authorities of secret information on him or her, it still remains the case that 'having regard to the area of discretion which must be left to the State in respect of the defence of the national security . . . [the interference was] . . . Necessary in a democratic society in the interests of national security'.[46]

The neat scheme of right/derogation that is embedded in the European Convention on Human Rights (ECHR) is constantly undermined by the experience that there is no unpolitical rule or standard that would set out when to apply the right and when the derogation. Why would letter-opening and wire-tapping, with limited judicial control, be 'necessary in a democratic society'? To answer such questions the Commission and the Court have developed a balancing practice that uses abstract notions such as 'reasonable', 'proportionate', 'public order', and 'morals' to justify reference either to the right or to the exception.[47] In this way, the scope of rights becomes conditioned by policy choices that seem justifiable only by reference to alternative conceptions of the good society.

The European Court of Justice has been quite express in this respect. Already, its early human rights jurisprudence was based on the assumption that a fundamental right was subject to restrictions inasmuch as 'the restrictions . . . correspond to the objectives of general interest pursued by the Community or whether, with regard to the aim pursued, they constitute a disproportionate and intolerable interference with the rights'.[48] It is now 'settled case-law that fundamental rights . . . are not absolute and their exercise may be subject to restrictions justified by objectives of general interest pursued by the Community'.[49] Such restrictions may even follow from 'proportionality' – a utilitarian test, if there ever was one.[50] It matters little if the Court holds the valid test to be that of 'disproportionate' or 'intolerable' effect. The point is that all such language indicates that the characterisation of social objectives in terms of the 'rights' of their beneficiaries adds little to the administrative pattern of dealing with them. This involves a political

---

[45] See S Marks, 'The European Convention of Human Rights and its "Democratic Society"'(1995) LXVI *British Year Book of International Law* 209–38. For an extension of the same point to recent international legal debate, see S Marks, 'The End of History? Reflections on Some International Legal Theses' (1997) 8 *European Journal of International Law* 449–77.

[46] *Leander v Sweden* (1987) Series A no 116, 18, 26–27.

[47] For one discussion and critique, see P Van Dijk and GV Van Hoof, *Theory and Practice of the European Convention on Human Rights* (The Hague, Nijhoff, 1990) 604.

[48] Case 44/79 *Hauer* [1979] ECR 3747.

[49] Case 84/95 *Bosphorus* [1996] ECR 3953.

[50] In *Internationale Handelsgesellschaft*, for instance, the Court concluded that the system of deposits imposed on cornflour exporters did not violate fundamental human rights because '[t]he costs involved in the deposit do not constitute an amount disproportionate to the total value of the goods in question'. Case 11/70 *Internationale Handelsgesellschaft* [1970] ECR 1136.

give-and-take and ad hoc decision-making in which no memory of pain or injustice is being articulated.

Indeterminacy of Rights

It is a truism that the linguistic openness of rights discourse leads to policy being determinative of particular interpretive outcomes. Discussing the concept of 'degrading' treatment, the European Court of Human Rights came to the conclusion that seems practically self-evident, namely that '[t]he assessment is, in the nature of things, relative: it depends on all the circumstances of the case and, in particular, on the nature and context of the punishment itself and the manner and method of its execution'.[51]

But indeterminacy exists far beyond such simple semantic openness. It is hard to imagine a standard that would seem more straightforward than the right to life under article 2 of the ECHR. Yet, even its application is revealed as a weighing standard. Does the right to life also include abortion? The European Commission's practice has been summarised as follows: 'even if one assumes that Article 2 protects the unborn life, the rights and interests involved have been weighted against each other in a reasonable way'.[52]

The same concerns the ending of life: 'the value of the life to be protected can and must be weighed against other rights of the person in question'.[53]

The normative limit of the right to life is established through an act of balancing with a view, supposedly, of attaining an aggregate good. It may seem hard to think of a context in which utilitarian approaches seem more out of place than this. Nonetheless, it seems equally clear that the right to life cannot be taken as an absolute standard but involves a prohibition against the arbitrary taking of lives, while what is 'arbitrary' depends on the context.[54]

Again, such assessment involves precisely the kind of discretion that the concept of rights (as 'trumps') was intended to do away with, including balancing between requirements of state security and individual interests.[55] The Strasbourg Court's much-criticised doctrine of the margin of appreciation, 'at the heart of virtually all major cases that come before the Court',[56] is from this perspective nothing more

---

[51] *Tyrer* (1978) Series A no 26, 15.

[52] Van Dijk and Van Hoof, *Theory and Practice* (1990) 220.

[53] ibid 220–21. On the proportionality standard in this context, see ibid 222–23.

[54] See the discussion of the International Court of Justice of the right to life in Art 6 of the International Covenant on Civil and Political Rights and of genocide in the *Legality of the Threat or Use of Nuclear Weapons* (1996) 35 ILM 809 (Advisory Opinion of 8 July 1996) [24]–[26]: 'after having taken due account of the circumstances of the specific case' [26].

[55] Van Dijk and Van Hoof *Theory and Practice* (1990), 232.

[56] R St J Macdonald, 'The Margin of Appreciation in the Jurisprudence of the European Court of Human Rights' in *International Law at the Time of Its Codification: Studies in Honour of Roberto Ago* (Milan, Giuffré, 1987) 208.

than a healthy admission that there is always interpretative indeterminacy in the construction of particular rights-claims and often it is local courts, and not Strasbourg organs, that are most competent to police the matter. The main point is that rights not only determine and limit policies, but that policies are needed to give meaning, applicability and limits to rights.

Between Myth and Bureaucracy

In a recent piece, Philip Alston has reviewed similar arguments I have made elsewhere as a 'standard post-modernist critique', noting that it is 'unduly focused on conceptions of rights as 'trumps''.[57] What he suggested is that human rights 'can provide a meaningful basis for social order without being rigid, absolute or forever enduring', and that they are 'Capable of partly transcending the institutions that gave birth to them, and those very same institutions (or their successors) which seek to exercise responsibility for their elaboration and interpretation'.[58]

For Alston, the above critique works with a straw-man conception of human rights, a conception that is impossibly rigid, and as such does not really exist anywhere. Of course rights are flexible and dependent on evaluation and process, but they are also partly reflective (and creative) of a political consensus without having to assume that they involve a banalisation of rights that would do away with 'their capacity to mobilize, to inspire and to exhort'.[59]

I am uncertain about the force of these arguments. I agree that in practice rights are downgraded from their status as 'trumps' to the level of soft policies in favour of this or that social objective. Like any other policies, they may or may not reflect a consensus of opinion within some part of the population, and being acknowledged as such may also help to mobilise political forces. Indeed, that they are often a policy is the gist of the argument of this chapter.

However, the point I want to make is that although this is true of a large number of those social goods that we tend today to call 'rights', none of us would wish that that to be true of certain limited number of 'core rights', namely those that we most commonly associate with the adjectives 'inalienable' or 'fundamental', and that are capable of articulating Klaus Günther's memories of fear and injustice. However, in order to uphold *that* distinction we must, I think, fall back on naturalist (or 'mythical') conception of basic rights whose special character depends on their not being subject to the kinds of legal-technical arguments and proof that justify – and make vulnerable – ordinary rights as policies. The right of property, for instance, is as strong or weak as the economic or social justification that its exercise has in a particular case. It may be assessed and, if necessary, overridden by

---

[57] P Alston, 'Introduction' in P Alston (ed), *Human Rights Law* (The International Library of Essays in Law and Legal Theory, Areas 27, 1996) xvi–xvii.

[58] ibid.

[59] ibid xv.

alternative political preferences. The right to be free from torture operates differently. Its validity is not relative to the force of any justification that we can provide for it, but is intrinsic in a manner that cannot be articulated through the forms of legal-technical argument.

We seem to have good reason to distinguish between two types of rights: those that are an effect of politics and those that constrain it. But upholding the distinction creates two difficulties. First, it seems difficult to defend special rights (memories of fear and injustice) on the basis of their intrinsic value, irrespectively of any arguments we can produce to support them – which means that they must be accepted outside rational convention: as part of our self-definition, as part of our identity as members of our communities; perhaps as taboo. Second, identifying the distinction compels an acceptance that *other* rights are no different from policies, in the sense that whether and to what extent they are applicable must be determined by reference to the kinds of 'balancing', 'proportionality', and other kinds of utilitarian considerations that are a commonplace of bureaucratic practice. The problem is that the rights of the former group seem too strong to be defensible within a democratic order, while the rights of the latter group seem too weak to constitute an effective constraint on policy. Indeed, they are indistinguishable from policy.

Rights discourse sometimes appears as an offshoot of inflexible (and, as such, Utopian) legalism:

> [t]o make a political issue that is deeply morally contested a matter of basic rights is to make it non-negotiable, since rights . . . are unconditional entitlements, not susceptible to moderation. Because they are peremptory in this way, rights do not allow divisive issues to be settled by legislative [or adjudicative] compromise: they permit only unconditional victory or surrender.[60]

The absoluteness of rights discourse is not, however, an accidental property in it, but follows from its justification within liberal theory, its purpose to create a set of unpolitical normative demands intended to 'trump' legislative policies or administrative discretion. The very point of rights as a special type of normative entitlement lies in their absoluteness, their uncontextual validity, and immediate applicability. Understood in such a way, rights discourse has three broad cultural effects on politics.[61]

One is the entrenchment of the idea of politics as already constrained by a non-political vision of the good society, understood as the sum total of individual rights that exist in a co-terminous relationship to each other. This is the core sense of liberal naturalism, the view that rights 'exist' outside political society and are then brought inside through legislation. Politics are thereby reduced to the declaration of truths already established elsewhere and the realisation of a society already in

---

[60] Gray, *Enlightenment's Wake* (1995) 22.

[61] For further discussion, see David Kennedy, 'The International Human Rights Movement: Part of the Problem?' in *Dark Sides of Virtue. Reassessing International Humanitarianism* (Princeton, Princeton University Press, 2004), 3–35.

virtual existence. As politics lose their creative, 'imaginative' character, they are transformed from their core sense as human *vita activa* into an exercise of technical competence by experts.[62] Exit from the tragedy of incompatible and contested goods is bought at the expense of the bureaucratisation of politics into balancing or the search of aggregate utility – paradoxically precisely the outcome that rights discourse originally sought to combat.

However, inasmuch as rights are not naturally given, but, as I have argued above, the result of the application of policies, then an offshoot is that politics become the politics of procedure, a struggle for the power to define, for jurisdiction: the question is not so much whether a weighing of interests has to take place, but rather which authority in the final analysis is empowered to do the weighing.

This aspect highlights the priority of process to substance in rights discourse. For those immersed in that discourse, the natural cultural preference is that 'only the Strasbourg organs are competent to conduct the weighing of interests involved in the Convention'.[63]

Second, rights are inescapably individualist. For even as they necessitate reference to social values and communal goods, rights always occupy the perspective of the single individual, slightly removed from those values and interests himself or herself. For rights discourse, the individual is a separable, unitary entity that has values or interests, and thus rights, only as external attributes to itself but whose identity is not formed by them or their underlying ideology.[64] Yet, it is not clear if a distinction can be made between the self and the values and interests it carries. The problem with the rhetoric of rights is that it fails to articulate the reality where our individual selves are (also) products of the contexts in which we live, of the values and interests of our communities. That is to say we are not fixed at birth but our identities change in interaction with others, and so do our preferences. Besides, often we are torn between competing values and interests, and no unitary standpoint beyond them can be found. Thinking of politics in terms of rights is unable to reach the process in which the interests of individuals (and their 'individuality') are formed, omitting the question whether having such interests is good in the first place, and failing to discriminate between interests that conflict but which we feel equally strongly about.

The very strong anti-sovereignty or anti-communitarian bias of rights fails to articulate the value of collectives to individual lives. We sometimes see this in the apparently puzzling conflict between rights of minorities and rights of the individuals belonging to them. But the issue is larger and has to do with the interest we all have in being part of self-determining communities where the value or preferences of the 'self' is more than an aggregate of the values or preferences of the individual members. The 'interest' we have in membership in such communities cannot be

---

[62] For this argument at greater length, see M Koskenniemi, 'The Wonderful Artificiality of States' (1994) *ASIL Proceedings* 22–29.

[63] Van Dijk and Van Hoof *Theory and Practice* (1990) 601.

[64] See generally M Sandel, *Liberalism and the Limits of Justice* (Cambridge, Cambridge University Press, 1982) 191.

translated to a right of any fixed 'self' for that interest may include the transforma-tion of our own self-perception, including our view of our entitlements.[65]

Related to this, rights individualism loses a creative conception of the political, reducing citizenship to passive reliance on rights and political decision-making to an oscillation between (individual) ethics and economics. No idea of civic virtue or political participation can be sustained through insistence on the priority of the right over the good, and, inasmuch as such ideas occasionally emerge, they find no resonance in a right-based political culture.[66]

A third general consequence of the proliferation of rights-rhetoric everywhere in administration is the inauguration of what could be called a *political culture of bad faith*. For liberal agnosticism, a conception of natural rights, situated outside political society, remains ultimately an unjustifiable, even mythical, assumption that cannot be brought within the conventions of liberal political debate as they would thereby lose their fundamental character. For seeking to justify rights makes those rights vulnerable to the objections that can be directed against the justifying reasons: should people have a right to free speech because that produces the largest aggregate utility, is in accordance with human nature, or corresponds to popular will? Each explanation condenses a contested theory about the political good. As providing such explanations will infect rights with the weaknesses that attach to those theories, they can no longer be used to overrule conflicts over them and their point is lost. Hence, paradoxically, rights seem effective only if they can be accepted by unquestioning faith – a faith, the absence of which provided the very reason for having recourse to them. If the critique of rights (as 'political') is correct, then the beneficiality of rights would seem to presuppose that the critique is not known![67]

But no such unthinking faith in rights can be taken for granted. Everyone knows that politics are not 'really' about translating natural rights into positive law; that at issue are struggle and compromise, power and ideology, and not derivations from transparent and automatically knowable normative demands. Nor can the critiques of formalism and realism be undone. Everyone knows that administra-tion and adjudication have to do with discretion, and that, however much such discretion is dressed in the technical language of rights and 'balancing', the outcomes reflect broad cultural and political preferences that have nothing inalien-able about them.

So, how does one deal with loss of faith? One response is simply to give up rights. This would be an unwarranted conclusion inasmuch as there does not exist any other language either, in which political conflict would already have been solved. Another and the more common response is to continue rights talk without actually believing in the a-political or foundational nature of rights:

---

[65] I have argued in defense of 'sovereignty' in many places, most recently in 'Conclusion: Vocabularies of Sovereignty – Powers of a Paradox', in H Kalmo and Q Skinner, *Fragments of Sovereignty. The Past, Present and Future of a Contested Concept* (Cambridge, Cambridge University Press, 2010) especially 239–42.

[66] See Mouffe, *Return of the Political*, (1993) 32–38 and 139–41.

[67] Tushnet, 'An Essay on Rights' (1984) 1386.

151

[d]o not mind that you cannot really defend your rights. If they effectively produce the political outcomes you wished to produce, just continue. Remember, no one else is in possession of a stronger or more convincing political language and if your justifications cannot withstand internal criticisms that are familiar from 200 years of liberal rhetoric, neither can theirs.

To succeed, however, such a strategy may require not disclosing your own loss of faith. For this might 'jeopardize the idea that human rights are fundamental and universally applicable which is a fiction Europe at least should try to adhere to'.[68]

In this way, you may be compelled – in order to advance the cultural politics of a 'Europe' – to choose a purely strategic attitude towards rights. Even as you know that rights defer to policy, you cannot disclose this, as you would then seem to undermine what others (mistakenly) believe to be one of your most beneficial gifts to humanity (a non-political and universal rights rhetoric). It is hard to think of such an attitude as a beneficial basis from which to engage other cultures or to inaugurate a transcultural sphere of politics.

The question would be then, not so much which rights we have, or should have, but what it takes to develop politics in which deviating conceptions of the good – whether or not expressed in rights language – can be debated and realised without having to assume that they are taken seriously only if they can lay claim to an a-political absoluteness that is connoted by rights as trumps.

---

[68] E Steyger, *Europe and Its Members: A Constitutional Approach* (Dartmouth, Brookfield, 1995) 49.

6

Human Rights, Politics and Love

The predominantly critical or negative tones in the previous chapter prompted me to explore the constructive, positive aspect of human rights in modern societies. This chapter is based on a talk given at the University of Oslo on the day before the attack on the World Trade Center in New York in September 2001. Since then, the message here, it seems to me, has become increasingly important: human rights are both impossible but necessary. The difficult, fascinating task of the lawyer is to manage the tension between those two aspects of human rights.

H UMAN RIGHTS ARE like love, both necessary and impossible. We cannot live without them, but we cannot have them, either. As soon as we are safely installed in a social order that promises to guarantee our rights, that order starts to appear oppressively totalitarian. We need new rights, our new interpretations of old rights. Routine kills love, as it does to rights-regimes. It is good to struggle for rights, or to reach them finally: in France between 1789 and 1791, in South Africa in 1994, East Germany or Russia for a brief period after 1989. As the tyrant falls, there is dancing in the streets. But the morning after is cold, and certain to come. Why?

In this chapter I want to discuss the paradox of international law that aims to create space for a non-political normativity that would be opposable to the politics of states but that is undermined by the experience that what rights mean, and how they are applied, can only be determined by the politics of states. This leaves reformist lawyers uneasily poised between a naïve enthusiasm and a suave cynicism. A familiar psychological trap, I suggest. In order to reconceive the emancipatory ethos of rights, it is necessary to grasp their open-endedness, their irreducibly political nature, the way they lead into a dialectic between universalism and particularism, individualism and community, and perhaps, like love, sometimes make the two seem the same, if only for a moment.

The Pedigree of Rights

What rights have we? A first paradox I want to examine has to do with the way we conceive of rights as an aspect of social life which, although very important, has come to us only recently. This allows me to describe the politics of rights in a historical perspective. The most common response to the question '*what rights have we?*' refers to the international reactions to the atrocities of the Second World War. A recent collection of essays claims that the Universal Declaration of Human rights:

> . . . represented a historical evolution in the norms of international society which from the seventeenth century onwards had maintained that the domestic practices of governments were not a subject of international concern.[1]

This is so patently problematic that it provides a good starting point for examining the peculiar weakness of human rights today. Of course, lawyers, kings and governments have always criticised foreign rulers for violating the rights of their subjects. Even if the scholastic conception of subjective rights was embedded in a firmly 'objective' frame of virtues and the good life, at least by Hugo Grotius (1583–1645) or perhaps the Spanish renaissance of the sixteenth century, the notion that humans have rights that their rules may not violate has become part of the early modern vocabulary of *jus naturae et gentium*.[2] In Francisco de Vitoria (1492–1546), for example, just war was not to waged out of ideological or religious reasons but to "defend the innocent".[3] The motives that used to take nations to war were, of course, mixed. But , there is no reason to think that the standard claim that one was fighting an unjust tyrant was always wrong or dishonest. The Western interventions in the Balkans or the Holy Land in the nineteenth century combine an imperial agenda with humanitarian concerns in a way that reveals much about the nature of both.[4] It is doubtful whether anything like a system of international norms existed before the end of the nineteenth century. However, when the first professional bodies, journals and university chairs in international law were established between 1870 and 1885, no important member of the new profession refrained from waving the flag of humanity when news about despotism made headlines in the day's paper. They were drawing from the late Victorian liberal sentiments, admired the *philosophes*, and spoke of inalienable rights that followed from human nature and were valid in Europe and colonies. These men were firm supporters of the *mission civilisatrice*, indissociable from their humanism.[5]

The pedigree of universal rights from Vitoria to Grotius, Kant to the United Nations, is highlighted in one of the first monographic treatments of the topic by a member of the international law profession, Hersch Lauterpacht in 1950. An immigrant in Britain from Galicia and Vienna in the 1920s, Lauterpacht had

---

[1] T Dunne and NJ Wheeler, 'Introduction: Human Rights and the Fifty Years' Crisis' in T Dunne and NJ Wheeler *Human Rights in Global Politics* (Cambridge University Press, 1999) 1.

[2] Out of a huge recent literature, see eg Annabel Brett, *Liberty, Right and Nature. Individual Rights in Later Scholastic Thought* (Cambridge, Cambridge University Press, 1997).

[3] Francisco Vitoria, 'On the American Indians', in A Pagden and J Lawrance (eds) *Political Writings* (Cambridge, Cambridge University Press, 1991) 288.

[4] For a contemporary view, see J Hornung, 'Civilisés et barbares'(1885) XVII *Revue de droit international et de législation comparée* 1–18, 447–70, 539–60 and (1886) 188–206, 289–96.

[5] See generally M Koskenniemi, *The Gentle Civilizer of Nations. The Rise and Fall of International Law 1870–1960* (Cambridge, Cambridge University Press, 2001) 98–178.

become Professor of International Law at Cambridge and in 1950 was among the most respected lawyers of his generation. His book consisted of two parts. One rehearsed the argument against state sovereignty that had become commonplace in the profession since the early 1920s. However, it did this by trying to recapture the Western canon of individual rights as derived not only from Enlightenment thinkers, but sixteenth century religious humanism and even Stoic dogma. The book's second part attacked the Universal Declaration of Human Rights because it provided no system of enforcement and was legally non-binding. Its adoption had perversely provided states with an opportunity to publicly declare that they were not legally accountable for violating human rights – something they would normally have shunned from saying in public. The Declaration was not only meaningless; it was harmful, a substitute instead of an example of action.[6]

The arguments deserve attention. In 1950 Lauterpacht was clear that human rights would have to form the core of a reformed international law. Arguing this, he claimed he was merely continuing a tradition of Western thought that originated in Greek philosophy. The diplomacy of states – that is to say, the Universal Declaration – could neither grant nor take away rights. That the Declaration was such a dangerous disappointment resulted precisely from the fact that this was what it suggested.

Now all of this contradicts the view that sees universal human rights as somehow grounded in 1948. Why, even as we are ready to recognise Lauterpacht as perhaps the most impressive international lawyer of the past generation, do we so blatantly disagree with him on this? The answer, I am afraid, is that unlike Sir Hersch international lawyers have never really taken seriously the literary tradition within which human rights grew up but 'have fragmented [it] . . . by appropriating parts of it while leaving behind crucial premises that gave these parts their underlying coherence'.[7] In the 1960s and 1970s rights penetrated everywhere in international institutions.[8] But this (new) tradition never seriously examined how it fitted the economic, social, and psychological worlds in which it had to live. As a result, rights became at best a sentimental memory of a political faith that we no longer have – a love that we had lost – but to which we hang on because of the absence of any more attractive alternatives, or for reasons perhaps best labeled aesthetic. They offer us a self-description that seems attractive and needs no deeper justification than that.[9] At worst, the novel language of rights became a façade for cynicism, and an instrument of empire.

The tradition that Lauterpacht sought to resuscitate in the aftermath of the Holocaust – in which most of his Polish family perished – received the meaning of human rights sometimes from scripture, sometimes from a concept of uniform

---

[6] H Lauterpacht, *International Law and Human Rights* (New York, Praeger, 1950) 475.

[7] I Shapiro, *The Evolution of Rights in Liberal Theory* (Cambridge, Cambridge University Press, 1986) 6.

[8] This 'recent' tradition has now been usefully accounted in Samuel Moyn, *The Last Utopia. Human Rights in History* (Cambridge MA, Harvard University Press, 2010).

[9] As argued in A MacIntyre, *After Virtue. A Study in Moral Theory*, 2nd edn (London, Duckworth, 1985) 68–71.

human nature, from a progressive philosophy of history or an autonomous concept of reason. However, today, naturalism, rationalism and religion have each become vulnerable to the hermeneutics of suspicion embedded in the same Enlightenment that gave us the notion of rights in the first place. The moral grounding of rights that was central to Vitoria, Grotius or Locke is not available in a world where morality has turned into subjective, historically conditioned 'value-systems' and where anthropologies of humanity have produced both liberal and racist conclusions. As the Italian political theorist Norberto Bobbio put it, ideas about human nature have turned out illusions. Not only can we not find a basis for human rights, 'any search for the ultimate foundations is itself without foundation'.[10] As a result, in the political marketplace, every preference claims the status of right, every romance parades as love – and we remain puzzled about whether it could ever be otherwise.

Here is the paradox of international human rights today. In a morally agnostic society, everyone should be entitled to decide on his or her own moral or political preferences. It is this realm of pre-political preferences that rights seek to protect. This is the meaning of the liberal principle of the priority of the right over the good, or the theory of rights as 'trumps' over policy, made famous by John Rawls and Ronald Dworkin.[11] To claim a right is different from claiming a benefit or advancing a policy. It sets limits to policy, however widely supported or useful such policy might be. The legislator may not order older citizens to be forcibly removed to nursing homes or an industrial area located in the lands of an indigenous tribe whatever economic advantages might ensue from such decisions to society at large. Aged persons or members of a minority have a *right* to live where they wish!

The special strength of rights lies in their being more than privileges endowed by legislation or emerging from some utilitarian calculation or other. They claim to set a *limit* to what may be legislated. In this sense, rights claim to exist beyond the political system. Here also lies their special appeal. In an ideological age, the advocates of human rights may be able to project rights as non-ideological, outside politics.[12] They appear as pure facts, objective, true and self-sufficient.

But what is there, beyond the political system, and how do we find access to it? In the older tradition, rights were part of a moral order that determined what the place of politics in society would be and what it could legitimately achieve. We no longer believe in such a moral order, or at least find it dreadfully difficult to tell what it might require – and are completely puzzled as to how to convince those who do not share our intuitions. Whatever philosophers might say, the social meaning of rights is exhausted by the content of legal rights, by the institutional

---

[10] Quoted in T Mazzarese, 'Judicial Implementation of Fundamental Rights. Three sorts of Problem' in *Recht, Gerechtigkeit un der Staat, Rechtstheorie, Beiheft* 15 (Duncker & Humblot, Berlin, 1993) 206.

[11] J Rawls, *A Theory of Justice* (Oxford University Press, 1971) 607; R Dworkin, *Taking Rights Seriously* (Cambridge, Harvard University Press, 1979) 371.

[12] See MW Mutua, 'The Ideology of Human Rights' (1996) 36 *Virginia Journal of International Law* 591 and generally 589–657. Likewise, D Kennedy, *A Critique of Adjudication (fin de siècle)*(Cambridge, Harvard University Press, 1997) 304–09.

politics that gives them meaning and applicability. From a condition or limit of politics, they turn into an effect of politics.

Human Rights as the Outcome of Politics

There are four ways in which rights defer to politics in the context of professional practice. I call them field constitution, indeterminacy, right-exception and conflicts of rights.[13]

First is field constitution, the process whereby an aspect of reality comes to be characterised in terms of rights. Think about the way the East-West relations were re-described in human rights language within the Conference on Security and Cooperation in Europe (CSCE) process on the way from the Helsinki Final Act of 1975 to the Paris Charter of 1990. What had been until then characterised as a problem of the security of frontiers, or a confrontation between two ideological blocks, started to be described in human rights terms. This involved a delicate politics, allocation of resources and struggle over institutional competencies. A striking example of the latter is provided by the way the European Court of Justice modified its jurisprudence in the late 1960s and 1970s under pressure from the Supreme Courts of Germany and Italy. To defend its legitimacy vis-à-vis constitutions with developed systems of rights-protection, the Court started to characterise aspects of market integration – especially the four freedoms in terms of 'fundamental rights'.[14]

Since then, many aspects of community policies have become characterised in terms of human rights – with the development peaking in the adoption of the EU Charter of Human Rights in December 2001 in Nice and their inclusion in the Lisbon Treaty in 2007. None of this is politically innocent, of course: only some aspects of reality become recognised in terms of rights while others do not; whether individuals may violate human rights remains still to be sanctioned by the European Court of Justice in Luxembourg[15] Also, free movement of persons has so far been described as a function of market integration rather than an aspect of personal choice.[16]

A *second* way in which rights defer to policy concerns the *indeterminacy* of rights-language. Discussing the concept of 'degrading treatment', the European Court of Human Rights came to the self-evident conclusion that: 'The assessment is, in the nature of things, relative: it depends on all the circumstances of the case

---

[13] This section summarises points made in chapter five above.

[14] This well-known story is summarised in B de Witte, 'The Past and Future Role of the European Court of Justice in the Protection of Human Rights' in P Alston et al (ed), *EU and Human Rights* (Oxford, Oxford University Press, 1999) 859–97.

[15] Ibid 874.

[16] See PM Maduro, 'Striking the Elusive Balance between Economic Freedom and Social Rights in the EU' in Alston, *EU and Human Rights* (1999) 462.

and, in particular, on the nature and context of the punishment itself and the method of its execution.'[17]

Open-ended language and 'dynamic' interpretation often produce interesting results. Article 11 of the European Convention on Human Rights provides for the right 'to form and join trade unions'. From this expression, the Court was able to receive the right of unions to be consulted over collective disputes.[18] However, even core rights such as the right to life receive sense only in a political context: think about abortion and euthanasia. The European Court of Human Rights has interpreted the right to life by deferring to the national authority's 'margin of appreciation' and by constructing a balancing standard. The Court's practice has been summarised as follows: '[. . .] even if one assumes that Article 2 protects the unborn life, the rights and interests involved have been weighed against each other in a reasonable way.' The same concerns the ending of life: 'the value of the life to be protected can and must be weighed against other rights of the person in question'.[19] In such cases, the right to life has no meaning independent from the way it is interpreted by the relevant authority. Here there is, of course, no guarantee of uniformity. While the European Court of Justice denies that companies might enjoy the right of privacy under article 8 of the European Convention of Human Rights, the European Court of Human Rights grants them such a right.[20] There is nothing in the rights itself that would decide such interpretations: they receive meaning only when they are viewed by reference to some context or purpose. But such assessment involves precisely the kind of discretion that the concept of rights (as 'trumps') was intended to do away with.

Third, rights always come with *exceptions* while the scope or conditions for the application of the exception are never clearly defined. In the United States, for instance, the right of free speech is conditioned by the balancing test of the 'clear-and-present danger' standard of the First Amendment. As a result, free speech has been confined to 'public forums' in a way that has excluded leafleting in shopping centres and prohibited the posting of signs on city-owned buildings. In the European system, the relation between rights and exceptions is conditioned by what may be 'necessary in a democratic society'. It is hard to think of a more politically loaded criterion than this.[21] There is nothing unpolitical in the conclusion that if a person loses his or her opportunity to work because of the disclosure by public authorities of secret information on him or her, it still remains the case that: [. . .] having regard to the area of discretion which must be left to the state in respect of the defence of the national security [the interference was] necessary in a democratic society in the interests of national security.[22] Why would letter-opening

---

[17] *Tyrer v United Kingdom,* ECtHR Series A no 26 (1978) 15.

[18] *Swedish Engine Drivers' Union v Sweden,* ECtHR Series A no 20 (1976) 15.

[19] Van Dijk-Van Hoof, *Theory and Practice of the European Convention of Human Rights,* 2nd edn (Deventer and Boston, Kluwer, 1990) 220–23.

[20] See, *Hoechst* [1989] ECR 2856 and *Niemietz* ECtHR A/251-B 1992.

[21] See, S Marks, 'The European Convention of Human Rights and its "Democratic Society"' (1995) LXVI *British Yearbook of International Law* 209–38.

[22] *Leander v Sweden* (1987) Series A no 116, 39 [26]–[27].

or wire-tapping by prison authorities or the security police be 'necessary in a democratic society'? To answer such questions, European human rights organs use notions such as 'reasonable', 'proportionate', 'public order' and 'morals' to justify reference either to the right or to the exception.[23] In this way, the scope of rights becomes conditioned by choices that seem justifiable only by reference to alternative conceptions of the good society.

Fourth and finally, in every important social conflict, the claims of opposing sides may be described as rights claims. A typical example involves conflict between a right-as-freedom and a right-to-security. If the state's authority to prohibit rape in marriage is seen in terms of 'right to privacy', then the husband's right to (sexual) freedom is privileged against the wife's right to security, or the other way around. Such conflicts cannot be resolved by mere rights-talk. The boundaries of freedom and security are not apolitically given. To the contrary, the debate reflects on culturally conditioned ways to think about family relationships and the function of the State.

In the practice of the European human rights organs, a conflict repeatedly dealt with involves an individual's right to privacy and the right of other individuals to security. Do prison authorities have the competence to censor prisoners' letters? Again, the matter turns on policy, or '[. . .]striking a balance between the legitimate interests of public order and security and that of the rehabilitation of prisoners'.[24]

However, there are no technical means to calculate the weights of the two interests. Whichever way 'balancing' is carried out, it will involve cultural and political assumptions about whether the good society should prefer the values of public order or those of rehabilitation. It is hard to think of a more openly politico-cultural divide than that. Besides, sometimes both sides are able to rely on the *same* right – as when the litigants in an Austrian case argued over the permissibility to limit the availability of magazines with prize competitions. In this case, however paradoxically, the motivation of the limitation of the freedom of the press lay in advancing the freedom of the press. The meaning of that freedom had to be construed by reference to (intrinsically contested) ideas about the effects of markets to freedom.[25]

The Contextuality of Rights

The projection of some aspects of social life in rights terms, the resolution of indeterminacies or rights conflicts (and every social conflict is amenable to a description as such) presumes a place 'beyond' rights that allows the limitation of the

---

[23] For one discussion and critique, see Van Dijk-Van Hoof, *Theory and Practice* (1990) 604.
[24] *Sliver* case (1987) Series B no 51, 75–76, Series A no 61.
[25] See FG Jacobs, 'Human Rights in the European Union. The Role of the Court of Justice' (2001) 26 *European Law Review* 336.

scope of the claimed rights and their subordination to some pattern, ideal or concept of what a good society is like. What this pattern might be in Community law was famously stated by the European Court in *Wachauf* (1989) as follows:

> The fundamental rights recognized by the Court are not absolute, however, but must be considered in relation to their social function. Consequently, restrictions may be imposed on the exercise of these rights, in particular in the context of a common organization of the market, provided that these restrictions in fact correspond to objectives of general interest pursued by the Community and do not constitute, with regard to the aim pursued, a disproportionate and intolerable interference impairing the very substance of those rights.[26]

The point is not that such a statement should be seen as mistaken or cynical but that recourse to the language of 'functions', 'objectives', 'general interest' and 'proportionality' which seems so far removed from our intuitive association of rights with an absoluteness, or 'trumping character', against social policies, is simply unavoidable. Rights do not exist as such – 'fact-like' – outside the structures of political deliberation. They are not a limit but an effect of politics.

Which is to say that rights depend on their meaning and force on the presence of institutions, histories and cultures, of people thinking in broadly similar ways about matters social and political. Freedom of speech is dependent on the systems of political decision-making and public information that prevail in society. Freedom of contract is limited by the conditions of the actually existing market. Rights protect autonomy but autonomy is possible only if society offers collective goods. In a society that offers no choices, autonomy is meaningless. The availability of collective goods, however, is a pure issue of political value; of struggle and compromise between alternative views about what a good society would be like. In terms of political theory, this vindicates Aristotle or Saint Thomas rather than Locke or the Universal Declaration. No right is 'given'; a right is what one is due as a result of political deliberation.[27] However, this is what rights tried to avoid. It was precisely because politics seemed to degenerate into a struggle for the advancement of particular interests that rights were introduced to protect those in weaker positions. If rights are a function of social arrangements, then this point is lost. They become just one more policy among others. There is no love, just a marriage of convenience.

Let me be clear about one thing. To reverse the insights of agnostic modernity provides no relief. Some do espouse the position that 'human rights are ineliminably religious' and that only a cosmological world-view can uphold the sacredness of the individual.[28] True, they say, agnostics may often be more conscientious human rights defenders than religious zealots. However, they lack an explanation for why it should be so: Kantians for instance, who derive the need to honour human rights from the rule of universality – do unto others as you would they do

---

[26] Case C-5/88 *Wachauf* [1989] ECR 2639 [18].
[27] See *also* M Villey, *Le droit et les les droits de l'homme* (Paris, PUF, 1983) 114–15.
[28] See MJ Perry, *The Idea of Human Rights* (Oxford, Oxford University Press, 1998) 11–41.

unto you – fail to explain why a masochist should not torture his or her children. This is correct. If one moves in a discursive universe inhabited by words such as 'sacredness', 'inalienable' and so on, religion is being connoted. Only God can fulfil the expectation of the firm ground.[29] But surely that is only a reformulation of the problem: faith – like love – is not borne out of a wish that we had it. However, nor is faith born out of reasons. This is easiest to see in the way attempts to justify rights makes those rights vulnerable to the objections that can be directed against the justifying reasons: do people have a right to free speech because that produces the largest aggregate utility, is in accordance with human nature, or corresponds to popular will? Each explanation encapsulates a contested theory of the political good. As providing such explanation will infect rights with the weaknesses that attach to those theories, they can no longer be used to overrule conflicts between them and their point is lost.[30] Surely we had a right to life even if article 6 of the Covenant on Civil and Political Rights had never been adopted? But, what might that right then be based on? Paradoxically, rights seem effective only if they can be accepted on faith – whose absence provided the very reason for having recourse to them.

Faith cannot be taken for granted. Everyone knows that politics is not 'really' about translating nature's commands into positive law; that at issue is struggle and compromise, power and ideology. The critiques of formalism cannot be undone. Everyone knows that administration and adjudication have to do with discretion and that the outcomes of 'balancing' reflect broad cultural preferences that have nothing inalienable about them.

None of this provides a reason to give up rights talks, for there exists no other language in which political conflict would already have been solved. Despite their incoherence, and the difficulty to justify them, human rights have functioned reasonably well in Western societies because they have been embedded in Western ways of life in the same way as, for example, wearing a tie or shaking hands when meeting. That we in the West feel rights important and are able to interpret them in broadly similar ways is a function of our common history, perhaps a result of our imagining our societies as moral communities – but certainly not any ability we have of grasping the meaning of human 'dignity' or 'sacredness' in some authentic, pre-social sense.[31] That we promote rights is based on nothing grander than satisfaction with the way our own political culture has been able to use them: the universality of human rights boils down to a call: look at us, and think for yourselves if you wouldn't like to live this way, too.[32]

---

[29] However, it is not certain that even God can. For in that case obligation would no longer exist as an atemporal universal but as a person-connected directive whose binding force would necessitate a further assumption about loyalty, MS Moore, 'Good without God' in RB George, *Natural Law, Liberalism and Morality* (Oxford, Oxford University Press, 2001) 260–61.

[30] In more detail, see chapter eight in this volume.

[31] For this argument, see also C Brown, 'Universal Human Rights: A Critique' in Dunne and Wheeler *Human Rights in Global Politics* (1999) 103–27.

[32] See R Rorty, 'Justice as a Larger Loyalty' in P Cheach – B Robbins, *Cosmopolitics: Thinking and Feeling beyond the Nation* (Minneapolis, University of Minnesota Press, 1998) 46, 56–57.

However, does this not take away the universality of rights and make them seem terribly Eurocentric, no longer naturally valid for all societies? Advocating universality now comes to seem just another way of trying to persuade other people to accept preferences I hold dear, social arrangements that I have come to think valuable. If my preferences are a product of my society, what basis do I now have to criticise practices that I find unacceptable in other societies? Between imperialism and indifference, is there anything?

Rights are a product of Western culture and history and their principal propagandists have been Western organisations, activists and academics.[33] But this is a problem only if one thinks that rights are universally good – for it is *that* position that tends to lead into thinking that Western culture is universally good, too. The legacy of rights in Europe – as everywhere – is ambivalent, however. After all, the very creation of a (subjective) rights doctrine in the twelfth and thirteenth century was part of a defence of the possessions of the Catholic Church against the Franciscan doctrine of natural poverty, and both Suárez and Grotius were able to use it to defend (consensual) slavery.[34] Rights, like any institutions, can be used for good and bad purposes; and it is precisely for this reason that they cannot be detached from political debate about such purposes.[35]

Instead of speaking of rights in abstract and universal terms, I prefer to connect them to the professional tradition. As Lauterpacht pointed out, as long as there has been something like an international legal profession, the call for respecting human rights has been a part of it. What he failed to mention was that this had always been in the context of a public law sovereignty of one or another type and this is no wonder. Human rights are rooted in the same terrain as sovereignty and self-determination. The Bill of Rights (1776) and the *Déclaration de droit de l'homme et du citoyen* (1789) were passed in the context of nation-building and claims for non-intervention against outside powers. This was not lost on nineteenth-century lawyers. John Westlake, the leading British internationalist of the period, thought that the State's duties and rights were 'only the duties and rights of the men who compose them'.[36] Johann Caspar Bluntschli, a leading continental public law theorist and cosmopolitan activist, certainly never imagined that there was any conflict between his Prussian nationalism and his defence of individual rights: each was defined in terms of the other.[37] Human rights and nationalism were reconciled in the view that allowed access to humanity through sovereignty. Both assumed that rights were part of national traditions – but also that there were

---

[33] Many have said this. However, useful data is contained in Mutua 'The Ideology of Human Rights' (1996) 607–40.

[34] R Tuck, *Natural Rights Theories. Their Origin and Development* (Cambridge, Cambridge University Press, 1979) 22–24, 56. See further B Tierney, *The Idea of Natural Rights: Studies on Natural Rights, Natural Law and Church Law 1150–1625* (Cambridge, Eerdmans 1997), especially 43–77 (the basis of rights in canon law).

[35] The indispensable work now is D Kennedy, *The Dark Sides of Virtue: Reassessing International Humanitarianism* (Princeton University Press, 2005).

[36] J Westlake, *Chapters on the Principles of International Law* (Cambridge, Cambridge University Press, 1894) 78.

[37] JC Bluntschli, *Das moderne Völkerrecht der civilisierten Staaten* (Beck, Nördlingen, 1887) 20.

universal rights that allowed intervention against tyrannies. Both supported the imperial policies of their homelands. The civilizing mission of the nineteenth century was closely related to the liberal ideology of human rights: the West used it to mold the 'orient' in its own image.

However, after the First World War nationalism became suspect and European intelligentsias turned to individualism. Key members of the profession in the inter-war period – Georges Scelle in France, Hans Kelsen in Austria and Germany and Lauterpacht in England – each saw the individual as the fundamental unit of the international society, too. Coming from sociology, formalism and natural law, each tried to integrate a liberal politics into the international institutions of the period. They did not succeed. However, to draw from this the conclusion that human rights were created in 1948 is to have no understanding of the embeddedness of human rights in liberal reformism that sought a balance between a right to nationhood – sovereignty – and the individual's right to be an equal member of a cosmopolitan world.

Rights in Historical Struggle

Now, this balance has been very fragile. Over again the scales have fallen on one side or another. Universalism has collapsed into imperialism and nationalism into chauvinism. It is easy to see this in four historical contexts.

1. In the sixteenth and seventeenth centuries, the universal pursuits of the Catholic Church were opposed by emerging secular sovereignty as papal ambition in religious disguise: hence the Westphalian system of *cuius regio eius religio*.
2. In the nineteenth century, French revolutionary nationalism upheld the flag of a universally valid *civilisation* against the emerging particularism of (German) national *Kultur* – revealing itself finally as imperial ambition in the neo-colonial wars of Indochina and Algeria in the 1950s and 1960s.
3. Until the First World War, the civilising mission drove a universal 'modernity' against the tribal backwardness of the 'Orient' – only to be later indicted as 'colonialism' against the universality of the right of self-determination in the Third World.
4. However, the right of self-determination, again, tended to turn into a celebration of (egoistic) particularity against the technological and economic modernity that now occupies the place of the universal under the banner of 'globalisation' – while that notion is under attack as merely a generalisation of certain Western habits and privileges against which perhaps a more determined 'identity politics' may seem necessary.

In each case, the claim for the 'universal' revealed a particular policy. To quote a sceptic: 'the intellectual theories and ethical standards of utopianism, far from being the expression of absolute and a priori principles, are historically conditioned, being both products of circumstances and interests and weapons framed for the furtherance of interests'.[38] This is not too far from the critiques put forward by Edmund Burke against the French Revolution in 1790, or Karl Marx in 1843 to temper Bruno Bauer's enthusiasm for 'purely political' emancipation.[39] The abstraction of rights, both argued, was their practical defect. As soon as they were applied in practice, they would support some groups over others. If applied as absolutes – or 'trumps' in the language of political philosophy – then they move the privileges of some from the realm of political contestation altogether: the ambitions of the Jacobins for Burke, the economic system for Marx.

From this perspective, the universality of rights is pure hegemony. A 'particular' takes on the garb of universality: humanitarianism, self-determination, equality of rights, global justice. But the choice is never between that which is universal and that which is particular. The choice is between different *kinds* of particular. To fail to see this is to remain blind to the way the political system makes such choices. If the question is never about realising rights that are 'out there', but always about whom we are to privilege, how scarce resources are to be allocated, then it becomes imperative to articulate the criteria of distribution that underlie such choices. This means not only constant attention to what outcomes political institutions produce and what claims can be heard in them but, in particular, to what extent the human rights vocabulary might contribute to one or another type of systemic bias in this regard.[40]

A Taxonomy of Rights Strategies

Let me finish by outlining five familiar legal strategies for the management of the tension between human rights and sovereignty, or the search for autonomy and community.

Human Rights Formalism

Human rights formalism examines rights as they are laid down in the international instruments adopted within the UN and other organisations since 1948. The question of the historical context or moral legitimacy of rights is deferred. Formal validity is enough, buttressed by commentaries on how rights have been implemented. This is not to say that human rights formalism would be devoid of political commitment. That commitment seeks to show that human rights are not

---

[38] EH Carr, *The Twenty-Years' Crisis 1919–1939* 2nd edn (London, Macmillan, 1946) 68.

[39] E Burke, *Reflections on the Revolution in France* (Stanford, Stanford University Press, JCD Clarke, 2001) 217–21; K Marx, 'On the Jewish Question' in *Early Political Writings* (Cambridge, Cambridge University Press, Joseph O'Malley, 1994) 42–50.

[40] For a useful 'pragmatic' critique, see D Kennedy, 'The International Human Rights Movement; Part of the Problem?' (2001) 3 *European Human Rights Law Review* 245–67. See also my 'International Law in Europe: Between Tradition and Renewal' (on the need to identity these aspects of international law that are today 'kitsch') (2005) *European Journal of International Law* 113–24.

simply parts of utopian morality but that they can be argued as technically as any other piece of law.[41]

However, formalism is not only blind to the problems of field-constitution, indeterminacy, right-exception and conflict. It instrumentalises human rights, making them a weapon of the hegemon in the precise Gramscian sense: the place left open to that which is universal is occupied by the particular interest that is in a position to do so. Think about the process of the UN Racism Conference in Durban in the fall of 2001. For once, the hegemon was neither the United States nor Europe. But this was the exception and nothing will follow from it. Think then about the hundreds of thousands of Africans, and soon perhaps Asians, who will march to an early death by sexually transmitted disease. The only formal rights that apply are those provided by an intellectual property system to multinational pharmaceutics companies to determine the price of their products.

Formalism finds no room for claims beyond the treaties that reflect the policies of states: Durban declaration, the Trade-Related Aspects of Intellectual Property Rights (TRIPS) Agreement. Well-meaning lawyers, of course, use techniques of teleological interpretation, customary law or Latin phrases such as *jus cogens* or *erga omnes* so as to respond to moral concerns – but this is vulnerable to technical arguments concerning the appropriateness of such interpretations. Formalism falls in a limbo: the lay public is non-formalist and unconvinced, while formalist colleagues know that with formal arguments, anything can be proved. Instead of love, exchange relations.

Human Rights Fundamentalism

Human rights fundamentalism feels nostalgia towards natural law. Although it admits that the door to classical humanism is no longer open, it uses language with essentialist notions such as 'liberty', 'human dignity' or 'sacredness'. But fundamentalism mystifies human rights. It uses arguments about natural essences that lead beyond the conventions, techniques and politics of modernity. In this way, it tragically loses its critical character. In trying to set a foundation to rights, it infects rights with the criticism that can be directed against those foundations. What is 'human nature', 'liberty' or 'reason' after all? To make rights conditional on responses to such questions, makes them vulnerable to the extreme. Again, no love – only romantic sentimentalism.

Human Rights Scepticism

Human rights scepticism knows that rights neither exist 'out there' nor can be proved in inter-individually valid ways. Hence, it views human rights as an

---

[41] See M Koskenniemi, 'The Pull of the Mainstream. Review Article on Theodor Meron, Human Rights and Customary International Law' (1990) 88 *Michigan Law Review* 1946–62.

irrationalist strand in liberal theory, 'nonsense upon stilts', to use Bentham's language. Scepticism uses critiques such as I did earlier and draws from them the conclusion that human rights have no role for politics whatsoever. However, scepticism takes its own critique too seriously. It assumes that the only defensible human rights are those that can live up to the extravagant validity claims that it has set. Scepticism is disappointed absolutism. It will fail to create or sustain commitment to anything but one's own (arbitrary) preferences. Rights become another strategic device in what is seen as an irreducible struggle for power. Instead of love, manipulation.

Formalism, fundamentalism and scepticism each believes that it is the task of law to establish, by means of rights, what the proper realm of individual autonomy is as against the demands of community. As each fails to set up such a limit, the opposite dangers appear. Rights either become completely overwhelmed by communal demands, or political culture is turned into an assertion of absolute rights – totalitarianism or identity politics. The lover either loses his or herself completely in the relationship, and is destroyed in the process; or is blocked from experiencing love through an obsessive concern of whether he or she now 'really' has it. *La Traviata* or *Sex and the City.*

Is it possible to deal with rights by reflection of the social context, still providing the rudiments of autonomy?

Cosmopolitan Democracy

Cosmopolitan democracy sees rights as one aspect of an expanding democratic international realm. As the international remains heterogeneous, this theory takes from Kant the view of the international as a confederation of independent republics, not a homogeneous world state. This procedural solution accepts that human rights depend on political decision-making and therefore insists on democratic international procedures and fair play. Three elements form its basis: constitutionalism, democracy and rights: constitution implies a balance of power and rule of law plus a republican commitment, democracy the search for the most inclusive participation of all concerned and rights lay down the moral principles that direct the deliberation within the established structure.[42] Such 'constitutional patriotism' seeks to provide a language through which even marginalised subjects may bring their experiences of pain and injustice to bear on the distribution of material and spiritual resources.

While cosmopolitan democracy has much to speak for the concept of rights embedded in it, it may underestimate the role of institutional power and bad faith. Institutions and procedures have their dangers, as Max Weber pointed out. They, too, may freeze into the justification of privileges. Without an active political realm they may be reduced into a formal façade of public decision-making behind which the private realm remains insulated from rights-claims.[43]

---

[42] See, eg C Niño, *The Constitution of Deliberative Democracy* (Yale University Press, 1996).

[43] See S Marks, *The Riddle of All Constitutions. Democracy, International Law, Democracy and the Critique of Ideology* (Oxford, Oxford University Press, 2000).

Democratic Radicalism

So, cosmopolitan democracy needs to be *radicalised* by an emphasis on the role of power in democratic processes. To assert a right will remain an attempt to fulfil the space of the universal (the meaning of 'right') by what is particular (by what is in one's own interest). There is no innocent space. Every democratic mechanism, too, builds on an exclusion (of the private, of the non-citizen, of the marginalised) and the task would be to bring the principle of exclusion within political contestation.[44] A radical democracy would attack the fixed and harmonious aspect of rights and highlight their role in the struggle for hegemony and in the articulation of antagonisms and exclusions. It would think rights valuable precisely because of the way they combine the particular with an attempt at the universal and thus provide resources for challenging existing hierarchies and exclusions. As said, to claim a right is, after all, more than claiming a benefit. It is to claim in the name of universality: this belongs not only to me but to *everyone in my position.* Thus, it always implies membership in a community, and having the benefit *because of that membership.* This takes nothing away from the contested nature of the particular substance being claimed. The ideal community – that is, the ideal constitution of rights – will remain a horizon that recedes as it is approached. This is why it is so important not to believe that rights can be fixed into permanent institutional structures, and to emphasise the flexibility of rights-rhetoric and its context-dependent usefulness. Rights may not always bring emancipation. But often they can because they are split against themselves: particular and universal at the same time, strong in waging hegemonic struggles, weak in maintaining hegemonic positions. In popular invocations of international law and justice against the faceless forces of globalization, rights are only ambiguously linked with any institutional reforms. Instead, whatever the institution, they imply a claim to hear those that remain outside, and to do this in good faith, and perhaps with an open heart.

Which is why rights are like love. They do not bring harmony or control – but it is for that very reason that even within a community, they may bring freedom.

---

[44] See E Balibar, 'Frontières du monde, frontières de la politique' in M Delbracco– B Pelloile *Du cosmopolitique* (Paris, Harmattan, 2000) 181–202.

167

Part IV

Limits and Possibilities of
International Law

7

Between Impunity and Show Trials

I have been concerned over the enthusiasm with which international lawyers have, over the past two decades, thrown themselves into the 'fight against impunity'. This chapter examines the dark sides of that project, in particular the fragility of the criminal law vocabulary in 'dealing with the past' in a justifiable way. Attention will be especially on the way criminal law will always buttress the hegemony of some contested narrative over others and the political power of those who rely on that narrative for the justification of what they do or have done. Much of the inspiration behind this piece comes from the debates in France about the uses of criminal trials to tell national histories. It was written at the time of the Milošević trial – but as I now follow the trial of Karadžić, or the painful efforts by the International Criminal Court (ICC) to intervene in African crises I find that these arguments remain no less pertinent.

WHEN FORMER PRESIDENT Milošević began his defence at The Hague on Tuesday, 12 February 2002, there was no reason to be surprised by his chosen tactics. By turning the accusing finger towards the West, in particular the members of the North Atlantic Treaty Organisation (NATO), for their alleged complicity in first destroying what Milošević called 'mini-Yugoslavia' (Bosnia-Herzegovina) and in 1999 conducting an aggression against his own country, he aimed to avoid conducting his defence under conditions laid down by his adversaries. At the same time, his manoeuvre highlights, once again, the difficulty of grappling with large political crises by means of individual criminal responsibility and gives reason to interrogate the ability of criminal trial to express or conserve the 'truth' of a complex series of events involving also the often erratic action by major international players, Great Powers, the European Union, the United Nations, and so on. The Milošević trial – like international criminal law generally – oscillates ambivalently between the wish to punish those individually responsible for large humanitarian disasters and the danger of becoming a show trial.

Why Punish?

Bringing Milošević to The Hague has been celebrated as the most significant event in the international efforts to end the culture of impunity, underway since the establishment of the Yugoslavian and Rwandan war crimes tribunals in 1994 and 1995, the adoption of the Statute of the International Criminal Court in 1998 and the commencement of criminal procedures in several countries against former domestic or foreign political leaders. The record of these events is mixed. However, there is no doubt that they manifest a renewed urge today to think about international politics in terms of domestic categories. The universalisation of the Rule of Law calls for the realisation of criminal responsibility in the international as in the domestic sphere. In the liberal image, there should be no outside-of-law: everyone, regardless of formal position, should be accountable for their deeds.[1]

Yet, as Hannah Arendt pointed out during the Nuremberg trials, '[h]anging Göring is certainly necessary but totally inadequate. For this culpability . . . transcends and destroys all legal order'.[2] What she meant, of course, was that sometimes a tragedy may be so great, a series of events of such political or even metaphysical significance, that punishing an individual does not come close to measuring up to it. In nearly all the criminal prosecutions having to do with the crimes against humanity committed during or after the Second World War, some observers have doubted the ability of the criminal law to deal with the events precisely in view of their enormous moral, historical, or political significance.

The philosopher Karl Jaspers, for instance, wrote to Arendt in 1960, a few months before the opening of the Eichmann trial, pointing to the extent to which the events for which he was accused 'stand outside the pale of what is comprehensible in human and moral terms' and that '[s]omething other than law [was] at stake here – and to address it in legal terms [was] a mistake'.[3] The same argument was heard occasionally in connection with the more recent trials in France of Klaus Barbie, 'the butcher of Lyon' in 1987, and of the two Frenchmen Paul Touvier and Maurice Papon, in 1994 and 1998 respectively. Today, it seems clear that even if Milošević had gone to prison that would have been in no way an 'adequate' response to the fact that over 200,000 people lost their lives – while millions more were affected – by the succession of wars in the former Yugoslavia. If the trial had significance, then that significance must lie elsewhere than in the punishment handed out to him.

As this is so plainly evident, it is often argued that trials involving genocide or crimes against humanity are less about judging a person than about establishing the truth of the events. While the prosecution of Adolf Eichmann in Jerusalem in 1961, for example, was almost universally held to be necessary, few thought that the necessity lay in the need of punishing Eichmann, the person. He was, after all, only a cog in the Nazi killing machine. Instead, the trial was held to be necessary

---

[1] The description of the campaign for ending the culture of impunity as an aspect of the legalist-domestic analogy is usefully discussed in G Bass, *Stay the Hand of Vengeance. The Politics of War Crimes Tribunals* (Princeton University Press, 2000) 8–36.

[2] Quoted in N Frei, 'Le retour du droit en Allemagne. La justice et l'histoire contemporaine après l'Holocauste - un bilan provisoire' in F Brayard (ed), *Le génocide des Juifs entre procès et histoire 1943–2000* (Brussels, Éditions complexe, 2000) 57.

[3] L Kohler and H Kohler (eds), *Hannah Arendt – Karl Jaspers. Correspondence 1926–1969* (New York, Knopf, 1996) 410. Quoted also in L Douglas, *The Memory of Judgment. Making Law and History in the Trials of the Holocaust* (Yale University Press, 2001) 174–75. Here Jaspers was undoubtedly drawing upon his *Die Schuldfrage* (1946).

in order to bring to publicity the full extent of the horrors of the 'Nazi war against the Jews',[4] especially as that aspect of the German criminality had, in the view of many, received only insufficient attention in the Nuremberg process. For the State of Israel, the trial was to bring to light a central aspect of the nation's history, and to take a step towards explaining how it all could have happened.[5] What was to be Eichmann's fate after the trial would be of secondary consequence. Indeed, Elie Wiesel suggested that Eichmann should be simply set free, while Arendt advocated handing him over to the United Nations.[6] His death would in no way redress the enormity of the crime in which he had been implicated. It might even diminish the extent to which the special nature of that crime lay in its collective nature as part of the official policy of the German nation.

The view of criminal justice – also the Milošević trial – as an instrument of truth and memory has been stated precisely in response to criticisms about criminal law's apparently obsessive concentration on the accused. This aspect of it was highlighted during the early years of the Yugoslavia Tribunal as it proved impossible to bring those accused of war crimes to trial in The Hague. The Tribunal resorted to the procedure that allows the reading of the indictment in open court and the issuing of an international arrest warrant in the absence of the accused.[7] The reasoning behind a 'tribunal de verbe' as the procedure was opened on 27 June 1996 against Karadžić and Mladić has been summarised as follows:

> Incapable jusqu'ici de rendre la justice, contraint de laisser sans châtiment des crimes contre l'humanité et un génocide, the travail du TPI prenait subitement une réelle consistance: la verité pouvait au moins être dite devant les juges et les victimes reconnues comme telles, face au monde.[8]

Recording 'the truth' and declaring it to the world through the criminal process has been held important for reasons that have little to do with the punishment of the individual. Instead, it has been thought necessary so as to enable the commencement of the healing process in the victims: only when the injustice to which a person has been subjected has been publicly recognised, the conditions for recovering from trauma are present and the dignity of the victim may be restored. Facing the truth of its past is a necessary condition to enable a wounded community – a community of perpetrators and victims – to recreate the conditions of viable social life.[9] Nuremberg, Eichmann and the three French trials (as

---

[4] In her *The Nazi War Against the Jews: 1933–1945* (New York, Bantam, 1975), Lucy Davidowicz stresses the extent to which the Holocaust was not an accidental offshoot, but a deliberate choice of the Hitler regime.

[5] This was certainly the perspective taken by the Prosecutor, Gideon Hausner, whom Arendt saw as simply 'obeying his master', David Ben-Gurion, the Prime Minister. H Arendt, *Eichmann in Jerusalem. A Report on the Banality of Evil* (New York, Penguin, 1963) 5. For an excellent recent discussion of this aspect of the trial, see Douglas, *The Memory of Judgment* (2001) 97, 150–82.

[6] Arendt, *Eichmann* (1963) 270–71.

[7] Rule 61 of the Rules of Tribunal: 'Procedure in case of failure to execute a warrant'.

[8] P Hazan, *La justice face à la guerre. De Nuremberg à la Haye* (Paris, Stock, 2000) 134.

[9] See, eg J Verhoeven, 'Vers un ordre repressif universel?' (1999) 45 *Annuaire français de droit international*, writing about criminal justice in terms of 'une fonction qui l'on dirait "consolatrice", d'ordre thérapeutique et pédagogique . . . la quiétude et la sérénité' 60. In regard to the Rwandan genocide of

well as more recent processes focusing on torture in Algeria) have each been defended as necessary for didactic purposes, for establishing an impartial account of the past and for teaching younger generations of the dangers involved in particular policies.[10]

It is hard to assess the psychological credibility of such justifications. In Germany, the didactic effects of Nuremberg have been obscure. At the time of the process itself 78 per cent of the German population regarded the trial as 'just', while a similar poll four years later showed that only 38 per cent had this opinion. Many reasons must have contributed to such change of perception: allied policy in occupied Germany, attitudes towards de-Nazification and the sense of Nuremberg as victor's justice.[11] German legal literature of the immediate post-war period treated the International Military Tribunal usually as an occupation court (*Besatzungsgericht*) rather than as an international tribunal.[12] The trials held in the American occupation zone during 1946–49, too, were intended 'to reform and re-educate the German people'.[13] However, they were compromised from the outset. Influential members of the US judiciary – including judges from the tribunals themselves – had serious doubts about the constitutionality and procedural fairness of the trials and congressional support for them was thin. Under such conditions, little sympathy could be expected for the trials from the German population.[14] In 1952, only 10 per cent of Germans approved of them:[15] 'To be tried by a Nuremberg Military Tribunal signified at least in the Federal Republic of Germany no dishonour.'[16]

Over the years, the German Government, communities and individuals have taken far-reaching steps to keep alive and come to terms with the memory of the crimes of the Hitler regime.[17] But criminal justice has not been at the forefront of

---

1994, DD Ntanda Nserko, 'Genocidal Conflict in Rwanda and the ICTR' (2001) 48 *Netherlands International Law Review* 62.

[10] For a summary of such justifications, see A Cassese, 'On the Current Trend towards Criminal Prosecution and Punishment for Breaches of International Humanitarian Law' (1998) 9 *European Journal of International Law* 2, 9–10.

[11] Frei, 'Le retour du droit en Allemagne' (2000) 62–67.

[12] S Jung, *Die Rechtsprobleme der Nürnberger Prozesse* (Tübingen, Mohr, 1992) 89–92, 109–11.

[13] FM Buscher, *The U.S. War Crimes Trials Programme in Germany, 1946–1955* (New York, Greenwood, 1989) 69.

[14] During 1946–49, 12 US military tribunals sitting in Nuremberg heard cases of 185–199 defendants (numbers vary according to source), while a US Army European Command set up its own process, conducted at Dachau that tried 1672 individuals. The trials were vehemently criticised by various United States and German organisations. Though the processes ended in a large number of convictions, most of the sentences were later reduced and a large number of the convicted amnestied in 1951. The summary of the historian of those trials is negative: '. . . the war crimes programme did little to change German attitudes. Cries of foul play and "victor's justice" accompanied the proceedings . . . The constant attacks against the Allies, especially the United States as the main instigator of the those proceedings in the late 1940's by Germany's church leaders, politicians, veterans' and refugee organizations demonstrated that the war crimes programme had not reeducated and democratized the Germans'. Buscher, *The US War Crimes Trials Programme* (1989) 22. For the domestic US critiques, see ibid 29–47. For the uses of administrative reviews and amnesties, see ibid 49–89.

[15] Buscher *The US War Crimes Trials Programme* (1989) 91.

[16] Jung, *Die Rechtsprobleme* (1992) 5.

[17] For a detailed review see, eg A Grosser, *Le crime et la mémoire* (Paris, Flammarion, 1989) 87–132.

Vergangenheitsbewältigung. The Auschwitz process that terminated in Frankfurt in 1965 had only slight popular response, despite widespread press and TV coverage. In that same year, the Ministries of Justice of *Länder* commenced a systematic effort to prosecute Nazi criminals: though the annual number of new dossiers arose in peak years to over 2000, the highest number of annual convictions was 39, and declined by 1976 to less than 10 a year.[18] Empirical confirmation about the positive effects of truth-telling is not much more available from other sources, either. The most significant effort in this regard, the South African Truth and Reconciliation Commission (TRC), was hugely controversial when it was set up, and much of that controversy persists. In a recent poll in South Africa, only 17 per cent of the interviewed persons felt that the process had had a positive effect, while altogether two thirds expressed the opinion that race relations after the TRC had deteriorated.[19]

Undoubtedly, many kinds of truth may be sought through criminal trials. The 'denial of the Holocaust', for instance, has been criminalised in a number of countries in part to honour the memory of the victims and in part to uphold the conventions of truthfulness and good faith that found the discursive basis of the State. The 1985 law in the Federal Republic of Germany that prohibits 'lying about Auschwitz' not only seeks to preserve the memory of the Holocaust but also, and perhaps above all, the legitimacy of the new Germany by keeping open the gap between it and its Nazi predecessor.[20] The more distant the events, the more fragile their truth becomes and thus, it may seem, the more necessary it will be to protect it by the law. Yet, as Lawrence Douglas points out, the agnostic formalism of the law that accepts all historical accounts as prima facie of equal value may, in an adversarial process, end up inadvertently legitimating 'negationism' as a position on which reasonable men may disagree.[21]

In a similar way, the strategy chosen by Milošević in The Hague reveals the danger of thinking about international criminal trials in historical or didactic terms. This was the gist of Arendt's controversial critique of the Eichmann trial. For her, the trial's problems arose from the introduction of historical, political, and educational objectives into it:

> The purpose of the trial is to render justice, and nothing else; even the noblest ulterior purposes – 'the making of a record of the Hitler regime . . .' can only detract from the law's main business: to weigh the charges brought against the accused, to render judgment and to mete out due punishment.[22]

---

[18] See A Rückerl, *NS-Verbrechen vor Gericht. Versuch einer Vergangenheitsbewältigung* (Heidelberg, Müller, 1984) 330; Grosser, *Le crime* (1989) 112–13, 121.

[19] E Kiss, 'Moral Ambition Within and Beyond Political Constraints. Reflections on Restorative Justice' in RJ Rotberg and D Thompson (eds), *Truth v Justice. The Morality of Truth Commissions* (Princeton, Princeton University Press, 2000) 88 and Rotberg ibid 19.

[20] L Douglas, 'Régenter le passé: Le négationnisme et la loi' in F Brayard (ed), *Le génocide des Juifs enter process et histoire et histoire 1943–2000* (2000) 218–23.

[21] Douglas, 'Régenter le passé' (2000) 227–38.

[22] Arendt, *Eichmann* (1963) 251.

By contrast, Arendt wrote, the Eichmann trial had become a 'show trial',[23] staged by the Prime Minister, David Ben-Gurion, to support political motives which had nothing to do with criminal trials as Arendt understood them, as being about the guilt or innocence of individuals.

But should Arendt have the final word? Many of the problems of applying criminal law in response to massive injustice have become evident in the reactions to her critiques. Surely, as many of those involved in the process that led to the signature of the Statute for the International Criminal Court in 1998 seem to have assumed, the value of the new court lies in its deterrent message, the way in which it serves to prevent future atrocities.[24] The force of this argument is, however, doubtful. In the first place, if crimes against humanity really emerge from what Kant labelled 'radical evil', an evil that exceeds the bounds of instrumental rationality, that seeks no objective beyond itself, then by definition, calculations about the likelihood of future punishment do not enter the picture. Indeed, there is no calculation in the first place. However, even if one remained suspicious about the metaphysics of 'radical evil' (as Arendt herself later became) the deterrence argument would still fail to convince inasmuch as the atrocities of the twentieth century have not emerged from criminal intent but as offshoots from a desire to do good.[25] This is most evident in regard to the crimes of communism, the Gulag, the Ukraine famine, liquidation of the 'Kulaks'. But even the worst Nazi nightmares were connected to a project to create a better world. Commenting upon the speeches of Heinrich Himmler to the SS in 1942, Alain Besançon concluded that even the death camps were operated 'au nom d'un bien, sous le couvert d'une morale'.[26] However, if the acts do not evidence criminal intent, and instead come about as aspects of ideological programmes that strive for the good life, however far in the future, or to save the world from a present danger, then the deterrence argument seems beside the point.[27] In such case, criminal law itself will come to seem a part of the world which must be set aside, an aspect of the 'evil' that must be eradicated.

As criminal lawyers know well, fitting crimes against humanity or other massive human rights violations into the deterrence frame requires some rather implausible psychological generalisations. Either the crimes are aspects of political normality – Arendt's 'banality of evil' – in which case there is no *mens rea*, or they take place in exceptional situations of massive destruction and personal danger when

---

[23] ibid 4–5.

[24] Thus one advocate: '... punishment of war criminals should be motivated primarily by its deterrent effect, by the impetus it gives to improved standards of international conduct'. CM Bassiouni, *Crimes against Humanity in International Law* (The Hague, Nijhoff, 1992) 14. A particularly thoughtful argument is in P Akhavan, 'Beyond Impunity. Can International Criminal Justice Prevent Future Atrocities?' (2001) 95 *American Journal of International Law* 7–31.

[25] See especially T Todorov, *Mémoire du mal – tentation du bien* (Paris, Robert Laffont, 2000).

[26] A Besançon, *Le malheur du siècle. Sur le communisme, le nazisme et l'unicité de la Shoah* (Paris, Fayard, 1998) 45.

[27] See J Klabbers, 'Just Revenge? The Deterrence Argument in International Criminal Law' (2000) 12 *Finnish Yearbook of International Law* 269–67.

there is little liberty of action.[28] This is not to say that in such cases, people act as automatons, losing capacity for independent judgment. Many studies have elucidated the way individuals react to pressure created by either normality or exceptionality, and are sometimes able to resist. However, it is implausible to believe that criminal law is able to teach people to become heroes, not least because what 'heroism' might mean in particular situations is often at the heart of the confrontation between the political values underlying the criminal justice system (perhaps seen as victors' justice) and the system that is on trial.

Then there is of course the very politics behind the establishment and functioning of a tribunal in the aftermath of a great crisis that may not always support the grandiloquent rhetoric that accompanies, on the victors' side, the work of justice so conveniently underwriting their views and post-conflict preferences. By the end of the 1940s, Allied preferences had shifted dramatically. There was no political support for the trials of German industrialists and proceedings against high-ranking professional soldiers were followed with some embarrassment. Fear of communism, Germanophilia, sometimes anti-Semitism, as well as administrative problems connected with further punishments, made the principal Allied powers wary of further purges in Germany and keen to establish normal relations with it.[29] At least some of this supported the widespread German opposition to the Allied war crimes trial programme of 1946–49: 'Germans saw themselves as victims and not as perpetrators'.[30]

In the Yugoslavian situation, too, it may not be exclusively the result of manipulation by the local leaders that the populations often seem to have little faith in the truth propounded by the Tribunal. The fluctuation of Western support, the visible impunity enjoyed by a large number of important Balkan war criminals, and the failure to prosecute the NATO bombings of Serbia of 1999 have provided space for cynicism and denial. Four years after the horrors of Srebrenica, Serbs residing in the area persist in claiming that '[n]othing happened here . . . It is all propaganda'.[31]

For such reasons, studies on the transformations of authoritarian regimes into more or less liberal democracies in central and eastern Europe, South America and South Africa have suggested a much more complex understanding of the role of criminal trials as not merely about punishment or retribution, nor indeed about deterrence, but as an aspect of a larger 'transitional justice' that, in the words of one commentator, sometimes 'perform[. . .] a successful "final judgement" in the religious sense, a performance that would ultimately enable the state itself to function as a moral agent'.[32] Under this view, it is the symbolism of the criminal trial

---

[28] For a recent analysis, see I Tallgren, 'The Sensibility and Sense of International Criminal Law' (2002) 13 *European Journal of International Law* 561–95.

[29] See D Bloxham, *Genocide on Trial, War Crimes Trials and the Formation of Holocaust History and Memory* (Oxford, Oxford University Press, 2001) 38–56.

[30] Buscher *The US War Crimes Trials Programme* (1989) 110.

[31] Hazan, *La justice* (2000) 245–47.

[32] J Borneman, *Settling Accounts. Violence, Justice and Accountability in Postsocialist Europe* (Princeton, Princeton University Press, 1997) 23.

– and the eventual judgment – that enables the community ritually to affirm its guiding principles and thus to become a workable 'moral community'.

But no uniform jurisprudence has emerged on the use of criminal trials of former political leaders in transition situations. Perhaps the main generalisation that can be made is that such trials have been few, they have been targeted very selectively, the convictions have been moderate and amnesties have been widely used.[33] The legal principles have been vigorously contested, the main controversy focusing on to what extent such trials are only political instruments to target former adversaries on the basis of laws that were not in force at the time they were acting. However, whether the trials use super positive law (such as the 'Radbruch formula' in Germany) or retrospective interpretation of pre-transition law,[34] it seems clear that in order to attain the symbolic, community-creating effect it is supposed to have, criminal law need not be applied to everyone. It is sufficient that a few well published trials are held at which the 'truth' of the past is demonstrated, the victims' voices are heard and the moral principles of the (new) community are affirmed.[35]

This may sometimes become a logistic necessity, too. In 1946, for instance, over 100,000 suspected war criminals resided in the British and American occupation zones in Germany. In 2001, the Rwandan prisons housed approximately 120,000 detainees. A full trial of each individual was, in both cases, an impossibility. In the Rwandan situation, an attempt was being made to use 'Gacaca courts', popular tribunals akin to truth commissions to expedite the work of justice and the prospect of reconciliation.[36] Clearly, at least sometimes victims do not so much expect punishment (although of course that is not insignificant) than a recognition of the fact that what they were made to suffer was 'wrong', and that their moral grandeur is symbolically affirmed.[37] For such purposes, 'show trials' are quite sufficient, especially if they are supplemented with other measures such as compensations, disqualifications, administrative measures, truth commissions, opening of archives, etc. However, such supplementary measures are not available at the international level. Here is the problem with the analogy between international courts and transitional justice. The reasons that make 'show trials' – that is to say, trials of only few political leaders – acceptable, even beneficial, at the national level, while others are granted amnesty, are not present when criminal justice is conducted at the international plane. When trials are conducted by a foreign prosecutor, and before foreign judges, no moral community is being affirmed beyond the elusive and self-congratulatory 'international community'. Every failure to prosecute is a scandal, every judgment

[33] See RG Teitel, *Transitional Justice* (Oxford, Oxford University Press, 2000) especially 51–59.

[34] For this controversy after German unification, especially in relation to the GDR border guard trials and the trials of Honecker and the former *Politbüro* members, see J McAdams, *Judging the Past in Unified Germany* (Cambridge University Press, 2001) 23–54.

[35] Teitel, *Transitional Justice* (2000) 46–49, 66.

[36] See KC Moghadli, 'No Peace without Justice. The Role of International Criminal and Humanitarian Law in Conflict Settlement and Reconciliation' paper given at a conference 'From Impunity to a Culture of Accountability' (Utrecht 26–28 November 2001).

[37] See, eg P Bouretz, 'Prescription: table ronde du 22 janvier 1999' (2000) 31 *Droits* 53.

too little to restore the dignity of the victims, and no symbolism persuasive to justify the drawing of a thick line between the past and the future.[38]

In other words, if the argument from deterrence is unpersuasive as a justification of international criminal justice, and if the symbolic, community-creative rationales can be invoked only with the greatest difficulty, the temptation is great to see the point of the Milošević trial in its truth-telling function, against the critiques by Arendt and others. Perhaps, the argument might go, the trial was important neither because it might have end up punishing Milošević , because it made potential dictators or their henchmen think twice, nor because it enabled the recreation of Balkan societies as moral communities. Perhaps, we might think, the significance of this 'trial of the century' lay in the way it brought to general knowledge the truth of what really happened – however and by whom that 'truth' may then have been used by anyone at the national or the international level.

Of Truth and Context

As criminal lawyers have always known, legal and historical truths are far from identical. The wider the context in which individual guilt has to be understood, and the more such understanding defers to the contingencies of historical interpretation, the more evident the limits of criminal procedure for reaching the 'truth'.[39] One of the few uncontroversial merits of truth commissions vis-à-vis criminal justice has been stated to lie in the way the former are able to canvass much more widely and deeply the criminality under scrutiny and thus to offer more 'opportunities for closure, healing and reconciliation'.[40] This is not to say that there would be no intrinsic relationship between the two types of truth, historical and criminal. In the domestic society, and in the context of a domestic criminal trial, that relationship rarely becomes questioned. Even if a crime is exceptionally shocking – 'serial killing' for example – there is normally little doubt about how to understand the relevant acts in their historical context. The only problem is 'did the accused do it'? No further question about how to understand what he did, how to place his behaviour in relation to the overall behaviour of those around him, emerges. The truth of the broader context is one, or at least relatively uncontested. In transitional periods, however, the debate about past normality takes on a contested, political aspect. How to deal with the routine spying by citizens of one another, shooting at those wishing to escape, or systematic liquidation of political opponents? How to judge the actions of individuals living and working in a 'criminal' normality (*Unrechtstaat*): how much 'heroism' is

---

[38] For this criticism in regard to the International Criminal Tribunal for the former Yugoslavia (ICTY), see Hazan *La justice* (2000) 239–63.

[39] See M Wildt, 'Des vérités qui diffèrent. Historiens et procureurs face aux crimes de Nazis' in Brayard (2000) 251–57. See also D Lochak, 'Prescription, remarques dans une table ronde du 22 janvier 1999' (2000) 31 Droits 49–54.

[40] Kiss, 'Moral Ambition' (2000) 69.

needed? What about (mere) passivity? And last but not least – can those who have not lived under such conditions judge?[41]

Much of this applies in the international sphere, too, where problems of interpretation are even more difficult. For any major event of international politics – and situations where the criminal responsibility of political leaders is invoked are invariably such – there are many truths and many stakeholders for them. In the Milošević trial, for instance, the narrative of 'Greater Serbia' collided head-on with the self-determination stories of the seceding populations, while historical assessments of 'socialism' and 'nationalism' competed with long-term historical and even religious frames of explanation. Much of the Western view depends on a (liberal) understanding of the sombre effects of the atavistic irrationalism underlying the different Balkan identifications – a view that dramatically plays down the political aspects of the conflict and the role of interest-groups (including the liberal one) in fomenting ethnic hostility. How to understand the actions of the leaders of the Yugoslav communities – whether they were 'criminal' or not – depends on which framework of interpretation one accepts.[42]

Political Realists such as Hans Morgenthau always highlighted the weaknesses of the legal process in coming to grips with large events of international politics. Already in 1929, Morgenthau concluded that the role of formal dispute settlement had to remain limited in the international context because it inevitably focused only on some, by itself, minor aspect of an overall situation. A legal 'dispute' for him was always just a part – and sometimes a very marginal part – of what he called a political 'tension'.[43] The narrower the focus, the less the process would convey any in-depth understanding of the situation and the less reason to think that it will bring about a credible political result. As the legal process inevitably distorted the political context, it was not only useless but counterproductive for the purpose of providing a basis for peace and reconciliation.

The effort to end the 'culture of impunity' emerges from an interpretation of the past – the Cold War in particular – as having taken an unacceptably political approach to international crises. Focusing on the individual abstracts the political context, that is to say, describes that context in terms of the actions and intentions of particular, well-situated individuals. Indeed, this is precisely what the Prosecutor in the Milošević trial, Carla del Ponte, said she was doing in the Hague in February 2002. The (Serb) nation was not on trial, only an individual was. The truth, however, is not necessarily served by an individual focus.[44] On the contrary, the meaning of historical events often exceeds the intentions or actions of particular

[41] For discussion of this difficulty in the German situation, see Bornemann, *Settling Accounts* (1997) 80–96, 99–100; McAdams, *Judging the Past* (2001) 47–54.

[42] For the role of such interpretations in the Milošević trial, see K Cavoski, 'Juger l'histoire' in PM Gallois and J Vergès (eds), *L'apartheid judiciaire au TPI, arme de guerre* (Lausanne, L'âge d'homme, 2002) 77–89.

[43] H Morgenthau, *Die internationale Rechtspflege, ihr Wesen und ihre Grenzen* (Leipzig, Noske, 1929) 62–72 and passim. For the general context and a discussion, see M Koskenniemi, *The Gentle Civilizer of Nations. The Rise and Fall of International Law 1870–1960* (Cambridge, Cambridge University Press, 2002) 440–45.

[44] Wildt 'Des vérités' (2000) 251.

individuals and can be grasped only by attention to structural causes, such as economic or functional necessities, or a broad institutional logic through which the actions by individuals create social effects. Typically, among historians, the 'intentionist' explanations of the destruction of European Jewry are opposed by 'functional' explanations that point to the material and structural causes that finally at the Wannsee conference of 1942 – but not until then – turned Nazi policy towards full-scale extermination. When Arendt and others were criticising the Eichmann trial, they pointed to the inability of an individual focus to provide an understanding of the way the Shoah did not come about as a series of actions by deviant individuals with a criminal mind, but through *Schreibtisch* acts by obedient servants of a criminal state.

This is why individualisation is not neutral in its effects. Use of terms such as 'Hitlerism' or 'Stalinism' leaves the political, moral and organisational structures intact that are the necessary condition of the crime.[45] To focus on individual leaders may even serve as an alibi for the population at large to relieve itself from responsibility. Something of this took place in the trials of Nazi criminals in Germany after World War II. The failure of the Allied powers to agree on a 'trial of industrialists' may have reflected emerging concern in the West about the appearance of a new enemy – the Soviet Union – and the need to enlist a democratic Germany on their side. But it dramatically downplayed the degree of participation by German economy and society in the Nazi crimes.[46] As the prosecutions moved to German courts, Allied legislation, particularly Control Council Law No 10, was set aside as contrary to the principle of non-retroactivity. Recourse was had to the German Penal Law whose relevant provisions had to do with murder and manslaughter. These described the relevant criminality in purely individual terms. Murder, under the interpretation of the *Bundesgerichtshof*, had to take place with a 'murderous intent' (*Mordlust*) or 'in a malicious and brutal manner' in a way that completely failed to grasp the kind of writing-desk action of which most Nazi criminality consisted and in which individuals could (rightly) believe themselves as fully replaceable if they did not carry out their tasks in accordance with the rules which were criminal.[47] By the time of the Auschwitz trials in Frankfurt in 1963–65, the crime of manslaughter had already been subject to the statute of limitations so that the defendants could only be tried for murder, and because of a definition of murder that referred to individual intent failed to apply to any but the most brutal operators of the extermination system, most of the Nazis not only escaped judgment but were integrated as loyal citizens of the Bonn Republic.[48]

The point here is not to try to settle the epistemological controversy about whether the individual or the contextual (functional, structural) focus provides

---

[45] As pointed out in Grosser *Le crime* (1989) 76–77.

[46] See Bloxham, *Genocide on Trial* (2001) 28–32.

[47] For an account of the procedural difficulties in prosecuting former Nazis in Germany under the common criminal law, see Rückerl, *NSVerbrechern vor Gericht* (1984) 261–88.

[48] See DO Pendas, '"Auschwitz, je ne savais pas ce que c'était". Le procés d'Auschwitz à Francfort et l'opinion public allemande' in Brayard (ed), *Le genocide des Juifs entre procès et histoire 1943–2000* (2000) 85–93. See also Douglas *The Memory of Judgment* (2001) 188–90.

the better truth but, rather, that neither can a priori override the other and that in some situations it is proper to focus on individuals, while in other cases – such as Nazi criminality, and perhaps in taking stock of Stasi collaboration in the German Democratic Republic (GDR) – the context provides the better frame of interpretation. However, if that is so, then there is no guarantee that a criminal process a priori oriented towards individual guilt such as the Milošević trial necessarily enacts a lesson of historical truth. On the contrary, it may rather obstruct this process by exonerating from responsibility those larger (political, economic, even legal) structures within which the conditions for individual criminality have been created – within which the social normality of a criminal society is created.

As the German historian Martin Broszat pointed out, the 'one-sided personalisation' and rigid conceptualisation of criminal categories may lead not only to a different kind of truth but also a different way of distributing accountability from that produced by a contextually oriented historical study in a situation such as Germany under the Hitler regime.[49] If one is participating in a collective venture with a sense of historical mission and a moral purpose ('happiness of mankind') such as 'communism', for instance, then little is gained by a retrospective interpretation of the effects of that effort – between 85 to 100 million innocent killed – in terms of the evil acts of some number of individuals. The logic of 'tentation du bien, memoire de mal' at work in communism can only be reached through trying to grasp the collective process that combines utopianism and scientism with a revolutionary spirit.[50]

In the end, however, individualisation is also impossible. After all, the defences available to the accused refer precisely to the context in which his or her acts were undertaken. Was there an acceptable motive or an alternative course of action? Did the victim contribute to the action?[51] What about the acts of the Croatian Militia in Krajina or Eastern Slavonia at the beginning of the war, or the UKC in Kosovo? What was the chain of command that led to the Omarska camp or the Srebrenica massacre? As a journalist commenting on the Račak inquiry during the Milošević trials observed:

> Even among experts who loathe Mr Milošević, there are worries over whether the proceedings may look like victors' justice and whether the prosecutor, Carla Del Ponte, can deliver the evidence that draws a direct line between Mr Milošević and bodies like those uncovered here.[52]

To create that chain will, in the absence of written orders, have to involve broad interpretations and assumptions about the political and administrative culture in

---

[49] H Graml and K-D Henke, *Nach Hitler. Der schwierige Umgang mit unserer Geschichte. Beitrage von Martin Broszat* (Munich, Oldenbourg, 1987) 47–49.
[50] Todorov, *Mémoire* (2000) 36–41; Besançon, *Malheur* (1998) 59–64.
[51] Even the individualisation of guilt is a policy – namely a policy of collective impunity. 'We have to individualize the guilt', said Ivan Djordjevic, a former dissident lawyer and an official in Serbia's Ministry of Internal Affairs. 'Otherwise we have this feeling of collective guilt, that this whole nation had the goal of eliminating other people and killing. Not all of us supported this', *New York Times* (11 February 2002).
[52] *New York Times* (11 February 2002).

the territory, including personal links and expectations between the various protagonists. In this way, even focus on individuals presumes a larger context in which
particular individuals rise to key positions and in which their choices and preferences are formulated and come to seem either as 'normal' or 'deviant'. The acts of
former Nazis or the Communist Party *Politburo* – or perhaps more mundanely,
Stasi agents or members of *apartheid* hit-squads – were not anti-social in the way
of regular criminality but part of the political 'normality' of criminal societies.
This is precisely why Milošević was able to reveal the hypocrisy in the Prosecutor's
position: the trial is a trial of the Serbian nation inasmuch as his acts were part of
(and not a deviation from) the social normality of Serbia's recent past.

It is at this point that the strategy chosen by Milošević receives its full significance, and tends to demonstrate the limits of the criminal trial as an instrument of
material truth and political reconciliation. When a trial concerns large political
events, it will necessarily involve an interpretation of the context which is precisely
what is disputed in the individual actions that are the object of the trial.[53] To accept
the terms in which the trial is conducted – what deeds are singled out, who is being
accused – is to already accept one interpretation of the context among those
between which the political struggle has been waged. This is what Jean-François
Lyotard has famously called a *Différend* – a situation in which to accept a method
or criterion of settlement is already to have accepted the position of one of the
disputing sides:

> A case of differend between two parties takes place when the 'regulation' of the conflict
> that opposes them is done in the idiom of one of the parties while the wrong suffered by
> the other is not signified in that idiom.[54]

In case of a differend, everything is at stake and the context is always a part of the
dispute itself. To understand the German bombing of Coventry and Birmingham
in November 1940, with over 1200 victims as a war crime, but not to see one in the
carpet bombing of Germany that resulted in perhaps 600,000 civilian deaths is
possible only if one already accepts the truth of the Allied view. Not to condemn
Germany, and only Germany, would have put into question the justice of the
Allied cause itself. The Nuremberg idiom presumed that the war had been launched
as Axis aggression and that every atrocity in the war came about as a consequence
of it.

If individual criminality always presumes some context, and it is the context
which is in dispute, then it is necessary for an accused such as Milošević to attack
the context that his adversaries offer to him. This is where a trial becomes inevitably
a history lesson and the dispute at the heart of it a political debate about the plausibility of the historical 'interpretations'. Blaming the destruction of Yugoslavia,

---

[53] As Charles Leben observed, the ordinary relationship between fact and context breaks down in
large political crimes. Judges may no longer confine themselves within the former, historians within the
latter: in judging the facts, judges also judge the context. 'Remarques dans un débat de table ronde le
22 janvier 2000' (2000) 31 *Droits* 64.
[54] J-F Lyotard, *The Différend. Phrases in Dispute* (translated by G Van Den Abbeele, University of
Minnesota Press, 1988) 9.

and the atrocities committed in what had been its territory, on Western policy, as Milošević did, plays upon complex structural causalities and long-term interpretations which are hard to consider within a formal trial. But it is imperative to notice that as long as the chain of causality to individual atrocities has not been established, to put the blame on Milošević plays upon equally complex assumptions and interpretations. The fact that Milošević was on trial, and not Western leaders, presumed the correctness of the Western view of the political and historical context. As the context is part of the political dispute, the trial of Milošević could only, from the latter's perspective, be a show trial participation in which will already mean the admission of Western victory.

There is no doubt that The Hague trials are an effect of Western policy. The Tribunal would not have come to existence without pressure from the Clinton administration and quarters in the French Government.[55] But the West should not be allowed to remain confident that its version of the recent history of the Yugoslavian populations will be automatically vindicated. A trial that 'automatically' vindicates the position of the Prosecutor is a show trial in the precise Stalinist sense of that expression. This, after all, was the source of the embarrassment of the Western judges at Nuremberg when their Soviet colleague at the beginning of the trial toasted to the prospect that 'they will all hang'.[56] To avoid looking like Vyshinsky, the judges not only must allow Milošević to speak, but take what he says seriously. They will have to accept being directed by Milošević into the context within which he will construct his defence in terms of patriotic anti-imperialism. As the political and historical 'truth' of the Balkans becomes one aspect of the trial, then the West must accept that some – perhaps quite a bit – of responsibility will be assigned to its weak and contradictory policy. The bombing of Serbia in the spring of 1999 that caused around 500 civilian casualties will become one of the relevant factors.[57] The Tribunal cannot ignore the question of whether that was a reasonable price to pay for flying at high altitudes so as to avert danger to NATO pilots.[58] But who can tell how far in the past the chain of political causality leads, Milošević had only lived to reveal his interpretation as to why the West rejected him as an acceptable interlocutor?

In the course of the trial Milošević conducted his defence less in order to save himself than in order to get his version of truth across to the public in Serbia, as well as to 'history' by and large. He portrayed himself not unlike the Armenian Tehlirian who in Berlin in 1921 shot to death Talaat Bey, one of those responsible

---

[55] For the diplomatic history, see Hazan *La justice face à la guerre*. (2000) 55–77.

[56] Vyshinsky, as reported in T Taylor, *The Anatomy of the Nuremberg Trials. A Personal Memoir* (Boston, Little and Brown, 1992) 211.

[57] For the view of the Prosecutor that although 'some mistakes' were made, no violations of humanitarian law were involved, see the Annual Report of the ICTY Doc A/55/273 (2000) 30–31 para 192. The legality of the bombing has, however, been severely contested within humanitarian organisations, among them the International Committee of the Red Cross (ICRC). For the contents of a confidential memorandum by the ICRC, see Hazan *La justice face à la guerre*. (2000), 219–23.

[58] See C Samary, 'Comparution de M Slobodan Milosevic, Les incohérences du Tribunal pénal international', *Le Monde Diplomatique* (20 juillet 2001) www.mondediplomatique.fr/cahier/kosovo/samary0701.

for the Armenian genocide of 1915, and gave himself up to the police so as to be tried and in the trial to have the occasion to give publicity the cause of the Armenian people. We may agree that the punishment of one man is incommensurable with the atrocities committed in the Former Yugoslavia. We are not, however, entitled to forget that this man, too, may share the sense of his own insignificance, and choose to play not for acquittal, but for truth and history.

Having finally moved away from the Scylla of impunity – however incoherently and in response to external pressure – the West is now heading either towards a lesson in history and politics in which its own guilt will have to be assessed, or to the Charybdis of show trials.[59] Whether or not Milošević was finally indicted only because the West had decided that it no longer needed him, and to provide support for its bombing campaign, once the trial had commenced, it had lost full control of where it might lead. The West may have erred in believing that the international 'truth' is the same as its domestic truth. As soon as the trial will be about the context, the West can no longer remain confident that its version will be automatically vindicated – unless, of course, it will prefer to have a show trial.

A Short History of History Lessons

The idea of the trial as a didactic process, a process of learning the truth about the events on trial has frequently been voiced. The French Prosecutor François de Menthon, for example, addressed the Nuremberg Tribunal with the following words:

> The work of justice is equally indispensable for the future of the German people. These people have been for many years intoxicated by Nazism . . . Their re-education is indispensable . . . The initial condemnation of Nazi Germany by your High Tribunal will be a first lesson to these people and will constitute the best starting point for the work of revision of values and of re-education which must be its great concern during the coming years . . .[60]

But the truth to which the Germans were to be educated at Nuremberg followed from controversial choices about how to focus the Allied case. In his four-hour indictment, De Menthon himself referred to the destruction of the Jews in only one sentence and not once to the Vichy régime, thus helping to build the Gaullist myth of the French nation united by la résistance.[61] Above all, however, the energetic pursuit of United States' priorities by Robert Jackson in preparing the trial

---

[59] For aspects of that guilt, see chapter four of the present volume.
[60] Quoted in M Marrus, *The Nuremberg War Crimes Trial 1945–46. A Documentary History* (Boston, Bedford, 1997) 90.
[61] ibid 88; Bloxham *Genocide on Trial*, (2001) 101–02. But de Menthon's alternate Edgar Faure went to great detail in researching and describing the persecution of the Jews and other crimes against humanity in the West. See A Wieviorka, 'La France et le procès de Nuremberg' in A Wieviorka (ed), *Les procès de Nuremberg et de Tokio* (Bruxelles, Complexe, 1996) 62–77.

led to the principal charge becoming that of the Nazis having prepared and carried out an aggressive war. As a consequence, the atrocities on the civilians – 'crimes against humanity' – were divested of an independent role and became relevant only to the extent they had been carried out after 1939 and 'in execution of any crime within the jurisdiction of the tribunal'. As Jackson himself put it in June 1945: 'Our case against the major defendants is concerned with the Nazi master plan, not with individual barbarities or perversions which occurred independently of any central plan.'[62]

Such an emphasis – until the end disputed by the French Judge Donnedieu de Vabres – downplayed the significance of the attacks on civilian populations and especially the racially motivated persecutions, carried out alongside and to a large extent independently of the war effort. As also the controversial charge of 'common plan or conspiracy' under which members of Nazi organisations were to be tried was finally and perhaps somewhat absent-mindedly linked only to the aggressive war charge (thus undermining the original idea of covering also the pre-1939 persecutions),[63] the result was an interpretation of the Nazi regime as predominantly one of aggressive militarists that put its racist and genocidal character in a secondary and at times almost invisible role.[64] For instance, Belzec, Sobibor and Treblinka, at which 1,7 million Jews were destroyed, shared between them only one fleeting reference during the trial.[65] The industrial mechanism of mass killings was completely overshadowed by the Prosecution's concentration on the 'common plan' and 'aggression' charges. As the historian Michael Marrus observed: 'Distortion and exaggeration were indeed the results – creating an unreal picture for subsequent historians'.[66]

The historical truth of Nuremberg came about through a complex play of national priorities, available evidence and interpretation. Among the trial's more embarrassing moments was a partial accommodation of the Russians' wish to avoid references to the Ribbentrop Pact that had divided the spheres of interest between Germany and the Soviet Union in August 1939 and whose existence was only indirectly affirmed through the examinations of Ribbentrop himself and Ambassador Ernst von Weizsäcker.[67] The British, too, had their skeleton in a closet, and it was only due to the defence counsels' persistence that it transpired in Admiral Erich Raeder's examination, that the reason for Germany's attack on Norway in 1940 was to forestall a planned attack by Britain. 'On these matters', Telford Taylor later observed, 'the tribunal was engaging in half-truths, if indeed there are such things'.[68]

---

[62] Jackson, '6 June 1945' as cited in Marrus, *The Nuremberg War Crimes Trial* (1997) 42.

[63] See Taylor, *The Anatomy of Nuremberg Trials* (1992) 75–76.

[64] For a critique, see Douglas *The Memory of Judgment* (2001), 48–56.

[65] Bloxham *Genocide on Trial* (2001) 108–10.

[66] Marrus, *The Nuremberg War Crimes Trial* (1997) 127. For a sustained description and criticism of the emphasis in the IMT and the successor trials, see Bloxham *Genocide on Trial* (2001) especially 57–128.

[67] Marrus *The Nuremberg War Crimes Trial* (1997) 134–39.

[68] Taylor *The Anatomy of Nuremberg Trials* (1992) 555. See also M Messerschmidt, 'La quête de la responsabilité . . .' in Wieviorka, *Les procès* (1996) 91–92. Other famous 'oversights' include the Allied

Nuremberg demonstrates the limits of criminal trial as an instrument of 'truth' above all in its treatment of the destruction of European Jewry. As Lawrence Douglas has recently shown, as the documentary *Nazi Concentration Camps* which was made directly after the liberation of the camps and which includes the famous images of mountains of naked bodies bulldozed into mass graves, was screened in Nuremberg for the first time, the voice behind the images spoke of excesses in war and political brutality, thus highlighting war crimes instead of crimes against humanity.[69] It is not necessary to interpret this as manipulation of the evidence. It took years until the full extent of the Jewish catastrophe was revealed to the victors. However, it does highlight the problem that as a trial writes history in the immediate aftermath of the events, its interpretation will be based on fragmentary evidence and influenced by interpretations by contemporaries with a concrete stake in the result.[70]

The *Eichmann* trial attempted to correct what was felt in Israel as insufficient weight given at Nuremberg to the Nazi policy against the Jews. This time, *Nazi Concentration Camps* was screened as evidence of the atrocities against Jews. However, this was not its only purpose and many observers have criticised the way the trial was used to bolster the self-confidence of the newly created Israeli State by focusing away from the image of Jews as helpless victims driven like lambs to slaughter and to bring to light stories of Jewish resistance and heroism.

In this regard, the story of the French use of the concept of 'crimes against humanity' in the controversial trial of Paul Touvier is perhaps even more illustrative. In 1964, when the prospect of former Nazi criminals escaping trial due to passing of the 20-years' prescription period appeared on the horizon, the French National Assembly enacted a law on the non-prescription of crimes against humanity.[71] What were to be held as such had been defined by the Cour de cassation in 1985 as:

all inhuman acts and persecutions which, in the name of a state practicing a policy of ideological hegemony, have been committed systematically, not only against persons because of their membership in a racial or religious group, but also against the opponents of this policy, whatever the form of their opposition.[72]

terror bombing of German cities and, of course, Hiroshima and (especially) Nagasaki. For the embarrassing treatment of the Katyn massacre, see A Viatteau, 'Comment a été traité la question de Katyn à Nuremberg' in ibid 145–55 and A Tusa and J Tusa, *The Nuremberg Trial* (London, Macmillan, 1983) 410–12.

[69] Douglas *The Memory of Judgment* (2001) 57–63.
[70] The increasing criticism and decreasing use by historians of Nuremberg documentation is pointed out for example in BF Smith, *Reaching Judgment at Nuremberg* (New York, Basic, 1977) xv–xvi. One aspect of the Cold War interpretation lay in the legend about the Wehrmacht's innocence in the crimes of the SS, necessary so as to prepare military cooperation with the West. Bloxham *Genocide on Trial* (2001) 129–33.
[71] Law No 64–1326 of 26 December 1964. For a discussion of the debates surrounding the adoption of this law, see A Laquièze, 'Le débat de 1964 sur l'imprescriptibilité des crimes contre l'humanité' (2000) 31 *Droits* 19–40.
[72] Cour de cassation, Judgment of 20 December 1985. For an extensive analysis of the drafting of this language, see L Sadat Wexler, 'The Interpretation of the Nuremberg Principles by the French Court of Cassation: From Touvier to Barbie and Back Again' (1994) 32 *Columbia Journal of Transnational Law* 338–42. See also G Binder, 'Representing Nazism: Advocacy and Identity in the Trial of Klaus Barbie' (1989) 14 *Yale Law Journal* 1321, 1337–38.

Now, Touvier was a Frenchman who had been at the service of the Vichy *Milice* and in this capacity participated in the shooting of seven hostages at Rillieux-la-Pape, close to Lyon, on 29 June 1944. His trial brought the nature of Vichy complicity in the atrocities during the German occupation to justice for the first time. As Leila Wexler points out in her detailed study of the case, there was a sense in which it was to be 'the trial of the whole French society and not just one man'.[73] Was French society ready to stand trial?

Touvier had been condemned to death in absentia in 1946 and 1947. After these sentences had prescribed in 1969, however, he surfaced in France and was granted pardon of the remaining convictions by President Pompidou two years later. He was again brought to trial in 1973 on the basis of the 1964 law and, after several turns, his case came to the Paris Court of Appeals which, in a decision of 13 April 1992, applied the above quoted definition by the Cour de cassation so as to conclude that there was no cause to prosecute him as the Vichy regime had not conducted a 'policy of ideological hegemony'. The decision caused a tremendous uproar, not least among French historians who were 'scandalised over the way the judges permitted themselves to write history and to characterise the ideological nature of the French State'.[74] The judgment was partially reversed by the Criminal Chamber of the Cour de cassation on 27 November 1992. However, in applying the definition, the Court did not attribute Touvier's acts to the Vichy France but to Germany, by pointing out that although Touvier was a member of the French Milice he was acting at the instigation of the Gestapo, and 'in the interests of the European Axis countries' as defined in article 6 of the Nuremberg Charter. Thus, finally, the Court managed to uphold an interpretation of the nature and role of the Pétain regime during the occupation period that did not conflict with the Fifth Republic consensus about an unbridgeable gap between France and the Hitler regime.[75]

This consensus was, however, fragile. Work by historians of Vichy contemporaneous to the trial brought out increasing evidence of the enthusiasm with which French administrators collaborated with the Nazis, initiating legislative action that disqualified Jews from public service and required their registration in a way that greatly facilitated rounding them up for transport to the death camps. The deportation of 75,000 Jews from France was largely organised by the French themselves, sometimes without pressure from Germany. Particularly notorious in this regard was the Vel d'Hiv roundup in July 1942 where 7,000 internees were held in a sports stadium in the 15th arrondissement in atrocious conditions over four days before being sent to the Drancy internment centre and then to the death camps.[76]

---

[73] Wexler, 'The Interpretation of the Nuremberg Principles' (1994) 346.

[74] Wieviorka, 'La France' (1996) 83.

[75] Touvier was finally condemned to life imprisonment by the Versailles Appeals Court on 19 April 1994. For the relevant part of the act of accusation, see S Chalandon and P Nivelle (eds), *Crimes contre l'humanité. Barbie, Touvier, Bousquet, Papon* (Paris, Plon, 1998) 160–63. For a description and critique of the 1992 judgments, see Wexler (1994) 344–53 and 361–67. See also Annex II of the article which contains the reasoning of the Paris Court, ending up in the conclusion that Vichy France was not exercising 'a policy of ideological hegemony' ibid 376–79.

[76] Especially M Marrus and RO Paxton, *Vichy France and the Jews* (New York, Scholem, 1983) 250–52.

The policy of Vichy France itself was brought to trial in 1997–98 when Maurice Papon, the Secretary-General of the Gironde prefecture in Bordeaux in 1942, was indicted for his role on the deportation of almost 1,600 Jews from the Bordeaux region. Papon, a Frenchman and, unlike Touvier, a white-collar administrator at the service of the 'L'État française', had organised the roundups, kept lists of Jews and provided transport and police protection to the convoys.[77] He had also enjoyed a successful career in post-war France, having been Prefect of Paris in 1958, member of the National Assembly in 1968 and even Minister of Finance in the French Government in 1978. There had been higher Vichy officials who had participated in the persecutions, such as René Bousquet and Jean Leguay, but both had died in the course of the proceedings in the 1980s. It was thus clear to most Frenchmen that to bring Papon to trial was to aim at Vichy France itself.[78] The fact that he was sentenced, on 2 April 1998, to only 10 years' imprisonment, and that French authorities anything but hurried with the execution of the sentence, throws only a slight shadow on the clarity of that message.

The cases of Eichmann, Touvier and Papon were each about avoiding impunity. However, they were also about historical truth and memory. As such, they entered the terrain where national identities are constructed out of interpretations of the national pasts – in these cases those of Israel and Fifth Republic France. However, there is no agreement on such identities. What 'Israel' or 'modern France' stand for are issues of fundamental political controversy among nationals and non-nationals. The engagement of a court with 'truth' and 'memory' is thus always an engagement with present political antagonism, and nowhere more so than in dealing with events of wide-ranging international and moral significance. Historians disagree on the interpretation of such events. So it is no surprise that judges may find it difficult to deal with them. However, how much judges may seek to proceed in good faith towards their judgments, the context of the trial cannot – unlike the history seminar – be presumed to manifest good faith on everybody's part. This is not a disinterested enquiry by a group of external observers but part of the history it seeks to interpret. Much is at stake for the protagonists – that is the nature of the trial – and no truth can remain sacred within it.

---

[77] L Sadat, 'The Legal Legacy of Maurice Papon' in RJ Golsan (ed), *The Papon Affair. Memory and Justice on Trial* (New York, London, 2000) 141–42.

[78] This theme is treated in most of the essays in Golsan, *The Papon Affair* (2000). However, see especially RO Paxton, 'Vichy on Trial' 169–70; A Lévy-Willard and B Vallaeys, 'Those who Organised the Trains Knew There Would be Deaths', Interview with RO Paxton in *Libération* (3 October 1997) ibid 181 and N Weill and R Solé, 'Today, Everything Converges on the Haunting Memory of Vichy', Interview with P Nora in *Le Monde* (1 October 1997) ibid 176–77. To judge Papon was to judge Vichy France was even an aspect of Papon's defence. See his final statement to the Bordeaux Appeals Court on 1 April 1998, see P Nivelle, 'Le procès papon' in Chalandon and Nivelle, *Crimes* (1998) 510–13, 515.

The Politics of Truth

In order to attain 'truth', and to avoid a show trial, the accused must be allowed to speak. However, this creates the risk of the trial turning into a propaganda show. This was the great concern at Nuremberg and remains a predominant worry as the United States will bring to trial the prisoners from its terrorism war in Afghanistan, presently detained in Guantanamo. One of the reasons for setting up a Military Court in 1945 instead of an ordinary civil procedure was precisely to avoid such embarrassment.[79] Employing military commissions and not ordinary US courts by the Bush regime was based on a significant precedent. In this regard, however, Nuremberg was only partly successful. As Jackson's cross-examination of Göring got out of hand, the latter later gloated with satisfaction: 'I had the best legal brains of England, America, Russia and France arrayed against me in their whole legal machinery – and there I was, alone.'[80]

There is no reason to think that historical truth in a trial of a political and military adversary – Milošević, Saddam Hussein, Radovan Karadžić – would come about through obedient cooperation by the accused. A criminal trial is defined by adversity and the construction of the historical context is part of the antagonism between the prosecutor and the defence. In the Milošević trial, the battle on the historical-didactic terrain clearly outweighed in importance the issue of whether or not the accused is found guilty. His behaviour well reflected this. Here is a reporter's summary:

> Il fait le spectacle, tantôt boudeur, tantôt blagueur, toujours aggressif et défiant face à des juges impassibles et des procureurs appliqués. Il bouscule chaque témoin produit par l'accusation. Il use et abuse des contre-interrogatoires au grand dam de l'accusation ... Parallèlement, l'accusé ne rate pas une occasion de s'emparer de cette tribune pour diffuser sa parole politique à son opinion publique.[81]

When the list of names that formed the group of Milošević' legal advisers was published, it was clear that much of the trial would be conducted on this terrain. That list included the name of the controversial French advocate Jacques Vergès, known not only as the counsel for Klaus Barbie, 'the Butcher of Lyon', the high-profile criminal 'Carlos' and a supporter of Palestinian activists, but also as the theorist of the 'trial of rupture' in which the defence is conducted entirely as an attack on the system represented by the prosecution case.[82] In contrast to the trial of 'connivance' in which the accused seeks merely to put the facts in question, a strategy of rupture starts from the existence of what I earlier referred to as a *différend* – two incompatible frameworks of interpretation, and directly attacks the opponent's framework:

---

[79] See Jackson's Report to the President, 6 June 1945 quoted by Marrus *The Nuremberg War Crimes Trial* (1997) 41.
[80] Quoted in Marrus *The Nuremberg War Crimes Trial* (1997) 118.
[81] C Châtelot, 'Le procès Milosevic s'enfonce dans la routine' *Le Monde* (25 Mai 2002) 15.
[82] J Vergès, *De la stratégie judiciaire* (Paris, Minuit, 1968).

'La rupture bouleverse toute la structure du procès. Les faits passent au deuxième plan ainsi que les circonstances de l'action; au premier plan apparait soudain la contestation brutale de l'ordre public.'[83]

The trials of Socrates, of Louis XVI, and of the Communist Dimitrov, accused by the Nazis of the *Reichstag* fire of 1934, each involve aspects of this strategy – as indeed does the posture of Prometheus, declining to defend himself under Divine law, or Zola's attack on the prosecutors of Dreyfus: *J'accuse*. Dimitrov's strategy was published in the *Pravda* on 4 March 1934 in terms of taking initiative, making the accusation, as well as the high representatives of the State called to the witness stand, seem ridiculous. The sole objective in the trial, as described by Vergès, was to advance the cause of the proletariat. Everything else, including Dimitrov's own fate – he refused to rely on an alibi of being away from Berlin on the night of the fire – was secondary.[84]

The trial of Klaus Barbie in Lyon in 1987 is an exemplary case of the use of such a strategy. For most observers, the prime significance of that trial, too, had to do with truth and memory, educating a new generation of Frenchmen in the facts of Nazi policy under the occupation. 'The trial was necessary' wrote André Frossard, member of *l'Académie française*, former member of the resistance and prisoner of war to the Germans, saved only by the fact of his ascendancy having been qualified as no more than 'three quarters' Jewish, in the immediate aftermath of the trial: 'la jeune génération d'aujourd'hui ne savait présque rien de la passé où l'histoire devenue folle était sortie du monde connu pour séjourner quelque temps en enfer. Le procès Barbie l'a instruite'.[85]

For giving this lesson, Barbie was an excellent candidate. He had been the head of the Information Section of the Gestapo in Lyon in 1942–44, managed to escape trial after the war by participating in US counter-intelligence in Germany and then fled to Bolivia 'where he spent the next three decades managing business and unapologetically touting Nazi and other militaristic causes'.[86] He was finally abducted by the French Secret Police from Bolivia in 1982 and the trial against him commenced a couple of years thereafter. Among the charges, two were particularly important. In April 1944 Barbie had organised the delivery to Auschwitz of 44 Jewish school children who had been staying at a religious *Foyer des enfants* in the village of Izieu, 75 km from Lyon, together with their five teachers. None of the children and only one teacher returned. He was known as the Gestapo officer having captured and tortured – sometimes to death – members of the resistance, among them the resistance hero Jean Moulin.

Two aspects of the Barbie trial bring strikingly to the surface the politics of a trial conducted for historical or didactic purposes. There was, on the one hand, the

---

[83] ibid 86–87.
[84] ibid 104–12.
[85] A Frossard, *Le crime contre l'humanité* (Robert Laffont, Paris, 1997) 40. On the reception of the Barbie trial in France, see also the very useful account in H Rousso, *The Vichy Syndrome. History and Memory in France since 1944* (translated by A Goldhammer, Harvard, Harvard University Press, 1991) 191–216. Interesting also is Binder,'Representing Nazism' (1989) 1322–23.
[86] Douglas *The Memory of Judgment* (2001) 187–88.

question of whether the French statute of limitations was applicable to Barbie's activities against the members of *la résistance*. That statute limited the prosecution for the most serious crimes of the common law (such as murder) to 20 years. An exception was, however, created by the 1964 law, referred to above, which integrated 'crimes against humanity' into French penal law and made them imprescriptible. In 1983, the Lyon court (*Chambre d'accusation*) interpreted the notion so as to allow only prosecution for the deportation of 'innocent Jews' – the children of Izieu, together with four other counts for action against Jewish civilians – but not for the torture and killing of Jean Moulin, the latter being a 'war crime' and thus not covered by 'crimes against humanity'.[87]

Under pressure from organisations of former resistance members, especially those close to Jean Moulin, the indictment was appealed to the criminal chamber of the Cour de cassation that chose a less restrictive interpretation of 'crimes against humanity'. As we have seen, the High Court defined the concept so as to include in the notion also crimes against the 'opponents' of a 'state practising a policy of ideological hegemony whatever the form of their opposition'.[88] This definition enabled the Court to focus not only on the Jewish victims, but also the action taken by the Gestapo against the resistance members, a determined preference for many politicians in the Fifth Republic. France was to be remembered not only as a land of victims and collaborators but also as a country of heroes and fighters as the civil parties in the Lyon hearings argued.[89] Through this means, however, as Frossard points out, the notion of 'crimes against humanity' was diluted so that almost any Frenchman could have invoked it against any German under the occupation.[90] Unlike the judgment of the Lyon Court, the broader view of the Cour de cassation was open to criticism on account of its equating the two historical facts that formed the background of the trial – the destruction of the Jews and the work of the resistance. By so doing, it seemed to erase the special horror of the Jewish genocide, captured in an understanding of 'crimes against humanity' as taking place only if, to quote Frossard once more, someone is killed 'under the pretext of having been born'.[91]

---

[87] Decision of 4 October 1985. For extracts from the act of accusation of the Lyon Court, see Chalandon and Nivelle *Crimes contre l'humanité* (1998) 17–28.

[88] Judgment of 20 December 1985. See also references in n 72.

[89] See, eg the account of the statement of the counsel for the *Ligue des droits de l'homme*, H Noguères, experiencing 'shock of witnessing a discrimination between the Jews and the non-Jews that had been thrown into the last train from Lyon to Auschwitz on 11 August 1944', one of the five counts available for the Lyon prosecutor, S Chalandon, 'Le procès de Klaus Barbie' in Chalandon and Nivelle *Crimes contre l'humanité* (1998) 125.

[90] Frossard, *Le crime* (1997) 17.

[91] ibid 70. In her thorough commentary of the case, Leila Sadat takes the position that Frossard's definition, which coincided with the Lyon Court's restricted view, was both 'illogical' and possibly 'insensitive'. L Sadat, 'The Legal Legacy' (2000) 137. Cassese, too, supports the wider definition – but oddly defends this on the basis that the targeted persons were chosen 'only because they belong to the enemy' (instead of being belligerents). A Cassese, *Law and Violence in the Modern Age* (London, Polity, 1986) 112. However, surely the Jews were not targeted because they were the enemy and surely that is precisely where the speciality of the Nazi genocide resides, as Frossard argues.

In effect, this confusion goes some way to supporting revisionist interpretations on Nazi policy that sometimes seek to explain the action against the Jews as directed against some kind of opposition or a 'danger' to Hitler's regime. When a German historian of international law, for instance, fails to say a word about the Shoah in an account of the conduct of the belligerent powers in the Second World War, instead pointing to actions against civilians by 'both sides', highlighting the 'sad role' that mass executions played in the activities against 'partisans', he is engaged in a particularly distasteful act of historical revisionism that could be bypassed as yet another negationist apology, would it not come from the discipline of international law from which the notion of 'crimes against humanity' once emerged.[92]

The second aspect of the politics of history in the Barbie trial is even more immediately relevant for the Milošević case. The declared tactics of Barbie's counsel, Jacques Vergès, was to use the trial for the purpose of attacking the hypocrisy of the French State in accusing Barbie of acts that had been routine parts of its own colonial warfare and particularly of French policy in the Algerian war (1954–62). Himself of Vietnamese origin, Vergès was an *ancien combattant* in the decolonialist cause who had married an Algerian woman once savagely tortured and condemned to death by the French military. In his pre-trial statements, Vergès had stated that the real battle lay not in attaining the release of his client but in achieving control of the historical and didactic aspects of the trial – far more important questions than the fate of an old Nazi.[93] In fact, he declared, the original indictment had been formulated so as to cover only acts against Jewish civilians so as to avoid the obvious parallel between Nazi action against resistance members and the French suppression of Algerian opposition, as well as to keep hidden the names of the resistance members – assumed to occupy high positions in contemporary France – that had delivered Moulin to the Gestapo on 21 June 1943.[94]

To conduct his 'trial of rupture', Vergès invited two African lawyers to accompany him on the defence bench, the Algerian Nabil Bouaïta and the Congolese Jean-Martin Mbemba, as if to suggest that whatever happened to the Jews in Europe was about intra-European guilt, 'a drop of European blood in the ocean of human suffering which, therefore, only concerned the white man'.[95] The Barbie team did not attempt to exculpate Barbie for what he had done, look for mitigating circumstances or point to his marginal role in the Gestapo. Its main concern was to develop the *tu quoque* to maximal public effect, to demonstrate that in essence, there was hardly any difference between what Barbie had done in Lyon and French racism during the years of its colonial wars. Why weep over the dead in the white colonialist's internecine struggles, arrogantly labelled a 'World War'? Did not the

---

[92] See W Grewe, *The Epochs of International Law* (translated by M Byers, Berlin, New York, De Gruyter, 2000) 626, and my book review in (2002) 51 *ICLQ* 746–51.
[93] For Vergès career and pre-trial statements, see Binder 'Representing Nazism' (1989)1356–59 and Cassese, *Law and Violence* (1986) 113–15.
[94] Rousso, *The Vichy Syndrome* (1991) 208–09.
[95] A Finkielkraut, *La mémoire vaine. Du crime contre l'humanité* (Paris, Gallimard, 1989) 51–52.

Barbie trial demonstrate that white man's pity extended only to another white man, his compassion turned into narcissism, exhausting his emotional energy and perpetuating his racism towards everything not-European?[96] 'Racism', Vergès argued in his closing statement to the Lyon Court, 'we know what it is. We bow our heads also in front of the martyrdom of the children of Izieu because we remember the suffering of the children of Algeria'.[97]

In the end, Barbie's counsel did not go into systematic detail in producing evidence of the tortures committed as part of the official policy of France in the Algerian war or reveal much that was unknown regarding Moulin's arrest. Yet, he restated his main argument over and over again. Acts of colonial brutality in Africa and Indo-China were brought in as aspects of the historical context within which Barbie's actions were to be interpreted: On the day of allied victory, on 8 May 1945, French troops massacred 15,000 Algerian demonstrators in the town of Sétif who joined the celebration of victory with a call for national self-determination.[98] There was no reason – apart from racist reasons – to single out Nazi policy from the historical patterns of continuing violence exercised by Europe on everyone. There was no reason to deny the Holocaust, only to put it in the correct historical frame – in which its significance became automatically relative.

The defence tactic in the Barbie trial was to accept it as being about historical truth. By then choosing an appropriate interpretative context – European colonialism – the actions of the accused would necessarily appear as a relatively 'normal' episode in the flow of racist persecutions and massive suffering of which European history has consisted. This was the choice of Milošević, in The Hague as well. By turning his accusing finger against the Tribunal and the forces that lay behind its creation and his own downfall, Milošević, too, sought to write the history of the most recent Balkan wars as a continuation of the Great Power policy that had over again torn the peninsula into pieces, throwing its peoples against each other as part of a ruthless game of European domination.

When the debate is moved at that level, then of course it becomes much harder to receive closure by the trial. The opposing evaluations and assessments about how to think about Balkan history will not cease to exist when the judgment is read. The judgment will not provide the only prism through which the events succeeding the dissolution of the former Yugoslavia will be read. On the contrary – and this gives the accused his idiom – the judgment will become part of the complexities of Balkan history. If Karadžić today succeeds in becoming a representative of one perhaps disputed but still respectable view of that history, then he will have attained two victories.

First, he will have escaped the full force of the legal judgment. The judgment will seem to manifest only one among several interpretations of the past and to receive its validity above all from the power of the forces that were behind it. It would be no more than '"victors" justice'. The condemnation of the accused would then not

[96] ibid 61–63.
[97] Vergès 1 July 1987, as reported in Chalandon and Nivelle (1998) 138.
[98] ibid 139–40.

seem to carry universal moral significance. It would seem that he was found guilty, as Goering put it in Nuremberg, 'because he was on the side that lost the war'.

In the second place, by articulating and giving concrete appearance to the particular historical vision that he claimed was on trial, he will have strengthened that vision, providing it with the aura of an iconoclasm that seemed critical enough to have been subjected to the extraordinary measure of a formal trial. The martyr-dom that will be the condemned man's private image will reflect on the historical truth that he represents as its secret critical force, its revolutionary power.

'Show Trial'?

It is precisely because Realist theorists such as Morgenthau or EH Carr had been right about the need to always look for the broad context that pure 'individualisa-tion' cannot be carried out. A legal system that did not hold the killing of the innocent a crime would be unacceptable. However equally, and more importantly, not every killing of the innocent is a crime. As the International Court of Justice observed in its *Legality of the Threat or Use of Nuclear Weapons* opinion in 1996, article 6 of the Covenant of Civil and Political Rights prohibits only the 'arbitrary' taking of lives and it cannot be determined whether the death of innocent civilians in some situation is an atrocious crime or an inevitable by-product of action that was necessary to protect some more fundamental interest.[99]

But as soon as the law tries to make an assessment about that larger interest, and evaluate the relevant contextual data, it will move onto an area of indeterminacy and political conflict. Are the Balkan wars to be interpreted by reference to ethnic animosities or the interests and alliances of the Great Powers in the region? It has been observed that a number of the altogether 271 historical facts of which the Tribunal took judicial notice in the 1998 Galić case involved contentious assump-tions that were disputed among historians.[100] A court cannot avoid taking judicial notice of a certain number of background facts. The moment it does this, however, it will seem to be conducting a political trial to the extent that what those facts are and how they should be understood is part of the conflict that is being adjudged.

Yet, success is not necessarily guaranteed by the opposite technique of refusing to take any of the disputed facts as granted, either. Trials against 'Holocaust deniers' have brought to the surface the dangerous weakness in the adversarial process: did the witness *really* see who gave orders to the massacre while he or she was hiding behind the barn? If nobody saw it, did the massacre take place at all? Nobody may have actually seen Jews gassed at Auschwitz and lived to tell about it:

[99] *The Legality of Nuclear Weapons* [1996] ICJ Rep 226, 239–40 [24]–[25]. See further M Koskenniemi, 'The Silence of Law/The Voice of Justice' in L Boisson de Chazournes and P Sands, *International Law, the International Court of Justice and Nuclear Weapons* (Cambridge, Cambridge University Press, 1999) 488, 490–98.
[100] Cavoski, 'Juger l'histoire' (2002) 77–89.

so did gas chambers really exist? Even Raoul Hilberg's extensive minutiae on the extermination process and Christopher Browning's detailed accounts of the participation of 'ordinary men' in the *Einsatzgruppen* are only 'hearsay' and thus perhaps inadmissible as evidence.[101] The more you try to prove such facts in court, the more fragile they become. Witnesses contradict themselves and each other, memories change, or remain inscribed in the words that have been used to give shape to them, and lose their immediacy and turn into myth. A vigorous cross-examination leads even the most reliable witness to a state of confusion. In the end, memory may not have been served but undermined – not to say anything of the dignity of the victims who, like the young woman who survived the Racak massacre in January 1999, testified about it in The Hague in May 2002, and whose evidence was reduced to a series of panicky 'I don't knows' by a bullying Milošević.[102] The Tribunal – any Tribunal – is here between the difficult choice of accepting some facts as commonly known (and integrating the controversies concerning the adequacy of what is 'commonly known') and constructing facts out of what the procedural techniques – including cross-examination – happen to bring forward. Here the line between justice, history and manipulation tends to become all but invisible.

The objective of 'educating' people of 'historical truths' through law emerges from our contemporary wish to accommodate the Realist insight about the need to take account of the context, but also from our rejection of the Realists' conclusion – namely that law cannot be of use here. To speak of a duty of memory is fine, but 'memory' may not be something that can be authoritatively fixed by a legal process. To document and to testify is necessary. However, documents and testimony are not memory as such. The organisation of archives and the interpretation of testimonies so as to construct coherent narratives involves selection and emphasis that are aspects of the historical craft. 'L'historien écrit et cette écriture n'est ni neutre ni transparente', writes the historian Pierre Vidal-Naquet in his polemic against Holocaust revisionism,[103] thus also making explicit the difficulty of conceiving courts as instruments of history and memory. A court rules – and must rule – over individual guilt and innocence and in so doing must strive for neutrality and transparency. Whether it succeeds can only be assessed from the outside, perhaps like in Nuremberg, only after decades of assessment and criticism. One type of memory involves precisely that assessment and criticism, an active interaction with the past from the perspective of one's personal recollection and

---

[101] See the account of the trial of Ernst Zundel, over his pamphlet 'Did Six Million really Die?' in Toronto, Canada, in 1988, in Douglas *The Memory of Judgment* (2001) 226–54. Through the aggressive cross-examination by Zundel's advocate, Douglas Christie, 'memory was ridiculed, the survivor transformed into an amnesiac at best, and outright liar at worst' 240. For the enormous risks involved in trying to prove 'sacred facts' through the banality of the legal process, see also DD Guttenplan, *The Holocaust on Trial. History, Justice and David Irving Libel Case* (London, Granta, 2001) especially 307–08.

[102] Cross-examination of Ms Drita Emini on 28 and 30 May 2002, Transcript of the Milošević trial 5747–64.

[103] P Vidal-Naquet, *Les assassins de la mémoire* (Paris, Découverte, 1987) 148.

experience, a memory that looks into the past but opens into the future, poised for transgression, possibly reconciliation. This contrasts with another kind of memory, labelled by the philosopher Alain Finkielkraut as 'vain memory', in which we outsiders admire our own moral sensibilities and capacity for quick compassion, a memory serving our personal and social projects, far removed from the events on trial[104] – perhaps the construction of an 'international community' out of the tragedies of others.[105]

So far, the dry and bureaucratic procedures at the International Criminal Tribunal for the former Yugoslavia (ICTY) have made little impression on the communities in the territory of the former Yugoslavia. There is not much evidence of a developed sense of culpability among the populations. The spectacle of the Milošević trial was followed with varying interest in the press and on the terrain. After many years now, other concerns seem to have set in. This is in the nature of the criminal trial, the famous tedium of Nuremberg so frustrating for a journalist but indispensable in a complex legal proceeding. Yet, one cannot fail to wonder to what extent a process conducted in front of foreign judges in The Hague is able to attain the didactic purposes hoped for; to what degree Balkan memory may be constructed or directed by an international process. Already antagonised by the absence of the death penalty, and the celebration as a hero of a condemned war criminal on his return to Zagreb after serving his two and half years' sentence,[106] the victims will have to accept being taught by a hypocritical West that has made sure its own guilt would not be formally adjudicated in the process. On the perpetrator side, the articulation of the Milošević or Karadžić side of the story gives it a measure of respectability that it might otherwise never have received. All this follows as a matter of course in criminal trial that looks for punishment. Anything more – 'truth', 'lesson', 'catharsis', 'reconciliation' – depends on how the Tribunal will be able to deal with a constitutive paradox at the heart of its job.

This is the paradox: to convey an unambiguous historical 'truth' to its audience, the trial will have to silence the accused. In such case, it ends up as a *show trial*. In order for the trial to be legitimate, the accused must be entitled to speak. But in that case, he will be able to challenge the version of truth represented by the prosecutor and relativise the guilt that is thrust upon him by the powers on whose strength the Tribunal stands. His will be the truth of the revolution and he himself a martyr for the revolutionary cause.

---

[104] See Finkielkraut, *La mémoire* (1989).

[105] It often seems that the memory for which the trial in The Hague is staged is not the memory of Balkan populations but that of an 'international community' recounting its past as a progress narrative from 'Nuremberg to the Hague', impunity to the Rule of Law. This 'community' would construct itself in the image of a 'public time' (in analogy with 'public space') in which it would contemplate its past and give a moral meaning to disasters such as Rwanda or Srebrenica as a rejected past and a promise of radiant future. On the idea of 'public time', see S Villavicencio, 'Sans même un procès. L'impunité et les identités collectives' in J Poulain, *Qu'est-ce que la justice? Devant l'autel de l'histoire* (Saint-Denis, 1996) 216–17.

[106] See Hazan *La justice face à la guerre* (2000) 243–47.

8

Faith, Identity, and the Killing of the Innocent: International Lawyers and Nuclear Weapons

I was among the few lawyers who found the declaration of a *non liquet* by the International Court of Justice in the *Legality of the Use by a State of Nuclear Weapons in Armed Conflict* Advisory Opinion (1996) intuitively right – though I did not have an immediate justification for this intuition. This chapter is an account of the reflections prompted by that intuition. At the same time, it is also an exploration of the limits of international law as professional language and a technique.

THE DICHOTOMY OF reason and passion is so deeply embedded in the construction of the 'legal' that it seems difficult even to imagine an international law that would not be entrenched in it. The very identity of international law seems based on its capacity to set itself on the side of reason, in opposition to the passionate, the irrational. Is not reason practically synonymous with order, and passion with chaos? Also, what is law for if not to bring about order, and to allow exit from our slavery under passion? Is it not reason which is universal and objective, while passion is particular and subjective? Is it not then the case that a law pretending to universality must perforce align itself with the forces of reason?

In the quest for a universally applicable law, international lawyers have always sought support from the universality of reason, developing theories and doctrines and engaging in debates about how to exclude from the law all that is subjective or partial. For some, this has meant trying to explain the law in terms of derivations from principles of universal validity or from internal relationships between rules. Others have sought to create as close a fit as possible between the law and the social processes it is supposed to reflect. Whether naturalists, formalists or realists, however, lawyers have derived their professional identity from their ability to manage a legal method enabling them to produce valid normative statements about the social world that bear no necessary connection to their personal beliefs.

The alignment of law with reason is under threat by the question of the legal status of the use or threat of use of nuclear weapons. As I hope to show below, a purely rational, legal-technical approach to the massive killing of the innocent –

198

the crux of the questions posed to the International Court of Justice in its 1996 advisory opinion – cannot be pursued without unacceptable moral and political consequences. It fails to attain a determinate regulation of the matter, cannot come to grips with the political and moral dilemmas involved and, above all, fails to articulate a defensible conception of what it is to engage in international law as a professional commitment. As such, it participates in 'a doctrinal practice that puts its hope in the contrast of legal reasoning to ideology, philosophy and political prophecy [and] ends up as a collection of makeshift apologies'.[1]

The Opinion

After intensive lobbying by an American-based non-governmental organisation, the International Association of Lawyers Against Nuclear Arms (IALANA), and at the formal initiative of the caucus of non-aligned states, the UN General Assembly adopted a resolution in December 1994 by which it decided to urgently request the International Court of Justice to render an Advisory Opinion on the following question: 'Is the threat or use of nuclear weapons in any circumstance permitted by international law?'[2]

The request followed another which had been made by the Assembly of the World Health Organisation (WHO) to the Court in May 1993, and which had focused on the health and environmental effects of possible use of nuclear weapons and its conformity with international law and especially the WHO Constitution.[3]

The Court rendered its opinions on both requests on 8 July 1996. It dismissed the WHO request on the grounds that it had not been made within the competence of the Organisation.[4] However, no such formal obstacle was present in regard to the General Assembly's request. Having also rejected the other objections to its jurisdiction, the Court responded to the Assembly as follows:

1. There is in neither customary nor conventional international law any specific authorization of the threat or use of nuclear weapons;
2. There is in neither customary nor conventional international law any comprehensive and universal prohibition of the threat or use of nuclear weapons as such;
3. A threat or use of force by means of nuclear weapons that is contrary to Article 2, paragraph 4, of the United Nations Charter and that fails to meet all the requirements of Article 51, is unlawful;

---

[1] RM Unger, *The Critical Legal Studies Movement* (Cambridge, Harvard University Press, 1986) 11.

[2] UNGA Res 49/75K (15 December 1994). For a good review of the handling of this controversial request by the General Assembly, see M Lailach, 'The General Assembly's Request for Advisory Opinion From the International Court of Justice on the legality of the Threat or Use of Nuclear Weapons' (1995) 8 *Leiden Journal of International Law* 401–11.

[3] WHO Res 46/40 (14 May 1993).

[4] *Legality of the Use by a State of Nuclear Weapons in Armed Conflict* (Advisory Opinion) [1996] ICJ Rep (hereinafter *Nuclear Weapons case*).

4. A threat or use of nuclear weapons should also be compatible with the requirements of the international law applicable in armed conflict, particularly the principles and rules of international humanitarian law, as well as with specific obligations under treaties and other undertakings which expressly deal with nuclear weapons;

5. It follows from the above-mentioned requirements that the threat or use of nuclear weapons would generally be contrary to the rules of international law applicable in armed conflict, and in particular the principles and rules of humanitarian law; however, in view of the current state of international law, as well as the factual elements at its disposal, the Court could not definitively conclude whether the threat or use of nuclear weapons would be lawful under extreme circumstance of self-defence, in which the very survival of a State would be at stake; and

6. There exists an obligation to pursue in good faith and bring to a conclusion negotiations leading to nuclear disarmament in all its aspects under strict and effective international control.[5]

Points 1, 3, 4, and 6 were unanimous; point 2 was decided by 11 votes to three; and point 5, the crucial part of the opinion, was decided by a split 7–7 decision, with President Bedjaoui casting the deciding vote.

The question and the Court's response, raise a number of questions of theoretical and practical interest for international lawyers. Did the form of the question – looking for permission instead of a prohibition – prejudice the response and seek to overturn the 'Lotus principle'?[6] If it could not be done here, when (if ever) is it feasible to object to the Court's exercise of advisory jurisdiction on the grounds that a matter is 'abstract' or 'political'?[7] What significance has the dispositive character of advisory jurisdiction? If a request falls within the competence of the requesting organ, is there any basis on which the Court should nonetheless decline such request? What is the consequence of the fact that the Court has now for the first time declared a *non liquet*?[8] Or more substantively: what is the normative meaning and relationship between the textbook categories (eg, use of force, law of armed conflict, rules and principles of humanitarian law) to which the Court has now given an official imprimatur? What is the relationship between the dismissal of arguments from *jus cogens* ([83]) and the Court's endorsement of 'intransgressible principles of international customary law' ([79])? What does it mean to say that the use or threat of use of nuclear weapons 'would be *generally* contrary to the rules of international law'? Is the obligation on states to achieve nuclear disarmament, which the Court characterised as an 'obligation of result' ([99]), merely the

---

[5] ibid [105].

[6] That is to say, the principle of the plenitude of sovereignty, or that everything is permitted that is not subject to a definite prohibition. The Court dismissed this question rapidly by noting that because states admitted that their right to use nuclear weapons was not unlimited, the matter could be dealt with through seeking out where, precisely, those limits were, ibid [20]–[22].

[7] For the Court's rapid dismissals of these points, see ibid [13] and [15].

[8] It has been argued with emphasis that there is a general principle prohibiting courts from declaring *non liquet* even in the apparent absence of law on a matter. See H Lauterpacht, *The Function of Law in the International Community* (Oxford, Clarendon Press, 1933) 63–65; 'Some Observations on the Prohibition on 'Non Liquet' and the Completeness of the Law' in JH Verzijl, *Symbolae Verzijl* (The Hague, Nijhoff, 1958) 196–221. However, in advisory proceedings the issue 'assumes a different complexion', ibid 199 fn 2. See also ibid 217–19.

old obligation to negotiate in good faith, or does something more definite follow from it?

My intention, however, is not to focus on any such (or other) individual problems which the opinion raises. I wish to examine and articulate the intuition I have had that the Court should not have been asked the question at all; an intuition strengthened by the particular response the Court now has given. Having argued, and being still convinced, that there is no essential distinction between 'law' and 'politics', the door is not, however, open to me to argue that the Court should have dismissed the request because of its 'political' character.[9] Instead, I shall argue that the legal reasoning available to the Court is unable to reach the core of the request – the massive killing of the innocent – and that to think otherwise would presume an image of international law and of ourselves as international lawyers we have good reason to reject. The argument is not – although it first seems as if it were – about a tension between 'law' and 'politics' and our ability to manage it, but about what we can be certain about and, consequently, who we are.

I shall examine the limits of (legal) reason and thereby inevitably look beyond those limits, towards the 'subjective' element – passion – to which reason is, as Hume always insisted, but a humble slave. For it is in that realm that the issues of what we can know (faith), and who we are (identity) are settled and linked with how we understand and argue about the killing of the innocent. The *Nuclear Weapons* Opinion raises existential questions of identity, community and responsibility that are prior to the conventional ways of legal reason and cannot beneficially be treated through it. To think otherwise, I shall argue, assumes a passive and tragic view about the human condition, and particularly of the condition of the international lawyer.

Law and Politics

The most immediate problem raised by the *Nuclear Weapons* Opinion concerns the apparent conflict between law and politics that it evokes and the difficulty in devising a convincing explanation of why the former should be able to overrule or encompass the latter. As a purely pragmatic, psychological matter, the political interests and values at stake in a decision to use or not to use nuclear weapons seem so overwhelmingly important that it is hard to believe that a statesman, having weighed them and having come to a conclusion one way or another, might still adopt for the contrary course of action because of a deviating legal assessment. On the other hand, if the legal assessment happens to coincide with the speaker's known political views, the doubt must always remain that the assessment is simply a rationalisation, in legal language, of a political position. Reason – as manifested in the legal process – seems not only unable to produce a credible counterweight

---

[9] See eg chapter two of this volume.

to politics, but is somehow compelled to succumb to it. This seems so no matter what the substantive outcome of the reasoning might be.

Imagine that the Court had declared the use and threat of use of force by nuclear weapons illegal in all circumstances. As the killing of the innocent is never allowed, and as nuclear weapons always entail that at least some non-combatants are killed, it is always illegal to use them. A threat to use them might have been prohibited on the simple *dictum* that it is always illegal to threaten to commit an illegal act. Quite apart from the fact that the law does accept the killing of the innocent in some circumstances (eg as an unintended but proportionate consequence of conventional self-defence), declaring such a rule would have put the Court and the whole system of law it represents in a collision course with the politico-military system of the nuclear age, ie the policy of deterrence. All nuclear powers base their policy on the eventuality of a strike at some extreme circumstance. In a conflict between the law (as declared by the Court) and the long-standing policy of the most powerful states, the law could hardly prevail. If (as argued above) it is pragmatically unthinkable that a statesman might be deterred from using the weapon in a situation of extreme national danger (for instance, in order to prevent the killing of his or her innocent compatriots) merely because of what the legal adviser might say, then an opinion underwriting an absolute prohibition would have condemned the law to irrelevance already in advance. This would hardly have been an appropriate consequence for the Court to attain, particularly as the defenders of deterrence could always formulate their dissent in legal terms as well. The opposition would then not have appeared as (good) law against (evil) politics but as one contested application of the law against another. The relative superiority between the two interpretations could not have been solved from within the (contested) law, but have remained a battle of prestige and influence to be fought out between the Court and the nuclear powers. Surely the Court's possibility to prevail in such struggle would appear rather slim.[10]

The Court also envisaged a contrasting scenario, the possibility that 'the "clean" use of smaller, low yield, tactical nuclear weapons might sometimes be permissible, or that the use of nuclear weapons might be permitted in an 'extreme circumstance of self-defence in which the very survival of a State would be at stake.'[11] In respect of all such scenarios, however, the Court declared a *non liquet*. It was unable to 'conclude definitively whether the threat or use of nuclear weapons would be lawful or unlawful in an extreme circumstance of self-defence, in which the very survival of a State would be at stake'.

It is easy to see why this seemed advisable. Envisaging any possibility for the *lawful* killing of the innocent by nuclear weapons would have collided head-on with powerful moral and political sentiments, humanitarian principles deeply

---

[10] The Court took a Delphic position, arguing, on the one hand, that it 'does not intend to pronounce here upon the practice known as the policy of deterrence' *Nuclear Weapons case*, [67], but observed nonetheless, that the existence of this policy 'hampered' the 'emergence, as a *lex lata*, of a customary rule specifically prohibiting the use of nuclear weapons as such' [73].

[11] ibid [94]–[95], [97].

entrenched in modernity's political discourse. Again, a collision between law and politics would have ensued. Again, as a practical matter, it would hardly have resulted in that world populations would have started to assume that some uses might, indeed, be lawful. In a conflict between the Court's view of the law and generally shared humanitarian sentiments, the Court would not have emerged as the victor. Again, it would have condemned itself – and the legal system it manages – into irrelevance.

In other words, both available solutions seemed excluded because of good pragmatic reasons. Both would have entailed a collision between law and politics, politics being understood either as the structure of the world's politico-military system or a generally shared politico-humanitarian ethics. In neither conflict could it confidently have been expected that the law would have prevailed. Nor can we be certain that the practical consequences of the law having been overridden by politics in one or another of its two disguises (power/ideas) would have been a less embarrassing outcome than the disappointment of its present indeterminate conclusion. Quite the contrary, open conflict with one or the other audience might have had a spill-over effect on the Court's less controversial jurisdiction, undermining whatever modest role it might seek to play in the world of diplomacy generally. The main issues at stake are not, however, about the pragmatic influence the Court (or its law) has. It is not a conflict between law and politics that is central to the case, but the law's inability to grapple with the massive killing of the innocent.

Limits of Rules

There are a number of reasons why the use or threat of use of nuclear weapons cannot successfully be treated by reference to formal rules and principles. The most obvious reason has to do with the banal fact that rules and principles always appear through language. Their application requires the use of interpretative techniques, typically such as those listed in articles 31–33 of the Vienna Convention on the Law of Treaties. These techniques, however, are considerably weaker than the values or interests at stake in the killing of the innocent whose conflict they seek to regulate. For example, even if there were agreement that the threat of use of nuclear weapons were illegal, such agreement would be soon dispelled by a controversy on what amounts to 'threat' in the first place. The normative force of such techniques is no match to the force of the values that demand a particular understanding of 'threat' in a particular context.

Would possession be 'threat'? Clearly, if it is intended to deter others, it is premised on the possibility of use and does amount to 'threat'.[12] On the other hand,

---

[12] See also H Shue, 'Conflicting Conceptions of Deterrence' in E Frankel Paul, FD Miller, J Paul, J Ahrens (eds), *Nuclear Rights, Nuclear Wrongs* (Oxford, New York, Blackwell, 1986) 45.

the same is true of the possession of conventional (and chemical) weapons – without this having engendered the argument that it is in violation of article 2 (4) of the UN Charter. Should threat of *first use* and *counter-use* be treated equally? The latter might seem permitted under the exception of self-defence under article 51 of the UN Charter, a possibility expressly left open by the Court's *non liquet*.[13] However, if possession is allowed under that exception, is it not then always allowed: it is impossible to distinguish between possession in preparation for first strike and possession in preparation of counterstrike. Besides, intentions change: a state with a deterrence doctrine premised on a massive counterstrike capability might find it more advantageous to embark on a limited pre-emptive strike.

On the other hand, any rule that makes reference to self-defence is, of course, marred by the large number of controversies regarding the scope of that concept. The application of self-defence is always premised on how the classical conditions of 'imminent danger' or 'proportionality' should be constructed and whether, for instance, a limited pre-emptive strike might be allowed in case that was the sole means to forestall a massive attack. As I will argue more fully below, these are matters that can be decided only by reference to concrete situations. The point here is only that no legal-technical argument that can be put forward to support one or another interpretation of the meaning of 'threat' or 'self-defence' can possibly attain the degree of determinacy, and pedigree that it could effectively structure the expectations on which the military doctrines of states are based or provide an argument so convincing that the moral views of the participants would be conclusively overruled. If that is so, then the dilemma about politics always overruling law is not only a consequence of pragmatic considerations but follows from a weakness internal to the law itself.

Aside from indeterminacy, however, an even more daunting problem is posed by the paradox of rules and standards. The paradox is this: you might think that the problem to be regulated is so grave that no interpretative difficulties should get in the way of the attainment of your objective, ie not killing the innocent. Therefore, you think it can only be dealt with by an absolute, unconditional prohibition, a rule that even a fool could unerringly apply.[14] Such absolute rules, however, are always both overdetermining and underdetermining: they will encompass situations you did not intend to be covered and exclude cases that you wished to cover. Therefore, absolute rules are usually accompanied by soft standards that allow the taking account of special cases and the balancing of interests. Such standards bring 'evaluation' within the law and highlight the position of law-applying agencies, courts in particular. The softer the standard, however, the greater the possibility of arbitrariness and political misuse and the more dramatic the consequences of the (mis)use of discretion. Let me now illustrate the workings of the paradox in the field of the Court's opinion.

---

[13] See *Nuclear Weapons case*, [97].
[14] Regarding such rules, see also TM Franck, *The Power of Legitimacy among Nations* (New York, Oxford University Press, 1990) 67–83.

I have already argued that an absolute prohibition is not pragmatically work-able: we cannot plausibly expect a politician to always sacrifice the innocent of his or her own country in order not to kill the innocent in the territory of a hostile neighbour. However, I cannot see such an absolute rule as rationally justifiable either (or, indeed, justifiable by reference to recent history of warfare).[15] If the law's purpose is to protect the innocent (and it is hard to see a more basic purpose for it in a system that excludes reference to personal virtue) and the launching of a nuclear strike would be the only means to attain this, then I cannot see how it could be excluded. In this sense, at least prima facie, the use of nuclear weapons in self-defence could not be excluded.

There is, of course, the argument that the use of nuclear weapons is 'qualita-tively different' from conventional warfare because of its 'unpredictable and uncontrollable human and environmental consequences'.[16] This is the bottom-line to which defenders of an absolute rule return: that due to their potentially apocalyptic consequences, nuclear weapons are in a class of their own.[17] However, I wonder about the strength of this argument. Quite apart from the (dubious) counter-examples of Hiroshima and Nagasaki, it fails to convince against using nuclear weapons in self-defence against a prior use. In such case, the extraordinary chain of causality postulated by the defenders of the absolute rule would already have been triggered by the adversary's action, and no *new* evil could ensue from trying to counter it. On the contrary, such use might perhaps have the 'unex-pected' consequence of preventing Apocalypse! Second, it is also powerless against the (paradoxical) argument that possession and deterrence are the sole means of *preventing* their use. Whether this argument is causally true or not may be debated, of course, but the absolute argument fails to address that causal assumption alto-gether. The conclusive point, however, against absolute view is that in fact it is only a relativist view in disguise. For the adherents of this doctrine, it is precisely their *consequences* that make nuclear weapons 'special'.[18] They rely (and must do so) on a relativist calculation – and cannot therefore be exempted from the kind of spec-ulation about alternative 'scenarios' that they wish to do away with. In this way, they lose the knock-out force of their argument against those whose very point is to prove that in some cases a limited use might be less devastating than remaining a sitting duck. The debate is about causality and foreseeable consequences after all. Even absolutists are compelled to entertain utilitarian calculations about the ratio

---

[15] I mean justifiable under *legal* reason. I can perfectly well understand a moral argument to the effect that in the choice between utilitarianism and absolutism, the latter is always the better inasmuch as war and massacre are concerned. See T Nagel, *Mortal Questions* (Cambridge, Cambridge University Press, 1979) 53–74.

[16] R Falk, L Meyrowitz, J Sanderson, *Nuclear Weapons and International Law* (Princeton NJ, Princeton University Press 1981) 78. See also, L Meyrowitz, *The Laws of War and Nuclear Weapons* in AS Miller, M Feinrider (eds), *Nuclear Weapons and Law* (Westport, Greenwood, 1984) 48.

[17] This is also the argument in the dissenting opinions of Shahabuddeen, Weeramantry and Koroma.

[18] See Shahabuddeen dissenting opinion 4–8; Weeramantry, dissenting opinion 11 ([I 7]) 13–31 ([II]) 58–62 ([IV]); Koroma, dissenting opinion 1 'Nuclear weapons are thus not just another kind of weapon, they are considered the absolute weapon and are far more pervasive in terms of their destruc-tive effects than any conventional weapon'.

of the innocent being killed under alternative scenarios.[19] It is the force of their very argument that compels the absolutists into the terrain of relativism.

However, the defenders of absolutism are right to point out that such a deliberation in a field of technical and causal uncertainty, secrecy, and changing military-political contexts tends to water down any determinate rule. In order to prevent that, it might be conceived that the inevitable exceptions should be couched in as absolute a fashion as possible. A good candidate might be an absolute prohibition of any *first strike*. This would be an easy-to-apply criterion that would keep the resort to nuclear weapons as a last alternative, to be employed only in the most extreme circumstance of self-defence, possibly only in retaliation of a prior nuclear attack.[20] However, I am not sure that such a rule would always be justifiable. It would exclude a non-dramatic first use – say, against a lone nuclear submarine in the Pacific – that might constitute the only means to prevent a foreseeable nuclear attack against your population centres.[21] Is it reasonable to expect a politician to commit suicide, together with large parts of the population, in deference to this kind of an absolute legal rule? Does the law allow the killing of the innocent by a nuclear attack conducted from a nuclear submarine in case the only means to forestall this would be a first use of nuclear weapons against it? Surely not. The application of the absolute rule would bring about precisely the consequences that its enactment was intended to prevent.

Regulation by absolute rules relies on the absolute value of rule-obedience. However, the application of a rule cannot always be detached from an examination of the presence of the reasons for which the rule was created. If those reasons are absent – as *ex hypothesi* they are in the case of the foreseeable attack on the lonely hostile submarine – then it cannot always be expected that the rule will be applied. Of course, in our daily lives we often expect that people obey rules even when their underlying reasons are absent. We expect drivers to stop at red lights even in the middle of the night where no other car or person can be seen within five miles. We do so because of two reasons. To leave it for individual drivers to decide when they might safely ignore the red light would, in some of the innumerable situations where red lights burn in the middle of distant crossings, create grave dangers anyway: perhaps a pedestrian in a dark coat is crossing the street but cannot be seen. Second, we want to honour the absolute character of the rules of the road in order not to induce people to judge for themselves. The proliferation of a sense that everything is up to individual decision might decrease general

---

[19] The absolutist language of the 'Apocalypse' sometimes smacks of dogmatism: it sweeps aside the relativist's causal-technical points assuming (without argument) the correctness of its own causal-technical assumptions.

[20] From the relatively undisputed criteria for the application of article 51 of the Charter (the presence of an 'armed attack' and the proportionality principle), Singh deduces the rule that the first use of nuclear weapons is always prohibited and that its use in retaliation would be permissible only against a nuclear attack. N Singh and E McWhinney, *Nuclear Weapons and International Law*, 2nd edn (The Hague, Nijhoff, 1989) 86–103. See also, D Rausching, 'Nuclear Warfare and Weapons' in *Max Planck Encyclopedia of International Law* (North-Holland, 1982) vol 4, 49.

[21] An example also referred to in Schwebel, dissenting opinion § 7.

security on the roads and endanger the application of other, perhaps more important rules. From the permission to decide for themselves in respect of red lights in
the desert, (some) motorists might draw the consequence that they could also
freely decide when to respect speed limits, or perhaps when to obey the law in
general. This might lead into a generalised non-obedience whose social costs
would be considerably greater than the costs of stopping at night in distant crossings even if no harm would seem to follow from just driving ahead.

Now, neither one of the explanations for honouring red lights in distant crossings
is present in the hypothesis of the first use against the lonely submarine. The danger
is not a consequence of the daily and repetitive character of the act, but arises from
the single situation. It is not a generalised social conduct that is being regulated, but
the behaviour of single individuals in a rare case of extreme gravity. The abstract,
generalising formulation of the rule against first strike (or of a full prohibition) fails
to account for (at least) this case and the arguments from the need to prevent marginal dangers (the pedestrian in the dark coat) or from the gradual erosion of rule-
obedience do not apply. The social need to honour the (empty) rule is considerably
weaker than the social need to prevent the individual submarine from striking first
now. No utilitarian calculation of gains and losses, however the costs of obedience
in this case may be conceptualised, could possibly yield the consequence that it
would be better to suffer the harm than to strike first.

An absolute rule (never a first strike) is unacceptable precisely because of its
absoluteness, because its application might (as in the case of the nuclear submarine) bring about precisely the consequence (the killing of the innocent) that it
aims to avoid. And because, in this case, the rule is no more valuable than the reason for which it was enacted, we are led to the paradoxical but, I think, compelling
conclusion that we must not apply it – a conclusion which, of course, undermines
its absolute character.

Absolute rules are easy to apply but cannot be applied because social contexts
are always more complex than the paradigm cases they are enacted to deal with.
Therefore, they must be softened by exceptions and broadly formulated standards
that allow the taking account of circumstances. Although contracts are binding
(absolute rule), it is sometimes necessary to release a party (standard of equity).
Even if equidistance normally creates a just settlement of a maritime boundary
delimitation, it is sometimes necessary to allow special circumstances to mitigate
the harshness of that rule. The relationship between the non-use-of-force rule in
article 2(4) of the UN Charter and the exception of self-defence under article 51
constitutes a similar case.

The problem in such cases is that even if the broad standard is originally
introduced only as an exception to the absolute rule, it tends to devour the rule
altogether. The introduction of equity into contracts or maritime delimitation
tends to reverse the hierarchy between the two: inasmuch as equity demands a
certain solution, there seems no good reason to avoid choosing it. The main rule
is relegated to the status of a (rebuttable) presumption about equity. The same is
true of the non-use-of-force/self-defence equation. In the absence of a criterion on

when to apply the rule and when the exception, self-defence tends to be applicable in all conceivable situations in which force is being used, buttressed by the reasonable argument that it must be up to the State itself to assess when its 'self' might be threatened.

The paradox of rules and standards is quite central in structuring the Court's Opinion. The Court avoided stating an absolute rule either way: it found neither an absolute permission nor an absolute prohibition specifically for the use or threat of nuclear weapons.[22] There was no rule that would have put nuclear weapons in a special category of means of warfare. It then had two alternatives available to it: silence (which, in fact, it chose) or trying to find out whether a permission or a prohibition might be deduced from the way in which the use of nuclear weapons might violate other rules of law. This meant, automatically, moving from a per se (absolute) prohibition to a relativist one, looking at nuclear weapons in terms of their consequences, ie whether they might be 'poisonous' or create unnecessary and indiscriminate suffering.[23] Embarking on the latter course, the Court first enquired whether a violation of the right to life or the commission of genocide might be involved. Neither rule could, however, be constructed as absolute: the right to life prohibited only *arbitrary* killing, while whether or not genocide was involved could only be appreciated 'after having taken account of the circumstances of the specific case'.[24] Even environmental law merely indicated 'important environmental factors' that were to be taken account in the overall assessment of the legality of any means of warfare.[25]

The bulk of the Opinion deals with two fields of law: the law on the use of force and international humanitarian law.[26] Neither contains an absolute rule against the killing of the innocent. Both construct the law in terms of contextual determinants that sometimes allow the (foreseeable although perhaps not intended) killing of non-combatants. The exception of self-defence looks for a balance between the threatening harm and the force to be used, while humanitarian law subsumes the legality of military action under a number of requirements intended to ensure a justifiable relation between the military objective to be attained and the damage caused (ie the prevention of unnecessary suffering). In both fields, the law can briefly be stated in terms of a search for *proportionality*.

In order to assess the proportionality of a proposed use of nuclear weapons in self-defence, assumptions about the 'imminence' of the coming attack and the gravity of the risk are involved. Relevant factors include at least the foreseeable consequences of a strike; the types of weapon employed; the gravity and foreseeability of the threat (nuclear or non-nuclear, limited or unlimited), the timing of

---

[22] Thus, the Court found that there was no specific prohibition of the use or threat of use of nuclear weapons in treaty law, *Nuclear Weapons case*, [53]–[63]) or custom (ibid [64]–[73]).

[23] See also Rausching, 'Nuclear Warfare and Weapons' (1982) 46–49.

[24] *Nuclear Weapons case*, [25] and [26].

[25] ibid [33].

[26] This consecration of two relatively autonomous fields of law is an important innovation by the Court and raises interesting questions about their relative superiority: what might happen if the rule on the killing of the innocent were different under the two?

the strike, the quality of the target (military or civilian), what other means are available, and the costs or consequences of non-use.

Other, less technical considerations might also seem relevant. What, for instance, is the 'self' that is a permissible object of defence?[27] Would it also extend to the protection of others? After all, collective self-defence under article 51 of the Charter is allowed, and it is hard to see the point of a rule that enables (an inno-cent) state to put its own life before that of the aggressor's but not that of anoth-er's.[28] Nor can it be assumed that subjective criteria regarding the *intended objectives* of a strike or objective factors about the *foreseeable effects* are irrelevant. A killing of civilians that is neither intended nor foreseeable would come under a different moral category from a massive strike against population centres. Failure to make a legal distinction between a defensive attack on a lonely submarine and an aggres-sive strike on a capital city would not only encourage expansionist tyrants (by putting them on the same level with conscientious politicians), but would be at odds with the very principle of protecting the innocent.[29]

Proportionality leads to an assessment of various alternative scenarios, taking account of technical data and making evaluations that cannot be carried out within any distinctly 'legal' form of reasoning. They involve highly abstract and contentious speculation about matters of uncertainty and grave political import-ance. Therefore, having first dismissed the argument that it was improper for the Court to give the opinion requested, as that would have necessitated the study of 'various types of nuclear weapons and to evaluate highly complex and controver-sial technological, strategic and scientific information',[30] the Court still came to the equivalent conclusion that:

> the Court considers that it does not have sufficient elements to enable it to conclude with certainty that the use of nuclear weapons would necessarily be at variance with the principles and rules of law applicable in armed conflict in any circumstance.[31]

It is easy to understand why the Court did not think it advisable to provide a deter-mined response. Having outlined the relevant law in terms of 'proportionality', going any further would have required an appreciation not only of uncertain tech-nical and factual information but also of alternative 'scenarios' involving 'factors' whose number cannot be limited and whose relevance cannot be assessed in advance. Had the Court arrived at some listing of the relevant 'factors', that would

---

[27] Answering this seems dependent on whether we identify the State in terms of its 'idea', its institutions or physical base. See B Buzan, *People, States & Fear*, 2nd edn (Boulder, Lynne Rienner, 1991) 57–107.

[28] See BA Brody, 'The International Defense of Liberty' in Franken Paul, Miller, Paul, Ahrens (eds), *Nuclear Rights, Nuclear Wrongs* (1986) 30–31.

[29] On the other hand, a nuclear policy based on retaliatory attacks on military targets only makes little military sense. As Henry Shue put it, 'An adversary who has decided to launch a nuclear attack is unlikely to be very cooperative about saving targets for you'. See Frankel Paul, Miller, Paul, Ahrens (eds), *Nuclear Rights, Nuclear Wrongs* (1986) 50. In order to constitute an effective deterrent, a second-strike based nuclear policy is pushed towards targeting non combatants.

[30] *Nuclear Weapons case* [15].

[31] ibid [95].

have been, like the definition of aggression, 'a trap for the innocent and a signpost for the guilty',[32] opening a mine of argumentative possibilities for *mala fide* statesmen in search of justifications.

Through proportionality (or 'equity', 'reasonableness' or 'good faith'), not only does the rule vanish into the background but we seem no longer able to make *any* distinction between the rule and the reasons for which it was enacted. The political or military leader is simply called upon to use his or her best judgment – which he or she would probably, in any case, do during a situation of such extreme gravity. The 'softening' of the absolute rule by a flexible standard ('proportionality') leaves everything ultimately up to the person with the button.

There is a related and, I find, a conclusive reason for why the Court was not in a position to provide the requested response in terms of a contextual judgment. Had it done so, it would have instituted a public and technical discourse for the defence of the killing of the innocent. By lifting the matter from the realm of passion to that of reason, the Court would have broken the taboo against any use of nuclear weapons. It would have opened a professionally honourable and perhaps even a tragically pleasurable way of addressing the unaddressable. The (massive) killing of the innocent would have become another contextual determinant, a banal 'factor' in an overall balancing of the utilities, to be compared with the equally banal factors of sovereignty, military objective, etc. As Thomas Nagel observed:

> Once the door is opened to calculations of utility and national interest, the usual speculation about the future of freedom, peace and economic prosperity can be brought to bear to ease the consciences of those responsible for a certain number of charred babies.[33]

Unlike taboo, rational argument cannot put nuclear weapons in a class of their own, to be treated outside the normal logic of identity and difference, legal analogy and 'distinguishing'. If the killing of the innocent by, say, conventional aerial bombing is allowed in some (exceptional) cases of self-defence, then reason insists that it should also be allowed by nuclear weapons in analogous cases, ie in cases where the proportionality rule yields the same ratio between gains and losses. *Thinking about the killing of the innocent in terms of gains and losses is not neutral, however.* It leads into a slippery slope of public discourse where deviating conceptions of 'gain' and 'loss' are constantly thrown against one another, and the final outcome always depends on a *fiat*, whether a tyrant's *Diktat* or – much more ominously – the anonymous routine of the bureaucrat.

---

[32] See J Stone, *Conflict through Consensus. United Aproaches to Aggression* (Baltimore, John Hopkins University Press, 1977).
[33] See Nagel, *Mortal Questions* (1979) 59.

The Sense of Silence

Discussing the use, or threat of use, of nuclear weapons through legal reason results in a general law on the killing of the innocent whose boundaries we should constantly have to patrol, not only against *mala fide* applications but genuine (though possibly mistaken) sentiments about the relative worth of values to be protected and destroyed. Only fear – the irrational image of the Apocalypse – puts nuclear weapons in a special category, detaching them from the banal logic of causes and consequences, gains and losses. If the prohibition against the killing of the innocent is not accepted as such – and it cannot be accepted as such within a legal reason that looks for proof – then it is always subjected to the balancing act of law's purposive-rational, bureaucratic ethos: '. . . divesting the use and deployment of violence from moral calculus, and [. . .] emancipating the desiderata of rationality from interference of ethical norms or moral inhibitions'.[34]

So whatever the reasons for the Court's silence, it was a beneficial silence inasmuch as it, and it only, could leave room for the workings of the moral impulse, the irrational, non-foundational appeal against the killing of the innocent.[35]

The use of legal reason to determine the normative status of the use or threat of use of nuclear weapons collapses at this: there is no more fundamental certainty that could be referred to in order to support the belief that the massive killing of the innocent is wrong. However much we seek to find supporting reasons for this belief, no such reason partakes an equivalent degree of convincing force as the statement itself. On the contrary, the more justifications are adduced to support the belief that the killing of the innocent is wrong, the weaker it starts to appear; the more it becomes contaminated by the uncertainties and qualifications that infect those justifying reasons. This is how rational argument breaks the taboo surrounding the use of nuclear weapons and thus, inadvertently, makes it easier to contemplate it.

This problem relates to an error regarding the status of the demand of not killing the innocent. If 'truth' is the quality of a proposition that can be supported by another proposition that is already known to be 'true', then the prohibition against massive killing of the innocent does not partake of it. Its validity is not dependent on the truth of any *other* proposition that could be cited as a justification for it. For a legal discourse that seeks the 'truth' about norms, this is a frustrating fact.

---

[34] Z Bauman, *Modernity and the Holocaust* (Ithaca, Cornell University Press, 1989) 28.
[35] The argument for the limitation of law understood as formal rules and principles draws inspiration from Emmanuel Levinas' seminal but difficult philosophical work, especially as developed in Z Bauman, *Postmodern Ethics* (Oxford, Cambridge Mass, Blackwell, 1993), D Furrow, *Against Theory. Continental and Analytic Challenges in Moral Philosophy* (New York, Routledge, 1995) especially 133–93 and (to a lesser extent, focusing on the continued relevance of judging actions by reference to their consequences) T May, *The Moral Theory of Poststructuralism* (Pensylvania State University Press, 1995). The most accessible introduction to Levinas remains: *Levinas, Ethics and Infinity. Conversations with Philippe Nemo* (Pittsburgh, Duquesne University Press, 1985).

The truth (or validity) of legal norms is always derived from the truth of other propositions that deal with their source or authority. Instead of a prescription, law starts from a denotation, inserting the norm into inverted commas: 'According to the UN Charter (or some other convention, custom or general principle of law) "nuclear weapons are illegal"'. The illegality of nuclear weapons – the *obligation* – is made conditional upon a cognitive argument about whether this is in fact what the UN Charter (or the other treaty, or custom, or a general principle) says. The denotation refers normally to either history or system. Can the proposed norm be proved by reference to a past legislative act? Can it be derived from a higher-level norm that we know to be valid? Neither avenue is open to verify the truth of the prohibition of the killing of the innocent. History is either too irrelevant or controversial to prove that the innocent ought not to be killed. Nor is the prohibition dependent on any more general or valuable norm or principle that would itself be truer. It cannot be 'derived' from a moral theory without becoming subject to apparently well-founded objections, derived from 3,000 years of argument in moral philosophy.

Legal reason is premised on the assumption that an obligation exists (or is valid) by virtue of there having been an anterior fact of a certain sort: an agreement, a behaviour, or a principle that embodies it. The obligation is invalid if no such anterior fact can be proved. The authority of that anterior fact or norm must then be traced to another, even more basic, fact or norm until we come at the law's ultimate justification that can no longer be proved but must be accepted as a matter of truth.[36] The prohibition of the massive killing of the innocent, however, cannot be derived in this way without losing its force. It is, in other words, not part of the linguistic practices of 'truth' or 'reason' as we know them and as we expect public authorities to follow. To think it is, is to subsume it under a set of particularly weak conventions that will cast doubt upon, and finally do away with, its binding force. Let me quote Lyotard from an analoguous context:

> [t]he tribunal whose idiom is that genre of discourse which is cognition, which therefore accepts only descriptive phrases with cognitive value as acceptable, asks of the one who claims an obligation: which is the authority that obligates you [. . .]? The obligated is caught in a dilemma: either he or she names the addressor of the law and exposes the authority and sense of the law, and then he or she ceases to be obligated solely by the mere fact that the law, thus rendered intelligible to cognition, becomes an object of discussion and loses its obligatory value. Or else, he or she recognizes that this value cannot be expressed, that he or she cannot phrase in the place of the law, and then this tribunal cannot admit that the law obligates him or her since the law is without reason and is therefore arbitrary.[37]

---

[36] This is, of course, what Kelsen called the 'transcendental hypothesis' and Derrida the 'mystical foundation of the authority of law'. See H Kelsen, *Reine Rechtslehre. Einleitung in die rechtswissenschaftliche Problematik* (Leipzig, F Deuticke, 1934) 66–67 (s 29) and J Derrida, 'Force of Law: The "Mystical Foundation of Authority"' in D Cornell et al, *Deconstruction and the Possibility of Justice* (New York, Routledge, 1992) 3.

[37] J-F Lyotard, *The Differend. Phrases in Dispute* (Minneapolis, Minnesota University Press, 1988) 117 para 176.

The request concerning the legality of the use or threat of the use of nuclear weapons gives rise to a situation where conflicting values are managed by reference to a cognitive idiom that not only fails to give effect to, but even to articulate, the meaning of the use of sophisticated modern technology to attain the massive and indiscriminate killing of the innocent living in far-off lands. In the legal argument about nuclear weapons, the enormity and the exceptional character, indeed the *unthinkability* of the threatening wrong, finds no signification and therefore cannot be taken into account. In Lyotard's theory of the *Differend*, this is typically the case in attempts to fit the Holocaust into the idiom of historical research and narrative and explains the frequent silence of concentration camp survivors. No historical explanation can possibly convey the experience – its personal or cultural significance. The sense in which the Holocaust transcends history is suppressed, cannot be expressed by the idiom of history. Hence, silence follows.[38]

We could also think about law's inability to give expression to the religious values of members of indigenous societies. The type of collective but transient linkage that Australian aborigine society has to land still remains largely unrecognised by a legal system that only acknowledges personal ownership to determined portions of territory. Remember, too, the argument about sexual violence against women being either completely outside the law or even at best recognised only in a limited and distorted way. Here as well, certain values cannot be translated to the idiom of legal reason.[39] Any settlement will in such cases fail to reflect the wrong subjectively suffered and may even be seen as a repetition, or rehearsal, of such wrong.

It is, of course, true that courts do not always follow the paradigm of legal reason but sometimes quite remarkably depart from the conventions of the juristic *genre*. In the *Reservations* case, for instance, the ICJ characterised genocide as

a denial of the right of existence of entire human groups, a denial which shocks the conscience of mankind and results in great losses to humanity, and which is contrary to moral law and to the spirit and aims of the United Nations.[40]

The Court added that 'the principles underlying the Convention are principles which are recognized by civilized nations as binding on States, even without any conventional obligation'.[41]

Such an argument about 'moral law' is unassailable from a technical point of view, because it is completely unsupported by technical argument. It can only be accepted or rejected because of what it says; not because of any evidence that was brought in to prove it. The Court appeals directly to the reader as a person who will immediately approve of the sentence and feels no need to prove it, to whom the illegality of genocide is not a matter of technical argument at all, to whom the

---

[38] ibid 9. See also Furrow, *Against Theory* (1995) 33–34, 161–93.
[39] See C Smart, *Feminism and the Power of Law* (London, New York, Routledge, 1989) 26–49.
[40] *Reservations case* [1951] ICJ Rep 21 (emphasis added).
[41] ibid. Note that the statement 'even without any conventional obligation' addresses precisely the issue of propositional truth to which I referred earlier. But now the Court rejects the need for establishing it. The prohibition of genocide was not true because of the truth of any other ('conventional') proposition.

contrary – the lawfulness of genocide – would be quite literally unthinkable. If the reader does not accept the statement *as it is*, he or she will not be convinced of its truth by any additional argument. And the Court makes no such argument. The sentence propounds a self-evidence that any 'proof' could only serve to weaken.

Genocide – or better, the unthinkability of genocide – brings to the surface the limits of rational argument and the character of normative knowledge. Chains of argument and proof can always be traced to a point at which something can no longer be proved but must be axiomatic, as something that we know because we could not think otherwise. This is what Kelsen meant when he characterised the norm that justifies the legal order – the *Grundnorm* – as a transcendental hypothesis, something that cannot be proved but must be assumed in order for everything else we know about the law to make sense.[42] Wittgenstein addressed the issue of receding justification in the following way: '[i]f I have exhausted the justification I have reached bedrock, and my spade is turned. Then I am inclined to say: "This is simply what I do"'.[43]

In this way, reason and justification refer away from themselves, into what is accepted outside as a matter of faith, and in particular to the social practices in which what we do is constitutive of who we are. By making an assertion about 'moral law', the Court in the *Reservations* case assumed that a (rudimentary) community existed between the parties to the conflict, the reader, and the Court. Questioning the Court's statement would have been to set oneself outside this community. From that moment, the argument could not go on. What is being evoked is not only the meaning of the statement *but also the self-evidence of that meaning*. Asking for proof is, to revert to Wittgenstein, to play another language game, to participate in a form of life that is not the one defined by the unthinkability of genocide. Such a break in communication cannot be repaired by more technical argument; a 'differend' ensues in which no language can bridge a gap between the competing forms of life.

In the *Reservations* case, however, the Court stepped outside legal reason and argument in an issue (the exceptional character of genocide) that was not in conflict. The case related to a technical point about the legal meaning of reservations and objections to them, not to whether or when genocide might be prohibited. The moral community defined by the unthinkability of genocide was never threatened; its affirmation was irrelevant for the technical argument regarding the operation of the object and purpose test which the Court outlined as the applicable rule. Its principal meaning was to reaffirm a constitutional value of the UN system in 1951 and to set up a mirror, less than a decade after the Holocaust, in which the members could recognise and redefine themselves.

In the *Nuclear Weapons* case, the situation was different. There was no anterior community that would have been defined by the agreement concerning the illegality or otherwise of the use of nuclear weapons. Any axiomatic statement about the

[42] eg Kelsen, *Reine Rechtslehre* (1934).
[43] L Wittgenstein, *Philosophical Investigations* (Oxford, Blackwell, 1958) 85 para 217.

impermissibility of the killing of the innocent would not only have been hypocritical (because unlike the commission of genocide, most states do accept the
killing of the innocent in a number of circumstances), it would have set up a
distorted self-image and an ideological screen over the public facade of the international system. Like Rousseau once remarked against Grotius, such use of morality may not be logical, but it is certainly favourable to tyrants.[44]

Abraham's Lesson

Let me conclude by reflecting on the implications of the request for legal faith and
the identity of the lawyer by reference to the familiar story of Abraham and Isaac.
One day an angel told Abraham to go to the mountain and prepare Isaac, his son,
as a sacrifice for God. Abraham complied without a question. He took Isaac to the
mountain, never telling him why he was not bringing a lamb with them (we are
not told whether Isaac knew what fate awaited him). As they arrived, Abraham put
Isaac on the unlit pyre that he had set up on a sacrificial rock and raised his knife.
At that moment, an angel's voice was heard: Lay down your knife; you have proved
your faith in God.[45]
   The images this story conveys of Abraham can be used to illustrate the situation of
the international lawyer in face of the god of law. Two very basic contrasting perspectives are open. One is the traditional, theological view of Abraham's behaviour as an
act of ultimate faith, a heroic, relentless faith that is prepared to go any length to
fulfil itself, regardless of any personal or human cost. This interpretation – the knight
of faith[46] – does not question Abraham's suffering as he prepares to sacrifice his only
son. Suffering is the very point of the act, proving as it does the strength of the faith.
Had Abraham been indifferent, no angel might have intervened.
   The other interpretation is the agnostic one for which the story is not one of
redemption but of foolishness and tragedy. It focuses on Abraham's renunciation
of personal responsibility and on his inability to protect the persons closest to him.
In the face of an anonymous command, Abraham is immediately prepared to lay
down human reason and conscience. His fate is sad, akin to that of Aischylos'
Agamemnon who does sacrifice his daughter Ifigenia to demonstrate his piety
towards Zeus. However, where Agamemnon's sacrifice is a cold, calculating, purposive-rational act, comprehensible and condemnable precisely for that reason,
Abraham appears simply as a lost human soul, living in a phantom land of subject-
less voices. And yet it is Abraham that is the more frightening of the two because

---

[44] JJ Rousseau, *The Social Contract* (translated and introduced by M Cranston, Harmondsworth,
Penguin, 1987) 51.
[45] The story is of course told in Genesis 22: 1–19. The moral-philosophical problems are famously
dismissed in S Kierkegaard, *Fear and Trembling*, edited by CS Evans and S Walsh (Cambridge University
Press, 2006 [1843]).
[46] ibid 32–46.

of the ease with which any of us might be led to complicity with cruelty induced by passive faith in authority and the bracketing of personal responsibility under an explanation of 'just following the rules'.[47]

The contrasting images of Abraham (heroic/tragic) depend, of course, from the reader's view of the status of the angel's words. If we can be certain that they did represent God's authentic will, we can only admire Abraham. Only then Abraham's act is revealed as an example to be followed. However, if our own faith is insecure and we can entertain the thought of the command not having come from God but from, say, the devil or from Abraham's own subconscious, or if the possibility cannot be excluded that the command was unclear or that Abraham misunderstood it, then his behaviour starts to seem as the height of foolishness, or dogmatic insanity.

The request concerning the lawfulness of nuclear weapons recalls the story by putting international lawyers in the position of Abraham, waiting passively for the command of the court, ready to suspend any requirements of personal conscience in order to execute it faithfully. Such an absolute loyalty may be a proper posture in case we have faith in the law and in the court's ability to know it. But inasmuch as the law may seem uncertain, full of exceptions and qualifications, references to contextual judgment – and this is what the previous sections have argued – the existence of such faith cannot be taken for granted. Discretion and 'evaluation', even error and misjudgment, are parts of the law however much it is dressed in the voice of universal reason.

But I do not think that many international lawyers feel themselves in the position of Abraham – although that is how the request portrays them/us. Many of us were never ready to accept and execute any statement the court might have given, but were quite prepared to condemn the court in case it gave the wrong opinion. The request dressed international lawyers as true believers in the image of Abraham. However, this was a dress of hypocrisy. Most international lawyers would have been prepared to sacrifice the court, and the law it propounded, but not their intuition because, in fact, they hold that intuition (instead of faith in the law) so central to their own self-image and identity as liberal 'progressives'.[48]

Such an attitude of hypocrisy has two perverse consequences. First, it reconfirms a structure of normative authority in which many lawyers do not believe and have no reason to believe. The court and the legal technique available to it are in no position to determine the status of the massive killing of the innocent. Portraying ourselves as faithful servants of the law, we in fact buttress the court as a puppet authority, and we are ready to reject it the moment it oversteps the moral walls around its paper castle. The image our behaviour conveys of the court, and

---

[47] For a famous experiment to this effect, see S Milgram, *Obedience to Authority. An Experimental View* (New York, Harper & Row, 1974). See also the discussion of its implications in Bauman, *Modernity and the Holocaust* (1989) 151–68.

[48] This point was made, somewhat more diplomatically, by Judge Oda, arguing that the request did not really seek the Court's opinion, but the 'endorsement of an alleged legal axiom', dissenting opinion para 3.

of ourselves, is profoundly distorted. We know this, yet keep the truth secret, because revealing it might altogether undermine a structure of authority which otherwise is so beneficial for ourselves and our public identity as the technicians of an objective legal reason.

Second, this attitude perpetuates the illusion of the existence of a privileged (legal) rationality that is able to resolve any political conflict without becoming political itself. Its bureaucratic attachment to legal technique allows the abdication of personal responsibility for anything that can be supported by this technique – and anything can. This is the path of Auschwitz and the key lesson expressed in Zygmunt Bauman's powerful dictum that 'the Holocaust was not an irrational outflow of not-yet-fully eradicated residues of pre-modern barbarity. It was a legitimate resident in the house of modernity; indeed one who would not be at home in any other house'.[49]

The *Nuclear Weapons* request emanated from an inability to articulate and to take seriously the moral impulse against the killing of the innocent. We may have been embarrassed for such impulse and regard it as a matter of 'subjective evaluation', incommensurate with competing moralities. Perhaps we feel that such an impulse is, as Alasdair MacIntyre has suggested, only a fragment of the moral consciousness of a past civilisation whose language is no longer with us so that we cannot publicly address our moral beliefs.[50] Perhaps we feel that fraudulence or hypocrisy are our only (unappealing) alternatives and that, even as we occasionally set argument aside to refer to 'moral law' we remain puzzled about what this really means and with what right we claim to extend our moral beliefs to other people.

But, this is so only under the assumption that the language of the law is a universal language, amenable to statements of rational principle that can be uniformly applied in essentially similar situations. This is, of course, the faith needed to sustain a legal technique through which the identity of the lawyer has been constituted vis-à-vis politicians, diplomats, or moral theorists. It is a faith created through the mistrust of politics, ideology, and the passions that have created so much human suffering. It is a faith, however, that never acknowledged itself as such, but was presented as the natural flow of an objective, impersonal reason.

So I come back to the story of Abraham and Isaac and the sense in which the issue of nuclear weapons relates to faith and the identity of international lawyers. The 'theology' of the law has prevented lawyers from seeing to what extent personal responsibility is involved, to what extent in every legal act – including the act of becoming a lawyer – a 'decision' and some kind of faith are implicated.[51] The fact that the massive killing of the innocent cannot be comprehended by reason is surely not a compelling argument against continuing to think of it as an extraordinary wrong. To say this is to recognise that at least one central fact of our existence is not the capacity to reason. Instead our humanness includes also the

---

[49] Bauman, *Modernity and the Holocaust* (1989), 17
[50] A MacIntyre, *After Virtue*, 2nd edn (Notre Dame, Ind, University of Notre Dame Press, 1984).
[51] See also M Davies, *Delimiting the Law: 'postmodernism' and the politics of law* (London, Chicago, Pluto Press, 1996) 93–99.

ability to recognise massive human suffering and to feel bound by the need to combat it without any more fundamental reason for feeling so.

Critical theory insists that identity is not something fixed but also, and sim-ultaneously, a project.[52] This is true of the identity of the lawyer as well. Is it better (I find no more relevant linguistic convention than the normative through which to address this question) to identify oneself on the basis of one's ability to manage a legal technique, one's unconditional loyalty to formal authority, or on the basis of one's sensitivity for the call of the innocent not to be killed? To look for rules, techniques or authority is to think of oneself as Abraham, sad and dangerous. As lawyers, we need to be able to say that we know that the killing of the innocent is wrong not because of whatever chains of reasoning we can produce to support it, or who it was that told us so, but because of who we are.[53] Without so defining ourselves, how could we possibly be trusted to do the right thing in the unique and precarious situations in which that passion is triggered?[54]

---

[52] J Habermas, *Autonomy and Solidarity: interviews with Jürgen Habermas* (London, New York, Verso, 1992) 243.

[53] As pointed out by Zenon Bankowski and Claire Davis, the story of Abraham and Isaac raises the question of the relationship of law and love, 'Living In and Out of the Law', in P OD Scott and V Tadros, *Faith in Law: Essays in Legal Theory* (Oxford, Hart, 2000) 33–51. Here is also the connection between the present chapter and chapter six of this volume.

[54] David Kennedy and I have continued this discussion in two essays in P Sands and L Boisson de Chazournes, *International Law and Nuclear Weapons* (Cambridge, Cambridge University Press, 1999), 462 and 488. In Kennedy's view, there is no point at which discourse 'ends', or should end. Even the discourse of spirituality (or theology) is a discourse and its merits cannot be measured outside some frame of costs and benefits and by reference to alternative discourses. I am willing to accept this but would insist on the need and possibility of 'temporary' silence, a point if reflective distancing from technical discourse itself, when its message is reduced, if not to silence then to no more than 'noise'.

9

International Law and Hegemony:
a Reconfiguration

The first text in this collection makes the point that international legal argument is a
'politics'. The present chapter extends this view by applying the theory of hegemony
by Gramsci and Laclau to the process of making international legal claims. The category of 'hegemony' used here is purely descriptive and covers the technique whereby
something particular (an interest, a preference) is presented as something universal
('the law', 'universal human right', 'community value', etc). The chapter describes the
use of hegemonic arguments in a number of areas of international law (use of force,
trade law, human rights law, law and globalisation). Its larger objective is to make the
point about the key role of polemics and contestation in law and how the law's 'universal' is also always a 'false universal'. It seemed particularly important to highlight
this at a time when the rhetoric of the 'international community' was everywhere and
very oddly clashing with the counter-vocabulary of the 'war on terror'.

INTERNATIONAL LAW APPEARS to be in trouble. The details are well
known. While the legality of the Afghanistan operations is still an object of
polite disagreement, the occupation of Iraq (2003–2006) was almost unani-
mously seen as illegal – occasioning the response from across the Atlantic that if
so, then so much the worse for law. Since the terrorist attacks of 11 September
2001, the United States had decided to go it alone. Others were welcome to join in
if they wished, and there may be advantages, but very little law, down that road.
The Guantanamo base was deliberately chosen to hold al-Qaida suspects under
full American control and has become a symbol of the US opposition to everything
that might check its liberty of action, from human rights treaty bodies to the
International Criminal Court, multilateral disarmament to the Kyoto Protocol.[1]
   However, this is nothing new. A few years ago the future Under-Secretary for
Disarmament Affairs of the Bush administration, John Bolton, asked his audience,
'Should we take global governance seriously?', went through the usual suspects –
International Criminal Court (ICC), International Court of Justice (ICJ), Test-
Ban Treaty (TBT), land mines, non-governmental organisation (NGO) activity in
human rights, trade and the environment – and responded, 'Sadly . . . yes.' For
him, globalism 'represent[ed] a kind of worldwide cartelisation of governments

---

[1] For a comprehensive discussion, see M Byers and G Nolte (eds), *United States Hegemony and the
Foundations of International Law* (Cambridge, Cambridge University Press, 2003) 531.

and interest groups', something the United States needed to combat with all energy:

It is well past the point when the uncritical acceptance of globalist slogans . . . can be allowed to proceed. The costs to the United States . . . are far too great, and the current understanding of these costs far too limited to be acceptable.[2]

Since 2000, that manifesto has moved firmly into the political centre. In his widely read pamphlet, Robert Kagan had this to say about transatlantic relations since 9/11: Where the Europeans are 'proselytising their doctrines of international law and international institutions, Americans have begun . . . turning back toward a more traditional American policy of independence, toward that uniquely American form of national universalism'[3]. Liberal internationalists were wrong: the world is still the way it was portrayed by Thucydides and Machiavelli. Leadership still 'demands a pagan ethos': 'The moral basis of our foreign policy will depend upon the character of our nation and its leaders, not upon the absolutes of international law'.[4]

How differently the Europeans see the world! 'Nowadays . . . the United Nations Charter has almost universally been recognised as the constitutional document of the international community of States'.[5] Antonio Cassese has this to say:

[A]t least at the normative level the international community is becoming more integrated and – what is even more important – . . . such values as human rights and the need to promote development are increasingly penetrating various sectors of international law that previously seemed impervious to them.[6]

Notice his optimism: the world is finally being organised by a law based on something grander than archaic forms of diplomacy: universal values are overriding the political wills of states. This is often discussed in terms of constitutional principles, the assumption that the international community will organise itself analogously to the domestic one, as a vertically constraining system of law manifested in notions such as *jus cogens* or universal jurisdiction over crimes against humanity.[7] The terms of the American-European debate seem clear: 'The crucial issue of dissent is whether justification through international law can, and should be replaced by the unilateral, world-ordering politics of a self-appointed hegemon.'[8]

---

[2] JR Bolton, 'Should we Take Global Governance Seriously?' (2000) 1 *Chicago Journal of International Law* 221.

[3] R Kagan, *Paradise & Power: America and Europe in the New World Order* (London, Atlantic, 2003) 88.

[4] RD Kaplan, *Warrior Politics: Why Leadership Demands a Pagan Ethos* (New York, Vintage, 2002) 131.

[5] B Simma and A Paulus, 'The "International Community" Facing the Challenge of Globalisation' (1998) 9 *European Journal of International Law* 266–77.

[6] A Cassese, *International Law* (Oxford, Oxford University Press, 2002) 45.

[7] For a brief overview of the discussion, see B Von Brun-Otto, 'Konstitutionalisierung des Völkerrechts und Internationalisierung des Verfassungsrechts' (2003) 42 *Der Staat* 61–76. For the tradition of reading the UN Charter as a constitutional document, see A Paulus, *Die internationale Gemeinschaft im Völkerrecht: Eine Untersuchung zur Entwicklung des Völkerrechts im Zeitalter der Glalisierun* (Munich, Beck, 2001) 292–318.

[8] J Habermas 'Interpreting the Fall of a Monument' (2003) 4 *German Law Journal* 706.

Despite this contrast, what is shared on both sides of the Atlantic is the view of international law as distinct from power, and that precisely because it is so, it needs either to be celebrated or discarded. Whatever view the speaker has taken on the 'absolutes of international law' the one thing each seems to agree upon is that they are indeed 'absolutes' and, as such, call for total commitment or total rejection.

My intention is to question the assumption that there is a set of substantive rules or principles of 'international law' that would be worthy of the kind of total commitment or rejection suggested. I shall describe international law as a process of articulating political preferences into legal claims that cannot be detached from the conditions of political contestation in which they are made. Instead of international law as strictly opposed to hegemony, I shall discuss it as a hegemonic technique. After an introductory section, I shall examine some of the themes under which it is employed, and end with a few words about its significance as a *legal* technique.

The Hegemonic Technique

There is a tradition of disagreement about whether the international world can be treated as a community, with views emphasising the heterogeneity of the interests represented therein clashing against theories of functional interdependence from the perspective of which the world indeed seems united. The pragmatic compromise to treat the international world as an 'anarchic society' finds its parallel in contemporary legal theories that juxtapose old diplomatic laws of coexistence and cooperation with incipient 'vertical' regulation about the protection of universal values.[9] The appearance is of the world at the same time as an aggregate of self-regarding units and as a functional whole.

In political terms, this is visible in the fact that there is no representative of the whole that would not be simultaneously a representative of some particular. 'Universal values' or 'the international community' can only make themselves known through mediation by a state, an organisation or a political movement. Likewise, behind every notion of universal international law there is always some particular view, expressed by a particular actor in some particular situation. This is why it is pointless to ask about the contribution of international law to the global community without clarifying first *what* or *whose* view of international law is meant. However universal the terms in which international law is invoked, it never

---

[9] This was the theme of a large symposium on the work of Wolfgang Friedmann, organised by the European Journal of International Law in 1997. Of the many explorations see, eg G Abi-Saab, 'Whither the International Community?' (1998) 9 *European Journal of international Law* 248–65. This oscillation between a description of the world in which sovereignty has been 'thinning out' and one in which 'the ramparts of old-fashioned sovereignty are still strongly manned' is also nicely manifested in T Farer, 'Toward an Effective International Legal Order: From Coexistence to Concert' (2004) 17 *Cambridge Review of International Affairs* 219–38.

appears as an autonomous and stable set of demands over a political reality. Instead, it always appears through the positions of political actors, as a way of dressing political claims in a specialised technical idiom in the conditions of *hegemonic contestation*.

By 'hegemonic contestation' I mean the process by which international actors routinely challenge each other by invoking legal rules and principles on which they have projected meanings that support their preferences and counteract those of their opponents. In law, political struggle is waged on what legal words such as 'aggression', 'self-determination', 'self-defence', 'terrorist' or *jus cogens* mean, whose policy will they include, whose will they oppose. To think of this struggle as *hegemonic* is to understand that the objective of the contestants is to make their partial view of that meaning appear as the total view, their preference seem like the *universal preference*.[10]

There are many examples of this contestation. The process that led into the definition of 'aggression' by the UN General Assembly in 1974 was about drawing a line between acceptable and unacceptable forms of coercion in a situation where different solutions put states in unequal positions. Every suggested definition seemed either under-inclusive or over-inclusive from some participant perspective, that is, covering cases one did not wish to cover (ie the behaviour of oneself or one's ally) or not covering cases that should have been covered (ie forms of behaviour of foreseeable enemies). Everyone participated in the nearly 20 year process with two (understandable) objectives: to encompass as much as possible of the behaviour of one's enemies, while making sure that nothing would limit the freedom of action of one's own country. Now when *all* participants acted on such premises the result could only be both completely binding ('Aggression is . . .', article 1 of the Resolution containing the definition) and completely open ended (a non-exhaustive list of nine examples with the proviso that the 'Security Council may determine that other acts constitute Aggression under the provisions of the Charter', article 4 of the Resolution containing the definition) simultaneously – a definition on which everyone could agree because it accommodated every conceivable meaning.[11]

The fact that the inability to define 'terrorism' broke up the negotiations for a comprehensive convention on terrorism in the United Nations in 2002 reflects an identical (hegemonic) logic: whose friends were to be branded as 'terrorists' and whose violence was to escape that denomination? Of course, there was no agreement on this. The world's uniform opposition to 'terrorism' is dependent on its open-endedness, the degree to which it allows everyone to fill the category of 'terrorist' with one's preferred adversary.

---

[10] See further E Laclau and C Mouffe, *Hegemony and Socialist Strategy*, 2nd edn (London, Verso, 2001) and E Laclau 'Identity and Hegemony: The Role of Universality in the Constitution of Political Logics' in J Butler, E Laclau and S Žižek, *Contingency, Hegemony, Universality: Contemporary Dialogues on the Left* (London, Verso, 2000) 44–89.
[11] See UNGA Res 3314 (1974) and the drafting history in J Stone, *Conflict though Consensus: United Nations Approaches to Aggression* (Sydney, Maitland, 1977) 234.

Likewise, for every understanding of a rule, there is a counter-understanding or an exception, for every principle a counter-principle and for every institutional policy a counter-policy. Law is a surface over which political opponents engage in hegemonic practices, trying to enlist its rules, principles and institutions on their side, making sure they do not support the adversary. In order to bring that perspective into focus, analysis must be shifted from rules to broad themes of legal argument within which hegemonic contestation takes place.

Basic Ambivalence: Between Unity and Diversity

The European-American controversy surveyed above suggests that two opposite projects characterise international law: one purports to lead from sovereign egoism into world unity, the other from the oppressive uniformity of global domination into self-determination and identity.[12] Each project starts from a negative characterisation of the political present and seeks to override it with a legal blueprint conceived alternatively as a project of unity or a project of diversity. No doubt, the project of unity has been rhetorically predominant. Here is the view of Judge Mohammed Bedjaoui from the Peace Palace:

> The resolutely positivist, voluntarist approach of international law . . . has been replaced by an objective conception of international law, a law more readily seen as the reflection of a collective juridical conscience and a response to the social necessities of States organised as a community.[13]

For this view, the problems of the international world crystallise under the weight of sovereign egoism over the rational administration of the world's affairs.[14] Today's human rights, environmental and trade law seeks to break through the 'artificial' boundaries of sovereignty so as to realise the promise of world unity articulated as the (hegemonic) universalisation of the values underlying human rights, environment or trade.[15]

Yet, 'world unity', precisely because it is hegemonic, can always be interpreted as dystopia, the imposition of special interests in the garb of general ones. 'Whoever invokes humanity wants to cheat', one of the paragons of political realism, Carl

---

[12] I have elsewhere called these the 'ascending' and 'descending' project, See M Koskenniemi, *From Apology to Utopia; the Structure of International Legal Argument* (1989) (Re-issue with a new Epilogue, Cambridge University Press, 2005) 59–60 and 474–512.

[13] M Bedjaoui, Declaration, ICJ, *Threat or Use of Force by Nuclear Weapons*, ICJ Reports 1996, 1345 para 13.

[14] The critique of sovereignty emerged with modern international law itself at the end of the nineteenth century and has remained one of its most conspicuous themes since. See M Koskenniemi, *The Gentle Civiliser of Nations: The Rise and Fall of International law 1870–1960* (Cambridge, Cambridge University Press, 2001) 569 and J Bartelson, *The Critique of the State* (Cambridge, Cambridge University Press, 2001).

[15] See further M Koskenniemi, 'The Wonderful Artificiality of States', *Proceedings of the American Society of International Law 1994* (Washington, ASIL, 1995) 22–29.

Schmitt, once wrote, and EH Carr even made a career (and possibly an academic discipline) out of preaching that 'pleas for international solidarity and world union come from those dominant nations which may hope to exercise control over a unified world'.[16] From this perspective, the call of 'old Europe' for law and international institutions seems to have little distance from the interests of once-upon-a-time imperial powers trying to achieve some control in a novel configuration of forces.

Stated in this way, both projects remain purely formal, allowing any substance to fill the space of that which appears to be either 'unity' or 'identity'. This provides the dynamic for hegemonic argument. Depending on what aspect of the world one's focus is on, it is possible to depict it as either egoistically anarchic or oppressively homogeneous and thus to buttress one's preference in terms of its ability to support binding law or sovereign freedom. If the problems of the world economy appear to result from protectionism (ie sovereign egoism), then our hegemonic recipe will lie in a uniform trade regime overriding national regulation.[17] But if the world's problems seem crystallised in the anonymous forces of globalisation, then we must buttress sovereign independence and cultural identity: 'The normative inhibitions associated with sovereignty moderate existing inequalities of power and provide a shield for weak states and weak institutions.'[18] Take away that shield and the international world will soon arrange itself hierarchically in response to the preferences of those in powerful positions.

The battle against 'homogeneity' sometimes makes for strange bedfellows. During the past half century, much of Third World rhetoric relied on sovereignty against Western dominance. Today, this is the ground for the US attack on the International Criminal Court, seen as 'some higher law on US military decision-making' that threatens the 'US Constitution [that is] in important ways, the common possession of the American people'.[19] Conversely, the battle cry *against* sovereignty has been sounded by market forces and environmentalists, advocates of international criminal law as well as experts in cyberlaw. But these positions do not remain permanently fixed. The State acting unilaterally is often condemned as 'the one that puts the triumph of its interests before that of the collective interest'.[20] However, there is a long history of unilateral action to protect generalisable environmental interests.[21] As neither sovereignty nor world community has any fixed

[16] C Schmitt, *The Concept of the Political* (translated by G Schwab, Chicago, University of Chicago Press, 1996) 54; EH Carr, *The Twenty-Years' Crisis 1919–1939*, 2nd edn (London, Macmillan, 1981) 86.

[17] For a useful description and critique, see K Rittich, *Recharacterizing Restructuring: Law, Distribution and Gender in Market Reform* (The Hague, Kluwer, 2002) 49–98.

[18] B Kingsbury, 'Sovereignty and inequality' in A Hurrell and N Woods (eds), *Inequality, Globalization, and World Politics* (Oxford, Oxford University Press, 2000) 86.

[19] J Rabkin, 'Worlds Apart in International Justice' (2002) 15 *Leiden Journal of International Law* 836, 843, and, quoting President Eisenhower, 'Sovereignty is never bartered among free men' 848.

[20] P-M Dupuy, 'The Place and Role of Unilateralism in Contemporary International Law' (2000) 11 *European Journal of International Law* 19–30, 20.

[21] For example R Bilder, 'The Role of Unilateral State Action in Protecting International Environmental Injury' (1981) 11 *Vanderbilt Journal of Transnational Law* 51 et seq; D Bodansky, 'What's So Bad about Unilateral Actions to Protect the Environment?' (2000) 11 *European Journal of International Law* 339–47.

content, the choice between the two cannot be made as a principled commitment, only as hegemonic strategy. For a labour rights activist, it may sometimes be better to choose the national way (if one works in a welfare state), sometimes to insist on global standards – just like the company seeking to maximise its profits may sometimes do best by seeking a country with particularly low standards, sometimes by insisting on a common standard of investment protection.[22]

Such claims receive meaning and force from the contrasting interpretations of what is useful and what is not in the world. Whether the international world seems governed by an anarchy of sovereignties or the uniformly constraining structures of 'capitalism', 'great power politics' or even 'human nature' depends on the conceptual framework that is normatively loaded. The projects of unity and identity are thus informed by perspectival choices that cannot trump each other in a general way. Both appear as surfaces on which political actors can reciprocally make and oppose hegemonic claims.

Despite the interminable character of the confrontation between claims seeking to advance world unity and claims to further independence and identity, it is possible to pinpoint areas of relative stability, moments when a mainstream has consolidated or is only marginally threatened by critique. Professional competence in international law is precisely about being able to identify the moment's hegemonic and counter-hegemonic narratives and to list one's services in favour of one or the other. The following is a brief overview of five themes under which political preferences are today articulated in legal claims.

The Law of Force: Imperial Themes

The hegemonic compromise over the use of military force through the Cold War consisted in the Charter system of one rule – non-use of force, article 2(4) of the UN Charter – and two exceptions: self-defence (article 51) and action under the Security Council (articles 39 and 42). This seemed cosmopolitan, since it provided for institutional supervision by the Security Council, deferring, however, simultaneously to sovereignty (territorial integrity and political independence) and entitling individual states to the necessary action to defend it.

Since 1989–90 that compromise has been breaking down in two directions. On the one hand, deference to sovereignty has been increasingly seen as a backward obstacle against humanitarian objectives. The North Atlantic Treaty Organisation (NATO) intervention in Kosovo in 1999 was patently illegal but widely approved owing to its successful projection in humanitarian terms. Teleology seemed prior to formal compromise, already shaken by the experience of Kigali and Srebrenica

---

[22] The controversy over the Multilateral Agreement on Investment (MAI) illustrates the ironic turn of companies insisting on regulation against the (finally victorious) group of states holding on to their sovereign freedom.

in 1994 and 1995 and China's awkward prevention of the renewal of the Macedonian peacekeeping operation in pursuit of its Taiwan policy in 1999. The opponents of the intervention did their best to point to its hegemonic nature, but had to do this from the uncomfortable position of defending either Serbia's formal sovereignty or the ineffective (and equally hegemonic) antics of the Security Council, sometimes accepting that if an intervention really was necessary, then its illegality could be excused by a kind of *post hoc* popular verdict.[23]

In other words, the humanitarian position successfully projected the Charter letter as an anachronistic shield over domestic injustice. After 9/11, however, this offensive stalled. The initiative launched by Canada in 2001 under the title 'Responsibility to Protect' was meant to develop a new law on intervention on the basis of a moderate extension of parts of the traditional compromise (International Commission on Intervention and State Sovereignty 2001). It was immediately overshadowed by the controversy over the 'war on terrorism' so that lowering the Charter threshold of humanitarian violence now seems excluded as likely to advance what the UN majority sees as the brutal *realpolitik* of the single super-power. Retreat from constructive debate in the United Nations has not, however, prevented regional organisations (NATO, European Union (EU)) from loosening the bounds of acceptable violence: 'inhuman non-intervention' has become a difficult position to defend. The Security Council's role has diminished while any authorisation by it may now have become 'one policy justification among others'.[24]

However, the pragmatic compromise is also challenged in the direction of expanding sovereign freedom to act in self-defence. The right of pre-emption declared in the US security strategy of 2002 had always underlain the relevant law. If the law should be interpreted by reference to its reasonable purpose, and if its purpose is to protect the State, then the expression: 'if an armed attack occurs' in article 51 may not be allowed to bring about the consequence that the law was intended to prevent – a successful attack.[25] Enlarging self-defence to cover threats or even 'potential threats' is both reasonable and dangerous. If the dangers were emphasised during the Cold War, the fate of the law will now depend on how diplomatic consensus will finally view the US-led attacks on Afghanistan and Iraq. However, a taboo has been broken and absent a serious reform of the UN's war system, the pragmatic reasonableness of coping with threats before they rise will turn the law on the use of force on its head.[26]

The developments in the EU must be seen in this light. Danish Special Forces were sent to Afghanistan in 2001–2 and the international force there came under

---

[23] MG Kohen, 'The Use of Force by the United States after the End of the Cold War and Its Impact on International Law' in M Byers and G Nolte (eds), *United States Hegemony and the Foundations of International Law* (Cambridge, Cambridge University Press, 2003) 219–20.

[24] S Chesterman, *Just War or Just Peace? Humanitarian Intervention in International Law* (Oxford, Oxford University Press, 2001) 236.

[25] For example A Sofaer, 'On the Necessity of Pre-emption' (2003) 14 *European Journal of International law* 209, 223.

[26] Among the wealth of literature see, eg M Bothe, 'Der Irak-Krieg und das völkerrechtliche Gewaltverbot' (2003) *Archiv des Völkerrechts* 255–71.

joint German-Dutch command. Poland accepted a role in Iraq, the EU took over NATO's peacekeeping and policing missions in Macedonia and Bosnia, and the French led the EU's first African venture in eastern Congo. The 'enhanced cooperation' that leads some EU members to establish integrated defence policies was included in the Lisbon Treaty, as was the promise by EU members to assist each other in self-defence action. There is no doubt, however, that the EU is moving towards a mutual defence pact.[27] The first European Security Strategy submitted to the European Councils in June and December 2003 was written in response to accusations of Europe's 'weakness' and, although otherwise unremarkable, does accept that threats must be countered before they materialise, that an effective defence starts outside Europe's frontiers and that the one thing to which European governments must resign themselves is to increase their defence spending.[28]

The pragmatic compromise over the law on the use of force has lost its hegemonic position. State violence has become increasingly accepted and political struggle is now waged on its justifications. While 'sovereignty' may be winning over 'humanitarianism', it is useful to remember that when extended to cover potential threats, it too may be invoked to support cosmopolitan causes.[29] Reacting to outside pressures, UN Secretary-General Kofi Annan established in November 2003 a 'High-Level Panel on Threats, Challenges and Change' with a remit, among other things, to 'recommend clear and practical measures for ensuring effective collective action' and in particular to look to the possibility of reviewing the conditions of application of the right of self-defence under article 51 of the Charter.[30] At the 2005 World Summit, the world leaders endorsed the responsibility to protect populations from genocide, war crimes, ethnic cleansing and crimes against humanity.[31] There is little likelihood of rapid progress, however. Widening the authority for unilateral use of force will not be acceptable for the majority of UN members. Attaining agreement on a definition of 'threats' that might trigger the right of pre-emption will remain hampered by the problem of its simultaneous over- and under-inclusiveness. Any formal criteria will allow the use of force in some cases where most states would not have wanted to allow it, had they only thought of those cases when the definition was adopted. In addition, it will exclude the use of force in other cases where decisive military action may seem absolutely called for. When is the development of a nuclear facility, for example or the establishment of

---

[27] See eg provision for the European Defence Agency, Act 28d TEU of the Treaty of Lisbon (OJ 17.12, 2007 C 306/35–36).

[28] J Solana, 'A Secure Europe in a Better World': *A European Security Strategy* (Brussels, Office of High Representative European Common Foreign and Security Policy, 2003) http://ue.eu.int/solana/docs/031208ESSIIEN.pdf. See further, Report on the Implementation of the Strategy, 11 December 2008 (S407/08).

[29] As illustrated by the fact that cases sometimes classed as humanitarian intervention (Indian intervention in Bangladesh in 1971 and the Vietnamese attack on Cambodia in 1978) were justified as self-defence measures.

[30] For the terms of reference, see www.un.org/News/dh/hlpanel/terms-of-reference-re-hl-panel.pdf.

[31] See P Niemelä, 'The Politics of Responsibility to Protect: Problems and Prospects' (2008) 25 *Erik Castrén Institute Research Reports* and the *World Summit Outcome*, UNGA A/RES/60/1 (15 September 2005), especially 138, 139. See also, UN, *Implementing the Responsibility to Protect*, Report of the Secretary-General, A/63/677 (12 January 2009).

a training camp for professional revolutionaries in a neighbouring country a 'threat' and when is it not? Such questions cannot be answered by rules or abstract definitions. In questions of national security, legal definitions and criteria do not work in the way they do in situations of domestic social routine. The need to act decisively *now* will always seem greater than any 'compliance pull' that abstract rules have.[32]

It is thus likely that discussion will turn from substantive criteria for assessing 'threats' to procedural safeguards for the control of pre-emptive strikes. The powers most likely to resort to unilateral force – the United States, Russia, members of NATO – will, however, insist that such safeguards should not hamper rapid action on the basis of classified information when necessary. Any development here will have to concentrate on strengthening the *ex-post-facto* role of the Security Council or, what is more likely, of the General Assembly. The Owl of Minerva will, unfortunately, only be allowed to spread its wings at dusk, when guns are already silent and the 'international community' is either scandalised by aggression or called upon to give legitimacy to a novel status quo.

The Law of Peace: Fragmentation Themes

Perhaps the most conspicuous recent theme in the law of peace has been the controversy over its 'fragmentation' into functional regimes. New institutions have been set up to manage particular problem areas (trade, environment, human rights, and international criminal law) by reference to interests and preferences that differ from those represented in the institutions of general law. Not surprisingly, the latter have sometimes reacted, seeing their position threatened by institutional proliferation and substantive fragmentation. The hegemonic theme of the need for 'unity' has been met by arguments about the need for innovation and specialisation. Three forms of fragmentation are worthy of note.[33]

First, new institutions have sometimes interpreted the general law in unorthodox ways. Thus, in the *Tadić* case in 1999 the Appeals Chamber of the International Criminal Tribunal for Former Yugoslavia (ICTY) replaced the standard of 'effective control', as the rule governing the accountability of foreign states over acts of parties in civil war laid down by the ICJ in the *Nicaragua* case in 1986 by the wider standard of 'overall control', thus significantly increasing such accountability in pursuit of the struggle 'against impunity' for which the ICTY has been one principal representative (*The Prosecutor v Dusko Tadić*[34]).

---

[32] See chapter four in this volume,

[33] This follows the debate conducted within the International Law Commission (ILC) at its session of 2003. See Report of the ILC from its 55th session (2003) UN Doc A/58/10 270–71 para 419. See also M Koskenniemi and P Leino, 'Fragmentation of International Law? Postmodern Anxities' (2002) 15 *Leiden Journal of International Law* 553–79.

[34] See ICJ, *Nicaragua* case, Reports 1986, 65 [para 115] and ICTY, *The Prosecutor v Dusko Tadić*

Second, functional differentiation has institutionalised firm exceptions into general law.[35] Human rights treaties, for instance, have been interpreted by human rights organs differently from the way 'regular' treaties have been interpreted under the Vienna Convention on the Law of Treaties. The departures have been justified by the 'object and purpose' of the treaties or their *effet utile* over the strict formalism of traditional law. If a human rights body understands its powers extensively,[36] or if the Court of Justice of the European Community develops a 'fundamental rights jurisprudence' in response to the challenges from certain Member States,[37] then these should be seen as hegemonic moves to support the special interests represented in those bodies against the (predominantly state-centred) interests represented by the ICJ or a national constitutional court.

A third fragmentation pits particular regimes against each other: trade against environment, human rights against humanitarian law, law of the sea against European community law. Whether some issue is qualified as a 'trade' or 'health' problem,[38] or whether its dominant concerns are those of 'human rights' or 'security', it involves a struggle for competence to decide. A fisheries issue may be seen in terms of the protection of natural resources or freedom of trade and contextualised either as part of a universal (World Trade Organisation (WTO) or law of the sea) or regional (EU) regime. Each classification points to a different authority that will decide, with preferences and practices deviating from those of competing bodies.[39]

Fragmentation reflects many levels of hegemonic contestation.[40] Again, there are two questions to ask: Who is entitled to project a legal rule with a meaning? What preferences does that meaning sustain? In Europe especially, lawyers have begun to worry about the 'unity of international law'.[41] If this worry is understood – as it should be – as a concern about the loss of influence with the institutions representing

[1999] 50 [122].

---

[35] See B Simma, 'Self-Contained Regimes' (1985) *Netherlands Yearbook of International Law* 111–36; LANM Barnhoorn and KC Wellens (eds), *Diversity in Secondary Rules and the Unity of International Law* (The Hague, Nijhoff, 1995).

[36] See Human Rights Committee, General Comment No 24 [52], CCPR/C/21/Rev.1/Add.6.

[37] See B de Witte 'The Past and Future Role of the European Court of Justice in the Protection of Human Rights' in P Alston (ed), *The EU and Human Rights* (Oxford, Oxford University Press, 1999) 863–66.

[38] See for example, WTO, *European Community – Measures Concerning Asbestos and Asbestos Products – Report of the Appellate Body* (13 March 2001) WT/DS135/AB/R, 61 [168].

[39] The MOX Plant case, for instance, having to do with an Irish complaint about the operations of the Sellafield nuclear facility in the United Kingdom, involves the competing jurisdiction of the Law of the Sea Tribunal, the Permanent Court of Arbitration and the European Court of Justice. For a brief overview, see P Weckel, 'Chronique de Jurisprudence Internationale' (2002) *Revue Générale de Droit International Public* 196–206.

[40] The technical terms of the debate are quite exhaustively laid out in the study by the International Law Commission. See ILC, 'Conclusions of the work of the Study Group on the Fragmentation of International Law: Difficulties arising from the Diversification and Expansion of International Law', *Yearbook of the International Law Commission*, vol II, Part Two, A/CN4/L.682, 13 April 2006.

[41] Out of a large contemporary literature see, eg P-M Dupuy, 'L'Unité de l'ordre juridique internationale: Cours général de droit international public' (2002) 297 *Recueil des Cours de l'Académie de Droit International de la Haye* (The Hague, Martinus Nijhoff, 2003) 9–489.

general international law (perhaps the ICJ especially), then the expectation of a constitutionalisation of the international system, advocated by those same lawyers, will
hardly be forthcoming – at least in the form of buttressing the positions of precisely
those institutions. Fragmentation is, after all, usually the result of a conscious challenge to the unacceptable features of the general law. The question of institutional
hierarchy will not be resolved in the near future. Even as there is agreement that some
substantive norms must have a hierarchically superior position (usually addressed
as *jus cogens* rules, or obligations *erga omnes*), this agreement is dependent on the
absence of an institutional link with those norms and their open-endedness that
allows all actors to project their preferences within their broad formulations. The
debate on the constitutionalisation of international law will not resemble domestic
constitution-making for the simple reason that not only does the international realm
lack a *pouvoir constituant,* but that if such a thing presented itself it would be empire
and the constitution it would enact would be one of not an international but an
imperial realm.

Trade: Utilitarian Themes

The establishment of the WTO in 1995 was a significant victory for the preferences
of free trade over nationally focused regulatory objectives. The domination of
Western interests was nowhere more visible than in the conclusion of the
Agreement on Trade-Related Intellectual Properties (TRIPS), designed to protect
copyrights, patents and trademarks overwhelmingly owned by Western companies. Since then, the high publicity received by HIV/AIDS-affected developing
states to free the production of generic drugs from pharmaceutical patent protection (of which 95 per cent are owned in the West) has given an increasing voice to
anti-globalisation lobbies.[42] It may have come as a surprise to the Uruguay round
negotiators – principally representatives of trade bureaucracies – that the adoption
of the Dispute Settlement Understanding (DSU) was understood to create a regular international court. This meant that WTO-covered treaties could no longer be
read 'in clinical isolation from public international law',[43] occasioning a debate on
the extent to which trade values could be adjusted by values represented by environmental, labour or social legislation. It is now widely accepted that WTO law
must be applied in the context of 'any relevant rules of international law applicable
in the relations between the parties' (Vienna Convention on Law of Treaties 1969
article 31[3][c]). The politics of interpretation now focuses on whether it suffices

---

[42] See, eg the Declaration on the TRIPS Agreement and Public Health of the Fourth WTO Ministerial
Conference, Doha, (20 November 2001) WT/MIN(01)/DEC/2.
[43] WTO, *United States - Standards for Reformulated and Conventional Gasoline* WT/DS2/AB/R (29
April 1996), 621.

that attention be given to WTO-compatible non-WTO rules or whether it might sometimes be possible to overrule the former with the latter.[44]

Thus, from the strict formalism of the *Tuna/Dolphin* cases (1991 and 1994) that declared unilateral US conservation measures illegal, the struggle in the WTO has developed significantly.[45] In the more recent *Shrimp/Turtle* case, the Appeals Body held it necessary to refer to international values: community, conservation and consensus that might sometimes justify adjustment of WTO rules.[46] Such inclusion of contested values leaves the field wide open for hegemonic manoeuvres. While it is often assumed that it would be 'good' if trade bodies took jurisdiction over environmental or human rights standards, it seems equally clear (though more seldom noted) that such 'mergers and acquisitions' may not always work in favour of environmental or human rights interests.[47] No wonder that the Doha Declaration of 2001 has sought to remove this struggle back to the political level.[48]

The polarisation of the opposition between the North and the South within the WTO (especially evident in the intellectual property realm) may have diminished possibilities for judicial innovation by the panels or the Appeals Body. Indeed, little has dispelled the concern that the Dispute Settlement Body is a rich men's club: by far most of the cases are still being brought to it by the United States or the EU. As the WTO treaties now are, they provide firm protection for the private rights of economic operators while leaving social or public policy concerns dependent on flexible adjustment standards or narrow exception clauses. A fundamental reorganisation is required in the economic law field so as to bring the 'empire of civil society' – transnational private economic relations – within the jurisdiction of the WTO if the intention is to provide an effective 'constitutional' grounding for the trade system. It is now quite unlikely that such a transformation might take place in the near future. As discussed below, by far most of the relevant rule creation and application is dependent on powerful private actors and interests. It may nonetheless be useful to note that at least in some Third World contexts social movements have had recourse to human rights standards as a strategy of resistance to a private law-governed economic 'empire'.[49]

---

[44] The (unsurprising) standard suggestion by trade law experts is that other rules may be taken into account to the extent that this can be done consistently with WTO law, but that in cases of irreducible conflict 'non-WTO law (including human rights law) cannot find direct application'. See G Marceau, 'WTO Dispute Settlement and Human Rights' (2002) *European Journal of International Law* 805; see also 753–814.

[45] United States - Restrictions on Imports of Tuna: Reports of the Panels: DS21/R, Report of the Panel, Sept. 3, 1991.and DS29/R, Report of the Panel, June 1994.

[46] United States - Import Prohibition of Certain Shrimp and Shrimp Products. Final Report. [WT/DS58/R, 15 May 1998]. For comments, see eg P Sands, 'Unilateralism, Values and International Law' (2000) 11 *European Journal of International Law* 291–302.

[47] P Alston, 'Resisting the Merger and Acquisition of Human Rights by Trade Law: A Reply to Petersmann' (2002) 13 *European Journal of International Law* 815–44.

[48] The Doha round will thus seek to clarify the relationship between WTO rules and the commercial rules in multilateral environmental agreements. See 'Ministerial Declaration' WT/MIN(01)/DEC/2.

[49] B Rajagopal, *International Law from Below: Development, Social Movements and Third World Resistance* (Cambridge, Cambridge University Press, 2003) 343.

Human Rights Themes

Human rights, it is often said, are the religion of (an agnostic) modernity. To be able to claim a benefit, not just as what one happens to prefer but as a right, is to make a political claim in the strongest available form. It is to seek to lift that claim from political contestation and from the discretion of the relevant authority. This would be no problem if an authoritative catalogue of rights existed. However, where would such a catalogue come from? Some have made the point that in order to possess the pre-political power that they claim, human rights must be understood as 'ineliminably religious'.[50] However, faith is not borne out of a wish to be religious. In modern conditions, rights can only be seen as legislative constructions, that is to say, the result of political priorities and, above all, contextual 'balancing'.[51]

This is why it is possible for every right to invoke a counter-right: my right of freedom against your right of security. As every significant rights claim involves the imposition of a burden on some other person, then the latter may invoke his or her right to be free from such a burden: even foreign investment and patent protection claims are made in human rights language.[52] In addition, because rights – like all rules – are over-inclusive and under-inclusive, they also need to be accompanied by exceptions. Even rights that cannot have exceptions (such as the 'right to life') are normative-ambiguous, leaving room for choice (is abortion or euthanasia covered?). There was nothing exceptional when the European Court of Human Rights (ECHR) assessed the permissibility of municipal interference in the 'fundamental rights' of certain French landowners in 1999 by seeking a 'fair balance' between the rights and 'the demands of the general interest of the community' (*Chassagnou v France*[53]). Such balancing is carried out in a routine way by human rights organs. It embeds rights in 'thick' political cultures – thus supporting the critique of their claimed 'universality' as a hegemonic strategy.[54]

However, the authority of rights bodies has been recently challenged by alternative preferences, notably those parading in the languages of 'security'. In Europe, the Strasbourg Court used to balance security with rights (to privacy, freedom of speech, and assembly) by the criterion of what was 'necessary in a democratic society' with a margin of appreciation lying with national authorities.[55] This

---

[50] MJ Perry, *The Idea of Human Rights: Four Inquiries* (Oxford, Oxford University Press, 1998) 11–14.
[51] See chapter five in this volume.
[52] R Wai, 'Countering, Branding, Dealing: Using Economic, Social and Cultural Rights in and around the International Trade Regime' (2003) 14 *European Journal of International Law* 42.
[53] ECtHR, *Chassagnou v France* (25088/94, 28331/95 and 28443/95), Reports 1999-III [75].
[54] C Brown, 'Universal Human Rights: A Critique' in T Dunne, NJ Wheeler (eds), *Human Rights in Global Politics* (Cambridge, Cambridge University Press, 1999) 103–23. See also M Ignatieff, *Human Rights as Politics and Idolatry* (Princeton, Princeton University Press, 2001) 187.
[55] I Cameron, *National Security and the European Convention on Human Rights* (Uppsala, Iustus, 2000) 479.

system may, however, now be undermined by an atmospheric change. In the *Banković v Belgium*[56] decision, the Court found it had no competence to deal with the bombing of the Serbian TV office in March 1999 by NATO countries. In the Court's view, the Convention had been designed in a regional context and not to be applied throughout the world, even with respect to the conduct of contracting states. This contrasts with its earlier jurisprudence where the Convention had been found to apply to acts by Turkish authorities in occupied Northern Cyprus: 'the responsibility of Contracting Parties can be involved because of acts of their authorities, whether performed within or outside national boundaries, which produce effects outside their territory' (*Drozd and Janousek v France and Spain*).[57] Whether bombing a civilian building is 'exercise of jurisdiction' may of course be debated. However, it may not be altogether a surprise that while the Strasbourg Court feels itself free to adjudge the acts of Turkish authorities, it does not feel so in regard to European great powers.

In *Al-Adsani v United Kingdom*,[58] the ECHR limited the scope of the article 6 right for a fair trial by reference to the 'generally recognised rules of public international law on state immunity' when the right being claimed (compensation) was formulated in the context of a civil case even though the original violation had been of a *jus cogens* rule (the applicant had been tortured abroad). This is in line with the International Court of Justice's decision in the *Yerodia [Arrest Warrant]* case, as it held Belgium to have violated the immunity of an incumbent minister of foreign affairs by having issued an arrest warrant against him. In these two cases, rights were trumped by traditional rules of diplomatic law. The reasoning of the International Court of Justice as it held immunity hierarchically superior to accountability for crimes against humanity is important. The arrest warrant 'effectively infringed Mr Yerodia's immunity . . . and was furthermore liable to affect the Congo's conduct of its international relations'.[59]

In the aftermath of 9/11, limitations of civil and political rights that would have been unimaginable earlier have been carried out in the United States, and also in Europe.[60] The story of the adoption of the EU Framework Decision on Terrorism of 2002 is both sobering and encouraging.[61] On the one hand, the Commission

---

[56] *Banković and others v Belgium* (Appl No 52207/99) Admissibility Decision 12 December 2001 ECHR 2001-XII .

[57] *Drozd and Janousek v France and Spain* (Appl No 12747/87) Judgment of 26 June 1992 ECHR Ser A 240. For a useful discussion of this and other recent cases, see A Orakhelashvili, 'Restrictive Interpretation of Human Rights Treaties in the Recent Jurisprudence of the European Court of Human Rights' (2003) 14 *European Journal of International Law* 529–68.

[58] *Al-Adsani v United Kingdom* (Appl No 35763/97) Judgment 21 November 2001 ECHR 2001-XI [56].

[59] *Arrest Warrant* Case, ICJ *Reports* 2002, 30–31 [71]. For an analysis of the clash between the duty to prosecute for international crimes and immunities of high state officials, see M Sassoli, 'L'Arrêt Yerodia: quelques remarques sur une affaire au point de collision entre les deux couches du droit international' (2002) *Revue générale de droit international public* 791–817.

[60] For a useful overview, see J Fitzpatrick, 'Speaking Law to Power: The War against Terrorism and Human Rights' (2003) 14 *European Journal of International Law* 241–64.

[61] See the Commission (EC), 'Draft Framework Decision on Terrorism' COM (2001) 521 final, 19 September 2001. The story is told in J Leino, *Human Rights and Terrorism*, a (non-published) study for the Finnish Ministry for Foreign Affairs (2003).

proposal of autumn 2001 made no reference to human rights and underwrote practically everything security experts wished to attain. Due to intervention from national parliaments and civil society, however, the draft was amended so that human rights became written into several of its provisions. That story illustrates the dangers and possibilities of hegemonic struggle in a moment of change.

Two decades ago such a moment provided the background for hegemonic moves under the 'extended notion of security'. In a landmark declaration in 1991, the Security Council classified economic, social, humanitarian and even ecological problems as 'threats to international peace and security'.[62] This constituted an unprecedented potential expansion by the Council of its competence – a coup d'état in regard to questions previously relegated to the General Assembly. At the time, conflict within the Council prevented further action. However, the intensity of the debate about whether the Security Council's Counter-Terrorism Committee set up to implement Decision 1373 (2001) should include a human rights expert is an illustration of the stakes involved. As 'anti-terrorism activities' are carried out by security experts, and conducted in secrecy, individuals will continue to find themselves blacklisted and embargoed without being heard or given effective remedy.[63]

The increasingly important position of security concerns may reflect a fallback on to something like a 'political questions' doctrine limiting the scope of judicial review. Although no such general doctrine has arisen in Europe (unlike in the United States), the exclusion of the European Court's jurisdiction in common foreign and security policy offers a basis for limiting its ambitions against the Commission – while at the same time the Court's power to classify a matter either within or beyond foreign policy offers some guarantee against the colonisation of other policy areas by the executive under the (hegemonic) argument that they have foreign policy implications.[64]

Finally, one should note the hegemonic trends within the spectacular rise of international criminal law. This does not only mean that the United States and Israel are probably right when they argue that under the universalistic banner of the ICC, it is their activities that are likely to be subjected to scrutiny. Nor is the main point ICTY's financial and ideological dependence on its Western supporters, manifested perhaps in the refusal of the Prosecutor to commence an investigation of the NATO bombings of 1999. The important point is that criminal law itself always consolidates some hegemonic narrative, some understanding of the political conflict which is a part of that conflict itself. In the Milošević trial, for instance, the Court must take 'judicial notice' of hundreds of facts that are disputed among the protagonists. Where Milošević depicts the Balkan crisis in terms of a long history of Western intervention, the Court can only focus on his guilt,

---

[62] S/23500 31 January 1991.
[63] J Fitzpatrick, 'Speaking Law to Power: The War against Terrorism and Human Rights' (2003) 14 *European Journal of International Law* 260–61.
[64] I have discussed this in detail in M Koskenniemi, 'Judicial Review of Foreign Policy Discretion in Europe' in P Helander, J Lavapuro and T Mylly (eds), *Yritys eurooppalaisessa oikeusyhteisössä* (Turku, Turku University, 2002) 155–73.

thus looking away from the context in which his behaviour may be constructed as either 'deviant' or 'heroic', 'criminal' or 'patriotic'. To focus on individual guilt instead of, say, economic, political or military structures, is to leave invisible, and thus to underwrite, the story those structures have produced by pointing at a scapegoat. Criminal law is a weak and vulnerable strategy to cope with large crises: the more we insist on its technical character, the more we look away from its role in strengthening one narrative over others, and the more the trial will ratify the hegemony of that power on whose shoulders justice sits.[65]

Globalisation Themes

'Globalisation' covers a large number of themes under which an even greater number of contestants seek to universalise their preferences over the body of sovereign statehood: economic and social development, liberal democracy, culture industries, environmental protection, human rights and so on – knowledge systems and types of expertise that compete for the occupation of 'global' space by making claims of legal right and principle within either forums of 'global governance' or those of informal 'transnationalism'.

In the 1990s, global governance presented itself in a series of global conferences organised under the auspices of the UN system.[66] One of its principal themes – 'sustainable development' – emerged in the Rio Conference of 1992 to encompass the hegemonic *modus vivendi* between the environmental concerns of the North and the economic development objectives of the South. Much of this compromise received legal form in the International Convention on Climate Change and the Convention on the Protection of Biodiversity. What could not be formalised was inserted in a Plan of Action to be implemented by the UN Commission on Sustainable Development (CSS). By the Johannesburg World Summit on Sustainable Development 2002, two trends emerged that still mark the development of the relevant law.

First has been the increase in non-binding ('soft law') regulation.[67] The Johannesburg Declaration was formulated in 'political' terms so as not to encroach on the principles adopted at Rio and its Plan of Action only sought to implement earlier engagements.[68] What critics sometimes label the tendency of 'delegalisation of international law' results from the absence of a strong hegemonic position.[69]

[65] See chapter seven in this volume.
[66] For an excellent overview and synthesis, see JA Lindgren Alves, 'The UN Social Agenda against "Postmodern" Unreason' (1999) 28 *Might and Right in International Relations. Thesaurus Acroasiarum* 56–105.
[67] D Shelton (ed), *Commitment and Compliance – The Role of Non-Binding Norms in the International Legal System* (Oxford, Oxford University Press, 2000) 560.
[68] For the Johannesburg Summit Declaration and Action Plan, see 'Report of the World Summit on Sustainable Development' UN Doc A/CONF.199/20 (26 August – 4 September 2002).
[69] For the term and a discussion, see V Barral, 'Johannesburg 2002: Quoi de neuf pour le développement durable?' 107 (2003) *Revue générale de droit international public* 415, especially 432.

Where Rio struck a deal between the environmental and development concerns, Johannesburg complicated the setting by bringing social development concerns onto the agenda and opening the negotiating table to a wide range of domestic and transnational private stakeholders. The result was that it became impossible to agree on universal standards. Instead, the commitments were formulated as 'selective incentives, differential obligations [that] are regionalised to become more open and flexible'.[70] The universal level, as it were, only identifies the authoritative concerns and actors, while material regulation will be decided contextually, often by setting up an informal 'regime' to manage the problem.[71]

An exemplary instrument of this type is the 1997 International Convention on the Non-Navigational Uses of International Watercourses.[72] The only material standard is the rule of 'equitable and sustainable use', defined in terms of a (non-exhaustive) listing of 'factors' that should be taken into account in deciding the rights and duties of states in regard to a particular river. More important are the procedural rules on information exchange, cooperation and negotiation that encourage parties to set up local, regional or issue-specific cooperative frameworks. Deference to contextual deal-striking in this and other similar conventions emphasises the role of stakeholder organisations and technical experts, lifting functional and economic arguments to a decisive position. Further examples are the system of emission permits under the Kyoto Protocol and the role of the World Bank's Global Environment Facility (GEF) in the administration of multilateral environmental treaties. The use of technical 'non-compliance procedures' instead of legal dispute-settlement to deal with breaches, highlights the 'soft' nature of the engagements. To become a party is to agree to continued negotiation.

Such transfer of decision-making power from the negotiating states to stakeholder organisations (corporations, environmental lobbies, representatives of local populations) and to technical, economic and legal experts modifies the terms of political contestation over 'sustainable development'. On the one hand, the bureaucratisation of the problems leads to erosion of the system's legitimacy basis and turns those interests into winners that usually prevail in the relevant functional context.[73] On the other hand, as problems are contextualised, possibilities for strategic action increase, including for counter-hegemonic contestation.

This leads to the second form in which globalisation affects international law through the transnational pooling of functional and technical interests in informal networks beyond public law regulation. First, the need of functional specialisation

---

[70] W Reinicke and JM Witte, 'Interdependence, Globalisation and Sovereignty: The Role of Non-binding International Accords' in D Shelton (ed), *Commitment and Compliance – The Role of Non-binding Norms in the International System* (Oxford, Oxford University Press, 2003) 89.

[71] The 'postmodern' turn of construing sustainable development as a technical management problem – the bureaucratisation of international environmental law – has been analysed usefully in T Kuokkanen, *International Law and the Environment: Variations on a Theme* (The Hague, Kluwer, 2002) especially 236–344.

[72] International Convention on the Non-Navigational Uses of International Watercourses UN Doc A/RES/51/229 (8 July 1997).

[73] This is, of course, an incident of the Weberian thesis of deformalisation as a prologue for bureaucratisation and the transfer of power from the legislator to the law applier.

leads into informal cooperation between governmental authorities and bureau-crats whose transnational caucuses have interests and preferences that are inde-pendent of and sometimes contradict those of national representatives.[74] Second, influential private actors assume a role not only as stakeholders but also as sources of new types of soft law regulation. Legislation for special interests develops out-side public law regulation, from those interests themselves and in response to purely economic and technical imperatives, accompanied by privatised dispute-settlement, informal sanctioning mechanisms and codes of conduct whose point is to pre-empt public law regulation.[75] The results of the attempt to forestall such developments by partnership programmes between companies and international organisations (such as the 'Global Compact') have so far remained unimpressive.

In other words, the space of the cosmopolitan previously occupied by inter-governmental, federalist public law schemes is taken up by a 'postmodern' process where the structural coupling between the political and the legal – constitutionali-sation[76] – takes place through fragmented and uncoordinated forms of normative specification at different levels of transnational activity.[77] Old law-making bodies, such as the United Nation's International Law Commission, find themselves increasingly jobless. Unable to identify stakeholder interests or regulatory objec-tives, 'generalist' law-making bodies will wither away to the extent that political commitment to that which is merely 'general' seems pointless. If human rights interests can best be advanced in human rights bodies, environmental interests in environmental bodies and trade interests in trade bodies, while transnational activ-ities create de facto practices that are as good (or even better) than formal law in regulatory efficiency, why bother with 'the codification and progressive develop-ment of international law' (Statute of the International Law Commission article 1) beyond tinkering with diplomatic immunities or technical treaty law?

Some analysts see this in terms of the emergence of a structural empire that is ruled from no single spot and by reference to no single, identifiable set of interests. Instead, the functional regimes would be relatively independent from each other and organised as a structure of checks and balances, not unlike an internation-alised version of the US Constitution.[78] In such a world, law would be a central

---

[74] See A-M Slaughter, 'Governing the Global Economy through Government Networks' in M Byers (ed), *The Role of International Law in International Politics: Essays in International Relations and International Law* (Oxford, Oxford University Press, 2000) 177–205.

[75] Underneath the voluntarist façade of the *lex mercatoria*, the global practices of a few influential (usually American) commercial operators turn into law. See E Loquin and L Ravillion, 'La volonté des opérateurs vecteur d'un droit mondialisé' in E loquin and C Kessedjian (eds), *La mondialisation du droit* (Paris, Litec, 2000) 91–148.

[76] This understanding of constitution comes from Niklas Luhmann and is articulated in interna-tional law by A Fisher-Lescano, 'Die Emergenz der Globalverfassung' (2003) 63 *Zeitschrift für auslän-disches öffentliches Recht und Völkerrecht* 717–60.

[77] G Teubner, 'Globale Zivilverfassungen: Alternativen zur staatszentrierten Verfassungstheorie' (2003) 63 *Zeitschrift für ausländisches öffentliches Recht und Völkerrecht* 1–28; as well as, more optimis-tically, H Brunkhorst, *Solidärität: Von der Bürgerfreundschaft zur globalen Rechtsgenossenschaft* (Frankfurt, Suhrkamp, 2002) 203–17.

[78] This is the vision of M Hardt and A Negri, *Empire* (Cambridge, MA, Harvard University Press, 2000) especially 304–50.

element, but only a small part of it would be of the traditional type: the voices of formal governments would be a minor aspect in a cacophony of spontaneous, often delocalised transnational claims made at several levels of action. 'Legal pluralism' may be a useful shorthand for this – as long as it takes account of the informal 'modelisation' taking place in the international juridical field: 'Certains parlent d'un nouvel imperialisme, d'un colonialisme juridique de la part du monde anglo-saxon, d'une tendence a` l'uniformisation de type hégémonique que pourront bel et bien conduire a` la mondialisation du droit américaine'.[79]

Conclusion: Between Hegemony and Community

The developments surveyed above do not give much reason to expect international law to play a more beneficial role in the future than it has played in the past. The expectations that arose after the fall of the Berlin Wall in 1989 and with the spread of the rhetoric of the rule of law, human rights and constitutionalisation have not been and are not likely to be met in the near future. A Kantian public law-based federation is no nearer than it was, say, fifteen years ago and recent events have emphasised power and national security concerns that underwrite the old realist critique of the domestic analogy. The international is in the relevant respects still the realm of the exceptional and thus a proper realm not for the application of rules but for statesmanship. However, it is in regard to the consequences of this fact that this chapter most decisively parts company with the perspective of US law schools that often share the same premise. For US lawyers, international law is thinned out into what the United States administration does or does not do, what the interests of American presidents may be, with the focus always on the use of (especially military) force. Even at its best, international law may only work as an instrument of a great power concert.[80]

Such a perspective too readily adopts the standpoint of the hegemon – perhaps the hegemon conceived as a democratic, sometimes even internationally minded United States – but nonetheless a great power with a political and legal agenda to impose on the world. Looked at from other points of view, however, the main problems of world order are not those the hegemon is obsessed with – use of force and national security – but economic problems, poverty being the most striking example, that is, problems the hegemon usually casts as outside regulation by public international law. Yet, it is important to see that as massive Third World poverty is sustained by the dealings of unrepresentative Third World governments with private transnational corporations, it is not unrelated to the international legal system that provides those governments with the competence to borrow

---

[79] A-M Serf, 'La modélisation des instruments juridiques' in Loquin, Kessedjian (eds), *La Mondialisation du Droit* (2000) 181.
[80] See eg Farer, 'Toward an Effective International Legal Order: From Coexistence to Concert' (2004) 219–38.

funds from the international financial markets and to conclude concession agreements with Western companies with binding force against the interests of their country and populations for decades to come. In this regard, the global public order – its principles of recognition of governments, binding force and non-intervention – is fully implicated in what can only be seen as a deeply unjust system of distributing material and spiritual values.[81] By focusing on war and great crises – the great power perspective – international law will continue to be implicated in the marginalisation of problems that touch by far the greatest and the weakest part of the world's population. It is therefore necessary that its agenda will be enlarged so as to cover questions that have been presently relegated to the unregulated, private network of transnational relations.

However, although international law, in this way, is a hegemonic politics, 'it is nonetheless a form of politics that has some particular virtues'.[82] Unlike claims of privilege or interest, claims of law constitute the claimants as members of a legal and thus also a political community. Engaging in legal discourse, persons recognise each other as carriers of rights and duties who are entitled to benefits from or who owe obligation to each other not because of charity or interest but because such rights or duties belong to every member of the community *in that position*. In law, benefits and burdens that belong to particular individuals or groups are universalised by reference to membership rules. What otherwise would be a mere private violation, a wrong done to *me*, a violation of *my interest*, is transformed by law into a violation against *everyone in my position*, a matter of concern for the political community itself.

One of the striking aspects of the worldwide condemnation of aspects of the American-led 'war against terrorism' is precisely the recourse to the vocabulary of law. Guantanamo and the war against Iraq were not just wrong, they were 'illegal'. The point of such claim lies in its implicit suggestion that at issue are not merely specific wrongs done to some Afghani or Iraqi individuals, but wrongs done to everyone in their position – and most people are able to imagine themselves in such a position. Through law, the special scandal of American action may be articulated in terms of its universal nature, being directed, in a sense, against the human species. This is also the sense of the frequent claim that the action appears 'imperial'. It denies any need for the United States to take a distance from its own cultural preferences and to articulate its claims in some language shared by humankind at large. It is a solipsism that resigns to the impulse of feeling threatened by 'terrorists' and those that 'harbour' them, believing they may be attacked or killed wherever and whenever it suits the empire.[83] The action is informed only by American laws and values that exclude those who are not recognised by those laws

---

[81] See T Pogge, 'The Influence of the Global Order on the Prospects for Genuine Democracy in the Developing Countries' (2001) 14 *Ratio Juris* 334–43; and generally T Pogge, *World Poverty and Human Rights* (Cambridge, Polity, 2002).
[82] R Wai, 'Countering, Branding, Dealing' (2003) 84. See further chapter ten in this volume as well as my 'What Should International Lawyers Learn from Karl Marx', in S Marks (ed), *International Law on the Left* (Cambridge University Press, 2008) 47–52.
[83] Habermas, 'Interpreting the Fall of a Monument' (2003) 707–08.

or do not share those values – with them, there is neither political community nor political contestation: they are 'outlaws' against whom any measure may be taken. Thus it is possible to understand, for example, the recent use of the ICJ by Paraguay, Germany and Mexico, or of the Inter-American Court of Human Rights by Mexico, in order to articulate claims about the treatment of their citizens in death row in US prisons as claims made on behalf of an international political community. This is particularly evident in regard to the pursuit of the German claim even after the two German brothers had been executed. The judgment no longer supported special interests: it was a voice of the community expressing and thus constituting itself, if always only for a moment.[84]

In a similar way, it is possible to see the expanding practice of making political claims in legal language by an increasing number of international actors in the human rights field, in trade and environment bodies, in regional and universal tribunals and organisations and, not least, in the struggles over the meaning and direction of globalisation, as both a technique of hegemony, and an effort to think in terms of what is shared – a community. In a secular, pluralistic world, there can be no transcendental basis for such community. All there is is language, and the performative act of invoking it with respect to some event or action. Inasmuch as that language and the (hegemonic) act of invoking it seem adequate or proper – that is to say, appropriate for the meaning that is being evoked – for all intents and purposes, we may speak of a community among its native-language speakers. To avoid speaking a language of empire, the members of that community need to conceive their words as open, revisable and contentious, while at the same time embodying an ambition of addressing humankind as a whole. But what else would it then be than a language of international law?

---

[84] M Pinto, 'De la protection diplomatique à la protection des droits de l'homme', *Revue générale de droit international public* (Paris, Pedone, 2002) 513–47.

10

What is International Law For?

This article is a reaction against the predominance of an overwhelmingly instrumentalist outlook in international legal theory today, ie the view that law is above all an instrument for the attainment of good objectives (the 'good life', 'utility', 'protection of "rights"', 'effective government', etc). The suggestion the article makes is that to think of international law in only instrumental terms will do away with its specificity vis-à-vis techniques of government on the one hand, and moral argument on the other. In both cases, law becomes a disposable tool of power. But international law also creates power and delimits it. And it offers a language for the defence of hegemonic and non-hegemonic practices equally. To give effect to its non-instrumental aspects, international law might also be understood as part of a 'culture of formalism', a tradition of cosmopolitan legalism that I have discussed at much greater length in my *The Gentle Civilizer of Nations. The Rise and Fall of International Law 1870–1960*.[1]

T HE FACT IS that the objectives of international law appear differently depending on one's standpoint. International law certainly seeks to realise political values, interests and preferences of various international actors. However, it also appears as a standard of criticism and means of controlling those in powerful positions. Instrumentalism and formalism connote two opposite sensibilities of what it means to be an international lawyer, and two cultures of professional practice, the stereotypes of 'the advisor' to a powerful actor with many policy alternatives and 'the judge' scrutinising the legality of a particular international behaviour. Beyond pointing to the oscillation between instrumentalism and formalism as styles of legal thought and practice, the question 'what is international law for?' also invokes popular aspirations about peace, justice, and human rights, including a desire for something like an international political community. As a langauage, it may serve many masters – but it will also socialise them in a culture biased in favour of participation over selectivity, transparency over secrecy, and responsibility for the choices it has been used to justify.

---

[1] M Koskenniemi, *The Gentle Civilizer of Nations. The Rise and Fall of International Law 1870–1960* (Cambridge, Cambridge University Press, 2001).

The Paradox of Objectives

Attempting to answer the question in the title, one first meets with a familiar paradox. On the one hand, it seems indisputable that international law 'has a general function to fulfil, namely to safeguard international peace, security and justice in relations between States'.[2] Or, as article 1 of the United Nations (UN) Charter puts it, the organisation has the purpose to 'be centre for harmonizing the actions of nations in the attainment of . . . common ends' such as international peace and security, friendly relations among nations, and international cooperation. Such objectives seem self-evident and have never been seriously challenged. On the other hand, it is hard to see how or why they could be challenged – or indeed why one should be enthusiastic about them – because they exist at such high level of abstraction that they fail to indicate concrete preferences for action. What do 'peace', 'security', or 'justice' really mean? As soon as such words are defined more closely, disagreement emerges. To say that international law aims at peace *between states* is perhaps already to have narrowed down its scope unacceptably. Surely it must also seek to advance 'human rights as well as the rule of law domestically inside States for the benefit of human beings . . .'[3] However, what if advancing human rights would call for the violent destruction of unjust peace?

In the end, very little seems to depend on any general response to the question, 'What is international law for?' The real problem seems always to be less about whether international law should aim for 'peace', 'security' or 'human rights' than about how to resolve interpretative controversies over or conflicts between such notions that emerge when defending or attacking particular policies. There is no disagreement about the objective of peace in the Middle East between Israel and Palestinian people. However, if asked what 'peace' might mean for them, the protagonists would immediately give mutually exclusive answers. Nor is the 'Asian values'[4] debate about being 'for' or 'against' human rights, but about what such rights might mean and how they should be translated into social practices in the relevant societies. Therefore, to inquire about the objectives of international law is to study the political preferences of international actors – what it is that *they* wish to attain by international law. As those preferences differ, the answer to the question in the title can only either remain controversial or be formulated in such broad terms as to contain the controversy within itself – in which case it is hard to see how it could be used to resolve it.

It would thus be wrong to think of the paradox of objectives as a technical problem that could be disposed of by reflecting more closely on the meaning of words such as 'peace', 'security' or 'justice', or by carrying out more sophisticated social or economic analyses about the way the international world works. Such notions

---

[2] C Tomuschat, 'International Law: Ensuring the Survival of Mankind on the Eve of New Century' (1999) *Recueil des Cours des Cours de l'Académie de droit international de la Haye* 23.

[3] ibid.

[4] See K Mahbubabi, *Can Asians Think?* (Singapore, Times Books, 1999) 37–94.

provide an acceptable response to the question 'what is international law for?' precisely because of their ability to gloss over existing disagreement about political choices and distributional priorities. If they did not work in this way, and instead permanently preferred some choices over other choices, they would no longer be able to do the service we expect of them. In accordance with the founding myth of the system, the Peace of Westphalia in 1648 laid the basis for an agnostic, procedural international law whose merit consisted in its refraining from imposing any external normative ideal on the international society. The objectives of that society would now arise from itself and not from any religious, moral or political notions of the good given externally to it. If there is an 'international community', it is a practical association not designed to realise ultimate ends, but to coordinate practical action to further the objectives of existing communities.[5] Sovereign equality builds on this: because there are no natural ends, every member of the international society is free to decide on its own ends, and to that extent, they are all equal. The law that governs them is not natural but artificial, created by the sovereigns through the processes that are acceptable because they are neutral.[6] To say that international law is for 'peace', 'security', and 'justice' is to say that it is for peace, security, and justice *as agreed and understood between the members of the system.*[7]

What this means for international legal argument can be gleaned, for instance, from the opinion of the International Court of Justice (ICJ) in the *Reservations* case (1951). Here the Court was called upon to examine the admissibility of reservations to the 1948 Convention on the Prevention and Punishment of the Crime of Genocide. The Court first outlined what seemed a natural consequence of the principles of neutrality and sovereignty, namely that no reservation should be effective against a state that has not agreed to it. To stay with this understanding, however, might have undermined the Convention by creating a system in which some reservations were in force in regard to some states (namely those accepting them) but not against others, while each non-accepting state would be free to regard the reservation-making state as not a party to the Convention at all. This would have gone against the universal nature of the Convention. Thus, the Court continued, a state having made a reservation that has been objected to by some of the parties may still be held a party to the Convention if the reservation is compatible with the 'object and purpose' of the Convention. At this point, then, the Court moved to think of law expressly in terms of its objectives. However, there were no

---

[5] This is why it is so easy to discuss it in terms of the ethics of Immanuel Kant, an ethics of universalisable principles of right action rather than as instrumental guidelines for attaining the Good. See, eg O O'Neill, *Bounds of Justice* (Cambridge, Cambridge University Press, 2000).

[6] eg T Nardin, *Law, Morality and the Relations between States* (Princeton, NJ, Princeton University Press, 1983).

[7] Henkin writes that instead of 'human values', the system is centred upon 'State values', L Henkin, 'International Law: Politics, Values and Functions' (1989) 216 *Recueil des Cours* 109. This polemical contrast undermines the degree to which states – including principles of sovereignty and non-interference – find their moral justification in late-eighteenth century liberal individualism and the ideal of national self-rule: 'State values' persist because they channel 'human values' within a political community. See also A Paulus, *Die internationale Gemeinschaft im Völkerrecht. Eine Untersuchung zur Entwicklung des Völkerrechts im Zeitalter der Globalisierung* (Munich, Beck, 2001) 69–97.

objectives to the Convention that were independent from the objectives of the *parties* to the Convention. Thus, it was up to each party to make the determination 'individually and from its own standpoint'.[8]

Such an argument defines the objectives of international law in terms of the objectives of the (sovereign) members of the international society – in this case the society formed by the parties to the Genocide Convention – bringing to the fore two types of problems: what will happen in cases where states disagree about the objectives? Also, why would only state objectives count?

Converging Interests?

If no antecedent order establishes a firm priority between what states want, then any controversy about them either will have to remain open or we shall have to assume that the procedure in which the disagreement is revealed will somehow be able to dispose of it to the satisfaction of all. The latter suggestion embodies the idea of the 'harmony of interests', the presence of an underlying convergence between apparently conflicting state interests. Under this view, any actual dispute would always be only superficial. At a deeper level, state interest would coalesce and the objective of international law would then be to lead from the former to the latter.[9]

It is difficult to defend this view against realist criticisms. Why would harmony, instead of conflict, be the true nature of international politics? What evidence is there that, rightly understood, the interests of states are compatible? Might the harmony not rather seem a form of wishful thinking that prevents people from clearly seeing where their interests lie, and acting accordingly? Hans Morgenthau, one of the fathers of realist thought, attacked the inter-war legalism precisely for having made this mistake. To believe in harmony under the League of Nations had left the world unprepared for Hitler's aggression in 1939.[10] EH Carr, another powerful realist thinker, described the harmony as an ideological smokescreen:

---

[8] *Reservations to the Convention on the Prevention and Punishment of the Crime of Genocide* (Advisory Opinion) [1951] ICJ Rep, 15, 26.

[9] This argument, always implicit in moral objectivism and theories of natural law, was made in a dramatic way by Hersch Lauterpacht, speaking at Chatham House in 1941, as bombs were falling over Coventry and his family was being destroyed by the Nazis in Poland: 'The disunity of the modern worlds is a fact; but so, in a truer sense, is its unity. Th[e] essential and manifold solidarity, coupled with the necessity of securing the rule of law and the elimination of war, constitutes a harmony of interests which has a basis more real and tangible than the illusions of the sentimentalist or the hypocrisy of those satisfied with the existing status quo. The ultimate harmony of interests which within the State finds expression in the elimination of private violence is not a misleading invention of nineteenth century liberalism', H Lauterpacht, 'The Reality of the Law of Nations' in *International Law, being the Collected Papers of Hersch Lauterpacht* (Cambridge University Press, 1975) Vol II, 26.

[10] H Morgenthau, 'Positivism, Functionalism, and International Law' (1940) 34 *American Journal of International Law* 261–84.

Biologically and economically, the doctrine of the harmony of interests was tenable only if you left out of account the interest of the weak who must be driven to the wall, or called in the next world to redress the balance of the present.[11]

International lawyers have responded to such criticisms in two ways. Some have accepted that only a marginal scope is left by power to law and defined any existing legal regimes as variables dependent on a central power,[12] or have developed purely instrumental accounts of the use of law in the defence of particular interests or preferences.[13] Others have sought to articulate the harmony under a more elaborate theory of interdependence or globalisation: 'International trade and commerce, international finance, international communication – all are essential to the survival of states, and all require an international legal system to provide a stable framework within which they may function.'[14] Institutional, procedural, and even linguistic theories have been used to argue that even the articulation of state interests is based on legal notions such as 'sovereignty', 'treaty', and 'binding force' that delimit and define what may count as state interest or even state identity in the first place.[15]

However, the opposition between 'realism' and 'idealism' is only of limited usefulness. The labels invoke contrasting political sensibilities and different jurisprudential techniques that often merge into each other. Even the hardest 'realism' reveals itself as a moral position (for example by highlighting the priority of the national interest) inasmuch as, 'philosophically speaking, realism is unthinkable without the background of a prior idealistic position deeply committed to the universalism of the Enlightenment and democratic political theory'.[16] On the other hand, any serious idealism is able to point to aspects of international reality that support it, and needs such reference in order to seem professionally credible. Much of the realism-idealism controversy is in fact about what element of a many-faceted 'reality' should be chosen as the starting point of one's analysis. Progress in the discipline of international law has typically occurred by a new generation of lawyers rejecting the previous one as either 'utopian' because it is excessively idealist or as 'apologist' because it is too impressed by sovereign power. These critiques

---

[11] EH Carr, *The Twenty-years' Crisis 1919–1939* 2nd edn (London, Macmillan, 1946) 50.

[12] C Schmitt, *Der Nomos der Erde im Völkerrecht des Jus Publicum Europaeum*, 3rd edn (Berlin, Duncker & Humblot, 1988); W Grewe, *The Epochs of International Law* (Berlin, DeGuyter, 2001).

[13] MS McDougal, 'International Law, Power and Policy. A Contemporary Conception' (1953) 82 *Recueil des Cours* 137–259; J Goldsmith and E Posner, *The Limits of International Law* (Oxford, Oxford University Press, 2005).

[14] Sir A Watts, 'The Importance of International Law' in M Byers (ed), *The Role of Law in International Politics. Essays in International Relations and International Law* (Oxford, Oxford University Press, 2000) 7.

[15] This is the 'constructivist' explanation of international law's impact on states, much used today in international relations studies. See, eg M Finnemore, *National Interests in International Society* (Ithaca, NY, Cornell University Press, 1996). For a discussion, see J Brunnee and SJ Toope, 'International Law and Constructivism: Elements of an Interactional Theory of International Law' (2000) 39 *Columbia Journal of Transnational Law* 19–74; F Kratochwil, 'How do Norms Matter?' in Byers (ed), *The Role of Law in International Politics* (2000) 55–59.

[16] S Guzzini, *Realism in International Relations and International Political Economy* (London, Routledge, 1998) 16.

are as available today as they were a century ago. Care must be taken not to associate any position or doctrine permanently with either: 'idealism' and 'realism' are better understood as forms of critique and channels for institutional manoeuvring than qualities of an independent international world.[17]

This is not to say that international law would not often be helpful for the limited resolution of conflicts, resulting in temporary accommodations or even settlement. This is, after all, why the General Assembly posed its question to the ICJ in the *Reservations* case in the first place. The Court was not asked to rule on the admissibility in particular reservations, but to indicate how to go about implementing the Convention so as to minimise any distorting effect that controversial reservations might have.

Many lawyers – and increasingly often political theorists – make a more ambitious defence of international law in terms of such practical effects. However neutral in regard to political principles, they would say, the structure is not devoid of normative direction. In their view, international law is accompanied by a cunning logic that slowly socialises initially egoistic states into the law's internationalist spirit.[18] It is possible (though not necessary) to picture this ethic as the 'inner morality of law' that accompanies any serious commitment to work in a legal system.[19] An alternative but parallel approach would be to characterise the system in terms of a 'culture of civility' shared by its administrators and excluding certain types of secrecy, dishonesty, fraud, or manipulation. Such an explanation resonates with international law's emergence in the late nineteenth century as an aspect of optimistic evolutionism among the liberal elites of Europe and North America. It is to assume that entering into the processes it provides, states come to define not only their objectives but perhaps even their identity by the language offered by international law.[20]

The Significance of Statehood

But the Westphalian myth leaves also unexplained why only *state objectives* count. At least since Immanuel Kant published his essay on the *Perpetual Peace* (1795),

---

[17] This is one of the central arguments in M Koskenniemi, 'International Law in Europe: Between Tradition and Renewal' (2005) 16 *European Journal of International Law* 113–24.

[18] A defence of the view that law socialises states not by constraint but by 'compliance strategies [that] seek to remove obstacles, clarify issues, and convince parties to change their behaviour', as well as by 'various manifestations of disapproval: exposure, shaming, and diffuse impacts on the reputations and international relationships of a resisting party', is found in A Chayes and AH Chayes, *The New Sovereignty. Compliance with International Regulatory Agreements* (Cambridge, Mass, Harvard University Press, 1995) 109–10. A more recent, proceduralist defence, insisting on the moral core of the international legal process, is J Habermas, *Der gespaltene Westen* (Frankfurt, Suhrkamp, 2004).

[19] The point about law necessarily containing certain 'aspirations of excellence' without which an order would not be recognised as 'law' in the first place, is made, of course, in LL Fuller, *The Morality of Law*, 2nd rev edn (New Haven, Conn, Yale University Press, 1969) 41–94.

[20] Koskenniemi, *The Gentle Civilizer of Nations* (2001).

philosophers, political theorists, and lawyers have routinely challenged the state-centrism of the international system, arguing that whatever instrumental value states may have for the coordination of affairs of particular communities, the 'ultimate' members of those communities are individuals and that many other human groups apart from states ('peoples', 'nations', 'minorities', 'international organizations', 'corporations') also play important roles.[21] Globalisation and the crisis of sovereignty have intensified the criticism of international law as state law from sociological, functional, and ethical standpoints. These critiques have often sought to project a material value or an idea of social justice outside statehood that they suggest should be enforced by international law.[22]

The universalising vocabularies of human rights, liberalism, economic and ecological interdependence have no doubt complicated inter-sovereign law by the insertion of public law notions such as *jus cogens* and 'obligations owed to the international community as a whole' and by 'fragmenting' the international system into functional institutions (see chapter fourteen below). However, no alternative to statehood has emerged in the centre. None of the normative directions – human rights, economic or environmental values, religious ideals – has been able to establish itself in a dominating position. On the contrary, what these values may mean and how conflicts between them should be resolved is decided largely through 'Westphalian' institutions. This is not to say that new institutions and regimes would not enjoy a degree of autonomy from the policies of states. Human rights and many economic and environmental regimes provide examples of such. The European Union has developed into an autonomous system that functions largely outside the frame of international law. How far these other regimes are from that of the European Union can, however, be gleaned from the characterisation of the World Trade Organisation (WTO) system by the Appellate Body in the *Japan – Taxes on Alcoholic Beverages* case:

> The *WTO Agreement* is a treaty – the international equivalent of a contract. It is self-evident that in an exercise of their sovereignty, and in pursuit of their own respective national interests, the Members of the WTO have made a bargain. In exchange for the benefits they expect to derive as members of the WTO they have agreed to exercise their sovereignty according to commitments they have made in the *WTO Agreement*.[23]

This outlook was reaffirmed by the ICJ in the *Legality of the Threat or Use of Nuclear Weapons* Opinion in 1996. In response to the question about the lawfulness of the threat or use of such weapons, the Court concluded that whatever the consequences, it could not exclude that such use would be lawful 'in an extreme circumstance of self-defence, when the very survival of a State would be at stake'.[24] 'Benefits' to the States and state survival remain the highest objectives of the

[21] J Westlake, *International Law*, 2nd edn (Cambridge, Cambridge University Press, 1910) vol 2, 16.
[22] M Koskenniemi, 'The Wonderful Artificiality of States' (1994) 88 *ASIL Proceedings* 22–29.
[23] *Japan – Taxes on Alcoholic Beverages* Report of the Appeals Body (AB-1996-2) DSR 1996:I 108.
[24] *Legality of the Threat or Use of Nuclear Weapons* (Advisory Opinion) [1996] ICJ Rep 226 [96], [101](E).

system. Likewise, bodies such as the European Court of Human Rights or the UN Human Rights Committee recognise that the treaties they administer function in a state-centred world: the margin of appreciation and the wide scope of derogations allow for national security reasons if 'necessary in a democratic society' to operate with notions of 'security' and 'democracy' that are embedded in a world of states.[25]

The defence of international law's state-centredness is thoroughly practical. 'Stated quite simply', James Brierly once wrote, 'what [international law] tries to do is to define or delimit the respective spheres within which each of the . . . States into which the world is divided for political purposes is entitled to exercise its authority'.[26] Little of this justification has changed. A form and a process is needed that channels interpretative conflicts into peaceful avenues. This is not to say that non-state values such as 'human rights', 'efficient economies', 'clean environment' or 'democracy' would be unworthy objectives of political action. Disagreement about them provides the life and blood of political community. The defenders of the state-system would only note that such values conflict and that 'States alone have provided the structures of authority needed to cope with the incessant claims of competing social groups, and to provide public justice essential to social order and responsibility.'[27] States may be set aside, of course, by consent or revolution but there are dangers in such transformations, some of which are well known, and something about those dangers results from the single-mindedness of the teleologies pursued by the institutions seeking to replace statehood.

On the other hand, there is no doubt that international politics is far from the Westphalian ideal. The informal networks and epistemic communities that influence international developments beyond the rigid forms of sovereign equality are populated by experts from the developed West. It is hard to justify the attention given and the resources allocated to the 'fight against terrorism' in the aftermath of the attacks on New York and Washington in September 2001 in which nearly 3,000 people lost their lives, while simultaneously six million children under five years only die annually of malnutrition by causes that could be prevented by existing economic and technical resources.[28] What becomes a 'crisis' in the world and will involve the political energy and resources of the international system is determined in a thoroughly Western-dominated process.[29]

[25] Or in other words, these mechanisms are only subsidiary: 'The [European Convention on Human Rights] leaves to each contracting State . . . the task of securing the rights and freedoms it enshires', *Handyside v UK* Series A No 24 (1979) 1 EHRR 737 [48]. As Susan Marks points out, liberal reformers conceive of 'democratization' in terms of reform of domestic (and not international) institutions, S Marks, *The Riddle of All Constitutions. International Law, Democracy and the Critique of Ideology* (Oxford, Oxford University Press, 2000) 76–100.

[26] J Brierly, *The Outlook for International Law* (Oxford, Oxford University Press, 1944) 3.

[27] O Schachter, 'The Decline of the Nation-state and its Implications for International Law' (1997) *Columbia Journal of Transnational Law* 22.

[28] FAO, 'The State of Food Insecurity in the World 2002', available at www.fao.org/DOCREP/005/Y7352e00.HTM.

[29] H Charlesworth, 'International Law: A Discipline of Crisis' (2002) 65 *Modern Law Review* 377–392; A Orford, *Reading Humanitarian Intervention. Human Rights and the Use of Force in International Law* (Cambridge, Cambridge University Press, 2003).

It is widely believed that the informal and fluid economic, technological, and cultural processes often termed 'governance' rather than 'government' strengthen the political position of the most powerful actors – transnational networks, large corporations, Western developed states – and marginalise public international law.[30] Weak states despair over their inability to hold on to achieved positions and privileges by the antiquated rhetoric of sovereignty. However, the latter's awkward defence of the conservative system of sovereign equality undermines the extent to which globalisation may also open avenues for contestatory transgovernmental action within international civil society, or by what Hardt and Negri call the 'multitude'.[31] There is room for conflict and consensus both *within* and *beyond* the Westphalian system and little political worth lies in deciding a priori in favour of either. Formal rules, as well as anti-formal objectives and standards may each be used for progressive or conservative causes.[32] The choice of technique must reflect a historically informed assessment of the effect of particular institutional alternatives.

In the following sections I will try respond to the question 'what is international law for?' by describing its role in a world that is not one of pre-established harmony or struggle but of both cooperation *and* conflict simultaneously. I will argue that international law operates – and should operate – as an instrument for advancing particular claims and agendas *as well as* relatively autonomous formal technique. This is not to claim political neutrality. Much instrumental thinking about international law today adopts the point of view of the decision-maker in a relatively prosperous state or transnational network, in possession of resources and policy-options and seeking guidance on how to fit their objectives within international legality – or to overrule legality with minimal cost. Clearly, international law exists 'for' such decision-makers. However, it should not exist exclusively for them. My argument is that there is often a reason to adopt a 'formalist' view on international law that refuses to engage with the question of its objectives precisely in order to constrain those in powerful positions. The question 'what is international law for?' needs to be removed from the context of legal routines to the political arenas where it can be used to articulate claims by those who are sidelined from formal diplomacy and informal networks and feel that something about the routines of both is responsible for the deprivations they suffer. In other words, there is a reason to defend a legal 'formalism' against a 'pragmatism' that views international law only in terms of its immediate outcomes. In order to do that, however, it is necessary first to outline the power of pragmatism.

---

[30] eg A Hurrell and N Woods, *Inequality, Globalization and World Politics* (Oxford, Oxford University Press, 1999); A-J Arnaud, *Critique de la raison juridique 2: Gouvernants sans frontières. Entre mondialisation et post-mondialisation* (Paris, LGDJ, 2003).
[31] M Hardt and A Negri, *Empire* (Cambridge, Mass, Harvard University Press, 1999) 393–413.
[32] For the varying use of the rule/principle, opposition in self-determination arguments about change, participation and community, see K Knop, *Diversity and Self-Determination in International Law* (Cambridge, Cambridge University Press, 2002) 29–49.

Into Pragmatism?

The paradox of objectives shows that the formal law of Westphalia cannot be replaced by social objectives or ethical principles without invoking controversies that exist in regard to the latter. 'Whoever invokes humanity wants to cheat', Carl Schmitt once wrote,[33] citing the nineteenth century French socialist Pierre Joseph Proudhon and making a useful point about the use of abstract humanitarianism to label one's political adversary as an enemy of humanity so as to justify extreme measures against him – a point that applied in today's context 'lacks neither lucidity nor relevance'.[34] One need not think only of the extreme case of the 'war against terrorism' to canvass the slippery slope from anti-formal reasoning to human rights violation. Quite everyday legal argument assumes the analytical priority of the reasons for the law over the form of the law in a fashion that underwrites Stanley Fish's perceptive dictum, 'once you start down the anti-formalist road, there is no place to stop'.[35]

For example, the right of self-defence under article 51 of the UN Charter is formally conditioned by the presence of an 'armed attack'. But what about the case of a *threat* of attack by mass destruction weapons? Here we are tempted to look for guidance from the objective of article 51. The rationale for allowing self-defence lies, presumably, in the objective of protecting the State. Surely we cannot expect a state to wait for an attack if this would bring about precisely the consequence – the destruction of the State – that the rule was intended to prevent. But the rule itself is no more valuable than the reason for its existence; we erase the condition of prior armed attack and entitle the State to act in an anticipatory way.[36] Or the other way around: surely formal sovereignty should not be a bar for humanitarian intervention against a tyrannical regime; in oppressing its own population, the State undermines its sovereignty. We honour 'sovereignty' as an expression of a people's self-rule. If there is oppression instead of self-rule, then it would seem nonsensical to allow formal sovereignty to constitute a bar to intervention in support of the people.[37]

Such arguments are based on a thoroughly pragmatic-instrumentalist view of the law, a view that highlights that we do not honour the law because of the sacred

---

[33] C Schmitt, *The Concept of the Political* (translated and introduced by G Schwab, Chicago, University of Chicago Press, 1996) 54.

[34] J-F Kervégan, 'Carl Schmitt and "World Unity"' in C Mouffe (ed), *The Challenge of Carl Schmitt* (London, Verso, 1999) 61.

[35] S Fish, *Doing What Comes Naturally. Change, Rhetoric, and the Practice of Theory in Literary and Legal Studies* (Oxford, Oxford University Press, 1989) 2.

[36] This is the argument of the 'Bush doctrine' of pre-emptive self-defence, as made in the United States security strategy, published on 20 September 2002. See the text in, eg *Financial Times* (London 21 September 2002) 4.

[37] This position is often combined with the argument for pro-democratic intervention. For useful analysis, see S Chesterman, *Just War or Just Peace? Humanitarian Intervention and International Law* (Oxford, Oxford University Press, 2001) 88–111.

aura of its text or its origin, but because it enables us to reach valuable human pur-poses. We follow the emission reduction schedule of chlorofluorocarbons (CFCs) in article 2 of the 1987 Montreal Protocol on the Protection of the Ozone Layer because we assume that it will reduce the depletion of the ozone layer and the inci-dence of skin cancer. We honour the domestic jurisdiction clause in article 2(7) of the UN Charter because we assume it upholds the ability of self-determining com-munities to lead the kinds of life they choose. However, what if it were shown that ozone depletion or skin cancer bears no relationship to the emissions of CFCs, or that domestic jurisdiction merely shields the arbitrary reign of tyrants? In such cases we would immediately look for an equitable exception or a counter-rule so as to avoid the – now unnecessary – costs that would be incurred by bowing to the empty form of the original rule. Article 10(1) of the European Convention on Human Rights provides for freedom of speech. If applying the right would enable the distribution of fascist propaganda, it is always possible to interfere and prohibit it by the counter-rule in article 10(2) that enables the 'prevention of disorder or crime' and to ensure 'the protection of morals' with a margin of appreciation lying with state authorities. Enabling those authorities to protect 'national security' is indispensable if they are to secure the liberal rights-regime. Yet, because setting the 'balance' between security and rights lies with the authorities against whom the rights-regime was established, the door to abuse remains open.[38]

We often allow the reason for the rule to override the rule. We do this because we believe the rule itself has no intrinsic worth. If it fails to support the purpose for which it was enacted – or worse, prevents its attainment – why should it be honoured? In domestic society, abstract law-obedience can be defended in view of the routine nature of the cases that arise, and the dangers attached to entitling citizens to think for themselves. Such arguments are weak in the international realm where situations of law-application are few, and disadvantages of obedience often significant. Few states that were economically or politically dependent on Iraq fully implemented the sanctions set up in 1990. Although they were in formal breach of articles 25 and 48 of the Charter, the UN preferred to look the other way. The European Union is not going to give up the prohibition of importation of hormone meat merely because the WTO dispute settlement organ may have decided it should do so. The importance of the interest in living peacefully with a powerful neighbour and of deciding on national health standards vastly outweighs any consideration about the importance of abstract law-obedience.[39]

And yet, there is a dark side to such pragmatic instrumentalism. A legal tech-nique that reaches directly to law's purposes is either compelled to think that it can access the right purpose in some politics-independent fashion – in which case it would stand to defend its implicit moral naturalism – or it transforms itself to a licence for those powers in a position to realise their own purposes to do precisely

---

[38] I Cameron, *National Security and the European Convention on Human Rights* (Stockholm, Iustus, 2000) 62–68.
[39] See M Koskenniemi, 'Solidarity Measures: State Responsibility as a New International Order?' (2001) 72 *British Year Book of International Law* 339–59.

that. In this way, pragmatism inculcates a heroic mindset: we *can* do it! It is the mindset of well-placed, powerful actors, confident in their possessing the 'right' purpose, the mindset that drove Stalin to collectivisation, or Israel to destroy the Osiriq nuclear power plant in 1981. It is the mindset of the civilising mission and of 'regime change' by force if necessary.

Instrumental action may or may not be acceptable in view of the circumstances and its advisability is typically the object of political controversy. However, the instrumentalist mindset – the readiness to act as soon as that seems what one believes to be useful or good – creates a consistent bias in favour of dominant actors with many policy-alternatives from which to choose and sufficient resources to carry out their objectives.[40] To always look for reasons, instead of rules, liberates public authorities to follow their reasoning, and their purposes – hence their frequent aversion against rules in the first place: the International Criminal Court, disarmament or human rights treaties, for example.[41]

The difficulty with the instrumentalist mindset is that there never are simple, well-identified objectives behind formal rules. Rules are legislative compromises, open-ended and bound in clusters expressing conflicting considerations. To refer to objectives is to tell the law-applier: 'please choose'. There is no doubt that article 2(4) of the UN Charter aims towards 'peace'. Yet it is equally certain that most people disagree on what 'peace' might mean in a particular case. This is not only about semantic uncertainty. Even apparently unobjectionable objectives such as 'peace' contain a paradox. To be in favour in 'peace' cannot, for example, mean that nobody can ever take up arms. 'Perhaps the most serious problem with outlawing force is that sometimes it is both necessary and desirable'.[42] The UN Charter expressly allows for the use of military force under the authority of the Security Council or in pursuance of the right of self-defence. The positive law of the Charter is both pacifist and militarist – and receives its acceptability by such schizophrenia. Without something like a right to use in self-defence, aggression would always be rewarded. The European Convention on Human Rights seeks to protect individuals' rights to both freedom and security. However, one person's freedom conflicts with another's security. Whether or not authorities should be entitled to censor prisoners' letters or prohibit the publication of obscene materials, for instance, cannot be reached through instrumental reasoning that would be independent from a political choice.[43] The will of the drafters *is* the language of the instrument. Beyond that, there is only speculation about what might be a good (acceptable, workable, realistic or fair) way to apply it.

Practitioners usually understand international law as being more about routine application of standard solutions, ad hoc accommodation and compromise than

---

[40] For a description of instrumentalism as a culture, see G Binder, 'Beyond Criticism' (1988) 55 *University of Chicago Law Review* 906–909.

[41] See M Byers and G Nolte *United States Hegemony and the Foundations of International Law* (Cambridge, Cambridge University Press, 2003).

[42] A Watts, 'The Importance of International Law' (2000) 10.

[43] See chapter five in this volume .

discourse about large objectives. Providing advice to a non-governmental organ-isation or drafting judgments at the ICJ are usually held to require pragmatic rec-onciliation of conflicting considerations, balancing between 'equitable principles', incompatible rights, or other prima facie relevant aspects of the case at hand. Settlement of the conflicts during the dissolution of the Former Yugoslavia in the early 1990s was understood to involve the balancing of conflicting considerations about stability of frontiers and expectations of just change, managing the *uti pos-sidetis* principle together with minority rights for populations left on the wrong side of the boundary.[44] The balance struck between these considerations was in no way dictated by the law but reflected the negotiators' pragmatic assessment of what might work.[45] At the European Court of Human Rights, individual freedoms are constantly weighted against the need for interference by public authorities. It is established case law that 'an interference must achieve a "fair balance" between the demands of the general interest of the community and the requirements of the protection of the individual's fundamental rights'.[46] In a like manner, the law con-cerning the delimitation of frontier areas or the sharing of natural resources resolves itself into a more or less flexible cluster of considerations about distribu-tive justice – sometimes described in an altogether open-ended fashion in terms of 'equitable principles' or 'equitable use' – in view of attaining a pragmatically acceptable end-result.[47] Also, hard cases within laws of war invariably turn into a contextual assessment of what number of non-combatant casualties might still be within the limits of proportionality by reference to the military objective (military experts and humanitarian lawyers agreeing on the need to 'calculate'.[48]

Few international lawyers think of their craft as the application of pre-existing formal rules or great objectives. What rules are applied, and how, which interpre-tative principles are used and whether to invoke the rule of exception – including many other techniques – all point to pragmatic weighing of conflicting consider-ations in particular cases.[49] What is sought is something practical, perhaps the 'fairness' of the outcome, as Thomas Franck has suggested. Under this image, law is not about peace *or* justice, freedom *or* security, stability *or* change, but always about both one *and* the other simultaneously. 'The tension between stability and change, if not managed, can disorder the system. Fairness is the rubric under

---

[44] See Opinions 2 and 3 of the Arbitration Commission of the Peace Conference on the Former Yugoslavia (1992) 31 *International Legal Materials* 1497–1500.

[45] MC Lâm, *At the Edge of the State: Indigenous Peoples and Self-determination* (Dobbs Ferry, NY, Transnational, 2000) 141–51.

[46] *Fredin v Sweden*, Judgment of 18 February 1991, Ser A, No 192 (1991) 13 EHRR 784 [51], *Lopez Ostra v Spain*, Judgment of 9 December 1994, Ser A, No 303-C (1995) 20 EHRR 277 [51].

[47] See, eg Separate Opinion of Judge Jiménez de Aréchaga, *Continental Shelf* (*Tunisia/Libyan Arab Jamahiriya*) (Judgment) [1982] ICJ Rep, 18, 103–108 ([11]–[31]) and, eg, the International Convention on the Non-Navigational Uses of International Watercourses (8 July 1997) A/RES/51/229. I have ana-lysed this 'turn to equity' in, among other places, M Koskenniemi, 'The Limits of International Law: Are There Such?' XXVIII *Thesaurus Acroasiarum: Might and Right in International Relations* 27–50.

[48] See D Kennedy, *The Dark Sides of Virtue. Reassessing International Humanitarianism* (Princeton, Princeton University Press, 2004).

[49] O Corten, *L'utilisation du 'raisonnable' par le juge international. Discours juridique, raison et con-tradictions* (Brussels, Bruylant, 1997).

which the tension is discursively managed.'[50] The lawyer's tasks are now seen in terms of contextual 'wisdom' or 'prudence', rather than the employment of formal techniques.[51] In a fluid, fragmented world, everything hinges on the sensitivity of the practising lawyer to the pull of contextually relevant considerations.

A Tradition of Anti-Formalism

The move to pragmatism emerges from a series of recurrent criticism of international law's alleged 'formalism'. It was supported in the last third of the nineteenth century by the use of a flexible notion of 'civilization' that enabled liberal lawyers to look beyond diplomatic protocol and an outdated natural law. The inter-war lawyers attacked the formalism of sovereignty they projected on pre-war doctrines and advocated (as conservatives) 'tradition' and (as progressives) 'interdependence' as bases for their pragmatic commitment. After the next war, reformist lawyers indicted what they described as the legalistic formalism of the League, basing their 'realism' on Cold War themes, either expressly in favour of the West or in a more social-democratic way to support international institutions.[52] Legal realism always had its Hawks and its Doves, but for both it seemed useful to criticise old law for its 'formalism' in order to support 'dynamic' political change.

Interdisciplinary studies in the 1990s highlighted the extent to which the formal validity of a standard was independent from its compliance pull.[53] As the law was seen instrumentally, its formality seemed to bear no particular merit: 'hard law' was just one choice among other possible regulative techniques, including soft standards or the absence of any standards at all in cases where the imposition of one's preference seemed within the limits of the possible and preferable given that it might 'minimise transaction and sovereignty costs'.[54] In such debates formal law

[50] TM Franck, *Fairness in International Law and Institutions* (Oxford, Oxford University Press, 1995) 7.

[51] For a celebration of judicial creativity in this regard, see H Lauterpacht, *The Development of International Law by the International Court* 2nd edn (London, Stevens, 1958).

[52] D Kennedy, 'When Renewal Repeats: Thinking Against the Box' (2000) 32 *New York University Journal of International Law and Politics* 380–87.

[53] See, eg D Shelton (ed), *Commitment and Compliance. The Role of Non-Binding Norms in the International Legal System* (Oxford, Oxford University Press, 2000).

[54] For a particularly straightforward instrumental approach, see R Posner, 'Do States have a Moral Obligation to Obey International Law?' (2003) 55 *Stanford Law Journal* 1901. An interdisciplinary research on the recent 'move to law' uses the method of assessing 'legalisation' by reference to the standards' obligatory nature, precision, and the presence of a centralised authority. The project examines 'legalisation' instrumentally, by concentrating on the conditions under which it constitutes a rational choice. See, eg K Abbott and D Snidal, 'Hard and Soft Law in International Governance' in JL Goldstein, M Kahler, RO Keohane and A-M Slaughter, *Legalization and World Politics* (Cambridge, Mass, MIT Press, 2001) 37–72. Such instrumentalism is not neutral: to assess law from the perspective of rational choice is to occupy the perspective of a small number of actors that actually may choose their options by agendas they set. It celebrates the managerial culture of Western experts at work to advance Western interests.

has nobody speaking in its favour and appears as a utopianism supporting conservative causes. Anti-formalism is always a call for transformation: to overrule existing law either because it does not really exist at all, or if it does, because it should not. The debate on soft law and *jus cogens* in the 1980s and 1990s manifested both of these criticisms and Prosper Weil's famous analysis of the pathological problems (the 'dilution' and 'graduation' of normativity) introduced in international law by such notions were unpersuasive to anti-formalist critics who wanted to realise the good society *now* and had no doubt that they knew how to go about this.[55] Avant-garde instrumentalism at the beginning of a new century reads like German public law conservatism a hundred years earlier: over every international rule hangs the sword of *clausula rebus sic stantibus*.[56]

What makes the formalism/anti-formalism debate suspect is the extent to which *any* substantive view may be and has been attacked as 'formalism'.[57] The following views, at least, have been so targeted:

- Rationalistic natural-law theories.
- Views emphasising the importance of (formal) sovereignty.
- Views limiting international law's scope to treaties or other (formal) expressions of consent.
- Views highlighting the importance of international institutions.
- Views emphasising 'rigour' in law-application.
- Views stressing the significance of formal dispute-settlement.
- Views insisting on clear boundary between law and politics.

The list is by no means exhaustive. In fact, any substance can be labelled 'formalism' because the term is purely relational. When a speaker advocates something (a norm, a practice) by its material fullness, the opposite view will inevitably appear to be holding fast to the dead weight of some 'form'. The almost uniformly pejorative use of the term 'formalism' in international law reflects the predominance of the instrumentalist mindset in diplomacy and international politics. The way the legal idiom constructs and upholds the structures of diplomacy and politics is left invisible.

The contrast between instrumentalism and formalism as cultures (instead of substances) is quite fundamental when seeking to answer the question 'what is international law for?' From the instrumental perspective, international law exists to realise objectives of some dominant part of community; from the formalistic perspective, it provides a platform to evaluate behaviour, including the behaviour of those in dominant positions. The instrumental perspective highlights the role of law as social engineering; formalism views it as an interpretative scheme. The

---

[55] See P Weil, 'Towards Relative Normativity in International Law?' (1983) 77 *American Journal of International Law* 413–42; J Tasioulas, 'In Defence of Relative Normativity: Communitarian Values and the Nicaragua Case' (1996) 16 *Oxford Journal of Legal Studies* 85–128.
[56] See E Kaufmann, *Das Wesen des Völkerrechts und die Clausula rebus sic stantibus* (Tübingen, Mohr, 1911).
[57] D Kennedy, 'Formalism' in *The International Encyclopedia of Social and Behavioral Sciences* (The Hague, Kluwer, 2001).

instrumental perspective is typically that of an active and powerful actor in possession of alternative choices; formalism is often the perspective of the weak actor relying on law for protection.

If instrumentalism today needs no particular defence, it may be useful to highlight the twin virtues of formalism. First, it is indispensable. Every standard is always substantive and formal at the same time. The very ideas of treaty and codification make sense only if one assumes that at some point there emerges an agreement, an understanding, a standard that is separate from its legislative background. When states enter an agreement, or when some behaviour is understood to turn from habit into custom, the assumption is that something that was loose and disputed crystallises into something that is fixed and no longer negotiable. The point of law is to give rise to standards that are no longer merely 'proposed' or 'useful' or 'good', and which therefore can be deviated from if one happens to share a deviating notion of what in fact is useful or good. In addition to their acceptability and effectiveness, legal rules are assumed to possess 'validity'. To accept that positive law enjoys that property is not to say anything about how it is recognised in individual rules or standards, nor indeed of whether any actual standard so recognised would possess any particular meaning as against some other putative meaning. Validity indicates a formal property that leaves the norm so characterised by a flat, substanceless surface – but a surface without which no 'law' could exist at all.

Second, the fact that the legal form is a 'flat substanceless surface' is not politically insignificant. It does something to those it accepts as legal subjects. In a world without or 'before' international law, the acting persons or entities exist as subjects of interests and preferences, both liberated and weighed down by their irreducible particularity. The logic of their relations is a logic of instrumentalism, each subject a *homo economicus*, poised to perpetuate the realisation of its idiosyncratic preferences. Such actors are completely controlled by the environmental conditions that make interest-fulfilment possible. For them, the external world – including other actors – has no meaning beyond interest-fulfilment: on its own, it is chaotic, incomprehensible. Paradoxically, however, a single-minded instrumentalism is bound to be frustrated in the end: at the mercy of a dangerous and incomprehensible world where every action creates unforeseen consequences, and always falls short of satisfying the ever intensifying interests.[58]

By contrast, as legal subjects, actors, as it were, give up their particularity in order to participate in what is general and shared. By recourse to the medium of law that claims 'validity', they are lifted from the tyranny of pre-existing interests and preferences: learning and change become possible. The *homo juridicus* in a way decentralises its own perspective, opening itself to the world at large. In other words, and as thinkers as diverse as Kant, Foucault, and Habermas have pointed out, the political significance of formal law – that is, of law irrespective of what interests or preferences particular legislation might seek to advance – is that it expresses the universalistic principle of inclusion at the outset, making possible the

[58] eg M Foucault, *Naissance de la biopolitique. Cours au Collège de France 1978–79* (Paris, Gallimard/ Seuil, 2004) 280–81.

regulative ideal of a pluralistic international world.[59] '[O]nly a regime of nonin-strumental rules, understood to be authoritative independent of particular beliefs or purposes is compatible with the freedom of its subjects to be different.'[60] The form of law constructs political adversaries as equals, entitled to express their sub-jectively felt injustices in terms of breaches of the rules of the community to which they belong no less than their adversaries – thus affirming both that inclusion and the principle that the conditions applying to the treatment of any member of the community must apply to every other member as well. In the end, competent lawyers may disagree about what this means in practice. But the legal idiom itself reaffirms the political pluralism that underlies the Rule of Law, however ineffi-ciently it has been put into effect. In fact, the failures in the international legal system are always recognised and constructive projects formulated by a prior (though often undisclosed) acceptance of the idea of the rule of formal law. Without that idea, much of the criticisms we all make of the international political world would no longer make sense.

Of course, formal law does not apply itself. Between that form and any decision to project on it meaning 'x' instead of 'y', is a professional technique that may be more or less successful in expressing these regulative ideals. In particular, there is a constant push and pull in the professional world between a *culture of instrumen-talism* and a *culture of formalism*. It would be wrong to associate this dialectic with fixed positions representing particular interests and preferences. Instrumental action by lawyers is a necessary part of the search for good rules or institutions beyond the status quo. Any present rules are always also mechanisms to support particular interests and privileges. 'Power' and 'law' are entangled in such complex ways that it is difficult to interpret particular events as manifesting either one or the other: power works through 'formal rules' – just like instead of 'naked power' we see power defined, delimited, and directed by rules everywhere.

However, the two cultures do play distinct political roles in particular historical situations. As the debates around the fluid dynamism of globalisation have demonstrated, formal standards and institutions are often called upon to provide protection for weak actors, and to pose demands on powerful ones.[61] Irrespective of its philosophical justification, there is no magic about formalism as a legal practice, however. It may also come to buttress privilege, apathy or both. Hence, it is important also to focus on instrumentalism and formalism as 'cultures', sensi-bilities, traditions and frameworks, sets of rituals and self-understandings among institutional actors. As pointed out above, the 'heroic' mindset of the *homo eco-nomicus* that sees law only as an instrument for *my objectives* often leads to collateral

---

[59] See I Kant, *Critique of Practical Reason* (M Gregor (ed), Introduction by A Reath) (Cambridge, Cambridge University Press, 1999) 24–25; M Foucault, *Naissance de la biolpolitique. Cours au Collège de France 1978–79* (Paris, Gallimard/Seuil, 2004) 280–81; J Habermas, *Der gespaltene Westen* (Frankfurt, Suhrkamp, 2004).

[60] T Nardin, 'Legal Positivism as a Theory of International Society' in DR Mapel and T Nardin (eds) *International Society. Diverse Ethical Perspectives* (Princeton, Princeton University Press, 1998) 31.

[61] Out of a burgeoning literature see, eg N Tsagourias, 'Globalization, Order and the Rule of Law' (2000) XI *Finnish Yearbook of International Law* 247–64.

damage, frustration and tragedy. Against it, I would invoke a practice of formalism, with its associated tropes about valid law, rights and constitutionalism, less as definite institutional models than as regulative ideals for a profession without which no community could rule itself by standards it recognises as its own (instead of those of some influential faction). The idea of a universal law needs servants that define themselves as administrators (instead of inventors) of universal standards – the class of lawyers. The traditions and practices of this class are significant only to the extent that they remain attached to the 'flat, substanceless surface' of the law.

Instrumentalism, Formalism, and the Production of an International Political Community

Modern international law puts the international lawyer at the heart of the legal system. It is possible to represent that position schematically by reference to the two types of logic at play in the international rule of law. Here is the international relations theorist Hedley Bull:

> The special interests of the dominant elements in a society are reflected in the way in which the rules are defined. Thus the particular kinds of limitations that are imposed on resort to violence, the kinds of agreements whose binding character is upheld, or the kinds of right to property that are enforced, will have the stamp of those dominant elements. But that there should be limits of some kind to violence, and an expectation in general that agreements should be carried out, and rules of property of some kind, is not a special interest of some members of a society but a general interest of all of them.'[62]

So described, law unites an *instrumentalist logic*, one that looks for the realisation of objectives through law, with a *formalist logic*, one that establishes standards of behaviour. Now it is obvious that neither logic is fully constraining. The instrumental logic is indeterminate as the objectives always leave a number of possible choices: what does 'peace and security' mean and how should it be realised in the Middle East, for example? Nor is the formalist logic ever fully formal, but always in practice somehow partial and biased. However general the rules of law are, their equal application may appear unjust because the reality to which they are applied is profoundly unequal: should large and small states, democracies, and dictatorships really be treated alike? The form of law is realised in particular rules and decisions that are no longer formal but that always institute a bias in favour of some substantive preferences.

In the *Nuclear Weapons* case (1996), the ICJ was requested by the UN General Assembly to give an advisory opinion on the legal status of nuclear weapons. From the perspective of the instrumentalist logic, the relevant regulation (human rights law, environmental law, humanitarian law, and the law concerning the use of

---

[62] H Bull, *The Anarchic Society. A Study of Order in World Politics* (London, Macmillan, 1977) 55.

force) sought to accomplish several types of objectives: above all protection of human life and the environment, as well as the survival of states. These objectives proved indeterminate, however, and both opponents and supporters of nuclear weapons argued by reference to them: are people better protected with or without nuclear weapons? The instrumental logic did set some limits to what the Court could say, but it did not – indeed could not – fully constrain it. A decision by the Court was needed to bring the instrumental logic into a conclusion.

The formalist logic was equally under-determined. To decide that nuclear weapons were *illegal* would have created a consistent material bias in favour of states in possession of conventional weapons or in de facto possession of undisclosed nuclear weapons. To require the dismantling of disclosed nuclear arsenals would have revolutionised the existing military-political relationships in unforeseen ways. However, to decide that nuclear weapons were *lawful* would have maintained the systemic bias in security policy in favour of the Great Powers and gone against the deep-rooted popular sense that the existence of such weapons constitutes a permanent hostage-taking by nuclear weapons states of most of the world's population. Neither illegality nor legality could remain fully within the formalist logic. Both broke through pure form and created one or another type of material preference. Indeed, it was impossible to decide either way without the decision seeming 'biased' from the opposed standpoints. As political choice in this case seemed too important for the Court to take, it chose the path of recognising the insufficiency of both logics: 'the Court considers it does not have sufficient elements to enable it to decide with certainty that the use of nuclear weapons would be necessarily at variance with the principles and rules applicable in armed conflict in any circumstance'.[63]

I have defended elsewhere the Court's silence inasmuch as it protected the need for a sustained *political* condemnation of the killing of the innocent, lifting it from the banal instrumentalism and formalism of modern law.[64] Irrespective of that position, however, the case illustrates the indeterminacy of both of the two types of logic behind the Rule of Law, as outlined by Bull above. Neither instrumental calculation nor a purely formal analysis could grasp the status of such weapons: a *decision* was needed that was irreducible to the two logics. Here the decision was silence. In other cases, the Court may have recourse to literalism, balancing, contextualisation, and bilateralisation, among a host of techniques, to complete the instrumental and formal structures with which it works.[65] Each of such techniques is, again, indeterminate. None of them explain why *this* argument was held relevant, why *that* interpretation was chosen. The decision always comes about, as a political theorist Ernesto Laclau put it, as a kind of 'regulated madness', never reducible to any structure outside it.[66]

[63] *Legality of the Threat or Use of Nuclear Weapons* (Advisory Opinion) [1996] ICJ Rep 226 [95].
[64] See chapter eight in this volume.
[65] M Koskenniemi, *From Apology to Utopia; the Structure of International Legal Argument* (Re-issue with a new Epilogue, Cambridge University Press, 2005) 462–67.
[66] E Laclau, 'Deconstruction, Pragmatism, Hegemony' in C Mouffe (ed), *Deconstruction and Pragmatism* (London, Verso, 1996) 58.

A court's decision or a lawyer's opinion is always a genuinely political act, a choice between alternatives never fully dictated by external criteria. It is even a *hegemonic* act in the precise sense that though it is partial and subjective, it claims to be universal and objective.[67] But it is this very partiality and political nature of the decision that ensures that it is an aspect of, or even a creative moment of, a political community. Here finally is the significance of the under-determination of the two logics behind the Rule of Law. The society upheld by international law is not an effect of instrumental reason, nor even (some conception) of formal reason *tout court*. It is an effect of decisions that invoke as their justification, and thus offer as valid points of criticism, an idea of (international) community beyond sectarial interests or preferences. An idea of solidarity informs that practice. Of course, such decisions are made under conditions of uncertainty and conflict. They are amenable for criticism from alternative standpoints: what after all does 'solidarity' mean in a world of lions and antelopes? However, that this decision-making practice is not the passive reproduction of some globalising (economic, environmental, humanitarian) structure, projects the international society as a *political community* that seeks to decide for itself what rules govern it. The practice of international law, as Bull suggested, seeks a union of 'dominant elements' with 'general interests'. As such, it remains a terrain in which the never-ending struggle between the two is being waged: hegemony, and critique of hegemony at the same time.

Beyond Instrumentalism and Formalism

In other words, although notions such as 'peace', 'justice', or 'human rights' do not fit well within the techniques of legal formalism, and are quite disappointing as behavioural directives, they give voice to individuals and groups struggling for spiritual or material wellbeing and seeking to express their claims in the language of something greater than merely their personal interests. Law – including international law – has a 'utopian, aspirational face'[68] expressed in large notions such as 'peace', 'justice', or 'human rights' that in countless international law texts appeal to solidarity within community. They do this in three distinct, but related ways.

First, they redescribe individuals and groups as claimants of rights or beneficiaries of entitlements, and in so doing provide them with an identity that they may assert against the homogenising pull of society's dominant elements. As Karen Knop has pointed out, the treatment of claims of self-determination by marginalised groups such as indigenous peoples in legal institutions has sometimes enabled those groups to be represented by an identity 'that might resonate with

---

[67] See chapter nine in this volume.

[68] R Cotterell, *Law's Community. Legal Theory in Sociological Perspective* (Oxford, Clarendon Press, 1995) 17.

those represented' and thus to 'equalize cultures in international law'.[69] Second, legal principles give an international voice to communities by allowing them to read their particular grievances as claims of universal entitlement, at the same level as claims made by other members of the community. To be able to say that some act is an 'aggression' or that the deprivation of a benefit is a 'human rights violation' is to lift a privately felt wrong to the level of a public law violation, of concern not only to the victim but to the community. Such notions – and the whole debate about the objectives of international law – act in the political realm to challenge what Norman Geras has termed the 'contract of mutual indifference' – the tendency to regard violations a private matter between the victim and the perpetrator, and therefore not of concern to others.[70] They challenge the way claims are blocked in the international realm as matters of 'security', 'economics', or, for example, 'private law', thus helping to contest dominant practices that seek to justify themselves by their a-political self-evidence. Thirdly, to make those claims as *legal* claims (instead of moral aspirations or political programmes) is to imagine – and thus to create – the international world as a set of public institutions within which public authorities should use their power in roughly predictable ways and with public accountability to the community at large.

The fact that public law notions such as *jus cogens* or of obligations *erga omnes* tend to be formulated in such large terms as to restate the 'paradox of objectives' has made them seem quite useless from an instrumental perspective. However, we may now assume, their role may be precisely to counteract the ideological effects of instrumentalism. Again, the *form* of those ideas – of an 'international legal community' – is important in allowing the articulation of the most varied types of claims as more than claims about personal preference, thus integrating the claimants as members of a pluralistic community. 'Self-determination', typically, may be constructed analytically to mean anything one wants it to mean, and many studies have invoked its extreme flexibility. Examined in the light of history, however, it has given form and strength to claims for national liberation and self-rule from the French Revolution to decolonisation in the 1960s, the fall of the Berlin Wall, and the political transitions that have passed from Latin America through Eastern Europe and South Africa. 'Peace' too may be an empty notion, perfectly capable of coexisting with economic deprivation and suppression of human rights. On the other hand, peace movements have been an invaluable aspect of political contestation inasmuch as they 'mobilise support and highlight the inconsistencies in international concepts of peace and security'.[71] Even if 'justice' does lie in the eye of the beholder, without a language of justice, the international struggles for resources, recognition, democracy or, for instance, 'ending the culture of impunity' would have seemed like so many meaningless games played by diplomats.

---

[69] Knop, *Diversity and Self-Determination in International Law* (2002) 210.
[70] N Geras, *The Contract of Mutual Indifference, Political Philosophy after the Holocaust* (London, Verso, 1998).
[71] H Charlesworth and C Chinkin, *The Boundaries of International Law. A Feminist Analysis* (Manchester, Manchester University Press, 2000) 272.

In other words, although the question 'what is international law for?' is seldom useful as an aspect of the deliberations over particular problems among international lawyers, it is absolutely crucial as a focus for international law's emancipatory potential. This is why it was significant that the demonstrations against the war in Iraq in 2003, for example, focused on the war's 'illegality'. In this way, the special scandal of Western military action could be articulated as not just the violation of the private interests of Iraqi citizens, but as directed against the (legal) community, and thus everyone. The manufactured character of the instrumental justifications invoked for the war further highlighted the significance of the claim of the war's formal illegality: behind the contrast between a morality of 'freedom' and a morality of 'law' there was a deeper question about who should be entitled to rule us and what can we take on trust.

None of this deviates from the need to recognise that while the culture of formalism is a necessary though often misunderstood aspect of the legal craft, as a historical matter, it has often provided a recipe for indifference and needs to be accompanied by a live sense of its political justification. To lift the debate about objectives from diplomatic instruments or academic treatises to the level of political debates – such as carried out during the Iraq war of 2003 and the resulting occupation – is a necessary counterweight to the bureaucratic spirit often associated with formalism. This will enable the reconstruction of international law as a political project. As modern international law arose in the last decades of the nineteenth century, it did so as a part of the elitist politics of European liberal internationalism that expected public opinion and democracy to pave the way for a rationally administered world.[72] The last articulations of the spirit date from the first decade following the Second World War.[73] Since then, a gap has been created between the utopian and the pragmatic parts of international law, the former becoming a rather grandiose justification over the latter. However, when formalism loses political direction, formalism itself is lost.[74] Hence the turn to pragmatism and instrumentalism surveyed above.

The question 'what is international law for?' needs to be resuscitated from the paralysis that it is infected with because of the indeterminacy of the responses given to it. However, this necessitates a reformulation of the relationship of international law to politics, in either of its two guises, as principles and doctrines on the one hand, and as institutional practices on the other. Both political realism and institutional pragmatism arose as reactions to failed expectations about international law's autonomy: realists rejected legal institutions as a sham and told politicians to aim directly at their objectives. Institutionalists were wary of such objectives and instead relied on techniques of adjustment and compromise.

---

[72] Koskenniemi, *The Gentle Civilizer* (2001); J-A Pemberton, *Global Metaphors. Modernity and the Quest for One World* (London, Pluto Press, 2001).

[73] See, eg H Lauterpacht, 'The Grotian Tradition in International Law' (1946) 23 *British Year Book of International Law* 1–53.

[74] For a useful reconstruction of Hans Kelsen's formalism in terms of the political project that inspired it, see J Von Bernstorff, *Der Glaube an das Universale Recht. Zur Völkerrechtstheorie Hans Kelsens und seine Schüler* (Baden-Baden, Nomos, 2001).

Between Hegemony and Fragmentation: a Mini-History

These reaction formations are intellectually disappointing and politically dubious. Neither provides space for anything but a most formal debate about 'what is international law for?' and no space at all for responding to that question by reference to popular aspirations about peace, order and justice. A first step in trying to account for such aspirations is to accept that these notions are subject to political controversy and that even as they are formulated in universal terms, they are constantly appropriated by particular agents and interests so as to support their agendas and causes. They are aspects of *hegemonic struggle*, that is to say part of an argumentative practice in which particular subjects and values claim to represent that which is universal.[75] That the question 'what is international law for?' is a terrain of such controversy is a natural aspect of a pluralist society and a precondition for conceiving its government in democratic terms.

The hegemonic nature of the debate about international law's objectives may be illustrated in terms of its history.[76] When Spain and Portugal, at the end of the fifteenth century, divided the non-European world between themselves by reference to a Papal directive, they claimed to be speaking as Christian powers on behalf of humankind as a whole. When the Spanish theologians, Vitoria or Las Casas, later claimed that God had given the Indians a soul, just as He had given it to the Spanish, a particular form of Christian scholasticism – Dominican theology – came to speak in terms of universal principles, which was equally constraining on the Princes and the Indians. When Hugo Grotius in 1608 challenged the Iberian claims, he was redefining the objectives of international law within a hegemonic struggle that opposed a Reformation-inspired commercial universalism against the *ancien regime* of (Catholic) Christianity. The narrative of international law from those days to the nineteenth century may be depicted as a succession of natural law arguments that were united by their always emerging from some European intelligentsia that claimed it was speaking on behalf of the world as a whole. When Emer de Vattel in 1758 formulated his 'necessary law of nations' in terms of the commands of natural reason, and found that it consecrated a balance of power between European sovereigns, he already filled the category of the 'universal' with a profoundly particular understanding that was a part of the (European) Enlightenment.

Since the first appearance of the (modern) international law profession in Europe in the late nineteenth century, that profession imagined itself as, in the

---

[75] See chapter nine in this volume.
[76] See also M Koskenniemi, 'Legal Universalism: Between Morality and Power in a World of States' in S Cheng (ed), *Law, Justice and Power. Between Reason and Will* (Stanford, Stanford University Press, 2004) 46–68; A Supiot, *Homo juridicus. Essai sur la function anthropologique de droit* (Paris, Seuil, 2005) 275–305.

words of the Statute of the *Institut de droit international* (1873), the 'juridical conscience of the civilised world'. This understanding, too, was born in a cultural environment that imagined its own experience – which it labelled 'civilisation' – as universal and postulated it as the end-result of the development of societies everywhere. The civilising mission enthusiastically propagated by late nineteenth-century international lawyers was a hegemonic technique, embedded in an understanding of the law as not simply a technical craft or a set of formal instruments and institutions. It was a spontaneous aspect of 'civilisation' which had the natural tendency to become universal.

If the First World War destroyed whatever was left of the civilising mission, it also gave rise to a series of efforts to articulate anew the universal basis of international law, sometimes in terms of a law-like movement of societies to ever more complex forms of division of labour and interdependence,[77] sometimes through a reinstatement of the hierarchical principles that were a natural part of legal systems.[78] Most of the reconstructive scholarship of the inter-war period, however, simply generalised the legal experience of European societies into the international level, bringing into existence a universal international law through private law analogies, conceiving the Covenant of the League of Nations as a constitution of the world and by allocating to the juristic class the function of 'filling the gaps' in an otherwise primitive-looking legal system.[79] The particular European experience with the Rule of Law became the placeholder for the aspirations of peace and justice that lawyers saw were demanded by populations struggling with industrialism and social conflict.

In the more recent post-war era, much of that kind of language – like the political liberalism with which it was associated – has lost credibility. When somebody today claims to be acting on behalf of the 'international community', we immediately recognise the hegemonic technique at work.[80] As against the diplomatic antics of public international law, new specialisations today often carry the ideals of universalism and progress. Recently, this has occasioned a lively debate about the 'fragmentation of international law' – the emergence and consolidation of special regimes and technical sub-disciplines: human rights law, environmental law, trade law, humanitarian law, and so on, each field projecting its preferences as universal ones.[81] The result has been increasing normative and jurisdictional conflicts. In its *The Prosecutor v Dusko Tadić* judgment of 1999, the International Criminal Tribunal of the Former Yugoslavia (ICTY) expressly deviated from the

---

[77] See, eg M Huber, *Die soziologischen Grundlagen des Völkerrechts* (Berlin, Rothschild, 1910).

[78] See, eg A Verdross, *Die Einheit des rechtlichen Weltbildes* (Tübingen, Mohr, 1923).

[79] See H Lauterpacht, *The Function of Law in the International Commununity* (Oxford, Oxford University Press, 1933); M Koskenniemi, 'Lauterpacht, The Victorian Tradition in International Law' (1997) 8 *European Journal of International Law* 215–63.

[80] See P Klein, 'Les problèmes' in O Corten and B Delcourt (eds), *Droit légitimation et politique exterieure: L'Europe et la guerre du Kosovo* (Brussels, Bruylant, 2001); M Feher, *Powerless by Design. The Age of the International Community* (Durham, NC, Duke University Press, 2000).

[81] See 'Fragmentation of International Law: Difficulties arising from the Diversification and Expansion of International Law' Report of the Study Group of the International Law Commission, Finalized by Martti Koskenniemi (13 April 2006) UN Doc A/CN.4/L.682.

practice of the ICJ, as laid out in its *Nicaragua* case in 1986 concerning the attribution of conduct by military irregulars to a state. To move from a standard of 'effective control' to one of 'overall control' significantly enhanced the accountability of foreign states indirectly involved in internal conflicts, constituting a shift of normative preference with respect to one set of international conflicts.[82] The continuing debate about the relevance of environmental, human rights, or labour standards within the WTO system reflects a search for the relative priority of political objectives within WTO institutions as those priorities have not been set at the level of the relevant agreements themselves. The autonomy invoked by human rights regimes constitutes a subtle manoeuvre by human rights implementation organs to universalise their jurisdiction. 'Dynamic' arguments and the object and purpose test allow the creation of a systemic bias in favour of the protected individuals that could be difficult to justify under traditional law.

Such 'fragmentation' is not a technical problem resulting from lack of coordination. The normative preferences of environmental and trade bodies differ, as do preferences of human rights lawyers and international law 'generalists' and each organ is determined to follow its own preference and make it prevail over contrasting ones. The result is, sometimes, deviating interpretations of the general law, such preferences reflecting the priorities of the deciding organ, at other times the creation of firm exceptions in the law, applicable in a special field.[83] Such fragmentation is also an aspect of hegemonic struggle where each institution, though partial, tries to occupy the space of the whole. Far from being a problem to do away with, the proliferation of autonomous or semi-autonomous normative regimes is an unavoidable reflection of a 'postmodern' social condition and a, perhaps at least to some extent, beneficial prologue to a pluralistic community in which the degrees of homogeneity and fragmentation reflect shifts of political preference.[84]

Legal Formalism and International Justice

Let me close by four responses to the question 'what is international law for?' Two are rather straightforward. First, international law exists to advance the repertory of substantive values, preferences, and practices that those in dominant positions seek to realise in the world. Second, it also gives voice to those who have been excluded from decision-making positions and are regularly treated as the objects of other peoples' policies; it provides a platform on which claims about violence,

---

[82] *The Prosecutor v Dusko Tadić* (Judgment) Case No IT-94-1-A, Appeals Chamber (15 July 1999) 57 [137].

[83] M Koskenniemi and P Leino, 'The Fragmentation of International Law: Postmodern Anxities' (2002) 16 *Leiden Journal of International Law* 533–79.

[84] B Stark, 'After/Word(s): Violation of Human Dignity and Postmodernism in Law' (2002) 27 *Yale Journal of International Law* 336–47. See also M Koskenniemi, 'Hegemonic regimes' in M Young, *Regime Interaction in International Law* (Cambridge University Press, forthcoming 2011).

injustice, and social deprivation may be made even against the dominant elements. To bring these two aspects of international law together means that there is no fixed set of objectives, purposes, or principles that would exist somewhere 'outside' or beyond international law itself, that they are always the objectives of particular actors involved in hegemonic pursuits. The law is instrumental, but what it is instrument for cannot be fixed outside the political process of which it is an inextricable part.

Third, this is why international law's objective is always also international law itself. For as I have tried to argue above, it is international law's formalism that brings political antagonists together as they invoke contrasting understandings of its rules and institutions. In the absence of agreement over, or knowledge of the 'true' objectives of political community – that is to say, in an agnostic world – the pure form of international law provides the shared surface – the *only* such surface – on which political adversaries recognise each other as such and pursue their adversity in terms of something shared, instead of seeking to attain full exclusion – 'outlawry' – of the other. In this sense, international law's value and its misery lie in its being the fragile surface of political community among states, other communities, individuals who disagree about their preferences but do this within a structure that invites them to argue in terms of an assumed universality.

However, there is a fourth response as well: international law exists as a promise of justice. The agnosticism of political modernity has made the articulation of this teleological view extremely difficult The justice towards which international law points cannot be enumerated in substantive values, interests, or objectives. It has no predetermined institutional form. All such languages and suggestions express inadequate and reified images, (partial) points of view. Even when acceptable in their general formulation, as soon as such principles are translated into particular policies, and start to prefer some interests or values over others, they become vulnerable to the critique of 'false universalism'. For the *homo economicus*, none of this is too important. All that count are the external objectives projected upon the law. If law fails in realising them, then it loses its authority. The image of law embodied in the metaphor of the *homo juridicus* is quite different. Now law itself – independently of the objective projected upon it – has authority. This authority comes from the way law describes the international world as a (legal) community where questions of just distribution and entitlement are constantly on the agenda, where claims of legal subjects receive an equal hearing and where the acts of public officials are assessed by a language of community standards. For the instrumental view, the constraint received from law is justified only in view of the authority of the law's (external) objectives. In the formalist view, law is used to compel because the violations cannot coexist with the aspirations of universality embedded in the legal form. Such violations are singular until the law lifts them from the purely subjective into public illegality:

> Law is the name of the semblance of order – the assembling, the ordering, the establishing of commonality – that is made of our otherwise (subjective) differences when we

take, or interpret them to be a world that can be judged, rather than mere subjective experiences.[85]

But the justice that animates political community is not one that may be fully attained. Not only is law never justice itself, the two cannot exist side by side. If there is justice, then no law is needed – and if there is law, then there is only a (more or less well-founded) *expectation* of justice. Here is the truth in instrumentalism about positive law being a pointer beyond itself. There is a Messianic structure to international law, the announcement of something that remains eternally postponed. It is this 'to-come' that enables the criticism of the law's own violence, its biases and exclusions. No doubt, law and justice are linked in the activity of lawyers, paradigmatically in the legal judgment. This is the wisdom grasped by legal pragmatism. But the judgment is always insufficiently grounded in law, just like positive law is always insufficiently expressive of justice. In the gap between positive law and justice lies the necessary (and impossible) realm of the politics of law. Without it, law becomes pure positivity, its violence a mere fact of power.

[85] M Constable, 'The Silence of Law: Justice in Cover's "Field of Pain and Death"' in A Sarat (ed), *Law, Violence and the Possibility of Justice* (Princeton, NJ, Princeton University Press, 2000) 95.

Part V

The Spirit of International Law

11

Between Commitment and Cynicism: Outline for a Theory of International Law as Practice

This is an attempt towards a sociology of the international law as a profession. It was inspired by Bourdieu's notion of the juridical 'field' and prompted by the grandiose but empty rhetoric surrounding the United Nations 'Decade of International Law' (1989–1999).

SOME TIME AGO, Professor David Kennedy pointed out the close connection between international law and a reformist-internationalist political agenda. According to him, international lawyers '. . . see themselves and their work favouring international law and institutions in a way that lawyers working in many other fields do not – to work a bank is not to be for banking'.[1] To me, this sounds true, important and enigmatic. Taking up international law as one's professional career simultaneously seems to opt for a politics that favours global governance over national sovereignty, human rights over domestic jurisdiction, integration over independence.[2] A powerful public rhetoric and a familiar historical narrative sustain the profession's association with such objectives, linked with Grotian humanism, Kantian cosmopolitanism and Wilson's institutionalist faith. International lawyers almost invariably see themselves as 'progressives' whose political objectives appear not merely as normative hopes, but as necessary insights into the laws of historical or social development: globalisation, interdependence, democracy, and the rule of law.[3] Coming from different national and legal cultures, international lawyers have

---

[1] DW Kennedy, 'A New World Order: Yesterday, Today, and Tomorrow' (1994) 4 *Transnational Law and Contemporary problems* 7.

[2] Hence M Reisman, for example, can so easily speak about globalisation as an 'optimistic prognosis' in 'Designing and Managing the Future of the State' (1997) 8 *European Journal of International Law* 411. Typically, 'American international lawyers and their professional associations share with the legal adviser a commitment to promoting effective United States participation in the international legal system'. 'The Role of the Legal Adviser of the Department of State. A Report of the Joint Committee Established by the American Society of International Law and the American Branch of the International Law Association' (1991) 85 *American Journal of International Law* 367. For an analysis of legal cosmopolitanism, see M Koskenniemi, 'Lauterpacht. The Victorian Tradition in International Law' (1997) 8 *European Journal of International Law* 215–63.

[3] The point about the 'objective' or 'necessary' aspect of this development in Wolfgang Friedmann's doctrine about the international law of cooperation is stressed in C Leben, 'Changing Structures of

little difficulty addressing each other in a common language of procedural objectives, public governance, social development and institutional renewal.[4]

While the cosmopolitan faith is regularly attested to by international lawyers in their United Nations speeches or opening chapters of their general courses at the Hague Academy of International Law, behind lies another, more humble understanding of international law as a rather marginal professional technique and culture, at best a handmaid to the national political leader or the colleague in a foreign ministry's operative division, with little connection to the philosophical tradition from which it claims to emanate or the academic theory that aims to articulate it as a system of general principles.

The enigmatic aspect of this lies in the relationship between these two understandings; one a matter of public faith, the other of private knowledge; one pushing in the direction of activism, the other towards passivity. One vision of the relations between theory and practice follow what could be called a *programme model*: the idea of practice as the implementation of normative ideals about the nature of world society or its ruling principles, portraying the practitioner, as Julius Stone has put it, as 'an unconscious or at least acquiescent vehicle of a historical process'.[5] The other vision reflects what might be termed a *reactive model* in which theory is rather more an instrument for responding to contingencies that arise in practical work. Moreover, such dichotomies are very familiar to the profession and continue to structure its discourse by opposing idealistic and pragmatic approaches to each other and occasioning interminable calls from the field and the academia for lawyers to balance the opposing forces, to try to mediate between cosmopolitan enthusiasm and the constraints of diplomatic routine.

In this chapter I want to argue, however, that no middle position is available; that to practice international law is to work within both strands of tradition: a sentimental attachment to the field's constitutive rhetoric and traditions, an attachment that I like to call 'commitment', and a pervasive and professionally engrained doubt about the profession's marginality, or even the identity of one's profession, the suspicion of its being 'just politics' after all, a doubt that I will call 'cynicism'. I shall aim at providing a somewhat impressionistic sketch of the structure of the psychological positions available to international law practitioners, as well as the emotional energies and dangers involved in a commitment to international law.

International Law Revisited. By Way of Introduction' (1997) 8 *European Journal of International Law* 401.

[4] R Jennings, 'An International Lawyer Takes Stock' (1990) 39 *International & Comparative Law Quarterly* 526–27.

[5] J Stone, 'Scholars in International Law', in *Of Law and Nations* (Buffalo, Hein, 1974) 253.

Work of Commitment?

In the accounts about international legal practice, reference is often made to the 'commitment' that taking up international law seems to require from its practitioners.[6] What is 'commitment'? As I see it, it involves a wholesale, ultimately unreflective or sentimental 'throwing-of-oneself' into one's work, an unthinking loyalty to one's profession, its constitutive rules and traditions, as well as an unwavering belief in its intrinsic goodness.

Despite the centrality of passion to, or the absence of calculating reason from, *genuine commitment*, we hold it to be a positive thing, a good in itself (that is to say, apart from the consequences that it produces). This, I suppose, is because it seems contrary to two of modernity's familiar negative effects: personal alienation and social nihilism. To have commitment is to be able to combine different aspects of one's life – private passion and public duty – into a whole that provides a stable personal identity and a meaningful social role, enabling one to overcome the threat that one's personality is split into private and public selves. Each now becomes an extension of the other; private faith and public profession link harmoniously – somewhat like Einstein's 'oceanic feeling' made it possible for him (though not to Freud) to have the experience 'of an indissoluble bond, of being one with the external world as a whole' – a sense of 'being in' religion without actually being religious.[7]

I wish to emphasise the a-rational character of commitment in three ways. First, a commitment, distinguished from mere 'work', has an aspect of heroism in that it works against all odds. One is committed to something, the success of which is not automatically guaranteed. Commitment involves danger, or risk of failure. Were it otherwise, mere self-interested calculation would provide a sufficient motivation. One may, of course, also succeed in what one is committed to, but the end may as well, or will perhaps more likely, be a disappointment. However, failure takes nothing away from the heroism of the commitment. Indeed, tragedy may even be its crowning achievement.[8]

In international law, this aspect of commitment is immediately evident. The hopes of the reconstructive scholarship of the inter-war era, as well as the projects for peaceful settlement and collective security within the League of Nations were easily dashed by Fascist aggression. Though tragedy is the name we apply to that period, we still admire the heroism of the profession's leading names: Anzilotti, Kelsen, Lauterpacht, Scelle. Their criticism of sovereignty, their methodological

---

[6] As pointed out in respect of the career of a governmental legal adviser: 'a lawyer's deep interest in and commitment to the law is most frequently the motivation for choosing a career as legal adviser', HCL Merillat (ed), *Legal Advisers and Foreign Affairs* (Dobbs Ferry, Oceana Publications, 1964) 27–28.
[7] S Freud, *Civilization and Its Discontents* (translated by J Riviere, edited by J Strachey, London, Hogarth, 1973) 2.
[8] See also O Korhonen, 'New International Law: Silence, Defence or Deferral' (1996) 7 *European Journal of International Law* 15–18.

individualism, their belief in public governance through international institution and the pacifying effects of interdependence remain part of the professional ethos today, while prospects for a public law governed global federation – the logical and sometimes expressly stated corollary of their writings – are no nearer today. Within diplomacy, the profession continues to speak from the margin to the centre. It is not at all certain that a judgment of the International Court of Justice (ICJ) will be complied with, or that the advice of the foreign office legal counsel will be followed. There is a wealth of writing about the utopianism that is indissociable from the profession. To struggle for 'world peace through law', 'world order models', the rights of future generations, 'fairness' or indeed global governance is far from a recipe for diplomatic success. But we could not recognise the profession for what it is if it did not hark back to such objectives.

Second, commitment is against one's own (immediate) interests, as well as the (immediate) interests of one's clan, party or nation.[9] Commitment overrides competing loyalties and normative demands. This is also an aspect of the heroism that we see in commitment; its unselfish generosity. Many aspects of international law practice appear to underscore this. After law school, a purely economic calculation will not convince one of the wisdom of choosing international law from the available fields of legal specialisation. To be a voice for no particular interest or position is not a lucrative affair; it calls for commitment! Yet, what one loses in salary, one may think one gains in one's ability to lead a life of commitment.[10]

This aspect of commitment has to do with the avoidance of politics, prejudice and everything else that appears as external, or strictly outside the law and is often described in terms of the good lawyer's particular 'integrity'. As Fitzmaurice expressed it:

> ... the value of the legal element depends on its being free of other elements, or it ceases to be legal. This can only be achieved if politics and similar matters are left to those whose primary function they are, and if the lawyer applies himself with single-minded devotion to his legal task ... By practicing this discipline and these restraints, the lawyer may have to renounce, if he ever pretended to it, the dominance of the rule of *lawyers* in international law, but he will establish something of a far greater importance to himself and the world – the Rule of Law.[11]

Third, commitment involves distance from both truth and faith. One is not committed to the proposition 2+2=4. One *knows* it to be true and knowing this involves

---

[9] I write 'immediate' because it is a part of the professional dogma that in the long run the interests of individual peoples, represented by states and the global cosmopolis coalesce. This seems often the last bridgehead in the battle with international law sceptics.

[10] '... the dedicated lawyer, while normally a sociable person, has little relish for the intensive representational activities inseparable from any diplomatic post', G Fitzmaurice, 'Legal Advisers and Foreign Affairs (Review Article)' (1965) 59 *American Journal of International Law* 84. He observes: 'the best lawyer is the dedicated lawyer – the man or woman who would never really be happy doing work that was not legal work and who, for the sake of doing that, is prepared to make considerable sacrifices in other desirable directions', ibid.

[11] G Fitzmaurice, 'The United Nations and the Rule of Law', *The Grotius Society, Transactions for the year 1952*, vol 38, 149.

no emotional attachment, and no risk. Nor was Aristotle 'committed' to the idea that the end of human life was virtuous action; he *knew* this to be the case in the same way that Benthamite utilitarians know that the end of political action is the production of maximum happiness. Knowing something is incompatible with being committed to it. Knowledge relies on the speaker's ability to support what one believes with evidence that, when laid out, will convince everyone sharing the speaker's concept of evidence and rational argument of the truth thus validated. No emotional attachment to such a truth is needed – emotional attachment may even disqualify a proposition from being 'true'.

Commitment to international law in the conditions of agnostic modernity is different from knowing a number of things to be true in the above, hard sense. The propositions of which the rhetorical stuff of international law consists do not possess, as philosophers would say, that kind of truth-value that rationally demonstrable propositions do. In what sense would 'sovereign equality' be true? What would constitute irrefutable proof for 'self-determination', 'equidistance', 'most-favoured nation clause' or 'domestic jurisdiction'? To work with such expressions involves acknowledged uncertainty, as well as semantic and evaluative indeterminacy. These expressions attain sense and applicability only through interpretive acts that involve the interpreter's 'life-view' or commitment to particular understandings of the world.[12]

Commitment to international law is, however, also different from genuine faith. St Augustine was not committed to belief in God. He believed in God even if his reason told him that it was absurd. A priest may be committed to a religion as a system. In such case, there is, or has been, a moment of doubt, a moment overcome neither by revelation nor by rational calculation but by an existential act; an act of will to join a tradition of priesthood to which one feels attached. In a purely faith-based political order, legal practice would become theology. As Vitoria argued in 1539, even if one took the right legal position, taking that position would be a sin if it were taken from other reasons than by deference to theological authority.[13] However much one might be committed to 'law', no such commitment could be determinative of one's action. The ultimate reference must always be to faith.

The identity of international law as a distinct practice depends on this distance from truth and faith. Without it, the legal profession would collapse into science or theology. That it is neither is nicely evident in the profession's ability to resist recurring academic calls to integrate rational means-end calculations or a greater sensitivity to moral axioms. While it is not absurd to describe, say, banking law as a form of 'social engineering', such a description for international law would seem strangely out of place. Providing legal advice to a delegation at an intergovernmental

---

[12] Here lies the modernist-agnostic basis of commitment. Rather like protest indignation, it emerges from a sentimental bond to a programme, an inability or unwillingness to seek further reasoned argument, a denial of even the *ex hypothesi* arguability of the opposite case. For further characterisation, see A MacIntyre, *After Virtue. A Study in Moral Theory*, 2nd edn (Duckworth, 1984).

[13] F de Vitoria, 'De Indis et de Jure Belli Relectiones', *The Classics of International Law* (Washington, Carnegie Institution of Washington, 1917) 116–17.

conference departs so far from empirical reality or moral discourse – without this of course making the advice any less useful – that describing it in terms of science or morality would not seem plausible.

Let me illustrate this by reference to the advisory opinion of the ICJ in the case concerning the *Legality of the Threat or Use of Nuclear Weapons*.[14] It would have been possible for the Court to discuss the matter by reference to quantitative-technical calculations about the effects of nuclear weapons: the number of (civilian) casualties under different scenarios and the relative effects of nuclear strikes compared to non-use ('sitting duck') and conventional warfare. Or it might have been possible for the Court to take a moral stand: it is inconceivable that the use or threat of use of such vicious weapons could be lawful! Surely democracy must be defended by any means! However, the Court chose neither tack, leaving the matter open in its unprecedented *non liquet*.[15] If law were silent, then no scientific or moral truth could speak in its stead. Otherwise, the service rendered would no longer have been legal.

To say that international law involves commitment in each of these three senses is to say that it involves an existential *decision*; that it is not a mechanical activity determined by power or interest, truth or faith. The decision is not arbitrary, however, but reflects the rituals of the tradition of liberal cosmopolitanism, its criteria of professional competence, and its narratives about the role of law and the lawyer in foreign affairs.[16]

Commitment under Stress

Yet, for all its psychological importance and its ability to create a sense of personal-professional identity, commitment to international law is fragile and difficult to sustain. How long, for example, can one be committed to a project to state responsibility that commenced in the United Nations in 1949 and is today no more than a set of controversial draft articles with no realistic prospect of being accepted as hard law in the foreseeable future?[17] Can one still be enthusiastic about a Common Heritage of Mankind after the redistributory goals of the III UN Convention on the Law of the Sea[18] were watered down in the 1994 Implementation Agreement,[19] concluded under the grandiose banner of the 'securing the universality of the

---

[14] *Legality of the Threat or Use of Nuclear Weapons* (Advisory Opinion) [1996] ICJ Rep 226.
[15] ibid.
[16] The argument draws inspiration from S Fish, *Doing What Comes Naturally. Change, Rhetoric and the Practice of Theory in Literature and Legal Studies* (Oxford, Oxford University Press, 1990).
[17] The Draft Articles on State Responsibility more adopted by the International Law Commission in 2001. For ten years, they have now been passive on the agenda of the General Assembly.
[18] III UN Convention on the Law of the Sea (10 December 1982) UN Doc A/CONF.62/122, vol XVII 151 (1982).
[19] Agreement relating to the implementation of part XI of the United Nations Convention on the Law of the Sea, General Assembly Resolution 48/263.

Convention', but in fact underwriting the demands of the developed West to create a cost-effective and market-oriented platform for private enterprise in the deep seabed?[20] Commitment to the United Nations may still feel appropriate as a vaguely left-leaning, public-law-oriented countermove to the increasing predominance in globalization of informal structures of the transnational private market.[21] Any such move is, however, undermined by the anachronistic pomp that surrounds the Organisation's daily activity against which successive cycles of reform proposals have turned into failures. The General Assembly never succeeded in growing into the kind of global *polis* that legal imagination always saw as its proper role. No new international economic or information order arose from the interminable debates in the Assembly in the 1970s. Who, apart from a few diplomats posted in New York, still remembers the 1982 Manila Declaration on Peaceful Settlement of Disputes, the 1987 Declaration on the Enhancement of the Effectiveness of the Principle of Refraining from the Threat or Use of Force in International Relations or the 1988 Declaration on the Prevention and Removal Disputes and Situations which May Threaten International Peace and Security and on the Role of the United Nations in this Field?[22] Even the contrived titles of such instruments testify to the futility of hopes about the efficient management of global affairs through the Organisation.

Commitment to collective security through the Security Council seems likewise troubled by procedural and ideological ambiguity. The debate about a 'legitimacy crisis' concerning the Council's action to define and forestall what counts as a 'threat to international peace and security' focuses directly on the question of determining agency: the practice of authorising powerful Member States to take action in the Gulf, Somalia, Haiti, Rwanda, Liberia, the Former Yugoslavia and Albania makes it doubtful whether these activities can be understood as an international community response to unlawful behaviour.[23]

There may be progress in such areas as environmental law, trade law, humanitarian law and outer space law. However, is the 'Kyoto process' and the interminable wrangles about national emission rates for greenhouse gases to be seen as a step towards an effective public regulatory regime for the global environment?[24] Can

---

[20] See M Koskenniemi and M Lehto, 'The Privilege of Universality. International Law, Economic Ideology and Seabed Resources' (1996) 65 *Nordic Journal of International Law* 533–55.

[21] As attempted, eg in G Abi-Saab, 'Cours général de droit international public', *Collected Courses of the Hague Academy of International Law, 1987-VII* (1996) vol 207, 9. See also S Sur, 'The State between Fragmentation and Globalization' (1997) 8 *European Journal of International Law* 429–31.

[22] See UNGA Res 37/10 (15 November 1982), UNGA Res 42/22 (18 November 1987) and UNGA Res 43/51 (5 December 1988).

[23] See in more detail M Koskenniemi, 'The Police in the Temple. Order, Justice and the United Nations: A Dialectical View' (1995) 5 *European Journal of International Law* 325–48 and the definitive study on the matter by I Österdahl, *Threat to Peace. The Interpretation by the Security Council of Article 39 of the UN Charter* (Stockholm, Norstedt, 1998) especially the discussion of NATO taking over the United Nations' role and of the Council's passivity in respect of African civil wars 128–39.

[24] One mainstream assessment of the United Nations Conference on Environment and Development (UNCED) follow-up process stated that, 'so far no crucial steps have been taken to save the global environment, nor has there been any significant move towards improving the development perspective

international lawyers be committed to the Energy Charter Treaty[25] or to the International Law Commission (ILC) Draft Convention on international liability,[26] with all the uncertainty they imply about who is to gain and who is to lose? What about the negotiations on reform of intellectual property regimes so as to provide for the commercial confidentiality needed by Microsoft or Nokia, while allowing access codes to the Pentagon or the FBI in their pursuit of international criminality? Which side should international lawyers commit themselves to in that struggle? What faith is left in the 'struggle against impunity' when, in 2010, after eight years of operation the International Criminal Court has not delivered one single judgment, while it seems that it is only African leaders that may be prosecuted in it?[27]

Examples about high hopes turning into frustration multiply to the point of parody. The elaborate provisions of the 1992 Conference on Security and Cooperation in Europe (CSCE) decision concerning the peaceful settlement of disputes have never been resorted to and no recourse has so far been made by anyone to the Court of Conciliation and Arbitration set up at the same time.[28] This is an ironic repetition of the silence that has surrounded the Permanent Court of Arbitration for the post-war era. Despite the increase in the workload of the International Court of Justice, it would seem quite misplaced to show the same enthusiasm about it as James Brown Scott did when the Assembly of the League of Nations approved the Statute of the Permanent Court of International Justice, exclaiming that: 'We should . . . fall upon our knees and thank God that the hope of ages is in the process of realization.'[29]

Was there not something comical about the *Decade of International Law* (1989–1999) that produced nothing of normative substance? Based on a Nicaraguan initiative within the Non-Aligned Movement in 1989, the Decade was routinely declared by the General Assembly later that same year; although by then a change of government in the initiating country had made it imprudent for it to continue its originally anti-American move.[30] Painfully aware of the fact that a decade once declared by the General Assembly could not just be set aside, dutiful

of most countries in the South', P Malanczuk, *Akehurst's Modern Introduction to International Law*, 7th edn (New York, Routledge, 1997) 252.

[25] *International Legal Materials* (ASIL, Washington, 1995) vol 35, 509 and eg E Paasivirta, 'The European Union and the Energy Sector: The Case of the Energy Charter Treaty' in M Koskenniemi (ed), *International Law Aspects of the European Union* (The Hague, Nijhoff, 1997) 197–214.

[26] Draft principles on the allocation of loss in the cases of transboundary harm arising out of hazardous activities, *Yearbook of the International Law Commission* (2006) vol II part 2, online http://untreaty. un.org/ilc/texts/instruments/english/draft%20articles/9_10_2006.pdf.

[27] See the internet site of the International Criminal Court: www.icc-cpi.int/Menus/ICC/ Situations+and+Cases/Cases/.

[28] *International Legal Materials* (1993) vol 35, 551 et seq. For a review of the ratifications (22) as of 18 September 1997 and a plea for the use of the mechanisms, see the statement by the President of the Court of Conciliation and Arbitration, Robert Badinter, 18 September 1997 (OSCE, PC.GAL/10/97). By 2010, it still has had no business. See http://www.osce.org/cca.

[29] J Brown Scott, 'Editorial Comment' (1921) 5 *American Journal of International Law* 55.

[30] UNGA Res 44/23 (17 November 1989). On the Decade, see also AHA Soons, 'The Hague Peace Initiative' in Al-Nauimi-Meese (ed), *International Legal Issues Arising under the United Nations Decade of international Law* (The Hague, Nijhoff, 1995) 53–54. See also UNGA Res 51/157 (16 December 1996) and UNGA Res 51/159 (16 December 1996).

delegations from a handful of legalist traditions sought to provide it with a sub-stantive programme – in vain. Year after year the only activity under the Decade was the setting up of a sessional working group and a procession of statements from Sixth Committee representatives about how much money their government had allocated to the teaching and study of international law – reports they would have provided anyway under the recurrent agenda item on the 'Teaching and Dissemination of Information on International Law'. The United Nations Congress on Public International Law in 1995 gathered nearly every prominent name in the profession at the United Nations Headquarters (on their own or their government's expense) to hear for five days roundly worded statements on general aspects of international law.[31] As the cliché goes, 'it is not the meeting but the opportunity to have private and confidential conversations . . .' As the embarrass-ment became simply too great, a few traditionalist governments decided to com-memorate international law in honouring the 'Centennial of the first International Peace Conference' by holding meetings in The Hague and St Petersburg in 1999.[32] Once again, this commemorative effort remained devoid of any definite substan-tive objective[33] and as such a fitting wrap-up for a century of recurrent enthusi-asms gone sour, a *fin-de-siècle* fireworks for the celebration of commitment to meaninglessness.

However, parody is a facile extension of journalistic accounts about 'Utopia Lost',[34] a fashionable post-modern trope. If it is not the United Nations, what is there for international lawyers to commit to? Does regionalism or specialisation provide relief? However, if law seems to work in the European Union, might this be precisely because of the 'special' character of the law and its success in distanc-ing itself from intergovernmental diplomacy? It is certainly possible to recognise the functioning of a legal system under the European Convention on Human Rights[35] – but do the Strasbourg Court's judgments on allowable detention peri-ods, rendered five years after the event, provide a stable focus for commitment?

Today's international dynamism looks elsewhere than at public international law, the United Nations and projects of formal governance. Its focus is on non-state-centered pragmatism, private economy and technocratic management of

---

[31] See *International Law as a Language for International Relations. Proceedings of the United Nations Conference on Public International Law*, New York 13–17 March 1995 (1996). The General Assembly Resolutions on the matter concentrate on encouraging the speedier publication of and providing wider access to various United Nations legal publications, on endorsing the activities of various other organ-isations and states, and in particular the Dutch-Russian Programme of Action, noting carefully, how-ever, that it 'does not entail budgetary implications for the United Nations'. See UNGA 'Official Records of the General Assembly, Fifty-second Session, Sixth Committee' (15th December 1997) UN Doc A/52/647.

[32] The Meeting in The Hague was held on 17–18 May 1999.

[33] Apart from the consideration of the 'Draft Guiding Principles for International Negotiations', Doc A/151/141. For the Dutch-Russian Programme of Action, see Doc A/C.6/52/3 (1997).

[34] Among the more interesting pieces in the genre, see R Righter, *Utopia Lost. The United Nations and World Order* (New York, The Twentieth Century Fund Press, 1995).

[35] *Convention for the Protection of Human Rights and Fundamental Freedoms*, 4 November 1950, United Nations, *Treaty Series*, vol 213, 221.

informal transnational regimes with a speed and flexibility for which rules and public governance are anathema and that need no specific commitment to anything to appear useful or convincing. It is also a world of unilateralism, 'liberal millenarianism', attempts to forge a new international order beyond sovereign equality through economic liberalisation, tactical recourse to international organisations and a globalising recourse to Western conceptions of political legitimacy.[36] It is a world where human life can sometimes be used as a symbol of the law's frustrating weakness.[37]

In this world, public international law, including the formal structures of sovereignty and treaties, is replaced by fluid transnational patterns of exchange between various types of more or less stable actors and interest groups. There, to quote Philip Alston, the public international lawyer's professional antics appear little other than 'exercises in nostalgia'.[38] Instead, now a professional technique seems needed that transgresses the limit between the international and the domestic, the public and the private, politics and economy, and becomes context-sensitive, short-term, market-oriented and ad hoc. Technical specialisation combines with what could be called 'fragmentation' only if there were a centre against which something would appear as a 'fragment'. From their position as managers of a global polity, international lawyers find their cosmopolitan fantasy increasingly as an old-fashioned cultural eccentricity, out of step with the needs of the liberal consensus, of globalising financial markets, regional economies and de facto principles of identification of human groups. As sovereignty breaks down, rules that used to be international become the professional stuff of all lawyers, while no rule remains exclusively linked to a domestic background or sphere of applicability. The management of the European Union's economic sanctions, for instance, becomes part of the commercial framework of the Community's external trade relationships that links together diplomatic decisions within the Council and domestic criminal law enforcement. Between 'liberal states' no inter-sovereign jurisdictional or immunity barriers seem justified; while precisely those rules are used to isolate not only 'rogue states', but much of the outside world from the benefits of increasing integration within the industrialised world.[39] Instead of a 'common law of mankind', international law becomes its ideological contrary; a divisive weapon; a protective shield under which the privileges of some can be upheld against the claims of others; and a unilateral weapon in the hands of the hegemon.[40]

---

[36] For a critical discussion of the 'Cosmopolitan Model of the Holy Alliance', see D Zolo, *Cosmopolis. Prospects for World Government* (Cambridge, Polity Press, 1997).

[37] As exemplified in the execution by the United States of Mr Breard, a Paraguayan citizen in (a completely pointless) act of defiance of the order for provisional measures in the case concerning the *Vienna Convention on Consular Relations (Paraguay v United States), Order of 9 April 1998* [1998] ICJ Rep.

[38] P Alston, 'The Myopia of the Handmaidens: International Lawyers and Globalization' (1997) 8 *European Journal of International Law* 447.

[39] A-M Slaughter, 'International Law in a World of Liberal States' (1995) 6 *European Journal of International Law* 503–38 especially 516–34.

[40] For a strong critique, see S Sur, 'The State between Fragmentation and Globalization' (1997) 8 *European Journal of International Law* 428–34.

If such is the disillusionment, and the remedy lies in shedding one's 'Victorian' optimism and meliorism, what then can be left of commitment? Let me sketch the dilemma. As what one is committed to cannot be proven as true or accepted as faith, the object of commitment always remains ambivalent and frequently changes to its contrary. While the lawyers' public rhetoric seems to imply a general preference for the international over the particular, often this preference cannot be maintained. It seems sometimes necessary to support sovereignty over attempts at international intervention. Statehood seems both a positive danger to human rights and an indispensible instrument for upholding them. Claims for self-determination are liberating as well as threatening. To fix the law's substance in some particular way seems to always require something more: a political decision. Whether to accept or reject extraterritorial jurisdiction, for example, depends on what one thinks are the basic values or interests represented by one's state.[41] What amounts to a 'threat to the peace' hinges on one's construction of 'peace'.[42] The law brings the committed lawyer to the brink of the (legal) decision, but never quite into it. If civil strife arises, the law tells the lawyer: 'Here are the two rules, "self-determination" and "uti possidetis". Now choose.'

There is a duality about international law rules and principles: they are sometimes applicable and sometimes not and whether or not they are (and how they are) depends on a (political) decision. In fact, this phenomenon is very familiar. As a former legal adviser at the Quai d'Orsay explains, in regard to the principle of *pacta sunt servanda*, Governments: '. . . déploient beaucoup d'ingéniosité pour découvri des moyens commodes de prendre des libertés avec le principes en question'.[43] This is no externally introduced distortion, however, but follows from the fluid character of international legal rules and principles: one is bound to make a choice and it is hardly unnatural that one's choice is for the alternative that is closest to oneself. However, this is a slippery slope. From the fact that law involves political decision it is tempting to move to where law is seen as an instrument of (particular) politics:

> Une certaine non-application des traités beneficie en fait d'une indulgence très générale comme si chacun comprenait fort bien, même s'il ne juge pas opportun de le dire officiellement, qu'il est imprudent de trop blâmer chez l'autre la recherche d'une liberté que l'on entend bien revendiquer pour soi.[44]

In this passage the former French diplomat and lawyer articulates a pragmatism that is only slightly removed from a cynicism that pits one's public faith against one's private scepticism. Now cynicism is precisely the reverse of commitment. As

---

[41] See R Malley, J Manas, Crystal Nix, Lomment, 'Constructing the State Extraterritorially: Jurisdictional Discourse, The National Interest and Transnational Norms' (1990) 103 *Harvard Law Review* 1273–1304.

[42] See in more detail M Koskenniemi, 'The Police in the Temple. Order, Justice and the United Nations: A Dialectical View' (1995) 5 *European Journal of International Law* 325–48 and I Österdahl, *Threat to Peace. The Interpretation by the Security Council of Article 39 of the UN Charter* (Stockholm, Norstedt, 1998) especially the discussion of NATO taking over the United Nations' role and of the Council's passivity in respect of African civil wars 128–39.

[43] G De Lacharrière, *La politique juridique extérieure* (Paris, Economica, 1983) 200.

[44] ibid 201.

commitment is identical neither with truth nor with faith, it always involves doubt, uncertainty about whether it is really warranted, whether it really provides a sufficiently stable practice and identity. This is an aspect of the danger that commitment involves, the danger that once the sentimental energy on which commitment works is exhausted, one is left with a voice that finds no support in inner emotion. The spoken or written word camouflages a self that secretly believes otherwise. This loses the heroism of commitment and transforms one's commitment acts into its contrary: advancement of private ends, partisan positions, group or national interests, complacency, manipulation, careerism.

Now each of the three aspects of commitment that I have sketched may well turn into or present itself as cynicism. The utopian aspect of commitment may be associated with a firm conviction that the object of one's public faith will never be realised. In such case, one's use of the rhetorics of global governance, democracy and human rights no longer emerges from a commitment that refuses to accept the reality of impending frustration but from, say, the speaker's wish to associate his or her interests or objectives with a positive value content drawn from a tradition of utopianism, an intent to camouflage what one knows will be the case or inertia.

Some of this, I suppose, is visible in the human rights field. The Convention on the Rights of the Child[45] was signed in September 1990 at a summit meeting attended by 71 heads of state and government – and the Convention has received an unprecedented number of ratifications. Nonetheless, it is far from evident what the effect of the Convention has been on the lives of children.[46] For many, the central issue in the *Case concerning the Gabčíkovo-Nagymaros Project (Hungary/ Slovakia)* was the environmental aspects of the large construction works in the Danube. The Court was well aware of this and included passages in the judgment that stress the need to take account of environmental considerations and the interests of future generations in the continuation of the works. These aspects of the judgment, however, stand out from the rest of the Court's reasoning and have nothing to contribute to the *ratio decidendi* that builds squarely upon the bilateral treaty aspects of the case.[47] The Rights of the Child Convention or the environmental passages in the *Gabčíkovo-Nagymaros* case are to be seen as formal deference to the utopian expectations of the general public that not only remain practically inconsequential but were never believed to attain the objectives they proclaimed. In a general way, even the discrepancy between the high rhetorics of United Nations human rights conventions and the dismal funds available to their implementation bodies may be understood in terms of a cynical distance between governmental faith and private willingness to depart from the privileges of sovereignty.[48]

---

[45] UNGA Res 44/25 (20 November 1989).
[46] At least judging the effectiveness of its reporting system see, eg J Lamotte – G Goedertier, 'Monitoring Human Rights: Formal and Procedural Aspects' in E Verhellen (ed), *Monitoring Children's Rights* (The Hague, Nijhoff, 1996) 102–11.
[47] *Case concerning the Gabčíkovo-Nagymaros Project (Hungary/Slovakia)* [1997] ICJ Rep [140].
[48] See the reports of the respective treaty bodies.

Likewise, commitment's avowed distance from self-interest or the interests of one's group may sometimes hide a consistent pattern of partiality in a way that we recognise as the cynical structure of hypocrisy. Despite its universal rhetoric, the practice of international law empowers governments in the international field to the exclusion of voices that are unable to secure governmental representation for themselves. As Philip Allott put it, 'Only international law is left speaking to Governments the words that Governments want to hear.'[49] In the Court's practice, this aspect may be illustrated by the *East Timor* case in which the brief and inconsequential reference to the right of self-determination of the Timorese people is overshadowed by the formal-procedural decision not to allow Portugal *locus standi* in a matter conceptualised as an inter-sovereign conflict in which one of the sovereigns (Indonesia) was asked to submit to a decision on the justifiability of its conduct without its formal consent.[50]

Finally, powerful arguments seek to replace commitment to international law either with scientific fact or moral truth. Yet, neither empiricism nor morality can live up to the law's cosmopolitan credo. The international relations approaches that envisage international law in terms of means-ends calculations either present the ends in such a general fashion that any interpretation of the law can be matched within them, or reveal themselves as rhetoric intended to support particular interests.[51] To think of law as a technical instrument for goal-values such as 'democracy', 'human dignity', 'fairness' or 'global governance', leaves unexplained uncertainties in the causal relations between technical norms and such goals and leaves open the question of who determines what such goals in practical terms mean.[52] An instrumentalist approach to the law that presents a claim of scientific objectivity disguises the fact that political decisions are needed to interpret the goal and to fix the chain of causality that leads from the norm to the goal.

Now the purpose of these examples about the dialectic of commitment and cynicism is not to throw doubt on the actual difficulties of settling international disputes in a workable fashion or the bona fides of individual lawyers or statesmen negotiating international treaties. My intention is to describe the work of *ambivalence* in the rhetoric of legal practice that enables the simultaneous justification

---

[49] P Allot, *Eunomia. New Order for a New World* (Oxford, Oxford University Press, 1990) 296.

[50] *East Timor (Portugal v Australia)* (Judgment) [1995] ICJ Rep 90, 105–106 [37]–[38]. Christine Chinkin characterised the Court's argument here as 'A form of procedural imperialism [that] accords absolute priority to States' interests', 'Increasing the Use and Appeal of the Court' in C Peck and RS Lee (eds), *Increasing the Effectiveness of the International Court of Justice, Proceedings of the ICJ/UNITAR Colloquium to celebrate the 50th Anniversary of the Court* (The Hague, Kluwer Law International, 1997) 49.

[51] This is typically argued to be the case in respect of the 'human dignity values' espoused as the law's naturalist basis by the 'New Haven School'. See the studies by K Krakau, *Missionsbewusstsein und Völkerrechtsdoktrin in den Vereinigten Staaten von Amerika* (Hamburg, 1967); B Rosenthal, *Etude de l'ouvre de Myres Smith McDougal en matière du droit international public* (Paris, 1970).

[52] See S Marks, 'The End of History? Reflexions on Some International Legal Theses' (1997) 8 *European Journal of International Law* 449–77 especially 470–75. Compare the 'liberal millenarianism' there critiqued with the 'third world traditionalist' view in C Pinto, 'Democratization of International Relations and its Implications for the Development of International Law', *International Law as a Language for International Relations* (The Hague, Kluwer Law International, 1996) 250–63.

and critique of particular normative outcomes.[53] Although that ambivalence is immediately visible in the open disagreement among lawyers and academics about such outcomes, I wish to argue that it is likewise present in the roles and mental structures of the practitioners whose task it is to produce them. In other words, the dialectic of commitment/cynicism is not just a result of external interpretations of the behaviour of particular agents, but structures the psychological reality of those agents themselves. It appears frequently as a doubt, often suspended but never wholly suppressed, that all practitioners share about the 'ultimate' justifiability of what they do. For although it is often silently assumed (especially by academic lawyers) that practitioners have a privileged access into the law's truth, being so close to the 'real world' where it all 'takes place', in fact practitioners live among the same uncertainty about the 'real character' of the problems they deal with and the consequences of their actions as anyone else. It is, I believe, precisely this sense of doubt, uncertainty, and occasional schizophrenia (is my work useful or not; does it produce the consequences that I say it does; am I Dr Jekyll or Mr Hyde) that is in the background when international lawyers describe their practice in terms of a *commitment*, instead of, say, a knowledge or a faith. Let me now sketch the way in which that dialectic is present in the four standard roles offered to practitioners.

The Judge

Few international lawyers ever become judges in the International Court of Justice or even members of an arbitral tribunal. Nonetheless, as Brownlie noted, 'The International Court of Justice stands at the centre of the world of the professional international lawyer.'[54] However much sociologists stress the marginality of formal dispute resolution and point to the conventional normality of conforming behaviour as occupying the largest amount of legally relevant behaviour, the activity of judging – or the eventuality of a judgment – still lies in the conceptual centre of international and, possibly, any law.[55] Without judging – and judges – something of the distinctiveness about law would be lost, something that cannot be replaced by sovereign power, conforming behaviour or effective enforcement. The judge personifies what in law is more than 'how nations behave', that can never be reduced to a partisan position, somebody's power and interest. When called upon to perform a legal service, even a non-judge (as adviser, academic, activist) must momentarily construct himself or herself as judge. One need not share a legal realist's ontology about law being (predictions about) what courts decide in order to

---

[53] See further M Koskenniemi, *From Apology to Utopia; the Structure of International Legal Argument* (1989) (Re-issue with a new Epilogue, Cambridge University Press, 2005) 474–512.

[54] I Brownlie, 'The Calling of the International Lawyer: Sir Humphrey Waldock and His Work' (1983) 54 *The British Year Book of International Law* 68.

[55] See Koskenniemi, *From Apology to Utopia* (2005) 24–28.

think that there is very little distance between the question 'what does the law say?' and the question 'how would a judge decide the case?' The judge personifies impartiality, rising above national and other group interests. Judges, writes Duncan Kennedy, 'are supposed to "submit" to something "bigger" and "higher" than "themselves"'.[56] This is the central aspect of their commitment. This 'bigger' and 'higher' is the 'legal system', more specifically the legal system as a system or an aggregate of *legal* rules. The judge's commitment is a commitment to the substance of the law as neutral and objective rules whose formal validity guarantees their distance from 'politics' whether in the guise of power, interest or ideology.

Commitment to rules, however, is as fragile as any other commitment. Much in the activity of judging testifies to the futility of thinking of judges in Montesquieu's familiar image as mouthpieces of (an impartial) law. Rules are indeterminate, open to interpretation and that interpretation involves 'subjective evaluation'. For every rule there is a counter-rule or a soft standard that allows the judge to choose. To quote Kelsen:

'Die Frage, welche der im Rahmen einer Norm gegebenen Möglichkeiten die richtige ist – voraussetzungsgemäss – überhaupt keine Frage der auf das positive Recht gerichteten Erkenntnis ist . . . sondern ein rechtspolitisches Problem.'[57]

Also international lawyers – including members of the International Court of Justice – have stressed the open-ended, artistic or political character of rule-interpretation, sometimes calling for an evaluative approach to it.[58] No less an authority than Sir Hersch Lauterpacht ridiculed the doctrine of the 'plain meaning' and advocated an openly flexible and goal-oriented approach to legal interpretation.[59] For Lauterpacht, as for many others, judging was inseparable from a progressive development of the law by means of balancing interests and having recourse to the law's purposes and internal values.[60] What Georges Abi-Saab has called 'justice transactionnelle'[61] has become an ineradicable part of the Court's practice, illustrated in the increasing use of equity and equitable principles and the bilateralisation of the cases brought to it even as general rules have been invoked by the parties.[62] Much of what we know of the practice of judging corroborates this vision. The negotiation between the judges at the International Court, for instance, is sometimes described almost as a diplomatic process of trying to reach a compromise between the differing positions. Counsel pleading for the parties know this and

---

[56] D Kennedy, *A Critique of Adjudication. Fin de siècle* (Cambridge, Harvard University Press, 1997) 3.
[57] H Kelsen, *Reine Rechtslehre. Einleitung in die rechtswissenschaftliche Problematik* (Tübingen, Mohr, 1934) 98.
[58] For a review of positions, see Koskenniemi, *From Apology to Utopia* (2005) 340–41.
[59] See H Lauterpacht, 'The Doctrine of Plain Meaning', *International Law. Being the Collected Papers of Hersch Lauterpacht* (Cambridge, Cambridge University Press, 1978) Vol 4, 393.
[60] See in particular, H Lauterpacht, *The Development of International Law by the International Court* (Cambridge, Grotius, 1958) and for an extended analysis, M Koskenniemi, 'Lauterpacht. The Victorian Tradition in International Law' (1997) 8 *European Journal of International Law* 252–57.
[61] Abi-Saab, 'Cours général de droit international public' (1996) 261–72.
[62] See Chapters 1–2 in this volume.

routinely formulate their arguments accordingly, knowing that while, in accordance with article 2 of the Statute of the ICJ, the judges must be 'independent', according to article 9, they also need to act in a 'representative' capacity.[63] We recognise this as we admire them if they rule ostensibly in favour of the underdog – Nicaragua or Libya against the United States or the United Kingdom – and are ashamed as they do the contrary – South Africa against Liberia and Ethiopia, for instance.

Here is the dilemma: the role of the judge is defined by reference to a commitment to neutral rules. The actual experience of judging, however, shows that rules never suffice but that evaluation and 'ideology' are part of the job. Judges are required, in other words, to believe and not to believe at the same time, oscillating between a public faith and a private scepticism. Peter Sloterdijk has analysed a similar phenomenon by reference to the condition of 'enlightened false consciousness'. What is this condition?

> It is that modernized, unhappy consciousness, on which enlightenment has laboured both successfully and in vain. It has learned its lessons in enlightenment, but it has not, and probably was not able to, put them into practice. Well-off and miserable at the same time, this consciousness no longer feels affected by any critique of ideology; its falseness is already reflexively buffered.[64]

In other words, commitment to rules cannot be sustained because the 'labour of enlightenment' has performed its task – the value-freedom or neutrality of rules and interpretation have revealed themselves as illusion. Privately, most judges are quite ready to admit that they are no automatons, that how they go about the work of rule application involves background assumptions, prejudices or commitments of various kinds, seeking compromises and trying to find a solution that is equitable or fair. The commitment to the law as rules then turns out to be not one that judges themselves would accept as a correct characterisation of the definition of judging.

Nevertheless, the public image of the judge has remained what it was before that 'labour'. The form of judicial activity, its rituals and its public justification are constructed as if rules were all there was to it. This is where, to follow Duncan Kennedy, the judge's cynicism or 'bad faith' – lies.[65] For despite his or her internal knowledge that what goes on under rule application is a 'politics of law', that knowledge does nothing to the public image of the judge's impartiality. However, the situation cannot really be remedied, either, provided that the judge wishes to remain a judge, to preserve loyalty to the profession and to the political society that builds upon a distinction between (objective) law and (subjective) politics, adjudication and legislation. The judge can only continue with this 'cognitive dissonance', seeking energy to suppress any possible anxiety thereby created in a

---

[63] A fact in which Abi-Saab detects 'a whiff (soupçon) of contradiction', 'Ensuring the Best Bench' in Peck and Lee (eds), *Increasing the Effectiveness* (1997) 168.

[64] P Sloterdijk, *Critique of Cynical Reason* (Minneapolis, University of Minnesota Press, 1988) 5.

[65] D Kennedy, *A Critique of Adjudication* (1997) chapters 8, 12 and conclusion.

mirage-like axiom that judging provides a useful – perhaps necessary – service to society as a whole. Denying the work of ideology, judges simultaneously have nothing but 'ideology' to explain their behaviour.[66]

Inasmuch as 'the judge' is at the heart of the law, this oscillation between commitment and cynicism also lies there and, not only in the eyes of external observers, but also, much more crucially, embedded in the roles and psyche of the practitioners themselves. If judging involves a schizophrenic consciousness and a kind of 'bad faith', buttressed by a sentimental loyalty to the ideological assumptions about the beneficiality of legal work in the international society, then that bad faith is indissociable from any legal practice. This situation ('enlightened false consciousness') is not to be got rid of without tremendous psychological and social cost. A public acknowledgement that what judges do is 'politics' would undermine the liberal ideal of the rule of law and transform the image of judges from faithful servants of social consensus to political manipulators. The ideal of fulfilling externally set social objectives would be lost. On the other hand, the critique of rules cannot simply be unlearned, either. From this existential schizophrenia the ways out may be no more appealing than the situation itself, namely either marginalisation in an arrogantly 'political jurisprudence' or opting for an elitism that says 'I know this is politics but it is better than the masses – for their own sake – live in ignorance of this fact'.[67]

The Adviser

Before university, I worked for a number of years as 'lawyer-diplomat'[68] employed by the Finnish Ministry for Foreign Affairs. Much of the writing about the work of the legal adviser in a Foreign Office concentrates on what appears as a tension between a commitment to the cosmopolitan pursuits of the profession and loyalty to one's government. That tension, however, alone fails to capture the sense in which the legal adviser's role is constructed, on the one hand, by critical projection from activist and academic lawyers and, on the other hand, from the 'political' colleagues in the operative departments of the home government. For legal advisers, the interplay of commitment and cynicism forms particularly complex patterns.

The perception of governmental legal advisers by their activist and academic colleagues is coloured by an ambivalent mixture of distancing and envy. From the perspective of cosmopolitan idealism, the governmental lawyer's position may seem like the paradigm of cynicism. To be professionally committed to always producing justifications for what one's government does may appear as an unappealing and unprincipled opportunism. What happens when equally competent

---

[66] ibid 191–92.

[67] For an outline of three coping strategies, 'tragedy', 'the noble fight for a lost cause' and 'phronesis', see Korhonen, 'New International Law' (1996) 15–26.

[68] The term is from Fitzmaurice, 'Legal Advisers and Foreign Affairs' (1965) 72–80.

governmental lawyers in the Sixth Committee of the United Nations General Assembly, for example, defend with equal rigor contradictory normative conclusions, each legal conclusion miraculously underwriting the policy of the adviser's government? Is that not the surest proof of the façade legitimation aspect of international law, the harnessing of a cosmopolitan language in the service of particular interests?

From the internal perspective of the adviser, things look different. Unlike the judge, the adviser is perfectly prepared to admit that legal rules are general and open-textured and leave much room for policy-choices. This does not lead cynicism, however, because what is good for my government is also usually good for the world at large – and what is good for the world cannot be bad for my country.[69] For the legal adviser, working for the government is a form of commitment to an international law that is more a (diplomatic) *process* than any set of substantive rules or axioms about world order, justice or human rights.[70] Providing advice to the government, the legal adviser sees his or herself often as a 'custodian and exponent of international law for the foreign ministry',[71] or a 'gentle civilizer' of national interest.[72] The legal adviser's commitment, often underlined by commentators, would in such case lie in not giving in to the temptation of pleasing the minister. Such recalcitrance is then sometimes seen from the political colleagues' perspective as the adviser's typical formalism and narrowness of vision ('finding a difficulty for every solution') – an attitude which the adviser is ready to accept ('heroically') as a necessary evil of the job and to which the adviser may reach by projecting the political colleague as an altogether superficial seeker of the quick pleasure.

The adviser's attitude towards the activist is ambivalent. On the one hand, that attitude is one of nostalgia, if not envy towards the activist's (innocent) commitment to substance. 'Oh I wish I could have said that' remarked a former colleague to me once after a meeting of a parliamentary committee that had discussed a bilateral investment treaty with Indonesia and in which I, as an academic, had been criticising the draft due to the absence of a human rights clause. Maybe such a wish was there. However, I could also detect the adviser's hidden pleasure at having fulfilled her professional commitment of bracketing – again, heroically, as it were – her private

---

[69] See in particular 'The Role of the Legal Adviser of the Department of State. A Report of the Joint Committee established by the American Society of International Law and the American Branch of the International Law Association' (1991) 85 *American Journal of International Law* 360; Also Merillat, *Legal Advisers* (1964) 16. This is also the spirit in which Daniel P Moynihan wrote his *On the Law of Nations* (Cambridge, Harvard University Press, 1989) as a critique of the United States administration's neglect of international legal justifications in the 1980s.

[70] As suggested in CW Jenks, 'Craftmanship in International Law' (1956) 50 *American Journal of International Law* 51.

[71] R St J MacDonald, 'The Role of Legal Advisers of Ministries of Foreign Affairs', RCADI 1977-III 386, 387.

[72] I have used this theme in *The Gentle Civilizer of Nations. the Rise and Fall of International Law 1870–1960* (Cambridge, Cambridge University Press, 2001). The expression of the 'gentle civilizer' is from G Kennan, *American Diplomacy 1900–1950*, Expanded Edition (Chicago, Chicago University Press, 1984) 54.

morality. I remembered the sense of satisfaction from my time in the Foreign Service of being committed to the good of one's country – a commitment which is never too difficult to turn into the more sophisticated (though perhaps morally dubious) position about this being also the general good 'of the long run'.

From the adviser's perspective, the academic's easy moralism (just like the political colleague's simple (if legally dubious) solution) looks like a facile and irresponsible indulgence in self-aggrandisement and ignorance of the lessons of diplomatic history. In the adviser's eyes, such moralism may be psychologically satisfactory but bears shades of an ultimately shallow and egoistic cynicism. By contrast, the adviser's difficult, perhaps painful bracketing of private faith and the defence of positions one thinks as untenable may not appear only as 'fully reconcilable with correct standards of professional conduct'[73] but is perhaps the clearest evidence of the adviser's commitment,[74] loyally acknowledged as such within the tight group of legal advisers, often one's principal (if invisible) audience.

The adviser's position oscillates between commitment and cynicism depending on whether the justification of governmental positions is seen from the inside through the rhetoric of process, 'gentle civilising' and the ultimate harmony of interests between the Government's (real) interests and those of the international community, or from the outside as a servile submission to the whims of national leaders, a short-sighted pursuit of every advantage that may appear, a diplomatic careerism that strives for those special privileges with which diplomacy is popularly associated, or a narrow and 'legalistic' obstruction of smooth policy-making.

The Activist

Some time ago, I published an article[75] defending the International Court's non liquet in the *Legality of the Threat or Use of Nuclear Weapons* Advisory Opinion.[76] For this, I was criticised by friends that were active in non-governmental disarmament organisations: how could I think that the law had (or should have) nothing to say in a matter of such vital importance? This was, I suppose, a variant of the cynicism critique: did I not see that such a position ended up supporting the intolerable threat to life that the existence of such weapons entailed? I shall use this critique to illustrate the role of the activist in international legal practice – a role of which I have no direct experience.

The activist participates in international law in order to further the political objectives that underlie his or her activism. The principal commitment of the serious activist is not to international law but to those objectives. If the law fails to develop in the right direction, or sets itself as an obstacle to it, then commitment

---

[73] Fitzmaurice ('Legal Advisers and Foreign Affairs' (1965) 77.
[74] MacDonald, 'The Role of Legal Advisers' (1977) 406–07.
[75] See Chapter 8 of this Volume.
[76] *Legality of the Threat or Use of Nuclear Weapons* (Advisory Opinion) (1996) ICJ Rep 240.

to policy will need to override the law. From the activist's perspective, a commitment to law only is a commitment to empty formalism or worse, taking a substantively conservative political position disguised as law. The lawyer's 'impartiality' now seems as being constrained by a professional convention and hierarchy where intrinsic merit appears as a political category.

To take an open attitude against international law, however, would put the activist in a strategically difficult position, running the risk of marginalisation. The eventuality of influencing or participating effectively in public decision-making in legal institutions will be lost. The activist therefore needs to dress his or her objectives as international law claims. This was, indeed, the point of the critics of the Court's opinion in the *Nuclear Weapons* case (and of my article): the law was not to be rejected in favour of a (controversial) policy, but the Court (and I) had simply made a professional mistake. Nuclear weapons were already condemned by positive international law. While professional lawyers regularly meet with the experience that equally competent lawyers routinely argue opposite cases, the activist interprets this as the profession's inherent cynicism and wants to attain more. It is not enough that legal technique has been applied. It must be applied for the correct result.

Arguing within the law, however, often makes the activist seem like an impossible *dilettante* in the eyes of legal professionals who have internalised the law's argumentative structures, the way it cunningly makes each position both justified and vulnerable to further criticism. To think, for instance, that the situation in East Timor may be influenced by setting up an (activist) jurists' platform in Lisbon and by adopting a resolution calling for the realisation of East Timorese self-determination, seemed as naïve as thinking that the activist's newly adopted formalism betrays a mere deference to the law's external antics.[77] Or it may perhaps seem like a (cynical) move in the in-fighting between non-governmental organisations for power and privilege. How easy it is to move from the moral high ground to the abyss of cynical word-play!

The more the activist learns the tricks of the trade, however, and starts to 'think like a lawyer' – that is, the more the activist's commitment shifts from political objectives to the law (with the resulting schizophrenia about believing and not believing at the same time) – the more the activist's old colleagues interpret this as a cynical betrayal of the common cause.

Now, the activist may try to deal with the dilemma (marginalisation/co-option) by arguing that the law has a moral basis and that the condemnation of nuclear weapons, for example, emerges directly from it. This commits the activist to a programme model of the law; it is a theological argument that is premised on faith in a moral reality and defines international law so as to always defer to it. Being based on faith (or knowledge, as the activist would have it), the position is incompatible with a commitment to international law and often leads the activist to

---

[77] See D Kennedy, 'Autumn Weekends. An Essay on Law and Everyday Life' in D Danielsen and K Engle (eds), *After Identity. A Reader in Law and Culture* (New York, Routledge, 1995) 191–209.

non-formalist positions (for example, about *jus cogens* or soft law) that traditional lawyers view with suspicion. Besides, to argue this way leads the activist back to marginalisation: if there is no agreement within the profession about what the law's morality says, or what consequences should be drawn from it, then an appeal to how deeply one personally feels about a decision is merely to shout louder. It has no convincing force to anyone not already committed to that moral truth.

Moreover, the activist's strong view on legal argument's ability to produce the (politically) correct result leads to another problem. What happens if a legal authority, say the International Court of Justice, arrives at a conclusion different from the activists? In such case, the activist will either have to yield – and face the critique of former friends in the cause – or he or she will have to believe that the authority has made a mistake. Such arrogance seems, however, psychologically implausible in the long run and tends to lead into marginalisation: what use is there in insisting on the authentic legal truth of *my* position is not held by legal authority?

Activism, too, functions within a dilemma. In case the activist is really committed to his or her political objectives, the emphasis on such commitment to legal argument runs the risk of naïveté and marginalisation, not being taken seriously by the profession. If the activist downplays the extent of his or her political commitment, and instead argues her preferred conclusion in terms of legal technique, then the risk of cynicism emerges in two forms. First, from the perspective of the *other* members of the activist's group: the activist has (cynically) allowed himself or herself to be co-opted by the mainstream, perhaps because of the activist's (secret) careerism. Second, his or her commitment to law may not be what the activist claims: he or she is prepared to accept a legal argument only if it accords with his or her political objectives – in which case the activist's legal rhetoric looks like a manipulative, cynical facade to those whose commitment is to the law.[78]

The Academic

The academic's position is much less stable than that of the activist or the adviser, hovering as it does between the two: a commitment to a rational and, if possible, scientifically argued vision of the rule of law; and a wish to be associated with those positions of influence that are available to governmental advisers. In any national community of academic international lawyers it is easy to distinguish between two groups. There are those 'visiting professors'[79] that are regularly consulted by the foreign ministry and who participate in governmental delegations as experts and

---

[78] For the strategic problems faced by legal activism, see further M Koskenniemi. 'Hegemonic Regimes', in M Young, Young (ed), *Regime Interaction in International Law. Facing Fragmentation* (Cambridge, Cambridge University Press, 2011 forthcoming).
[79] Fitzmaurice 'Legal Advisers and Foreign Affairs' (1965) 77; M Lachs, *The Teacher in International Law*, 2nd edn (The Hague, Nijhoff, 1987) 199–207.

publish commentaries on topics that enjoin governmental policies with the creation and administration of legal rules. Then there are also those professors, whose principal loyalty is to their activist or bureaucrat friends, who hold themselves aloof from governmental positions and tackle, in their sometimes interdisciplinary writings and lectures, large issues about world order, international justice or human rights, often taking a critical view of public diplomacy.

The academic's ostensible object of commitment is to the discipline of international law, its truth and its 'objectivity'.[80] From the inside, the academic's commitment lies in his or her often somewhat marginal role in the legal faculty. The academic is also the one who from the isolation of his or her study speaks *truth to power* in the fashion that Hans Morgenthau characterised Kelsen, or as described by Julius Stone, standing: '. . . on the mountain of all human knowledge, with his eyes open to the vistas that all others have seen'.[81] From this perspective, both the activist's politics and the adviser's governmental connections appear as forms of cynicism: they must know better than that! With all the academic's reading, interdisciplinary techniques, his or her scientific orientation, the academic is able to show the errors of the activist's politics and the self-betrayal of governmental justifications. Choosing a sociological language, for instance, the academic may think that he or she can penetrate appearance to perceive a 'reality' that remains hidden from those who advocate governmental or political causes.

The academic's (relative) isolation from government and activism may, however, also cast doubt on the academic commitment itself. How easy it is to write a critical article on almost anything from one's ivory tower – with no social objectives that one would need to pursue, and no professional responsibility within any political hierarchy! Moreover, legal indeterminacy may occasion a doubt about the academic pursuit altogether; is not law precisely about the daily practice of political/governmental decision-making, weighing pros and cons in a world of limited time and resources, and not about the academic's abstract norms? In such case, academics could never have practical relevance, nor even the ability to articulate the intuitive distinctiveness of the legal practice that practitioners themselves *feel*.[82] Yet, when they do engage in practice as advisers to governments or representatives of litigators, as many of them do, their academic colleagues may deridingly look at their scholarly work and conclude that they have given up commitment, that they, too, have began to howl with the wolfs, , that their 'pragmatism has supplanted theory'.[83]

Hence the academic, too, is always liable to be criticised as a cynic from both the activist's and the adviser's perspective. For the activist, the academic is but an activist *manqué* who hides behind the ivory-towerish edifice of technical rhetoric

---

[80] Stone, 'Scholars in International Law' (1974) 255–56.

[81] ibid 260.

[82] See D Kennedy, 'A Rotation in Contemporary Scholarship' in Joerges and Trubek (eds), *Critical Legal Studies – an American-German Debate* (Baden-Baden, Nomos, 1989) 358–63.

[83] C Warbrick, 'The Theory of International Law: Is there an English Contribution?' in Allot and others (eds), *Theory and International Law: An Introduction* (London, The British Institute of International and Comparative Law, 1991) 53.

and at crucial moments defers to diplomacy. Although (as explained above) the adviser may envy the academic's ability to 'speak truth to power', he or she can still see the academic as really an *amateur*, delighting in speaking the language of public governance without responsibility to anyone about his or her statements. For both the activist and the adviser, the academic may seem like the true cynic, falling short of a commitment to ideals or to power, enjoying both the privilege of academic freedom, which elevates the academic to the status of the truth-speaker, and occasional counseling work that satisfies the academic's quest for practical relevance.

* * *

International law is what international lawyers do and how they think. The dialectic between commitment and cynicism that I have surveyed in the preceding pages is part of the psychological reality of being an international lawyer.[84] This is not to say that what international lawyers do or think today is terribly wrong. It is to highlight the emotional aspect of the ambivalences of yet another period of transformation at the end of a century of successive 'transformations' that have led to unforeseen failures, to enthusiasms grown stale, to normative or institutional ideals resulting in bitter disappointments. If international lawyers are now wary of being enlisted as whole-hearted protagonists of globalisation, the end of the nation-state, the proliferation of liberal markets and Western political rhetoric ('democracy'), then this should not be too great a surprise. History provides little support for the belief that revolution or happiness could survive the first moments of enthusiastic bliss. The morning after is cold, and certain to come. As we pick up the pieces of yesterday's commitment, we might perhaps fight tomorrow's cynicism by taking ourselves lightly, for a change.

---

[84] The four roles I have outlined are, of course, ideal-typical. I am aware that, for instance, feminist critiques have sought to challenge them. But although such challenges nuance the strategies embedded in particular roles, I am not convinced that they go beyond the commitment/cynicism dialectic.

12

Style as Method: Letter to the Editors of the Symposium

This letter was written in response to an invitation by Anne-Marie Slaughter (Princeton) and Steven Ratner (Texas) to contribute an exposition of 'critical legal studies' to a Symposium of 'Methods in International Law', published in the *American Journal of International Law* in 1999 and in a book in 2004 with the same title. It is both an attack on the liberal legal theory represented by the editors' approach to the Symposium and a discussion of some of the basic themes of my own work, especially work published since the 1990 article on 'The Politics of International Law'.which is now reprinted in a slightly modified form as chapter 1 of this volume.

A S I STARTED to think about how to respond to your kind invitation to write on the 'methods of international law', I soon noticed that it was impossible for me to think about my – or indeed anybody's – 'method' in the way suggested by the Symposium format that you offered. This was only in part because I felt that your (and sometimes others') classification of my work as representative of something called 'critical legal studies', failed to make sense of large chunks of it whose labeling as 'CLS' might seem an insult to those in the American legal academy who had organised themselves in the 1970s and early 1980s under that banner. You may, of course, have asked me to write about 'CLS' in international law irrespectively of whether I was a true representative of its method (whatever that method might be). Perhaps I was only asked to explain how people generally identified as 'critics' went about writing as they did, but I felt wholly unqualified to undertake such a task. Dozens of academic studies had been published on the structure, history and ideology of critical legal studies in the United States and elsewhere. Although that material is interesting, and often of high academic quality, little of it describes the work of people in our field sometimes associated with critical legal studies – but more commonly classed under the label of 'new approaches to international law'.[1] In fact, new writing in the field was

[1] For overviews, see D Kennedy, 'New Stream of International Law' (1988) 7 *Wisconsin International Law Journal* 1; N Purvis, 'Critical Legal Studies in Public International Law' (1991) 32 *Harvard International Law Journal* 81; O Korhonen, 'New International Law: Silence, Defence, or Deliverance?' (1996) 7 *European Journal of International Law* 1; and the essays in M Koskenniemi (ed), 'Special Issue: New Approaches to International Law' (1996) 65 *Nordic Journal of International Law*. See also D Kennedy and C Tennant, 'New Approaches to International Law – A Bibliography' (1994) 35 *Harvard Journal of International Law* 417.

so heterogeneous, self-reflective, and sometimes outright ironic, that the conventions of academic analysis about 'method' would inevitably fail to articulate its reality.

I had a difficulty with the suggested shopping mall approach to 'method', the assumption that styles of legal writing are like brands of detergent that can be put on display alongside one another to be picked up by the customer in accordance with his or her idiosyncratic preferences. It is not only that, like many others, I dislike being labeled and marketed in accordance with the logic of consumer capitalism. I am aware that from your perspective, such an attitude may seem a rather predictable and boring product of an overblown ego, the offshoot of an elitist unwillingness to put oneself up for popular scrutiny, perhaps disguising the fear that the market's preference will not be for oneself.

However, at least since Marx and McLuhan, it has been conventionally accepted that the form of the market and the value of the commodity are not independent from each other. The liberal-pluralist approach to method, suggested by the image of the shopping mall or the electoral campaign, is a reifying matrix that makes apparent from the plethora of styles through which we approach and construct 'international law' only those qualities that appear commensurate so as to allow comparison. In the case of this Symposium, the commensurability criterion suggested in your letter was contained in the request 'to explain how your method helps a decision-maker or observer appraise the lawfulness of the conduct at issue and construct law-based options for the future'. To participate in the Symposium on those terms, however, would have been to subsume what I think of as a variety of different, yet predominantly anti-instrumentalist, legal styles into an instrumentalist frame: 'who is going to be the diplomat's best helper?' This seemed to make no sense.

The main reason for my unease, however, may be rephrased as follows: what is the method through which I should write about the 'CLS method'? The problem, I think, should be apparent. It has to do with the very structure of a liberalism from the perspective of which the Symposium and the shopping mall seem eminently beneficial contexts of human interaction. The difficulty lies in the assumption that there is some overarching standpoint, some non-methodological method, a non-political academic standard that allows that method or politics to be discussed from the outside of particular methodological or political controversies. Just as political liberalism assumes itself to be a non-political, neutral framework within which the various parties can compete for influence in society, so your question – your *initial* question – assumed the existence or accessibility of some perspective or language that would not itself be vulnerable to the objections engendered by the academic styles that carry labels such as 'positivism', 'law and economics', 'international law and international relations', 'legal process', 'feminism' or 'critical legal studies'. There is no such neutral ground, however: like the shopping mall, the Symposium is a mechanism of inclusion and exclusion; of blindness and insight (where were the methods of 'ethics', 'natural law', or 'postcolonialism' . . .?). The problem, as I see it, is not about which of the brands of detergent is best, most useful, accessible or whatever. The problem lies in the shopping mall, or the Symposium format, the way it flattens out difference and neutralises critique, silently guaranteeing the victory of an apathetic consumerism.

Your Memorandum did, however, canvass the possibility that 'some of' the contributors might not wish to adopt the shopping mall approach. Those who did not were then called upon to explain themselves. The foregoing has, I hope, provided the beginnings of an explanation. To elaborate, I need to start from elsewhere. If there is no (credible) external perspective on 'method', then I need to commence from the inside, biographically as it were, and in the course of my discussion hope that my occasional substitution of the word 'style' for your chosen signifier – 'method' – in the above text was no slip of the pen.[2]

Early on, I assumed that there were available to academic lawyers several different methods from which they were to choose one or two in order to carry out their scholarly pursuits. My legal education certainly suggested to me that I needed some such method that would provide me with a standpoint (a set of problems, intellectual tools, a language) that was external to my subjective idiosyncrasies, political preferences or layman's prejudices. This method would allow me to develop the distance between myself and the object of my study – international law – that would enable the production of neutral, objective, perhaps even scientific statements about it. (This is how most of the contributors to the Symposium, too, have understood their task[3] – with the exception of Hilary Charlesworth.[4]) The method would guarantee that the results of my work would enjoy scientific reliability or professional respectability (which always seemed to denote one and the same thing).

The Finnish legal academy was (and still is) liberal and pluralist and readily accepted that there was no one method through which one could approach international law. One could be a positivist, a hermeneutic, a Marxist, a legal realist, a critical positivist or whatever. The main thing was that one had to be *something* other than what one was in the pureness or corruption of one's heart in order to be a good participant in the common venture of (international) jurisprudence. This was the call for objectivity, or putting aside one's idiosyncratic ideas, passions

---

[2] The following text draws on my 'Tyyli Metodina' ('Style as Method'), which appeared in J Häyhä (ed), *Minun Metodini* (Helsinki, WSOY, 1997) 173.

[3] Dunoff and Trachtman hope to find in 'law and economics' 'a firmer and less subjective basis for argumentation'. Simma and Paulus opt for a positivist reliance on formal sources in order to avoid 'arbitrariness of administrative technicians or postmodern relativism'. O'Connell chooses 'legal process' as a response to realists, seeking to demonstrate how law 'constrain[s] inevitable judicial lawmaking so that it should not be done with the view of realizing a judge's personal view of policy'. Abbott is enthusiastic about international relations inasmuch as it enables the reproduction of the distinction between 'science' and 'norms' and the reliable prediction of future events and design of institutions. Wiessner and Willard maintain that 'policy-orientation' makes it possible to address systematically the contextual concerns of the various participants in the relevant processes, while its 'conscious' taking of the observer's standpoint does amount to 'complete subjectivization' but, on the contrary, increases critical awareness. For these articles, see S Ratner and A-M Slaughter (eds), *The Methods of International Law* (Washington, ASIL, 2004).

[4] Her feminist methodologies 'may clearly reflect a political agenda rather than strive to attain an objective truth on a neutral basis'.

and desires. Method connoted science and science drew – so I assumed – on what is universal, not on what was particular.

Yet, this academic discourse was normatively tinged. Some choices were held in more esteem than other choices. There was a story about progress in our discipline that one needed to learn in order for one's science to get going. This was a narrative about a series of methodological transformations that went somewhat like this: The origins of (international) jurisprudence lay in a naturalism that was initially theological but became secularised in the course of the Reformation. This was superseded in the nineteenth century by a historical school and theories of sovereignty that were themselves overtaken by a positivism of the pure form in the early twentieth century. Formal or logical approaches fell, however, under the attack of various 'realistic' schools, an orientation toward law as process or as a means of social engineering.

The alternative orientations of method implied in this story stood in contrast to the dominant domestic legal theory of the time. The most up-to-date jurisprudential debates as I went to law school in the 1970s espoused a continental hermeneutics that stressed the quality of legal truth as a meeting of interpretive horizons, adopting a complex *Verstehen*-language that aimed at reflecting the uncertainty that was embedded in any effort to make general statements about the law, whether understood as texts or forms of social behaviour. The move from an empirical-technical to a softer, 'humanist' understanding of the law, emphasis on language and on law as literature, empathy towards social agents and the ready acceptance of social or linguistic indeterminacy – all that seemed to respond adequately to the complexity of late modern social reality. Law became argumentation, 'language-games', rhetoric – a linguistic practice oriented towards social reality.[5]

Examined from the perspective of this jurisprudential debate, international law seemed a hopelessly old-fashioned repertoire of formalist argumentative dicta. Where was complexity, the fusion of horizons, *Vorverständnis*, indeterminacy or social critique? The only methodological arguments one encountered in international legal writing seemed to be those that conventionally classed scholars as more or less 'formalists' ('idealists') or 'realists', depending on the degree to which they added references to treaties or policies in commenting upon recent diplomatic events. Either 'method' equaled discussion about formal sources or it referred simply to techniques of finding the collections of documents from which authoritative statements about the law could be found.[6] On the other hand, however, from the perspective of international law as practice, much of such high-brow methodological debate seemed quite pointless. Legal disputes arose and were settled routinely; states and international organisations seemed to be quite satisfied with the services that international lawyers had to offer – however unsophisticated their methodologies might appear to the academics.

---

[5] See, eg A Aarnio, *Denkweisen der Rechtswissenschaft* (Vienna, Springer, 1979).
[6] See, eg M Bos, *A Methododology of International Law* (Asterdam, Oxford, North-Holland, 1984); S Rosenne, *Practice and Methods of International Law* (London, Oceana, 1984).

Style as Method

As I wrote *From Apology to Utopia: The Structure of International Legal Argument* Helsinki, 1989) at the end of the 1980s, my aim was to examine international law from a standpoint that would be in some ways systematic, perhaps even scientific. My starting point was an observation I had made in the course of having practiced international law with the Finnish Ministry for Foreign Affairs since 1977 that, within the UN and elsewhere in international fora as well as legal literature, competent lawyers routinely drew contradictory conclusions from the same norms, or found contradictory norms embedded in one and the same text or behaviour. I never thought that this was because they were simply cynics, manipulating the law to suit the ends of their governments. In some ways what I learned to call the law's indeterminacy was a property internal to the law itself, not introduced to it by 'politics' from the outside. As I learned from David Kennedy, the legal argument inexorably, and quite predictably, allowed the defence of whatever position, while simultaneously being constrained by a rigorously formal language. Learning to speak that language was the key to legal competence. Such competence was not mere imagination. It was not possible to say just anything that came to one's mouth and pretend that one was making a legal argument. Among other practitioners I had the ability to distinguish between the professionally competent and incompetent uses of legal language – but this ability had little or nothing to do with the identity of the norm or the behaviour to be justified or criticised.

I wanted to describe this property of international legal language – its simultaneously strict formalism and its substantive indeterminacy – in terms of a general theory. Hermeneutics was helpful inasmuch as it allowed focusing on law as language. Its interpretative orientation, however, proved disappointing. To search for a 'fusion of horizons' seemed altogether too vague and impressionistic to sustain a solid 'method'. Looking elsewhere, I found that much in the way critical legal scholars in the United States argued sought to grasp precisely this aspect of the law: its formal predictability and substantive indeterminacy.[7]

In search of a method with a critical bite and with some degree of resistance to the most obvious criticisms from recent social and linguistic theory and post-analytical philosophy, I became attached to (classical) French structuralism, its differentiation between *langue/parole* (or 'deep-structure' and 'surface') and its ability to explain in a hard and positivist – 'scientific' – way the construction of language or cultural form from a network of limited possible combinations. Following mainstream structuralism, I described international law as a language that was constructed of binary oppositions that represented possible, but contradictory, responses to any international legal problem. I then reduced international legal argument – what it was possible to produce as professionally respectable discourse in the field – to a limited number of 'deep-structural' binary oppositions and transformational rules. To this matrix I added a 'deconstructive' technique

---

[7] As early examples, I am thinking particularly of D Kennedy, 'Theses about International Law Discourse' (1980) 23 *German Yearbook of International Law* 353; and D Kennedy, *International Legal Structures* (Baden-Baden, Nomos, 1987); as well as the work of Duncan Kennedy and, for example, Clare Dalton's, 'An Essay in the Deconstruction of Contract Doctrine' (1985) 94 *Yale Law Journal* 997.

that enabled me to demonstrate that the apparently dominant term in each binary opposition in fact depended on the secondary term for its meaning or force. In this way, an otherwise static model was transformed into a dynamic explanation as to how the binary structures of international law (rule/exception; general/particular; right/duty; formalism/realism; sovereignty/community; freedom/constraint, etc) were interminably constructed and deconstructed in the course of any argument, through predictable and highly formal argumentative patterns and allowing any substantive outcome. I felt I had reached a scientific optimum where I had been able to reduce a complex (linguistic) reality into a limited set of argumentative rules.

Now, however, a new problem emerged. If international law consisted in a small number of argumentative rules through which it was possible to justify anything, what were the consequences of that finding to legal dogmatics (the description and systemisation of valid law) or indeed to my practice in the legal department of the Foreign Ministry? Or more accurately: I posed no question but continued writing articles about valid law and memoranda to the Minister, arriving at definite interpretive statements. The rule R and not $-R$ was valid and it was to be interpreted in situation X in the way Y and not $-Y$. This seemed puzzling to my academic colleagues. Had I not just argued that international legal arguments were indeterminate and that the rule $-R$ was in every conceivable situation as valid as the rule R because, in fact, R and $-R$ entailed each other? How come I now produced texts in which I interpreted treaties and practices just like any other lawyer? – as if my materials were somehow free of the indeterminacy that I claimed elsewhere to be the most striking reality of international law.

This was the problem of the relationship between academic theory/doctrine (I always have difficulty in distinguishing the two from each other) and practice, or of the relations between my (external) description of the structure of legal argument and my (internal) participation in that argument. It soon seemed clear that, however that relationship might be characterised, there was, at least, no direct logical entailment between the one and the other: external description did enhance the facility to make a professionally persuasive argument, but it did not 'produce' its outcomes. Such theory/doctrine did not provide ready-made solutions for social conflict, or suggest institutional arrangements that could only be 'applied' and that would then have the consequences they were supposed to have. Which way one's argument as a practitioner went still depended on what one was ready to think of as the 'best' (or least bad) or workable, reasonable, humane solution – as well as on what one's client wanted. It was a merit of this theory, however, that it demonstrated that to achieve these strategic goals, the contexts of legal practice offered many different styles of argument. It was sometimes useful to argue as a strict positivist, fixing the law on a treaty interpretation. At other times it was better to conduct an instrumentalist analysis of the consequences of alternative ways of action, while at other times moral pathos seemed appropriate. Each of such styles – or 'methods' in the language of this Symposium – was open-ended in itself, amenable to the defence of whatever position one needed to defend. None of them, however, gave the comfort of allowing the lawyer to set aside his or her 'politics', his or her subjective fears and passions. On the contrary, to what use they were put depended, in some crucial way, precisely on those fears and passions.[8]

None of this is to say that lawyers are, or should become, manipulative cynics – apart from the sense that it is a crucial part of professional competence for the lawyer to be able to construct his or her argument so as to make it credible to his or her targeted audience. Outside the relationship between the argument and the context, however, there was no external 'method', no 'theory' that could have proven the correctness of one's reasoning, the standpoint that one was called upon to take as part of one's professional practice.

What works as a professional argument depends on the circumstances. I like to think the choice lawyers are faced with as being not one of method (in the sense of external, determinate guidelines about legal certainty) but of language or, perhaps better, of style. The various styles – including the styles of 'academic theory' and 'professional practice' – are neither derived from nor stand in determinate hierarchical relationships to each other.[9] The final arbiter of what works is nothing other than the context (academic or professional) in which one argues.

From this perspective, the tension between academic theory and practice disappears: they too are styles that are taken on in a particular context. The 'deconstruction' I used in my book provided an effective language and a technique – but only in the academic environment that thinks highly of the linguistic conventions and cultural connotations of deconstruction. More precisely: the academic context is defined by the kinds of cultural conventions – styles – of which that kind of critique forms a part. By contrast, the languages of legal sources, 'base-values' or economic efficiency are effective in those contexts of legal practice that are identified precisely through those styles. To write a deconstructive memorandum for a permanent mission to the United Nations would be a professional and a social mistake – not unlike ordering a beer in a Viennese Heurigen. European rule-positivism might seem hopelessly old-fashioned in front of a post-realist American audience – while informal American arguments about policy goals or economic efficiency associate with European experience in bureaucratic authoritarianism. 'Process' language might find a positive echo when debate is about the jurisdiction

---

[8] There is a nice contrast in the papers of this Symposium between the tropes used to connote scientific objectivity and those for moral pathos. Objectivist associations are created by the personification of the method (instead of the lawyer) as the speaker (sometimes by the use of an informal acronym: ILP, L&E, IR – perhaps also 'CLS') – 'ILP speaks', 'L&E asks', 'IR theory reminds us'. The erasure of the author's voice is precisely the consequence 'method' expected to attain. On the other hand, all authors desist from normative closure: positivist rules receive substance through (moral) interpretation; law and process awaits morality to give substance to soft law and general standards; law and economics is silent about conditions of market access; international relations only 'helps' normative analysis; and the base values of policy orientation are 'posited' and not defined. Only TWAIL appears to adopt an authorial voice – though not its own. Instead, it claims to speak for 'the lived experience of Third World peoples'. However, to decide whether it has succeeded in this is made no easier by the unwillingness of the TWAIL authors to reveal their theory of representation.

[9] See also M Koskenniemi, 'Hierarchy in International Law. A Sketch' (1997) 8 *European Journal of International Law* 566.

of international functional organisations, yet feminist styles might better articulate the concerns of activists of non-governmental organisations, and so on.

It is hard to think of a substantive or political position that cannot be made to fulfill the condition of being justifiable in professionally competent legal ways through recourse to one or another of the legal styles parading through this Symposium. The 'feel' of professional competence is the outcome of style, more particularly of linguistic style. For international law in all its stylistic variations always involves translation from one language to another. Through it, the languages of power, desire and fear that are the raw materials of social conflict are translated into one or another of the idiolects expounded in the contributions to the Symposium. Translation does not 'resolve' those claims, but it makes them commensurate and susceptible to analysis in the professional and bureaucratic contexts in which it is used. But translation is not completely devoid of normative consequences, either.

When Kenneth Abbott, in his contribution, moves to speak about acts of massive injustice and responses to them in terms of 'atrocities regimes', it is not only language but also the world which undergoes a slight transformation. When Dunoff and Trachtman translate 'criminal law' as 'a pricing mechanism', they simultaneously effect a change in the way we understand and interpret the relevant acts. Wiessner and Willard expressly observe that their conceptual 'mapping procedures' can identify 'particular features and combinations of features that are problematic in specific contexts' – presumably features that 'normal' legal analysis would miss. Indeed, Hilary Charlesworth's feminist methodologies expressly focus on the ways such alternative languages create silences that sustain gendered practices. However, let us not make the mistake of thinking that there is a natural legal language which these idiosyncrasies seek to pervert. As Sir Robert Jennings has reminded us, all legal argument is reductionist. International lawyers

> need this *reduction* of the matter to a series of issues, dictinct from the arguments supporting or attacking the parties' contentions . . . This reduction, concentration, refinement, or processing (many expressions suggest themselves) of a case is also to an important extent to modify its character. It looks different from how it was before being reduced to, and embroidered in, the submissions.[10]

Though necessary, sometimes reduction (or translation) loses what is significant so that a conclusion that proceeds on that basis will seem irrelevant, unable to articulate a relevant understanding or perhaps positively distorts a participant value. One need not be a Marxist in order to perceive that as the law compels wage labourers to think of parts of themselves – their labour, their time – as a commodity, it cannot but miss many of the aspects of their lives that are suspended by the labour contract. The sentimental relations with family are severed, their ability to cater to their needs diminished by the contract. Analogously, it has been argued,

---

[10] R Jennings, 'The Proper Work and Purposes of the International Court of Justice' in AS Muller, D Raic, JM Thuranszky (eds), *The International Court of Justice. Its Future after Fifty Years* (The Hague, Nijhoff, 1997) 33–34.

for example, that systems of international copyright or protection of cultural property have excluded or failed to articulate indigenous understandings of ownership and possession, underwriting biased assumptions about art and culture.[11] It is a commonplace that many key notions of international law – the concepts of sovereignty, legal subjects or sources – fail to give voice to communities or informal understandings of the good in a way that many experienced as unjust. In their different ways, the papers of this Symposium suggest alternative languages that seek to deal precisely with such problems.

The distinctive contribution of alternative styles lies in their ability to shed light on mainstream law's hidden priorities, the way legal translation articulates some participant values but fails to do so for other values. Much feminist and post colonial writing has undertaken precisely this task. The introduction of human rights or environmental claims into the law is a familiar outcome of such renewalist 'imagining' earlier in the century. Nonetheless, struggle is always involved and, just as a novel legal articulation may strengthen some voices, so may it limit and weaken other voices, undermining their passionate appeal by including them as parts of bureaucratic routine.

In this way, any style of legal argument may work as a mechanism of blindness. There is, for instance, something about genocide, or massive attack on core community values, that makes the application of formal legal language about it not only irrelevant but positively harmful.[12] To submit such values to legal demonstration is to infect them with the uncertainties and indeterminacies that inhabit all such demonstration – the play of the rule and the exception, principle and counter-principle, or the 'canons of interpretation'. How should 'base values' be understood? What price should be given to the values protected or destroyed in alternative courses of action? The harm lies in the suggestion that law – in any of its stylistic transformations – may condemn evil, however massive, only if legal technique allows this – when this technique always contains a justifying principle as well: perhaps genocide by nuclear weapons resulted from self-defence, was an unintended consequence of action or necessary to prevent some greater evil. Perhaps the acts did not fall under some definition of 'war crime' or 'torture', the claimant lacked *locus standi*, or the lawyer was devoid of jurisdiction.

In such cases, available professional styles are by definition unable to provide a translation to the experiences, fears and passions that are involved.[13] An appeal from the bench, however articulate and sincere, is always an appeal from formal authority, defined by its claim for universality and neutrality. Where the conventions about universality and neutrality break down, however – as they do at that undefined point where the very conditions of rationality are put to question,

---

[11] RJ Coombe, 'The Properties of Culture and the Politics of Possessing Identity: Native Claims in the Cultural Appropriation Controversy' in D Danielsen, K Engle, *After Identity. A Reader in Law and Culture* (New York, Routledge, 1995) 251.

[12] I have argued this point in greater detail in chapter eight of this volume.

[13] This is not to say that any other specific language would necessarily provide a more reliable or authentic translation of those experiences, fears and passions.

where events are singular and their objective meaning cannot be detached from their subjective sense – there a neutral (juridical) humanism becomes, as George Steiner once remarked, 'either a pedantic artifice or a prologue to the inhuman'.[14] What could be sillier – or more dangerous – than to argue, for instance, that the validity of the prohibition of torture outside specific conventional frameworks is dependent on the presence of the formal conditions of customary international law?

The problem lies with the inverted relationship between what we think can be presented as legal conclusion and what as evidence for it. In legal rationality, we hope to establish the truth or a normative proposition by linking it to a factual proposition that we already assume to be true. In this way:

(1) Does X have the obligation O?
(2) X has concluded a treaty that reads that X should do O.
(3) Hence, X is obliged to do O.

The validity of the normative conclusion (3) depends on our ability to prove that (2) is indeed true. (By 'proof', I mean only a subjective sense or a 'feel' of certainty.) However, sometimes such proof is not forthcoming. We are in fact more certain of the conclusion than of the evidence. In such a case, insisting that our conclusion (3) is nonetheless a consequence of the truth of our evidence (2) will infect (3) with all the uncertainty we have about (2). We 'know' that torture is prohibited. But is there in fact a treaty, binding on X, that would allow us to characterise the acts of certain persons, alleged to be members of the secret police of X, as 'torture'? A host of uncertainties arise: Is the treaty applicable? Does what we can prove of the acts amount to 'torture'? Were the persons in fact acting as agents of X? Proceeding through legal language, the fears and passions linked with 'torture' are transformed. Torture becomes another 'atrocity regime' (Abbott), a part of bureaucratic formalism – this form of violence is torture, that not. In an institutionalised 'torture discourse', all the normal legal exceptions and defences are available – and must be so – and we as lawyers are called upon to employ them. It can only be speculated what it may mean, socially and for ourselves, to integrate 'torture' as part of the routines of bureaucratic culture instead of holding it as an exceptional evil, defying technical articulation, and grasping us, as it were, through our souls.

Legal styles are styles of argument, of linguistic expression. The accounts of method contained in the Symposium readily accept this and seek to establish a firm relationship between that language and the world that it is assumed to reflect. In order to describe or assess the relationship between language and the world, however, there should be some way that is independent of language to which the forms of language could be compared. There is, however, no such way. The languages create worlds and do not 'reflect' them. However, if legal method, too, is (only) a set of linguistic conventions and relations between them, then the attempt

---

[14] G Steiner, *Language and Silence* (New York, Faber & Faber, 1985) 87.

by any method to show why it is better than its competitors in a non circular fashion becomes impossible. *Methodenstreit* takes place (as Thomas Kuhn and others have shown) through a ritualistic exchange of expressions between closed ('autopoietic') systems that can only justify themselves by reference to their own conclusions. None of the protagonists can be convinced by the force of the arguments of the others because one's own premises allow only the acceptance of one's own conclusions.

The reality of law, as of science, is, in this sense, historically and synchronically discontinuous. There is no methodological development that could be explained by reference to improvement, judged from the perspective of some non methodological standpoint; transformations of legal style are linked (in non linear ways) to more general changes in the contexts of social and cultural identification. For example: 'I do deconstruction because I associate it with the kinds, of friendship, literature and cinema that I like.' Or: 'I argue as a positivist because I value effective action and do not wish to waste my time in useless babble.' Instrumentalism will win the day where connotations to economic efficiency and exact measurability are preferred to moral pathos or strictures of administrative form. Positivist distinctions between law and not-law carry conviction where traditions of professional solidarity and responsibility are valued.[15]

It also follows that different legal language-games do not possess greater or smaller distance to something that could be called an independent 'reality'. The methods create their own 'realities'. They exist as linguistic conventions – styles – that have as such no hierarchical relationship to each other. As we are not entitled to presume the existence of a 'metastyle', it is pointless to be anxious, for example, about the relationship of academic theory/doctrine and diplomatic practice. Incommensurate objects cannot enter into contradiction: a novelist need not face an identity crisis when drafting an income tax declaration.

It follows, finally, that no special 'method' exists somewhere outside the contexts of practice or theory that would lead these into some particular direction. 'Method' is a style of speaking, writing and living in a relationship with others. It is not a superficial phenomenon, but it is what unifies and identifies a group of people as a community (of diplomats, practitioners, academics). It is not necessary (but is in fact altogether pointless) to assume that behind such styles there would exist individuals or communities that would 'choose' their styles in accordance with what they 'will' – as suggested by the image of the shopping mall (or that of a 'veil of ignorance'). A group of people does not first exist as a minority and only then start to speak a minority language. It speaks a minority language – and therefore feels itself a minority.

---

[15] Such connotations are, however, culturally embedded and not fixed; hence, stylistic associations may sometimes take surprising turns. Strict formalism may sometimes be avant-garde – just as policy orientation may be the language of cultural conservatism. This is also why – as the TWAIL authors note – formalism may sometimes be enlisted as an anti-imperial devise irrespective of its substantive indeterminacy. The 'internal morality' of formalism may only be a set of cultural conventions. However, this does not mean that those conventions would not be politically innocuous. See further chapter ten of this volume.

The same applies to the various styles of law – including international law. The distant and impersonal language of authority employed by the International Court of Justice stands in sharp contrast to the passionate advocacy of Amnesty International or Greenpeace. To mix up the contexts would be a professional mistake – witness the way Bosnia was compelled to replace its initial American counsel because of the style of presentation he elected to use.[16] The style of a law review article on the law of the sea cannot be identical with that of a doctoral dissertation examining the argumentative structures of international law – however much having done the former might increase the facility of doing the latter. The end result falls short of being a contribution to the 'law of the sea' (whatever other merit it may have) if practitioners in that field never recognise it as such.

To describe legal method as style is to bracket the question of law's referential reality. As such, it may be assumed to lead into an 'anything goes' cynical scepticism, the giving up of political struggle and the adoption of an attitude of blasé relativism. This would, however, presuppose the internalisation of an unhistorical and reified conception of the postmodern in which the truth of scepticism would be the only truth not vulnerable to that scepticism. However, 'deconstruction', too, is only a cultural or historical convention, a style with an emancipatory potential but which – just like Kantian universalism – is always in danger of being transformed into a means of status quo legitimation.

Today this universalism and the conventions of science, technique and economy associated with it are being developed into a globalised, liberal lingua franca. Not to fall under the spell of that shopping mall requires focusing on its dangers, discontinuities and mechanisms of exclusion. If 'deconstruction' is able to bring out that dark side, the reality of the mall at night, it may provide a means for critical identification and practice. That liberalism – like the shopping mall – can be placed under critical scrutiny only by adopting a style that breaks the liberal conventions, by adopting an ironic distance. This may be done by replacing the conventions of formalism or pathos with a radically personalising language: by looking at legal process in terms of the play of ambition, influence and insecurity never far below the surface.[17]

No style is neutral. A legal language-game has no difficulty to express hegemony – indeed, this is what it is supposed to do. However, it is also expected to articulate experiences of injustice. No language-game, however, can express every subjectively felt violation. In order to articulate violations that are repressed in the dominant language-game, a change of style may be necessary. Martha Nussbaum once pointed out that justice may sometimes be realised only by giving up the conventions of

---

[16] For Bosnia's initial team, its application and its submissions, see Application of the Convention on the Prevention and Punishment of the Crime of Genocide, Provisional Measures, ICJ Rep 3, 4–25, and 325, 326–50 (8 April and 13 September). For the new team and reformulated submissions, see ibid Judgment, Preliminary Objections (11 July 1996).

[17] For brilliant examples, see D Kennedy, 'Spring Break' (1985) 63 *Texas Law Review* 1377; and his 'Autumn Weekend' in Danielsen, Engle (eds), *After Identity* (1995) 191. See also the concluding reflections in H Charlesworth's contribution to the 'method' Symposium in (1999) 93 *American Journal of International Law* 379, 392.

generalisability and commensurability that are typical of law – and perhaps by writing a novel.[18] It is not always necessary to aim that high: a letter may sometimes suffice. But, a break is needed if what is sought is critical distance from that diplomatic or academic consensus to the articulation of which the styles of international law have been devoted.

---

[18] M Nussbaum, *Love's Knowledge. Essays on Philosophy and Literature* (Oxford, Oxford University Press, 1990) especially 35–50. See also her *Poetic Justice. The Literary Imagination in Public Life* (Oxford, Oxford University Press, 1995).

13

Miserable Comforters: International Relations as New Natural Law

In his *Perpetual Peace*, Kant indicts the natural law tradition (Grotius, Pufendorf, Vattel) as 'miserable comforters', whose principles and doctrines 'cannot have the slightest legal force'. The indictment emerges from Kant's critique of natural law in both its empirical and rationalist variants as unable to uphold a really 'binding' notion of cosmopolitan legality. Since the early 1990s a new literature has emerged in the International Relations field that speaks about the effectiveness and legitimacy of international law as a form of supranational 'governance'. This chapter argues that that literature raises precisely the same problems that Kant detected in early modern natural law. Like the latter, this literature is best seen as an attempt to appropriate the voice of international legality to fully instrumentalist discipline dedicated to serving the interest of power.

Introduction

WORDS ARE POLITICS. When vocabularies change, things that previously could not be said are now spoken by everyone; what seemed obvious yesterday, no longer finds a plausible articulation. With a change of vocabularies, new speakers become authoritative. When everyone speaks English, those who do this as their native tongue will feel entitled to correct everyone else. Some vocabularies address the same aspect of the world, but in specialised ways. Ethics and economics for example: they both speak about human life, but from different perspectives, with different consequences. Which is why their jurisdiction must be clearly demarcated: in hospitals, ethical vocabularies rule; in shopping-malls, economics. Or so we have reason to hope. Periods of social transformation often involve clashes of vocabularies. Old languages begin to seem inadequate. They begin to ring like the voice of corruption of old elites. This is true of law as well: a new legal idiom challenges an old one; new lawyers become authoritative.

I would like to compare here two moments of international change in which legal vocabularies clashed against each other. One moment is what the Belgian historian

Paul Hazard called the 'Crisis of European Conscience', the end of the seventeenth century, the period after the Thirty Years' War, the consolidation of the modern states system.[1] The other moment is that of the early twenty-first century, namely the post Cold war era, when the inherited language of the modern states system, and of international law, no longer seems able to give voice to important groups and interests. The point is not to argue that we are now like they were then. What links the two moments is the form the clash takes: on the one side, an anachronistic scholasticism, and an old elite clinging to its privileges; on the other side, complex technical words seeking to penetrate the tired surface of political life to give expression to the dynamic forces underneath. Modern international law was born from a defence of secular absolutism against theology and feudalism. The international world became an extension of sovereign rule. Today, political sovereignty is challenged by the new idioms of globalisation and transnational governance. In both moments, the 'old' seems artificial and fragmented while the 'new' appears natural and universal. Now as then, change is represented as a natural necessity. This is what prompted Immanuel Kant to indict the founders of modern international law – Grotius, Pufendorf and Vattel – as 'miserable comforters'. I would like to turn this indictment against the novel vocabularies of international power parading under International Relations.

The chapter is in three parts. I will begin by describing the vocabulary of state power and international law that emerged in the late seventeenth and early eighteenth century from a brand of German public law, represented by the natural lawyer Samuel Pufendorf. In the second part, I will describe the new language of transnational governance that tells, at an international level, the story early modern natural law recounted at home. The third part seeks to remind us why Kant thought that the new languages of peace, security and effective government left something unarticulated, namely what he, perhaps enigmatically, chose to call freedom.

Samuel Pufendorf: Natural Law as the Science of the Social

The crisis of the late seventeenth century was felt most acutely in Germany. The Thirty Years' War had done away with up to 50 per cent of the rural and around one-third of the urban population.[2] The cultural life of local communities was largely wiped out, their economic base destroyed. The Westphalian peace consolidated the fragmentation of the Holy Roman Empire into a patchwork of estates – larger and smaller territorial units enjoying de facto independence from the imperial centre. It located the confessions – Lutheran, Calvinist and Catholic – within particular territorial regimes, thus fostering 'doctrinal distinctiveness,

---

[1] P Hazard, *La crise de la conscience européenne (1680–1715)* (Paris, Boivin, 1935).

[2] The number of inhabitants in Germany declined from 15–16 million in 1620 to 10 million in 1650. R Vierhaus, *Germany in the Age of Absolutism* (Cambridge University Press, 1988) 3. It took until the 1720s for the population levels to reach pre-war status, ibid 14.

distrust and misunderstanding' in a way that 'forced a search for meaning and created profound anxieties about the meaninglessness of existence'.[3] Since the late sixteenth century, many vocabularies had offered a promise of a better future. The confessions provided hope for personal salvation although, of course, not stable frameworks of social life. Religious orthodoxy was challenged by various kinds of scepticism with the confessional side reacting by a return to metaphysics.[4] However, clerical rule was opposed by various off-shoots of Renaissance humanism: Neo-Stoicism and Tacitism, Machiavellism and the Reason of State, *Staatsklugheit*, that projected politics as a wholly autonomous sphere of society, with its own intrinsic laws analogous to those drawn from nature.[5] The advances in natural sciences in the early seventeenth century – Galilei and Bacon, Newton some decades later – and in metaphysics – Descartes above all – suggested completely new ways to think about truth and superstition, public authority and private faith that might have interesting applications in politics and law.

From such materials, Samuel Pufendorf, the holder, at the University of Heidelberg, of the first chair in the Law of Nature and of Nations, developed in 1672 a first vocabulary of government by law that we recognise as modern, and as ours.[6] International law was an inextricable part of that vocabulary. For the old, Aristotelian school, 'law' participated in the search of the good that resided in the essence of things. By contrast, for Pufendorf, it spoke about social relations within and between communities sharing *different* notions of the good – the situation of the Post-Westphalian Empire *par excellence*. The new legal language articulated into existence a notion of 'civil society', ruled by principles reasonably analogous to the ones natural sciences operated to govern the physical world.[7] It universalised

---

³ ibid 6. The importance of this background for the understanding of Pufendorf's project is highlighted in M Seidler, 'Introductory Essay' in S Pufendorf, *On the Natural State of Men* (Michael Seidler, translated, annotated and introduced, Lewiston, Mellen, 1990) 3–12.

⁴ I Hunter, *Rival Enlightenments. Civil and Metaphysical Philosophy in Early Modern Germany* (Cambridge University Press, 2001) 58 (referring to Althusius).

⁵ For the variety of political vocabularies in sixteenth century Germany, with influence extending into the formation of public law in the seventeenth century, see M Stolleis, *Geschichte des öffentlichen Rechts in Deutschland I* (Munich, Beck, 1988) 88–125. For the situation at German universities, see H Meier, 'Die Lehre der Politik an den deutschen Universitäten vornehmlich vom 16. Bis 18. Jahrhudert' in D Oberndörfer (ed), *Wissenschaftliche Politik. Eine Einführung in Grundfragen ihrer Tradition und Theorie* (2. Aufl. Freiburg, Rombach, 1966) 59–116. See also R Tuck, *Philosophy and Government 1572– 1651* (Cambridge University Press, 1993).

⁶ S Pufendorf, *De jure naturae et gentium, libri octo*, translated as *On the Law of Nature and Nations. Eight Books* (2 vols W Oldfather transl, Oxford, Clarendon, 1934). This is not to say that Pufendorf would not in many ways have continued older traditions of political thought. See S Goyard-Fabre, *Pufendorf et le droit naturel* (Paris, PUF 1994) 43–44 and passim. The point about his modernity focuses on the technique whereby he was able to explain the origin and functioning of society from principles immanent in society itself.

⁷ See, eg H Medick, *Naturzustand und Naturgeschiche der bürgerlichen Gesellschaft* (Göttingen, Ruprecht & Vandenhoeck 1973) 40–63. Pufendorf did not (unlike Hobbes) think that human affairs were governed by the same laws as the natural world. The opening section of *On the Law of Nations* create, alongside the world of natural entities, that of 'moral entities' – a distinction foreshadowing that between natural and human sciences, creating space for 'freedom' in the latter. Nevertheless, Pufendorf's 'resolutive-composite' method provided for 'certainty' in moral science at the price of often collapsing that space into 'sovereignty'.

the image of society composed of what Marx called bourgeois men for whom '[t]he one tie that holds them together is natural necessity, need and private interest, the conservation of their property and their egoistic person.'[8] This view of social relations was accompanied by Pufendorf with an image of the modern state – the state of the Westphalia system – as a moral person, whose ruler was expected to achieve two things: (a) *pax et tranquillitas*, peace and security; as well as (b) *conservatio status*, the protection and strengthening of government and the accumulation of the welfare of the people.[9] In domestic as well as in international law, this would be attained by sovereign commands whose binding force was received from, and limited by, natural law.

Such a law was neither religious nor metaphysical, but a 'social' phenomenon. Its native speakers were neither theologians nor philosophers, but lawyers. But as Pufendorf expressly underlined, these would not be experts of this or that positive law, Roman, Greek or German law. They would be experts of *universal law*.[10] This vocabulary articulated an intellectual, political and a professional project.

The *intellectual project* was in two parts. One had to do with certainty, the other with universality. The coincidence of scepticism, confessional antagonism and civil war in early seventeenth century Europe made it tempting to try to use the language of natural science so as to speak confidently of human matters. Pufendorf first tried to create a universally applicable jurisprudence out of mathematical formulae – definitions, axioms and observations.[11] Although many contemporaries were impressed, Pufendorf himself became dissatisfied with its youthful abstractions. In his mature work of 1672, abbreviated in the following year in what became the most widely used treatise of natural law in late seventeenth and early eighteenth century Europe, he turned in a new direction. Now he hoped to develop a distinct science that would account for what he chose to call *socialitas*, sociability. Aristotle and Grotius had written of sociability as an *innate* quality of human beings – love – reachable through metaphysical reflection. Pufendorf had read his Hobbes, however, and although he refrained from the most extreme conclusions the latter had drawn from his analysis of human nature, he had no faith in innate sociability. Whatever directives for behaviour existed, they were artificial, human creations.[12] They were not arbitrary for that reason, however, but emerged from the application of reason on empirical data. The most basic datum about human beings was their self-love, connected with an intense drive for self-preservation in the conditions of pathetic weakness. For such creatures, reason dictated one over-

---

[8] K Marx, 'On the Jewish Question' in *Early Political Writings*, (Cambridge University Press, 1994) 46.

[9] On these two tasks, see further T Simon, *'Gute Policey' Ordnungsleitbilder und Zielvorstellungen politischen Handels in den frühen Neuzeit* (Frankfurt, Klostermann, 2004) 218 et seq.

[10] S Pufendorf, *On the Duty of Man and Citizen According to Natural Law* (J Tully ed, M Silverthorne transl, Cambridge University Press, 1991) Author's Preface, 6–13.

[11] *Elementorum jurisprudentiae universalis, libri duo*, transl as *Elements of Universal Jurisprudence* (2 vols, W Oldfather transl, Oxford, Clarendon, 1931).

[12] Although, as he says, some of these precepts are so plain that we can easily mistake them for being innate, Pufendorf, *On the Duty* (1991) 37

riding rule: it commanded sociability: 'Man, then, is an animal with an intense concern for his own preservation, needy by himself, incapable of protection without the help of his fellows, and very well fitted for the mutual provision of benefits.'[13]

From self-love, weakness and sociability, a number of conclusions could be drawn – such as the necessity to have laws and taxes to ensure the regular functioning of society and to have a sovereign that would enforce those laws and police the boundary between behaviour that was to be regulated in order to maintain social peace and the freedom within which self-love could be directed to spontaneous pursuits within the civil society, productive work and commerce. In this, sociability was not to undermine individual interest – on the contrary, as Adam Smith would later conclude with express reference to Pufendorf – it would make the realisation of that interest possible.[14]

The argument explained the universality of the law. For Aristotle, the good had no universal form. On the contrary, sound moral judgment needed to take good account of the character of each specific type of case. On this, scholasticism had built a complex casuistry of the different forms of good that were appropriate for particular categories. This accorded with the sceptical observation of the wide variety of human societies and human laws and questioned the possibility of norms enjoining humankind as a whole. By contrast, Pufendorf's truths were valid universally. How come? By resort to the hypothesis of the state of nature that collected what we knew of people everywhere – namely that they were motivated by self-love, characterised by weakness but in possession of reason that dictated to them the duties of sociability. There was nothing locally specific about these features; they had the same universal power as the laws of geometry or gravity. The effort to examine political states by recourse to the idea of the natural state, then, was comparable to the effort of natural scientists as they sought to understand nature by analysing it to its component parts.[15]

The political project was to find a technique for the maintenance of social peace on a durable basis. True, natural laws provided that 'every man ought to do as much as he can to cultivate and preserve sociability'.[16] But the mere statement of this – however reasonable – was insufficient. Pufendorf came from the family of a Lutheran priest and knew that human beings were full of sin, and incapable of seeing reason clearly. Even as they accepted the need to cultivate sociality, they would still in real life understand this obligation differently, unless guided by a superior authority. A secular sovereign was needed that would enforce the

---

[13] Pufendorf *On the Duty* (1991) 35.
[14] Pufendorf *On the Law of Nature* (1934) 210–13 (bk II, ch III, § 16). See further I Hont, 'The Languages of Sociability and Commerce: Samuel Pufendorf and the Theretical Foundations of the "Four Stages Theory"' in *Jealousy of Trade. International Competition and the Nation-State in Historical Perspective* (Harvard University Press, 2005) 164–84.
[15] Pufendorf *On the Natural State* (1990) 109. See also *On the Law of Nations* 154–78 (bk II, ch II) and commentary in Goyard-Fabre *Pufendorf* (1994) 63–88.
[16] Pufendorf *On the Duty* (1991) 35.

commands of natural reason through positive laws to which subjects owed a duty of unconditional obedience.[17] What this entails for the relationship of universally certain natural law and locally binding positive law is important. As positive law arose from sovereign command, it did not bind the sovereign.[18] Later liberals have felt this scandalous. Pufendorf does not, however, think the sovereign ethically – and what is crucial here, *legally* – unbound.[19] He is bound by natural law. 'The safety of the people is the supreme law', Pufendorf writes and engages in extensive discussion on the good laws and just punishments that are needed for *pax et tranquillitas* and *conservatio status*.[20] The Prince has a natural law obligation, not only to keep his own treaties but also those of his predecessors when they concern the commonwealth as a whole.[21] Liberals have not been impressed. Because natural law does not have sanctions, it is not *really* binding. When Pufendorf writes that the command of a superior is obligatory when it has 'just reasons', critics from Leibniz onwards have indicted him of contradiction. Either duties are born of will, or from a justice that precedes will.[22] Not so for Pufendorf. Between the utopia of scholastic justice and the apology of arbitrary will lies the *social rationality* of *natural law*. Its commands are articulated by a science of government, the techniques of peace, security and welfare. If these are lost, then social power is lost; the link between protection and obedience is broken.[23] The sovereign ceases to be such as a simple rational conclusion from his or her failure to govern properly.

The critique that focuses on the absence of a superior body that would enforce natural law against the Prince overlooks the character of natural law. Its directives are not addressed to magistrates to enable them to control other branches of government. There are no two legal systems, one natural the other positive. There are moral situations, 'offices', which respond to different social needs. Positive law is natural law applied in a particular situation, namely that of the magistrate.[24] By contrast, natural law is what enjoins the Prince to govern wisely – including to rule wisely on the magistrates. The people cannot have a right to enforce natural law against the Prince for the simple reason 'that he whose peculiar task it is to care for the state, and who is most thoroughly conversant with the reasons of the

---

[17] See Pufendorf *On the Law of Nature* (1934), 1055 (bk VII ch VI § 6); Pufendorf *On the Duty* (1991), 146–47.

[18] Pufendorf *On the Duty* (1991) 146.

[19] The definition of supreme authority (sovereignty) in terms of not being bound by one's own commands comes from Roman law and was expressed in a modern form in Jean Bodin's *Six livres de la republique*. This provides for absolutist rule but a kind of 'constitutional' absolutism, the King ruling in the interests of the people. See further FH Hinsley, *Sovereignty*, 2nd edn (Cambridge University Press, 1988) 111–16.

[20] Pufendorf *On the Law of Nature* (1934), 1118 (bk VII ch IX § 3); Pufendorf *On the Duty* (1991) 151, 151–57.

[21] Pufendorf *On the Law of Nature* (1934) 1337 (bk VIII ch IX § 8).

[22] For on overview of the debate see, eg TJ Hochstrasser, *Natural Law Theories in the Early Enlightenment* (Cambridge University Press, 2000) 79–83 and passim.

[23] Hunter, *Rival Enlightenments* (2001) 156, 158–63.

[24] See, eg Pufendorf *On the Duty* (1991) 155–57.

Commonwealth, surely sees more clearly than private citizens what is for its benefit'.[25] The recognition of this, after all, is the heart of the social contract. The same principles of *socialitas* applied in the international world, now seen as an extension of the resources the Prince should use in order to advance the security and welfare of the people. The argument from self-love and weakness gave a ready portrait of Europe as a set of egoistic but interdependent sovereign entities whose interest was to cooperate, not to fight. Unlike Grotius, Pufendorf rejected the view that princes had the authority to enforce natural law if no direct injury to them was involved.[26] No war was to be waged on the American Indians on the basis of their alleged cannibalism – only if they actually caused injury.[27] Wars were not punishment – 'since they neither proceed from a superior as such, nor have their direct object the reform of the guilty party but the defence and assertion of my safety, my property, and my rights'.[28] Also, the evils we do in war must be compatible with future peace and security. International law is a matter of human relations, outside the jurisdiction of religion or conscience. However, it does not fall into the purview of secular magistrates either – for that would be to grant them the right to speak in the name of the sovereign. Magistrates rule on matters having to do with relations between citizens and citizen and sovereign under positive law, not on relations of princes under natural law.[29]

These are powerful arguments and it is no wonder that the entry on the law of nations in Diderot's *Grande encyclopaedie* observes that, although Grotius had written of some aspects of the laws of war in a useful way, it was Pufendorf who ought to be seen as the father of the law of nations – international law. These were rules of natural law, of course, because they were based on the self-preservation and self-love of nations – understood as Pufendorf proposed – as moral entities, the compacts between which were emanations of what was necessary for that purpose.[30]

This answers the *professional project*. Ruling is a complicated business: 'the science of government is so difficult that it requires all of men's ability'.[31] To carry it out properly sovereigns should 'make friends of wise men and such as are skilled in human affairs, and hold at distance flatterers, useless fellows, and all who have learned nothing but folly'.[32] Natural lawyers now emerge as the experts in the authoritative vocabulary operating the post-Westphalian, post-confessional order, marked by the extreme complexity of the imperial constitution, assisted at the universities by studies on the techniques of modern government (*Staatskunst*), sometimes based on comparative exercises: *ius publicum universale*.[33] Natural law

---

[25] Pufendorf *On the Law of Nature* (1934), 1146 (bk VIII ch I § 8).
[26] ibid 1293 (bkVIII ch VI § 2).
[27] ibid 1297 (bk VIII ch VI § 5). See also R Tuck, The *Rights of War and Peace. Political Thought and the International Order from Grotius to Kant* (Oxford University Press, 1999) 159–60.
[28] Pufendorf *On the Law of Nature* (1934), 1298 (bk VIII ch VI § 7).
[29] ibid 1301 (bk VIII ch VI § 10).
[30] 'The Entry on The Law of Nature' in *La Grande encyclopaedie raisonné* ...; http://diderot.alembert. free.fr.
[31] Pufendorf *On the Law of Nature* (1934), 1118 (bk VII ch IX § 2).
[32] ibid.
[33] See, eg Stolleis, *Geschichte* (1988) 291–97.

came to be seen as foundational to other civil sciences,[34] an indispensable technique of scientific government, and the proper vernacular for a counsellor to the Prince. The qualities that the counsellors would need were received by Pufendorf from Hobbes. Government 'requires great knowledge of the dispositions of Mankind, of the rights of Government, and of the nature of Equity, Law, Justice and Honour, not to be attained without study'.[35] Also knowledge of the rights of all nations is needed; this is more than ordinary study – what is needed is 'intelligence and letters' [but also] 'all records of Treaties and other Transactions of States between them'.[36] And yet, as Pufendorf explains in *On the Natural State of Men*, the binding force of international law is not independent from the more fundamental objectives of *pax et tranquillitas* and *conservatio* status:

> [T]he prime obligation of leaders to seek the preservation of their own states surely forbids them to endanger their own status for another's sake, except in so far as a coincident advantage permits. Thus all treaties are understood to contain a hidden restriction: 'insofar as it will not jeopardize the safety of our state'.[37]

The natural lawyer as the Prince's counsellor is, then, not merely the magistrate reading treaties but one that has a wide knowledge of the condition and intentions of other states – achieved inter alia through the ambassadorial network, as well as the results of the novel forms of academic *Staatskunst* – so as to enable an accurate assessment of necessary action (for example, for distinguishing between innocuous and threatening changes in the balance of power).[38] The right course of action might, after all, often consist of breaching a treaty rather than following it.

At the time of finishing his main work on natural law, Pufendorf himself was employed at the Court of Sweden from where he moved to Prussia, focusing his work on a study of the statecraft of particular monarchs. Enlightened absolutism meant close cooperation between the academic adviser and the Monarch – *Doctor et Princeps*.[39] For this purpose, natural law developed in the eighteenth century into increasingly more specialised governmental sciences such as Cameralism and *Polizeywissenschaft* – a science of politics as a technology of government, peaking in the historical and comparative studies carried out especially at the University of Göttingen, such as Gottfried Achenwall's *Statistik* that emerged in the 1760s as a technique of collecting and comparing information from all states so as to account for the reasons for their strength and weakness and to be able to develop scientific

---

[34] As Hunter states, *De jure naturae* 'functions as a clearing-house for the other civil sciences – Lipsian political philosophy, Helmstedt political Aristotelianism, Hobbesian anti-clericalism, Bodinian sovereignty theory, positive Staasrecht' Hunter, *Rival Enlightenments* (2001) 150.
[35] T Hobbes, *Leviathan* (Harmondsworth, Penguin, 1981 [1651]) ch 25, 308.
[36] ibid.
[37] Pufendorf, *On the Natural State* (1991) 131.
[38] ibid 131–33.
[39] W Schneiders, 'Die Philosophie der Aufgeklärten Absolutismus. Zum Verhältnis von Philosophie und Politik, nicht nur in 18. Jahrhundert' in HE Bödeker and U Herrmann, *Aufklärung als Politisierung – Politisierung der Aufklärung* (Hamburg, Meiner, 1987) 36–37.

principles of government.[40] In an important 1750 work that he prepared together with a younger colleague, the leading public lawyer Johann Stephan Pütter, Achenwall also laid out an ambitious justification for a universally valid science of (natural) law that included international law within an overall scheme of self-preservation and the search for the common good. Here, international affairs coincided with the good of each people (*Gens*), and *salus populi* and war and diplomatic relations were treated as elements of a utilitarian statecraft that sometimes (*ex ratione status extraordinarii*) authorised going against one's (legal) duty.[41] Pufendorf created a secular vocabulary of politics and law that sounded like natural science in its rigorous empiricism – but differed from the latter by its moral tone; and that also resembled philosophy by being rigorously rationalist – but differed from it by claiming practical applicability in government. This move into something 'in between' (it was called 'eclectic philosophy' in Germany) had important conclusions for international law. It consolidated political authority around a notion of secular sovereignty, and made official the anthropomorphic metaphor of states acting in the international world as 'moral entities', seeking self-preservation and self-fulfilment under the dictates of natural reason. This was neither the high heaven of theology nor the dark reason of Machiavellianism. It was premised on a *social concept of law* that could be used to explain any present rule as a reflection of deeper human necessities. The international world could now be seen in terms of the Government of the equilibrium of states, made official in the diplomatic language of the balance of power in the Peace of Utrecht, 1713.

The Hidden Career of Natural Law

I have spent a lot of time on a historical period long ago and with an obscure person with a funny name. Moreover, the career of that person lay in the field of natural law and, as I was taught at law school in the 1970s, natural law is dead. Yet, as I specialised in international law at the Finnish foreign ministry or the United Nations, every doctrine, every legal institution would lean back on assumptions such as those articulated by Pufendorf. It was impossible to exorcise natural law because the alternative seemed to be always a wholly arbitrary scholasticism of the legal form – in particular what seemed the wholly question-begging form of 'sovereignty'. A credible law needed to express some 'deeper' logic of social life itself.

---

[40] See, eg J Brückner, *Staatswissenschaften, Kameralismus und Naturrecht. Ein Beitrag zu Grundlagen der politischen Wissenschaft in Deutschland der späten 17. und frühen 18. Jahrhunderts* (Munich, Beck, 1977).
[41] G Achenwall and JS Pütter, *Anfangsgründe des Naturrechts (Elementa juris naturae)* (J Schröder ed, Frankfurt, Insel, 1996) 302–303 (§ 911) and generally 298–324 (895–976).

From the late nineteenth century onwards, international lawyers have been critics of 'sovereignty' as egoism, arbitrariness and absolute power.[42] The opposite of sovereignty was binding international law. But was international law really binding? The most influential response to this question was given by the Austrian public lawyer Georg Jellinek in 1880 as follows. States are bound by treaties because they will so. However, this does not mean that they could discard their obligations by changing their will. For that will is not free. It is limited by what Jellinek called the *Staatszweck* – the purpose of the State, namely to provide protection and welfare to its people. This was possible only in cooperation with others. The nature of the international world – *Natur der Lebensverhältnisse* – required that states keep their word.[43]

Jellinek, a friend of Max Weber's later in life, like generations of international lawyers after him, followed Pufendorf in employing a sociological vocabulary to understand international law's force: it is binding because that is socially necessary.[44] Law – as I, too, learned to say – was a 'social phenomenon', and it was only how one conceived the 'social' that explained whether one would join the ranks of the optimists or the pessimists: altruism or egoism? Grotius or Hobbes? This was Pufendorf's question too. In the 1950s and 1960s, jurists from Yale and Columbia Law Schools, or Julius Stone from Sydney, sought to produce a robust sociological language to support international law against what they saw as the anachronism of formal diplomacy among sovereign equals.[45] Their efforts became first hostage of the Cold War controversy, and were then embraced in deceptively simple formulas such as Wolfgang Friedmann's 1964 distinction between the old law of coordination and the new law of cooperation. For Friedmann, the increasing institutionalisation of the social, economic and humanitarian interests of states in treaty networks and international organisations bound them into novel progressive Zeitgeist.[46] In the 1970s and 1980s, human rights, environmental protection and international trade began to institutionalise into an independent international social realm, to be managed in accordance with functional needs. The question of the 'binding force' of the new treaties and institutions continued to be answered by some sort of sociological generalisation: interdependence and enlightened self-interest would ensure the usefulness of international law as an instrument for managing modern states. But few lawyers actually took the trouble to examine

---

[42] See M Koskenniemi, *The Gentle Civilizer of Nations. The Rise and Fall of International Law 1870–1960* (Cambridge University Press, 2001).

[43] G Jellinek, *Die rechtliche Natur der Staatenverträge* (Vienna, Hölder, 1880).

[44] Behind a few generalities about *ubi societas, ibi jus*, most international lawyers have persisted in speaking in formal terms about treaties, customary laws and general principles law – the three legal sources referred to as applicable positive law in article 38 (1) of the Statute of the International Court of Justice.

[45] See MS McDougal, 'International Law: A Contemporary Conception' (1953) 82 *Recueil des cours de l'Académie de droit international* 133–259; J Stone, *Legal Controls of International Conflict. A Treatise on the Dynamics of Disputes- and War-law* (New York, Rinehart, 1954) especially 37–49, with many further references to calls for sociological studies in international law.

[46] W Friedmann, *The Changing Structure of International Law* (New York, Columbia University Press, 1964).

whether this was true, or what it meant. It was sufficient to work with the formal materials thus produced – treaties, reports, cases, decisions and so on – by rationalising them as the product of something like a social contract between sovereigns, oscillating between a scientific hypothesis and a historical fact. If pressed, lawyers said that how this worked was not their task to explain but that of sociologists. Yet, they could remain confident that it would be they who held the Prince's ear, not *those* people.

For – and this is the crux of my 15-year experience at the legal department of a European foreign ministry and then in the academy – despite their constant use of a vocabulary of interdependence and occasional recourse to sociological generalisation about 'real interests', lawyers never took these very seriously or examined them in any depth. They were adopted as articles of faith rather than matters of argument or proof – or if not really faith, then at least as professional mannerisms reflecting the lawyers' self-deprecatory assumption that the only respectable modern vocabulary of 'theory' was some kind of sociology and that by deferring to the assumed regularities of international life they could avoid two mortal dangers: to be branded either as 'moralists' or 'formalists'. To be viewed in such terms, they would assume, would be to condemn oneself to complete marginalisation.

There was, in other words, a dissonance between the proto-sociological (in fact, naturalist) vocabulary grasped at by international lawyers to demonstrate the respectability of their craft and the deeper but unarticulated sense that international law was not really a sociological project at all, that it did not have to do with functions, structures, or instrumental action in search of the *pareto optimum*. Instead, it was a political project that aimed at something more important than helping the diplomats out of whatever crisis had emerged, but also more difficult to describe in the canons of academic (or indeed diplomatic) respectability.[47] The only vocabularies approaching that self-understanding were those of humanitarian decency, peace and enlightenment – 'gentle civilising' – words that connoted sentimental, perhaps 'Victorian' moralities of repressed desire sublimated by a wholly intuitive faith in human goodness.[48] With that baggage, one could not advance very far in administrative or academic environments populated by a 'realist' spirit that equated successful speech with the production of policy proposals that sounded convincing to those in high positions. International lawyers thus imposed a kind of double speak on themselves: superficial use of (Pufendorfian) generalisations that had little (really nothing) to do with competent legal speech about the 'validity' of treaty or customary obligations or the jurisdiction of this or that international actor.

---

[47] I have also discussed this in chapter 14 in this volume.
[48] See M Koskenniemi, 'Lauterpacht: the Victorian Tradition in International Law' (1997) 8 *European Journal of International Law* 215–63.

The New Natural Law

After the end of the Cold War – 1989 and all that – the attack on the idioms of formal international law – sovereignty, diplomacy and foreign politics was everywhere. Sovereignty had always been a problem for liberal minds. Now it seemed a positive obstacle for the natural development of social and economic life: too wide to encompass claims of human groups inside the State; too narrow to respond to global threats and opportunities. Alternative vocabularies mushroomed: trade and human rights, environment and security, the fight against impunity and terrorism, integration, migration, religion. Each had its native speakers, institutions and political project. Old law spoke the language of sovereignty, and it was off. Take the debate on humanitarian intervention. Surely sovereignty should not hinder action if lives of thousands were at stake. It was no mantra or taboo. We respect it inasmuch as it enables us to reach valuable purposes, such as *pax et tranquillitas*, happiness and security of the population. If it is the point of sovereignty to provide all this, then surely it cannot be invoked to *undermine* it. Or think of environmental problems. When addressed in the vocabulary of sovereignty, the source State's right to undertake economic and technological activities will be simply posed against the right of the target State to a clean environment. No solution will be available. A vocabulary *above sovereignty* is needed. But where would it come from?

The traditional response would have been to legislate new and better rules – treaties, resolutions, declarations and so on. There is, however, a grave problem with rules – namely their inflexibility, their failure to take into account the particular circumstances. 'Rules' will always cover cases we would not wish them to cover and fail to attach to situations to which we would have wished to apply them, had we only known of them at the moment of rule-creation. A rule on humanitarian intervention – whatever its content – will always discriminate arbitrarily between the cases that cross the atrocity threshold set up in the rule and those that fail to do so by the tiniest margin. It will always implicitly authorise human rights violations up to that very point. A rule on 'no pollution', on the other hand, will seem reasonable if applied to a developed state with a competitive economy, but completely off the mark if used to prevent a poor country from developing technologies others had always used.[49]

For such reasons, the effort to legislate never went very far. Diplomacy was not replaced by legalism. Treaties became 'cooperative frameworks' with flexible provisions and specialised implementation bodies were vested with a wide margin of discretion. A complex managerial vocabulary emerged that spoke neither about

---

[49] I have discussed the difficulties of universal rules in M Koskenniemi, 'International Legislation Today: Limits and Possibilities' (2005) 23 *Wisconsin Journal of International Law* 61 et seq. The best legal theory account of the problems with rules is F Schauer, *Playing by the Rules. A Philosophical Examination of Rule-Based Decision-making in Law and Life* (Oxford University Press, 1991).

sovereignty nor about rules but about 'objectives', 'values' and 'interests' behind them. It took seriously the use by international lawyers of sociology, and instrumentalist political theory. Do not remain enchanted by the legal or the institutional form, this language suggests. Look behind rules and institutions. Figure out the costs and benefits. Streamline, balance, optimise, calculate. When the social is fluid, a social concept of law – that is, a 'realist', or 'pragmatic' concept – must become fluid as well. Everything must become negotiable, revisable in view of attaining the right outcome. The bomb is ticking and torture might save lives . . . The new vocabulary was inaugurated in six steps.

From Institutions to 'Regimes'

The first step lies in thinking about rule complexes not in terms of formal public law institutions but as informal 'regimes', that is norms, practices and expectations within specific 'issue-areas', defined by the distribution of available technologies of knowledge production.[50] Where the law of international institutions focused on formal competence, representation and accountability, regime theory is thoroughly functional, comparing outputs against inputs by reference to alternative behavioural 'models' so as to 'derive testable hypotheses about what would explain co-operation under which conditions and in what circumstances'.[51]

'Regimes' do not come about through formal procedures but by way of converging practices and consolidating knowledge patterns. They create redescriptions of the world through novel languages that empower novel groups. Think, for example, of the spectacular rise of 'environmental regimes' out of an outdated vocabulary of territorial sovereignty, or about the characterisation of certain interests or preferences as the 'human rights' of those claiming them.[52] Against the tired antics of 'public international law', vaguely associated with Cold War multilateralism and the Third World-oriented diplomacy at the United Nations, up-to-date expertise in 'environmental governance' or 'human rights regimes' or indeed 'trade' or 'security' regimes offer a promise of entry into the professional avantgarde, mastery of technical idioms with global penetrating power. *Lex mercatoria* may still lack the orthodox textbook and case collection – but look inside transnational law firms and you will find an unproblematic routine of transcribing contract terms under new standard formulas to articulate the voices of dominant clients whose field of operation transcends any territorially limited system of control.[53]

---

[50] See, eg S Krasner, *International Regimes* (Cornell University Press, 1983) and A Hasenclever, P Mayer and V Rittberger, *Theories of International Regimes* (Cambridge University Press, 1997).
[51] A Hurrell, 'International Society and the Study of Regimes: A Reflective Approach' in V Rittberger and P Mayer (eds), *Regime Theory and International Relations* (Oxford, Clarendon Press, 1995) 55.
[52] For the former example see, eg P Haas, 'Epistemic Communities and the Dynamics of International Environmental Co-operation' in Rittberger and Mayer (eds), *Regime Theory* (1995) 168–201.
[53] C Kessedjian, 'La modélisation procédural' in E Loquin and C Kessedjian (eds), *La mondialisation du droit* (Paris, Litec, 2000) 237–56.

What is a world of many (functional) regimes like? It is a world nervously characterised by international lawyers through the language of 'fragmentation', articulating (as the word always did) a sense of loss of the secure ground of tradition, memory of the time when everything still seemed somehow coherent (and international lawyers held the Prince's ear). By contrast, regimes act as special systems of truth and value, idiolects ready to encompass the whole world, but from their own perspective, with their own (structural) bias.[54] Should the importation of hormone meat or genetically modified organisms (GMOs) to Europe be articulated in terms of the global trade regime or the global environmental (or health) regime? Should boundary-crossing humans be thought of as a human rights problem or a security problem? To decide on such questions in some rational way, there ought to be a superior system, a regime of regimes – a 'constitution' in the legal idiom. There is none, however. This is why regimes will continue to deal with whatever they can lay their hands on. In the end, that regime will win whose application will, for whatever reason, no longer be challenged. The world of regimes is a world of hegemony, of pure power.[55]

These vocabularies are written in the grammar of strategic action: they are used to decide on a case-by-case basis. Hence the concern with 'regime design': membership, scope, degree of centralisation, control by members and flexibility so as to bring about optimal results.[56] As noted by one of its fathers, it is the point of regime theory to focus on observational behaviour so as to avoid 'slipping into formalism' (the expression is his), exemplified (for him) by the scandalous way in which instruments such as the 1927 Kellogg-Briand Pact had been thought of as 'law', 'even though they had no behavioural implications'.[57]

From Rules to 'Regulation'

A second step collapses the distinction between law and regulation. In regimes, 'legalisation' is a policy choice sometimes dictated by strategic interests, sometimes not. The new literature is full of analyses of harder and softer techniques of regulation, using variables such as 'obligation', 'precision' and 'delegation' to canvass the alternatives.[58] As targeted audiences are assumed to behave as strategic

---

[54] The best discussion on this is A Fischer-Lescano and G Teubner, *Regime-Kollisionen: Zur Fragmentierung des globalen Rechts* (Frankfurt, Suhrkamp, 2006); see also M Koskenniemi, 'Fragmentation of International Law: Difficulties arising from the Diversification and Expansion of International Law' (Report of the Study Group of the International Law Commission, Finalised by Martti Koskenniemi, 13 April 2006) UN Doc A/CN.4/L.682.

[55] I have argued this at greater length in chapter nine in this volume .

[56] See B Koremenos, C Lipson and D Snidal, 'The Rational Design of International Institutions' (2001) 55 *International Organization* 761–99, 763.

[57] R Keohane, 'The Analysis of International Regimes. Towards a European-American Research Programme' in V Rittberger (ed), *Regime Theory and International Relations* (Oxford University Press, 1993) 27.

[58] See, eg C Lipson, 'Why are Some Agreements Informal?' (1991) 45 *International Organization* 495; KW Abbott and D Snidal, 'Hard and Soft Law in International Governance' (2000) 54 *International Organization* 434–54; D Shelton, 'Introduction' in Shelton (ed), *Commitment and Compliance. The Role of Non-Binding Rules in the International Legal Order* (Oxford University Press, 2000) 10–17.

actors, the inducements must become equally strategic: sometimes sticks, sometimes carrots. Soft law alternates with hard, private constraint with public as the idiom of legislation is replaced by what the experts call 'new global division of regulatory labour'.[59]

Academic research on regulation is thoroughly instrumental. Its outcomes are presented as variables to strengthen the regime. As proudly exclaimed by a recent study on international institutions, 'our approach also provides an appropriate formulation for prescribing policy and evaluating existing institutions'.[60] Pufendorf would have been thrilled.

From Government to 'Governance'

A third step consists in a move from a vocabulary of formal 'government' to informal 'governance'. If 'government' connotes administration and division of powers, with the presumption of formal accountability, 'governance' refers to de facto practices and is – like those corporate enterprises in which the term originates – geared to the production of maximal value.[61] Sometimes disagreement is managed ('problems are resolved') through assistance or 'facilitation', sometimes by negotiation or administratively ordered sanctions, rarely through formal settlement. Under this vocabulary, indefinite detention may take place by administrative degree, while the ability to suspend the law consecrates the ultimate victory of governance over government.[62]

From Responsibility to 'Compliance'

Fourth is the move away from the backward looking obsession lawyers have with breach and illegality, declared in formal dispute settlement, courts in particular. As a mechanism of deterrence, responsibility fails in an international context where routines are few, situations idiosyncratic and interests great. However, even more: invoking responsibility might be often counter-productive. It would undermine solidarity and commitment to regime objectives. Instead of 'breach', environmental and economic treaties now speak of 'non-compliance' and 'non-violation complaints'.[63] Instead of courts, they set up mechanisms for reporting, discussion and

---

[59] RO Lipschutz and K Vogel, '"Regulation for the Rest of Us?" Global Civil Society and the Privatization of Transnational Regulation' in RB Hall and TJ Bierstaker (eds), *The Emergence of Private Authority in Public Governance* (Cambridge University Press, 2002) 117.

[60] Koremenos, Lipson and Snidal, 'The Rational Design' (2001) 767.

[61] The literature on global governance is too wide to be reflected here. Nevertheless, it might be useful to note that lawyers have sometimes reacted to this change of vocabulary, for example by re-imagining governance in terms of an international administrative law, see B Kingsbury, N Krisch, RB Stewart and JB Wiener, 'The Emergence of Global Administrative Law' (2005) 68 *Law and Contemporary Problems* (Special Issue nos 3 and 4) 1–377.

[62] See J Butler, *Precious Life. The Powers of Mourning and Violence* (London, Verso, 2004).

[63] For the former, see M Koskenniemi, 'Breach of Treaty or Non-Compliance? Reflections on the Enforcement of the Montreal Protocol' (1992) 3 *Yearbook of International Environmental Law* 123–62.

assistance: informal pressure and subtle persuasion as socially embedded guarantees for conforming behaviour.[64]

From Law to 'Legitimacy'

The previous steps point from normative to empirical vocabularies that cannot distinguish between coercion and the law, the gunman and the taxman. How do we make that distinction? How – to put it in a manner that Pufendorf would have understood – do we accept Hobbes but sound like Grotius? We do this through the vocabulary of 'legitimacy'.[65]

Conceptual history tells us that the earliest uses of 'legitimacy' coincided with 'legality'. Something was legitimate if it was lawful. However, the regime analyst asks for something different: Why *should* law be obeyed? When Western experts claimed that the intervention in Kosovo in 1999 might have been illegal, but was quite legitimate, their point was precisely to find a normative vocabulary overriding formal validity. This was not so as to move back into the pre-modern notion of the political 'good', however. As Thomas Franck rhetorically asks in a leading work on international legitimacy: '. . . When different belief systems contend, what can one say about the justice of rules?'[66] Regimes, governance and compliance are needed precisely between morally disagreeing agents. In his later work, Franck speaks of legitimacy as procedural 'fairness'.[67]

'Fairness' and 'legitimacy' are mediate words, rhetorically successful only so long as they cannot be pinned down either to formal rules or moral principles. Ian Hurd writes in a Weberian tone of legitimacy as 'a kind of feeling' about authority and 'a sense of moral obligation'.[68] As such – as a psychological 'feeling' – it opens itself to empirical study. The political scientist only describes the 'operative process' whereby this 'feeling' emerges though 'internalization by the author of an external standard'.[69] As such, legitimacy is indifferent to the conditions of its existence: fear, desire, manipulation, whatever.

Legitimacy is not about normative substance. Its point is to *avoid* such substance but nonetheless to uphold a *semblance* of substance. Therefore, it is suitable for production within the communications industry, including the academic publication industry. Listen to how Chayes and Chayes put it in their widely used book on compliance with international agreements:

[64] A study on informal norms in the international system in 2000 received the title 'commitment and compliance' – the functional equivalents to 'law' and 'responsibility'. See Shelton (ed), *Commitment and Compliance* (2000).

[65] The following text is in part from M Koskenniemi, Legitimacy, Rights and Ideology: Notes towards a Critique of the New Moral Internationalism' (2003) *Associations: Journal for Legal and Social Theory* 349–74.

[66] TM Franck, *The Power of Legitimacy among Nations* (Oxford University Press, 1990) 210–11.

[67] TM Franck, *Fairness in International Law and Institutions* (Oxford University Press, 1995).

[68] I Hurd, 'Legitimacy and Authority in International Politics' (1999) 53 *International Organization* 383–89, 388. Note the difference between the political philosophy question about 'moral obligation' and the empirical question about the 'sense' of moral obligation.

[69] ibid 388.

The American people have not always understood that even when the United States has the military or economic power to act alone, the effectiveness of its actions might be undermined if it did not seek and achieve a degree of international consensus to give its actions legitimacy.[70]

The perspective is control. The normative framework is in place. Action has been decided. The only remaining question is how to reach the target with minimal cost. This is where legitimacy is needed – to ensure a warm feeling in the audience.

From Lawyers to International Relations Experts

The sixth, final move is a shift in the authoritative speaker. In the 1990s lawyers began to hear an invitation to collaboration with international relations experts at US universities.[71] Only little collaboration took place, probably because it remained unclear what place would be left to notions such as 'sovereignty' or 'law'. If, as regime experts argue, 'governments will negotiate agreements and establish institutional rules that they intend to follow in any case',[72] then law becomes fully epiphenomenal. Why should anyone care?

In a book published a few years ago, Jack Goldsmith – the author of a memo on transferring prisoners from Afghanistan to locations where they can be tortured,[73] but now Professor at Harvard Law School, and Eric Posner from Chicago argue that the traditional defence of international law – that most states abide by most international law rules most of the time – is true only because of the way lawyers dress actual behaviour as law. However, this provides no explanation for why states behave as they do. If, as they argue, state behaviour is caused by, and should be explained by reference to 'coincidence of interest and coercion', then to say that it is 'law' is an irrelevant decoration.

For these analysts, like for Pufendorf, treaties are bargains between rational egoists seeking to resolve coordination or cooperation problems so as to minimise transaction costs resulting from unclear communication of their expectations under customary law.[74] States do not comply because treaties have 'binding force', but 'because they fear retaliation from the other state or some kind of reputational loss, or because they fear a failure of coordination'.[75] Treaties are surfaces over which parties exercise pressure against each other. For example, the provisions on

---

[70] A Chayes and A Chayes, *The New Sovereignty. Compliance with International Regulatory Agreements* (Harvard University Press, 1995) 41.

[71] See, eg A-M Slaughter, AS Tulumello and S Wood, 'International Law and International Relations Theory: A New Generation of Interdisciplinary Scholarship' (1998) 92 *American Journal of International Law* 367–97.

[72] M Kahler, 'Conclusion. The Causes and Consequences of Legalisation' (2000) 54 *International Organization* 673.

[73] J Goldsmith III, 'Memorandum for Alberto R Gonzales, Counsel for the President' in K Greenberg (ed), *The Torture Papers. The Road to Abu Ghraib* (Cambridge, Cambridge University Press, 2004) 367.

[74] J Goldsmith and EA Posner, *The Limits of International Law* (Oxford University Press, 2005) 84–85.

[75] ibid 90.

the use of force in the UN Charter constitute a bargain states once made to have protection. That bargain is now undermined by the possession of weapons of mass destruction by terrorists of 'rogue states'. Hence, for states as rational egoists, the 'costs of strict adherence to the UN Charter in a world of new security threats' has just become too great.[76]

The vocabularies of 'consent', 'validity' or 'dispute settlement' are replaced by the social science vocabularies of 'explaining' behaviour and attaining 'compliance'. Also, because achieving compliance is all that counts, the interdisciplinary call is not really about cooperation but conquest. Let me quote from Goldsmith and Posner: 'There is a more sophisticated international law literature in the international relations subfield of political science.'[77]

Words are politics – and in the past 20 years or so, new words have emerged to articulate the reality of international life. Technical expressions such as 'regulation', 'compliance', 'governance' and so on hark back to new political and legal sensitivities and priorities, lifting new experts into positions of authority. I have wanted to analyse this change in language by drawing a parallel to an analogous moment in the late seventeenth century. Then, as now, a new empirically oriented 'realist' language (natural law/international relations) emerged to give voice to new preferences, forms of authority and hierarchy of influence. The new vocabulary – a new natural law – gives voice to special interests in functionally diversified regimes of global governance and control. This feeds on the habit of international lawyers to articulate the founding certainties of the profession in sociological, instrumental terms. The new orientation takes these articulations seriously and, like seventeenth century *ius naturae et gentium*, builds on a state of nature that it abstracts from observation of human beings as they are now. In the most sophisticated form available, the state of nature is articulated today in the anarchy of autonomous functional systems: trade, human rights, environment, security, diplomacy, and so on. As there is no truth superior to that provided by each such system or vocabulary, each will re-create within itself the sovereignty lost from the nation-state. Hence managerialism turns into absolutism: the absolutism of this or that regime, this or that system of preferences.[78] The lawyer becomes a counsel for the functional power-holder speaking the new natural law: from formal institutions to regimes, learning the idiolect of 'regulation', talking of 'governance' instead of 'government' and 'compliance' instead of 'responsibility'. The normative optic is received from a 'legitimacy', measured by international relations – the Supreme Tribunal of a managerial world.

---

[76] J Yoo and W Trachman, 'Less than Bargained for: the Use of Force and the Declining Relevance of the United Nations' (2005) 5 *Chicago Journal of International Law* 384.
[77] Goldsmith and Posner, *Limits* (2005) 15.
[78] This parallel is further discussed in chapter 14 in this volume.

Kant and International Law Today

International lawyers have always been surprised to find that in the middle of his *Zum ewigen Frieden* (1795), Kant dismissed the fathers of international law – Grotius, Pufendorf and Vattel – as *leidige Tröster*, miserable comforters.[79] Why would Kant wish to attack their attempt to humanise the relations between nations at war and to construct what Pufendorf called 'universal jurisprudence'? Surely Kant did not quite mean what he was saying . . .

However, Kant's critique of early modern natural and international law reso-nates with themes in today's world. For Kant, unlike for Pufendorf, law is not yet another vocabulary of governmental skill. It is a project, or better, the object of a political project to bring about what Kant – perhaps somewhat obscurely – called the 'Kingdom of Ends'. True, there is an instrumental aspect in law, as there is in economics or in technologies of security. However, unlike those other disciplines, law is not *only nor even predominantly* instrumental. Instead, it is a surface over which we carry out our projects and assess and criticise those of others. It is the platform over which, Kant would say, we make reality of our freedom.[80] For Pufendorf, the relevant legal relation was always between the sovereign and the subject, for Kant it is between citizens.

Here is Pufendorf, writing in 1673, about the purpose of the State and the law of the State:

> The over-riding purpose of states is that, by mutual cooperation and assistance, men may be safe from the losses and injuries which they may and do inflict on each other. To obtain from those with whom we are united in one society, it is not enough that we make agreement with each other not to inflict injuries on each other, nor even that the bare will of a superior be made known to citizens; fear of punishment is needed and the capacity to inflict it immediately. To achieve its purpose, the penalty must be nicely judged, so that it clearly costs more to break the law than to observe it; the severity of the penalty must outweigh the pleasure or profit won or expected from wrongdoing. For men cannot help choosing the lesser of two evils.[81]

Everything about this language was objectionable to Kant: the reduction of states into mechanisms for avoiding 'losses and injuries'; the view of obedience to law based on a calculation of costs and benefits; and the image of human beings as passive slaves to their pleasures. Kant seems to be saying that natural law offered security and wellbeing at too high a price, human freedom. This, I think, applies to the new language of legitimate governance as well.

---

[79] I Kant, 'Perpetual Peace. A Philosophical Sketch' in *Political Writings* edited by H Reiss, 2nd edn (Cambridge, Cambridge University Press, 1991) 101, 103.
[80] For a discussion of the instrumental and intrinsic aspects of freedom in Kant's work, see P Guyer, 'Freedom as the Inner Value of the World' in Guyer, *Kant on Freedom, Law and Happiness* (Cambridge, Cambridge University Press, 2000) 96–125.
[81] Pufendorf *On the Duty* (1991) 139–40.

The gist of the managerial critique of international law is that it is unable to bring about security and happiness in the conditions of globalisation. A new language is needed that will translate the interest in happiness and security into globally effective policies. However, if that vocabulary aims directly at security and happiness, then it must be less than universal, and hopelessly speculative. What access do we have to the fears and hopes of others? More importantly, what guarantee have we got that it would not be precisely the happiness of some that is the cause of the insecurity or the unhappiness of others? Or vice-versa? Is humanitarian intervention allowed under the UN Charter? Well, yes and no, the lawyer would respond. The Charter speaks both of peace and human rights. Beyond that, there is only speculation about what should be a useful, good, way to apply it. Not that this question could not be decided. Of course it can. However, it cannot be decided by the vocabularies of peace or human rights themselves *without assuming that we have already made a choice*. The same goes for all the other new vocabularies: trade and environment, security and rights, and so on. If the conflicts of the world are articulated in terms of a clash of functional languages, then those languages cannot be used to solve those conflicts – that is, they cannot be so used without at the same time doing away with what Kant thought of in terms of human freedom.

Like the late seventeenth century, the present moment is one of clashing vocabularies – trade against human rights, technology against environment, security against liberty, governance against diplomacy.[82] The managerial intuition would go for 'balancing'. But, what items would go into the 'balance'? How would they be measured? Would future benefits count the same as present – and what about the benefits of those who are absent? This is the world of regimes not of law but of truths, each computing compliance in accordance with its special logic, outside political contestation: the hubris of instrumental knowledge. In the end, which language will prevail is simply a question of power: which experts think they can get away with it?

So understood, clash of instrumental languages under globalisation repeats the clash of sovereignties in traditional diplomacy. As political realists from Moses Mendelssohn (Kant's target) and Hans Morgenthau to Robert Kagan have seen it, the world is pure immanence – the eternal recurrence of the same: struggle for power.[83] From Thucydides to Rumsfeld, nothing has changed. The iron cage of human nature: rulers change, but the character of rule does not.

Against this, Kant puts the famous condition of right. It is a condition of indeterminacy. As Kant insists, rules do not spell out the conditions of their application.[84] Judgment is needed. It is this fact that is so difficult for natural lawyers to come to terms with – indeed, against which that vocabulary once was conceived.

---

[82] International lawyers address this in terms of the fragmentation of international law. See Koskenniemi, 'Fragmentation of International Law' (2006).

[83] H Morgenthau, *Politics among Nations. The Struggle for Power and for Peace* (New York, 1946); R Kagan, *Paradise and Power. America and Europe in the New World Order* (London, 2003).

[84] I Kant, *Critique of Pure Reason*, edited by V Politi (London, Everyman's, 1991) 140–41.

Judgment is replaced by the fiction that the technical vocabularies are controlling – a fiction intended to ensure that the novel vocabularies will hold the Prince's ear. This was precisely the target of the critique of pure reason. The point of Kant's attack on rationalist utopia (the Leibnitz-Wolff school) and the apology of empirical civil philosophy (Pufendorf, Vattel) was to privilege practical over theoretical reason, judgment over instrumental calculation. When truth vocabularies run out, one judges only particulars. Let me finish by looking at what this might mean.

Conclusion

In the Appendix to the Perpetual Peace, Kant makes a distinction between the 'political moralist' and the 'moral politician'.[85] The former, he writes, 'makes the principles subordinate to the end'.[86] The political moralist is the manager of functional systems, speaking in the instrumental idiom. However, because these idioms are indeterminate and they conflict with each other, recourse to them turns out to be, in Kantian language, *Schwärmerei*. Choices have to be made; judgment has to be exercised. However, the use of the instrumentalist vocabulary hides this, turning political judgment into an exercise of technical skill. As a result, nobody seems to rule. While power remains, responsibility disappears. This is the 'realism' of what Foucault called 'governmentality', the exercise of power by technical discourses that appear justified owing to their ability to bring about the security and welfare of the population. In Kantian language, again, this is to put 'man into the same class as other living machines which only need to realise consciously that they are not free beings for them to become in their own eyes the most wretched of all earthy creatures'.[87]

Kant did not think that the fidelity to law meant fidelity to any particular substance but irrespective of such substance. Everything was left up to the judgment of the law-applier. Yet, he proposed no legal hermeneutics, no model vocabulary in which the judgment should be voiced. Kant has nothing to say about technical lawyers – apart from dismissing some of them as 'miserable comforters'. However, he has much to say about the 'moral politicians' whose task it would be to employ language so as to respect the ideal of the 'Kingdom of Ends', translated into practical politics as a scheme of Perpetual Peace. Law is the language that holds both of these as standards of individual judgment and political contestation.[88]

---

[85] For this link, see A Tosel, *Kant révolutionnaire. Droit et politique* (Paris, PUF, 1990) 19–21.

[86] Kant, 'Perpetual Peace' (1991) 118–21.

[87] Kant, 'Perpetual Peace', (1991) 123.

[88] The view of Kant as seeking internal moral regeneration and thus prolonging the tradition of school metaphysics against the externally oriented civil philosophy of Pufendorf and Thomasius is interestingly, though perhaps one-sidedly (there are practically no references to Kant's openly political writings), discussed in Hunter, *Rival Enlightenments* (2001) 274–376.

Judgment is located in the institutional act of applying the law in one way rather than another, choosing one among many alternative meanings offered by the available vocabulary. Kant has this moment in mind when he endorses the mindset of the moral politician, conscious that the right judgment cannot be derived from instrumental reason and who, in judging, aims to act as a 'genuine republican', encompassing the perspective of the whole.[89] As is well-known, Kant's political theory is complemented by his analysis of the faculty of imagination operative in aesthetic judgment.[90] The nature of the aesthetic judgment – neither rational subsumption under a rule, nor fully subjective expression of emotion – captures also the plight of the moral politician as the law-applier, approaching a particular situation in a way which, although undetermined by any rule still claims general assent – the difference between saying 'this is good' and 'this is valid law', the distance between nature and freedom, a closed particular and a horizon of universality.

Liberal jurisprudence has tried to articulate the rules for the use of that imagination in a series of hermeneutic techniques. Yet Kant suggests something different – to expand towards universality, one must penetrate deeper into subjectivity, law not in opposition to, but as a crystallisation of personal virtue. This suggestion cannot be detached from enlightenment notions such as *Bildung* and the public sphere, the vocabulary of law as also the language of self-improvement, spiritual maturity and all the virtues of the 'inner morality of law': honesty, fairness, concern for others, avoidance of deceit, injury and coercion.[91] If the lawyer persists in using words such as the 'perfect civil constitution', 'perpetual peace' – or indeed the UN Charter – it is not because they constitute a positive programme, even less a set of ideal institutions but as they invoke a shared standard of criticism.[92] The legal judgment may of course go wrong. Kant's view of the imaginative ability of lawyers was not too flattering.[93] However, this does nothing to undermine the *cultural* and *political* significance of law as a language about what standards of criticism a community ought to have, and then using them.

But, legal vocabularies do not just frame the professional world of lawyers. They inform political struggles. International law has increasingly begun to appear in slogans and public speeches as that which is not yet another technique of global

---

[89]   See the Appendix to Kant, 'Perpetual Peace' (1991) 116–25, especially 122.

[90]   I Kant, *Critique of the Power of Judgment,* edited by Paul Guyer (Cambridge, Cambridge University Press, 2000). For the suggestion that the Third Critique forms the core of Kant's political theory, see especially H Arendt *Lectures on Kant's Political Philosophy* (edited and with an interpretative essay by R Beiner, Chicago University Press, 1982). See also A Renaut, *Kant aujourd'hui* (Paris, Aubier, 1997) 405–15.

[91]   For alternative formulation of this 'inner morality' see famously L Fuller, *The Morality of Law* (Rev ed Yale University Press, 1964) and eg JB Schneewind, 'Autonomy, Obligation and Virtue: An Overview of Kant's Moral Philosophy' in P Guyer (ed), *The Cambridge Companion to Kant* (Cambridge University Press, 1992) 320–21; O O'Neill, *Bounds of Justice* (Cambridge University Press, 2000) 65–79 and passim.

[92]   On this, see especially S Goyard-Fabre, *Philosophie critique et raison juridique* (Paris, PUF, 2004) 68–70, 79–84.

[93]   Kant, *Critique of Pure Reason* (1991) 140–41. The exercise of judgment, Kant notes, requires 'mother wit' for which there are no rules and 'the want of which no schooling can compensate'. Although Kant here says in a footnote (fn 1 p 140) that '[d]eficiency in judgment is properly that which is called stupidity', in later writings, especially in the Third Critique, his assessment is less harsh.

governance. Look at recent debates about the Iraqi war, or on torture, or on trade and environment. International lawyers are not expected to engage in hair-splitting technical analyses. Instead, they are called upon to soothe anxious souls, to give voice to frustration and anger. The vocabularies of moral pathos or religion find limited audiences. Institutional politics connotes party rule. For such reasons, I think, international law has suddenly become almost the only public vocabulary connected with a horizon of transcendence, the expression of a kind of secular faith. When transnational companies wreck havoc on the environment, powerful states engage in imperial wars or globalisation dislocates communities, I often hear an appeal to international law. Astonishingly – and somewhat embarrassingly – philosophers such as Jürgen Habermas and Jacques Derrida or globalisation critics such as Joseph Stiglitz appeal to international law. Not for this or that rule or institution but as a placeholder for the languages of goodness and justice, solidarity and responsibility. I think this is Kant's cosmopolitan project rightly understood: not an end-state or party programme but a project of critical reason that measures today's state of affairs from the perspective of an ideal of universality that cannot itself be reformulated into an institution, a technique of rule, without destroying it. It is a project of freedom in at least two senses. First it holds political judgment open to different, even opposing, alternatives, highlighting the (legal) accountability of the one who makes the judgment. Second, its concept of legal expertise is not that of instrumental skill but a mindset – a 'constitutional mindset' – that is constantly measuring any judgment or institutional alternative against the ideal of universality embedded in the very idea of rule by law (instead of by expert decision).[94] Kant's abstract universality may no longer seem an attractive way to think about the world's varied cultural vocabularies. Nothing, however, has undermined the need for translating between them, and learning through such translations. This is never simply about functional needs of collaboration between vocabularies but, to put it perhaps contentiously, about the meaning of life.

Words are politics and vocabularies are manifestos. In the late seventeenth century, the poetry of sovereignty joined the grammar of secular statehood to produce a new type of authoritative speech and a class of competent speakers. The language of natural law possessed a reality effect against which the old idioms of love and piety appeared as nostalgia, or cynicism or both. Kant was a good reader of the new poetry, but he was not enthusiastic about the pretence that reality itself spoke in it. He wanted to celebrate the creative voice instead of the Saxon romance that Pufendorf delivered by it. It was not enough to sound *true*. One would also need to sound *right*. This was more ambitious, of course, and it was perhaps impossible to express it directly as a blueprint, or architecture. This, I think is why Kant wrote 'Perpetual Peace' as an ironic commentary on the sign of a Dutch innkeeper. The double meaning of Perpetual Peace was employed to acknowledge that one is writing – as present day theorists would have it – under erasure.

[94] I have discussed this also in my 'Constitutionalism as Mindset: Reflections on Kantian Themes about International law and Globalization' (2007) 8 *Theoretical Inquiries in Law* 9–36.

The best argument for international law is like that. It speaks neither of empiri-cal, nor analytical truths. It signals commitment to work in a setting of competing vocabularies with full knowledge of their indeterminacy and a sense of account-ability for the choices one makes. It also sets up a standard of universality and peace – a standard felt always as a lack in present institutions but still irreducible to a project of institutional reform. Kant was not a poet, far from it. But a delight-ful passage in the *Metaphysics of Morals* expresses this objective well:

> So the question is no longer whether perpetual peace is something real or a fiction, and whether we are not deceiving ourselves in our theoretical judgment when we assume that it is real. Instead, we must act as if it is something real, though perhaps it is not; we must work for establishing perpetual peace and the kind of constitution that seems to us most conducive to it . . . And even if the complete realization of this objective always remains a pious wish, we still are not deceiving ourselves in adopting the maxim of working incessantly towards it. For this is our duty, and to admit that the moral law within us is deceptive would call forth in us the wish, which arouses our abhorrence, rather than to be rid of all reason and to regard ourselves as thrown by one's principles into the same mechanism of nature as all the other species of animals.[95]

---

[95] I Kant, *The Metaphysics of Morals*, edited by M Gregor (Cambridge, Cambridge University press, 1996) 123.

14

The Fate of Public International Law: Between Technique and Politics

Public international law hovers between cosmopolitan ethos and technical specialisation. Recently, it has differentiated into functional regimes such as 'trade law', 'human rights law', 'environmental law' and so on that seek to 'manage' global problems efficiently and empower new interests and forms of expertise. Neither of the principal legal responses to regime-formation – constitutionalism and pluralism – is adequate, however. The emergence of regimes resembles the rise of nation states in the late nineteenth century. But, if nations are 'imagined communities', so are regimes. Reducing international law to a mechanism to advance functional objectives is vulnerable to the criticisms raised against thinking about it as an instrument for state policy: neither regimes nor states have a fixed nature or self-evident objectives. They are the stories we tell about them. The task for international lawyers is not to learn new managerial vocabularies but to use the language of international law to articulate the politics of critical universalism.

The Project of Modern International Law

PUBLIC INTERNATIONAL LAW is rules and institutions but it is also a tradition and a political project. If you view it only as rules or institutions, you will be struck by how different it looks from the rules and institutions you know from the domestic context. Of course, there was always the suspicion that what international lawyers do is not like domestic attorneys or judges reading dossiers, interviewing clients or handing out decisions. Compared with the sophisticated techniques of domestic law, international law seemed primitive, abstract and above all political, too political. It was against this attitude that international lawyers have defended their project by seeking to show that, despite appearances, it is not really so different. States could, after all, be conceived as legal subjects in a system where their territorial possessions were like property, their treaties like contracts and their diplomacy like the administration of a legal system.[1] That

[1] This way of thinking about international law emerged together with the professionalisation of the field and its integration into the law school curriculum in the late nineteenth century. One powerful

strategy was quite successful. However, I would like to suggest that the problems faced by public international law today – marginalisation, lack of normative force, a sense that the diplomatic mores that stand at its heart are part of the world's problems – result in large part from that strategy, the effort of becoming technical.

The strategy, I may report, was developed with particular force at the London School of Economics (LSE) in the course of the first meetings between the lecturer, as he then was, Arnold Duncan McNair, and the immigrant doctoral student from Galicia and Vienna, Hersch Lauterpacht, in 1923 and 1924.[2] The publication of the International Law Reports from 1929 onwards that resulted from those meetings helped one to think of inter-state arbitration and the work of the recently established Permanent Court of International Justice (PCIJ) as 'cases' and precedents. The setting up of the British Year Book of International Law created a forum where those cases could be commented on like domestic cases in domestic law reviews. McNair's manual of treaty law offered a methodology for reading treaties like domestic statutes, while Lauterpacht projected the League Covenant as 'Higher Law', comparable to a domestic constitution.[3] His editorial work in the 1930s and thereafter for Oppenheim's International Law assured him control of the contents of the most widely used legal manual in the world's foreign offices. In addition, his magnum opus from 1933 – The Function of Law in the International Community – summarised the view of international law as a complete, common law type of legal system with a single right answer to every problem.[4]

Some 60 to 80 years ago, a small group of cosmopolitan-minded lawyers translated the diplomacy of states into the administration of legal rules and institutions. This was a progressive, liberal project, conceived originally in nineteenth century Germany from where immigrants such as Lassa Oppenheim or Hersch Lauterpacht brought it into the English-speaking world.[5] It combined a political realist reading

---

text that reads treaty law as no different from domestic constitutional law is G Jellinek, *Die rechtliche Natur der Staatenverträge. Ein Beitrag zur juristischen Construction des Völkerrechts* (Vienna, Hölder, 1880). The 'dualist' approach of understanding international and domestic law as separate legal systems and introducing the former in legal education and practice through its incorporation into domestic law was instrumental to the process of professionalisation. The publication of ratified treaties in domestic code books opened the way to their interpretation and application analogously to domestic law.

[2] I have told this story in 'Hersch Lauterpacht 1897–1960' in J Beatson and R Zimmermann, *Jurists Uprooted. German-Speaking Emigré Lawyers in Twentieth-Century Britain* (Oxford, Oxford University Press, 2004) 601, 613–14.

[3] AD McNair, *The Law of Treaties* (Oxford, Clarendon,1938); H Lauterpacht, 'The Covenant as the Higher Law' in *International Law. Being the Collected Papers of Sir Hersch Lauterpacht* (Cambridge, Cambridge University Press, 1978) vol 4, 326–36.

[4] H Lauterpacht, *The Function of Law in the International Community* (Oxford, Clarendon Press, 1933).

[5] The predominance of German legal thought in the development of international law in the nineteenth century is striking. One of the (insufficiently examined) reasons for this may be suspected to lie in the ease with which the techniques developed by German public lawyers to deal with the fragmented structures of the Old Empire could be applied to problems of European organisation after the Napoleonic wars. After all, many of the classic naturalists elaborated imperial law under the label of *jurisprudentia universalis*. At least, this is what I suggest in 'Into Positivism Georg Friedrich von Martens (1756–1821) and the Origins of Modern International Law' (2008) 15 *Constellations. An International Journal of Critical and Democratic Theory* 189–207.

of statehood with a strong anti-sovereignty ethos through a historical reading of modernity, a reading once forcefully expressed in Immanuel Kant's 1784 essay on 'The Idea for a Universal History with a Cosmopolitan Purpose'.[6] Everybody agreed that although statehood was important, it was also problematic. Lawyers sought to deal with those problems by thinking of states as intermediate stages in a historical trajectory that would lead to the liberation of individuals enjoying human rights in a global federation under the rule of law.[7]

This project always had its ups and downs. The experience with the League of Nations turned out to be particularly traumatic and deterred abstract speculation about the United Nations as an incipient world government.[8] Nevertheless, in the 1960s, the cosmopolitan ethos found a new home in the expanding human rights institutions and the welfare and development activities in the UN and other inter-governmental organisations. Scholars like Wilfred Jenks in Britain – also a high official of the International Labour Organisation (ILO) – or Wolfgang Friedmann – another refugee from Germany to the LSE, among other places – read these developments as the transformation of international law from a law of coordination to a law of world-wide cooperation to further shared ends.[9] The main limiting factor was the Cold War. But the federal ambition remained protected by the fact that it was impossible to realise under conditions of ideological conflict.

Then came 1989 and all the enthusiasm about a global rule of law – human rights, trade, environment, criminal law, sanctions and a world police. The end of the Cold War was understood – especially in Europe – as the removal of obstacles on the way to history's natural progress towards a universal federation. Western statesmen even resorted to the (German) vocabulary of the 'international community' as they defended North Atlantic Treaty Organisation (NATO) bombings of Serbia in 1999.[10] Where American international relations analysts added footnotes to Hegel, Europeans fell back on Kant.[11] Somehow, international law appeared to find its home in a (Germanic) language of universal reason

---

[6] I Kant,'The Idea for a Universal History with a Cosmopolitan Purpose' in H Reiss (ed), *Political Writings*, 2nd edn (Cambridge, Cambridge University Press, 1991) 41–53.

[7] Thus, quite strikingly, at the end of his magnum opus that seeks to interpret international law as analogous to any other law, Lauterpacht appeals for a realistic admission of its 'present imperfections' and its being 'in a state of transition to the ¢nite and attainable ideal of a society of states under the binding rule of law', *The Function of Law* (1933) 432. I have sought to map this sensibility in M Koskenniemi, *The Gentle Civiliser of Nations. The Rise and Fall of International Law 1870–1960* (Cambridge, Cambridge University Press, 2002).

[8] The new spirit of 'realist' modesty in the profession was well articulated in J Brierly, *The Outlook for International Law* (Oxford, Clarendon Press, 1944).

[9] W Jenks, *The Common Law of Mankind* (London, Stevens, 1958); W Friedmann, *The Changing Structure of International Law* (London, Stevens, 1964).

[10] Arguing about the international world as a legal community harks back to the widespread – predominantly German – debates during the inter-war era and since about the world as a *Rechtsgemeinschaft* – a legal community. For a useful overview, see A Paulus, *Die internationale Gemeinschaft im Völkerrecht.Eine Untersuchung zur Entwicklung des Völkerrechts im Zeitalter der Globalisierung* (Munich, Beck, 2000).

[11] F Fukuyama, *The End of History and the Last Man* (London, Penguin, 1992); J Habermas, 'Hat die Konstitutionalisierung des Völkerrechts noch eine Chance? in *Der gespaltene Westen* (Frankfurt am Main, Suhrkamp, 2004) 113–93.

Fragmentation

But the new developments in the law did not point to unity. The more powerfully they dealt with international problems – problems of economics, development, human rights, environment, criminality, security – the more they began to challenge old principles and institutions. Specialisations such as 'trade law', 'human rights law', 'environmental law', 'criminal law', 'security law', 'European law' and so on started to reverse established legal hierarchies in favour of the structural bias in the relevant functional expertise.[12] Even though this process was often organised through intergovernmental organisations, the governmental delegations were composed of technical (economic, environmental, legal) experts in a way that transposed the functional differentiation at the national level onto the international plane.[13] Moreover, the resulting regimes have often been formulated in an open-ended manner, leaving power to decide – above all, to decide on how scarce resources should be distributed – to the legal and technical experts appointed to the supervisory organs. It is this change to which international lawyers have reacted by speculating on the 'dangers' of incoherence, forum shopping and, perhaps characteristically, 'loss of overall control'.[14]

One example of this would be the Tadić case of 1999 from the Appeals Chamber of the International Criminal Tribunal for Former Yugoslavia (ICTY). The Chamber replaced the standard of 'effective control' laid down by the International Court of Justice (ICJ) in the Nicaragua case in 1986 as the rule governing the accountability of foreign states over acts of parties in civil war by the far wider standard of 'overall control'.[15] Judged against the criminal lawyers' professional struggle 'against impunity', the old law seemed conservative and state-centric, part of the problem rather than of its solution.

But open challenges to established law have remained rare.[16] It is normally sufficient for a regime to introduce itself as an exception so as to avoid the old rule or

---

[12] On 'structural bias', see M Koskenniemi, *From Apology to Utopia; the Structure of International Legal Argument* (1989) (Re-issue with a new Epilogue, Cambridge University Press, 2005) 600–15.

[13] For the unitary state 'disaggregating' into functionally organised networks of governmental experts, see A-M Slaughter, 'Governing the Global Economy through Government Networks' in M Byers (ed), *The Role of Law in International Politics* (Oxford, Oxford University Press, 2000) 177–205 and ibid, *A New World Order* (Princeton NJ, Princeton University Press, 2004) 12–15 and passim.

[14] For a discussion of the positions and overview of literature, see M Koskenniemi and P Leino, 'Fragmentation of International Law? Postmodern Anxieties' (2002) 15 *Leiden Journal of International Law* 553; A Fischer-Lescano and G Teubner, 'Regime-Collisions: The Vain Search for Legal Unity in the Fragmentation of Global Law' (2004) 25 *Michigan Journal of International Law* 999; A Fischer-Lescano and G Teubner, *Regime-Kollisionen. Zur Fragmentierung des globalen Rechts* (Frankfurt, Suhrkamp, 2006). The discussion below draws upon 'Fragmentation of International Law. Problems caused by the Diversification and Expansion of International Law' Report of the Study Group of the International Law Commission. Finalised by Martti Koskenniemi, UN Doc A/CN4/L.682 (13 April 2006).

[15] *The Prosecutor v Dusko Tadić* [1999] ICTY 50, 122.

[16] P Weckel, 'La CIJ et la fragmentation du droit international' in RH Vinaixa et K Wellens (eds), *L'influence des sources sur l'unité et la fragmentation du droit international* (Brussels, Bruylant, 2006) 167–85.

the established preference. In this way, for example, human rights treaties have been read by human rights organs differently from 'regular' treaties so as to enable human rights bodies to assume a wider jurisdiction than regular treaty organs and to prioritise human rights over formal state consent.[17] The European Court of Human Rights (ECHR) justified its special approach to the Vienna Convention on the Law of Treaties by pointing to:

> ...a fundamental difference in the role and purpose of the respective tribunals [ie of the ICJ and the ECHR], [that], coupled with the existence of a practice of unconditional acceptance [. . .] provides a compelling basis for distinguishing Convention practice from that of the International Court.[18]

The point of the emergence of something like 'international criminal law' or 'international human rights law' (or any other special law) is precisely to institutionalise the new priorities carried within such fields. As a result, political conflict will often take the form of conflict of jurisdictions. Who shall decide? This, again, will depend on how a matter will be described, which of its aspects are seen as central and which marginal. Should the importation of hormone meat, for example, be understood principally as a trade question, or an environmental (health) question? In the 1998 Beef Hormones case, the Appellate Body of the World Trade Organisation (WTO) considered the status of the 'precautionary principle' under the WTO covered treaties, concluding that whatever its status was 'under international environmental law', it had not become binding for the WTO.[19] If legal principles that emerge in certain fields may be inapplicable in others, the crucial question will be to determine under which regime they should be decided.

A standard way to go about this would be to try to find the regime that is most relevant, or specific, to a matter.[20] Thus, in the *Legality of the Threat or Use of Nuclear Weapons* case (1996), the ICJ observed that both human rights law (namely the International Covenant on Civil and Political Rights) and the laws of armed conflict applied 'in times of war'. Nevertheless, when it came to deciding what was an 'arbitrary deprivation of life' under article 6(1) of the Covenant, this fell 'to be determined by the applicable *lex specialis*, namely the law applicable to armed conflict'.[21] The Court avoided assuming any general priority between the regimes. Both were applicable – although only to the extent they converged. To the extent there was conflict – as there was in regard to the applicable standard of killing – humanitarian law ought to be applied because it was the more specific of the two.

How so more 'specific'? It was more specific only if one thought that the most characteristic aspect of nuclear weapons is that they are a strategic weapon to be

---

[17] *Belilos v Switzerland* (App no 10328/83) ECtHR A/No 132, para 60.
[18] *Loizidou v Turkey* (App No 15318/89) Preliminary objections, 23 March 1995, ECHR A/No 310, para 67 .
[19] European Communities – Measures Concerning Meat and Meat Products (Hormones) (13 February 1998) WT/DS26/AB/R,WT/DS48/AB/R, 123–25.
[20] This technique – lex specialis – is treated extensively in Koskenniemi and Leino, 'Fragmentation of International Law?' (2002) 30–114.
[21] *Legality of the Threat or Use of Nuclear Weapons* (Advisory Opinion) (1996) ICJ Rep 240, 25.

used in armed conflict. This view, however, presupposed what was to be decided. For the advocates of the illegality of those weapons, they were in fact useless as a means of warfare and the most central aspect of their use was the massive violation of the human rights of non-combatants this would entail.

The choice of one among several applicable legal regimes refers back to what is understood as significant in a problem. The question of significance also refers back to what the relevant institution understands as its mission, its structural bias. If the WTO Appellate Body dealt with hormone beef as a trade (instead of a health) issue, this follows from the fact that it was constitutionally mandated to treat it in that way. Analogously, if the Inter-American Court of Human Rights described consular protection as a human right, this was perfectly coherent from the perspective of the interests it was called upon to protect.[22] Yet, such priorities may not be so obvious when the institution is one of general jurisdiction. When the ICJ gave its Opinion in *Legal Consequences of the Construction of a Wall in the Occupied Palestinian Territory* (2004), it had the choice to do this from the perspective of the laws of self-determination, self-defence against terrorism and human rights/ humanitarian law. The fierce disagreements about the Opinion focus precisely on whether it had made the right choice.[23] Likewise, the occupation of Iraq was routinely addressed through the vocabularies of 'human rights' and 'security' that point to very different legal regimes and it is only once we know which of them applies that we know how to assess the occupation. In a recent case before the High Court of Justice in Britain, the claimant – a dual citizen of Iraq and Britain – contended that the fact that he had been detained for 10 months without being charged violated his rights under the Human Rights Act of 1998. The Court, however, dealt with the matter from the perspective of 'security' while reading 'human rights' as subsidiary to it:

> The Security Council, charged as it is with primary responsibility for maintaining international peace and security, has itself determined that a multinational force is required. Its objective is to restore such security as will provide effective protection for human rights for those within Iraq. Those who choose to assist the Security Council in that purpose are authorised to take those steps, which include detention, necessary for its achievement.[24]

There was no doubt that the matter could be examined from the perspective of 'security' as well as 'human rights'. The choice of the frame determined the decision. But for determining the frame, there was no meta-regime, directive or rule. The Court's reading of the applicant's rights from the perspective of considerations of security may or may not be approved. However, it can only be understood once it is viewed in terms of the Court's bias towards security.

[22] Inter-American Court of Human Rights, *The Right to Information on Consular Assistance* (Advisory Opinion) (1 October 1999) OC-16/99.

[23] *Legal Consequences of the Construction of a Wall in the Occupied Palestinian Territory* (Advisory Opinion) (2004) www.icj-cij.org/docket/files/131/1671.pdf. See the discussion in F Mégret, 'A Sacred Trust of Civilization' (2005) 1 *Journal of International Law and International Relations* 307.

[24] Case CO/3673/2005 *The Queen (on the application of Hilal Abdul-Razzaq Ali Al-Jedda) v Secretary of State for Defence* [2005] EWHC 1809 (Admin) 104.

Now fragmentation may not seem too serious as long as the bias is well established, widely known, and resonates in the community to which the institution speaks. After all, the development of special fields of law never posed a fundamental challenge to domestic legal orders owing in part to the recognised benefits of specialisation, in part to the way in which domestic jurisprudence was able to neutralise these developments by systemic interpretation.[25] The matter becomes more contentious when several institutions seek to deal with a problem differently and there is no such robust consensus or interpretative practice. The question of the possible environmental effects of the operation of the 'MOX Plant' nuclear facility at Sellafield, United Kingdom, has been raised at three different institutions: an Arbitral Tribunal set up under the United Nations Convention on the Law of the Sea (UNCLOS), another Tribunal under the Convention on the Protection of the Marine Environment of the North-East Atlantic (OSPAR Convention) and within the European Court of Justice (ECJ) under the European Community and Euratom Treaties. Three rule-complexes – the UNCLOS, the OSPAR Convention, and EC law – each address the same facts. Which should be determinative? Is the problem principally about the law of the sea, about (possible) pollution of the North Sea, or about inter-EC relationships? To pose such questions already points to the difficulty of providing an answer. Surely the case is about all of these matters? Yet, a choice has to be made between the institutions, and its significance did not escape the UNCLOS Arbitral Tribunal:

> ... even if the OSPAR Convention, the EC Treaty and the Euratom treaty contain rights or obligations similar to or identical with the rights set out in [the UNCLOS], the rights and obligations under these agreements have a separate existence from those under [the UNCLOS].[26]

Even if the institutions were to apply the same rules, they would apply them differently owing to 'differences in the respective context, object and purposes, subsequent practice of parties and *travaux preparatoires*'.[27]

Everything depends on the bias of the institution. It may be suggestive that while the UNCLOS Arbitral Tribunal held that according to 'dictates of mutual respect and comity' it should defer the treatment of the matter until its implications under EC law had been clarified,[28] the ECJ in 2006 simply condemned Ireland's initiation of proceedings against Britain under international law as breaches of Community law.[29]

In a world of plural regimes, political conflict is waged on the description and re-description of aspects of the world so as to make them fall under the jurisdiction

---

[25] See K Tuori, *Oikeuden ratio ja voluntas* (WSOY, 2007).
[26] *MOX Plant case, Request for Provisional Measures Order* (*Ireland v the United Kingdom*) (3 December 2001) ITLOS Reports (2005) 126 ILR vol 273, 50.
[27] ibid 273–74 [51].
[28] MOX Plant Case, Statement by the President of the Arbitral Tribunal, 13 June 2003, 11.
[29] Case C-459/03 *Ireland v the United Kingdom* (30 May 2006). For a commentary, see N Lavranos, 'The MOX Plant and Ijzeren Rijn Disputes: Which Court Is the Supreme Arbiter?' (2006) 19 *Leiden Journal of International Law* 223.

of particular institutions. Think, for example, about the way the ECJ adopted a fundamental rights vocabulary in the 1970s and 1980s to meet the challenge certain national courts had posed to its jurisdiction and in particular to the principles of supremacy and direct effect of community law. Those national courts had argued that it would be inconceivable that the bills of rights in their national constitutions would be inferior to what were merely rules organising a customs union. In response, the ECJ began to read community law as a regime for protecting the fundamental rights of community citizens. Through this reading, Community law was transformed from an economic regime into a rights-regime and its hierarchical position over national laws was finally consolidated.[30]

Opportunities are endless here as any significant problem may be defended as a 'human rights' problem, a 'security' issue – or indeed an 'environmental', 'trade' or 'health' problem. In the United Nations (UN) for example, wide readings of 'security' have buttressed the competence of the Security Council, while the boundary between 'environmental' and 'development' expertise remains a topic of constant negotiation within institutions tasked to deal with 'sustainable development'.[31] A case concerning the maritime carriage of hazardous substances, for example, may be defined as a problem of trade, or maritime transport, or environmental protection, or of the law of the sea, and thus may be subsumed to any such regulatory regime. Such characterisations are not intrinsic to the relevant problem, but emerge from the interest or preference from which it is examined. This is where, as I have elsewhere written, fragmentation becomes struggle for institutional hegemony.[32] Which institution will have the authoritative voice? According to which bias will a matter be resolved? If there are no regime-independent ways of describing an issue, the door is open to the unilateral assumption of jurisdiction by experts who feel themselves powerful enough to have the last word.

Today, few experts conceive of themselves as part of the Lauterpacht tradition of a public law oriented global federalism. Instead, they may work for private or public-private institutions, national administrations, interest groups or technical bodies, developing best practices and standardised solutions – 'modelisation', 'contractualisation' and mutual recognition – as part of the management of particular regimes.[33] The vocabularies of constraint are cognitive rather than normative. They emerge from economic, military, or technological facts and calculations – recasting problems of politics as problems of expert knowledge.[34] The resulting

---

[30] I have discussed the strategy of 'field constitution' in chapter six of this volume.
[31] For a recent comment on the broad reading of security see, eg E Hey, 'The High-Level Summit, International Institutional Reform and International Law' (2005) 2 *Journal of International Law and International Relations* 5. For the contrast between the (economically oriented) international resources law and the international law of the environment, see T Kuokkanen, *International Law and The Environment. Variations on a Theme* (The Hague, Nijhoff, 2000).
[32] See chapter nine in this volume.
[33] See K Nicolaidis and G Schaff, 'Transnational Mutual Recognition Regimes: Governance without Global Government' (2005) 68 *Law & Contemporary Problems* 263.
[34] The thesis about power in the West, since the eighteenth century, turning increasingly from formal government to informal 'governmentality', the regulation of the way in which 'freedom' unfolds in society, is at the heart of Michel Foucault's late work and its themes, although relevant to this chapter,

regulation may also be more geared towards enabling private power than limiting it.[35] Consumer protection within e-commerce, for instance, must take place in the informal mechanisms of the web – anything else would be commercially and technically impossible.[36]

In such (and other) ways, traditional international law is pushed aside by a mosaic of particular rules and institutions, each following its embedded preferences. As a result, the project of Lauterpacht and his generation is left dangling in an empty space, the ninth edition of Oppenheim's *International Law* (1992)[37] reduced into nostalgia, together with such other inter-war enthusiasms as functional architecture, conveyer-belts or European rule as 'sacred trust of civilization'. Ideals turn into rituals, like the unending debates about UN reform, divested of political meaning.

Deformalisation

None of this would matter too much if the new regimes were amenable to political control. However, even where they are based on formal international law rule-making (typically through the device of a multilateral treaty), they lead into contextual ad hocism that further strengthens the position of functional experts. This is the difficulty with formal, universal rules.[38] Any rule with a global scope will almost automatically appear as either over-inclusive or under-inclusive, covering cases the law-maker would not wish to cover, and excluding cases that would need to be covered but were not known of at the time when the rule was made. To forestall this, most law with a universal scope refrains from rule-setting and instead calls for 'balancing' the interests with a view of attaining 'optimal' results to be calculated on a case-by-case basis.

cannot be dealt with here. See in particular his *Securité, territoire, population. Cours au Collège de France 1977–1978* (Paris, Gallimard/Seuil, 2004) especially from 91 (lecture of 1 February) onwards and the whole of *Naissance de la biopolitique. Cours au Collège de France 1978–1979* (Paris, Gallimard/Seuil, 2004). For the application in the analysis of late modern global law, see A Supiot, *Homo juridicus. Essai sur la fonction anthropologique du droit* (Paris, Seuil, 2005) 223–73 and M Delmas-Marty, Trois défis pour un droit mondial (Paris, Seuil, 1998) 78–84.

[35] Out of the burgeoning literature see, eg C Cutler, *Private Power and Global Authority. Transnational Merchant Law and the Global Political Economy* (Cambridge, Cambridge University Press, 2003); R Lipschutz and C Vogel,'"Regulation for the Rest of Us?" Global Civil Society and the Privatization of Transnational Regulation' in RB Hall and TJ Biersteker (eds), The Emergence of Private Authority in Public Governance (Cambridge, Cambridge University Press, 2002) 115–39. Particularly useful are the essays in E Loquin and C Kessedjian, *La mondialisation du droit* (Paris, Litec, 2000).

[36] See T Puurunen, Dispute Resolution in International Electronic Commerce (University of Helsinki, Doctoral thesis, 2005).

[37] Sir Robert Jennings and Soir Arthur Watts, *Oppenheim's International Law* 9th edn (Oxford, Oxford University Press, 1999).

[38] The best account of this difficulty is still F Schauer, *Playing by the Rules: A Philosophical Examination of Rule-Based Decision-Making in Law and in Life* (Oxford, Oxford University Press, 1991) 31–34, 47–52 and passim.

Take, for example, the law of territory, the former heartland of international legality. Looking for a just allocation of maritime resources, or drawing a terrestrial boundary, it is hard to generalise. Hence the law in instruments such as the 1982 UN Convention on the Law of the Sea or the practice of the ICJ points to the need to attain an equitable result.[39] In conflicts of jurisdiction or state succession, the law goes little further than a call for balancing the interests.[40] International situations tend to be seen as idiosyncratic and fact-intensive. Any single rule might spell injustice in some of the future cases where it will be applied. Thus, the failure of international efforts to find universal 'criteria' for humanitarian intervention,[41] for the identifying of 'aggression', or for singling out human groups that ought to be treated as 'terrorists'.[42] Everyone participates in such efforts with two concerns in mind: to agree on nothing that might prejudice the future interests of my country, but to try as hard as possible to attain a definition that will strike at every conceivable future adversary. Where everybody participates on those premises, the result can only be inconclusive: an agreement to leave such determination for decision as the situation arises (with the hope, of course, that one will then be in a position to decide for oneself). This is so even in areas where policy arguments for rules are otherwise strongest. The complexity of modern warfare makes humanitarian law unable to say more than 'proportionality' and 'necessity', reasonable calculation of gains and losses, with the vocabularies of humanitarian and military experts becoming finally indistinguishable.[43]

It is not that finding the equitable solution or knowing who the aggressor is or when to launch a humanitarian operation would be impossible or even necessarily difficult. But, little about such decision-making can plausibly be seen in terms of employing a legal vocabulary of rules and principles, precedents or institutions. Instead, the relevant considerations always seem to require technical expertise, calculations of the data produced in the context in order to figure out the best outcome. The law defers to the politics of expertise: for what might be 'reasonable' for an environmental expert is not what is 'reasonable' to a chemical manufacturer; what is 'optimal' to a development engineer is not what is optimal to the representative of an indigenous population; what is 'proportionate' to a humanitarian specialist is not necessarily what is proportionate to a military expert.

---

[39] I have made this argument at length in Koskenniemi, *From Apology to Utopia* (2005) 258–302, 576–83.

[40] For a discussion of the 'good sense and reasonableness' needed in conflicts of jurisdiction, see R Jennings and A Watts, *Oppenheim's International Law vol I Peace*, 9th edn (London, Longman's, 1992) 463–66. On contextualism in state succession, see the reports of the directors of studies in PM Eisemann and M Koskenniemi, *La succession d'États: La codification à l'épreuve des faits/State Succession: Codification Tested against the Facts* (The Hague, Nijhoff, 2000).

[41] I have discussed the futile search for 'determining criteria' for humanitarian intervention in chapter seven of this volume.

[42] For the indeterminacy of the discussion on the definition of 'terrorism' in connection with the drafting of a 'general' UN Convention on the matter, see J Petman, 'The Problem of Evil and International Law' in J Petman and J Klabbers (eds), *Nordic Cosmopolitanism. Essays in International Law for Martti Koskenniemi* (Leiden, Nijhoff, 2003) 128–37.

[43] See especially D Kennedy, *The Dark Sides of Virtue. Reassessing International Humanitarianism* (Princeton NJ, Princeton University Press, 2004) 272–96.

Let me give a few examples from the recent work of a UN body of which I have been a member, the International Law Commission (ILC). The Commission was set up in 1948 by the General Assembly for the 'codification and progressive development of international law'. The Commission's first programme of work was drafted at the invitation of the UN Secretary-General by Hersch Lauterpacht.[44] After two busy decades, the Commission has been increasingly sidelined as treaty-making has moved within specialised institutions.[45] However, one set of problems has continued to call for global solutions: the government and protection of the world's natural resources. At its session in 2006, the Commission finalised a 'Draft Convention on the Law of Transboundary Aquifers' – the rights and obligations with regard to the world's groundwater resources, an immensely important issue.[46] The main substantive provision of the draft invites states to construct a 'plan' for each aquifer system, taking into account 'the present and future needs and alternative water sources for the aquifer states'. The 'relevant factors' that should be taken into account include items such as 'the natural characteristic of the aquifer system', 'the social and economic needs of the States concerned' and 'the existing and potential utilisation of the aquifer' and so on, with the ultimate paragraph providing that:

> The weight to be given to each factor is to be determined by its importance with regard to a specific transboundary aquifer or aquifer system in comparison with that of other relevant factors. In determining what is equitable and reasonable utilization, all relevant factors are to be considered together and a conclusion reached on the basis of all the factors. However, in weighing different utilizations of a transboundary aquifer or aquifer system, special regard shall be given to vital human needs.[47]

This pattern is repeated in countless recent instruments.[48] To agree to a treaty is to agree on a continued negotiation with the reference to contextual deal-striking, stressing the role of technical experts, and lifting functional interests to decisive position.

For example, the Draft Articles on the 'Prevention of Transboundary Damage from Hazardous Activities', presently under consideration in the UN General

---

[44] Survey of International Law in Relation to the Work of Codification of the International Law Commission document A/CN.4/1 (United Nations publication, Sales No 48.V.1) reissued under the symbol A/CN.4/1/Rev.1 (United Nations publication, Sales No 48.V.1(1)), also published in E Lauterpacht (ed), *International Law. Being the Collected Papers of Sir Hersch Lauterpacht* (Cambridge, Cambridge University Press, 1970) vol I, 445–530.

[45] I have also discussed the Commission's work in 'International Legislation Today: Limits and Possibilities' (2005) 23 *Wisconsin International Law Journal* 61.

[46] ILC, 'Draft Report of the International law Commission on the Work of its Fifty-Eighth Session, Chapter VI: Shared Natural Resources. C. Text of the Draft Articles on The Law of Transboundary Aquifers adopted by the Commission on First Reading' (4 July 2006) UN Doc A/CN.4/L.694/Add.1.

[47] Draft article 5(2), ibid 4.

[48] See also the 1997 UN International Convention on the Non-Navigational Uses of International Watercourses, UNGA Res 51/229 (Annex) (21 May 1997). The main standard in the Convention is that of 'equitable and sustainable use', defined in terms of a (non-exhaustive) list of economic, environmental, geographical and other 'factors'. More important are procedures on information exchange, cooperation and negotiation that encourage parties to negotiate local, regional or issue-specific regimes.

Assembly, calls upon states to 'take all appropriate measures to prevent significant transboundary harm or at any event to minimise the risk thereof'.[49] In case problems emerge, '[t]he States shall seek solutions based on an equitable balance of interests'.[50] For this purpose, the Draft produces a (non-exhaustive) list of 'all relevant factors and circumstances' that is perhaps useful to reproduce *in extenso*:

(a) the degree of risk of significant transboundary harm and of the availability of means of preventing such harm, or minimizing the risk thereof or repairing the harm;

(b) the importance of the activity, taking into account its overall advantages of a social, economic and technical character for the State of origin in relation to the potential harm to the State likely to be affected;

(c) the risk of significant harm to the environment and the availability of means of preventing such harm, or minimizing the risk thereof or restoring the environment;

(d) the degree to which the State of origin and, as appropriate, the State likely to be affected are prepared to contribute to the costs of prevention;

(e) the economic viability of the activity in relation to the costs of prevention and to the possibility of carrying out the activity elsewhere or by other means or replacing it with an alternative activity;

(f) the standards of prevention which the State likely to be affected applies to the same or comparable activities and the standards applied in comparable regional or international practice.[51]

The commentary prepared by the Commission explains that suggestions to provide a blanket obligation to prevent certain (intrinsically harmful) activities had been considered inappropriate because 'Any such list of activities is likely to be under inclu[sive] and could become quickly dated from time to time in the light of fast evolving technology.'[52]

At its session in 2006, the ILC also adopted a 'Draft Declaration on International Liability for Damage Caused by Hazardous Activities'.[53] This is the outcome of more than 30 years of work on the question of environmental damage, the source of which lies elsewhere than where the damage is suffered. In accordance with the managerialism animating its work on 'prevention', the Commission entitled its work on 'liability' to read 'allocation of loss in case of transboundary harm arising out of hazardous activities'. The draft declaration recommends that states conclude issue specific regimes of operator liability, insurance and funding schemes with no fixed points apart from a softly formulated objective not to leave victims uncompensated. None of the language is phrased in terms of rights or obligations.

---

[49] ILC, 'Draft Articles on the Prevention of Transboundary Damage from Hazardous Activities', Report of the International Law Commission of its Fifty-Third Session' GAOR 56th session Suppl.10 UN Doc A/56/10, 390.

[50] Article 9 (2) ibid 409.

[51] Article 10 ibid 374. For the non-exhaustive nature of this list, see also ILC Commentary to the Draft Articles on Prevention of Transboundary Harm from Hazardous Activities, ibid, 413–18.

[52] ibid 381 para 4.

[53] ILC, 'Draft Report of the International law Commission on the Work of its Fifty-Eighth Session, Chapter V: International Liability for Injurious Consequences of Acts not Prohibited by International Law, E: The Text of the Draft Principles on the Allocation of Loss in the Case of Transboundary Harm Arising out of Hazardous Activities' (2006) UN Doc A/CN.4/L.693/Add.1.

The vocabulary is that of law and economics – 'allocation of loss' – on case-by-case basis with the view to reaching an optimal result.

Most environmental law is like this. In the 1992 Framework Convention on Climate Change (FCCC), states agreed to stabilise their greenhouse gas emissions at 1990 levels within a reasonable time.[54] The Convention lists such principles as inter-generational equity, common but differentiated responsibility and the precautionary principle, all of which should be applied in a manner that is 'cost-effective so as to ensure global benefit at the lowest possible cost' (article 3(2)). However, even where the obligations are clearly formulated – as for example in the 1997 Kyoto Protocol to the FCCC – they are supplemented by secondary rules that lift violations from the compass of breach of treaty or state responsibility. A 'Multilateral Consultation Process' has been set up to 'facilitate the implementation' of the commitments. The formal dispute settlement mechanism is unlikely to be used as most parties have only accepted a 'non-adversarial' non-compliance procedure.[55] Like the corresponding procedure under the 1987 Montreal Protocol for the Protection of the Ozone Layer, this focuses on technical and financial assistance, not sanctions or liability. Even for persistent violations, the only sanction is that of publicity.[56] In this way, even formally rule-like provisions (emission reduction standards) become negotiating chips in an unending process of balancing, adjusting and managing.

The same ethos has penetrated formal dispute-settlement. In the 1997 *Gabčíkovo Dam* case, the ICJ found that both Hungary and Slovakia had breached a 1977 Treaty that had provided for the construction of large water diversion project in the *Gabčíkovo* -Nagymaros region in the Danube river. Contrary to what had been maintained by Hungary, the 1977 Treaty remained in force. As a result, the Court held that the parties were to 're-establish the co-operative management of what remains of the Project'.[57] As both parties had breached their obligations, both owed each other reparation. Such 'intersecting wrongs' could, however, only be satisfactorily resolved 'in the framework of an overall settlement'.[58] The Court indicated that the 1977 Treaty 'not only contains a joint investment programme, it also establishes a régime'.[59] As the Treaty was in force and the régime was its

---

[54] 'within a time frame sufficient to allow ecosystems to adapt to climate change, to ensure that food production is not threatened and to enable economic development to proceed in a sustainable manner', article 2, Framework Convention on Climate Change (FCCC) (1992) 31 ILM 851.

[55] On problems relating to such soft enforcement, see M Koskenniemi, 'Breach of Treaty or Non-Compliance? Reflexions on the Enforcement of the Montreal Protocol' (1992) 3 *Yearbook of International Environmental Law* 123.

[56] The deformalisation of state responsibility as non-compliance has thereafter become 'standard practice in the environmental context', T Kuokkanen, 'Putting Gentle Pressure on Parties. Recent Trends in the Practice of the Implementation Committee of the Convention on Long-Range Transboundary Air Pollution' in Petman and Klabbers (eds), *Nordic Cosmopolitanism* (2003) 316. See also S Maljean-Dubois, 'Une mécanisme originale: La procedure de "non-compliance" du protocole relatif aux substances appauvrissant la couche d'ozone' in C Imperiali (ed), *L'effectivité de droit international de l'environnement* (Paris, Economica, 1998) 225–47.

[57] *Gabčíkovo Dam* case, ICJ Reports (1997) 80, 150.

[58] ibid 81, 153.

[59] ibid 79, 144.

basic element, that régime had to be restored. This was to take place by taking into account the changed economic and environmental circumstances: 'in such a way as to accommodate both the economic operation of the system of electricity generation and the satisfaction of essential environmental concerns'.[60] This, the Court noted, will also 'reflect in an optimal way the concept of common utilization of shared water resources for the achievement of the several objectives mentioned in the Treaty'.[61] In other words, the Court saw the legal problem in terms of making adjustments in a 'régime' that would guarantee an equitable balance of interests between the parties. Because it was not itself in possession of the relevant data, it sent the parties back to negotiate and to agree on the details in view of what technical experts would be able to produce.

Such references from law to 'regime' testify to an increasing predominance of a mindset in which 'disputes' appear as 'management problems' and in which the proper response is always technical or economic.[62] For this mindset, rights and obligations are rules of thumb or presumptions subject to adjustment with a view to reach optimal results. This is nicely visible in the recent practice of inserting clauses in multilateral treaties to deal with possible regime conflicts. The Preamble to the Cartagena Protocol on Biosafety to the Convention on Biological Diversity (2000) addresses the relationship of the Protocol to the obligations under the WTO covered agreements as follows:

> *Recognizing* that trade and environment agreements should be mutually supportive with a view to achieving sustainable development,
>
> *Emphasizing* that this Protocol shall not be interpreted as implying a change in the rights and obligations of a Party under any existing international agreements,
>
> *Understanding* that the above recital is not intended to subordinate this Protocol to other international agreements.[63]

What a 'mutually supportive' reading might mean in a conflict between the Protocol and the WTO (or any other) treaty is anybody's guess.[64] However, it does open the Protocol (and the conflicting treaty) for interminable managerial adjustments in view of administrative coherence and the structural bias of the relevant institution.

---

[60] ibid 80, 146.

[61] ibid 80, 147.

[62] This move was powerfully advocated some years ago under the call for 'interdisciplinary' cooperation between lawyers and empirical social scientists. For an incisive critique, see J Klabbers, 'The relative Autonomy of International Law, or the Forgotten Politics of Interdisciplinarity' (2005) 1 *Journal of International Law and International Relations* 35.

[63] Cartagena Protocol on Biosafety on the Convention on Biological Diversity, Depositary notification C.N.251.2000.TREATIES-1 of 27 April 2000. See also (2000) 39 ILM 1027.

[64] This idea of 'mutually supportive' reading appears in many instruments and is presented in the relevant literature as a kind of managerial antidote to 'formalist' or 'literal' readings of the relevant provisions. See especially the very useful N Matz, *Wege zur Koordinierung völkerrechtlicher Verträge, Völkervertragsrechtliche und institutionelle Ansätze* (Berlin, Springer, 2005). Likewise, R Wolfrum and N Matz, *Conflicts in International Environmental Law* (Berlin, Springer, 2003) especially159–208. See further the sources in Koskenniemi and Leino, 'Fragmentation of International Law?' (2002) 138–43.

Lauterpacht and other inter-war lawyers were right to assume that statehood would be slowly overcome by the economic and technical laws of a globalising modernity. This is what functional differentiation in both of its forms – fragmentation and deformalisation – has done. But they were wrong to believe that this would lead into a cosmopolitan federation. When the floor of statehood fell from under our feet, we did not collapse into a realm of global authenticity to encounter each other as free possessors of inalienable rights. Instead, we fell into watertight boxes of functional specialisation, to be managed and governed by reading our freedom as the realisation of our interest. As our feet hit the ground, we found no Kantian federation but the naturalism of Pufendorf and Hobbes – powerful actors engaged in strategic games with their eye on the Pareto optimum.

Constitutionalism

International lawyers – especially European international lawyers – have responded to fragmentation and the emergence of anti-formal expert regimes by starting to think of international law in constitutional terms.[65] This continues their effort to move away from diplomacy and politics – the politics of sovereignty in the early twentieth century, the politics of functional diversification in the early twenty first – by reading the international legal system through definite (though perhaps implicit) hierarchies of rules or institutions reflecting choices of value often expressed in Latin formulas such as *jus cogens* or obligations *erga omnes*.[66] This is an understandable suggestion, one that closely follows the way domestic lawyers have abstracted general principles to safeguard the 'coherence' of the domestic

---

[65] For the debate among international lawyers, see for example, J Klabbers, 'Constitutionalism Lite?' (2004) 1 *International Organizations Law Review* 31. For a representative collection of writings on international constitutionalism, see R St J Macdonald and D M Johnston (eds), *Towards World Constitutionalism: Issues in the Legal Ordering of the World Community* (Boston, M Nijhoff Publishers, 2005). For the suggestion to develop the ICJ into a 'constitutional court of the world community', see FO Vicuna, *International Dispute Settlement in an Evolving Global Society. Constitutionalization, Accessibility, Privatization* (Cambridge, Cambridge University Press, 2004) 18–28.

[66] For an early twentieth century suggestion to deal with international law in a constitutional way, see A Verdross, *Die Verfassung der Völkerrechtsgemeinschaft* (Vienna, Springer, 1926). Today, Christian Tomuschat writes of international law as a 'comprehensive blueprint for social life' in his 'International Law: Ensuring the Survival of Mankind on the Eve of A New Century, General Course on Public International Law' (2001) 281 *Recueil des Cours de l'Académie de droit international* 63–72. See also the commentary and elaboration in A von Bogdandy, 'Constitutionalism in International Law. Comment on a Proposal from Germany' (2001) 47 *Harvard International Law Journal* 223. For a Francophone version, see P Dupuy, 'L'unité de l'ordre juridique international, Cours général de droit international public' (2002) 297 *Recueil des Cours de l'Académie de droit international* especially 269–313 (on *jus cogens*). See also S Kadelbach, 'Ethik des Völkerrechts unter Bedingungen der Globalisierung' (2004) 64 *Zeitschrift für ausländisches öffentliches Recht und Völkerrecht* 1–20 and E de Wet, 'The Emergence of International and Regional Value Systems as a Manifestation of the Emerging International Constitutional Order' (2006) 19 *Leiden Journal of International Law* 611.

legal system in the face of novel legal fields and a fickle legislator.[67] But which would be the relevant international values? No doubt, free trade for trade bodies, human rights for human rights organs, environmental values for environmental regimes, security for the Security Council, each such 'value' again sub-divided into a mainstream understanding of what its practical implications might be and a minority challenge to that understanding. Constitutionalism, as we know it from the national context, relies on some basic understanding of the common good, some sense of a law as a shared project for a reasonably clearly defined (and often historically informed) objective.[68] In the international world, there is no semblance of this beyond the languages of diplomacy and positive law whose very fragmentation and indeterminacy provided the starting-point for the search for an (implicit) constitution. The undoubted increase of law in the international world ('legalisation') does not translate automatically into a substantive constitution in the absence of that sense of shared 'project' or objective.[69] If deformalisation has set the house of international law on fire, to grasp at values is to throw gas on the flames.

A more plausible constitutionalism remains formal. It suggests that system and hierarchy are intrinsic to juristic thought and thus also to international law. From this perspective, the suggestion according to which international law's speciality would lie in its consisting only of scattered diplomatic compromises here and there, while it would lack the 'secondary rules' that characterise national law as a legal 'system', fails to reflect international practice.[70] No special regime has ever been understood as independent from general law. In an early but typical case from 1928, for example, a claims commission interpreting a treaty did not hesitate to state as follows:

> Every international convention must be deemed tacitly to refer to general principles of international law for all the questions that it does not itself resolve in express terms and in a different way.[71]

Inter-war lawyers used this and other cases to argue for the systemic nature of public international law, the way its rules referred to other, hierarchically superior rules for their meaning or force.[72] No lawyer will refuse to regard states as states, or ask for evidence for the rule of *audiatur et altera pars* merely because a treaty or a regime is silent on such matters. They are structurally given, not positively

---

[67] A key task of domestic legal doctrine has always been to safeguard the systemic unity of the domestic legal system in response to changes in positive law. See, eg A Aarnio, *Denkweisen der Rechtswissenschaft* (Vienna, Springer, 1979) 50–159. The origin of this tradition in German nineteenth century *Begriffsjurisprudenz* is discussed in Tuori, *Oikeuden ratio ja voluntas* (2007).

[68] As articulated eg in TRC Allen, *Constitutional Justice. A Liberal Theory of the Rule of Law* (Oxford, Oxford University Press, 2001) 21–25.

[69] D Grimm, 'Ursprung und Wandel der Verfassung' in J Isensee and P Kirchhof (eds), *Handbuch des Staatsrechts*, 3rd edn (Heidelberg, CF Müller, 2003) 42.

[70] This suggestion is most famously made in HLA Hart, *The Concept of Law* (Oxford, Clarendon Press, 1961) 229–31.

[71] *Georges Pinson Case (France v Mexico)* (1928) 5 *Reports of International Arbitral Awards* 422.

[72] See especially Lauterpacht, *The Function of Law* (1933).

enacted. In its very first case, the Appellate Body of the WTO observed that the WTO agreements 'should not be read in clinical isolation from public international law'[73] and later specified that '[c]ustomary international law applies generally to the agreements between WTO members'.[74] Regimes such as the European or Inter-American human rights convention make constant reference to general international law without any act of incorporation.[75] After all, the Vienna Convention on the Law of Treaties provides that every treaty must be interpreted, taking into account 'any relevant rules of international law applicable between the parties' – a provision used in 2003 by the ICJ to tie Iran and the United States into the general law on the use of force by a reading of a bilateral friendship treaty.[76]

In 2001, the UN General Assembly, having heard the alarmist reports by the Presidents of the ICJ, requested the International Law Commission to give consideration to the problem of fragmentation. In 2003 the Commission set up a Study Group on the matter and, in 2006, at the end of the five-year mandate of the present Commission, the Group produced a 250 page report, plus a set of conclusions drawn from international practice with relevance to the question of international law's break-up into specialised 'boxes' of functional differentiation. The Report found no legal regimes outside general international law. Many of the new treaty regimes in the fields of trade, environmental protection or human rights did have special rules for rule creation, rule application and change. This is what made them special after all. When the rules run out, however, or regimes fail, then the institutions always refer back to the general law that appears to constitute the frame within which they exist.[77] Here is a battle European jurisprudence seems to have won. Law is a whole – or in the words of the first conclusion made by the ILC Study

---

[73] WTO, *United States – Standards of Reformulated and Conventional Gasoline* (20 May 1996) WT/DS2/AB/R, DSR1996:I, 16.
[74] WTO, *Korea – Measures Affecting Government Procurement* (19 January 2000) WT/DS163/R [796].
[75] In the *Bankovič v Belgium* case (1999), the ECHR 'recall[ed] that the principles underlying the Convention cannot be interpreted and applied in a vacuum. The Court must also take into account any relevant rules of international law when examining questions concerning its jurisdiction and, consequently, determine State responsibility in conformity with the governing principles of international law, although it must remain mindful of the Convention's special character as a human rights treaty. The Convention should be interpreted as far as possible in harmony with other principles of international law of which it forms part' *Bankovič v Belgium* (Decision of 12 December 2001, Admissibility) ECHR 2001-XII, 351 [57] (references omitted). For a discussion, see L Caflisch and C Trindade, 'Les conventions américaine et européenne des droits de l'homme et le droit international général' (2004) 108 *Revue Generale de Droit Internationale Public* 5.
[76] *Oil Platforms* case ICJ Reports 2003, 161 [41]. The Court applied art 31(3)(c) of the Vienna Convention on the Law of Treaties. For a comprehensive recent discussion, see C McLachlan, 'The Principle of Systemic Integration and Article 31 (3) (c) of the Vienna Convention' (2005) 54 *International and Comparative Law Quarterly* 279.
[77] 'Fragmentation of International Law. Problems caused by the Diversification and Expansion of International law, Report of the Study Group of the International Law Commission' finalised by M Koskenniemi A/CN4/L.682 (13 April 2006) (Analytical Report). The way allegedly 'self contained' regimes link to general international law is discussed at 65–101. The 42 conclusions prepared by the Study Group on the question of fragmentation on the basis of the 'Analytical Report' are contained in Fragmentation of international law: difficulties arising from the diversification and expansion of international law: Report of the Study Group of the International Law Commission' A/CN.4/L.702 (18 July 2006) (Conclusions) 7–25.

Group, 'International law is a legal system'. You cannot just take one finger out of it and pretend it is alive. For the finger to work, the whole body must come along.[78] But how useful is this victory? Constitutionalists are right to say that functional regimes or expert systems do not float in a normless vacuum. They do not, however, have definite hierarchies to resolve conflicts between them – they have a vocabulary, in other words, but nothing definite to say with it. While the ILC Study Group discovered that no regime, however special, was autonomous from international law, it did not feel it appropriate to give an indication of whether in cases of normative conflict the special rule or regime should be read as an exception to or an application of the general law. In fact, practice showed examples of both solutions and it was impossible to determine which way the equation should go in the abstract. Of course, an EU rule might derogate from law of the sea, or a regime on the use of force might conflict with a principle of humanitarian law. But what to do in such situations would have to depend on the circumstances.[79] On the one hand, conflicts between special regimes and general international law express the tension between particularism and universalism and the mere speciality or generality of a rule or a regime gives no conclusive reason to prefer it.[80] On the other hand, there is the question of what 'general' and 'special' mean in this context. It may be natural for international lawyers to think of their specialisation as 'general'. But it is equally unsurprising that other lawyers see it as a particularly exotic craft relevant mainly for the quaint traditions of diplomacy.

Likewise, it is quite unclear what it means for a WTO organ or a human rights body to say that its law does not apply 'in a vacuum'. It suffices to read the dissenting opinions in the recent cases at the ECHR concerning its treatment of the clash between human rights law and the law of diplomatic immunities, to realise to what extent regime conflict is a conflict of political preference.[81]

Legal practice may be read in a systemic light: everything is always already regulated. There are no clear cases of *non liquet* in international practice. Law has integrity as a system, either in the Anglo-American image, through the constructive operations by which lawyers decide cases, or in the continental perspective, through the systematising efforts of legal science. However, the system only says that everything should be decided according to it – which is to say no more than

[78] For two more recent examples in a burgeoning literature, see, A Lindroos and M Mehling 'Dispelling the Chimera of 'Self-Contained Regimes' International Law and the WTO' (2005) 16 *European Journal of International Law* 857 and B Simma and D Pulkowski, 'Of Planets and the Universe: Self-Contained Regimes in International Law' (2006) 17 *European Journal of International Law* 483.

[79] See especially Report of the Study Group of the International Law Commission' A/CN.4/L.702 (18 July 2006) (Conclusions).

[80] For the inconclusive discussion in international law of the status of regional versus universal regimes and for the conclusion on 'general law'/'special law' relations, see Report of the Study Group of the International Law Commission' finalised by M Koskenniemi A/CN4/L.682 (13 April 2006) (Analytical Report)102–15.

[81] See *Al-Adsani v the United Kingdom* (Judgment of 21 November 2001) ECHR 2001-XI. Especially instructive is the Dissenting Opinion of Judge Ferrari-Bravo. For a discussion of these conflicts from the point of view of 'fragmentation', see H Fox, 'State Immunity and other Norms of International Law: Possible Methods of Accommodation' in J Erauwet al (eds), *Liber memorialis Peter Sarcevic, Universalism, Tradition and the Individual* (Munich, Sellier, 2006) 552–64.

that whatever the decision, it should be made by legal institutions, in particular institutions populated by public international lawyers. But if that is all the law says, it only underwrites the structural bias of its institutions. This may seem fine if one is a member of those institutions oneself. If one does not share their bias, however, but rather thinks of them as part of the problem, then constitutionalism has no compelling force. Surely what matters is whether it is a *good* constitution, whether it empowers the *right* people, whether it allocates resources in accordance with the *right* bias.

A constitutional vocabulary itself has little to show why it should be preferable to the vocabularies of, say, economics, technology, socialism, nationalism, or Christianity. They, too, come with their own experts and embedded preferences. There is no reason to think of them as a priori worse than the institutions constitutionalists typically prefer – courts in particular, especially courts populated by Europeans. In fact, constitutionalism can defend itself only by recourse to some such vocabulary – typically that of liberal political theory – that is itself subject to ongoing political contestation.[82] If there seems reason to prefer constitutionalism – with the institutions and practices that this entails – this can only come about as a political project that identifies the political objectives the constitution intends to enhance.[83] Saint-Just did not celebrate the revolutionary Constitution because it was such, but owing to what it did for what he called tyranny and feudalism.[84] Also, if Kant thought of this as a phenomenon that *can never be forgotten*, this was owing to the way it manifested both the liberation of the people and the end to wars of aggression.[85]

Constitutionalism responds to the worry about the 'unity of international law' by suggesting a hierarchical priority to institutions representing general international law (especially the United Nations Charter).[86] Yet it seems difficult to see how any politically meaningful project for the common good (as distinct from the various notions of particular good) could be articulated around the diplomatic practices of United Nations organs, or notions such as *jus cogens* in the Vienna Convention on the Law of Treaties. Fragmentation is, after all, the result of a conscious *challenge* to the unacceptable features of that general law and the powers of the institutions that apply it. This is why there will be no hierarchy between the various legal regimes in any near future. The agreement that some norms simply *must* be superior to other norms is not reflected in any consensus in regard to who should have final say on this. The debate on an international constitution will not

---

[82] See especially J Habermas, 'Eine politische Verfassung für die pluralistische Weltgesellschaft?' (2005) 38 *Kritische Justiz* 223 and at more length, 'Hat die Konstitutionalisierung des Völkerrechts noch eine Chance?' in *Der gespaltene Westen* (Frankfurt, Suhrkamp, 2004) 113–93.

[83] Goyard-Febre identifies two objects for every constitution: to keep away monarchic absolutism and rule by the masses, S Goyard-Fabre, *Les fondements de l'ordre juridique* (Paris, PUF, 1991) 137–39.

[84] A de Saint-Just, *Esprit de la révolution et de la constitution de la France* (Paris 10/18, 2003 [1790/91]) 27–42, 66–67.

[85] Kant, 'The Contest of the Faculties' in *Political Writings* (1991) 184.

[86] See especially B Fassbender, 'The United Nations Charter as a Constitution of the International Community' (1998) 36 *Columbia Journal of Transnational Law* 530.

resemble domestic constitution-making. This is so not only because the international realm lacks a *pouvoir constituant*, but because if such presented itself, it would be empire, and the constitution it would enact would not be one of an international but an imperial realm.[87]

Legal Pluralism

The alternative to constitutionalism is legal pluralism. International lawyers have not done much to explore this. This is perhaps understandable as it is their opponents – political realists – whose 'anarchophilia' has cast them as always de facto pluralists.[88] Whereas domestic legal pluralism has, however, been a project on the political left, the pluralism *malgré soi* of realism has usually been conservative in method and policy.[89] For example, in inter-war France, the solidarist constitutionalism of Georges Scelle or Nicolas Politis was developed on the basis of Third Republic radical liberalism, even socialism. Against them, realist historians such as Charles Dupuis ridiculed the effort at getting away from sovereignty as naïve and pointless – without sense for the law's cultural and historical moorings. The League's cosmopolitan facade failed because it had no contact with the material power of nations or the spiritual power of the public opinion. Only a balance between those plural points of political power called states would be reflective of the diversity of the international realm.[90]

A famous manifesto of pluralism *avant la lettre* was Hans Morgenthau's legal swan song, his article on 'Positivism, Functionalism and International Law' of 1940 that indicted the whole of the inter-war legal system for its lack of a sociological grounding on the one hand, and its insensitivity to the actual divergence of moral values in the world, on the other. Its fixation on one single centrist model was a receipt for failure.[91] But Morgenthau's plea for sociologically sensitive anti-formalism led to no serious sociology of international law. This is perhaps understandable. If law is a 'reflective' mirror of social or psychological phenomena, ambitious minds will turn away from it. With his *Politics Among Nations: The Struggle for Power and Peace* of 1948, Morgenthau himself abandoned the field and set up International Relations on the ruins of constitutional thinking in world affairs.[92]

---

[87] This is why international constitutionalism has always been dependent on the constructive efforts of the international law profession.

[88] The realist view of the international system as 'anarchic' is labelled 'anarchophilia' by M Shaw, *Theory of the Global State: Globality as an Unfinished Revolution* (Cambridge, Cambridge University Press, 2000) 263–65.

[89] This is largely due to the fact that while domestic pluralism is critical of the State, international pluralism adopts the standpoint of the State for its critique of internationalism.

[90] C Dupuis, 'Regles générales du droit de la paix' (1930) 32 *Recueil des Cours de l'Académie de droit international* 5.

[91] H Morgenthau, 'Positivism, Functionalism and International Law' (1940) 31 *American Journal of International Law* 261.

[92] See further Koskenniemi, *The Gentle Civiliser* (2002) 445–74.

It would be wrong to say that there has been no effort at all to build international law on a sociology of pluralism. Lauterpacht, after all, knew Harold Laski well – the father of pluralism – at the LSE, and participated in the School's famous sociological club together with eminent sociologists and anthropologists such as Bronislaw Malinowski or Edward Westermark and international relations scholars such as CAW Manning or Martin Wight. Nevertheless, it was not Lauterpacht – whose project was not pluralism but federalism – but his critics who grasped at something like sociological jurisprudence. Georg Schwarzenberger, among others, used the distinction between 'community' and 'society' to canvass the 'social background of international law' in terms of an irreducible hostility between states, expressed in the various forms of 'power politics' which international law could only facilitate and symbolise but not limit.[93] Julius Stone publicly attacked Lauterpacht's federalist ideas, arguing that the idea of the completeness of international law was a counterproductive piece of legal utopianism. Peace and justice themselves required that international law should be aware of its limits.[94] Stone had collaborated with Roscoe Pound in Harvard and in a 1957 course he enquired about the prospects of a sociological analysis in international law in terms of the study of the attitudes, perceptions and evaluations communicated between significant policy-makers in the world. He was not optimistic. The sociology of international law, he concluded, 'must move still in a difficult and unknown land, with conditions unknown and paths unblazed'.[95]

It may now be possible to historicise the effort to integrate political realist understandings in international law in the 1950s and 1960s as the product of a post-war moment of disillusionment for which a turn to sociology gave expression.[96] It failed to transform the field, however, leading to little more than the habit of prefacing normative analyses by ritual reference to interdependence and the balance of power. If McDougal and his Yale followers used a vocabulary of process, this imported some of the insights of sociological jurisprudence, as mediated by American legal realism, into the 1970s and beyond.[97] The ideological commitments

---

[93] See, eg G Keeton and G Schwarzenberger, *Making International Law Work*, 2nd edn (London, Stevens, 1946) 14–48 ('The Social Background of International law' and 'The Functions of International Law'). On Schwarzenberger's sociology of international law, see S Steinle, *Völkerrecht und Machtpolitik. G Schwarzenberger (1908–1991)* (Baden-Baden, Nomos, 2000) 108–23. On Schwarzenberger's (tense) relationship with Lauterpacht, see ibid 216–18.

[94] J Stone, 'Non-Liquet and the Function of Law in the International Community' (1959) 35 *British Year Book of International Law* 124.

[95] J Stone, 'Problems Confronting Sociological Analyses in International Law' 89 *Recueil des Cours de l'Académie de droit international* (1956-I) 141.

[96] Among the more significant works were P Corbett, *Law and Society in the Relations of States* (New York, Harcourt, Brace, 1951) and C deVisscher, *Théories et réalities en droit international public* (Paris, Pedone,1953). These were written by experts in international law and diplomacy. Works produced from the inside of the US political science establishment never attained that kind of influence. See, eg MA Kaplan and N Katzenbach, *The Political Foundations of International Law* (New York, Wiley, 1961) and WD Coplin, *The Function of International Law. An Introduction to the Role of International Law in the Contemporary World* (Chicago, University Press, 1966).

[97] For a recent overview, see S Wiessner and A Willard, 'Policy-Oriented Jurisprudence and Human Rights abuses in Internal Conflict: Toward a World Public Order of Human Dignity' in SR Ratner and A-M Slaughter, *The Methods of International Law* (Washington, ASIL, 2004) 47–77.

of that part of the US international law establishment prevented it, however, from developing a robust pluralist statement. Nor did the 'Manhattan school', more inclined as it was to support mainstream international organisations, use its legal realist training with a view to sociological enquiries so much as to develop a defence of the UN that would resonate credibly for US policy-makers.[98] Neither of these has been so much pluralist as constitutionalist in a Schmittian sense, focusing on the 'legitimacy' developing out of the public order ('nomos') for which either the American Constitution or the UN Charter would provide a centre.

Today, a well developed vocabulary of pluralism in law schools has emerged from three sources: the study of local laws and de facto practices in modern society; the experience of native law's coexistence with imported metropolitan laws in the colonial encounter, and globalisation.[99] In the huge literature on this last phenomenon, two concerns have been predominant: a wish to develop a descriptively accurate image of the ways of influence in today's world and a normative desire to rethink the nature of the legal profession whose task it is to manage the new forms of regulation beyond the State.[100]

Much could be said about the effort to develop pluralistic models of global governance that would focus on the transnational mechanisms of informal rule setting, rule-administering and conflict management. I am uncertain if present discussions of *lex mercatoria*, or of the informal networking by private industries, non-governmental stakeholder groups and national administrations have produced a stable basis for a formal pluralist statement.[101] I rather doubt this. On the one hand, much of the relevant literature is in fact critical of the developments it discusses.[102] On the other hand, inter-legality and polycentrism sound very much like another constitutional – though de-politicised – vocabulary. As Jens Bartelson concludes: 'the attempt to throw the state concept out was futile as this concept was invariably replaced with others that were semantically equivalent'.[103]

By far the most advanced pluralist statement has emerged from the sociology of Niklas Luhmann that embraces not only openly normative but also scientific,

---

[98] The expression 'Manhattan school' refers to the strong multilateralist international orientation around Columbia and New York Universities. For a discussion, see D Kennedy, 'Tom Franck and the Manhattan School' (2003) 35 *New York University Journal of International Law and Politics* 397.

[99] For a useful recent overview, see S Roberts, 'After Government? On Representing Law Without the State' (2005) 68 *Modern Law Review* 1.

[100] For two examples from quite different political sensibilities, see J Braithwaite and P Drahos, *Global Business Regulation* (Cambridge, Cambridge University Press, 2000) and B de Sousa Santos, *Towards a New Common Sense: Law, Science and Policy in the Age of Paradigmatic Transition* (London, Routledge, 1995).

[101] For a representative collection of essays, see P Schiff Berman, *The Globalization of International Law* (Aldershot, Ashgate, 2005).

[102] This applies in particular to the extensive French literature on law and globalisation. See especially the useful analyses in E Loquin and C Kessedjian (eds), *La mondialisation du droit* (Paris, Litec, 2000) and the somewhat less analytical but very critical M Chemillier-Gendreau and Y Moulier-Boutang, Le droit dans la mondialisation (Paris, PUF, 2001).

[103] J Bartelson, *The Critique of the State* (Cambridge, Cambridge University Press, 2001) 124. He detects a secret 'ontologisation' of the State (really the state form as a normative base) behind the various efforts to develop descriptively accurate sociologies of pluralism, 103–13 and passim.

technological and economic regimes, each of which possesses the resources for explaining the whole world from its perspective, and an inbuilt tendency to maximise its proper rationality.[104] Under this view, legal globalisation means the globalisation of the functional differentiation that has taken place in national society. Transnational regimes would replace territorial states. Far from unifying the world, this would intensify the clash of legal regimes, each internally hierarchical, some more central than others. Conflicts between, say, trade and human rights regimes; economic development and the environment; scientific and political expertise; can never really be settled because, in the absence of the nation state, no meta-rationality allocates to each its respective place. Although no hierarchy is established, however, the centre moves. Yesterday, we looked to the UN General Assembly as the focus for our reforms, today perhaps to Beijing's economic policies or non-governmental organisation (NGO) networks dealing with human trafficking.[105]

The centre moves because each regime is hegemonic. Each seeks to make its special rationality govern the whole – to transform its preference into the general preference, its institution into the institution of general jurisdiction. The experience is familiar that once one knows which institution will deal with an issue, one already knows how it will be disposed of. Luhmannians such as Teubner and Fischer-Lescano derive from this the experience of law's epiphenomenality: 'a legal reproduction of collisions between the diverse rationalities within global society'. A part of the problem and not of its solution, law has no argument to defend its ambition to be anything but 'a gentle civiliser of social systems'.[106]

The problem with legal pluralism lies in the way it ceases to pose demands on the world. Its theorists are so enchanted by the complex interplay of regimes and a positivist search for an all-inclusive vocabulary that they lose the critical point of their exercise. This is visible, for instance, in the habit of collapsing the distinction between law and regulation, a favourite technique of international relations studies, and describing law as another regime in thoroughly instrumentalist terms: 'legalisation' as a policy choice sometimes dictated by strategic interests.[107] I like to think of this as a hegemonic move on the part of international relations experts as an effort to occupy the voice of normativity previously held by lawyers. A sociology of complexity articulates a project of technological reason that seems, after all,

---

[104] This is now available in English as N Luhmann, *Law as a Social System* (Oxford, Oxford University Press, 2004).

[105] See A Fischer-Lescano and G Teubner, *Regime-Kollisionen. Zur Fragmentierung des globalen Rechts* (Frankfurt, Suhrkamp, 2006). Earlier versions of this include A Fischer-Lescano and G Teubner, 'Regime-Collisions: the Vain Search for Legal Unity in the Fragmentation of Global Law' (2004) 25 *Michigan Journal of International Law* 999.

[106] Fischer-Lescano and Teubner, *Regime-Kollisionen* (2006) 170.

[107] For an extended analysis, see J Goldstein, M Kahler, R Keohane, and A-M Slaughter, *Legalization And World Politics* (Cambridge, Mass, MIT Press, 2000). I have criticised the turn to political science vocabularies of 'governance', 'legitimacy' and so on in 'Legitimacy, Rights and Ideology: Notes towards a Critique of the new Moral Internationalism' (2003) 7 *Associations: Journal for Legal and Social Theory* 349 and 'Constitutionalism as Mindset. Reflections on Kantian Themes on International Law and Globalization' in (2007) 8 *Theoretical Inquiries in Law* 9.

so much more up to date than the Victorian antics of international law. Normative politics is replaced by what the newspeakers call 'new global division of regulatory labour'.[108] When I hear this language I recognise the blank stare in the eyes of my European colleagues – and share it.

The wider the laws grasp, the weaker their normative force. Until, finally, one becomes unable to distinguish between the gunman and the policeman, the regime of corruption from the regime of contract. Of course, each may have its merits. Each certainly empowers a distinct group of people. By pointing out de facto powerful regimes, legal pluralism may be descriptively powerful. But its accuracy occasions the same response as constitutionalism did: 'So what?' Pluralism's main contribution lies in the awareness it brings of the biases of different legal vocabularies; but it cannot sustain a project of law in its own right. For it, the image of the lawyer is always the image of the regime-manager, their search for a balance between 'efficiency' and 'legitimacy', the pluralist equivalent to the 'integrity' of constitutionalist.[109]

Constitutionalism and pluralism are abstract responses to the emergence of multiple legal regimes. Each comes with a disciplinary tradition – one associated with law, the other with political science – split against itself. In its self-confident, ruling mode, constitutionalism appears as centralism, rights and order, supported by histories of state-building. From a pluralist perspective, however, it often means bureaucratic authoritarianism and rule by the *ancien regime*. By contrast, pluralism's major mode highlights diversity and freedom, spontaneous development. But that is surely vulnerable to the constitutionalist retort: it accepts de facto rule merely because it is there.

Constitutionalism and pluralism are generalising doctrines with an ambivalent political significance. Each may support and challenge the existing state of affairs. Together they provide alternative orientations to deal with, and to reduce, complexity. This is why I think of them as two tendencies in a single set of problems the need for centralism and control on the one hand, diversity and freedom on the other. In practice, they often converge in intermediate forms: federalism, limited autonomy, interpretations reconciling the particular with the general – 'systemic integration'. But they are external, academic vocabularies that remain at a birds-eye distance from law as professional commitment, even a 'calling'.

Narrative Perspectives

I would like to think of constitutionalism and pluralism less as aspects of the world than as experiences of it, reproducing in legal practice what are in fact stereotypical

---

[108] Lipschutz and Vogel, 'Regulation for the Rest of Us?' (2002) 117.

[109] See, eg the discussion of 'accountability problems' in private governance, in J Koven Levit, 'A Bottom-Up Approach to Law Making: The Tale of the Trade Finance Instruments' (2005) 30 *Yale Journal of International Law* 194.

reactions to modernity. International law and sociology both arose in the late nineteenth century to map the breakdown of a traditional world – on the one hand into sovereign states, supported by narratives of national history, culture and spirit, and on the other into increasingly specialised, functionally organised ways of life emerging from narratives about economic and technological progress. Sociology – like international law – described this initially in sombre tones – anomie, suicide, the iron cage. But it soon developed reassuring counter-narratives: modernity as complexity, dynamism, freedom, even utopia.[110] Dadaism once gave voice to a perception of chaos in a world whose verities had been blown to pieces by 1914. But a depiction of absence of sense, too, may create sense. Soon no tourist could leave Paris without a reproduction of a Dada artwork. The logic of capitalism turned plurality into a surface underneath which the invisible hand would reproduce the conditions of bourgeois accumulation. The same with international law: the catastrophe of the Great War created the narrative of the world of sovereigns as an 'anarchic society'.[111] Political theorists and lawyers may, in the twentieth century, have understood the world in realist terms of 'struggle for power'. However, this never prevented them from describing this as a well-ordered 'system'.[112] Think, for instance, about our intuitive habit today of looking back to the Cold War as the tranquil normality of tradition.

This play of narratives of unity and fragmentation is quite central for the self-understanding of Western law, often expressed in the tension between historical 'positivity' and rational 'system'. Developments in seventeenth century law were told as a story about progress from civil war to the unified nation, as well as descent from the Christian community to sovereign states. Eighteenth century natural jurisprudence – Samuel Pufendorf in Germany, Adam Smith in Britain – turned the Reformation fear of individualism and human self-love into a scientific explanation for enlightened absolutism on the one hand, and the wealth of nations on the other, while the Kantian postulate of the 'unsocial sociability' from 1784 remained the last refuge for the faith of many a liberal internationalist until well into the twentieth century.[113] Today, when every unifying deep-structure has been subjected to demystifying deconstruction what will be left is demystification deconstruction as the great unifying myth.

Fragmentation and unity are matters of narrative perspective.[114] What from one angle looks like a terribly chaotic image of something, may from another appear just as a finely nuanced and sophisticated reflection of a deeper unity. *E pluribus unum.*

[110] See especially H Liebersohn, *Fate and Utopia in German Sociology 1870–1923* (Cambridge, Mass, MIT Press, 1988).

[111] As famously depicted in the analyses of the 'English school' and peaked in H Bull, *The Anarchical Society. A Study of Order in World Politics* (London, Macmillan, 1977).

[112] See, eg the discussion in J Donnelly, *Realism and International Relations* (Cambridge, Cambridge University Press, 2000) 81–130.

[113] I Kant, 'Idea for a Universal History with a Cosmopolitan Purpose' in H Reiss (ed), *Political Writings* (Cambridge, Cambridge University Press, 1991) 47.

[114] See further the discussion of 'variations of world order' in Koskenniemi, *From Apology to Utopia* (2005) 474–512.

Dozens of national myths tell the story of how separateness and individuality express togetherness and community. Or think of European constitutional patriotism today – the effort to bridge social conflict by focusing solidarity on a constitutional text. Constitutionalism and pluralism provide vocabularies that make sense of a new world from alternative perspectives and thus establish the authority of those forms of expertise whose home lies in the respective vocabularies.

German Analogies

The force and the apparent novelty of today's fragmentation debate have obscured the degree to which it captures a classical international law problem. 'How is law between sovereign States possible?' is not too different from the question 'how is law between multiple regimes possible?' In the course of the professional life of public international law – perhaps around 150 years – there have been many responses to that question. As always, however, a good place to begin is late nineteenth century German legal thought. Writing in the aftermath of German unification in 1871, the Hegelian legal philosopher Adolf Lasson argued that international law could make no constitutional demands on states. It was an empty abstraction, possible only as a *Koordinationsrecht* binding for reasons of prudence and strategy. Its force lay in its instrumental usefulness.[115] This was later reflected in Heinrich Triepel's dualist – in fact pluralist – view of the relations between national and international law which for most practising lawyers meant the primacy of the national because that was the regime in which their law jobs were situated.[116] You could make reference to a treaty only once it was incorporated into your domestic law.

The coordination view is of course equally applicable to the management of the relations between transnational regimes.[117] As such, it implies a view of legal practice as the faithful reproduction of the rationality of each regime also in its external relations. Trade or human rights lawyers would accept the need to coordinate their actions with each other when and to the extent that might be rationalised under the respective logics of trade and human rights. The lawyer would be a fully instrumentalised cog in the respective machine, while any constraint received from coordinating arrangements would be constantly renegotiated in view of the present calculation. This is the content of what I described above as the managerial mindset.

The managerial view has, however, exactly the difficulty of nineteenth century nationalism, in Germany and elsewhere. Even as Lasson was writing, the regime of the – German – nation was showing itself conflictual, indeterminate, open: Protestant

---

[115] A Lasson, *Princip und Zukunft des Völkerrechts* (Berlin, Herz, 1871).
[116] H Triepel, *Völkerrecht und Landesrecht* (Leipzig, Hirschfeld, 1899).
[117] This is the suggestion in Fischer-Lescano and Teubner *Regime Kollisionen* (2006).

or Catholic, Marx or Bismarck? The 'nation' was not an iron cage but a myth, the 'national interest' not a firm datum for resolving policy conflicts but a platform for waging them.[118] This was as true of the German empire in the late nineteenth century as it is of the regimes of trade, human rights, environment, European Union. Nationalism was always dependent on universalist principles – interpreted in different ways by the various national parties and groups. In a similar way, trade regimes, for example, are themselves conflict-ridden, open-ended and contingent on other regimes – for example, social welfare and environmental regimes, regimes of public decision-making and those of the particular market. A regime is as indeterminate as the nation – its founding principles contradictory and amenable for conflicting interpretations and its boundaries constantly penetrated by adjoining rationales.

The view of international law as a coordination law had come to an end well before Wolfgang Friedmann declared it dead in the 1960s.[119] Sovereignties were cut across by innumerable functional, moral, legal and other rationalities so that it was no longer possible to distinguish the national from the cosmopolitan: Finland – a land of cell phones. My own nationalism is a construct of poetry written in Swedish, German music, Russian landscapes and American technology, all transmitted through a cosmopolitan culture industry. Everyone can say the same about their nationalism and their sense of the 'national interest' – these are not natural, but subject to constant political (de)construction.[120]

The demise of nationalism comes to mind when one hears the suggestion that multiple legal regimes should be managed by a system of regime coordination. History suggests that this would have a surprising consequence. It would compel the internal hierarchisation of the regimes. Eighteenth century absolutism stood on the shoulders of a coordinating view of the international world. For the nation to have a policy of single interest, it needed to have a single spot from which it was ruled.[121] So it is not only that the nation is an open-ended field of political contestation, we have reason to wish it to be such in order to check its slide into authoritarianism. The same applies to functional regimes: to inaugurate a practice—especially a practice looking outside the regime—that would think itself an automatic consequence of regime-rationality would be tantamount to sending out the ethnic cleansers. That has been the tragedy of nationalism—and its principal lesson for thinking about multiple regimes.

The view of future law as a system of regime coordination compels the regimes into the image of billiard balls poised against each other in the Hobbesian image

---

[118] One of the reasons for the demise of 'classical realism' in international relations has been the experience that focus on the 'interests' of actors collapses at the experience of the instability and indeterminacy of particular interest-descriptions.

[119] W Friedmann, *The Changing Structure of International Law* (London, Stevens & Sons, 1964).

[120] For two classics, see E Hobsbawm and E Ranger (eds), *The Invention of Tradition* (Cambridge, Cambridge University Press, 1992); B Anderson, *Imagined Communities* (London, Verso,1983).

[121] The point about the jus publicum Europaeum being able to coordinate the actions of European sovereign efficiently because those sovereigns were seen as morally neutral managers with full control is made in C Schmitt, *Der Nomos der Erde. Im Völkerrecht des Jus Publicum Europaeum*, 3rd edn (Berlin, Duncker & Humblot, 1950) especially 111–86.

of 'gladiators', constantly ready to occupy any territory left vacant by the other. But regimes, like states, are no billiard balls. Every regime is always already connected with everything around it. We know this from practice. Environmental law may be best supported by market mechanisms through introducing pollution permissions. For the market to fulfil its promise, again, a huge amount of regulation is needed, not merely on the conditions of exchange or the terms of ownership or banking. A market with no provision for social or environmental conditions will fail. Human rights may be best advanced by looking away from strict human rights criteria and, for example, insisting on early accession of Turkey in the European Union. Regimes of security may be re-described – as was done recently by a British High Court – as regimes of rights protection and vice-versa. The prize of victory in re-description is jurisdiction to decide. Extended to a world of multiple regimes, this highlights the contingency of regimes, their dependence on other regimes, the politics of *regime definition.*

Contesting Governance

When Lauterpacht and his generation devised their legal politics in the aftermath of the First World War, they looked for a technically sophisticated international law, on a par with the domestic, from which they could attack the totalitarian reason of statehood. For them, sovereignty had become the problem, and they aimed to overcome it by occupying the place of the international, imagined as a technically complex web of rules and institutions that would tie the State down like Gulliver was – liberating individuals from the prison of inter-war hegemonic nationalisms.

Today, however, the 'international' is no longer a meaningful space for progressive politics. Which 'international' would it be? That of free trade or of human rights? Security, science, or mass media? The international of the EU or Nokia; of Amnesty or Al-Qaida? The transformations since 1989 have hardly advanced the Kantian project of cosmopolitan community. Instead, we seem to have been thrown back to the early modern natural law of Hobbes and Pufendorf, against which Kant conceived universal law in the first place. The natural lawyers developed a vocabulary that inaugurated law as a technique for governing human beings by manipulating their fears and desires. They were, of course, theorists of absolutism. What they thought of as the appropriate space for governing was the territorial state. Now, that space has been occupied by de-territorialised regimes. But the vocabulary of absolutism has remained, the absolutism of disciplinary truth, declared by technical institutions with claim to a universal reason, an absolutism of speculative reason as *Schwärmerei* whose limits Kant traced in the Critique of Pure Reason (1781):

> Unfortunately for speculation – but perhaps fortunately for the practical interests of humanity – reason, in the midst of its highest anticipations, finds itself jostled by claims

and counterclaims, from which neither its honour nor its safety will permit it to draw back.[122]

So what ought to be done? One alternative must be discounted immediately. This is the conservatism of statehood. Even if the way back to sovereign states were open it would lead nowhere as the State itself has been functionally fragmented. Try to find out the national position on a matter and you will hear a different answer depending on whom you ask: the policy of the Ministry of Finance, declared in Washington, is not identical with that of the Ministry of the Environment, declared in Geneva. The official position cannot be distinguished from the position of the national representative of some 'international' (truth) regime or other. We are stuck in the 'international', with no guarantee that this would be beneficial. In order to begin re-imagining international law, it is first necessary to see in what way the internationalism of Lauterpacht and his generation is no longer plausible.

The old international law project aimed to replace sovereignty by an international system of rights presumed as authentic, pre-political and coterminous with each other. No struggle was needed. The rights would realise themselves as soon as the obstacle of sovereignty to 'freedom' was lifted. Yet, this did not happen. Instead, the international was occupied by an enormous number of policies with a plethora of institutions in which every claimed benefit parades as a 'right' of this or that group.[123] Priorities and choices must be made. In the absence of political institutions, however, the choices will be made by experts and advisors, economists, technicians, scientists and lawyers, all having recourse to the technical vocabularies of ad hoc accommodation, coordination and optimal effect. Utilitarianism is the political constitution of a de-politicised world. However, if functional systems are as indeterminate as law, religion, or nationalism, the question is not so much which regime should rule us, but whose understanding of it should be authoritative, or more concretely, which experts should possess jurisdiction.

The great achievement of Lauterpacht and his generation was to create space for progressive law outside the vocabularies of nationhood. That achievement came at a cost. Thinking of international law in apolitical and technical terms opened the door for expert rule and managerialism, not in competition with politics as in the domestic realm, but as a *substitute* for it. What we now see is an international realm where law is everywhere – the law of this or that regime – but no politics at all; no parties with projects to rule, no division of powers, and no aspiration of self-government beyond the aspiration of statehood – aspirations identified precisely as what we should escape from. Managerialism was the dark side of the inter-war project of imagining international law in technical terms. So I think it is no surprise that international relations experts – particularly strong at US universities – have suggested replacing international law's archaic mores by a political

---

[122] I Kant, *Critique of Pure Reason* (London, Everyman's, ed, 1934) 342 [A463/B491].
[123] For the way in which any legal regime may be narrated as a rights regime ('field-constitution'), see chapter six of this volume.

science-inspired language of governance, regulation, compliance and legitimacy.[124] International law as a strategic game to realise self-interest – that is to say, the interest of those who are represented in its institutions, and their academic advisors. However, the more one conceives of international law in those terms, the sillier it begins to look. The world's causalities are too complex, the strategic simplifications too crude. The functional 'interest' is not a solid policy datum but an object of struggle. When technical vocabularies encompass the whole world, they begin to look like religions with no distance from priestly rule.

There is reason to reconceive international law today. However, instead of changing its vocabulary into coordinating governance though empirical political science – a recent article described international lawyers as 'architects of global governance'[125] – it must be redeemed as a political project. There are two aspects to this. One is the development of a professional sensibility that feels at home in all regimes, yet is imprisoned in none of them. This would be what cosmopolitanism can be today: the ability to break out and connect, participate in the politics of regime definition by narrating regimes anew, giving voice to those not represented in the regime's institutions. To politicise governance means to re-think the activity of expert institutions not as the technical production of pre-determined decisions by some anonymous logic, but choices by well-placed men and women at various spots where power happens: not only in diplomacy or intergovernmental organisations but transnational corporations, interest-groups, banks, armies, development agencies, universities and so on.[126] Instead of bringing law to bear on politics, as Lauterpacht and his generation aimed, it is time to re-describe managerial governance as politics with a particular bias.

But there is another aspect to this re-imagining. International law increasingly appears as that which resists being reduced to a technique of governance. When international lawyers are interviewed on the Iraqi war, or on torture, or on trade and environment, on poverty and disease in Africa – as they increasingly are – they are not expected to engage in hair-splitting technical analyses. Instead, they are called upon to soothe anxious souls, to give voice to frustration and outrage. Moral pathos and religion frequently fail as vocabularies of engagement, providers of 'empty signifiers' for expressing commitment and solidarity.[127] Foreign policy may connote party rule. This is why international law may often appear as the only available surface over which managerial governance may be challenged, the sole vocabulary with a horizon of transcendence – even if, or perhaps precisely because,

---

[124] See, eg Goldstein et al, *Legalization and World Politics* (2000), and for a more recent example, J Goldsmith and E Posner, *The Limits of International Law* (Oxford, Oxford University Press, 2005).

[125] K Abbott, 'Toward a Richer Institutionalism for International law and Policy' (2005) 1 *Journal of International Law and International Relations* 11.

[126] This project of expanding the notion of rulership is at the heart of recent writings by D Kennedy. See especially *The Dark Sides of Virtue .Reassessing International Humanitarianism* (Princeton NJ, Princeton University Press, 2004).

[127] On the need for 'empty signifiers' – that is, vocabularies of political contestation, see E Laclau, *Emancipation(s)* (London, Verso, 1996) especially 36–46 but also passim.

that horizon is not easily translated into another institutional project.[128] I often think of international law as a kind of secular faith. When powerful states engage in imperial wars, globalisation dislocates communities or transnational companies wreck havoc on the environment, and where national governments show themselves corrupt or ineffective, one often hears an appeal to international law.[129] International law appears here less as this rule or that institution than as a placeholder for the vocabularies of justice and goodness, solidarity, responsibility and – faith.

I do not think international law is often invoked because of the sophistication of its rules or institutions. Those rules or institutions are as vulnerable to criticism as any other rules of institutions. The fact that they are 'international' is no proof of their moral value. But the tradition of international law has often acted as a carrier of what is perhaps best described as the regulative idea of universal community, independent of particular interests or desires. This is Kant's cosmopolitan project rightly understood: not an end-state or party programme but a project of critical reason that measures today's state of affairs from the perspective of an ideal of universality that cannot be reformulated into an institution, a technique of rule, without destroying it. The fate of international law is not a matter of reemploying a limited number of professionals for more cost-effective tasks, but of re-establishing hope for the human species.

---

[128] This I suppose also encourages appeals to international law by philosophers such as Jürgen Habermas and Jacques Derrida. See G Borradori (ed), *Philosophy and Terror: Dialogues with Jürgen Habermas and Jacques Derrida* (Chicago, University of Chicago Press, 2003) 27, 38–40, 114–20.

[129] International law's constitutional role though giving voice to 'scandalization' processes ('colère public internationale') is usefully discussed in A Fischer-Lescano, *Globalverfassung. Die Geltungsbegründung der Menschenrechte* (Göttingen, Velbrück, 2005) 67–99.

INDEX OF NAMES

Index of Names

INDEX

Index

False necessity, 65
Field constitution, 140–1, 157, 165
Finnish Ministry of Foreign Affairs, 287, 298, 317
First Amendment (US Constitution), 145, 158
First World War, 37, 41, 79, 163, 264, 358
Fisheries Jurisdiction case, 50, 57
Formalism, 73, 79, 99, 109, 111–8, 128–9, 130–5, 151, 161–6, 175, 229, 231, 241, 249, 254–67, 288, 290, 298–9, 303–5, 320
  anti-formalism, 254–8, 350
  formalist logic, 258–9
  human rights formalism, 164–5
  non-formalist, 165, 291
Former Yugoslavia, 82, 85, 108, 113, 134, 172, 185, 194, 197, 253, 277
  Bosnia, 84, 85, 94, 171, 227, 305
  Serbia, 112, 114, 115, 120, 125, 129, 177, 180, 183, 184, 226, 233, 333
  Srebrenica, 125, 177, 182, 225
Fragmentation, 65–7, 228–30, 263–5, 280, 308, 320, 334–9, 344–9, 353–6
Framework Convention on Climate Change (FCCC), 343
France:
  Fifth Republic France, 188, 189, 192
  Third Republic France, 350
French revolution, 162–4, 261
  Déclaration de droit de l'homme et du citoyen (1789), 162
French statute of limitations, 192
Friendly Relations Declaration (1975), 116
From Apology to Utopia: The Structure of International Legal Argument, 35, 64, 298
Functional regime, 69, 228, 237, 320, 331, 348, 357
Fundamental rights, 123, 134–6, 141–6, 156, 157, 160, 229, 232, 253, 338

G
Gabčikovo-Nagymaros case, 282, 343
Gacaca courts, 178
Galić case, 195
Genocide, 101, 108, 126, 172–7, 185–7, 192, 208, 213–5, 227, 243–4, 302
Genocide Convention, 244
Gentle civilizer (of Nations), 110, 111, 241, 288–9, 316–7
Gestapo, 188, 191–3
Global governance, 65, 68, 219–20, 235, 271, 274, 282, 283, 321–4, 352, 360
Globalisation, 66, 69, 72, 90, 163, 219, 224, 230, 235–8, 245–9, 257, 271, 293, 308, 326, 329, 352, 353, 361
GMOs, 320
Good faith, 52–6, 60, 138, 167, 175, 189, 200–1, 210
Governmentality, 327

Grogan case, 141, 144
Grundnorm, 214
Guantanamo, 190, 219, 239
Gulf of Maine case, 50, 53

H
Hague Academy of International Law, 272
Handyside case, 139, 140, 248
Harmony of interests, 244, 245, 289
Hegemony, 111, 164, 167, 171, 187, 188, 192, 219–41, 232–6, 260, 263–5, 305, 320, 338
  counter-hegemonic, 225, 236
  institutional hegemony, 338
  world unity, 223, 225
Helsinki Final Act (1975), 157
Hermeneutics, 35, 63, 118, 119, 156, 297, 298, 327
Hiroshima, 205
Holocaust, 155, 172–7, 194–6, 211–7, 261
Homo economicus, 256, 257, 266
Homo juridicus, 256, 266
Human rights, 65–71, 81, 83–6, 99, (104), 113–23, 131–67, 176, 219–40, 241–65, 271, 279, 281, 282, 288, 292, 302, 316–20, 324–6, 331–9, 346–8, 353, 356–9
  formalism, 164–5
  fundamentalism, 122–3, 165
  law, 65–71, 219, 258, 264–5, 331, 334, 335, 348, 356
  skepticism, 165–6
  universality of human rights, 161
  violations, 83, 117, 122, 176, 318
Human Rights Act, 336
Human Rights Committee, 248
Humanitarian, 58, 83, 85, 90, 114–22, 126, 128, 142, 154, 171, 200–3, 208, 225–9, 234, 250, 253, 258, 260, 316–8, 326, 340
  crisis, 94, 95
  exemptions, 87
  intervention, 85–86, 116–26, 248–50, 318, 326, 340
  law, 67, 68, 99, 142, 200, 208, 229, 253, 258, 264, 277, 335, 336, 340, 348
Humanitarianism, 86, 125–28, 162–4, 227, 250

I
Idealism, 43, 245, 256, 287
  idealists, 45, 297
Ihlen declaration, 47
Immanent critique, 35, 64
Impunity, 65, 108, 113, 171–98, 228, 261, 278, 318, 334
Indeterminacy, 35, 63, 67–9, 79, 101, 103, 110, 112, 140, 157, 165, 195, 204, 259, 262, 275, 292, 297–9, 304, 326, 330, 346
  of rights-language, 147–8, 157–9
Indigenous societies, 137, 213
Individual criminal responsibility, 171–83

Index

368

Index

Lightning Source UK Ltd.
Milton Keynes UK
UKOW06f0743200516

274640UK00007B/144/P